BRITISH QUAKERISM
1860–1920

Fig. 1   John Wilhelm Rowntree (1868–1905), *c.* 1900

British Quakerism
1860–1920

The Transformation of a Religious Community

THOMAS C. KENNEDY

OXFORD
UNIVERSITY PRESS

OXFORD
UNIVERSITY PRESS

Great Clarendon Street, Oxford OX2 6DP

Oxford University Press is a department of the University of Oxford.
It furthers the University's objective of excellence in research, scholarship,
and education by publishing worldwide in

Oxford New York

Athens Auckland Bangkok Bogotá Buenos Aires
Cape Town Chennai Dar es Salaam Delhi Florence Hong Kong Istanbul
Karachi Kolkata Kuala Lumpur Madrid Melbourne Mexico City Mumbai
Nairobi Paris São Paulo Shanghai Singapore Taipei Tokyo Toronto Warsaw

and associated companies in Berlin Ibadan

Published in the United States
by Oxford University Press Inc., New York

First published 2001

British Library Cataloguing in Publication Data

Data available

Library of Congress Cataloging in Publication Data

for

Kennedy, Thomas C.
British Quakerism, 1860–1920 : the transformation of a religious
community / Thomas C. Kennedy.
p. cm.
Includes bibliographical references and index.
1. Society of Friends–Great Britain–History–19th century.
2. Society of Friends–Great Britain–History–20th century. I. Title.
BX7676.3 46 2001
289.6′41′09034–dc21   00–068615

ISBN 0–19–827035–6

1 3 5 7 9 10 8 6 4 2

Typeset by Kolam Information Services
Private Ltd, Pondicherry, India

Printed in Great Britain by
Biddles Ltd, Guildford & King's Lynn

The night is far spent,
The day is at hand:
Let us therefore cast off the works of darkness,
And let us put on
The armour of light.

Romans 13: 12

In loving memory of Roger Cowan Wilson,
1906–1991
Historian, friend, great Friend
and
With grateful thanks to
Edward H. Milligan,
the peerless Ted

Acknowledgements

Many individuals and institutions have made invaluable contributions to this study, but no one offered so much or delivered so abundantly as the late Roger C. Wilson, one of the great leaders of twentieth-century British Quakerism, to whom the book is dedicated. I never felt worthy of his inexhaustible kindness, let alone his absolute confidence, and can only hope this study is in some way worthy of his memory. My dedication also includes another astute, generous, and able Friend, Edward H. Milligan, former Librarian of the Society of Friends. Ted showed me where I ought to look, helped me to understand what I had found, and, by reading and correcting the manuscript, saved me from innumerable embarrassing errors and egregious misinterpretations; I owe him more thanks than I can adequately express. Malcolm Thomas, current Librarian at Friends House and his wonderfully competent and helpful staff, especially Josef Keith, have cheerfully and efficiently dealt with all my requests, despite the problems and inconveniences I often caused for them. They have been good Friends indeed.

I am grateful for the friendship and insight so abundantly conferred by Edwin B. Bronner, former curator of the Quaker Collection at Haverford College, and his staff, especially Elizabeth Potts Brown, Dianna Franzusoff Peterson, and Nancy Magnesson (now librarian of Goucher College), during the year I spent at Haverford as T. Wistar Brown Fellow. During the intervening years Emma Lapsansky, the current curator, has maintained this Friendly tradition. Two other Friends who have given unstintingly of their knowledge, hospitality, and good will are Jean Rowntree and Mary Hoxie Jones, daughters who have maintained and expanded the legacies of their fathers. In conversations, correspondence, and published works, John Punshon has shared his always penetrating and often moving insights into Quaker religious thought. If I have been half so good a student as he is a teacher, I will not lead the innocent or uninitiated far astray. Other Friends who provided hospitality, information, or good counsel include numerous members of the Rowntree family, the late Ormerod Greenwood, Mollie Grubb, the late Horace Alexander, Robin and Mary Hodgkin, Mary Barlow Millor, the late Richard Braithwaite, Knightsbridge Professor of Philosophy, University of Cambridge, Thomas Hamm, Director of the Earlham College Quaker Collection, Philip Radley, Henry Ecroyd, Stephen and Olive Peet. I am deeply indebted to the Wardens and Fellows of Woodbrooke College, Birmingham for their assistance and generosity.

I need also to express gratitude to the directors and staffs of the John Rylands Library, University of Manchester, Manchester Archives and Local Studies, Manchester Central Library, Hardshaw East Monthly Meeting, the Brotherton Library Special Collection, University of Leeds, the Lancashire County Record Office, the Yorkshire General Meeting, Lancashire and Cheshire Quarterly Meeting, the Bertrand Russell Archives, McMaster University, the University Library, Cambridge, and to Graham Pollard, former librarian of Wolfson College, Cambridge, and his associate Ruth Webb. Beth Juhl, Reference Librarian of Mullins Library, University of Arkansas, saved me considerable time and discomfiture providing answers I should already have known and others I would never otherwise have found.

My mentor and friend Richard Rempel originally conceived of the idea of a study of the renaissance of British Quakerism and collaborated in its early stages until ill-health combined with his duties as an editor of the Bertrand Russell Editorial Project made it impossible for him to continue. He has, none the less, persisted in giving of his time and insight, reading the manuscript and providing wise counsel and invaluable criticism. Martin Ceadel, the historian of the British peace movement, also read the manuscript, offering shrewd advice and warm friendship without hope of recompense. Jo Vellacott, an esteemed colleague and friend, has contributed her knowledge of Quakerism and insights as a historian. Peter Clarke, Master of Trinity Hall, Cambridge, has been a role model, no less for his kindness than for his erudition. Peter Brock, Boyd Hilton, Chris Hollingsworth, Fred Leventhal, Brain Phillips, and Jay Winter have helped me in various ways and I am grateful to each of them. I also owe special thanks to Sir David Williams, former President of Wolfson College and Vice-

Chancellor of the University of Cambridge, and to the Fellows, students, and staff of Wolfson College, where my wife and I spent a memorable year while I was Fulbright College Visiting Fellow, a happy circumstance made possible by the patience and goodwill of the History Department of Fulbright College and its Dean, Bernard L. Madison. My research assistant Michael Martin was a wonderfully efficient proof-reader and bibliographer. I apologize for any omissions from the above lists and for any errors I have failed to correct despite all the assistance and good will lavished upon me.

Jim Whitehead practically abandoned his own work for a time to concentrate his knowledge of Christian thought and history, and his passion to have it rightly told, on the final draft of this book, providing, beyond the enduring gift of his friendship, reverent insight and irreverent laughter when both were badly needed. R. J. Q. (Quince) Adams, David Edwards, and Bill Lubenow are special friends who have inspired me, encouraged me, and made me laugh—wondrous gifts, freely given, that I can never repay. My children and grandchildren may not always be sure of what I am up to but I can always be sure of their loyalty and affection. Finally, my great historical friend, Mary Lynn, the light of my life, has comforted me when I was despondent, corrected me when I was wrong, ignored me when I was impossible, and loved me in spite of it all. Dazzling blessings that never cease to amaze.

T.C.K.

Fulbright College, University of Arkansas
Fayetteville
February 2001

Contents

List of Illustrations

Abbreviations

A.B.B.	A. B. Brown
AF	*The American Friend*
AFC	All Friends Conference
A.N.B.	A. Neave Brayshaw
ARF	*A Reasonable Faith* (London, 1886)
AOSA	Ackworth Old Scholars Association
A.S.R.	Arnold S. Rowntree
ASRP	Arnold S. Rowntree Papers
BDMPL	*Bibliographical Dictionary of Modern Peace Leaders* (Westport, Conn., 1985)
BF	*British Friend*
BFP	Braithwaite Family Papers
BL	Brotherton Library, Leeds
B.R.	Bertrand Russell
C.E.M.	Catherine E. Marshall
CEMP	Catherine E. Marshall Papers
CH	*Church History*
CIS	Council for International Service
CO	conscientious objector
COIB	Conscientious Objectors Information Bureau
CPBR	Collected Papers of Bertrand Russell
C.R.K.	Caleb R. Kemp
DMM	Darlington Monthly Meeting
DORA	Defence of the Realm Act
DQB	*Dictionary of Quaker Biography* (Library of the Society of Friends)
E.E.	Edith Ellis
E.G.	Edward Grubb
FAU	Friends Ambulance Unit
FCFU	Friends Christian Fellowship Union
FFDSA	Friends First-Day School Association
FFMA	Friends Foreign Mission Association

FHMC	Friends Home Mission Committee
FHS	Friends Historical Society
FLNC	Friends League of Nations Committee
FOR	Fellowship of Reconciliation
FQ	*Friends Quarterly*
FQE	*Friends Quarterly Examiner*
FSARC	Friends South African Relief Committee
FSC	Friends Service Committee
FSU	Friends Social Union
FWVRC	Friends War Victims Relief Committee
G.C.	George Cadbury
GCP	George Cadbury Papers
GDH	*The Gospel of Divine Help* (London 1886)
HEMM	Hardshaw East Monthly Meeting
HMC	Home Mission Committee
H.T.H.	Henry T. Hodgkin
HMHP	Herbert M. Hodgkin Papers
H.W.P.	Hubert W. Peet
ILP	Independent Labour Party
ITNAC	*Is There not a Cause?*
JFHS	*Journal of the Friends Historical Society*
J.B.B.	Joseph Bevan Braithwaite
J.P.F.	J. P. Fletcher
J.R.H.	J. Rendel Harris
J.W.G.	John William Graham
JWGP	John William Graham Papers
J.W.R.	John Wilhelm Rowntree
LNU	League of Nations Union
L&CQM	Lancashire and Cheshire Quarterly Meeting
LPA	Local Peace Association
LRO	Lancashire Record Office
LSF	Library of the Society of Friends
LYM	London Yearly Meeting
MCL	Manchester City Library
MF	*Manchester Friend*
NAM	National Army Museum
NCF	No-Conscription Fellowship
NFCC	National Free Church Council
P&G	*Peace and Goodwill*
PDP	*The Present Day Papers*

PS	*The Ploughshare*
PRO	Public Records Office
QH	*Quaker History*
QM	Quarterly Meeting
QRT	*Quaker Religious Thought*
QS	*Quaker Studies*
RFP	Rowntree Family Papers
R.G.	Richard Graham
R.M.J.	Rufus M. Jones
RMJP	Rufus M. Jones Papers
R.O.M.	Robert O. Mennell
SACC	South African Conciliation Committee
SQS	Socialist Quaker Society
SSCC	Summer School Continuation Committee
SSS	Scarborough Summer School
TF	*The Friend* (London)
W.C.B.	William Charles Braithwaite
W.E.L.	Wilfred E. Littleboy
WL	Woodbrooke Library
WLP	Wilfred Littleboy Papers
WOP	War Office Papers
WSOC	War and the Social Order Committee
WSPU	Women's Social and Political Union
YM	Yearly Meeting

Introduction

My first serious encounter with Quakers occurred in the midst of a study on British conscientious objectors during the First World War. At the time I was particularly struck by a group of no-compromise (absolutist) war resisters who were members of something called the Friends Service Committee (FSC), a group appointed to assist Quakers of military age who were determined to resist the implementation of compulsory military service. My being drawn to these young men was, no doubt, related to my own opposition to the American intervention in Vietnam, then in its most intense and deadly phase. I admired the courage and tenacity of all the men who faced imprisonment and worse for refusing, for conscience's sake, to partake in Britain's war effort, but the FSC Friends, exuding unwavering confidence in the rightness of their stand, impressed me most. What was it about the Society of Friends that inspired these men to remain so steadfast in their resistance to the demands of both public opinion and the warrior state? My curiosity about the nature of this tiny body of believers (20,000 in 1914) was the beginning of a process which has culminated, after many years, in the completion of this book.

I did not, to be sure, begin with the idea of embarking upon an intellectual, and I must say, spiritual journey which would encompass nearly two decades of intermittent but sometimes obsessive toil. My initial aims were modest: to investigate ideas and actions which might help to account for the depth and persistence of Quaker resistance to the Great War and conscription. Because of my previous work, I already knew some things about Quakers. I was aware of the odd organizational structure of British Quakerism, wherein an annual Spring gathering called London Yearly Meeting[1] gave guidance and direction to subordinate but largely

---

[1] London Yearly Meeting, with final constitutional authority for the Religious Society of Friends in Great Britain, outside Ireland, was comprised of about two dozen quarterly

self-governing monthly meetings located throughout the country. I knew of the quaintly-named Meeting for Sufferings, a body of 'weighty' Friends who acted as a sort of executive committee when Yearly Meeting was not in session.[2] These and other Quaker meetings conducted business in a unique way, being presided over by a combination interlocutor/autocrat called the Clerk who unobtrusively directed discussion on various topics and then arbitrarily determined the 'sense of the meeting' concerning these matters, without ever taking a vote. I had also discovered that the Quaker penchant for silent religious worship seemed to allow Quaker prisoners of conscience more easily to withstand the calculated cruelty of solitary confinement in the third division of the English prison system.[3] Finally, I was particularly cognizant of the historic Quaker peace testimony as the basis for their confrontation with the British State. My sense that this pacifist legacy caused Friends as a group to be uncommonly gentle and humane seemed to be confirmed by my impressions of the Quakers I had met or corresponded with. All of this, I suppose, contributed to my initial, naïve sense that the British Society of Friends was a sort of seamless web, enduring in largely unbroken sequence from its seventeenth-century origins to its fearless stand against the Great War. It took time and some embarrassment for me to discover how wrong I was about that.

When, thus unawares and ill-equipped, I sought instruction on the origins of Quakerism, diving into the religious turmoil of the mid-seventeenth-century world of Civil War, Puritan Commonwealth and millenarian fanaticism that produced the Society of Friends, I initially stayed afloat by hanging with a death grip to

meetings which, in turn, encompassed some eighty monthly meetings. The latter, representing two or more local meetings for worship, were largely autonomous administrative bodies, responsible for matters of membership, finance, property, discipline, and the resolution of disputes as well as 'the preliminaries to and solemnisation of all marriages "according to our usages" '.

[2] Meeting for Sufferings dates from 1676 when, amidst considerable persecution by local authorities, a body of Friends was created to make pleas on behalf of their suffering brethren to Assize Judges meeting in London. In time, this body met on the first Friday of each month and evolved into the operating executive committee of the Society of Friends.

[3] I also became aware of the fact that the silence system in English prisons was in part a response to the vision of the early nineteenth-century Quaker prison reformer, Elizabeth Fry, who believed that enforced silence would lead prisoners to repentance and rehabilitation.

Christopher Hill's captivating *World Turned Upside Down*.[4] Quakers loomed large in this topsy-turvy milieu, emerging among the most radical representatives, socially as well as spiritually, from that most eccentric and iconoclastic of eras. Only after absorbing the riveting picture of early Friends created by Hill and his students did I turn to the official and monumental Quaker histories.[5] These painted a different though not contradictory picture, emphasizing the religious rather than social radicalism of the first 'Children of the Light'. The sum of books and perspectives I digested was sufficient to convince me that the followers of George Fox were a far more complex and diverse crowd than I had at first imagined. Early on, their beliefs and actions were sufficiently revolutionary to cause them to become a feared, hated, and persecuted minority, especially following the Restoration which most of them initially opposed. Still, after overt persecution ceased and George Fox died, the maturing Society of Friends, no longer threatened or perceived as a threat, gradually turned from a vibrant, proselytizing movement to an inward-looking sect which, while continuing to nourish the spiritual lives of its adherents, largely ceased to seek new converts or otherwise mingle with the sociable world of men. The results of this withdrawal were paradoxical. Quakers consciously adopted peculiarities in their style of worship, dress, speech, and living which marked them as unworldly people; at the same time, many of them succeeded in commerce, banking, manufacturing, and even brewing and distilling to a degree that aroused the attention and envy of their most worldly neighbours.

My investigations of the early periods of Quakerism, sobering in the sense of exposing previous and presumptive ignorance, did give me some confidence that I was at last sufficiently prepared to begin a serious inquiry on the roots of the twentieth-century Quaker war-resistance which had so aroused my admiration and curiosity. My earlier work on wartime dissent had concentrated on the secular and mainly socialist No-Conscription Fellowship,[6] but much of the Quaker material I discovered added another

---

[4] *The World Turned Upside Down: Radical Ideas During the English Revolution* (London 1972). Also see Barry Reay, *The Quakers and the English Revolution* (London 1985).

[5] William Charles Braithwaite, *The Beginnings of Quakerism* (London 1912; 2nd edn. 1955) and *The Second Period of Quakerism* (London 1919; 2nd edn. 1961).

[6] See *The Hound of Conscience, A History of the No-Conscription Fellowship, 1914–19* (Fayetteville 1981).

dimension, at once militant and unworldly. This was especially true of the papers of the Friends Service Committee which were covered with a half century's dust when first brought to my attention by Ted Milligan, a walking encyclopaedia of Quaker lore, then the Librarian at Friends House in London. These papers also made me aware of the considerable and at times intense differences among British Quakers, some of whom were not at all meek and docile, regarding their Society's response to the wartime crisis. Most Friends opposed the war and conscription (although about a third of British Quakers openly supported the war effort), but there was a wide range of opinions about what form and scope Quaker resistance should take. I discovered that the no-compromise stand assumed by the Friends Service Committee, and confirmed at various times by both Meeting for Sufferings and Yearly Meeting, represented, in fact, a distinctly minority position within the Society. I also came to appreciate the significant contribution made by Quaker women who took charge of the Friends Service Committee when most of its male members were in State custody. These women, many of them veterans of the Edwardian suffrage campaign, were fully as unyielding as their male counterparts and some of them shared their more radical menfolk's attachment to socialism, a political and economic position far removed from the diligent Liberalism I had previously identified with Quakers.

After completing one brief study of the unique and controversial stand taken by the absolutists of the Friends Service Committee,[7] I set out to look more deeply into the historical roots of Quaker war-resistance. Working backwards through the Edwardian period, I found a gratifying abundance of material on the peace testimony but also discovered a deep division within the Society over the war in South Africa, which was supported by some prominent Friends. Early twentieth-century materials also revealed strong opinions on questions of social reform, many of these critical of Quaker philanthropy, so highly praised during the Victorian decades, for its failure to come to grips with the underlying afflictions of modern industrial society. At this point, I also began to acquire some understanding of various self-defining categories

[7] 'Fighting About Peace: The No-Conscription Fellowship and the British Friends' Service Committee, 1915–1919', *Quaker History* (*QH*), 69/1 (Spring 1980), 3–22.

of Friends—evangelical, conservative, liberal—and the ways in which these groups delineated serious, and at times even bitter, differences, intellectual and theological as well as social and economic. In this regard, certain names and ideas appeared with increasing regularity, all associated with what certain historians of Quakerism were calling a Quaker renewal or renaissance. According to its partisans, this renaissance of Quakerism combined freshly evolving liberal theology and progressive social activism with a new-found knowledge of and attachment to traditional Quaker beliefs which had been largely discarded by the evangelicals who dominated the Society of Friends throughout most of the nineteenth century, especially the concept of the Inward Light of Christ. Although, in the beginning, I had little understanding of the issues involved, it did seem to me that the liberal agents of Quaker renewal were fresh, vital, and compassionate while their evangelical rivals appeared stodgy, desiccated, and rigid. In any case, I decided that my focus would be the Quaker Renaissance and that my survey of its influence should begin at about 1890 when, as it seemed to me, the ideological struggle for control of the Society had gotten underway. Wrong again, as time would tell.

Having selected a theme, I soon discovered a hero in the person of John Wilhelm Rowntree (1868–1905). A ubiquitous presence in Quaker circles during the 1890s and early twentieth century, J. W. Rowntree was handsome, fun-loving, energetic, intellectually acute, and remarkably influential for one so young; he was perhaps doubly attractive because he died too soon and at the height of his influence, leaving an inspiring if unfulfilled vision for his contemporaries to realize. With the generous support of my University and Haverford College, I set out to elucidate the Quaker Renaissance and thereby to provide answers to relevant questions about the nature and importance of twentieth-century British Friends. In the course of my year as T. Wister Brown Fellow at Haverford, I wrote an essay on John Wilhelm Rowntree's sense of the importance of comprehending the Quaker past in order that Friends might fully grasp their future possibilities.[8] Through the good offices of Mary Hoxie Jones, daughter of John Wilhelm's great friend and fellow renewer, Rufus M. Jones, this paper was placed

[8] 'History and the Quaker Renaissance: the Vision of John Wilhelm Rowntree', *JFHS*, 55/1–2 (1986), 35–56.

into the hands of Jean Rowntree, John Wilhelm's surviving daughter, and she passed it along to Roger Cowan Wilson, a former Clerk of London Yearly Meeting. After reading my essay, Roger asked if we might meet for a talk the next time I was in England. Our talk took place the following summer in the garden of the Penn Club in London. For me, at least, that meeting changed everything.

Roger Wilson told me that he had maintained an enduring interest in the meaning and importance of Quakerism's metamorphosis from a tiny, self-isolated body of peculiar people in the early nineteenth century into a spiritually-driven association of activists defined by a strong social commitment and enduring pacifist ethic. With this in mind, he had long thought about the possibility of undertaking a study of this transformation, but his own work as an educator and as a leader in the Society had caused him to defer launching the project until recently when, after making a beginning, he realized that, nearing 80, he had neither time nor energy to complete the task.[9] 'Somebody has to do it', he said, 'and I think you're the man.' When I protested that the study he seemed to have in mind might be better done by a Quaker, he replied that insofar as he was concerned, a history of the evolution of modern British Quakerism could best be done by a non-Friend unburdened by any institutional or ideological baggage.

Deeply flattered if still uncertain, I succumbed to Roger Wilson's wiles and in so doing began the process of learning the great deal he could teach me. Ever a font of wisdom, he was also the soul of generosity. During the following summer Roger personally arranged a series of interviews with mainly elderly Friends who might have personal insight into the development of their Society in the early twentieth century. He was also decisive in persuading me that a proper study of the changes in Quakerism that culminated in its struggle against the Great War and the British State should not begin in the 1890s when the contest for control of the spiritual direction of London Yearly Meeting reached its climax. Rather, he said, it ought to commence much earlier, in the 1860s, during that crucial time when the majority of Quakers had been convinced by their evangelical brethren that changes in the world

---

[9] See 'Friends in the Nineteenth Century', *FQ*, 23/8 (October 1984), 353–63, 405.

as well as in their own perception of how God wished to be worshipped required that their religious Society break out of its spiritual isolation and begin moving toward the mainstream of evangelical Protestant Christianity. It was at this moment of apparent triumph that the evangelical leadership of British Quakerism was peremptorily challenged by an group of mainly young men espousing modern ideas and a liberal theology.

That critical crossroads was encountered about 1860, a round and balanced point from which to set forth. The story that follows begins as a tale of conflict, a paradoxical circumstance, perhaps, for one of the few Christian churches which has officially sustained its pacifist doctrine. But, in fact, British Quakerism was transformed as a result of a long and intense ideological and theological struggle involving some of the fundamental questions which had troubled Christians from the days of Paul and Augustine. When, in the early nineteenth century, weighty Friends began to absorb and embrace the central doctrines of the evangelical revival—salvation based upon the necessary belief in Christ's redeeming sacrifice and strictly guided by a literal interpretation of Scripture—they had, perforce, to de-emphasize or even discard many of the peculiar beliefs and practices inherited from early Friends, most especially the idea of an Inward Light which appeared to place the individual conscience above scriptural authority.

During the initial decades of the nineteenth century, evangelical Quakers were forced to struggle for ascendancy within their religious Society against the stubborn resistance of traditionalist Friends who might more accurately be called radical than conservative. The contest, which had personal as well as theological dimensions, was difficult, at times even agonizing. Still, evangelicals might take comfort in the knowledge that the views they promulgated were considered both sound and fashionable within the broad mainstream of non-conformist Protestantism. Thus, evangelical Quakers could feel sure of their doctrinal soundness as well as their modernity. By the time evangelical Friends had achieved effective control of the machinery of London Yearly Meeting, the views they espoused had come under serious attack from the combined, if not precisely allied, forces of religious liberalism and godless scientism. Thereafter, the aggressive mode evangelical Friends had maintained for nearly half a century rapidly became defensive and those who had so recently promoted

significant changes within the Quaker canon became the
determined enemies of innovation and modernism, seeking to
prevent dangerous new ideas from penetrating the walls of their
meeting houses.

The ensuing struggle followed familiar lines. In the early stages,
young, hot-blooded but outnumbered and ill-organized rebels
were decisively repelled. But the initial triumph of orthodoxy
and good order was neither complete nor without its Pyrrhic
qualities. Dissent continued to flourish and, in time, was marked
by both a swelling alienation among the younger generation and
the creeping defection of evangelical moderates. There was,
furthermore, a growing perception of organizational high-
handedness and intellectual complacency among the evangelical
leadership of Yearly Meeting. All of this would seem to point to
the inevitability of a liberal/modernist victory, but evangelical
Friends were not without virtues or resources. They continued
the struggle, driven by the spectre of a religious Society, bereft of
scriptural guidance and sound doctrine, alternatively drifting without compass or storm-tossed by successive and destructive waves of
modern thought, rooted in nothing. Indeed, had it not been for
the intellectual acuity, leadership ability, and spiritual depth of
liberal/modernist Friends, the evangelicals might have prevailed
as did their cousins in the American Midwest and South. Still, by
the beginning of the twentieth century the contest for control of
London Yearly Meeting became increasingly uneven and, in a
sense, even unfair. Quaker liberals marched to the sound of a
drum beating time for progress throughout the Western world.
They were not only, in the main, young, earnest and energetic;
they were *au courant* as well. Beside them, evangelicals, however
reasonable their fears and arguments, invariably looked old, tired,
and backward. So, in the years of the Quaker Renaissance between
1890 and 1914, liberal Quakers succeeded in their quest to mod-
ernize and invigorate London Yearly Meeting. Their victory was
decisive although not unconditional since a goodly number of
British Friends remained staunchly evangelical well into the twentieth century. But the mould of twentieth-century British Quakerism was shaped by men and women who led the parade toward
modernity of thought and spirit. Liberal theology returned the
Inward Light to its central position in the pantheon of Quaker
beliefs and liberal thought opened the way to the sort of social and

political activism that would have been unthinkable for nineteenth-century Friends.

The most important product of the Quaker Renaissance was the revitalization of the Society's peace testimony. The young men and women who so ardently resisted the Great War and the imposition of conscription did not suddenly and conveniently discover Quaker pacifism once the war began; the principles they lived out and suffered for had been an integral part of their moral and spiritual training during the Edwardian years. For them the Great War was an opportunity to demonstrate to the world the dimensions and depth of their Quaker faith as means of nourishing life rather than, as was the case of nearly every other religious community, simply ministering to death.

Quaker resistance to the Great War not only caused the public perception of Quakerism to be inexorably linked to pacifism rather than, as in the past, to various other peculiarities of belief and practice, it also raised the stature of the Society of Friends in the post-war world to a higher plane than it had ever previously occupied. One of the remarkable features of the post-war period was the fact that, almost as soon as the guns fell silent, this minuscule religious community, despite their proscribed condition as supposedly unpatriotic pariah, began to manifest a remarkable moral influence. One prominent former British Liberal politician called Quakers the 'religious body which came through the war least tainted' and a German journalist asserted that British Friends, 'who really regard religious freedom seriously', stood highest among those who still professed to be Christians.[10]

By 1920 when the British Society of Friends hosted Quakerism's first world-wide conference, London Yearly Meeting had, to borrow Yeat's contemporaneous phase, changed utterly from the time six decades earlier when Friends first began to compromise with the modern world. The wings of both conservative and evangelical factions had been clipped by a soaring liberal theology that would remain dominant throughout the remainder of the twentieth century. Quakerism's inward-looking propensities had been replaced by a devotion to social activism; its allegiance to laissez-faire

[10] Charles Masterman to Lucy Masterman, quoted in L. Masterman, *C. F. G. Masterman, A Biography* (London 1939), 290 and Alfon Paquet, 'The Quakers', pamphlet reprinted from *Frankfurter Zeitung*, 12.

capitalism and the Liberal Party had been shaken to the roots; its peace testimony had become a badge of identity rather than vague historical baggage; finally, some of its most devoted followers had come to believe, as George Fox and early Friends had believed, that theirs was truly a Prophet Society which might lead in the struggle to bring about the Kingdom of God on earth.

The years traversed in course of this study are some of the most momentous in the history of British Quakerism. They began with the struggle to determine the nature of authentic George Fox Quakerism or even, in the case of some Victorian evangelical Friends, to decide if George Fox was an authentic Quaker; they ended with a ringing authentication of George Fox's radical message through the witness of a small body of Friends who refused to surrender conscience to Caesar. During the intervening years, a great many things occurred within the Society of Friends and between Quakers and the rest of the world upon which this work is chiefly silent. The boarding and day schools which formed a private educational system of which Friends were justly proud are mentioned mainly in passing.[11] This is because of my sense that the lessons brought to action by movers and shakers of the Society were, by and large, not learned in notoriously cautious Quaker schools but in the larger world of ideas Quaker academies were reluctant to embrace. Similarly, little attention is given to the Quakers who successfully pursued political careers in the British Parliament. These men certainly gave prestige to the Society and were on hand when necessary to look to its special interests, but their influence, as politicians and as Friends, on major developments within the Society seems marginal at best. Finally, there is the question of the role of businessmen in the evolution of Quaker ideas and attitudes. Alliances between and among Quaker families were, most assuredly, vital to the success of numerous Quaker enterprises. Wealthy Friends often donated generously to Quaker religious and charitable activities and many Quaker entrepreneurs retired from business in early middle age to devote themselves to the well-being and advancement of their religious Society. Still, any serious attempt to evaluate the influence of Quaker religious

---

[11] Standard studies on Quaker schools are W. A. Campbell Stewart, _Quakers and Education_ (London 1953) and John Reader, _Of Schools and Schoolmasters: Some Thought on the Quaker Contribution to Education_ (London 1979).

principles on Quaker business practices would require a separate and different sort of book.[12] I can only hope that, for the reader, the book that follows will suffice.

[12] A recent study which emphases the importance of business connections in the developments of eighteenth and nineteenth-century Quakerism is James Walvin, *The Quakers: Money & Morals* (London 1997). But see the critical review of Walvin by Michael Rowlinson in *Historical Studies in Industrial Relations*, 6 (Autumn 1998), 163–198. Rowlinson's own work on the employment practices of Quaker businessmen is eagerly awaited.

I

The Condition of Friends

WHITHER THE LIGHT? ORIGINS AND DIVERGENCES

I preached from the expression 'the heart of man is deceitful above all things and desperately wicked' [Jeremiah 17:9] setting before the people our loss thro' the fall, the mission of Jesus Christ, the object of power of the gospel, inviting them to lay hold of the hope set before us—that submitting to the operations of the Holy Spirit they might be brought for themselves availing to behold the Lamb of God who took away the Sins of the world...

Caleb Rickman Kemp (1836–1908)

Friend Caleb Kemp's ministry in September 1860 echoed his vision of the Quaker faith, set out earlier that same year, and incorporating 'what I understand to be the Gospel, i.e., the power of God unto Salvation to every one who believeth...'

I believe that man, through the fall of our first parents, is naturally prone to evil, born into the world sinful & lost...salvation & redemption are offered him through Jesus Christ—as he yields to these touches of Heavenly Love his heart is contrited, baptised, humbled, broken before his God...on his repentance for sin & faith...in the Coming, Sufferings, death, Resurrection & Ascension...of Christ Jesus...as he experiences of this faith which...may be described as the substance of things hoped for...he is 'justified'—well does he know that without faith it is impossible to please God, also that without holiness no man shall see the Lord.[1]

---

[1] Caleb R. Kemp, 'Journals, 1853–1908', six manuscript volumes, 7 June 1860 (hereinafter C. R. K., 'Journals', with volume and date), Library of the Society of Friends (LSF), London.

Kemp's confession of faith embodied the central doctrines of mid-Victorian evangelical Protestantism: a vital religion of the heart whereby depraved humanity, weighed down by original sin, is offered the possibility of salvation through Christ's atoning sacrifice on the Cross. Only unyielding faith in that Atonement could justify and sanctify the sinful human soul; the believer's attachment to the literal truth of the Scriptures was the test of the soundness of his faith.[2] At the same time, Kemp defined himself as 'a Quaker to the back bone' and his life and thought, mirrored in the extensive 'Journals' he kept, give ample demonstration of the sincerity of his convictions. Furthermore, the principles Kemp professed coincided with those of the dominant leadership element among British Quakers in 1860. He himself was scarcely more than a callow youth when his local monthly meeting recognized his special gifts by recording him as a minister,[3] and, in honoured old age, he would preside as Clerk of London Yearly Meeting for most of a decade (1890–98). For all of this, a sizeable minority of Kemp's fellow Quakers, calling themselves 'old-fashioned' Friends, would have argued that his convictions contained little that was distinctively Quaker. Indeed, conservative Friends would, no doubt, have aligned Kemp with those self-appointed 'leaders of the people' whom they believed to be bent on so redesigning Quakerism as to make it 'unworthy to retain the honoured designation—the Society of Friends'.[4]

The authenticity of his Quaker principles aside, Caleb Kemp, pious and earnest to a fault, recognized in 1860 that his beloved Religious Society was at a critical crossroads. With every fibre of his being, he was uniting with other evangelical Friends in the effort to lead British Quakerism, alarmingly diminished in numbers and stature,[5] down a path that would eventually intersect with the

---

[2] For the general topic of the impact of evangelical Protestantism on the middle and upper classes in early nineteenth-century British society see Boyd Hilton's brilliant study, *The Age of Atonement: The Influence of Evangelicalism on Social and Economic Thought, 1785–1865* (Oxford 1988).

[3] Because of early Friends' devotion to spiritual equality, Quakers rejected the idea of a separate, trained, and privileged clergy. Still, the special gift of vocal ministry was always recognized and, from the early eighteenth century, inspired preachers, both male and female, were acknowledged and 'recorded' by their monthly meetings, a practice continued until 1924.

[4] William Irwin, *Brief Remarks On the Past and Present Condition of the Society of Friends* (Manchester 1867), pp. v–vii.

[5] A total of 14,016 Quakers attended morning meeting on Census Sunday in 1851; ten years later, according to the Society's own 'Tabular Statement', there were a total of 13,859

high road of Victorian Protestantism. Kemp and his allies were convinced that only by incorporating the evangelical principles they had embraced could the Society of Friends be extricated from the spiritual torpor and social isolation into which it had drifted and, thus, reclaimed as a vital and vibrant community of believers. Still, the route evangelical Friends were determined to follow was strewn with obstacles and pitfalls. Conservative Quakers believed that adherence to an evangelical creed would inexorably force them to abandon many of the traditional practices and tenets they believed were fundamental to maintaining Quakerism as a separate Christian communion.

Why did Kemp and his go-ahead evangelical associates believe that Quakerism had strayed so far down the path toward spiritual desolation that only a strong jolt of biblically-based evangelical Christianity could restore its spiritual vitality? What were the Quaker beliefs and practices, so cherished by traditional Friends, that evangelicals believed must be set aside as irrelevant or even dangerous to the salvation of Quaker souls?

To begin, conservative Friends in 1860 believed that they continued to practice authentic Quakerism. Furthermore, they were convinced that their faith, as set out by George Fox (1624–91) and reiterated (evangelical critics might say distorted) by Robert Barclay (1648–90), the most systematic early Quaker theologian, was a genuine revival of primitive Christianity. In the early 1640s Fox had abandoned the Puritanism of his youth and set out as an itinerant preacher 'to turn people from darkness to the light that they might receive Christ Jesus'.[6] In what can only be called a mystical vision, Fox perceived that not only was Christ alone able to speak to the human condition but that through the infinite love of God, Christ might also speak directly to every believer by way of an Inward Voice or Light without the intervention of any human minister or sacred book. In effect, Christ himself was come to teach his people and the Light of Christ gave all human beings the capacity to discern their sinful condition (darkness) and by surrendering to openings or 'leadings' from the Light, they might 'come into the state of Adam which he was in before he

members in London Yearly Meeting, cited by Elizabeth Isichei, *Victorian Quakers* (Oxford 1970), 112–13. Alan D. Gilbert, *Religion and Society in Industrial England: Church, Chapel and Social Change, 1790–1914* (London 1974) puts the number at 13,384.

   [6] *Journal of George Fox*, ed. John Nickalls (London 1952), 34.

fell'.[7] Matters of dogma which inspired or divided other Christians—the relationship of the historical Jesus to the divine Christ, biblical infallibility, clerical authority, rituals, etc.—were of little import to Fox and he denounced 'those temples, tithes, priests and rudiments of the world' which had led the people away from primitive Christianity. For him and most early Friends, it was enough to say that the Light would lead souls away from sin and into righteousness. Through the aggressive evangelism of Fox and other 'first publishers of the Truth', a considerable band of adherents was gathered.[8]

When Fox taught that every human person had access to God's saving gift of Light, it followed that all souls, male and female, rich and poor, lord and labourer, King and commoner, were equal before God and, thus, should be before men. As a result, these Children of the Light, as they first called themselves, embraced a sweeping brand of egalitarianism. They refused to doff their hats to any man or woman of whatever worldly station; they declined to swear oaths before earthly judges; they addressed persons of all ranks as 'thee' or 'thou', a form commonly used in the seventeenth century when speaking to children or inferiors[9] Early Quakers considered no hallowed ground, no day of the week, no title of honour, no feast or season superior to any other. For them, neither 'steeple house' nor 'hireling priest' was necessary for a gathered meeting of the faithful to seek and find the redeeming Word.

This was a radical business, even in the tumultuous decades of the 1640s and 1650s, and certainly after the Restoration of the monarchy. For their eccentric beliefs and practices, the first two generations of Quakers were widely hated and severely persecuted, by both ecclesiastical and secular authorities. Two centuries later mid-Victorian conservative Friends still believed they faithfully practised 'those sound views of Christian truth handed down to us by our persecuted or martyred predecessors...'[10] They also believed that the most efficacious means through which the faithful might receive illumination from the Light was to wait in silent

---

[7] Ibid. 27.

[8] Ibid. 109. Quaker membership in 1680 has been estimated at 60,000. See John Punshon, *Portrait in Grey* (London 1984), 190.

[9] Hugh Barbour and J. William Frost *The Quakers* (New York 1988), 41 note that seventeenth-century gentlemen said thee 'only to God, lovers, children and servants'.

[10] Irwin, *Brief Remarks*, pp. vi–vii.

meeting wherein gathered believers might share saving revelations. For them, conviction of sin came, not primarily through outward means such as the preaching of ministers or the written words of Scripture but through *inward* 'openings from the Light'. They did not deny the efficacy of the Bible as an outward guide to right living, but the saving radiance of inward leadings from the Light was superior to Scripture in teaching righteousness and holiness. On the other hand, these conservatives did not believe that mere recognition of one's sins resulted in extinguishing the spiritual damage done by the sinner. The process of sanctification, or freeing oneself from the consequences of sin, was a life-long struggle, and justification, becoming free from the guilt of sin and reconciled with God, was possible only for the sanctified.

If conservative Friends did, as they claimed, still practice Quakerism as it was taught and practiced by Fox and his early followers, how did they come to be an embattled minority within their own religious Society? This is a long story which, here, must be briefly told.

In the face of serious adversity, the spiritual inspiration and organizational skill of George Fox helped to secure the survival of the Society of Friends in its earliest days. After the Glorious Revolution and the passage of the Toleration Act (1689), the persecution of Quakers faded to mild disability, and public animosity dwindled to curiosity or indifference. With the death of George Fox in 1691, Quakerism gradually lost touch with its radical roots. In a peculiar combination of relief and drift, Quakers, as one historian put it, 'like a rowing crew after a fierce race, rested on their oars'.[11] In marked contrast to the vigorous and successful evangelizing activities of early Quakers, eighteenth-century British Friends largely ceased to proselytize, drawing inward and establishing a social exclusivity which effectively discouraged converts to the fold. In their subsequent quest for simplicity Friends rejected music, dancing, and other forms of public amusement, while retaining both the plain speech and arcane dress of their forebears. This drawing away from the larger society of non-believers has caused the eighteenth century to be dubbed as Quakerism's 'quiet-

---

[11] John Wilhelm Rowntree (J. W. R.), 'The Rise of Quakerism in Yorkshire', in *John Wilhelm Rowntree: Essays and Addresses*, ed. Joshua Rowntree (London 1906), 64–5.

ist' era.[12] Although Friends of that period never used this expression to define themselves, there seems to have been an increasing propensity among them to deprecate 'dependency on words', leading to a marked decline in the sort of spontaneous, emotional ministry which had characterized early Quaker meetings. In time, many meetings for worship became distinguished by long periods of silent waiting upon the Light, only occasionally broken by the peculiar sing-song discourses of ministers who always took care to empty their minds of worldly thoughts and distractions before daring to speak. Indeed, the idea of preparing one's remarks rather than waiting upon unrehearsed 'gifts of the spirit' was anathema.[13] To ensure that ministers remained properly submissive to leadings from the Light, a system of elders and overseers was devised to guide or censure what, given the awesome sense of responsibility felt by those who dared to speak at meeting, became a diminishing corps of preaching ministers. In this regard, the emphasis of the Yearly Meeting *Epistle* of 1740, issued for the guidance of subordinate meetings, is clear:

The immediate teaching of the Holy Spirit [the Light] is the foundation of all gospel worship and ministry; and those who depend entirely thereon shall not be disappointed through the failure or the absence of instrumental means. Wherefore, we beseech you, wait in silence with reverence and singleness of heart, in all your meetings, that you may witness the ... refreshing influence of the Holy Spirit by which you will be strengthened in the inward man ...[14]

So, in the course of a few generations, Quakers turned from an 'apostolic vision of the Kingdom of God into the prose of Quietism and Commerce',[15] passing from a Prophet Society seeking to establish God's Kingdom on earth to a peculiar people abjuring earthly pleasures in their quest for the Kingdom of Heaven.

---

[12] The universality of this spiritual withdrawal has been challenged by Nicholas Morgan, *Lancaster Friends and the Establishment, 1660–1730* (Halifax 1993), Chap. 7 and *passim*. Also see H. Larry Ingle, 'The Future of Quaker History', *JFHS*, 58/1 (1997), 5–6, 10.

[13] For critical discussions of the nature of Quaker quietist ministry see John S. Rowntree, *Quakerism Past and Present*, (London 1859), 66, 103–4 and Robert Barclay, *The Inner Life of the Religious Societies of the Commonwealth* (London 1879), 509–14.

[14] *Epistle*, 1740 quoted by John Kitching, 'On the Rise and First Principles of the Society of Friends', *TF* (April 1859), 61.

[15] [John Wilhelm Rowntree], 'The Outlook', *The Present Day Papers* (*PDP*), II, (1899), 9.

Rejecting any spiritual expression which lay outside their unique if narrow conception of the true Christian way, some conservative Friends might be justly accused of making the peculiarities they lived by central manifestations of their faith.

Quietism dominated Quakerism for nearly a hundred years, but by the beginning of the nineteenth century a new and vital spiritual vision, inspired by the Evangelical Revival, at last began to break through the Quaker 'hedge' that had been constructed during the quietist period. By 1860 this vital evangelical spirit was still moving Friends like Caleb Kemp and his allies in their quest to rejuvenate and reform British Quakerism. To fully grasp the issues and interests involved in the long-standing struggle of evangelical Friends to rescue their Society from its somnolent recent past and deliver it to a vigorous future, a discussion of major developments during the first half of the nineteenth century is in order.

THE BATTLE JOINED

Thomas Clarkson's *Portraiture of the Society of Friends* (1806) at one point described his Quaker contemporaries as a peculiar people remarkably unaffected by the whirling political, social, and intellectual currents of a tempestuous time.[16] In this regard, Clarkson's picture was incomplete and misleading for there were serious tensions among early nineteenth-century Quakers which reflected the drawing of more thoughtful and active members towards the opposing attractions of Enlightenment rationalism and the Evangelical Revival. The latter influences had a somewhat delayed arrival among Friends, although the appearance of evangelical influence in London Yearly Meeting was sufficiently timely to raise the alarm against agents of rationalism, scepticism, and deism who, in the view of some anxious Friends, seemed to be making inroads into their Religious Society.

As it transpired, the bearers of these unsound sentiments sprang forth from two geographical centres of revolutionary thought and action, Ireland and America. The first of these was Abraham Shackleton (1752–1818) who provoked a small but bitter schism

---

[16] Thomas Clarkson, *Portraiture of the Society of Friends*, 3 vols. (London 1806), cited by Edward Grubb, 'The Evangelical Movement and Its Impact on the Society of Friends', *FQE*, Jan. 1924, 8.

in Dublin Yearly Meeting in the late 1790s by questioning the accuracy of sections in the Old Testament which asserted that God had commanded the Hebrews to attack and slaughter their neighbours. Reason, Shackleton said, would not support the omnipresence of a Divine Being who in one era ordered the massacre of innocents and in another commanded his followers to turn the other cheek. Shackleton believed that these scriptural passages must be misguided or mistaken and that adherence to them by Friends was a manifestation of their abandoning Inner Truth and embracing corrupting outward symbols. Concerns raised by Shackleton's disturbing rationalist revolt obviously influenced the decision by leaders of London Yearly Meeting in 1801 not to endorse the travelling ministry of a popular American minister, Hannah Barnard. Barnard seemed to British Friends not only to support Shackleton's Old Testament doubts, but even to call into question parts of the Christian Gospels relating to the Virgin Birth and the miracles of Jesus, defending her position as based upon 'leadings from the Light'. Later, Barnard's censure and eventual disownment by New York Yearly Meeting threw into stark relief the question of biblical authority as against individual openings from the Light.[17]

The first evangelically-inspired theological salvos to be fired against the rationalism and incipient deism of thinkers like Shackleton and Barnard were let off by Henry Tuke in *The Faith of the People called Quakers* . . . (1801) and *Principles of Religion as professed by the* . . . *Quakers* (1805). These works, particularly the latter which ran to twelve editions, were influential in disseminating among Friends the doctrine of the absolute infallibility and unqualified authority of Scripture. The degree to which this emphasis deviated from the beliefs and practices of early Quakers became and remained the basis for a long-standing debate.[18] Clearly, however,

---

[17] The accusations against and eventual disownment of Hannah Barnard are discussed in *BF*, October 1902, 257–60 and David Maxey, 'New Light on Hannah Barnard, A Quaker "Heretic"', *QH* Fall, 1989, 61–86. A recent discussion of Abraham Shackleton's case is Mollie Grubb, 'Abraham Shackleton and the Irish Separation of 1797–1803', *JFHS*, 56/4 (1993), 262–71. Also see *BF*, December 1902, 313 and Rufus M. Jones, *The Later Periods of Quakerism*, 2 vols. (London 1921), i, 293–8.

[18] Rufus Jones in *Later Periods* maintains that Tuke's interpretations 'entirely altered' the original perspective of Quakerism and raised 'evangelical doctrines into unprecedented prominence', i, 285–6. Edward Grubb, 'Evangelical Movement', 21, agrees that Tuke's books 'are important landmarks showing the direction in which the Society was moving'.

the works of Henry Tuke as well as John Bevan's *A Defence of the Christian Doctrines of the Society of Friends against the charge of Socinianism* (1805), which refuted Hannah Barnard point by point, brought Quakerism into touch with the main currents of thought in the Age of Atonement early in the nineteenth century. It was during the succeeding generation, in the life and work of Joseph John Gurney (1788–1847), the first writer since Robert Barclay to attempt a comprehensive exposition of the Quaker faith, that evangelical thought among Friends came into full flower.

J. J. Gurney was born into a large and prosperous merchant-banker family, widely accounted to be 'gay' Quakers. For Friends, that adjective retained its original English meaning, signifying members who were more citizens of the world than solemnly withdrawn from it. In their magnificent Norfolk home, Earlham Hall, the Gurneys sang and danced and rode to hounds, while dressed in the latest London fashions. They were illustrative of John Punshon's belief that many eighteenth-century Friends, particularly if they were wealthy, had no compunctions about ignoring Quaker oddities while feeling perfectly comfortable within their self-defined boundaries of Quaker theology and culture.[19]

The second youngest of twelve Gurneys (his older sister was the prison reformer Elizabeth Fry), Joseph John had an agile mind, finely honed under the guidance of a sound and conscientious but unQuakerly private tutor at Oxford. Even before the death of his father in 1809, Gurney's magnetic personality had attracted a number of important Anglican evangelicals, including Edward Edwards, Henry Venn and especially Charles Simeon, who brought their increasingly serious young charge solidly into the evangelical camp.[20] Also important was Gurney's friendship with the abolitionist William Wilberforce which sharpened his social awareness and expanded his range of philanthropic activities to include the campaign against the slave trade. But while he received his theological underpinnings from these prominent churchmen,

Mollie Grubb, 'The Beacon Separation', *JFHS*, 55/6 (1988), 190 has asserted that Tuke differed from Barclay's *Apology* only in his detailed description of the eternal damnation of sinners and his insistence upon the unimpeachable authority of Scripture as against Barclay's position that the Bible was not the 'fountain' of Divine knowledge but only the declaration of the fountain and, therefore, secondary to the Light.

[19] Punshon, *Portrait in Grey*, 148, 151, 157.

[20] For Simeon, see Hilton, *Age of Atonement*, 286–378, *passim*.

his spiritual home remained within the known and beloved circle of Friends. Recognized as a minister before he was thirty, Gurney's special 'fire and vision' evangelism made him the most popular and influential preacher among Quakers on both sides of the Atlantic. Beginning in the mid-1820s, he published a series of books and tracts which provided the Society of Friends with what Rufus Jones later called 'a complete system of evangelical theology'.[21]

Gurney, indeed, seemed to have thoroughly embodied the spirit of the Age of Atonement. Viewing humanity after the Fall of Adam—ruined, depraved and dominated by sin—Gurney could find hope only in the atoning blood sacrifice of Jesus by which human kind, incapable of rising from its fallen state through any pitiful personal effort, was justified by the mercy and love of God. This was, of course, the standard Augustinian line reaching into the nineteenth century via Calvin as modified by Wesley and finally by moderate evangelicals of the Clapham Sect who had such a strong personal influence on Gurney.

So far so good for the ordinary slacking Protestant in need of honest fear and trembling. But Gurney's critics, both during and after his lifetime, believed that his preaching and teaching set the original principles of George Fox and his associates, as confirmed and systematized by Robert Barclay, on their head. For early Friends the Light was the *means* to justification through recognition of sin, whereupon the faithful were sanctified as they grew in spiritual life and power by following its leadings. By Gurney's spiritual calculus, said his detractors, the Inward Light was reduced to a non-essential adjunct, another expression for the Holy Spirit's sanctification of those who maintained an unremitting faith in the Atonement, a faith confirmed by strict adherence to the letter of Holy Scripture.[22]

Gurney's critics, while praising his sincerity of purpose and recognizing his vital contribution to conveying the Society of Friends beyond the limitations of quietism, complained that he 'never really understood what the early Friends had discovered'. By changing the basis for Quaker religious authority from the inward

---

[21] Jones, *Later Periods*, 1, 501–2.

[22] For insightful comments on Gurney's version of the Inward Light, see Thomas Hamm, 'The problem of the Inner Light in Nineteenth Century Quakerism', in *The Lamb's War: Quaker Essays to Honor Hugh Barbour*, eds. Michael L. Birkel and John W. Neurman ([Richmand] 1992), 110–12.

revelation of the Light to the outward creed of biblical literalism, he 'recalled the Society from the Quakerism of Fox and his friends to the position of their Puritan opponents'. Whether or not this depiction was entirely accurate, Joseph John Gurney's vision of Quakerism is still adhered to by more than half of those who call themselves Friends, although, ironically, few of these live in Gurney's native land.[23]

While J. J. Gurney was the most popular and influential prophet of the evangelical message that would, during the 1820s and 1830s, begin to sweep Anglo-American Quakerism toward the Protestant mainstream, he was by no means alone. There was a regular transatlantic exchange of travelling evangelical ministers 'liberated' by their own meetings for missions of religious concern. Their ministry was generally aimed at inducing the sort of individual conversion experience so essential to the evangelical creed. This was accomplished by vigorous preaching based upon biblical texts. Such an approach, of course, contrasted dramatically with the quietist meeting for worship which, when not completely silent, demanded a ministry that was entirely unpremeditated. The incongruity of both style and spirit between these two versions of Quaker ministry planted the seeds of suspicion and distrust that would in time bear bitter fruit.

In 1820 William Forster (1784–1854), Gurney's close friend on a travelling mission in America, expressed his anxiety about Friends in Long Island who seemed to be infected with many of the same notions that had influenced Abraham Shackleton and his followers.[24] The leader of these New York Friends was Elias Hicks (1748–1830), whose name would soon become synonymous with the largest and most rancorous 'Separation' in Quaker history, an upheaval that would also have profound effects on the development of nineteenth-century British Quakerism.

William Forster was not alone in expressing concern about the growing and, as he saw it, subversive influence of Elias Hicks. Soon after the Hannah Barnard affair, the American Quaker Stephen Grellet (1773–1852), a transplanted Frenchman and former freethinker fully aware of the dangers of rationalism and deism, had warned that Hicks was spreading doctrines 'repugnant to the

---

[23] Quotations are from Grubb, 'Evangelical Movement', 32.

[24] Benjamin Seebohm (ed.), *Memoirs of William Forster* (London 1865), I, 267. Also see Grubb, 'Evangelical Movement', 24–5.

Christian faith, [and] tending to lessen the authority of the Holy Scriptures....'[25]

As the evangelical stream in America became a torrent during the first two decades of the nineteenth century, British visitors continued to voice their fears about Hicks. Recent historians of the Hicksite Separation have generally made the point that differences among American Friends were seriously exacerbated by travelling British ministers who saw in Hicks's preaching a growing tendency towards Unitarianism, pantheism, and even 'the spirit of AntiChrist'.[26] One English visitor, Anna Braithwaite (1789–1859), published a tract accusing Hicks of denying the truth of the Scriptures, the Virgin Birth, the Atonement, and other essential Christian doctrines. For his part, Hicks asserted that he was defending traditional Quaker beliefs—the Inward Light, silent worship and the rejection of outward sacraments—from an insidious onslaught of evangelical innovation.[27]

The obvious doctrinal point of collision between Hicksites and those who assumed the mantle of a new Quaker orthodoxy was the seat of ultimate religious authority. Did this reside in the letter of Scripture or the inspiration of the Light? Most of the American Friends who followed Hicks into exile probably agreed that evangelical dependence on scriptural authority threatened the primacy of the Inward Light, but many did not share Hicks' extreme mysticism or his apparent depreciation of the Scriptures as a 'dead letter'.[28] Indeed, British Friends seemed to have little sense of the degree to which the Hicksite Separation was not only a doctrinal dispute but also a political and social revolt against the narrow oligarchies who controlled most American Yearly Meetings. There was, in fact, a fairly wide variety of opinions among the

---

[25] Benjamin Seebohm, (ed.), *Memoirs of the Life and Gospel Labours of Stephen Grellet* (London 1860), 1, 142.

[26] This point is stressed by H. Larry Ingle, *Quakers in Conflict: The Hicksite Reformation* (Knoxville 1986), 32–7 in a staunchly pro-Hicksite account. Also see Edwin B. Bronner, 'The Other Branch': London Yearly Meeting and the Hicksites, 1827–1912 (London 1975), 5–7.

[27] Barclay, *Inner Life*, 557–60; J. S. Rowntree, *Quakerism*, 131; Bronner, *Other Branch*, 5–7; and Grubb, 'Evangelical Movement', 22–4.

[28] Probably the most significant actual division between Orthodox and Hicksite Friends was the Orthodox insistence that belief in the propitiatory doctrine of the Atonement was a necessary precondition to availability of the Holy Spirit in the soul; Hicksites believed that such a view transformed and distorted the spiritual authority of the Light to an outward 'head-matter', i.e., the necessity of accepting a particular interpretation of the Bible in order to be saved. See Barclay, *Inner Life*, 564–6 and Punshon, *Portrait in Grey*, 174–5.

breakaway elements, but the generally one-sided versions of the struggle most British Friends received deepened their anxieties about the pernicious effects of Hicks's teaching.[29] Indeed, Hicksism, although representing as many as 60,000 American Quakers, became a sort of spiritual bogey, embodying all that was deceitful, pestilent, and 'unsound'. When various Hicksite Meetings attempted to establish communications with London through *Epistles* emphasizing their devotion to the Trinity, to the Divinity of Jesus Christ, to His essential role in human redemption and to the divine inspiration of Scripture, such messages were peremptorily rejected and connections with Hicksite Meetings were severed for generations.[30]

Within London Yearly Meeting the shock of the Hicksite Separation had the effect of bringing to the fore evangelical arguments concerning the necessity for right belief to challenge the conservative emphasis on right worship. Quietist meetings, addressed sporadically by ministers speaking without notes or other preparations, might become profoundly moving spiritual experiences when the minister stirred the gathered faithful to the depths of their souls. But more often, the Spirit remained inward and the meeting silent, sometimes for weeks on end. This form of ministry, said evangelicals, not only tended to create an atmosphere of somnolent indolence but, more significantly, it also depended on demonstrably unreliable, and possibly dangerous, inward leadings. They held that the divinely inspired message of the Scriptures, preached by ministers of acknowledged insight and ability, was a far more efficacious spiritual guide than the possibly 'delusive' notions of the Light, representing the sort of spiritual anarchy which had been a continuing source of difficulty and confusion for Friends since James Naylor's aberrant behaviour at Bristol in 1656.[31]

---

[29] During the 1860s British Quaker historian Robert Barclay alleged that 'irresponsible' and 'oligarchical' church leadership was the major cause of the division and that 'to a very large extent traditional religion prevailed' among Hicksites. Still, London Yearly Meeting did not restore even partial communication with Hicksites until 1908. See Barclay, *Inner Life*, 561–2, 579 and Punshon, *Portrait in Grey*, 174–75.

[30] For extracts from Hicksite messages to London, see Samuel M. Janney, *History of the Religious Society of Friends* (Philadelphia 1860), 4 vols., IV, 339–40. Also see Bronner, *Other Branch*, 9–10.

[31] For Naylor, see William G. Bittle, *James Naylor, 1618–1660: The Quaker Indicted by Parliament* (York 1986) and Leo Damrosch, *The Sorrows of the Quaker Jesus: James Naylor and the Puritan Crackdown on the Free Spirit* (Cambridge, MA. 1996).

Obviously, the question of authentic ministry and the authority upon which it should be based will always be a problem for a religious body which eschewed the concept of a professional priesthood. William Penn (1644–1718), ever the diplomat and peacemaker, had attempted to resolve this dilemma by citing 'the double and agreeing testimony of God within and Holy Scripture without'. For much of the nineteenth century, however, conservative Friends, by exclusively embracing the first of Penn's testimonies, could turn their meetings 'towards two hours of empty silence'; and evangelicals, by adopting only the second, might steer theirs 'towards the worship of texts'. Conservatives blamed evangelicals for concentrating on 'head matters' and for compromising with things of the world that were not 'in the life'. For their part, Gurneyites accused conservative Friends of becoming so self-absorbed as to lose touch with both basic Christian principles and the idea of corporate worship.[32] They also complained that lack of knowledge of the Scriptures, a product of conservative resistance to all 'outward' things, was the single greatest cause of the 'desolating heresies' which had racked their Society in Ireland and America.[33] During the 1830s, attempts to resolve this lingering question created the possibility that Britain might be visited by similar desolation.

In 1833 the annual *Epistle* or letter of instruction and guidance from London Yearly Meeting asked Friends to 'seek an enlightened sense of the various delusions', an evangelical code-word for the misleading or dangerous interpretations of leadings from the Light. Responding to the tone of this Yearly Meeting, conservative diarist Richard Cockin also perceived dangers, but for him they came in the guise of those who would place the letter of Scriptures above 'our reverent watchful dependence upon...the Holy Spirit'.[34] Cockin doubtless would have agreed with the Friends who had objected to William Boulton's formation of a Quaker Bible-study group in Manchester Meeting because they believed

---

[32] Roger C. Wilson, 'Friends in the Nineteenth Century, *FQ*, 23/8 (Oct. 1984), 353–63', 355 and *Manchester, Manchester, and Manchester Again*, Presidential Address to the Friends' Historical Society, 1989 (London 1990), 7. On this point, also see Doreen Rosman, *Evangelicals and Culture* (London 1984), 211.

[33] J. S. Rowntree, *Quakerism*, 55. Also see Barclay, *Inner Life*, 502–13 *passim*.

[34] Quoted by Wilson, *Manchester*, 12, 14.

such activity was 'calculated to promote the growth of a *branch* rather than the deepening of the root'.[35]

The vehemence of these deep-seated objections to merely studying Scripture justifies Roger Wilson's description of Yearly Meeting in 1834 as sitting in 'confused gloom, hope, anger, self-righteousness, and...spiritual commitment'. Obviously British Friends were on the edge of a 'volcanic explosion' and this was duly set off in January 1835 by the publication of Isaac Crewdson's (1780–1844) little book, *A Beacon to the Society of Friends*.[36]

At one level, Crewdson's tract was a straightforward attack on the seeming Unitarian tendencies of the Hicksites, but its underlying meaning was clearly to connect Hicksism with Robert Barclay's 'central error' in presenting the Inward Light as independent of and superior to Holy Scripture. According to Crewdson, not only the concept of an Inward Light, but nearly all of the phraseology traditionally used by conservative Quaker ministers—'dwelling deep', or 'gathering home to the gift of God in our hearts [in the] absence of all creaturely exertions'—had no biblical authority nor legitimacy in Christian practice.[37]

Isaac Crewdson, formerly a supporter of traditional views, had embraced evangelicalism late in life, and he exuded all the single-minded fervour of the newly converted. He was, most assuredly, a man with a mission: to rescue Quakerism from the dangers of Hicksite scepticism as well as from the snares of stifling quietism and to carry a united and scripturally sound Society into the mainstream of vital evangelical Protestant culture.[38] Crewdson's *Beacon*, however, became not so much a rallying point for the faithful as a barricade to compromise which in the end, despite the Quaker genius for backing and filling, had to be battered down lest it create an insuperable division.

---

[35] Barclay, *Inner Life*, 574.   [36] Wilson, *Manchester*, 17.

[37] For summaries of the *Beacon's* message, see Jones, *Later Periods*, 1, 490–2; Barclay, *Inner Life*, 573–5; and A. Neave Brayshaw, *The Quakers: Their Story and Message* (London 1919; reprinted 1982), 230–32.

[38] Roger Wilson recounts how Crewdson moved by 'something akin to a vision' was able through the sheer force of personality and influence to convince Hardshaw East Monthly Meeting in Manchester to build a local meeting house with a seating capacity (1900) equal to about 10 per cent of the total Quaker population in all of Great Britain. Wilson, '*Manchester*', 18–19.

Shortly after the publication of the *Beacon*, a young Friend wrote to his fiancée describing the scene he had witnessed in Manchester Meeting: 'I never beheld a meeting in such a state. Very many were in tears on both sides of the meeting and it was really a most distressing season.' Such disorder and weeping were occasioned by charges from conservative Friends that Isaac Crewdson, present at the meeting, had 'published a book which contained principles contrary to those of our Society...'[39] When Crewdson's own followers leaped to his defence, neither the Clerk's exhortations nor Crewdson's own plea for calm could prevent an acrimonious upheaval that set the pattern for a short-lived but deeply disturbing rift which briefly threatened to pull British Friends asunder. Many of those who were present at Manchester would probably have supported the young witness's opinion that the differences expressed were not 'sufficient to warrant... a separation between Christians'. But the dispute had a fiery momentum of its own which belied all attempts at mediation.[40]

When London Yearly Meeting gathered in May 1835, the first order of business was to rescue the concept of the Holy Spirit (for obvious reasons moderates avoided the use of Inward Light) from the *Beacon*'s attempt, admitted even by Crewdson's close friend J. J. Gurney, 'to undermine the precious doctrine of the immediate guidance, and government of the Holy Spirit'.[41] To achieve this objective, officers of the Yearly Meeting proposed that, in addition to the regular annual *Epistle*, an 'Epistle of Counsel', which both supported the idea of the immediate guidance of the Holy Spirit and endorsed the writings of early Friends, be approved.[42] At the same time, after long and uneasy consideration of the crisis, Yearly Meeting decided upon the appointment of a Committee to visit Manchester with a view to resolving the escalating row.

This Visiting Committee, incorporating a well-balanced representation of traditional, moderate, and evangelical views, including J. J. Gurney himself, visited Manchester eight times during the following year and a half. While a majority of the Committee were, like Gurney, probably sympathetic toward Crewdson, they

---

[39] Quoted in J. Edmund Clark, ' "The *Beacon*" Letters of James Clark,' *JFHS*, 16/1 (1919), 129–30.
[40] Ibid. 133. Also see Mollie Grubb, 'Beacon Separation', 193.
[41] From J. J. Gurney's unpublished diary, cited by *TF*, 1 Nov. 1870, 257.
[42] See William Irwin, 'Brief remarks', pp. iii–iv and Brayshaw, *The Quakers*, 232.

were disturbed that his assertive, self-assured style and ceaselessly aggressive ministry had created deep resentment within Manchester Meeting, and not just among hide-bound conservatives.[43] In these circumstances, the Committee first asked Crewdson to help ease tensions by withdrawing the *Beacon* from circulation. When he refused to acquiesce, they suspended him from exercise of his ministry. It seemed a harsh penalty, but in reaching this judgement, the Committee attempted to avoid a debate on doctrinal questions and to focus instead on resolving the personal differences that divided Manchester Friends.

Yearly Meeting itself took a somewhat different tack. Responding to a provocatively pro-Beaconite Declaration offered by Westmoreland Quarterly Meeting (and subsequently rejected) that the Bible be certified as 'the paramount rule of faith and practice', Yearly Meeting issued an *Epistle* which stated that 'the Holy Scriptures... were given by the inspiration of God... and there can be no appeal from them to any other authority whatsoever', adding that any act or belief contrary to Scripture, even 'under profession of the immediate guidance of the Spirit, must be reckoned... a mere delusion'. Such phraseology, in light of the Westmoreland Declaration, seemed to lean heavily toward Crewdson's theological position, but it not only fell short of satisfying the Manchester dissidents, it seriously offended the beliefs and sensibilities of traditional Friends.[44]

Outsiders attempting to discern the precise position of British Quakerism in 1836 with regard to either Scripture or the Holy Spirit might be excused for being puzzled. Contemporary accounts provide a wide variety of impressions but very little enlightenment. For example, in summarizing the stand taken by J. J. Gurney during the 1836 Yearly Meeting, the notes of Josiah Forster (1782–1870), a weighty evangelical, implied that while Gurney upheld the supremacy of Scripture as a guide to Friends beliefs and practices, he also testified as to 'the true soundness of Frds.' views in regard to silent mtgs' and declared that if the Society 'were to give way in our mtgs. for worship to any ministry except that which flows immediately from the Lds.' anointing, we should

---

[43] See Edward Ash, M. D., 'The *Beacon* Controversy and the Yearly Meeting Committee of 1835–37', *TF*, 1 Sept. 1870, 207–8 and Wilson, *Manchester*, 21–3.

[44] Wilson, '*Manchester*', 24–5 and 'Friends in the Nineteenth Century', 355–6 and '[John Southall's Account of] London Yearly Meeting, 1836', *JFHS*, 17/2 (1920), 87–8.

suffer loss'.[45] John Southall (1788–1862), a conservative Friend, responded very differently. Gurney's views, he said, did not 'correspond in principle and profession with our Society'. When, for example, Gurney asserted that any attempt to place 'the impressions received from our own minds' over the Scriptures would lead to deism, Southall cited an unnamed Friend who had argued that the 'question was not the exaltation of the Scriptures but the exaltation of the human interpretation of the Scriptures' which would leave Friends 'under the ban of...Theologians'. Some evangelical 'theologians', he said, had already indeed gone so far as to call for the renunciation of 'questionable' works by early Friends.[46]

The upshot of such exchanges, not surprisingly, was that 'the mtg. grew dark...was greatly unsettled...and...separated uncomfortably'.[47] For the longer range, the *Beacon* struggle returned to its starting place in Manchester, where the Yearly Meeting Committee and Hardshaw East Monthly Meeting, filled with Crewdson's partisans, gathered for a momentous five-day debate which turned, according to Roger Wilson, on questions of style rather than doctrine. In the end an unbending Isaac Crewdson could find no satisfaction and resigned from the Society.[48] He was followed into the wilderness by a body of seceders variously estimated at from fifty to three hundred. Those who withdrew formed a shorted-lived body of 'Evangelical Friends', stressing that strict adherence to a biblical creed necessitated the introduction of 'water baptism' and Lord's Supper which early Friends abhorred as vain outward rituals. Most of Crewdson's followers eventually drifted into the Plymouth Brethren or Low Church Anglicanism, but their loss was long lamented by many evangelicals who felt that they had been shamefully and needlessly driven from the fold.[49]

---

[45] Josiah Forster, 'Accounts of Yearly Meetings', 1836, 34–5, 38, MS. Vol. S26, LSF.

[46] [Southall], 'London Y. M., 1836', 86–9 and Forster, 'Account of 1836', 39, MS Vol. S26, LSF.

[47] Forster, 'Account of Y. M., 1836', 39–40, MS Vol. S26, LSF.

[48] A line-by-line account of this contest is *The Crisis of the Quaker Contest in Manchester* (Manchester, London & Bristol, 1836/7), two hundred pages of apparently verbatim text. Also see Wilson, *Manchester*, 26–9.

[49] See Barclay, *Inner Life*, 571–8 *passim.*; Ash, 'Beacon Controversy', 210–11; and William Tallack, *George Fox, the Friends and the Early Baptists* (London 1868), 36.

Although the *Beacon* Separation had grievous personal effects that divided families and shattered friendships,[50] Mollie Grubb holds that, in the long term, it mattered little to the life and development of British Friends. In her view, the moderate evangelical party, led by J. J. Gurney, guided the Society away from the shoals of ritual sacraments, programmed meetings, revivalism and hymn singing along a course parallel to but differing from the mainstream evangelical churches.[51] But, if important aspects of traditional Quakerism such as silent meeting and the guidance of the Holy Spirit, along with the marriage regulations and other peculiarities, remained as part of the mid-Victorian Quaker lifestyle, how much of the intense evangelicalism of the Crewdson connection was also retained?

Writing in the 1870s, Quaker historian Robert Barclay asserted that: 'All the views of Isaac Crewdson's followers which would bear discussion took root in the Society... in England and America.' Barclay's contemporary, William Tallack also believed: 'The main body of the friends—aided especially by the influence of Joseph John Gurney, and the most intelligent and philanthropic men of the Society—have subsequently come round, with little exception, to the very views for which their *Beacon* brethren were obliged to secede.'[52]

Did those Friends cited by Barclay and Tallack really need to 'come round'? Or were their differences from the Beaconites always more strategic or emotional than strictly theological? The case of Joseph Bevan Braithwaite (1818–1905), the leading Gurneyite evangelical during the latter half of the nineteenth century, may be illuminating in this regard. Early in 1836, when J. B. B. was not yet twenty, his earnest but self-assured letters would seem to indicate an imminent defection, bag and baggage, to the Crewdson läager. He revealed to a friend that he had become convinced of the 'radical unsoundness' of early Friends.

---

[50] See Jean Mortimer, 'Leeds Friends and the Beaconite Controversy', *JFHS*, 54/2 (1977), 52–66 and Lawrence Darton, 'The Baptism of Maria Hack, 1837: An Episode in the *Beacon* Controversy', *JFHS*, 46 (1954), 67–77.

[51] Mollie Grubb, 'Beacon Separation', 196–7.

[52] Barclay, *Inner Life*, 580 and Tallack, *George Fox*, 37. Also see Grubb, 'Evangelical Movement', 27–8.

We clung to them as long as possible, but experience has convinced us that one thing they lacked—faith. With them everything was inward. Their hope was inward—their righteousness was inward—the blood by which they were cleansed was within—the water by which they were washed was within—their Christ was within—and George Fox even declares their heaven was within.[53]

Despite this apparently Crewdsonian alienation from the founders of the Society and despite the fact that many of his immediate family left with Crewdson, J. B. Braithwaite remained with Friends, not because his theological views had changed but because his cultural attachment to Quakerism, with all the personal consolation it provided, had not. Braithwaite's subsequent mission was to ensure that his beloved Society would become and remain doctrinally sound as well as emotionally satisfying. The degree to which J. B. B. and other devout evangelicals were successful bears further examination Were the theological principles to which evangelical Friends adhered, for all the patina of traditional Quakerism that surrounded and obscured them, truly at odds with the spirit and teachings of George Fox and his early followers?

THE STRUGGLE SUSTAINED

In the years following the *Beacon* Controversy, tensions between conservative and evangelical Friends continued to seethe but generally below the surface and, according to one recent account, at the periphery rather than the centre of the Society's affairs.[54] Historians generally agree that control of the machinery of London Yearly Meeting fell increasingly into the hands of moderate evangelicals who shuddered at the prospect of inducing another shattering separation by pushing the still sizeable conservative element too far, too fast.

For one thing, J. J. Gurney was himself removed from the British scene in the immediate aftermath of the Beaconite struggle. In 1837 Gurney asked for and received a certificate of liberation to travel in the ministry to the United States where he remained for

---

[53] *Joseph Bevan Braithwaite: A Friend of the Nineteenth Century*, by his children (London 1909), 71.
[54] Mollie Grubb, 'Beacon Separation', 193.

three years. His wide-ranging American tour, which took on some characteristics of a revival, was enormously successful. In many areas, especially frontier Yearly Meetings like Indiana, Gurney's evangelical message was the harbinger of a startling transformation for American Quakerism.[55] But while the Gurneyite gospel carried many Orthodox (non-Hicksite) American Yearly Meetings by storm, in some places, Ohio, Philadelphia, and especially New England Yearly Meetings, Gurney encountered substantial and determined resistance to his reforming campaign.[56] In New England, the opposition was led by a single-minded, strong-willed conservative of great integrity and authority, John Wilbur (1774–1856). Wilbur's antagonism arose from a general concern about the 'unsound doctrines' and unseemly 'departures' from true Quakerism that he detected in Gurney's teaching as well as from the 'uncivil usage' to which he had been subjected by Gurneyites during his own two-year visit to England and Ireland in the early 1830s. An unrepentant quietist, whose views were impressively set out in his *Letters to a Friend...* (1832), Wilbur voiced the familiar complaint that Gurney and his allies were shifting the fundamental basis for Quakerism by placing scriptural authority before the Inward Light and by assigning to the Atonement 'the *whole* covenant of salvation'. The difference between Wilbur and other opponents of Gurneyism was the vehemence and tenacity with which he assailed his powerful and influential adversary.[57]

The upshot of John Wilbur's fierce and continuing opposition to Gurneyite ideas was an unseemly power-play by wealthy and prominent leaders of New England Yearly Meeting. When his own monthly meeting refused to censure him at the behest of the Yearly Meeting, Wilbur was gerrymandered into a more compliant body which subsequently disowned him for 'disobedience'. The outrage over the misuse of this obviously troublesome but entirely righteous man, as much as the doctrinal differences that precipitated it, brought on still another small but bitter American Separation, with its concomitant anguish for British Friends.[58]

[55] See Thomas D. Hamm, *The Transformation of American Quakerism, Orthodox Friends, 1800–1907* (Bloomington 1988) for the long-range impact of Gurney's mission.

[56] For a summary of J. J. Gurney's mission to America, see Jones, *Later Periods*, 1, 515–21.

[57] See ibid. 511–15 and Punshon, *Portrait in Grey*, 196–7.

[58] In 1854 Ohio Yearly Meeting divided between the minority adherents to John Wilbur's views and the Gurneyite majority. Philadelphia Yearly Meeting also had a decidedly Wilburite flavour.

While Joseph John Gurney was in America, British conservatives, who had bestirred themselves to oppose his going in the first place, showed strength in the Yearly Meeting, especially in the continuing assaults of Sarah Lynes Grubb and her allies on both the innovative doctrines and 'pharisaical spirit' of evangelical Friends. After hearing Sarah Grubb denounce those who had adopted 'money-getting as . . . the very end and object of their existence' while simultaneously denying the 'divine Power' of the Light, one sympathetic observer of Yearly Meeting in 1838 noted: 'It was worth the journey to London to participate in the feelings excited by this address . . . fully convinced as I am that the true Christianity as professed by early friends is founded upon an immutable rock.'[59]

A decade later, with Sarah Lynes Grubb deceased and J. J. Gurney soon to follow, that rock still stood, unmoved and immovable, but the major aspects of Quaker corporate life had surged around and passed it, leaving many conservative Friends high and dry. In 1846 the Manchester quietist John Harrison complained to a correspondent in Philadelphia about the conduct of evangelical Friends who successfully conspired to get their own way at Yearly Meeting: 'Everything had been cut and dried by the Table Friends prior to our coming together . . .'[60]

In having their way, the evangelicals who dominated the administrative machinery of the London Yearly Meeting were wont to emphasize the infallible, unimpeachable, immutable nature of Holy Scripture. But, unlike the Beaconites, who had denounced early Quakers for their failure to embrace Scriptural authority, the adherents of this new orthodoxy took pains to illustrate how the first generation of Friends had, in fact, taken 'their stand upon the Holy Scripture as the only ground of their religious faith . . . .' For the first Friends, said one evangelical account, the Spirit operated in perfect conjunction with the Word, 'interpreting its meaning, and solemnifying its application'. Insofar as early Quakers may have differed from other Christians, said another

---

[59] '[John Southall's Account of] London Yearly Meeting, 1838', *JFHS*, 18/1 (1921), 90–1.

[60] John Harrison to William Hodgson, 2 June 1846, in *Life and Memoirs of William Hodgson* (Philadelphia 1856), 95, reprinted as 'A "Conservative" View of London Yearly Meeting, 1846', *JFHS*, 18/1 (1921), 28. The Table Friends were evangelicals who assisted the Gurneyite Clerk round the table where Yearly Meeting documents were kept. Also see Clark, '*Beacon* Letters', 129–30.

evangelical publicist, '*their doctrines were scriptural*'.[61] Thus, according to these accounts, it was only after the ministry of Fox and the
'First Publishers of the Truth' that certain Friends began to give
'undue prominence to the inward illumination of the Holy Spirit'
and to adopt the unscriptural term 'inward light' as a description of
this supposed process. In so doing these misguided, if sincere,
Quakers left themselves open to accusations of setting up the
individual conscience or mere human reason 'as an all-sufficient
guide'. To avoid the future possibility of such misunderstandings,
evangelicals recommended that all Friends recognize, as William
Penn had done, that the light of which they spoke was the Light
and Spirit of the crucified Christ, never meant to supersede the
Scriptures but 'to credit and confirm them'.[62]

Evangelicals also looked to William Penn to give credence to
their interpretation of the Atonement. Jesus Christ, Penn declared,
was 'our holy sacrifice, atonement and propitiation . . . he bore our
iniquities and . . . by his stripes we are healed of the wounds Adam
gave us . . . nothing we can do, through the operation of the Holy
Spirit, is able to cancel old debts, or wipe out old scores; it is the
power and efficacy of that propitiatory offering, upon faith and
repentance, that justifies us from the sins that are past.'[63] Thus, they
maintained that early Quakers believed as firmly as themselves that
it was solely through the Atonement, 'our Lord's death on the cross
as a propitiatory sacrifice for sin . . . [that] all who truly believe in
his name receive the Divine forgiveness'.[64]

Because evangelical Quakers asserted that the basic principles of
the Society, as they understood and practiced them, were set forth
in Scripture as well as confirmed by early Friends, and because they
feared that the 'element of ambiguity' caused by the use of the term
'Inward Light' might induce an individual Friend, even with the
highest motives, to 'compromise the reputation of our Society . . . by putting forth his own views as an expression of the
principles of the society at large', they counselled their brethren

---

[61] Quotations are from John Kitching, M. R. C. S., 'On the Rise and First Principles of
the Society of Friends' (three lectures), printed in *TF*, Jan.–April 1859, 1–5, 19–22, 39–41, &
59–64 and from an editorial 'What Is Quakerism?', ibid., April and May 1861, 88–9 & 118–20.

[62] Kitching, 'The Scriptures: The Basis of the Beliefs of Friends', ibid., Feb. 1859, 19 and
'What is Quakerism?', ibid., April 1861, 88–9 and May 1861, 119.

[63] Quoted in 'What is Quakerism?', *TF*, April 1861, 88–9.

[64] Robert Charleton, *Brief Thoughts on the Atonement* (Bristol 1869), 5. Cf. Joseph Bevan
Braithwaite, 'Thoughts on the Atonement', 11 April 1872, MS. Port. 8/126, LSF.

to 'avoid all merely human theory and speculation, and . . . confine ourselves to what is plainly taught in the Holy Scriptures'.[65]

The degree to which the theological views of evangelical Friends, once they had abandoned any attachment to the Inward Light, differed from the bed-rock position of any mainstream Protestant non-conformist denomination would seem to be subtle at best. Yet Quaker evangelicals maintained their beliefs within the context of a unique culture which provided the social and psychological assurance that true Christianity was also, as Caleb Kemp believed, 'pure and undefiled Quakerism—as the Society of Friends has ever held it—I pray God we may not let go one iota thereof. . . .'[66]

While it appears accurate to describe Quaker ministry during the 1840s and 1850s as predominantly evangelical, leavened by some 'of a more mystical character',[67] it remains difficult to estimate with any assurance the relative numerical size of the conservative and evangelical wings. Still, the 'leaven' of traditionalism seems to have been sustained in many local meetings. As late as 1873, Caleb Kemp was flustered and disconcerted by an elderly conservative Friend who voiced 'strong disunity with my ministry', warning Kemp that he was on 'the brink of a precipice'. Friend Caleb's discomfiture could not have been relieved when his critic, upon being asked what precisely he objected to, replied that, among other things, he disapproved of the way Kemp brushed his hair. 'It may be wise, it may be Christian to treat it silently,' Kemp told his 'Journal', 'but it is not easy.'[68]

Jonathan Grubb (1808–94), another widely travelled evangelical minister, expressed a growing distaste for the rigidity of some of his more traditional brethren: 'The more I see of that self-satisfied spirit which accompanies the fierce contending for what people call orthodoxy [quietism], and the extremely uncharitable way in which such [people] conduct themselves, the more convinced I am that it will never gather the fold, or build up Quakerism, but is of all things most calculated to pull it down.'[69]

[65] Charlton, *Brief Thoughts*, 5 and in a letter to *TF* 'On the Inward Light', Feb. 1859, 32–3.
[66] C. R. K. 'Journals', III, 7 June 1860.
[67] T. Edmund Harvey, 'Looking Back', *JFHS*, 45/2 (Autumn 1953), 51–9. Also see Wilson, 'Friends in the Nineteenth Century', 358.
[68] C. R. K., 'Journals', IV, 2 Feb. 1873.
[69] Quoted by Edward Grubb, 'Seventy Years Ago', *FQE*, 1928, 298–9.

Whatever the relative strength of the two opposing wings of the Quaker communion, it seems clear that insofar as their Society manifested any tendencies toward a 'fresh concentration of life' and a readier response 'to the claims of necessitous souls', the impetus came from its evangelical wing.[70] As one appreciative commentator noted: 'All through the nineteenth century that [evangelical] voice as been awakening the Society... out of a complacent and spurious quietism... and raising it above pedantic fears of "creaturely activity" to the overmastering realisation of the service of love, which is the birthright of all who enter upon the higher life.'[71]

Although many traditional Friends were deeply involved in philanthropic activities, much of their contribution to the life of the Victorian Society was distinctly negative, reflecting a devotion to the 'weight of dead [and] traditional forms' that lacked any spark of spiritual or social vitality.[72] Certainly, one continuing complaint concerned the conservative approach to meeting for worship. Evangelicals believed that a gathering of the faithful should be a period of renewal, a reaffirmation and strengthening of their faith in Christ crucified as inspired by the saving Gospel message of Scripturally sound ministers. The contrast between this active religious service and the conservative attachment to 'dwelling-deep' during long periods of silence was reflected in the story of an elderly Manchester Friend who, upon returning to his home from First-Day Meeting, told his landlady, with radiantly beaming face: 'We have had a glorious time this morning at the meeting: not one spoke.'[73]

For many local meetings the results of such attitudes were deeply disturbing. In the late 1850s one writer contrasted the vital, aggressive ministry of early Friends, to whom conservatives claimed to be devoted, to the condition of many quietist-dominated meetings 'which are absolutely silent sabbath after sabbath for months if not for years!' A survey of British meetings in 1868 revealed that only two Quaker meetings in five had regular and active ministry,

---

[70] The quotations are from ibid. *306* and from a review of John Wilhelm Rowntree and Henry B. Binns' *A History of the Adult School Movement* in *PDP*, 5/50 (15 Sept. 1902), 262.

[71] [John Wilhelm Rowntree] *PDP*, v/50 (15 Sept. 1902), 262.

[72] J. W. R., 'Rise', in *Essays and Addresses*, 65–6.

[73] Septuagenarian [Thomas Tonge], 'Fifty Years Ago', *Manchester City News*, 3 August 1921, Vol. vv/75, LSF.

usually of the evangelical character. For the rest, 20 per cent had only 'fitful' ministry and fully 40 per cent had little or none.[74]

Conservative influence in local meetings was also reflected in the common complaint of evangelical Friends concerning 'the practical exclusion of the holy scriptures from our meetings'. Resistance to 'Biblically-based contributions' in meeting for worship was justified on the grounds that the regular introduction of Scripture would give rise to the 'growth of formality' and 'routine religious services', thus undermining the spontaneous nature of the meeting, even when such spontaneity resulted in two hours of 'unconsecrated silence'.[75] Nor was that silence to be broken by the strains of a hymn, for the traditional Quaker rejection of music had the double-barrelled force of being prohibited inside the meeting as premeditated and outside as creaturely activity that might easily lead to more serious 'disorderly walking'. John S. Rowntree noted that music was not referred to in the official publications of London Yearly Meeting until 1846 when the annual *Epistle* warned against 'the unprofitable and injurious tendency of music'. As late as 1880, the *British Friend* reprinted an article on 'The Temptations of Choir-Singers' which traced the fall from grace of a former chorister-boy 'to the *unreality* of constantly chanting words which were not the genuine expression of his heart'.[76]

Of course, not all conservative activity was so peripheral to the main currents of Victorian religious life and thought. Quietist authors, responding to all hints of innovation by evangelically inspired 'Babel-builders', made a sizeable contribution to an enormous body of Quaker pamphlet literature produced during the period. A number of these efforts were ably written and effectively argued. One fascinating, and pertinent, example of this genre is a treatise entitled 'Barclay Vindicated . . .', privately published by William Lamb Bellows (1802–77) of Gloucester. In this paper, Bellows challenged *Thoughts On Barclay's Apology* by Robert Charlton (1809–72), an evangelical Friend. Charlton's tract was an attack on the major theses of Robert Barclay's *Apology*, especially his seeming devaluation of Scripture in relation to the Inward

---

[74] J. S. Rowntree, *Quakerism*, 108 and Wilson, 'Friends in the Nineteenth century', 354–8.
[75] Edward Ash, *Quakerism* (London 1865), 20; J. S. Rowntree, 'The Friends' Book of Discipline', *FQE*, Oct. 1898, 494; and Wilson, 'Friends in the Nineteenth century', 354.
[76] J. S. Rowntree, 'Discipline', 493 and *BF*, 1 Dec. 1880, 220.

Light. Bellows felt obliged to respond to Robert Charlton's 'mistake . . . of limiting the saving power of the Most High to the letter of Scripture. . . .' by naming the Bible as *the* 'divinely appointed means' to true knowledge of God rather than *a* means to such knowledge, Bellows asserted that Charlton contradicted God's promise of salvation for all humanity, confining that possibility only to those with knowledge of the Scriptures. What, he asked, 'is the use of offering salvation to all, unless there be something *in all* predisposing them to receive it?'[77]

Charlton objected, Bellows noted, to Barclay's representation of Christ 'not with reference to his propitiatory sacrifice—but as an internal principle of light common to all men'. How, Bellows asked, could this be wrong '*in the case of those who had never had the Scriptures*', but were, like all other human souls, recipients of God's promise to provide the means for salvation? Barclay, Bellows concluded, had possessed the insight to grasp that the internal principle of Divine Light was not merely *a* foundation Truth of Quakerism: it was emphatically *THE* foundation Truth. To make outward knowledge of Scripture an absolute necessity for salvation was not only to cut off heathens, without access to the sacred texts, but apparently Christians as well when, through weakness of memory, they forgot the required texts.[78]

William Bellows' plea for the universality of the saving Light was pitched at a higher level than the more frequent quietist contributions concerning the maintenance of Quaker peculiarities and the enforcement of *The Discipline*.[79] And, as they chiefly

[77] William L. Bellows, *'Barclay Vindicated': A Review of Robert Charlton's 'Thoughts'* (Manchester 1868), 3, 16. Emphasis in original. Bellows's query was taken from Thomas Hancock's earlier critique of Isaac Crewdson.

[78] Bellows, *'Barclay Vindicated'*, 11, 29–30. A decade earlier one of Bellows' contemporaries had made the same point that 'it is no derogation to the character of Holy Scripture . . . to maintain that some measure of the light or Spirit of God has been immediately granted to man ever since his fall . . . and . . . [is] the *spring* and *principle* of all true knowledge and holiness. . . .' *TF*, March 1859, 52–3.

[79] *The Discipline* was first established to allow local meetings to seek advice from Yearly Meeting as to whether or not certain practices were 'in accordance with Truth'. Early-on this advice was issued as seemed appropriate, but by the 1730s a felt need for codification resulted in the issuance of a manuscript volume 'Christian and Brotherly Advices'. Revisions to these 'advices' were made periodically and results were increasingly referred to as the 'books of extracts' or 'books of discipline'. From 1783 the *Extracts from the Minutes and Advices*, periodically revised and reissued, became one of the few 'official' publications of the Society. A copy of these 'extracts and advices' meant to embody the past decisions, current rules, and general principles to 'be in future observed by the respective Quarterly, Monthly

evoked *The Discipline* to remind 'the unfaithful, the immoral, and the libertine professors . . . of their danger and their duty', its tone was often more prescriptive than inspirational.[80] If conservative Friends were anxious to keep the Bible out of their meetings and music out of their hearing, many were equally devoted to ensuring strict enforcement of all those essentially negative aspects of the *Discipline* that demonstrated Quakerism's 'testimony . . . against certain ideas and practices found in other sectors of the church'. In the 1850s Monthly Meetings disowned not only 'disorderly walkers' who broke the commandments but 'individuals of irreproachable conduct and undoubted piety' who violated traditional proscriptions against the payment of tithes, undergoing the rite of 'water baptism', or suffering bankruptcy. The most common cause for removal from highly-prized membership, however, was 'marrying out, that is, marriage to a non-member'.[81] While this proscription was not at the centre of differences between traditional and evangelical Friends, it proved the proximate cause of a series of monumental changes relating to the 'Rules of Discipline' within London Yearly Meeting of Friends.

As late as the 1850s many Friends apparently still interpreted St Paul's warning against being 'unequally yoked with unbelievers' in a strictly denominational sense, but there were also legal constraints to Quakers marrying outside the fold. Since the passage of Lord Hardwicke's Act (26 Geo. 2 c. 33) in 1753, which permitted special dispensations for Quaker and Jewish marriage ceremonies, the legitimacy of marriages according to the usages of Friends (that is, in Quaker meeting in the sight of witnesses but without a presiding clergyman) was recognized only if both contracting parties were Quakers.[82] In effect, this meant that a member of the Society of

and other meetings and by the several members of our Society', was to be retained in every local meeting affiliated with London Yearly Meeting. See Edward H. Milligan, 'How We Got our Book of Discipline: the Revision of 1921—From Doctrine to Experience', *FQ*, 25/3 (July 1988), 110–17 and J. S. Rowntree, 'Discipline', 457–98.

[80] See Jones, *Later Periods*, 1, 142–4 and J. S. Rowntree, 'Discipline', 469.

[81] J. S. Rowntree, *Quakerism*, 25–42 *passim* and Ash, *Quakerism*, 12. Quaker disdain for 'water baptism' as against 'baptism of the spirit' is reflected in the words of a Victorian Friend who noted that 'a sprinkling, or water-sprinkled, sacrament taking Quaker is a sort of incongruous medley I can neither classify or [sic] understand'. Quoted in Jean Mortimer, 'Leeds Friends and the Beaconite Controversy', *JFHS*, 54/2 (1977), 66.

[82] According to section 18 of Lord Hardwicke's Act, Quakers and Jews were relieved from the general provision that all marriages be solemnized in the parish church after the issuing of banns. This exemption was not extended to other non-conformists or Roman

Friends who married a non-Quaker, presumably in the presence of a minister or 'hireling priest', would be automatically disowned. In one way at least the prohibition against marrying out had served an extremely useful purpose. Marriage alliances among Quaker families often strengthened economic ties and sometimes shared capital or expertise provided the necessary means for the success of a Quaker enterprise.[83] But by the 1850s, the strictures against marrying out had become a major contributing factor to a continuing, and for some, ominous, decline in the Society's membership. It was, indeed, the question of dwindling numbers that was an important catalyst for the wave of changes that swept through London Yearly Meeting around 1860.

In 1859 an anonymous donor offered the considerable prize of one hundred guineas for the best essay on 'The Causes of the Decline in the Society of Friends'.[84] From amongst one hundred and fifty entries judged by three non-Quaker referees, the winning essay was *Quakerism, Past and Present* by 25-year-old John Stephenson Rowntree (1834–1907). Rowntree's essay proved to be a work of seminal influence in the transformation of British Friends. With all the exuberance of youth, Rowntree presented a broad-based attack on the narrow vision of contemporary Friends, conservative and evangelical alike. In their narcissistic concentration on the narrow concerns about differing visions of belief and practice, Quakers, he said, had turned from that service to truth and their fellow Christians which was the essence of the message powerfully delivered by the Children of the Light. Friend's educational vision, Rowntree asserted, was as narrow as their sphere of influence in the British society. To ever again become the sort of dynamic spiritual force their ancestors had been, he said, Quakers needed more knowledge of the wider world, deeper comprehension of the Bible as a guide to living in that world and stronger appreciation of the necessity for liberty of thought and action for both working

Catholics until the Marriage and Registration Acts of 1836. See Milligan, 'Quaker Marriage Procedure', a lecture to the annual conference of the Institute of Population Registration, Carlisle, 7 June 1993, 6–7 as well as his pamphlet on *Quaker Marriage*, a part of the 'Quaker Tapestry Booklets' series (London 1994), [10, 12].

[83] For examples, see James Walvin, *The Quakers Money and Morals* (London 1997), 66–72.

[84] The concerned donor was probably the wealthy Birmingham Friend George Sturge (1798–1888). See John S. Rowntree to Norman Penney, 10 Oct. 1905, MSS Port. 8/135, LSF.

through their own differences and providing a healing spirit for others. As for the specific means by which British Friends might begin the process of rejuvenating their Society, Rowntree first recommended that serious steps be taken to enhance the quality of Quaker ministry, especially where the abyss of silence threatened to extinguish both the ideal and the reality of worship services. Next he called for relaxation of the *Discipline*, especially with regard to the peculiarities and marriage regulations. He identified the latter as a 'deliberate...act of suicide' driving energetic young people out of the Society and perhaps preventing the most pious Friends from marrying at all.[85] Rowntree believed that these were essential steps if Friends were ever to recover their spiritual depth and renew their influence on the life of the world.[86]

Young Rowntree had emphatically delivered the right message to the right audience at the right time. Even as his call for dramatic changes was being published and read, London Yearly Meeting was making the first tentative steps toward the modification of its *Discipline*. Actually, the process had began in 1856 when Yorkshire Quarterly Meeting, urged on by J. S. Rowntree's father Joseph (1801–1859), proposed the revocation of the penalty of disownment for marriage to a non-Quaker.[87] The proposal concerning marriage was talked about but not acted upon at Yearly Meeting in 1857. But a proposition to send a Salutation 'in Gospel love to the members of our religious Society, and also to those who bear the name of Friends, wherever resident' was agreed upon after lengthy and heated discussion. Decoded, this proposal meant that Hicksites as well as others who had left the Society would receive an official communication from British Friends. As these proceedings moved forward one agitated conservative Friend felt bound to announce his 'solemn duty...to stem the torrent of innovation' flooding through the Society.[88] He was, however, thwarted, for the tide of

---

[85] See J. S. Rowntree to Elizabeth [his wife], 14 July 1858, MSS Port 42/56, LSF in which he described his own Monthly Meeting's attempt to disown a young woman for marrying out as 'injurious to the individual, hurtful to the Society, [and] unauthorized by Scripture'.

[86] J. S. Rowntree, *Quakerism*, 51, 65–7, 98–104, 108, 153–8 and *passim*.

[87] Edward Milligan, 'Quaker Marriage Procedure', 6–7, gives Joseph Rowntree major credit for persuading Yearly Meeting to accept the change.

[88] Josiah Forster, 'Memoranda Respecting London Yearly Meeting from 1828–1870 (with some exceptions)', MS., Vol 76, LSF.

novelty was further advanced with the agreement to print the *Minutes and Proceedings* of subsequent Yearly Meetings so that they might be read at leisure by the general membership.[89]

Late in 1859, Joseph Bevan Braithwaite, now a London barrister, corresponded with Quaker MP John Bright concerning the introduction of a private member's Bill to establish the legitimacy of marriage ceremonies 'according to the usages of Friends' when one of the parties was not a Quaker. This legislation had been made necessary by the recent decision of London Yearly Meeting, after four years of cautious discussion, to alter its marriage regulation 'to allow marriages to be solemnised in our meetings for worship . . . only one [or neither] of the contracting parties being a member of the Society'.[90] Conservative Friends remained adamant that the ban against mixed marriages not be lifted, but John Bright correctly anticipated no difficulties in obtaining parliamentary approval of what would become the Marriage (Society of Friends) Act, 1860 (23 & 24 Vict. c. 18). He was pleased to play a part in revising this draconian custom, which he described as 'one of the many inconveniences the Society has suffered . . . ' arising from 'the disposition of . . . Friends . . . to fence in the Membership of the Body, as if it were some exclusive & privileged club rather than a Christian Church'.[91]

The impetus for reform carried over to 1860 when Yearly Meeting agreed to a suggestion under consideration since 1857 to make adherence to the Fourth Query on simplicity (plainness of speech and dress) optional. In addition, all of the 'Queries and Advices' annually sent by Yearly Meeting to Quarterly and Monthly Meetings were revised with a view to adapting Quakers practices to life in modern society. For example, the Seventh

---

[89] *Extracts from the minutes and proceedings of the Yearly Meeting of Friends Held in London, 1857* (London 1858), 9–10. (Hereafter LYM, with year). While most evangelical Friends welcomed the forthcoming changes, Wilson, *Manchester* notes that J. B. Braithwaite opposed the printing of the Yearly Meeting *Minutes* lest they distract Friends from the message embodied in the annual *Epistle*; Braithwaite was a member of the *Epistle* drafting committee for over thirty years. The ever-cautious Caleb Kemp may have expressed his fear that some changes might cause 'great hurt to our society' for the same reason. C. R. K., 'Journals', 11, 26 May 1858.

[90] Milligan, 'Quaker Marriage Procedure', 6–7 and *Quaker Marriage*, [12].

[91] John Bright to J. B. Braithwaite, 26 December 1859, Temp. Box 10a/11, LSF. The *British Friend* organ of Conservative Friends in London Yearly Meeting, stated in June 1859, 151 'that the testimony of our Society against marriage between individuals not united in religious view should remain *unimpaired*.'

Query, enjoining Friends against 'all vain sports, and places of diversion...' was shifted into the list of merely cautionary Advices. Finally, in 1861 Yearly Meeting approved the recommendations of a conference called to oversee a complete revision of the *Discipline*, the first since 1833. Later that same year a new volume entitled, for its three parts, *Christian Doctrine, Practice and Discipline* was published, claiming in its Preface to have preserved 'the *form* of our discipline' while bearing 'abundant testimony to the *spirit* in which it should be conducted', and embracing that 'wisdom, patience, forbearance and love, which ought ever to prevail among Friends'.[92]

Some conservative Friends found it impossible to forbear. J. S. Rowntree, pleased that Friends were beginning to come to grips with modernity, was, on the other, distressed by the remarks of a 'very trying convinced Frd.' (probably William Irwin of Manchester) who denounced 'change and its promoters in [such] strong language' that there seemed a 'danger of the meeting getting into disorder'. Over half a century later the famed Quaker jurist Sir Edward Fry (1827–1918) recalled how 'the miserable questions about dress and address, and... disputes about orthodoxy... produced a chasm... between myself and systematic Quakerism which I have never got over'.[93]

There was a small body of conservative 'purists' who were also unable to bear 'the oppression... of the enemy who has, it appears to some amongst us, taken his seat in the Church... [and] brought forth fruits so incompatible with Truth's dictates... that we... a poor and afflicted remnant... cannot join with them.'[94] Eventually, this 'poor and afflicted remnant', broke free from 'that lapsed body which *calls* itself the Society', and established a 'true

---

[92] *Christian Doctrine, Practice and Discipline* (London 1861), v. Until 1861, London Yearly Meeting was technically restricted to a limited number of official representatives from Quarterly Meetings, such recorded Quaker ministers as might be in London and the members of Meeting for Sufferings, the executive body of Yearly Meeting. In practice, Yearly Meeting had long since become open to any Friend who had the time and inclination to attend. See Edward H. Milligan, ' "To Friends Everywhere": Reflections on the Epistle in the Life of London Yearly Meeting', *FQ*, 22/11 (July 1982), 729.

[93] J. S. Rowntree, 'Account of Y. M., 1859', MS. vol. S–368, LSF and Anges Fry, *A Memoir of Sir Edward Fry* (Oxford 1921), 168.

[94] *Selections from the Diary and Correspondence of John G. Sargent*, 104, quoted by Edward H. Milligan, '"The Ancient Way": The Conservative Tradition in Nineteenth Century British Quakerism', *JFHS*, 57/1 (1994), 74. 'Purists' is Milligan's term.

conservative' meeting at Fritchley in Derbyshire which maintained itself as a separate entity for over a century.[95]

Continued conservative rumblings not withstanding, by the end of 1861 the Society of Friends had so far recognized the necessity of coming to grips with the modern world that Quakers could, without fear of sectarian censure, marry a non-Friend in their local meeting house dressed in ordinary clothing. They could keep abreast of developments and opinions within their Religious Society by reading printed copies of the *Minutes and Proceedings* of Yearly Meetings as well as an up-to-date version of *Christian Doctrine, Practice, and Discipline*. By and large, members of this tiny, and still declining, if slightly less peculiar, body of believers supported these changes as necessary means for propelling Quakerism into the modern world. In point of fact, however, few Friends of any theological stripe were adequately prepared to deal with the eventualities that awaited them. For even as British Quakers instituted minor modifications in their long-standing procedures, Darwin's *Origins of Species* was running through half a dozen editions and the first translations of German 'Higher Criticism' of biblical texts were being published in England. And while these first stages of the assault on the structure of Victorian Christian values were gathering force, in 1860 the Yearly Meeting of British Friends was spending 'the largest part of an hour ... discussing whether the word preceding *Christian* in the sixth new Query [peace testimony] should be *a* or *our*'.[96] Quakerism had determined to enter the modern world, but the means whereby it might continue to defend itself from the dangers of that world were nowhere apparent.

There was, however, one notable and creative social effort to which Friends, especially those of the younger generation, might attach themselves. In 1845 Joseph Sturge (1793–1859) of Birmingham founded the first Friends' Adult School, followed two years later by the joining of this institution with sixteen other Quaker Adult Schools in the Friends First Day School Association (FFDSA). These Adult Schools, built around the concept of developing or improving basic skills of working-class men through Sunday instruction centred on biblical texts, gradually expanded

---

[95] The quote is from *Selections from the Correspondence of William Hodgson, with Memoirs of his Life* (Philadelphia 1886), 350. Also see Walter Lowndes, *The Quakers of Fritchley, 1863–1980* (London 1980).

[96] *TF*, 8 June 1860, 104.

in size and in the range of their activities and services. For many reasons, including the inherent traditionalist fear of being swept away by a tide of '*superficial* applicants', ill-equipped to absorb Quaker cultural traditions and religious practices,[97] Adult Schools brought few new recruits into the Society. But they did widen the social and religious horizons of several generations of mainly evangelical young Friends. Perhaps even more important, they gave younger Quaker males some meaningful activity outside the still severely limited confines of their tiny, self-contained, and frequently self-absorbed religious community.[98]

The impetus for the 'life-giving influence' of the Adult Schools and other religious and philanthropic activity was almost entirely evangelical and it unquestionably increased the influence of that theological position among members of the younger generation. If most Quakers born in the middle years of the Victorian period had their first religious instruction at the feet of a more open, active, and involved evangelical ministry which encouraged increased contact with and appreciation for spiritual developments outside the Religious Society of Friends, many of these same young people were also drawn into a world of ideas from which their spiritual mentors could only recoil with horror. For as conservative orthodoxy had sought spiritual security by building a defensive hedge around ancient, sacred but nebulous truths, the evangelicals thought they had found an impregnable fortress in the infallible, irrefutable message of Holy Scripture. The work-a-day world of mammon had been largely unaware of or, at best, mildly amused by the reclusive Friend with bonnet or collarless coat of grey, but the more refined world of modern thought could swoop down upon the supposedly invulnerable evangelical stronghold of biblical inerrancy in an undifferentiated assault on unquestioned testimonies, old and new.

One insightful contemporary observer, Frederick Maurice, caught the point exactly in his diagnosis of Quaker infirmities. Once the Society of Friends began to reach out and join with other

---

[97] Irwin, 'Brief Remarks', v, 18–20.

[98] The standard study is John Wilhelm Rowntree and Henry B. Binns, *A History of the Adult School Movement* (London 1903). This work has recently been reprinted with a new introduction and some new material by Christopher Charlton. Also see Wilson, 'Nineteenth Century Friends', 357 and *Manchester*, 34–5 and Edward Grubb, *Quakerism in England: Its Present Position* (London 1901).

groups in socially significant corporate acts, Maurice noted, it was forced to abandon the role assigned to it by its founders as *the* single Divinely-constituted means for achieving God's Kingdom on earth. Henceforth, Maurice said, their previously exclusive educa-tion would have 'to be conducted upon principles precisely the reverse of those . . . [formerly] proclaimed to be the only spiritual principles'.[99]

Quakerism is threatened from without on two sides—on the Evangelical side and on the Unitarian . . . one or the other . . . will be henceforth predominant; Quakerism will have less and less a basis of its own. All its great pretensions are at an end; its greatest defenders speak of it now not as the . . . Kingdom of God, but as the best of the sects which compose the religious world. Such language can never satisfy those who retain any of the old Quaker spirit. They must believe that there is a spiritual Kingdom somewhere; if they cannot find it in the Society of Friends, they will look for it in those opposing systems of which I have spoken.[100]

In the end, Maurice thought, historical Quakerism, caught between the demythologizing force of evangelical dogmatism and the liberating power of modern scepticism, would succumb to 'slow decay' and cease to be of account among those seeking the Kingdom of Christ. It was, for Friends, a gloomy prediction and for a time seemed about to be fulfilled.[101]

---

[99] Frederick Maurice, *Kingdom of Christ*, 2 vols. (London 1958; rep. of 1842 edition), I, 65–7.
[100] Ibid. I, 67, 70.   [101] Ibid. I, 26.

2

Spiritual Rebellion

'A CASE OF DIFFICULTY' IN MANCHESTER

One of the warnings issued by John Stephenson Rowntree in
Quakerism, Past and Present concerned the precarious circumstances
of younger Friends with improved educations and enlarged opportunities who were migrating from rural areas to larger towns and
cities. Because the previous experience of these young people had
usually been 'isolation from evil, rather than preparation to resist
evil', they seemed particularly vulnerable to the beguiling snares of
modern city life, and thus presented the Society of Friends with
still another possible cause for its precipitous numerical decline.[1]

Leaders of urban Quaker communities were naturally anxious to
provide an environment in which younger Friends 'could get what
was needful and useful without leading them into temptation', but
the average Quaker meeting, dominated by serious, older, and
often wealthy Friends, had little to offer active and curious young
adults. Edward Vipont Brown (1863–1955) remembered an
oppressive ambience in meetings of his youth where amongst the
gathered bonnets and broad-brimmed hats much of the talk was
concerned with 'God's justice and being "washed in the blood"'.
Even the most dutiful young Friend might hesitate to choose such
an atmosphere over the alternatives offered by a modern city.[2]

In the late 1850s, Caleb Kemp (1836–1908) confided to his
'Journal' a deep concern about choosing companions, especially
as a young man 'living away from his parental roof, mixing with
men of the world... who know little, or nothing of religious
feeling...' Sadly, Kemp's earnest scrupulosity meant that in his
adopted home at Mitcham, near Croydon, he had 'no one with

---

[1] J. S. Rowntree, *Quakerism*, 176–7.
[2] Richenda C. Scott, 'Authority or Experience: John Wilhelm Rowntree and the
Dilemma of 19th Century British Quakerism', *JFHS*, 49 (Spring 1960), 77 and E. Vipont
Brown, 'The Renaissance of Quakerism', *Friends Quarterly*), 5/4 (Oct. 1951), 201–2.

whom to take a walk—no one to open my mind to, upon subjects . . . either temporal [or], spiritual . . . ' He attempted to put the
best possible face on his isolation, but eventually had to admit that
'my comfort and happiness much depends [sic] upon Christian
fellowship . . . with persons who see in religious things as I
see . . . .'[3] Where was such companionship to be found?

In some meetings well-intentioned older Friends like Josiah
Forster (1782–1870) might make the guidance of youth the special
concern of their ministry. But Forster's 'Letters to Younger Members', emphasizing such themes as how 'the evil propensities of
the natural heart, the temptations and allurements of the devil, the
associates to whom some are exposed . . . powerfully attract to
the unhallowed pleasures of the world that lie in wickedness',
were unlikely to provide soothing balm for lonely and restless
young souls.[4]

Manchester, with its burgeoning trade and diverse manufacturing as well as a sizeable Quaker community, was one of the cities
that attracted mobile younger Friends. When these young people
attended a meeting such as Mount Street in central Manchester,
they were not likely to be inspired by the religious services which
have been described as mildly evangelical and generally stodgy, but,
at the same time, attendance at meeting for worship offered the
possibility of encountering old schoolmates, family friends, or even
strangers close to their own age with whom they might socialize.
Indeed, older members of the Mount Street congregation became
alarmed when local residents began referring to certain public
houses as 'Friends Meeting Houses' from the frequency with
which young Quakers gathered in them.[5] The determination to
correct this situation was, doubtless, one of the inspirations for the
founding in March 1858 of the Manchester Friends' Institute as a

---

[3] C. R. K., 'Journals', II, 6 Jan. 1857 and III, 4 Dec. 1859.
[4] Josiah Forster, *Letters to Younger Members of the Religious Society of Friends* (London
[1869]), I, 5–6.
[5] 'Notes on Interviews' Second Day Morning at 9:30, MS. Box 9.5(1), LSF. It should be
noted that even though there was an evangelically inspired temperance movement among
Friends, the Society, many of whose most prominent families had made fortunes in the
brewing trade, had never censured the moderate use of alcohol. Even so pious a Quaker as
Caleb Kemp long resisted the call to make abstinence a corporate testimony of the Society,
noting: 'I take but little of these things but I think that little does me good . . . ' Only in later
life, when Kemp was running for local political office, did he take the 'total abstinence'
pledge. See C. R. K., 'Journals', III, 5 June 1867 and V, 18 Jan. 1889.

'congenial place of resort for... young people belonging to Manchester Meeting'.[6]

By 1860, the Friends' Institute, with its club rooms (including a special room for young women), its library and its teas, had become, as one member recalled, 'an active centre of social and intellectual life', where young people could find convivial fellowship and also enjoy, in the words of William Thistlethwaite (1813–1870), schoolmaster and inaugural speaker in the Institute's ambitious lecture series, 'the benefits of continued study and self-culture' whose inevitable end would be 'the discovery of truth'.[7] But could this Institute, innocently erected as a safe and comfortable refuge from the lurking moral dangers of big city life, also lead young Friends along paths too dangerous to tread? That question became the focus of a bitter and far-ranging dispute that for a time disturbed, distressed, and divided British Friends.

As it happened, the Manchester Friends' Institute embarked upon its lecture series just as the struggle over the extent and meaning of changes within London Yearly Meeting was reaching a crucial stage. The Institute's monthly course of presentations attempted to avoid controversial subjects, but audience discussions elicited by even the most innocent of topics inevitably revealed two antagonistic schools of thought in the Manchester Quaker community: 'the advanced or Evangelical', which favoured 'a nearer approach to the orthodoxy of other professing Christians', and the conservative, 'which opposed all innovation in practice, and held fast to Barclay in doctrine'.[8]

Post-lecture discussions often ended as heated debates which, according to one participant, were contrary to the original intentions of the Institute's founders and the harbingers of 'evil consequences'. One of those consequences was, evidently, the arousal of interest among some members of the Institute in reading contemporary religious literature. When it came to the question of acquiring a library to support such interests, controversy flared

[6] Frederick Cooper, *The Crisis in Manchester Meeting: With a Review of the Pamphlets of David Duncan and Joseph B. Forster* (Manchester 1869), 2. Also see *TF*, May 1859, 94.

[7] Septuagenarian Thomas Tonge, 'Fifty Years Ago', *Manchester City News*, 3 August 1921, Vol. VV/74, LSF and Wilson, *Manchester*, 29–30.

[8] *The Manchester Friend* (hereafter *MF*), I/1, 15 Dec. 1871, 7, microfilm copy, Mullins Library, University of Arkansas, Fayetteville and Joseph B. Forster, 'Memoranda in reference to the action of the Committee of the Manchester Friends Institute, 1858 to 1869', 25 Sept. 1870, MS. Box 9.6 (2), LSF.

anew. Conservatives objected to the acquisition of the *Life* of J. J.
Gurney and evangelicals to the works of John Wilbur. Still, in the
end, these and other books were purchased by the Institute Committee and read by those who claimed to be less concerned about
the partisan nature of the books than their insights into the historic
meaning of Quakerism. Such readers would, no doubt, have
agreed with Joseph Rowntree's plea at Yearly Meeting in 1856
that while mere intellect might not fully grasp Divine truths, there
was 'a danger of discouraging the employment of the intellectual in
the things of God'.[9]

This was where events stood in April 1861 when the Friends'
Institute Lecture Committee, faced with a last minute cancellation,
asked David Duncan (1825?–1871), a local merchant and manufacturer, to step into the breach. Duncan, a Scotsman who had
joined Friends upon marriage to a Quaker and who had once
trained for the Presbyterian ministry, agreed to speak provided
his topic, a discussion of *Essays and Reviews*, the recently controversial collection of theological studies by seven prominent Angli-
cans, was deemed acceptable. The lecture committee exhibited
serious Quakerly caution even in an emergency, but the Institute's
General Committee eventually gave its support, influenced, no
doubt, by the high esteem in which Duncan was held at the
Institute, especially by younger members.[10]

For a figure who ultimately commanded serious attention as
leader of a troublesome band of rebellious Friends, Quaker
archives contain remarkably little about David Duncan's life or
even his physical appearance. His published work, nearly all of
which related to the controversies in which he became embroiled,
is neither extensive or profound, but a brief, posthumously published fragment may serve as a summary of his views concerning
Friends' beliefs and practices:

We are a voluntary movement for the promotion of truth, and we
acknowledge the spirit of truth in each individual as the highest and
ultimate ground of authority... in the meeting of worship... all prepared

---

[9] Cooper, *Crisis*, 2–3; Joseph B. Forster, 'Memoranda...' MS Box 9.6 (2), LSF; and
Josiah Forster, 'Accounts of Yearly Meeting, 1856', MS. Vol. S. 26, ibid.

[10] Joseph B. Forster, 'Memoranda...'; *MF*, I/1, Dec. 15, 1871, 7–8 and Wilson,
Manchester 30–1. Also see *TF*, May 1859, 94. Duncan had lectured previously at the Institute,
without alarming evangelical members.

reflections or expositions of doctrine ... are excluded, and the only recognized teaching is the expression of the individual, supposed to be inspired by the power and wisdom of God ... [T]he Scriptures ... are subordinate to the spirit of truth in the individual, and are dependent on that spirit for their efficacious application in enlightening the mind.

We must resist the domination of those who have lost the tradition of our fathers, who are sacrificing the genuine principles of Quakerism, and putting in their stead the hollow sounding phrases of a pretentious and pharisaical formalism.[11]

One admirer recalled Duncan as 'a very talented man ... half worshipped by some who knew him closely'. He was, to be sure, an earnest and outspoken Victorian intellectual, sensitive to new ideas and stimulated by them. Some young people at the Friends' Institute obviously considered him to be on the cutting edge of modern spiritual thought, but Duncan's own view of his role never clearly emerged. He claimed to have no religious contacts or interests outside Manchester Friends, but, in keeping with a long-standing Quaker tradition, he took care to have all of his carefully prepared lectures and addresses published and circulated. Perhaps he believed, not without a touch of vanity, that he could play a useful role in heightening the level of discourse, not only at Manchester Friends' Institute but among Friends in general.[12]

By the time Duncan presented his lecture on 12 April 1861, the preponderant weight of British Protestant judgement had already fallen heavily upon *Essays and Reviews*. Evangelicals in particular decried the book's 'infidelity' which arose, in their view, from the insistence of its seven Broad Church Anglican authors—in the light of modern scientific and historical discoveries—on treating the Bible, however Divine its inspiration, 'like any other book' written

---

[11] David Duncan, 'Quakerism Past and Present', *MF*, I/4, 15 March 1872, 57–8. In many ways Duncan's views seemed to echo those of conservative Friends, but as controversy grew, conservatives were often in the vanguard of those attacking Duncan and his followers. The crucial difference was that for Duncan only the principle of the Inward Light was unassailable; he appears to have believed that most other Quaker traditions and eccentricities were as irrelevant as evangelical attachments to the experience of salvation by faith alone, Biblical inerrancy or the concept of propitiatory Atonement. For a similar view by an anonymous contemporary, see 'Lover of Truth' to *TF*, 1 March 1859, 53–4.

[12] Tonge, 'Fifty Years Ago'. In the early twentieth century John Wilhelm Rowntree, while outlining his proposed definitive history of Quakerism, planned to devote an entire chapter to the 'Lancashire Trouble', but there is no mention of Duncan or the controversy surrounding him in Rufus Jones' *Later Periods of Quakerism*.

by human beings.[13] Duncan felt that these so-called 'seven against Christ' had been unfairly judged and he intended to use the Friends' Institute as a forum for putting questions they had raised into proper perspective.

In setting forth his objectives, Duncan noted that his lecture was first of all, 'a protest against the intolerant spirit' in which *Essays and Reviews* had been attacked; secondly, he wished to bring to the attention of Friends its authors' unanimous 'Testimony... to an "Inward Guide" superior to the Outward Testimony—although in the main concurrent with it'; finally, he hoped to inform and enlighten those who were perhaps not fully apprised of the questions that the contentious volume had raised.[14] Duncan asserted that most criticism of the book was based upon the mistaken belief that Christianity was comprised of a precise and definable set of unchallengeable dogmas. 'If the principle were more generally admitted that Christianity is a life rather than a formula,' he asserted, 'theology would give place to religion... and that peculiarly bitter spirit which actuates religionists would no longer be associated with the profession of religion.'[15]

Early Protestant reformers, Duncan said, had claimed to be striking a blow for human freedom in matters divine, but while men like Hus, Luther, and Calvin correctly denied 'the supremacy of any ecclesiastical authority in persons', they unwisely transferred that authority to a single book and thus instituted the practice of Bibliolatry which had burdened Protestantism from its inception. One of the great virtues of *Essays and Reviews*, he believed, was its attempt to progress beyond 'the Judicial spirit of worshipper of the Book to the advanced ground of critical investigation'. The authors' purpose, he said, was not to deny Scripture but to advance human knowledge in relation to it. Their book had 'been puffed into a temporary notoriety' which would soon 'pass out of fash-

[13] *Essays and Reviews* was published early in 1860 but received little attention until the appearance of Frederic Harrison's comments in the *Westminster Review* under the title 'Neo-Christianity' in October 1860; in April 1861 Bishop Samuel Wilberforce published a scathing attack in the *Quarterly Review*, 109, 248–305. For the ensuing national controversy, see Desmond Bowen, *The Idea of the Victorian Church* (Montreal 1968), 161–172 and M. A. Crowther, *Church Embattled: Religious Controversy in Mid-Victorian England* (Newton Abbot 1970), *passim*. Also see Mark Francis, 'The Origins of *Essays and Reviews*: An Interpretation of Mark Pattison in the 1850s', *Historical Journal*, 17/4 (1974): 797–811.

[14] David Duncan, '*Essays and Reviews*: A Lecture delivered at Manchester Friends Institute' (Manchester 1861), [5].

[15] Ibid. 8

ion', but the honesty and courage with which the authors had addressed questions that all young believers would sooner or later have to consider were, in Duncan's view, most admirable. He also reminded his audience of the curious parallel between the opprobrium heaped upon the 'seven against Christ' and 'the attacks with which our early Friends were assailed,' all such assaults being 'characterized by . . . reckless assertions of impiety and heresy.'[16]

Duncan concluded on a conciliatory note, admitting that while he was 'fearful of the responsibility of addressing Friends' on such a topic, he was not conscious 'of having written a line which could, or need give pain to any of my brethren, the most sensitive or the most careful'.[17]

After the lecture was printed and distributed, initial responses in the Quaker press seemed to bear out Duncan's plea of moderation. *The Friend*, a weekly journal solidly linked to the Quaker evangelical establishment, barely took notice of his remarks, at least initially, and the *British Friend*, sounding-board for traditional Quakerism, remarked that there was 'nothing in the lecture at all calculated to create . . . controversy, and . . . much that meets our entire approbation'.[18] The tone of reactions began to change in late May at the annual gathering of London Yearly Meeting where Duncan's views were seriously challenged.[19] Shortly thereafter an anonymous pamphlet expressed deep distress at Duncan's having made the Society of Friends 'the only section of the Christian Church which has furnished an advocate' for *Essays and Reviews* and accused him of leaning 'towards neo-Platonism, pantheism and finally . . . toward infidelity'.[20]

Duncan's friends at Manchester did not allow such criticism to go unanswered. Among his strongest advocates was Joseph Binyon Forster (1831–83), a sugar refiner and secretary to the General Committee at Friends' Institute. Forster, a disciple of J. S. Mill

[16] Ibid. 6–8, 23, 29–30.

[17] Ibid. 30.

[18] *BF*, May 1861, 116–17. Both *The Friend*, published in London, and *The British Friend*, issued from Edinburgh, were established in 1843.

[19] *BF*, June 1861, 133. Also see Wilson, *Manchester*, 33. David Duncan was not present to defend his position as he was not 'a Yearly Meeting Friend'; his involvement in the Society had apparently been limited to the Manchester area.

[20] [Anon.], 'Observations on a lecture delivered at the Manchester Friends' Institute by David Duncan, entitled "*Essays and Reviews*",' (London 1861), 28–9. One intriguing aspect of Quaker internecine struggles is the speed with which contending arguments could be got into print.

passionately devoted to the cause of free expression, might be described as 'Duncan's bulldog', so fiercely and tenaciously did he leap to his friend's defence. Late in 1861 Forster not only addressed a specific rejoinder to Duncan's critics but also issued a general plea that Friends recognize the creative possibilities offered by the venting of controversial views:

> Is it not to be regretted that we are any of us unable to tolerate, or benefit by that difference of opinion and earnestness of original investigation which in literature and science are held to be so invaluable?... I have no fear but that the good sense of our members will ever guard us from the evils of controversy, whilst the admission of all questions of interest will also serve to broaden the grounds of Christian charity, teaching us that differences of opinion ought never to separate men bound together by the love of Christ.[21]

If Forster's intention was to bring underlying differences into the open, he failed. No responses were forthcoming, at least not in any public forum. Still, men like Forster and Duncan did represent a new sort of threat to the largely evangelical hierarchy that dominated Manchester meeting. Louder, better educated, more widely read than the brooding quietist faction, they were also more dangerous because, for them, no subject was out of bounds and no idea unworthy of consideration. Another of their associates was Charles Thompson (1819–1903), a wealthy cotton manufacturer, Justice of the Peace and Manchester City Councillor as well as a recorded minister at Ashton-on-Mersey (Sale) Meeting. Thompson has been identified as a 'vocally active conservative voice' at Yearly Meeting,[22] but his brand of conservatism, while fiercely anti-evangelical, seems not to have been anti-modern. Neither was Thompson shy in his assertions: 'Believers were not to stand still... for there was a large, *or even a larger, amount of divine authority* and outpouring of the Spirit *now* than there was in the days when the Scriptures were written.'[23]

---

[21] J. B. Forster, 'David Duncan and His Reviewer', *BF*, 2 September 1861, 224–5 and 'Dread of Controversy', ibid., 2 Dec. 1861, 287–8.

[22] See Milligan, '"The Ancient Way": The Conservative Tradition in Nineteenth Century British Quakerism', *JFHS* 57/1 (1994), 74–101.

[23] Quoted by Scott, 'Authority or Experience', 79.

At the Friends' Institute these men of advanced views obviously encouraged the young people they met to investigate aspects of modern thought, including biblical criticism and Darwinian science, in their attempts to come to grips with fundamental questions of life and faith. As Kirk Willis has pointed out, it was through German biblical criticism that Hegel's religious views, which 'went to the heart of the Victorians' intellectual preoccupations and cultural assumptions', were first introduced to British students, including those at the Friends' Manchester Institute.[24]

Most of the younger people who gathered at the Institute were in their late teens or early twenties, an impressionable age, especially for those brought up in the sheltered confines of Victorian Quaker homes and schools. The natural tendency towards youthful rebellion could only have been exacerbated by the presence of outspoken modernists like Duncan and Forster who glorified, as God's greatest gifts, reason which led human beings to ask questions, and free will which permitted them to pursue the answers.[25] No doubt these were exhilarating times for young Manchester Friends, probing, as they imagined, at the frontiers of human knowledge while secure in the rightness of their quest, whatever the cautious or elderly might say.

Thus, although the Manchester Friends' Institute's public lecture series aimed at avoiding controversy and if anything, leaned toward evangelical presentation, one of its apparent results was to turn the Institute into a centre for liberal, anti-evangelical religious inquiry. If many of the parents of David Duncan's young admirers had, under Gurneyite influence, thought of the Bible as a single, if heavily fortified, line of defence against unbelief, agnosticism and despair, their sons and daughters learned at the Institute that they had a solid spiritual position to fall back upon. Where Scripture proved inadequate, obscure, or frankly unbelievable, they could take up the writings of either early Friends or modern theologians

---

[24] Kirk Willis, 'The Introduction and Critical Reception of Hegelian Thought in Britain, 1830–1900', *Victorian Studies* 32/1 (Autumn 1988), 87, 94–5. Also see, Terry G. Harris, 'Matthew Arnold, Bishop Joseph Butler, and the Foundation of Religious Faith', ibid. 31/2 (Winter 1988), 189–208. For the impact of 'modern thought' on mid-Victorian Friends, see Isichei, *Victorian Quakers*, 29–43 and 'From Sect to Denomination Among English Quakers', in *Patterns of Sectarianism*, edited by Bryan R. Wilson (London 1967), 174–6.

[25] For an expression of the view that reason was 'the highest talent we possess' and the means by which humanity could put the world to rights, see letter from 'Philotheorus' to *TF*, Sept. 1861, 236–7.

to find their way. Like old-fashioned Quakers, these young liberals generally had a strong affinity for the writings of early Friends, particularly those passages from Barclay's *Apology* that emphasized the saving power of the Inward Light rather than the absolute authority of Scripture. Unlike conservatives, however, they were also willing to consider modern ideas as a means of freeing them from what many felt was a stifling atmosphere of ignorance and fear.[26]

Still, while events would show that some of the mature leaders of this simmering spiritual rebellion were tending toward Unitarianism or even some sort of vague theism, few of the earnest young 'progressive' Manchester Friends harboured any desire to leave the comfortable confines of Quakerism; they only wished that their religious Society, in keeping with what they perceived to be its original historical practice, would open itself to free enquiry and loosen the bounds of doctrinal restraint. No great concessions were necessary to keep the overwhelming majority of callow Manchester liberals in unity with Friends.

Compromise was, indeed, at hand. One Quaker scholar has identified a group of weighty moderates who were working, largely from within the evangelical fold, to modify more extreme views regarding absolute biblical inerrancy or the propitiatory Atonement as a blood sacrifice to appease an angry God.[27] Unfortunately, these moderates revealed themselves too late and too timidly to stave off serious upheaval in Manchester. By the time the *Friends' Quarterly Examiner* was established in 1867, partly as a medium to propagate a middle-of-the-road version of modern Quakerism, the trouble at Mount Street Meeting had taken a fateful turn toward open confrontation. When that contest was joined, few, if any, of the moderate faction chose to align themselves openly with the sort of modernism and liberty demanded by David Duncan and his friends.

However reflective of deep-seated differences among Manchester Friends, the public controversy over David Duncan's defence of *Essays and Reviews* was short-lived. During the next few years only an occasional ripple disturbed the apparent calm at Manchester

---

[26] Isichei, *Victorian Quakers*, 30, 35–6; Punshon, *Portrait in Grey*, 212–3; and Scott, 'Authority and Experience', 79–80.

[27] Edwin Bronner, 'Moderates in London Yearly Meeting, 1857–1873: Precursors of Quaker Liberals', *Church History*, 59/3 (September 1990), 356–71.

Friends' Institute. One such flutter occurred at the end of 1862 when the Institute's library committee approved, in the face of the 'urgent remonstrances of many well-concerned Friends', the purchase of books 'of a very hurtful tendency', including Bishop J. W. Colenso's commentaries on the books of the Pentateuch, which had caused him to be excommunicated by his superior in South Africa. Supporters of this library expansion later called it a victory for both democratic procedure and free enquiry since 'it may be fairly concluded that the liberal views with which the Institute has been carried on from its commencement have been those of the generality of its members...' Perhaps this was so, but the liberal triumph also had a Pyrrhic quality for it was won at the cost of resignation by three dissenting members of the Institute's General Committee, including its president.[28]

A letter of resignation from one of the three, James Hodgkinson, an elder of Mount Street Meeting, survives among the *Minutes* of Hardshaw East Monthly Meeting and provides a somewhat different perspective on the growing division. For while Hodgkinson admitted that he could not agree with the policy of simply purchasing '*any* book... which is not decidedly immoral or a well known novel', a more compelling motive for his resignation was the fact that his 'feelings were very much wounded by the remarks made on the friends who happened to take a different view from some of the speakers... I suppose I am one of those alluded to who tries to get through this world in an easy way anxious for nothing except getting money, and not fit to judge of what is suitable for the young friends of the present day.'[29]

Other evangelicals protested that books which questioned the literal truth of Scripture, Old or New Testament, should not be conveniently placed to test the faith of young Friends. There was also a more personal, human reason behind their growing distaste for the situation at the Friends' Institute. Historically, many champions of liberty have been demonstrably more devoted to the ideal of humane learning than to the sensibilities of individual human beings. Perhaps it was the half-arrogant pride of righteous youth

[28] Cooper, *Crisis*, 2–3 and *MF* I/I 15 Dec. 1871, 7–8. For Bishop Colenso, see Peter Hinchcliff, *John William Colenso* (London 1964), especially chap. 5.

[29] James Hodgkinson to John Hargrave, 24 Feb. 1863, *Minutes*, Hardshaw East Monthly Meeting, (hereinafter *Minutes*, HEMM, with date), M 85/6/5/6, Manchester City Library (MCL).

that contributed, as much as any doctrinal difference, to the growing distance between the factions in Manchester. There is considerable evidence that David Duncan, for one, was not only earnest and outspoken but also prideful and self-assured. A Manchester Friend who was largely in sympathy with Duncan's views noted in 1864 her uneasiness with the fact that he had on occasion boasted 'that no one dared to take him to task'.[30]

In any case, David Duncan felt that Friends had nothing to fear from the revelations of any biblical scholar, critical or otherwise. With other modernist thinkers, Duncan had discovered the entrancing concept of 'progressive revelation'. Truth, he said, was eternal and immutable, but God's revelation of that truth to finite human minds was gradual. As humanity came to understand more about the nature of the world, so could they more clearly discern the nature of God's truth. Thus, he concluded, a practical, ethical faith based upon the ever expanding understanding of God's will must replace narrow doctrines and formulas devised in times when the Divine message was less clear.[31] Duncan took pains to emphasize this position in a lecture at the Friends' Institute in 1863, subsequently published as *Can an Outward Revelation be Perfect?* He obviously chose the title to contrast the outward authority of Scripture with what he perceived to be the more fundamental principle of the Inward Light: 'The Bible as a whole is a revelation of the Divine Will . . . It is an unveiling of that mystery which has puzzled and distracted the highest minds; and like the unveiling of the laws of the natural world, it has been adapted to the wants and necessities of men. The revelation has therefore been gradual and progressive.'[32]

Duncan's views may have been broad-minded, but his style seemed deliberately provocative. True believers in Divine goodness, Duncan said, would embrace those biblical 'principles which accord with the teachings of Jesus . . . undisturbed by the ignorance and cowardice of those who dare not doubt the letter, because they have not known the spirit'. The posture taken by 'so-called "Evangelical" Friends' was, he believed, 'fatal to all spiritual life

[30] Mary Hodgson to Elizabeth [Green], 7 March 1864, Port. A 58, LSF.

[31] For discussion of this viewpoint see Isichei, *Victorian Quakers*, 33–4; Punshon, *Portrait in Grey*, 212–3 and Brayshaw, *The Quakers*, 256–7.

[32] David Duncan, *Can an Outward Revelation be Perfect? Reflections Upon the Claim of Biblical Infallibility* (2nd edn., London 1871, 1st edn. 1863), 23.

and all faith in God and truth'.[33] Quakers who upheld such narrow views were 'moving Heaven and Earth to resist the march of intelligence, which is substituting for a traditional belief, a living faith rich in results for the future.' 'Are we right', Duncan asked, 'in striving to reduce faith in God to faith in a book?' What was needed, he answered, was a new reformation marked by 'the abolition of any authority short of God, as He reveals himself to the spirit of the individual. This is the only practice worthy of the name of faith.'[34]

Again, if Duncan's blunt and sweeping denunciation of the evangelical spirit was calculated to draw out his antagonists, *Can an Outward Revelation Be Perfect?* was a failure. The speech elicited no open response, even in Mount Street Meeting. Perhaps, this silence reflected the hope of cautious Friends, evangelical and otherwise, that Duncan's self-induced theological storm would blow over without serious damage.[35] Still, as one concerned Manchester evangelical noted: 'the Committee of the Institute found themselves ... unable to prevent the evil which gradually, but with certain steps, advanced its sway, largely influencing the religious opinions of many of our members, especially those of the younger class.'[36]

By 1866 the 'sceptical opinions' increasingly expressed by younger Friends during the discussions that followed Institute lectures (most of them on non-religious topics)[37] caused some members to make a backhanded attempt to ban all lectures at the Institute during the following year. When this minority effort was overturned at a subsequent meeting, a somewhat larger group, including all but one of the ministers, elders, and overseers at Mount Street advertised their desire 'to promote the harmonious working of the Institute', by prohibiting 'verbal discussion of Biblical or theological questions' following lectures. After this proposition was also defeated by a 'considerable majority',[38]

---

[33] Ibid. 8, 25.   [34] Ibid. 24, 25.   [35] Wilson, '*Manchester*,' 39.

[36] Cooper, *Crisis*, 2.

[37] Joseph B. Forster's analysis of the content of 131 lectures presented at the Institute between 1858 and 1869 indicated that a hundred of these were 'neutral', twenty could be classified as evangelical and only eleven as heterodox or 'unsound' by orthodox evangelical standards. Forster lists lecture topics as follows: Science 28, Religion 15, Politics 13, Biography 12, History 11, Travel 10, Literature 9, Bible 7, Poetry 5, Reading 5, Art 5. See J. B. Forster, 'Memoranda...', MS Box 9.6 (2), LSF and *MF*, 1/1, 15 Dec. 1871, 8.

[38] Apparently, the Friends Manchester Institute did not follow the usual Quaker practice of determining a sense of the meeting without taking a vote.

Charles Thompson, in the flush of triumph, proclaimed that 'the religious teachings at this Institute were of decidedly more value than what we heard over the way,' i.e., at Mount Street Meeting.[39]

Following this incident, ministers and elders from Mount Street ceased to attend lectures at the Institute. Whether that was because they were, as Charles Thompson believed, 'almost isolated' in the Monthly Meeting or because they could no longer countenance the scent of apostasy in the Institute's proceedings, the division grew apace and could scarcely remain simply a local concern.[40]

In the eyes of Manchester Meeting's evangelical leaders, the provocations of the Duncanites continued unabated. In April 1867 Joseph B. Forster, with clear reference to recent attempts to limit free expression at the Institute, lectured 'On Liberty'. Picking up the threads of David Duncan's previous address on 'Outward Reve- lation', Forster stated that 'liberty of thought and *Bible worship*' could not co-exist in the religion of George Fox and Robert Barclay. The 'true children of the Early Quakers', Forster argued, were men like Colenso and the authors of *Essays and Reviews* who understood that the only way to grasp the full realization of God's progressive revelations was in an atmosphere of complete liberty of thought. Only by re-establishing 'absolute freedom within the borders of the Society of Friends', Forster said, could Quakers again become what early Friends had been, 'the reconcilers of Religion with the advancement of Man in Knowledge of every kind'.[41]

In this instance, the Manchester liberals did not go unanswered. Fielden Thorp (1832–1921), an evangelical minister educated at University College, London and eventually headmaster of Bootham school in York, published a stinging rebuke to Forster's 'On Liberty' in the *Friends Quarterly Examiner*, accusing Forster, 'and those who think with him', of 'promulgating substantially the same doctrines as those preached by the originator of the Hicksite schism...' which were a 'fertile source of doubt and scepticism'. Thorp believed that the liberty advocated by the Manchester dissidents was 'the liberty of impugning the fundamental truths of

---

[39] J. B. Forster, 'Memoranda...', MS Box 9. 6 (2); Letter to the Secretary of the Friends Institute, n.d. [1866], HEMM, M 85/6/5/6. MCL; and *MF*, 1/1 15 Dec. 1871, 8. Also see Wilson, *Manchester* 39–40 and Cooper, *Crisis*, 3.

[40] J. B. Forster, 'Memoranda...', MS Box 9. 6 (2), LSF and Cooper, *Crisis*, 3.

[41] Joseph B. Forster, *On Liberty: An Address to the Members of the Society of Friends* (London 1867), 23–32 *passim*. Also see *BF*, 1 Jan. 1869, 19–20 and 1 Feb. 1869, 48 for a continuation of the dispute about the views of early Friends.

Christianity. . . .' There could be, he said, 'no safe standing ground between the plain old Gospel as preached by the Apostles and the wildest speculations of mystical Deism. If we forego our simple Bible faith, we may ultimately find ourselves reduced to universal scepticism.'[42]

Another attack on J. B. Forster was carried into the very citadel of the rebellious modernists. In January 1868, Thomas Hodgkin (1831–1913), a lawyer and banker who would earn an international reputation as the historian of *Italy and Her Invaders*, delivered a paper at the Friends' Institute directly challenging Forster's insistence on absolute liberty of expression. According to one sympathetic observer, the burden of Hodgkin's remarks was to illustrate why every religious body, however tolerant, must 'insist upon its members not openly proclaiming and propagating views *on essential points* opposed to its well known Principles and Doctrines'.[43]

Upon completion of his remarks, Hodgkin was shocked by the storm of indignant protest that ensued. David Duncan led the charge, noting that if Hodgkin's view of *essential* included the same 'over-strained estimate' of scriptural authority insisted upon 'by the Evangelical party,' then he could only respectfully disagree for 'as to many things the Scriptures tell us, it is *impossible* they can command our assent'. George Fox himself, Duncan said, 'did not hesitate to denounce the high pretensions claimed for the Scriptures as an authority and communication direct from God'. When an elderly Friend in the audience questioned the accuracy of Duncan's remarks, he struck back vehemently at what he termed an attempt to 'sit in judgment on . . . [my] conscience . . . You need not wonder at your low condition as a Church,' Duncan concluded, 'so long as you have amongst you a man with an ill-educated and illogical mind, professing to preach the glorious gospel.'[44]

---

[42] Fielden Thorp, *A Review of a Lecture on 'Liberty'* (London 1867), 6–7, 16–17, 19. Edwin Bronner lists Thorp among the 'less active Moderates' in London Yearly Meeting, noting: 'He became more moderate as he grew older.' Bronner, 'Moderates', 9.

[43] Cooper, *Crisis*, 4 italics in original and J. B. Forster, 'Memoranda . . .' MS Box 9.6 (2), LSF. Edward Milligan believes this address was distinctly out of character for Thomas Hodgkin, who was later a leader of progressive Quaker opinion, and more in keeping with the views of Hodgkin's father John, a strong evangelical. But also see Hope Hewison, ' "Human Progress and the Inward Light",' *JHFS*, 56/2 (1991), 135 for an earlier article by Thomas Hodgkin attacking one of the authors of *Essays and Reviews*.

[44] Cooper, *Crisis*, 4–5.

The 'most significant and painful' circumstance of this incident, said the scandalized observer, was the fact that the young men who were present overwhelmingly supported Duncan's intemperate outburst. One of them even went so far as to say that while the speaker's remarks might have been acceptable twenty-five years earlier, the influence of the Institute had changed Manchester Friends and they would never again go backwards despite the unenlightened views of certain evangelical ministers.

This 'censorious criticism of the Ministry... quite unparalleled at any former period' took place in the wake of still another confrontation between liberal youth and elderly authority. John B. Edmondson (1831–87), a Friend of some standing in Manchester Meeting (he was both an overseer and assistant clerk of Hardshaw East Monthly Meeting),[45] had, in private conversation with an elder, revealed doubts concerning biblical miracles because he did not believe God would contravene the laws of nature to perform magic tricks. This elder, upon hearing such an unsound exposition, attempted to block Edmondson's reappointment as assistant clerk. But despite the elder's assertion of 'heresy in an office-holder', Edmondson was reappointed.[46]

In the midst of these struggles and travails, George Satterthwaite (1822–91), a minister, formerly in Hardshaw East Monthly Meeting, wrote to Thomas Hodgkin's father, John (1800–75) deploring 'the state of things in Manchester... Both in and out of meeting. I could not', Satterthwaite noted, 'but be aware of a spirit of opposition, criticism and *free thinking*,' obviously reflecting 'the extreme views of D. Duncan & his friends'. This faction, he said, was rapidly gaining influence and even threatening dominance at Mount Street: 'I cannot but state how deeply I feel the existence and spread of this heresy[,] for I can call it nothing else *now*... This is a sad state of things & I trust in some shape the Quarterly Meeting must take it up.'[47]

Even as Satterthwaite was writing, a *Minute* reached Lancashire and Cheshire Quarterly Meeting asking that it appoint a commit-

---

[45] *MF*, 1/3 15 Feb. 1872, 41–2; Cooper, *Crisis* 7–9; and Wilson, *Manchester*, 40. According to E. H. Hankin, 'The Mental Ability of the Quakers,' *Science Progress*, 16 (1921–22), 659, J. B. Edmundson's father 'devised the present [1920s] effective system of railway tickets, and likewise invented the machine... for stamping them...'

[46] *MF*, I/3, 15 Feb. 1872, 41–2; Cooper, *Crisis* 8–9; and George Satterthwaite to John Hodgkin, 13 Jan. 1868, Port. C. 136, LSF.

[47] George Satterthwaite to John Hodgkin, 13 Jan. 1868. Emphasis in original.

tee to visit Manchester to assist 'in a case of difficulty'. Several of those attending Quarterly Meeting, including John Bright, 'strenuously resisted' this proposal. Bright warned that 'the consequences would be most disastrous, the unity of the Society would be broken, its manhood discouraged, its youth disgusted and deadly wounds inflicted, which years would not suffice to heal'.[48]

The famous orator's plea notwithstanding, a committee of visitors was appointed 'to render such assistance as may seem to be required'. Its seven members, not all strong evangelicals,[49] began regular attendance at the proceedings of Hardshaw East Monthly Meeting. After observing a series of rancorous meetings for business, including an unsuccessful attempt, initiated by the overseers of Mount Street Meeting, to create a committee to investigate whether David Duncan was professing 'unsound doctrine', the Clerk of the QM committee, William Thistlethwaite, expressed the view that 'the Friends of Manchester Meeting have far more to fear from ... strifes ... divisions ... and disputations, than *from any errors in doctrine*'.[50]

Thistlethwaite's comments were obviously intended to shame the leaders of Hardshaw East into putting their own house into a more harmonious condition, but it soon became apparent that his view of the Manchester situation was seriously disputed. At London Yearly Meeting in May 1868, evangelical Friends accused the Lancashire Visitors' Committee of failing 'to secure ... the right exercise of discipline,' even as 'the poison was spreading' among the young and innocent. A month later at a gathering of Lancashire and Cheshire QM, Samuel Jesper, an evangelical member of the Visiting Committee, asked to be removed from that body because

[48] J. B. Forster, 'Memoranda ...', MS Box 9.6 (2), LSF; *MF*, I/3, 15 Feb. 1872, 41–2; and Cooper, *Crisis*, 9. It is not clear if the requesting *Minute* was sent by Mount Street Monthly Meeting or by the Quarterly Meeting of Ministers and Elders.

[49] *Minute 7*, 16 Jan. 1868, *Minutes*, Lancashire and Cheshire Quarterly Meeting, Lancashire Record Office (LRO) lists the members of the committee as does Cooper, *Crisis*, 9, with apparent disapproval. Bronner, 'Moderates', names two of its members, W. E. Turner and William Thistlethwaite, in his list of influential moderates.

[50] Cooper, *Crisis*, 10–14, emphasis in original and *MF*, I/3 15 Feb. 1872, 42–3. *Minute 14*, 13 Feb. 1868, *Minutes*, HEMM, 1861–1870, MCL records, without note of thanks or regret, J. B. Edmondson's resignation as overseer and Assistant Clerk. *MF*, I/3, 15 Feb. 1872, 42 noted that Edmondson resigned 'for the sake of peace'. But peace was an illusive quality in Manchester Meeting. In March 1868 after the sense of the meeting was not to appoint a committee to investigate charges of unsoundness against David Duncan, Charles Thompson stated that the Manchester 'Select Meeting' of ministers, elders, and overseers, was '*an unmitigated evil*'. Cooper, *Crisis*, 13.

he did not believe its actions were 'calculated...to check the growth of unsound doctrine in Manchester Meeting: I am quite convinced', he continued, 'that Infidelity exists in that large Meeting...and that the most sacred doctrines of our holy religion are treated with contemptuous levity.'[51]

One observer thought that Samuel Jesper's words made a 'very serious impression' on the Quarterly Meeting, but he was not, in any case, allowed to be relieved and the Committee continued with the same divided membership. When the Quarterly Meeting assembled again a few months later, the Visitors offered a second report. The substance of their findings was that while some Manchester Friends were 'accustomed to exercise considerable freedom of speech, at times exceeding...the limitations which a more watchful spirit would enjoin, nevertheless, it is a satisfaction to believe that no outward breach of Love has occurred.' Friends in Manchester, the report concluded, 'with one or two exceptions ...claim for their views unity with the religious doctrines as held by our Society'.[52]

The announcement of this decidedly tepid verdict brought down a chorus of consternation and derision upon the committee. One evangelical Friend noted that the report provided 'no light whatever' on the state of Manchester Meeting. The staunch conservative William Irwin called the report 'the most delusive document...ever...presented to a [Friends'] meeting'. When a member of the Committee referred to his words as 'intemperate', Irwin replied that he was 'prepared to prove...that at least six members of Manchester Meeting hold...unsound opinions' and that one had only to read the published works of David Duncan and J. B. Forster to verify the 'truth and soberness' of his words.[53]

Despite these and other attacks, the Committee's Report was eventually accepted by the Quarterly Meeting.[54] Still, the issue was clearly unresolved and the presence of unsoundness in Manchester was rapidly becoming a national concern. *Minutes* of both the Quarterly and Hardshaw East Monthly Meetings, mention the

[51] The quotations are from Cooper, *Crisis*, 15–29 *passim*.

[52] Cooper's quotations in *Crisis*, 31–4 differ in precise wording but not in substance from the QM *Minutes*, 17 Sept. 1868, L&CQM, LRO.

[53] Cooper, *Crisis*, 35, 38–40.

[54] Ibid., 34–40; *Minutes*, 17 Sept. 1868, L&CQM, LRO; and *MF*, I/3 15 Feb. 1872, 43.

presence of the weighty evangelical leader, Joseph Bevan Braithwaite at their deliberations during the autumn of 1868.[55]

AN ANTIDOTE FOR POISON

Early in 1869 Frederick Cooper of Manchester, an evangelical Friend who had been among the most outspoken critics of the Quarterly Meeting Committee, privately published a sizeable pamphlet on 'The Crisis in Manchester'. Cooper described his tract as an 'account of the rise, progress and the development of Unsound Doctrine in Manchester Meeting' and he included in it long extracts from the writings of David Duncan and J. B. Forster. 'Before we can recover the healthy vitality of the Church,' Cooper said, 'we should understand its disease...and then, under the guidance of the Great Physician, such measures may be taken as will result in the cure of its wounds....'[56] Wounds, however, come in various forms. Although Friend Cooper claimed to be seeking a solution to division in Manchester Meeting, it soon became obvious that Cooper himself was part of the problem. For while more and more charges of apostasy were being hurled at the Manchester liberals, with Cooper among the foremost accusers, he himself was becoming implicated in a scandal with far more serious social consequences.

When former female servants in Cooper's household brought charges of 'gross immorality' against him, these accusations were, for some time, either ignored or swept under the carpet by the leaders of Manchester Meeting. Charles Thompson, whose hostility toward the leadership of that meeting had already been amply demonstrated, testified that 'to the last they had done all they could to stifle enquiry'.[57] Cooper was eventually disowned after an investigation revealed 'several cases of great impropriety', including two instances of 'criminal intercourse with young women in his service', one of whom became pregnant as a result. There seems to have been no criminal prosecution brought against Frederick

---

[55] *Minute 1*, 17 Sept. 1868, *Minutes*, L&CQM, LRO and *Minute 1*, 8 Oct. 1868, *Minutes*, HEMM, MCL.

[56] *MF*, I/3, 15 Feb. 1872, 43 and Cooper, *Crisis*, i.

[57] *Minute 9*, 11 Dec. 1870, in *Minutes*, HEMM, MCL and 'Notes of Interviews with members of Hardshaw East Monthly Meeting', 4–5, MS Box 9.5 (1), 5 LSF.

Cooper, but it seriously rankled the liberal faction that the officers of the meeting seemed more intent on pursuing heresy than on punishing crime.[58]

When London Yearly Meeting assembled in 1869, the Quarterly Meeting Committee's controversial report was again subjected to much critical scrutiny. After Samuel Jesper had repeated his consistent disagreement with his colleagues' conclusions and described the situation in Manchester as 'a fearful heresy', others also expressed concern. Prominent among these was Henry Hipsley (1810–89) of London, a leading evangelical spokesman. When persons claiming to be Friends 'openly disseminate heresy in printed form' on behalf of the Manchester Friends' Institute, Hipsley noted, the time for disciplinary measures had long since passed.[59]

Speaking for the QM Committee, William Thistlethwaite asserted that interviews with persons accused of unsoundness had revealed no grounds for disciplinary action despite 'some objectionable passages' written a few years earlier. The committee, he said, had met with many members of the Friends' Institute and counselled them against presenting 'certain kinds of lectures'. This advice, Thistlethwaite added, had been 'kindly received and adhered to' and as a result, the committee believed that 'a better feeling existed' in Manchester. Another committee member, William Ecroyd (1796–1876), a former clerk of Lancashire and Cheshire QM, concluded that 'there had been...a much greater amount of apprehension to the prevalence of unsound views than the facts warranted, and that the young men were generally of sound mind and not disaffected towards the Society'. The need,

---

[58] *Minute 11,* 13 Jan. 1870, *Minutes 13 and 14,* 1 July 1871, *Minutes,* HEMM, MCL provides a detailed description of this 'painful enquiry' and the committee's conclusion that there had been 'a case of seduction of a virtuous young woman' which required that Cooper be separated from the Society of Friends. For a decidedly partisan account of the controversy over Cooper's private life, see *MF,* I/7, 15 June 1872, 102 which emphasized 'the public feeling arrayed against Ministers, Elders, and Overseers...on account of the attempt to shield immorality because they feared that its exposure would have scandalized orthodoxy...' In January 1870 Cooper resigned from Hardshaw East Monthly Meeting, but his resignation was refused pending an investigation by a committee of the Meeting. After another 'painful enquiry', this committee, believing that the charges against Cooper had been proven, recommended that he be disowned.

[59] From a summary of Yearly Meeting proceedings in *TF,* June 1869, 121–26. Also see *BF,* 3 June 1869, 132–39. Henry Hipsley visited Lancashire and Cheshire early in 1870 with a certificate for religious service. *Minute 3,* 20 Jan. 1870, *Minutes,* L&CQM, LRO.

Ecroyd said, was not discipline but rather 'forbearance, kindness and consideration'.[60]

For the moment, this view, while hotly contested, still prevailed and Yearly Meeting took no further action. Still, the discussion closed on a somewhat ominous note as Joseph Bevan Braithwaite, a recent visitor to the troubled area, noted that the decision not to act should 'not be considered a retreat from the foundation of the prophets and apostles'. Even more to the point were lines from the yearly *General Epistle*, of which Braithwaite was the chief drafter:

To claim to be a Christian, and to declaim the testimony and the authority of Christ Jesus, either as to the truth declared concerning Him in the inspired record of Holy Scripture or as to his right to reign over us, involves an obvious contradiction. We would caution our members against all writings, the tendency of which may be to weaken their allegiance to Christ, to create a disesteem . . . for Holy Scripture or in any other way to enfeeble their capacity for engaging in sober earnestness on the duties of life.[61]

If indeed J. B. Braithwaite and his allies intended to sound a final note of warning to the Manchester rebels, their admonitions were unheard or unheeded.[62] During the following winter, Mount Street Meeting was visited by James Owen, a travelling minister from Iowa Yearly Meeting, whose preaching of what one critic called 'pure dogmatic theology' upset both liberal and conservative Friends. An ill-advised, though thoroughly Quakerly, attempt to reconcile differences ended with Owen proclaiming 'he could have no charity for any one who did not agree with him . . . on the miraculous Conception and birth of Christ'. In addition to a lack of charity, some dissidents also claimed a breach of trust when notes of the conference, clearly intended to be confidential,

---

[60] *TF*, June 1869, 121–2.

[61] Ibid. 126 and *LYM*, 1869, 28. In July 1869 Caleb Kemp attended Manchester Meeting 'under some feeling of concern & think we had evidence that I was not in any wrong place. The faithful there are much troubled by the prevalence of unsound religious views obtaining amongst some of their fellow members'. C. R. K., 'Journals', July 1869.

[62] In its final report before being discharged, the ever optimistic QM Committee reported 'that moderation and rightmindedness are more manifest' in Manchester Meeting than for sometime past. *Minute 7*, 16 Sept. 1869, *Minutes*, L&CQM, LRO.

were printed and circulated by evangelical members of the meeting.[63]

In the wake of this new upheaval, perhaps partly in response to it, David Duncan, despite the earlier agreements to avoid controversial subjects, again mounted the rostrum at Manchester Friends' Institute to present an address on 'National Life'. Duncan's lecture revealed, among other things, his republicanism (monarchy and royalty, he said, were 'quite irreconcilable with an advanced rule of reason'), his social radicalism (there could 'be no national life worthy of the name until the nation... means the body of the people, until simplicity of life enables the workers to take their ground according to their qualifications, and not according to their wealth') and his irreverent free-thinking ('Obsolete dogmas will be swept aside and the bigots, who are at present prejudicing the claims of rational religion, will possibly live to admit their folly, in the demolition of the whole structure... ').[64]

One critic, reviewing Duncan's lecture in *The Friend*, noted that his views seemed 'calculated to repel' rather than convince.[65] When London Yearly Meeting met in May 1870, it quickly became obvious that Duncan's pronouncements would no longer be ignored. After receiving a minute from Lancashire and Cheshire Quarterly Meeting pleading for assistance in dealing with 'the *want of love*' among Manchester Friends, Yearly Meeting Clerk Joseph Storrs Fry (1826–1913) expressed the sense of the Meeting that, in view of the gravity of the situation, immediate steps should be taken for the appointment of 'suitable Friends to visit the Quarterly Meeting...' At the suggestion of the venerable Josiah Forster, responsibility for the nomination of this committee was given over to the Epistle Committee of which he was himself a member. This decidedly evangelical body was increasingly dominated by Forster's protégé J. B. Braithwaite, soon to become the Hammer of Unsound Manchester Friends.[66]

---

[63] *Minute 1*, 20 Jan. 1870, *Minutes*, L&CQM, LRO; *MF*, I/6, 15 May 1872, 88–9; and Wilson, *Manchester*, 41. J. B. Forster, for one, believed that the printing of these notes was perfectly acceptable and in keeping with the principles of free speech and enquiry he espoused. See J. B. Forster, *Memoranda . . .*, MS. Box 9.6 (2), LSF.

[64] David Duncan, *National Life* (London 1870), 9, 15, 21.

[65] Review of 'National Life', *TF*, 1 July 1870, 170–1.

[66] *LYM* 1870, 16; Harrison Penney, 'Account of Yearly Meeting, 1870', MS Box P 1/8, LSF; *TF*, 2 June 1870, 126; and *MF*, I/10, 15 Sept. 1872, 152.

Lawyer, linguist, biblical scholar, minister, J. B. Braithwaite has been variously described as a sort of ' "Quaker Bishop" keeping the Society sound in doctrine' and as 'the towering Friend in the evangelical stream and indeed in the Society itself' for over half a century.[67] Not surprisingly, Braithwaite was named on the Committee to visit Lancashire as were Joseph Storrs Fry and fifteen others, a dozen of whom were also members of the appointing body.[68] Ignoring vigorous protests and warnings about the Committee's possibly disruptive influence, J. B. Braithwaite's 'Journal' recalled the Yearly Meeting as 'a time of renewed exercise and helping' during which he had been 'much aware of the Lord's directing hand'.[69]

There were, however, some Friends who believed that something besides the hand of the Lord was at work. One of the most arresting tracts to appear during this crucial stage of the Manchester difficulty was *Thoughts on the Toleration of Important Differences of Opinion in the Same Religious Community*... Its author, adopting the *nom de plume* 'Trust-to-Truth', warned the Yearly Meeting Committee against confusing 'the correctness or soundness of certain religious opinions, and the justice or wisdom of forcibly repressing...those who published the sentiments in question'. The matter of doctrinal soundness, he said, was not so uncomplicated as some Friends apparently thought; Quakerism lacked a written credo and thus any consensus as to what was sound. He reminded readers that thirty-five years earlier the visitation of a similar committee to Hardshaw East Meeting had resulted in the silencing and subsequent withdrawal of Isaac Crewdson and his Beaconite followers because they rejected the writings of early Friends and would accept *only* the authority of the Bible.[70] Some of David

[67] A. T. Alexander, 'Yearly Meeting Attenders—Familiar Personalities', *JFHS*, 27 (1930), 15–6 and Wilson, *Manchester*, 42.

[68] *TF*, 2 June 1870, 126; *MF*, I/10, 15 Sept. 1872, 152; and Wilson, *Manchester* 41–3.

[69] Joseph Bevan Braithwaite, 'Journals and Commentaries' (hereinafter J. B. B., 'Journals', with date), 1865–76, 21 June 1870, 153, LSF. Braithwaite gives the names of some Committee members; a fuller but incomplete list is given in a letter from C. Brightwen Rowntree to John Nickalls, 26 Aug. 1934, MS Box 9.1 (2), LSF. Also see, *Minute 1*, 16 June 1870, *Minutes*, L &CQM, LRO and *LYM*, 1870, 16.

[70] In September and November 1870, *The Friend* published a series of articles on the 'Beacon Controversy and the Yearly Meeting Committee of 1835–7', by Edward Ash, M. D., the last surviving member of that Committee. Ash took the position that he and the other committee members had been mistaken in their treatment of Isaac Crewdson because 'the nature and state of the case was not such as to justify either the Committee in suggesting,

Duncan's severest critics, noted Trust-to-Truth, were as extreme in their dismissal of early Friends as the Beaconites had been. 'If anyone merits discipline,' he declared, 'it would manifestly be the Evangelical or Calvinist party;' yet no committee had set about investigating them. Nor did Trust-to-Truth advocate that one be established. The important point, he said, was that the Society had suffered so grievously from 'this easy cry of unsoundness that it ought to be scrupulously careful how it employs...a weapon so unfair, yet so frequently and effectively used, simply because it is so easy to wield'.[71]

When the Yearly Meeting Committee gathered at Manchester in mid-August 1870 to commence its deliberations, there were no signs that its members had heard Trust-to-Truth's admonition. Under the guiding hand of J. B. Braithwaite, they decided that because of their 'confidence in one another' they would forgo the usual practice of conferring with a representative group from the Monthly Meeting as to how they should proceed. Thus, they were, in Braithwaite's words, 'left at liberty to pursue our own course'. Some dissidents, however, believed that the effect of the Committee's decision had been 'to declare martial law amongst Friends...and set at nought the securities provided in the Book of Discipline against religious persecution'.[72]

The Committee proceeded with its charge to assist Hardshaw East Monthly Meeting by interviewing groups and individuals chosen to represent a cross-section of ideas and opinions within the Meeting. By J. B. Braithwaite's account some of these exchanges produced powerful manifestations of 'the work of harmony', while others were filled with 'a sorrowful want of harmony'.[73] The Monthly Meetings' elders and overseers were 'full of anxiety', while several of the nearly twenty groups that waited upon the Committee blamed local difficulties on the fact that leaders of the Meeting 'gave no room for thinking minds' nor scope for consultation between members of different generations.

---

or the Monthly Meting in taking, so extreme a course as that of suspending the exercise of Isaac Crewdson's ministry'. Ibid., 1 Sept. 1870, 207–11 and 1 Nov. 1870, 256–7.

[71] Trust-to-Truth, *Thoughts*...(London 1870), 3, 7–9. 12. The author of this article has not been identified.

[72] J. B. B., 'Journals', 19 Aug. 1870, 167–8 and *MF*, I/1, 15 Dec. 1871, 2.

[73] J. B. B., 'Journals', 17 Aug. 1870 [this date is probably in error as it follows after entries for 19 Aug.], 170, 174; *MF*, I/10, 15 Sept. 1872, 152–3; and Wilson, *Manchester*, 44–5.

As a result, they said, serious discussion of religious subjects were, by default, carried over into the freer atmosphere of the Friends' Institute.[74]

One evening the visitors 'met about 35 of our young friends under 30: some of whom painfully illustrated the spread of Modernism and sceptical views'. Braithwaite called the meeting 'a very painful opportunity'. There was a similar encounter with female Friends, including David Duncan's wife, Sarah Ann, and Maria and Jane Atkinson, wherein the Committee discovered that not only was Mrs Duncan in full sympathy with her husband but that the Atkinsons were openly avowing Unitarian sentiments. J. B. B. was 'deeply pained'.[75]

The Committee found J. B. Edmondson to be 'loving and tender', but when J. B. Forster was interviewed, he 'boldly stated his views [sic] . . . that each member of X[Christ's] Church was at liberty to believe what influenced him'. Braithwaite reported that 'on being referred to our Rules, he said that the Society was at liberty to change its faith'.[76]

The most important conference was with David Duncan himself, who, Braithwaite noted, received them 'with openings and candor' but no repentance. The Committee's notes make clear that while Duncan wished to be conciliatory because 'the position of Antagonism in which he had been placed . . . had been injurious to his own mind', he would not alter his views nor cease to speak them when the spirit moved him. Not surprisingly, J. B. Braithwaite concluded that Duncan's 'views were not those held by Friends on the authority of Scripture, on the person of Jesus Christ and on the efficacy of his saving sacrifice'.[77]

Another member of the Committee, while admitting that many younger Manchester Friends had given 'Painful evidence' of 'Socinian, or rather Hicksite' beliefs, also noted the widespread dissatisfaction with 'the alleged incompetence, errors of judgement and partisan conduct of the Friends in official station'. In the end, however, these many and detailed complaints 'shared by a

[74] See 'Notes of Interviews with members of Hardshaw East Monthly Meeting', two parts, MS, Box 9.5 (1)–(2). Wilson, *Manchester*, 44–6 provides a summary of the nineteen meetings held by the Committee.

[75] J. B. B., 'Journals', 17 and 19 Aug. 1870, 168–70, 173 and 'Notes on Interviews . . .' MS Box 9.5 (1)–(2), LSF.

[76] Ibid. and J. B. B., 'Journals', 17 Aug. 1870, 170, 172.

[77] Ibid. 172 and 'Charles Fox's notes', 26 Aug. 1870, MS Box 9.2 (1), LSF.

considerable number', most of whom disclaimed any sympathy with Duncanite views, were ignored in the Committee's official communications.[78]

Withal, the work did not go well. The Committee found some solace in the 'very powerful ... manifestation ... of harmony' among 'our *Christian* friends'[79] but could claim little progress in bringing youthful strays back into the fold. When J. B. Braithwaite returned to London in September, he confided to his 'Journal' distress not only with the 'weight of the Manchester difficulty' and its effect on the Society but also with 'this sin stricken, stormtossed world' graphically reflected by war and upheavals in 'poor desolate France' where the fires of the Communards blazed even as he wrote: 'Keep me Christ for I cannot keep myself.'[80]

In October several members of the Yearly Meeting Committee returned to Manchester, conferring again with both Duncan and Forster as well as representatives of the Monthly Meeting. One of the latter, expressed the view that David Duncan's apparent devotion to the young people of the Meeting reflected 'a strong determination in D. D. to be the conqueror in this meeting'. This, he said, was more Duncan's object than spreading truth or establishing liberty: 'His heat and impetuosity of mind is very painful ... carried on in a loud tone & a very dogmatic manner while objecting to all dogmas.'[81]

J. B. Braithwaite, apparently recovered from his recent melancholia, called these meetings 'favoured seasons' which further convinced him of the need to deal with the crisis by setting forth 'the Testimony of the Evangelical Brethren [as] to the person and character of our Lord & Saviour ...'[82] By mid-January 1871, Braithwaite had convinced the Committee that they should prepare a document stating 'our settled concurrence as to Christian doctrine ... and our determination to uphold it—as a basis of future action, if such action were called for'. Clearly, then, the

[78] 'Impressions on the State of Manchester Meeting by a member of the Committee', 9th month 1870, MS Box 9.4, LSF.

[79] J. B. B., 'Journals', 17 Aug. 1870, 174, italics added.

[80] Ibid. 3 Sept. 1870, 175–6 and 18 Sept. 1870, 177 f.

[81] 'Interview with Joseph H. King', 14 Oct. 1870, MS Box 9.6 (1) and J. B. B., 'Journals', 16 Oct. 1870, 182–4.

[82] J. B. B., 'Journals' 16 Oct. 1870, 183–4.

committee had decided to proffer this 'Declaration' as a test of soundness or unsoundness rather than make an further attempts to reconcile the dissidents in Manchester.[83] As the Society of Friends had never adopted any formal credal statement, this was a novel procedure, but because the Committee had been appointed by London Yearly Meeting, there was the implication that such a document, heavily laced with evangelical views and supported by quotations from the writings of early Friends as well as Scriptural references, might henceforth be recognized as a doctrinal standard for the entire Society.

The Committee characterized its 'Declaration' as setting forth 'some of those fundamental principles of Christian Truth which have always been professed by our religious Society'. These principles included the Trinity, the sinfulness of man as a consequence of Adam's fall, the immediate influence of the Holy Spirit through Jesus Christ (but always separated from both conscience and 'the natural facility of reason'), the acceptance of the Old and New Testaments as 'the authentic testimony of the Spirit', an unwavering allegiance to the Divinity of Jesus Christ 'whom God hath set forth to be a propitiation through faith in his blood...' and who was 'the Shepherd and Bishop of Souls...' And, finally: 'the revelation of God to man, in the Gospel of Jesus Christ, is given, not as material for speculation, but to teach us all necessary truth in regard to our relation with our Creator, and the means whereby we may become reconciled to Him.'[84]

Prior to the publication of the 'Declaration', the Committee also circulated an 'Address... To Hardshaw East Monthly Meeting' which summarized its proceedings to date, noted its discovery in Manchester of 'opinions freely propagated, tending to throw discredit upon Holy Scripture' and set forth its views on doctrinal soundness as supported in *Christian Doctrine, Practice and Discipline*, recently promulgated (1861) by London Yearly Meeting. The 'Address' concluded with a frank warning: 'We entreat those who, from whatever cause, may have relaxed their hold on any of the truths of Divine revelation to be willing, in fear of the Lord, and in a wise distrust of... their finite powers, seriously to review

---

[83] Ibid. 6 and 11 Jan. 1871, 186–8. J. B. B.'s notes on the meeting of 11 January strongly suggest his decisive influence.
[84] The *Declaration* was reprinted in *LYM*, 1872, 32–4.

their position, both as regards themselves and the Christian community with which they are connected.'[85]

After this sombre address had been printed and circulated, one correspondent to the *British Friend* called it 'truly valuable and weighty... written under the sweet influences of... Christian concern for the spiritual welfare of those among whom the Committee has been labouring'.[86] High praise, from the converted, but apparently without effect on its intended audience. For scarcely had the ink dried upon the pages of the 'Address' when David Duncan delivered still another controversial lecture at the Manchester Friends' Institute. On this occasion, his subject was 'John Woolman', the saintly eighteenth-century American Friend and abolitionist, whose example of courageously living his faith so as to change the moral climate of his time Duncan contrasted with 'the Godless condition of feeling' of later men who would 'idolize the New Testament and at the same time ridicule those who endeavor to carry out its directions and precepts...' Such deluded persons, said Duncan, would do well to learn from John Woolman's example that

the great work of life is to live... to make pleasant the duties of the part assigned to us... the world will dispense with a religion which exists only as a kind a rampart against the artillery of the soldiers in the war of human freedom. Christianity was not intended as a system of abstract thought... it never contemplated state intrigues and court cabals as means of propagating its principles...'[87]

Duncan's provocative words brought new letters of concern or outrage to the Yearly Meeting Committee;[88] more significantly, it brought the Committee to a decision to confront him personally once more and 'if our interview proved unavailing to bring his case under the notice of the Mo[nthly] M[eetin]g'.[89]

---

[85] 'Address from the Yearly Meeting Committee to Hardshaw East Monthly Meeting' reprinted in ibid., 58–61 and in *BF*, 1 March 1871, 65–6. Opponents of the Committee's actions pointed out that the *Discipline*, so recently transformed regarding speech, dress, marriage customs, etc. was always a 'working paper', never a fixed creed.

[86] J[ohn] H[odgkin] to *BF*, April 1871, 92.

[87] '*John Woolman': A Paper at the Friends' Institute Manchester', 20 January 1871* (London and Manchester 1871), 19–20, 25.

[88] For example, see Alfred Brayshaw to committee, n.d., MS Box 9.3 (1), LSF.

[89] Braithwaite, 'Journals', 20 April 1871, 194–5.

On 14 April 1871 the Committee again interviewed Duncan, assuring him of its desire 'to act in a spirit of love ... to restore the harmony of the Meeting on the right foundation'. In light of this, they hoped that he might in some way modify positions he held which were 'at variance with the recognized views of the Society of Friends'. Speaking for the Committee, J. B. Braithwaite noted especially Duncan's apparent denial of the 'Divine authority of the Holy Scriptures & the Deity of our Saviour,' sentiments 'incompatible with membership in the Society'.[90]

After a long silence, Duncan responded by asking why, when individuals made accusations against him, the Committee had not admonished 'those busy bodies' about the moral dangers of 'tale bearing and detraction'. As for the *Discipline*, Duncan stated that when parts of it ceased to speak to the time, they should be altered. Why, in any case, he asked, should he be charged with departing from the views of the Society when, for instance, members of Hitchin Meeting 'read the Scripture in their meeting,' a complete departure from any traditional form of worship practiced by Friends. The Committee replied that they were not appointed to consider the case of Hitchin but to deal with disturbances in Manchester of which Duncan appeared to be the principle author.[91]

At this point, Duncan came 'under much excitement' declaring that there should be only public meetings in these matters since it was a waste of time to hold private conferences with men who were 'shut up in narrow, sectarian literal views and could not grasp the scope of the Gospel'. He had been called an infidel who denied Christ but his own conscience convicted him of nothing and 'he would die for what he felt to be truth'. Furthermore, he could not repress his views, 'for if he attempted it they would ooze out of his coat tail'. The Committee, he said, was 'blasphemously endeavouring' to drive from the fold all who did not believe precisely as they did. With that outburst, Duncan stormed out of the room, leaving the shaken committee to draft its recommendations to the Monthly Meeting.[92]

[90] 'Interview with D. Duncan on 6th day 4 Mo. 14 [Friday, 14 April 1871]', MS Box 9.3 (8), LSF.

[91] Ibid.

[92] Braithwaite, 'Journals' 20 April 1871, 194–5 and 'Interview with D. Duncan ... 14 April 1871', MS Box 9.3 (8), LSF.

Three days later, the Committee brought notice to Hardshaw East that it had found David Duncan's views at variance with those of the Society and added that it was prepared to see the case through to final resolution. In effect this meant that the Visiting Committee, having accused Duncan of heresy, was offering to act on behalf of the Monthly Meeting in determining his guilt or innocence.[93] Thus, an outside investigating body would serve as the internal judiciary for the local meeting, although no members of that meeting would partake in its final determination. This recommendation was 'very fully deliberated upon' by a badly divided monthly meeting. J. B. Braithwaite noted that twenty-eight opposed the document while thirty-four or thirty-five supported the committee 'which the Clerk...pronounced to the judgment of the Meeting'. What he failed to mention, however, was that the voices of the Committee members in attendance had, in effect, overborne the majority opinion of regular members of the Meeting, an innovation not lost upon the Duncanite faction.[94]

Before any action was taken, however, the Committee presented an interim report to Yearly Meeting stressing that the situation at Hardshaw East was still claiming the Committee's 'most serious deliberation and care' with regard to matters 'of fundamental Christian truth' and, therefore, it asked to be allowed to continue its work. Response to this request mirrored the divisions that the Manchester difficulty had exposed. Evangelicals praised the Committee for upholding 'the great doctrines...[that] made Friends a Christian Church' while detractors, mainly from Manchester, accused the Visitors of unwarranted interference in the affairs of a local meeting. J. B. Forster went so far as to say that the Committee's unChristian treatment of some Manchester Friends reflected the unhealthy state of their entire Religious Society. But this protest availed him nothing. Because 'the tide of confidence in the Committee ran sharply for an hour or more', its work was continued in hopes of bringing some final resolution to the Manchester difficulty which, in J. B. B.'s words, 'seethed like a cauldron'.[95]

[93] *Minute 4*, 17 April 1871, *Minutes*, HEMM, MCL.

[94] *MF*, I/10 15 Sept. 1872, 153; George S. Gibson (for the Committee) to David Duncan, 19 April 1871, MS Box 9.3 (3), LSF and Braithwaite, 'Journals', 20 April 1871, 195.

[95] Charles Fox, 'Notes of visit to David Duncan and his family', 19 May 1870 [sic], MS Box 9.2 (1), LSF; *LYM*, 1871, 21–3; J. S. Rowntree, 'Account of Yearly Meeting, 1871, MS Vol. S 370, LSF and *TF*, 8 June 1871, 125–6.

Shortly after the close of Yearly Meeting, the cauldron boiled over. In mid-June J. B. Braithwaite and Robert Alsop informed the Committee of a new outrage perpetrated by David Duncan and his followers. It seemed that the Manchester dissidents had taken a hand in inviting Charles Voysey (1828–1912), an Anglican vicar recently deprived of his living for publicly denying, among other things, eternal punishment for sin and biblical infallibility, to speak in their city (though not at the Friends Institute).[96] Duncan, who doubtless saw Voysey as an embattled comrade in the struggle for free expression, not only chaired the second of two Voysey lectures but also hosted a reception in his honour. The lectures, characterized by one scandalized Manchester Friend as 'awfully profane', were widely reported in the local press which did not fail to note the prominent role played by Friends, especially Duncan and Charles Thompson.[97] For the Committee, this was the final straw.

THE RECKONING

On 22 June 1871, J. B. Braithwaite, Isaac Brown (1801–76) and Charles Fox (1797–1878), acting for the Committee, wrote to David Duncan assuring him of 'feelings of personal regard toward thyself', but noting with dismay 'a serious aggravation of the charge now pending against thee'. Not only had he endorsed the views of a man widely known to be 'altogether opposed to the Divine authority of Holy Scripture and the Deity of our Lord', but he had also invited many people, including young Friends, to meet with Charles Voysey in the Duncan home. 'Painful as it is to our feelings,' the letter concluded, 'it is our duty to inform thee that the public countenancing of the dissemination of such principles is altogether . . . inconsistent with thy position as a Member of our religious Society.'[98]

[96] R. Alsop and J. B. B. to Friends, 17 June 1871, MS Box 9.1 (6), LSF. For an account of Voysey's career, see *Dictionary of National Biography, Twentieth Century, 1912–1921* (London 1927), 545–6. Also see Edward H. Milligan, 'In Reason's Ear'; Some Quaker and Anglican Perplexities', *FQ*, 23/8 (October 1984), 384–96.

[97] Braithwaite, 'Journals', 13 Aug. 1871, 197–200 and R. Alsop and J. B. B. to Friends, 17 June 1871, MS Box 9.1 (6), LSF.

[98] Isaac Brown, Chas. Fox and J. B. Braithwaite to David Duncan, 22 June 1871, MS Box 9.3 (9), LSF.

Because of these new developments, the Committee travelled to Manchester to meet with Hardshaw East Monthly Meeting a month earlier than originally planned. There, on 13 July, 'after full deliberation, during much of which D. D. was present, the Monthly Meeting came clearly to the judgment to disown him'.[99] In reporting this result, *The Friend* used its editorial columns to provide full particulars on the case and to deliver a solemn message to its readers: 'We earnestly hope that any of our members, and especially those in younger life, who may have lost their hold on doctrines of the gospel in their fullness, will be led seriously to reconsider their position, for it is only by the exercise of true faith in Christ on the part of the members... that the Church herself can be maintained.[100]

It seemed that evangelicals had succeeded in making David Duncan an object lesson on the fate of Friends who failed to exercise true faith, but few expected the matter to end there. Within a week of Duncan's disownment, J. B. Forster published a pamphlet on 'The Society of Friends and Freedom of Thought in 1871' in which he charged that Duncan had been unjustly and unconstitutionally driven out from Friends 'in order to gratify resentment or allay fear'. It was, Forster said, bad enough that the Society no longer permitted liberty of opinion but even worse 'when it adds to the narrowness of its Discipline a disregard of the provisions made therein for the protection of its members from the unjust accusation of passion or fanaticism'.[101] Many in Manchester and elsewhere believed, with Forster, that the Yearly Meeting Committee, in its desire to quell what looked to be an incipient spiritual rebellion, had by-passed normal procedures to ensure that nothing was left to chance. Thus, after reporting Duncan's unsoundness to Hardshaw East, the Committee had arranged to represent the Monthly Meeting in investigating its own accusations and having verified these charges to its own satisfaction, it had persuaded Hardshaw East to sustain its recommendation of disownment. Duncan's supporters asserted that, by so acting, the Committee had violated the principles of both common decency and English jurisprudence, charging Duncan with heresy, demanding that he disprove their accusations and, when he refused to co-

[99] Braithwaite, 'Journals', 13 Aug. 1871, 199–200.   [100] *TF*, 1 Aug. 1871, 193–4.
[101] (Manchester 1871), 10, 26–8.

operate, using the *ex post facto* evidence of his appearance at the Voysey lectures to sustain the original charges.[102]

After his disownment, Duncan claimed that while he would not fight merely for the sake of his own membership, failure to invoke his right of appeal to Yearly Meeting would mean that 'no Friend's liberty or membership would be safe'. A prolonged and bitter contest was anticipated.[103]

Then, less than a month after his disownment, David Duncan died suddenly from an attack of 'virulent small pox'.[104] J. B. Braithwaite immediately wrote to members of the Visitor's Committee noting that 'it would be a matter of deep regret and pain, if it were supposed that any of us regarded the event with any other feelings than of heartfelt sympathy with those who mourn the loss of a much loved and valued friend'. But in his 'Journal', Braithwaite took a rather different stance. The fact that Duncan's death had resulted in the immediate resignation of eleven of his supporters and ended the threat of an appeal was, said J. B. B., 'a marvelous winding up of D. D.'s case ... How wonderful are the ways of Providence! Last year he stood in what appeared to be proud defiance; now laid low in the dust. How clearly may we trace the Hand that has graciously guided and thus far protected our little Society from the inroads of a dangerous scepticism ... that he Himself may have all the praise.'[105]

While Duncan's grief-stricken family and friends were not privy to J. B. Braithwaite's private jottings, many would not have been surprised by their tone or sentiments. For Duncan's sudden death had clearly 'deepened ... the feeling that he had been dealt with in a harsh and vindictive spirit'. Claiming that a dogmatic creed had become the test for membership, his wife and closest associates determined to withdraw from the Society while still believing themselves 'as fully entitled to the name Friends as the Evangelical

---

[102] *MF*, I/1, 15 Dec. 1871, 2; 1/7, 15 June 1872, 101–2; 1/10, 15 Sept. 1872, 153–4; and 11/6, 15 June 1873, 101.

[103] Ibid. 1/10, 15 Sept. 1872, 154.

[104] S[hipley] N[eave] to J. B. Braithwaite (copy), 7 August 1871, MS Box 9.3 (4), LSF.

[105] J. B. Braithwaite to Friends [Yearly Meeting Committee], 8 August 1871, ibid. and J. B. B., 'Journals', 13 August 1871, 197, 200–1. Cf. J. B. B. to my dear Cousin [probably Shipley Neave], 11 Aug. 1871, MS Box 9.4 (1), LSF: 'I have felt the event deeply ... In looking back, I can see nothing, *substantially*, that we could have done differently;—though very sensible of my own short-comings. Thankfulness clothes my spirit in the sense of the *Guidance* which has, I think, been graciously afforded from step to step–not for our sakes, for that of the cause ...'

party, who consider the most characteristic ideas of early Quakers to be dangerous exaggeration of truth'.[106]

Besides the fourteen who eventually resigned their membership, there was another group of forty-two Manchester Friends, who, while not wishing to leave the Society, signed a letter of 'unqualified protest' against the 'irregular, hasty and arbitrary' handling of Duncan's case. They expressed the hope that their protest would bring to a halt 'the attempt to fix a doctrinal standard of orthodoxy amongst us and so avert the calamity of further strife and ultimate dispersion'.[107]

One of the Friends who signed this protest was Mary Jane Hodgson, an artist and poet, whose brother Joseph Spence Hodgson was a prominent member of the Friends' Institute and a close friend to David Duncan. The letters of this thoughtful conservative Friend provide a candid and heartfelt response to the tragedy that had befallen her religious community. She recounted to a friend that Sarah Ann Duncan, who had been 'out of her mind since sometime after the funeral', had received many letters of sympathy, some even from men on the Yearly Meeting Committee who 'wrote very kindly'. But J. B. Braithwaite, she said, had written 'coldly, more so than any. He is considered very hard and lawyer-like by many here'. Mary Hodgson deeply resented what she felt to be Braithwaite's 'special pleading to get D. D. disowned'. Outsiders, she said, were 'amazed at Friends sending persons to override a meeting to which they do not belong...like the Pope excommunicating Dr. Dollinger for not believing in his "infallibility"'.[108]

Hodgson added that while she and all her family thoroughly disapproved of the Committee's actions, they would not resign from Friends. 'We are *born* members and consider our rights equal to those of any in the society on that ground.' But if the Hodgsons would not leave the fold, they found little peace within it.

---

[106] *MF*, 1/1, 15 Dec. 1871, 2 and 11/6, 15 June 1873, 101. Of the twelve members of the meeting who initially submitted their resignations, the officers of Hardshaw East Monthly Meeting accepted eleven without an expression of regret; Sarah Ann Duncan's resignation was held in abeyance and then quietly accepted. Two others subsequently resigned. For the complete list of names see *Minute 1*, 10 Aug. 1871, 70, 73, 82 & 88, *Minutes*, HEMM, MCL and Braithwaite, 'Journals', 13 Aug. 1871, 197–8 and 20 Sept. 1871, 214. Also see *MF*, 11/6, 15 June 1873, 101.

[107] *MF*, 11/6, 15 June 1873, 101–2.

[108] Mary Hodgson to Elizabeth Green, 12 Aug. 1871, Port. 59, LSF.

We ... consider that the whole Society of Friends ... has forsaken the Faith of its forefathers ... and gone over to other Dissenters. . . . There is no question that the Society is narrowing itself to a creed. . . it is impossible for me to express to thee what a cruel thing I feel this to be and how little hope there is that such action will ever draw us nearer together or turn the hearts of the children to the fathers. . . . I feel that if I went to J. B. Braithwaite ... with a statement ... of some theological tenets, I should be told that my notions were 'inconsistent' with my position as a member, but that if I went to Christ ... he, the greatest heretic of his time, would welcome me to his society, and not excommunicate me for what is, after, all but a head matter. . . . Oh, that our preachers would leave off harping on doctrinal head matters and speak to the heart & soul—I feel no satisfaction in these outward credenda ... the best worship seems to be striving after duty, poorly and weakly as one strives, and the best peace a little quiet alone with God where outward things are but hindering ones.[109]

Mary Hodgson's distraught plea sounded in stark contrast to Joseph Bevan Braithwaite's triumphant tones in celebrating the victory of righteousness over heresy. From the perspective of 1871, it would be difficult to image any other prospect than of stern evangelicalism marching from victory to victory until the Society of Friends had 'become submerged in the rising tide of "Evangelical" sentiment'. Indeed, within two years of Duncan's death, Edward T. Bennett (1831–1908), after an unsuccessful appeal to Yearly Meeting in 1873, was, like David Duncan, expelled from the Society of Friends for supporting views of the infamous Charles Voysey 'which were entirely opposed to the Divinity of Christ and to the doctrine of His atonement'. Caleb Kemp found it 'a painful affair', but J. B. Braithwaite recorded his 'humble thanksgiving' that the disposition of Bennett's case had provided 'a decisive testimony against the promulgation of Voyseyism'.[110] Another witness to Bennett's disownment also believed it to be 'a memorable event in the history of ... Friends', not as a victory over heresy but 'as a blunder we should be glad, were it possible, to efface from our history'. If the expelling of Edward

---

[109] Ibid., 12 August and 15 Nov. 1871, Port. A 59 & 60, LSF.

[110] C. R. K., 'Journals', iv, 2 Feb 1873; *MF*, 11/8, 15 Aug. 1873, 128; and J. B. B., 'Journals', 22 June 1873. 223. Also see *LYM*, 1873, 3–7; *MF*, 11/1, 15 Jan. 1873, 2, 11/6, 15 June 1873, 112–4 and 11/8, 15 Aug. 1873, 127–9; and Milligan, '"In Reason's Ear"', 393–4.

Trusted Bennett was indeed mistaken, the mistake was never repeated; he was the last British Quaker to be disowned for holding unsound views.[111]

Even before the decision in Bennett's case, the tragic outcome of David Duncan's expulsion and death seems to have served as a warning to moderately inclined Friends that further extreme actions, inspired by evangelicals zealots flush from recent triumphs, might lead to disastrous consequences for their Society. The first example of this more circumspect approach occurred when, at J. B. Braithwaite's prompting, an attempt was made to censure Charles

Fig. 2   Joseph Bevan Braithwaite (1818–1905) *c.* 1900

[111] *MF*, 11/6 15 June 1873, 114 and Bronner, 'Moderates', 24n.

Thompson for his connection with the Voysey lectures in Manchester. When a Committee of Hardshaw East Monthly Meeting, which included J. B. B. and two other outside visitors, sought some sort of retraction from Thompson, they were greeted with his defiant refusal to 'make a confession of faith . . . even . . . to save his Membership'.[112] The case dragged on for months amidst growing complaints that some seemed bent on driving 'all independence and individuality' out from Friends and turning the Society into 'the smallest and narrowest of sects, requiring implicit submission to whatever Church authority choose to exact'. Even J. B. Braithwaite began to have '*very mingled feelings*' about Thompson's unwillingness to compromise and the monthly meeting's obvious reluctance to discipline him.[113]

In the end, after Thompson admitted—but only to overseers from his own meeting, not to any representatives of the Yearly Meeting Committee—that if he had known that his involvement in the Voysey lecture would cause pain to Friends, he would not have participated, the case was removed from the meeting books. Charles Thompson, who left Manchester for his ancestral home in Westmoreland in 1874, remained a Friend and minister of 'sometimes unconventional views' until his death in 1903.[114]

After the thwarted attempt to remove Charles Thompson, the Yearly Meeting Committee took no further measures against individuals. But when it asked Hardshaw East Monthly Meeting to endorse and circulate its previously published *Declaration of Some Fundamental Principles of Christian Truth . . .* the proposal was so strongly resisted that the Clerk decided it could not be adopted. Thwarted by those who thought the Committee's 'Declaration' was 'an infringement of constitutional usage', that body issued a farewell message admonishing Friends of Lancashire and Cheshire Quarterly Meeting not to 'mistake the false liberty of the natural

---

[112] *MF*, I/1, 15 Dec. 1871, 3, 9–11 and J. B. B. to my dear Cousin, 11 Aug. 1871, MS Box 9.4 (1), and J. B. B. to Charles Thompson, 18 Aug. 1871, MS Box 9.3 (4), LSF.

[113] *MF*, I/1, 15 Dec. 1871, 10 and J. B. B., 'Journals', 31 Dec. 1871, 208.

[114] See MS Box 9.7 (1–8), LSF; *Minute* 5, 9 Nov. 1871, and *Minute* 5, 11 Jan. 1872, *Minutes* HEMM, 1870–78, MCL; *MF*, I/2, 15 Jan. 1872, 27; and 'DQB', LSF. Mary Jane Hodgson called Thompson 'one of the best men . . . and most hard working philanthropists I know . . .', M. J. Hodgson to Elizabeth Green, 15 Nov. 1871, Port. A, 60, LSF

will for the liberty which is only to be known in subjection to Christ and his truth'.[115]

In the wake of this local rejection of the now tarnished 'Declaration', evangelical Friends leaped to its defence as 'a most powerful & impressive address on the Divine attributes of the Saviour against what is called *Modern Thought*'. When the Committee reported to Yearly Meeting, feeling, perhaps, somewhat chagrined by the treatment it had received at the hands of subordinate meetings, it asked that British Friends act as a body to remove 'any doubts as to the vital importance which the Society of Friends attaches to the acceptance and upholding of these great truths' by approving the 'Declaration'.[116] But a strong current of hostility ran against that document. When one Friend announced that the 'Declaration' smacked of Calvinism, J. B. Braithwaite responded 'at considerable length' on its foundation in Scripture and the words of early Quaker prophets. Another Friend stated that absolutely nothing was to be gained from endorsing quotations from Scripture and that however interesting seventeenth-century testimonies might be, they were irrelevant since the faith of early Friends 'was not in doctrine but in the Lord Jesus Christ'. In the end, the Committee had to settle for the unendorsed 'Declaration' being printed as an Appendix to the *Proceedings* of Yearly Meeting.[117]

So ended the brief spiritual rebellion in Manchester. The Duncanite remnant, calling themselves the 'Free Society of Friends', met for a time in a rented upper room in Manchester's Memorial Hall to worship, quietly and without controversy, according to the traditional manner of Friends; for two years they also published, under the editorship of J. B. Forster, a weekly newspaper, *The*

---

[115] *MF*, I/2, 15 Jan. 1872, 27–9. Lancashire and Cheshire Quarterly Meeting also refused to adopt the 'Declaration'. See *Minute 3*, 17–18 April 1872, *Minutes*, L&CQM, LRO and *MF*, I/6 (15 May 1872), 93–4.

[116] *LYM*, 1872, 20–2, reprinted in *MF*, I/9 (15 Aug. 1872), supplement.

[117] Ibid., 32–5; J. B. B., 'Journals', 28 Jan. 1872, 215; William Rowntree of Scarborough, 'Yearly Meeting, 1872', Box P 1/5, LSF; *MF*, I/7 15 June 1872, 109–10; and Wilson, *Manchester*, 48–9. The Manchester difficulty was not mentioned in the memoir on Braithwaite published by his children, *J. B. Braithwaite: A Friend of the Nineteenth Century* (London 1909), but Braithwaite did draw upon the 'Declaration' fifteen years later when he acted as chief drafter for the Richmond Declaration of Faith. See below, Chapter 3 and William Pollard to *BF*, May 1888, 117.

Manchester Friend.[118] Eventually, they drifted off to Broad Church Anglicanism, to the Unitarians or into the vague theism of some Voysey-like splinter movement, forever lost to Friends. Mount Street Meeting, still one of the largest Quaker congregations in Britain, quickly regained its equilibrium, aided in no small way by the arrival of William Pollard (1828–93). A former master at Ackworth Friends' School and a stalwart, but diplomatic, upholder of 'Old-Fashioned Quakerism',[119] Pollard was destined to play an important role in the future transformation of British Quakerism.[120]

Any uneasiness that Joseph Bevan Braithwaite and his allies, 'the self-constituted high priests of the Society of Friends' as one of the Manchester seceders described them,[121] may have felt over the rejection of their vaunted 'Declaration' does not emerge from their public or private pronouncements. A recent study of the *General Epistles* notes that after 1870 there was a newly discernible fundamentalist impulse in these annual pastoral letters whose composition was presided over by J. B. Braithwaite while others have identified the increasing influence of moderate and progressive Friends during the same period.[122] These conclusions are not necessarily contradictory since both describe individuals working at different levels within the Society and with obviously different objectives. One discernible influence that might have troubled the dreams of men like Joseph Bevan Braithwaite was embodied in the earnest plea of one troubled commentator on the Manchester Difficulty: 'dogmatic Quakerism is actually a thing inconceivable... the spurious... authority of the dogmatist will be superseded by the legitimate and permanent authority of Truth; and the now difficult and painful question: how best to deal with heretics and heresies, will never have to be answered, because it will never need to be asked.'[123]

---

[118] See Mary Hodgson to Elizabeth Green, 12 Aug. 1871, Port. A 59, LSF and *MF*, I/7 (15 June 1872), 99–100.

[119] See Pollard's tract *Old-Fashioned Quakerism: Its Origins, Results and Future* (Philadelphia 1889).

[120] See below, Chapter 3.

[121] Joseph Atkinson, 'Institutionalism, the Last Stronghold of Priestcraft', *MF*, I/9 (15 Aug. 1872), 136.

[122] Mollie Grubb, 'Tensions', 11–13 and Bronner, 'Moderates', 18–21.

[123] A.B.C.D., 'Ideal Quakerism or Undogmatic Theology', *BF*, 1 Aug. 1871, 201.

3
An Angry God or *A Reasonable Faith?*

[It] seems at least tolerably certain that the Society of Friends must soon either cease to exist as a separate Christian sect, or put itself in harmony with the forces of liberal opinion around it.

Manchester Friend, 15 August 1873

ADVANCING INTELLIGENCE

During Yearly Meeting in 1871 leading conservative Friends joined their evangelical brethren in supporting the decision of the Committee Visiting Lancashire and Cheshire Quarterly Meeting to deal swiftly and firmly with the Manchester heresy. These old-fashioned Quakers readily agreed with evangelicals concerning Christ's Divinity, human sinfulness and the finality of eternal punishment for those who refused God's offer of salvation.[1] Still, agreement as to the presence of evil within did not necessarily imply agreement on the most efficacious means of overcoming its influence. In the course of Yearly Meeting proceedings, conservative and evangelical members clashed repeatedly. For example, after conservative stalwarts William Graham (1823–1911) and Daniel Pickard (1828–1905) failed to secure the exclusion of an offending Epistle from staunchly evangelical Indiana Yearly Meeting, J. B. Braithwaite appeared to rub salt on the wound by pointedly repeating parts of the document and emphasizing their importance for spiritually 'sound' Friends. If Braithwaite's high-handedness was irksome, the refusal of the evangelically dominated Printing Committee to approve a new reprinting of Robert Barclay's *Apology*, because it did not present 'Friends' views in such a

---

[1] See Edward Grubb, 'Seventy Years Ago', *FQE*, 62 (1928), 301–02.

simple and scriptural manner as to recommend it for widespread distribution' caused deep offence.[2]

The indignation expressed by conservatives over this implicit rejection of their most treasured theological text was a manifestation of their frustration over increasingly assertive evangelical domination of Yearly Meeting. Among the most vehement protesters was William Irwin, the Manchester printer. Although he had been a fierce opponent of the Duncanites, Irwin had previously circulated a pamphlet in which he characterized the ' "Evangelical" mind' as 'so susceptible to delusion on questions of "Faith and Doctrine" that it is ready to class those who firmly adhere to the ancient views of the Society, with Unitarians or Hicksites'.[3]

Irwin's accusations were apparently confirmed a few months later with the publication of William Tallack's *George Fox, the Friends and the Early Baptists* (1868). Tallack's book clearly supported the Beaconite position that George Fox had been consistently unwilling to 'enforce some of the fundamental principles of the Gospel' and that he clearly rejected such doctrines as the 'vicarious atonement and imputative righteousness'. Thus, Tallack negatively confirmed the claims of American Hicksites that they were 'the most faithful followers and representatives of Fox and his coadjutors'.[4] However closely Fox and his early followers identified themselves with 'primitive' Christianity, Tallack said, they had misinterpreted the real objective of the apostolic preaching of early Christians which had not been to reveal an Inward Light to humanity but to lead them, through the Scriptures, to faith in the redeeming sacrifice of Jesus of Nazareth. Tallack concluded: 'The excessive spiritualism of Fox and his fellow founders of Quakerism was ... carried to perilous lengths ... there was in the theology of Fox, Barclay, and Penn a dangerous defect, a Deistical *tendency*.'[5]

William Irwin responded with vigour and even venom to Tallack's 'infamous charges against the Christian character of the

---

[2] Quoted in John S. Rowntree's Account of 1871 Y.M.', MS. Vol.S 370, LSF.

[3] William Irwin, *Some Suppressed Facts Respecting the Recent Conference on Christian Work* (Manchester 1867), 27–28.

[4] William Tallack, *George Fox, the Friends, and Early Baptists* (London 1868), 61–63 and Samuel H. Janney *An Examination of the Causes which Led to the Separation of the Religious Society of Friends in America in 1827–28* (Philadelphia 1868).

[5] Tallack, *George Fox*, 61.

illustrious dead'.[6] Tallack's allegations, said Irwin, rested on no authority except 'perverted judgment, Isaac Crewdson's hypercritical, Calvinistic "Beacon"' and Hicksite sophistry. Irwin concluded that Tallack

exhibits so large an amount of inaccuracy of detail, of reasoning from false premises, and positive opposition to the authorized views which the Society of Friends has maintained for upwards of 200 years, that it may be justly placed in the same category as those works which have been written by the avowed enemies of our Faith; but with this difference . . . he is an enemy. . . within the camp.[7]

William Irwin was a loud and persistent voice of opposition to the expanding influence of evangelical Friends, demanding, not reform, but reversion. For him and his conservative allies, the crisis of Quakerism was not that it was changing too slowly but that it had changed at all. Friends of Irwin's stripe had no interest in reconciling Quakerism to either evangelical theology or modern thought. Rather, they wished to return their Society to what they believed to be its original inspiration while simultaneously insulating it from all temptation to or desire for innovation.[8] Thus, for all the differences between evangelical and conservative Friends, what they did have in common, according to Roger Wilson, was 'the rejection of the role of thought in the life of the Society'.[9]

Whether or not this assessment is entirely accurate or fair, it certainly reflects the opinion of the 'third force' within Victorian Quakerism, most obviously represented by the Duncanites. The breakaway meeting of 'Free Friends' established in Manchester following the tragic ending of the Duncan affair claimed 'to represent the Liberal party within . . . the Society which believes in . . . perfect liberty of thought and expression . . . .'[10] Their chief means of propagating this view was *The Manchester Friend*, a lively weekly, which consistently adhered to the theme that what really

[6] William Irwin, '*A Refutation of William Tallack's remarks on Barclay's* Apology *and the Manchester Schism as contained in the book entitled* George Fox, the Friends, and the Early Baptists', (Manchester: William Irwin, 1868), 4.

[7] Ibid. 5–10 *passim*. Cf. with *MF*, I/1, 15 Dec. 1871, 4, which accused evangelicals of a 'determination to make early Friends answerable for their new faith'.

[8] Grubb, 'Seventy Years Ago', 301–2.

[9] Wilson, 'Friends in the Nineteenth Century', 356.

[10] *MF*, I/2, 15 Jan. 1872, 18.

threatened Quakerism was neither investigation of new ideas nor adherence to old ones, but the insistence, by any faction, that their particular brand of faith represented all that Friends needed to know. One writer in the *Manchester Friend*, lamenting the ascendancy of 'bigoted intolerance' among British Friends, noted that it should come as no surprise when 'earnest and thoughtful young persons, whose aspirations are towards a higher life than that identified with the observance of traditional codes,' leave the Society of Friends and join other religious associations.'[11]

The fact that the author of those sentiments was an American Hicksite seemed appropriate since the Manchester dissidents felt a strong affinity for their proscribed Americans cousins. Just as the British 'rational' party saw their movement as 'identical, *in aim*, with that of Fox, Barclay and Penn', they believed that in America this same position had been maintained only in 'the theology of the Hicksites...' Joseph Atkinson, one of those who resigned after David Duncan's death, declared that America was 'the only country where William Penn Quakerism exists, under what is known in England by the name of Hicksism'.[12]

Manchester liberals were also impressed by the endorsements David Duncan had received from prominent Hicksites, including the noted reformer Lucretia Mott (1793–1880). For them this support reflected the Hicksite recognition 'that Christianity... [was] a life and not a creed'. The *Manchester Friend* believed that 'Free Friends' shared with their Hicksite brethren the belief that the Atonement was not a blood sacrifice to appease a vengeful God but rather 'at-one-ment, men becoming, though obedience to the Spirit of God and participation in the life of Christ, at one with God'.[13]

Beyond any theological connections, the Manchester liberals saw themselves as one with the followers of Elias Hicks in 'bearing aloft the banner of... intellectual and spiritual liberty' in the struggle for human progress. The *Manchester Friend* pointed out that it was not until Hicks had spoken in defence of liberty that his theological views were challenged 'by the Orthodox party who, backed by their English allies, sought to bind the Society with the

[11] Ibid. I/2, 15 Jan. 1872, 18; I/4, 15 March 1872, 63; and I/5, 15 April 1872, 75–76.

[12] Ibid. I/2, 15 Jan. 1872, 18–19 and I/11, 15 Oct. 1872, 170.

[13] *MF*, I/2, 15 Jan. 1872, 29–30. For references to L. Mott's support for D. Duncan see ibid. I/1, 15 Dec. 1871, 1.

fetters of a creed, and lead it captive into the morass of Evangelicalism'.[14]

Late in 1872 the *Manchester Friend* began to print a series of articles by Hicksite Thomas H. Speakman (1820–1904) which, in imitation of J. S. Rowntree's *Quakerism, Past and Present*, sought to account for the continuing numerical decline of British Quakers.[15] Speakman pointed out that recent developments, including the disownment of both David Duncan and Edward Trusted Bennett, illustrated how far British Friends had embraced the 'narrow-minded bigotry and sectarian intolerance' of evangelical doctrine at the very time that liberal Christian thought was 'undermining the foundations of Evangelicalism'. Similarly, Speakman believed that conservative Friends, far from offering a meaningful alternative, remained and entirely negative force, responding to the modern world by clinging with a death grip to outworn ideas and practices that had even less relevance than the evangelical creed. In a long list of 'Causes of Declension' of Quakerism, Speakman concentrated on the refusal of any body of Friends, save English liberals and American Hicksites, to address 'the advancing intelligence of the age'. In its present state, Speakman said, British Quakerism was an unhealthy combination of 'popular theology' drawn from the evangelical churches and 'morbid conservatism' which turned local meetings from a religious experience to a tribal ritual consisting largely of empty silence. Speakman characterized Quaker ministers and elders, regardless of their theological stance, as persons of middle age or beyond who generally addressed younger Friends as if their very time of life was evil, insinuating that spiritual understanding could reside only with those who had 'gotten over' the temptations of youth.[16]

Evangelical Friends might have responded to Speakman's charges by pointing to a suggestion in the Yearly Meeting Epistle on Meetings for Discipline for 1868 that older Friends 'look all round and see if any...younger friends...in the freshness of religious feeling, may not perform much of the needed service'.[17] Furthermore, had it not been Mount Street Meeting's attempt to

[14] *MF*, I/4 15 March 1872, 60 and I/9, 15 Aug. 1872, 143.
[15] Speakman's articles were printed in the *Manchester Friend* from October 1872 through December 1873.
[16] *MF*, I/12, 15 Nov. 1872, 186.
[17] See *LYM 1868*, 11.

attract and hold young people through the experiment of the Friends' Institute that had led to disorder and disaster? But, according to the *Manchester Friend*, the crisis at Mount Street had arisen because young Manchester Friends had actually become interested in new ideas causing the meeting's alarmed evangelical leadership to respond by expelling or silencing those members who sought to encourage independent thinking. The British Society of Friends, said the *Manchester Friend*, had insidiously developed its own priestly caste, educated on the same 'false basis' as clergymen of churches with formal hierarchal structures, equally dedicated 'to the duty of suppressing all inquiry' and just as irrelevant to the needs of believers for whom thoughtful inquiry was the first rule of faith. To extract itself from the quagmire of stunted theology into which it had stumbled, the Society needed 'an educated ministry of life and power; graduates of the school of Christ, baptized with a missionary spirit, to spread the glad tidings far and wide'.[18]

Speakman's view was seconded in pages of the *Manchester Friend* by George Stewardson Brady (1833–1913),[19] a scientist and future fellow of the Royal Society. Brady accused his Quaker brethren of settling for

a slightly Quakerised version of the prevailing evangelical theology— nothing to justify the existence of the Society as a separate body... unless this Society shows in coming years more capacity to discern the signs of the times than it has recently shown, unless it can be brought to see that religious belief... must advance with... advancing knowledge, it will inevitably fall back, even further than it has already fallen, from its old position in the advanced guard of religious freedom.[20]

The central issue for liberal Friends like G. S. Brady was continuing evangelical devotion to a literal interpretation of Scripture. He believed that their rejection of any form of biblical criticism was inexorably linked to a general Quaker ignorance of or disdain for modern ideas. During the same time that events in Manchester were moving towards their sorrowful conclusion, increasing numbers of more intelligent, better-educated individuals were ceasing

[18] *MF*, I/3, 15 Feb. 1872, 33–34.
[19] For Brady, see Harkin, 'Mental Ability of Quakers', 654–64.
[20] George S. Brady, 'State of the Society of Friends', *MF*, II/10, 15 Oct. 1873, 168. Also see Brady's *Lumen Siccum...* (London 1868).

to place blind faith in biblical commentaries which modern science or critical history had exposed as charming fables.[21] Brady's *Essay on the Exercise of the Intellect in Matters of Religious Belief* (1868) was a plea for free thought, for the legitimacy of biblical criticism and for the need to reconcile modern scientific principles with traditional religious beliefs. There was, among Friends, Brady noted 'a very widespread disinclination to accord a patient hearing, much less a careful examination, to arguments which threaten to undermine long-cherished beliefs and traditions, and it is probable that the relation in which such beliefs stand to modern knowledge has received but little attention amongst us.'[22]

Brady continued this same theme in a piece written for the *Manchester Friend* on 'Thoughts Suggested by Darwin's *Origin of Species*', asserting that since Darwin's work was by that time (1872) 'beyond the pale of general criticism', Friends had, of necessity, to face up to the implications of evolutionary theory for Christian cosmogony.[23]

Actually, Brady gave less credit than was due. Some evangelical Friends had, in fact, attempted to address questions of biblical criticism and scientific knowledge within the context of acceptably orthodox beliefs. For example, in 1868 while the Manchester controversy still raged, Fielden Thorp, who had already launched a fierce attack the Duncanites, published a long article on the nature of the scriptural authority. The burden of Thorp's essay was to declare that whatever errors of translation or transcription might exist in various versions of the Bible, there was, finally, 'no escape from the conclusion that the Scripture narratives—miracles and all—are true'.[24] William Tallack seconded this point, noting that Christianity had absolutely nothing to fear 'from real Science ...fully, fairly, broadly and *scientifically* carried out' because 'the God of creation, whose interpreter therein is Science, cannot contradict, or be out of harmony with Himself...'[25]

[21] See Brady, *Lumen Siccum, passim* and editorial comments in the *MF*, I/7, 15 June 1872, 97–98.

[22] Brady, *Lumen Siccum*, pp. v–vi and *passim*.

[23] *MF*, I/5, 15 April 1872, 73–75.

[24] Thorp, 'Considerations on the Genuineness...of Holy Scripture', *FQE*, (1868), 71–104.

[25] William Tallack, 'Christian Positivism', *FQE*, (1874), 557. In time Tallack became an advocate of social and theological reform. He was for many years Secretary of the Howard Society for Prison Reform.

Such escapes into Natural Theology may have been comforting to some Friends, but they were scarcely an advance from the initial reaction to Darwin in the Quaker press a decade earlier.[26] In August of 1861 the 'Scientific Notes' column of *The Friend* commented at length on Darwin's evolutionary hypothesis. The author, identified only as 'I. K.', admitted that Darwin's 'luminous reasonings and multitudinous facts' easily overbore those theological critics who sought to attack him with a Bible in one hand and a copy of *The Origin of Species* in the other, but I. K. was pleased to note that a recent article in *The Zoologist* had exposed Darwin's thesis as false 'because his conclusions are at variance with the teachings of science'. I. K. therefore recommended that his readers peruse, not Darwin's dangerous book, but a pamphlet which summarized the argument from *The Zoologist*. According to I. K., this brief exposition would provide the faithful with 'a logical and satisfactory refutation to those—and, alas their name is legion!—who openly advocate Darwin's views . . . The Bible itself, that citadel of truth, needs no defence: but the timid and wavering often derive comfort from the conviction that the teachings of true science are in perfect harmony with those of revealed religion.'[27]

I. K.'s conclusions embodied the standard response of official Quaker publications to Darwinian science. During the following decade the Quaker press made few forays into the field of scientific speculation.[28] Whether Darwin was ignored out of fear for his conclusions or simply from a remarkable lack of curiosity, this apparent refusal to address the question of evolution represented just the sort of know-nothingness that frustrated and infuriated Quaker liberals.[29]

---

[26] W. A. Campbell Stewart, *Quakers and Education*, 118 points out that Paley's *Natural Theology* was widely used at Quaker schools, including Bootham, where Fielden Thorp was headmaster from 1865 to 1875.

[27] *TF*, August 1861, 210, 212. Also see *The Zoologist*, 19 (1861), 7580–611, especially 7609. I have been unable to identify I. K.

[28] Alvar Ellegard's study of *Darwin and the General Reader: The Reception of Darwin's Theory of Evolution in the British Periodical Press, 1859–1872* (Chicago 1990, 2nd edn.), 374 indicates only two further references to Darwin in *The Friend* during the next ten years. The *Friends Quarterly Examiner* included discussion of Darwinian science in three articles published between 1867 and 1871.

[29] The *History of Bootham School* (York 1926), 75 recounts that in 1865 one lad of 15 read the *Origin*, obviously without permission, 'and became a convert to the abhorred doctrine of evolution'.

In the early 1870s amidst the furore over the Vatican Council's declaration of Papal infallibility, the *Manchester Friend* ventured the opinion that 'Romanism and Quakerism stand upon a common level of bigoted intolerance when they tell us, "we have all the truth man . . . needs to know, and if you doubt our infallibility, it will be at your peril".' Nothing, said editor J. B. Forster, 'would induce us to return again to that hedged in ground'. The 'free views' held by dissenting Friends were, he said, 'the direct result of that spirit of enquiry and impatience of all outward authority which have for years pervaded the literature of this and other countries . . .'[30]

The *Manchester Friend* concluded that readers, especially inquiring religious readers, could learn more from the ideas of Matthew Arnold, Thomas Henry Huxley and even Julia Ward Howe, than from a modernized version of 'Jewish mythology' whose very preservation was as great a miracle as any of the fantastic, if captivating, stories it contained. The sort of narrow orthodoxy which currently held sway among Quakers, said the *Manchester Friend*, was an 'unsatisfactory explanation of God's relation to his works'. 'We know that we are the creatures of the infinitely perfect and good, and we think that Jesus Christ was the teacher who taught us thus to regard God as his Father and ours . . . we feel at liberty to say that we are Christians out of acknowledgment to a life given to the world by God and . . . in its obedience to the convictions given to it, Divine.'[31]

REASON AND THE WILL OF GOD

The new emphasis on Jesus as man rather than Lamb, on religion as a guide to living as well as a passport to Paradise, is probably connected with the rise of social action during the second half of the nineteenth century.[32]

---

[30] *MF*, I/1, 15 Dec. 1871, 8; I/4, 15 March 1872, 56; and II/12, 15 Dec. 1873, 190.

[31] *MF*, I/1, 15 Dec. 1871, 3 and II/8, 15 Aug. 1873, 117. The *Manchester Friend* made much of the fact that when Julia Ward Howe visited Manchester, the only Friends that would provide her a platform for her message of peace were the breakaway faction, noting that her remarks were perhaps not sufficiently 'Scriptural' to suit the local Quaker establishment. *MF*, I/8, 15 July 1872, 121 and I/9, 15 Aug. 1872, 134–5.

[32] Boyd Hilton, *The Age of Atonement*, 5.

Boyd Hilton's estimate that the Age of Atonement ended about 1860 somewhat misses the mark for British Quakerism, but by about 1870 Quaker evangelicals had began to become seriously concerned about inroads of the new liberal theology. Mollie Grubb has asserted that it was only in the 1870s that annual *Epistles* began to show a distinctly evangelical tone and to 'move steadily towards the austere and earnest piety of late Victorian England'.[33] Grubb believes that until about 1870 these annual messages (which, in her view, 'most accurately reflect the changes in [Quaker] religious thought') exhibited, not biblical fundamentalism, but 'an almost desperate desire to find refuge from the traumatic years of the early part of the century in a return to the principles and practices of early Friends'.[34]

Quaker scholar Edwin Bronner has taken issue with Mollie Grubb on the grounds of her failure either to appreciate the evangelicals' use of early Friends to support scriptural authority or to distinguish between the evangelical usage of Holy Spirit in the sense of a conversion experience and the traditional Quaker use of 'Inward Light' as consistent and universal Divine Indwelling.[35] Still, there is no question that during the 1870s and 1880s prominent evangelicals like J. B. Braithwaite made repeated efforts to secure the support of Yearly Meeting for some standardized doctrinal statement mirroring the 'Declaration of Some Fundamental Principles of Christian Truth', issued in response to the Manchester difficulty. Even before this alleged benchmark for 'sound doctrine' was rejected as a credal statement in 1872, Braithwaite had privately set out his 'Thoughts on the Atonement', perhaps with a view to adding these to a growing canon of sound Quaker doctrine. For lawyer Braithwaite, the Atonement represented not simply the literal blood sacrifice of 'one altogether innocent' in propitiation for the sins of humanity but also a revelation of God's wrath. Because God's law had been violated by human sinfulness, the atonement for such transgressions had to be accompanied by the shedding of blood, 'without which there was no remission'; this was not, Braithwaite believed, Divine revenge but rather the

---

[33] M. Grubb, 'Tensions', 10.
[34] Ibid. For an opposing view, see Wilson, *Manchester*, 4–5.
[35] Unpublished comments seen by courtesy of Professor Bronner.

'active manifestation of that holiness wholly consistent with His Love...'[36]

One Quaker liberal later expressed the view that by such pronouncements evangelical Friends 'not only called men back to the very theology against which Quakerism itself was a protest but committed themselves to a position which brought its own retribution'.[37] And retribution was not long in coming. Roger Wilson has cited the proceedings of a widely-attended 1873 Conference on the 'State of the Society' to illustrate the growing resistance to 'timid submission to the power of routine and custom'.[38]

These sentiments were expressed by William Pollard, who had arrived in Manchester shortly after the disownment and death of David Duncan and who has been credited with bringing a healing influence to Mount Street Meeting.[39] During the two decades left to him, Pollard consistently voiced strong aversion to the 'gradual drifting of the Society towards Evangelicalism'. He was a leading opponent of what he termed the 'sharply defined masses of dogmatic teaching' contained in the abortive Declaration of 1872.[40] At the 1873 Conference, Pollard emphasized the 'wonderful educating power' of free and open forums 'in promoting enlightenment and useful thought'. At the same time, he took the lead in resisting evangelical attempts to introduce Bible reading and congregational singing into meetings for worship. These innovations, would, according to Pollard, 'both disturb the worship and restrict the teacher' in Friends' meetings. In 1874 Pollard's view was confirmed by a Minute from his Monthly Meeting, Hardshaw East, to Yearly Meeting cautioning against the reading of Scripture in meetings for worship, lest such practice 'weaken our testimony to the spirituality and simplicity of true worship, and the right authority of Gospel ministry'.[41]

---

[36] J. B. Braithwaite, 'Thoughts on the Atonement', 11 April 1872, lithographic copy of handwritten original, MS Port 8/126, LSF. A longer version of these 'Thoughts' was published nearly twenty years later in the *FQE*, 24 (1890), 103–120.

[37] Edward Grubb, 'Yearly Meeting, 1836', *FQE*, (1895), 116–17.

[38] *Manchester*, 29. Also see William Pollard, 'The Recent Friends Conference in London', *FQE*, 8 (1874), a separately published pamphlet version is in Box 474/22, LSF.

[39] See Wilson, *Manchester*, 30 and the entry for Pollard in 'Dictionary of Quaker Biography', LSF.

[40] William Pollard, 'Recent Friends' Conference' 13–24.

[41] Pollard, 'Recent Friends Conference', 10; Minute 3, 15–16 April 1874, *Minutes*, Lancashire and Cheshire Quarterly Meeting, Lancashire Record Office (LRO), Preston. Also see Wilson, *Manchester*, 30.

Pollard's concern about evangelical influences within the Society was reflected in an article of 1875 expressing deep anxiety about the uncertain drift of the Society as it broke loose from the moorings of 'isolation and quietism'. Pollard was fearful that evangelicals, as they attempted to steer Quakerism into the Protestant mainstream, would take as their watchword the old saying that 'a live Methodist is better than a dead Quaker'. Friends, he said, should never forget that while the evangelical churches 'declare . . . their foundation truth to be the Death of Christ', Quakerism, 'not clogged and mystified with theological verbiage', was founded upon something more substantial: 'the Living Saviour—the same yesterday, today and forever. . . We have a place assigned for us among the tribes of spiritual Israel. . . As such, we may safely leave the propagation of Methodism to the Methodists themselves and in all faithfulness mind our own calling'.[42]

Soon after Pollard's cautionary warning, Francis Frith (1822–98), a retired Liverpool merchant and pioneer of Victorian photography,[43] published a tract which aggressively sought to establish a clear differentiation between two 'utterly opposed. . . perfectly irreconcilable' beliefs, Quakerism and evangelicalism. The latter movement, Frith said, embraced a 'manifestly. . . extreme creed; reproducing some of the worst errors of Calvinism, and those fearful Antinomian heresies, which have at various periods devastated the Church'.[44] In setting out these views, Frith spoke from his own experience and, perhaps, from a sense of guilt as well. He had been a member of the committee of Reigate Friends' Meeting that had been instrumental in the disownment of Edward Trusted Bennett, the last British Quaker to be cast out for heresy.[45]

However Bennett's disownment affected Frith, by 1877 he had come to the conclusion that the evangelical doctrine of salvation solely through a biblically-based faith, without reference to the Inward Light, had led to the drawing of a distinct line separating the converted from the unconverted. By contrast, Frith said, early

---

[42] William Pollard, 'The Present Crisis in the Society of Friends', *FQE*, (1875), 323–6.

[43] For a brief discussion of Frith's life and ideas, see Beryl Williams, 'Francis Frith (1822–1898)', *FQ*, 23/8 (October 1984), 364–70. Bill Jay's, *Victorian Cameraman: Francis Frith's Views of Rural England, 1850–1898* (Newton Abbot 1973) is an excellent introduction to Frith's pioneering contributions to photography.

[44] Francis Frith, *'Evangelicalism' From the Stand Point of the Society of Friends* (London: Samuel Harris & Company, 1877), 8, 27–28.

[45] See Williams, 'Francis Frith', 366–7; Milligan, 'In Reason's Ear' and Chapter 2 above.

Quakers not only recognized the necessity for righteous acts to prepare the way for the coming of the Lord and His Kingdom but also held that the grace of God—the Light—could come to all 'however comparatively dark and ignorant they may be (including the Heathen . . .).' Furthermore, Frith added, a second cornerstone of evangelicalism, the substitutionary doctrine of the atonement, whereby one who believed, though permanently steeped in sin, gained justification through the 'imputed' righteousness of Christ, was the very opposite of traditional Quaker view. '[W]e maintain that the believer is called to the attainment of real holiness' and that '[w]hat a man *does* . . . has really more to do with saving faith than what he merely believes'.[46] Frith concluded by asking: 'Will you have Quakerism or Evangelicalism? They are not both right. Unless the former has been throughout an utter delusion and mistake, the latter is so to a very serious extent.'[47]

This sort of overt attack on the continued promulgation of evangelical doctrine within the Society was also manifested in a growing sense of alienation from evangelical ministry, especially among younger Friends. At about the time Frith published his anti-evangelical pamphlet, Caleb Kemp, among the most earnest and active of evangelical ministers, confided to his 'Journal' a continuing concern about 'the want of unity with my doctrinal teaching'. Some members of his own meeting had expressed particular objection to Kemp's insistence on denying the possibility of salvation to those 'without the household of faith'.[48] Although deeply troubled by this 'divergence', Kemp was 'perfectly clear that in this, the Society at large is with me . . . ' When he visited J. B. Braithwaite in London, Kemp was relieved to discover that this '*wise counsellor* . . . who walked with God [was] with me in doctrinal truth'. Despite such reassurances, however, complaints and objections continued to trouble Caleb Kemp and other evangelical ministers.[49] Thus were the lines drawn for a struggle to determine the spiritual direction of British Quakerism that would continue throughout the last two decades of the nineteenth century.

[46] Ibid., 8, 10–14, 22, 28. The 'second-experience' holiness movement had enormous influence on American Quakerism west of Philadelphia during the 1870s and 1880s, but never gained a strong foothold among British evangelical Friends.

[47] Ibid. 28.

[48] Caleb Kemp, 'Journals', IV, 31 Dec. 1876, 107–08 and 18 Feb. 1877 116, MS Vol S7, LSF.

[49] Ibid. 31 Dec. 1876, 108, 16 Jan. 1877, 112–14 and v, 5 Aug. 1883, 30.

An clear demonstration of this struggle was revealed at Yearly Meeting in 1880 when Henry Hipsley, an influential minister of Holloway Meeting in north London, rose to condemn dancing, drinking, card playing, and novel reading as well as to deplore the growing tendency among younger Friends to depreciate the terrors of eternal punishment. For Hipsley, these ominous developments reflected the spread of 'infidelity' among Quaker youth, especially those possessing an advanced education. One of these, Edward Vipont Brown, a medical student at London University in the early 1880s, chaffed under Hipsley's ministry at Holloway and recalled being admonished there for refusing to believe in the fires of hell. 'It was not Quakerism that we listened to in Holloway meeting', Brown concluded.[50]

Among Quaker youth of lesser education or advantage than the future Dr Brown, Henry Hipsley's concern about young members losing the fear of hell-fire may have been premature. One example of the persistence of that terror is set out in the 'Reflections' of Laura Jane Moore (1870–1955), describing her exposure as a motherless Quaker child to a 'primitive and dreadful kind of religion of fear...' In the custody of an uncle and aunt, character-ized as 'Friends of the prevalent type of the time, a mixture of old-fashioned Quakerism... and then modern evangelicalism of the later years of the Evangelical Revival', Laura Jane was made abun-dantly aware of the terrible fate of sinners. 'Heaven and Hell', she recalled, 'were ever-present realities and entered into all the details of our lives.'[51]

Among Laura Jane Moore's most vivid recollections were nightly bedtime readings from a children's devotional book called *Little Pillows*, especially the story of John, the deaf-mute boy. This parable told how John, despite his handicap, loved and followed Jesus until one night, in a dream, God showed this apparent innocent a book listing all his sins—'so many and so black'—and let him glimpse the awaiting hell-fire. Then, as poor terrified John tottered on the brink of despair, Jesus appeared and placed his hand, dripping with the blood of the Cross, on the

---

[50] *BF*, 1 June 1880, 128 and E. V. Brown, 'Renaissance of Quakerism', *FQ*, (Oct. 1951), 202–3. Also see Wilson, 'Friends in the Nineteenth Century', 359.

[51] Laura Jane Moore, 'Reflections', [4], typescript acquired from Henry Ecroyd and used with his permission; copy available at LSF.

book of John's sins and with '[t]hat dear red hand . . . blotted them all out'.[52]

In this instance at least, Henry Hipsley could rest easy. For her part Laura Jane Moore was at pains to indicate that she was not an untypical Quaker child of the time. At age 10 she was sent to Ackworth, a Quaker boarding school in Yorkshire, where, she remembered, 'Evangelical and Fundamentalist religion was rife'. While at Ackworth, Laura Jane witnessed an incident involving a 'much loved teacher' who, upon reaching the climax of the scriptural story of Balaam's ass, discreetly concluded: 'And then we are told the ass spoke . . .' This young women, Caroline Woodhead, had, it seems, come under the influence of 'higher criticism', and, having thus inadvertently revealed her secret adherence to modernist thought, was duly reported to school authorities by zealous evangelical students. Subsequently, after a meeting with the headmaster, Caroline Woodhead admitted her apostasy to an assembly of students. She was not among the teachers who returned to Ackworth the following term.[53]

Laura Jane Moore's disquiet over the consequences of unsoundness was apparently widely shared by younger Friends Early in 1881 John William Graham (1859–1932), then a student at University College, London, wrote to his parents with the ominous news of an acquaintance who had become an agnostic and resigned his membership: 'he is by no means a solitary instance. In fact, the young men in our Society who think much are passing through a very serious time of conflict in religious matters; a good many fellows have talked to me who have many most painful doubts . . .'[54]

A few months later, Graham, reported to an older Friend that after one speaker at Holloway Meeting had expressed sympathy for the 'young fellows who are being compelled to dig upon beliefs and see what they grow from', Henry Hipsley had responded by casting a 'severe eye' upon such 'erratic believers'. During the same meeting, J. B. Braithwaite denounced all forays against 'the truth of

---

[52] Moore, 'Reflections', [5–8].

[53] Ibid. [10–12]. I am grateful to Edward Milligan for having uncovered Caroline Woodhead's identity.

[54] John William Graham to his parents, 27 Feb. 1881, Box 1, John William Graham Papers (JWGP), John Rylands Library, Manchester University. Also see E. V. Brown, 'Renaissance of Quakerism', 203.

Fig. 3 John William Graham (1859–1932), leader in the Quaker
Renaissance

God' inculcated by 'this or that fashionable notion' which would
soon pass away.[55]

John W. Graham's own doubts concerning what evangelical
Friends thought to be 'the truth of God' did not pass away so
easily. Immediately after Yearly Meeting in 1883, a deeply concerned female Friend advised the apparently despairing Graham:
'thou *must* cling to past experience of God's love & goodness.' One
source of Graham's spiritual malaise may have been the 'clear
Evangelical tone of. . . doctrinal teaching' expressed by the Yearly
Meeting *Epistle* of 1883 in which Caleb Kemp saw 'much cause for
thankfulness'.[56]

Two years later on the opening day of Yearly Meeting, J. B.
Braithwaite confided to his 'Journal' that he had just finished

[55] J. W. Graham to Mr. [Roderick ?] Clark, 19 May 1881, Box 1, JWGP.
[56] Lucy Linney to J. W. Graham, 8 June 1883, Box 1, J.W.G.P. and C. R. K., 'Journals',
Vol. V, 7 June 1883, 62–63, LSF.

reading 'the pamphlet *A Reasonable Faith*—which struck me as a very shallow performance however well-intended. It did not disturb my mind.'[57] But, in fact, J. B. B. was neither undisturbed nor unconcerned. For this 'pamphlet' had already begun to cast its shadow among British Quakers. Indeed, the little book J. B. Braithwaite had affected to scorn became a *cause célèbre* that would not only alter the tone of the Yearly Meeting in 1885 but would, in time, become a major catalyst for the transformation of British Friends.

By the time Yearly Meeting gathered in 1885, *A Reasonable Faith*, published anonymously late in 1884, was already the subject of considerable controversy in the Quaker press. A reviewer in *The Friend* had recognized the book as 'an honest attempt to uphold the truth of the religion of Christ, and to show its power to bring pardon, peace and purification...' Some readers of *The Friend* supported that sympathetic assessment, but most letters agreed with the writer who characterized the book as 'radically unsound in doctrine'.[58]

During the course of Yearly Meeting, J. B. Braithwaite delivered his usual lengthy oration, quoting '[w]ith great power one Scripture passage after another', at the same time, he 'carefully avoided any... allusion to the pamphlet... but several of our dear friends followed with pointed allusions... which did not, in my view, help the matter'.[59] These negative references, in fact, brought a full-fledged debate of *A Reasonable Faith* on to the floor. Sensing danger, J. B. B. attempted 'to lift the consideration above the arena of controvarsy [sic] to the great Foundat[io]n of Truth & Unity,' but his would-be allies proceeded to condemn the book and its anonymous authors as heretical, especially as regards the doctrine of the Atonement, and to demand that they reveal and defend themselves.[60]

[57] J. B. B., 'Journals', 7 June 1885, 189.

[58] See *TF*, 1 Dec. 1884, 303–04 for the review. On 1 Jan. 1885, 8–9, Henry Hipsley condemned the unsoundness of both the book and a sympathetic reviewer. Of six letters published on 2 Feb. 1885, 32–36, four were unfavourable and two supportive. *The Friend* refused to publish John William Graham's defence of the book. See JWGP, Box 1 for a copy of his letter. The book was also strongly condemned by evangelical Friends in America; see *The Christian Worker*, 27 July 1885, 431–32.

[59] *TF*, 6 June 1885, 132 and J. B. B., 'Journals', 7 June 1885, 190, 192.

[60] *TF*, 6 June 1885, 142–43 and J. B. B., 'Journals', 6 June 1885, 192. Over forty years later, one eye-witness to the discussion recalled 'a strong sense of resentment' because the authors had not signed their work; G. H. Braithwaite to *TF*, 15 July 1927, 663–4.

At that point the book's three authors, William Pollard, Francis Frith, and William E. Turner (1836–1911), rose, one by one, to rebut the attacks on their collaborative effort. Pollard spoke first, noting that the writers had been moved to act through an increasing awareness of growing scepticism, among younger Friends. Previous attempts to belay such questions and doubts had been for the most part reassertions of traditional authority or ideas, with little discernable effect. Their book, Pollard said, was founded on the premiss that there need not be any contradiction between sound reason and Gospel faith. Its purpose was to bring 'the wandering ones . . . back to the truth of the Gospel of Christ, by presenting . . . this Gospel in its simplicity and spirituality'. Whatever wrath might fall upon them, Pollard said, the authors of *A Reasonable Faith* took consolation in knowing that they had to some degree succeeded in giving solace to doubtful believers. Pollard himself claimed to have personal knowledge of fourteen Friends who, under the influence of the book, had returned to 'rejoicing in the Gospel of Christ'.[61]

After responses to Pollard's statement, both positive and negative, the Clerk, Joseph Storrs Fry, attempted to bring the discussion to a halt, but before this could be done, Francis Frith rose to speak. Frith began by noting that he believed those who opposed the book were 'God-fearing and Christ-loving men' whose faith he had no wish to disturb, but the book had not been written for them. Rather, its intended audience was those who wished to adhere to Christian Quakerism but could not accept the evangelical interpretation of doctrines like the Atonement. The authors, said Frith, were attempting to offer an alternative between agnosticism and evangelical fundamentalism which was, as they believed, fully in accord with the teachings of the founders of their Society.[62]

After William Turner also acknowledged his share of responsibility for *A Reasonable Faith*, the debate ended with a poignant comment from Jonathan Grubb, an elderly and much admired

---

[61] TF, 6 January 1885, 143–4.

[62] *TF*, 6 June 1885, 144. J. Ormerod Greenwood *Quaker Encounters*, vol. 1, *Friends and Relief* (York 1975), 169, 169n notes that Frith, who had in his youth suffered a serious spiritual crisis over 'the legalistic view of the Atonement and the doctrine of eternal punishment', wrote the first draft of *A Reasonable Faith* which was then revised by Pollard and W. E. Turner. Pollard's son later recounted that his father, rather than Frith, wrote the chapter on the 'Inspiration of the Bible'. See Arthur B. Pollard to *TF*, 29 July 1927, 703; also see Egbert Morland to ibid. 22 July 1927, 681.

evangelical minister, which underscored the human dilemma central to such theological disputes. Twenty years earlier, said Jonathan Grubb, he had, in the midst of despair, found hope in the concept of the forgiveness of his sins through Christ's Atonement, but now 'he could not but feel that an attempt was being made to sweep away the ground of his hope'.[63]

What tenets of Jonathan Grubb's belief did *A Reasonable Faith* attempt to undermine? Its authors would have denied any such negative designs. They claimed that the book's message was intended for those who desired 'a Faith at once Scriptural and reasonable' in contrast to an 'emotional' evangelical creed which they viewed as a modern form of the Calvinistic theology against which the founders of Quakerism had initially rebelled.[64]

The *Reasonable Faith* envisioned by the book's authors explicitly rejected the necessity for accepting a creed based on literal interpretation of the Scriptures. They recognized the Bible as a divinely-inspired 'Record of a Progressive Revealing of Spiritual Truth' but denied that it was the sole source of Light along the path to salvation. If it were, they said, those human beings who, by accident of time and place, had no access to Scripture would have no possibility of being saved. Since 'sound reason and common sense' dictated that a loving and merciful God would not withhold from any person, Christian or heathen, 'some measure of the same Divine Influence which "inspired" the religious element of the Bible', there must be some other means through which all humanity could have hope of salvation.[65]

The means prescribed by *A Reasonable Faith* was the Inward Light, the most distinctive and distinguishing of traditional Quaker beliefs. Through the Divine inspiration of the Light, all human beings could gain 'access to the same spirit which inspired the sacred writers...' and receive the 'primary source of all religious light and duty'.[66] 'The reasonable Truth... is that God's revelation has ever been a continuous and progressive one, and the stage to which it has now developed... is that of God more fully manifest

---

[63] *TF*, 6 June 1885, 144.

[64] *A Reasonable Faith. Short Essays for the Times by Three 'Friends'*. (London 1886, revised edition), 3, 7. Hereafter cited as *ARF*, with pages.

[65] *ARF*, 19, 43–4, 104–5.   [66] *ARF*, 11, 43, 100–101.

in the Spirit . . . the Divine Voice Within . . . [which] is and ever has been present . . . to the human soul as a real experience, although often an obscure and almost unconscious one.'[67]

Beyond evangelical attempts to replace the warm spirit of the Inward Light with the cold hand of biblical literalism, *A Reasonable Faith* singled out another 'false teaching' of the evangelical creed which drove 'logical and thinking minds . . . [into] a region of darkness and despair': the substitutionary or propitiatory doctrine of the Atonement which required the shedding of Christ's blood for forgiveness of human sin. The authors agreed that '[m]en *must* have a personal Saviour', but insisted that Jesus's suffering and death were not to atone for the sins of humanity or to impute righteousness to them but to illustrate 'Divine pity . . . and . . . Divine forgiveness' as well as to provide a 'perfect example, a true ideal' for human beings. In other words, Jesus had not died merely for the sins of Mankind; rather, He had lived to give humanity hope by His example. The Cross saved from sin all those whose hearts were touched by Christ's sacrifice, but it did *not* represent simply vicarious suffering to atone for sin. Instead, Christ's passion and death was 'a supreme declaration of God's infinite love for sin-stricken souls . . .'[68]

In the post-Niebuhrian twentieth century, the views set out in *A Reasonable Faith* may leave an impression of 'feel-good' Christianity, promising much and demanding little. But among late-nineteenth century Quakers, the book's effect seems to have been electrifying, especially for young people. Over two decades after its publication, W. E. Turner, the last surviving author, recalled:

During the Eighties we had many letters of a deeply encouraging nature, full of grateful recognition of the help the book had been . . . under Providence of winning them back to Christ & Christianity from whom they had been driven by the distorted teaching which was so popular years ago . . . I have lived to see still greater progress in the march of our intelligent grasp of divine truth, & the education of a large part of our people along the lines . . . of . . . the 'Reasonable Faith'.

---

[67] *ARF*, 39–40.   [68] *ARF*, 29, 31–3, 44–5, 48, 59, 69.

More than fifty years after its publication, the book was still being credited with saving 'the reason and faith of that generation of Quaker youth'.[69]

Early in 1886, with the controversy over *A Reasonable Faith* continuing in the Quaker press, John William Graham told his parents of his recent correspondence with Edward Worsdell (1852–1908), who had been one of his teachers at Bootham, concerning a book Worsdell had just completed. Graham thought well of the result but believed the title, 'The Gospel of Divine Helpfulness', was too bland to catch the attention of the casual reader. Graham had a point. Worsdell's slim volume, which appeared a few weeks later with a slightly altered title, apparently did not even catch the attention of Quaker editors, for none of the Society's major journals reviewed or even gave notice of the book's publication.[70] Still, despite this cold official reception, *The Gospel of Divine Help* was warmly read by a considerable range of Friends. The American Quaker poet John Greenleaf Whittier wrote to tell Worsdell that the book had been a great joy to him; and Laura Jane Moore, who surreptitiously received a copy as holiday reading from a sympathetic Mount School teacher, remembered that Worsdell's work, along with *A Reasonable Faith*, had been 'very helpful to me and cleared my doubts wonderfully for some time'.[71]

Edward Worsdell's recollection of his own doubts had, in fact, been his chief inspiration for writing *The Gospel of Divine Help*. After experiencing the classic evangelical conversion experience in late adolescence, Worsdell had spent the following decade in a state of spiritual distress, overwhelmed by human depravity and helplessness in the face of an angry God demanding blood sacrifice and eternal punishment of the wicked as satisfaction for sin. His growing sense of despair was exacerbated not only by his inability to find solace in the Scriptural dogmatism that seemed to prevail among evangelical Friends but also from the fact that there seemed

[69] W. E. Turner to J. J. Green, 13 April 1907, Port. C 27, LSF and Egbert C. Morland in *TF*, 22 July 1927, 680–81.

[70] J. W. Graham to his parents, 20 March 1886, Box 1, JWGP; Wilson, 'Nineteenth Century Friends', 361; and Worsdell's entry in 'Dictionary of Quaker Biography', LSF. Quaker journals may have been running for cover after the controversy caused by *A Reasonable Faith*.

[71] E. Vipont Brown, 'Renaissance of Quakerism', 203 and Moore, 'Reflections', [13–14]. Whittier wrote a prefatory note to the second edition of *The Gospel of Divine Help* (London 1888).

to be no older person with whom he or his friends felt able to discuss their fragile spiritual condition. As a result, Worsdell had seen many of his own small circle of friends drift into Unitarianism or agnosticism, 'largely through failing to distinguish between the teachings of Christ and the assertions of theologians'.[72]

Worsdell's own deliverance from mental and spiritual anguish had come as a result of a sudden insight when 'he saw in Christ "the revelation of the Father of Lights in whom there is no darkness at all" '.[73] Furthermore, his subsequent contact with younger Friends at Bootham had convinced him that most of them still suffered from the same sort of lonely travail through which he had passed and for the same reasons. This affinity for young people was apparently reciprocated; over seventy years after Worsdell's death, Horace Alexander recalled that he was the minister young Friends most liked to hear at York Meeting. Alexander remembered Worsdell calling the Society of Friends a ship that had remained in dry dock too long and exhorting young people to ensure that Quakerism again ventured out into spiritual depths not navigated since the days of George Fox.[74]

Because Worsdell wanted *The Gospel of Divine Help* to speak specifically to the concerns of educated Christians torn between the demands of biblical literalism and the revelations of modern thought, he concentrated on God's saving gift of Light as the means of reconciling religious faith with reason and conscience. In this effort Worsdell set out along the trail already blazed by the authors of *A Reasonable Faith*, but he proceeded further and produced a more effectively realized statement of liberal theology.

Worsdell believed that since all higher religions were informed by the idea of Divine Goodness and since reason prescribed that what was virtuous for human beings must be a reflection of that Divine Goodness, Christians could be assured 'that truth, justice and compassion' are the same for God as for humanity.[75] Such a view was, however, entirely contradicted by the two chief premises of the evangelical creed that dominated Protestant Christianity.

---

[72] *The Gospel of Divine Help: Thoughts on Some First Principles of Christianity* (London 1886), pp. iii and 68–71; hereafter *GDH*, with page. Also see Rowena Loverance, 'Edward Worsdell (1852–1908)', *FQ*, 23/8 (October 1984), 382–8.
[73] Wilson, 'Nineteenth Century Friends', 361 and Worsdell's entry, 'DQB', LSF.
[74] Interview with Horace Alexander, Kenett Square, PA., November 1980.
[75] *GDH*, 9

For if unquestioning faith in the literal truth of the entire corpus of scriptural texts was, in fact, the necessary means to salvation, then not only was salvation utterly denied to the 'unenlightened conscience', however morally and ethically sound, but even the 'enlightened conscience' which was forbidden to apply God's gift of reason to religious experience. Thus, any attempt to interpret even the Old Testament in other than a literal sense was effectively a refutation of the faith required for one to be saved.

Furthermore, the evangelical insistence that Jesus's Atoning act required the shedding of blood in order that God should be propitiated for the sins of humanity meant that Christians were worshipping a Divine Being whose code of morality was of a lower order than that which He demanded of His followers. This seemed to Worsdell to involve a fundamental logical contradiction, one that any thinking believer would ultimately find impossible to maintain. On the other hand, such a substitutionary doctrine, which according to Worsdell, had 'no place at all in early Christian theology' until the fourth century, had the advantage of imputing righteousness to those who had undergone the saving experience of conversion. Thus, even though their lives subsequently remained 'ungenerous, unlovely and unprogressive', living not in imitation of Christ but in outward conformity to a rigidly legalistic concept of Divine law, evangelical believers might continue to assume an aura of spiritual superiority that inevitably led to arrogance and stagnation.[76]

Worsdell believed that this evangelical version of the Gospel had been explicitly rejected by first generations of Friends, only to be revived on the wave of early nineteenth-century enthusiasm. Having insinuated itself into the Quaker communion, evangelicalism had created serious tensions between 'reformed' followers and traditional Friends and even raised questions as to the relevance of their Society as a separate religious community. As the century drew toward a close, Worsdell said, evangelicalism, increasingly feeble and inadequate in the face of new religious and scientific revelations, was in its dotage as a spiritual force. Within their Society, however, a still powerful evangelistic influence was threatening to drive the flower of Quaker youth away from Friends and perhaps from Christianity altogether. Since the purpose of

[76] *GDH*, 92, 108, 112–13, 115, 121, 151.

Worsdell's essay was to speak to the condition of those Friends, especially the young, who were troubled by both the content and spirit of the sort of teaching that predominated in their Society, he desired 'to promote *true thinking* as well as *true feeling*' while remaining 'in entire agreement with the . . . spirit of Early Quaker-ism.'[77] For just as George Fox and the other first publishers of the truth 'spoke as . . . they were moved by the Spirit, not as schooled by theologians', Worsdell wished to consider religious ideas with-out 'accepting as authoritative any asserted teaching of Scripture' that contradicted 'the testimony within' or violated God's gifts of reason and conscience.[78]

Early Friends had understood, Worsdell said, what many latter-day Quakers, had forgotten, i.e., that the Bible was not 'law delivered as an infallible document for the government of men's lives, but a series of records describing successive stages of God's self-revelation,' which was continuing and providing progressive or 'gradual spiritual discernment . . .'[79] 'From very rever-ence . . . we must not allow His gifts of reason and conscience to be overborne by accepting as authoritative any asserted teaching of Scripture which contradicts them.' Reason and conscience, Wors-dell said, must always be taken into account in order that the Divine helpfulness revealed by the Christian Gospel might operate undeterred.[80]

Worsdell believed that 'the only essential element of Christianity to which nothing analogous is found in any other religion of the world, is this power of the Example of Self-Sacrifice . . . *on the part of a Divine and everlasting Being*'. It was, therefore, Jesus's life, not His death, that was central to the Christian experience. The faith that brought salvation began, not in adherence to certain creeds, but in human striving to follow Christ's example. '[M]oral earn-estness,' Worsdell asserted, 'is to the individual of more importance than accurate moral perception.' Because Quakerism was 'less fretted by a creed . . . than perhaps any other religious body which accepts the Divinity of our Lord', Friends had not only a special advantage but also a special responsibility in the work of creating God's Kingdom on earth. The spirituality and universality of this Kingdom were clearly revealed in the New Testament

---

[77] *GDH*, 11, 13.   [78] *GDH*, 14, 17, 39.   [79] *GDH*, 42, 65.
[80] *GDH*, 29, 38, 51.

accounts of Christ's life, not by the narrow and negative creeds subsequently developed by theologians. Quakerism, Worsdell said, was first and foremost an experiential religion based not upon a set of doctrines but upon the living, growing presence of God in every human person and the example of Jesus Christ as to the best means of expressing that presence.[81]

One Friend who had been young when *The Gospel of Divine Help* appeared, later recalled that Worsdell 'found his way to many of our hearts and helped us to realise that God is not only to be loved but actually loveable...'[82] If Worsdell's book got little public notice from his fellow Quakers, it seems to have made something of a splash among other non-conformists. In 1905 the president of the Leeds Free Church Council noted that *The Gospel of Divine Help*, which had been made required reading at his theological training college, was 'one of the greatest things Quakerism had given to the Church'.[83] Despite such praise, Worsdell's little book continued to be viewed by many Orthodox evangelicals as symptomatic of the radical forces bent on further dividing the world-wide Quaker communion. Its author received little credit and less support from influential contemporaries. The story persists, though apparently unconfirmed by any hard evidence, that the book cost Worsdell the Headmastership of Lancaster Friends' School.[84]

Within London Yearly Meeting, modernist thinkers like Worsdell and the authors of *A Reasonable Faith*, adhering to an emerging liberal philosophy, were determined to harmonize traditional Quaker principles and practices with the main currents of modern thought. In the United States divisions among orthodox American Friends ran in a different direction. There was, as in Britain, a nascent liberal element and Philadelphia Yearly Meeting retained a strong flavour of Wilburite conservatism, but during the post-Civil War period the nearly universal triumph of revivalism in western and southern Yearly Meetings had given rise to a strain of Quakerism which non-evangelical British Friends found to be alien and

---

[81] GDH, 14, 28–32 *passim*, 56–61, 122.

[82] Harold J. Morland to *TF*, 16 July 1927, 664.

[83] Quoted by Hope Hewison, 'The Way Forward', *FQ*, 23/8 (Oct 1984), 400.

[84] See Isichei, *Victorian Quakers*, 40 and Punshon, *Portrait in Grey*, 192. Apparently, Worsdell himself believed that he was denied the position on account of the book, see Loverance, 'Edward Worsdell', 384.

even dangerous.[85] Some digression is necessary to explain the impact of American developments on actions and dispositions of London Yearly Meeting.

THE RICHMOND DECLARATION

As American Friends migrated westward both their physical circumstances and the example of their fundamentalist Protestant neighbours led many of them to adopt novel practices that produced interesting and, for some, disquieting results.[86] One of these innovations was the replacement of silent meetings by worship services, which, though they might begin with a brief period of silence, incorporated all the accoutrements of Protestant denominational worship—readings from the Bible, hymn singing, and prepared sermons based on biblical texts. In time, revival meetings, emphasizing the spoken word and the experience of immediate conversion, sprang up and included what more traditional Friends considered unQuakerly displays of extreme emotion. The results were often impressive with respect to bringing new sheep into the fold—never, since the seventeenth century, one of Quakerism's strong suits. Such soul-saving, soul-gathering methods had a price and, ultimately, as congregations grew in size and complexity, that price, for most American Friends west of Philadelphia, was the laying aside of the traditional Quaker admonition against hireling ministers and the gradual establishment of a pastoral system, and 'programmed' meetings wherein a paid pastor became the authority figure to whom members looked for guidance to the probable exclusion of any leadings from the Light.

As the revival movement expanded, some Holiness Friends, not content with merely relinquishing traditional practices, sought to make optional even the prohibition against vain outward forms, especially the sacraments of 'water Baptism' and partaking in the Lord's supper, both of which appeared to have Scriptural

---

[85] See Thomas D. Hamm, the *Transformation of American Quakerism* (Bloomington 1988), 146–7 on the nearly solitary modernist position of Nereus Mendenhall among Orthodox (non-Hicksite) American Friends. Mendenhall, an educator from North Carolina, privately held views in the 1860s that were similar to those of David Duncan and his followers.

[86] What follows owes much to Hamm, *Transformation, passim* and Punshon's *Portrait in Grey*, 199–204.

sanction.[87] The challenge of this Ordinance or 'water party' led moderately evangelical leaders of Midwestern and Western American Yearly Meetings to summon an international Conference of all Orthodox Yearly Meetings, including Dublin and London, which convened in Richmond, Indiana in September 1887. The proceedings of the Richmond Conference, although not free from controversy, upheld the traditional Quaker rejection of outward sacraments. But, for the organizers, its crowning achievement was the promulgation of a Declaration of Faith, setting out a corpus of Quaker beliefs in the hope of halting the tendency among Friends towards dissension, division and, perhaps, ultimately, disintegration. Seeking both weighty authority and broad consensus, the Conference turned to Joseph Bevan Braithwaite, attending as one of the delegates from London, to frame its statement of spiritual principles. J. B. B.'s theological views may have been unpopular among progressive British Friends, but he was widely recognized as a world spokesman for Orthodox Quakerism of the sort represented at Richmond.

Swiftly and almost single-handedly,[88] Braithwaite produced what he described as 'simply a gathering up from existing authenticated documents of the testimony of Friends . . . to the fullness which is in Christ'. J. B. B. held that, far from being a novelty, such 'declaratory statements of Christian doctrine' had been issued by Friends from the earliest period of their history.[89] A century later some Quaker historians attest to the validity of Braithwaite's view, characterizing his Declaration as 'a clear, scripturally based statement of belief . . . far more traditional . . . than its critics often allow' or as 'a monument to the impact of evangelical thought in the Society'.[90] Recently, one American Friend called the Declaration 'a valiant effort to bring unity among the then largest segment of

---

[87] For an illuminating discussion of the so-called Ordinance controversy, see Hamm, *Transformation*, 130–37. Also see Barbour and Frost, *The Quakers*, 201–18 and James H. Moon, *Why Friends (Quakers) do not Baptize with Water* (Fallsington, Pa. 1909).

[88] J. B. Braithwaite was assisted by James E. Rhoads, President of Bryn Mawr College, and James Carey Thomas of Philadelphia, but it seems clear that the Declaration was largely conceived before the Conference began and that it owed more than a little to the Declaration produced fifteen years earlier by J. B. B. and other members of the Lancashire Committee in the wake of the David Duncan affair.

[89] J. Bevan Braithwaite, 'Notes on the Richmond Conference, 1887', *FQE* (1888), 272–88, see especially 280, 285.

[90] Punshon, *Portrait in Grey*, 203 and Hamm, *Transformation*, 137.

Friends in America...' containing much that could be affirmed 'on sound historical grounds'.[91] Contemporary critics were, however, likely to see the document in a more partisan, less generous light. In his *Later Periods of Quakerism* Rufus M. Jones, who became the leading American spokesman for liberal theology, recalled the Declaration as 'a relic of the past... [which] made no effort to interpret Christianity to this age... [and] reflected no sign of the prevailing intellectual difficulties over questions of science and history'. The distinguished Quaker historian Thomas Hodgkin called it a 'goody, goody, determined-to-be-orthodox, vapid and diffuse Confession of Faith...'[92] Certainly, it is of interest to note that while the Declaration confirmed that the Holy Spirit dwelt in the hearts of believers, it denied any 'principle of spiritual light, life or holiness inherent by nature in the mind of heart of man...' effectively denying the Inward Light.

The Richmond Declaration was endorsed by most American Yearly Meetings although Ohio, Iowa and Western rejected it for varying and sometimes contradictory reasons; Philadelphia (Orthodox) would not even consider it. When J. B. B. brought his 'creed', as critics immediately termed it, back to England for certification, he stirred up a nest of opposition which would eventually prove to be a decisive factor in the overthrow of the evangelical oligarchy which dominated British Quakerism for half a century.

During the fall of 1886, in the period between the publication of *The Gospel of Divine Help* and the opening of the Richmond Conference, J. B. Braithwaite's 'Journals' recount a trip to Cambridge to meet with 'our undergraduates, of whom there are 10 to 15—among them Roger Fry...'[93] There is a certain irony in this apparently innocent passage, for while Roger Fry's Quakerism did not long survive his Cambridge experience, other young Friends who came down from Cambridge or some other institution of higher education were thereafter almost certainly hostile to the brand of evangelicalism that J. B. B. undoubtedly offered in his

---

[91] Wilmer A. Cooper in *QRT*, #78, 25/4 (July 1992), 43; Cooper adds that for all its virtues, the Declaration was 'less than a desirable statement of faith for Friends'. The fullest consideration of the Richmond Conference and Declaration is Mark Minnear, *Richmond 1887: A Quaker Drama Unfolds* (Richmond 1987).

[92] Jones, *Later Periods*, ii, 931: T. Hodgkin to Joseph Rowntree, 17 May 1888, in Louise Creighton, *Life and Letters of Thomas Hodgkin* (London 1917), 337.

[93] J. B. B. 'Journals, 1883–1890', 31 Oct. 1886, 219.

inevitable ministry to their meeting for worship.[94] Generally speaking, when young Quakers returned from University to their local meetings, they brought with them not only an extraordinary sense of confidence but also renewed dedication to make explicit the sort of Quaker faith they had learned from the likes of Edward Worsdell and the authors of *A Reasonable Faith*.

Late in 1887, before J. B. Braithwaite had returned from America, John William Graham, B. A. London, M. A. Cambridge, and newly appointed tutor at Dalton Hall, Manchester, expressed concern to his parents about J. B. B.'s 'trying to give us a *creed*'. 'It would be a grievous calamity and would split the Society if carried; but *everybody* is against it, including Evangelicals such as W. S. Lean and J. B. Hodgkin, so I think there is not much fear. Still, the Y. M. should be strengthened by genuine Friends going up . . . It will mean a presidential defeat when Bevan returns.'[95]

However confident of victory for the forces of progress, Graham was determined to leave no stone unturned. A few weeks prior to the gathering of London Yearly Meeting, he wrote to Roger Fry, still at Cambridge, asking his help in enlisting the support of, among others, his father Sir Edward, the renowned jurist, 'to strike a blow for religious freedom at the approaching Yearly Meeting'.

we *must* exert ourselves if the battle for truth and progress is not to be lost. It is terrible to think that the sublime carelessness of dogma, and most potent insistence on spiritual *life* that Early Friends exhibited should be lost, just at the time when a creedless Fellowship for a higher life is so much the one thing needful for the age.[96]

When the younger Fry passed Graham's letter along to his father, his comment that 'the creed . . . would be a death blow to Quakerism in its present form . . . ' adds to the accumulated evidence that well-educated younger Friends formed an obvious and

---

[94] See J. W. Graham, 'Reminiscences of the Beginning of Cambridge Meeting', *BF*, Feb. 1895, 31–2 and March, 59–60 and Laurel Phillipson, 'Quakerism in Cambridge from the Act of Toleration to the end of the Nineteenth Century (1689–1900)', *Proceedings of the Cambridge Antiquarian Society*, 77 (1988), 1–33.

[95] J. W. Graham to parents, 5 Nov. and 4 Dec. 1887, Box 7, JWGP. William Scarnell Lean (1833–1908), principal of Flounders Institute, 1870–99 is listed as an 'active moderate' in Bronner, 'Moderates', 367; Jonathan Backhouse Hodgkin (1843–1926) was an influential evangelical minister and author, often associated with J. B. Braithwaite.

[96] J. W. Graham to Roger Fry, 3 May 1888, Temp. MSS. 587/3, LSF.

Fig. 4　Edward Grubb (1854–1929), with unidentified women at the
Scarborough Summer School, 1901

vociferous element of opposition to the Richmond Declaration.
Certainly, men like J. W. Graham and Edward Grubb (1854–1939),
M. A., London, have subsequently been given considerable credit
for finally convincing London Yearly Meeting that the Declaration
should be rejected. But it may be that a bit of Quaker
mythology, partly self-constructed, has given these younger members more celebrity and acclaim for the decisiveness of their contributions than they deserve, at least insofar as they have been
depicted as leaders of a beleaguered minority rousing the forces
of progress in a do-or-die struggle against evangelical reaction. In
fact, resistance to the adoption of any sort of credo appears to have
been broadly based from the beginning and to have included, as
Graham noted, many older and at least moderately evangelical
Friends.

　　In the spring of 1888 Richard Westlake (1827–1915), editor of
the *Friends Quarterly Examiner*, published an editorial warning

against approval of the Declaration which, in his view, might be less a basis for doctrinal unity than a blunt instrument for 'enforcing the claims of orthodoxy'. 'Let us ... be cautious', he said, 'in adopting such precise terms of belief as would unduly limit minds that with all reverence and humility are reaching out [through the Scriptures] to the infinite love of God as revealed therein.'[97]

Joseph Rowntree (1836–1925), the York chocolate manufacturer, also published, at his own expense and in a time of financial uncertainty for his firm,[98] a 'Memorandum on the Declaration ... ' setting out at considerable length the reasons for his opposition to 'elaborate dogmatic creeds'. Noting the considerable historical differences between the development of American and British Quakerism, Joseph Rowntree made clear that he wished neither to deprecate what the evangelical American Yearly Meetings had done nor to comment adversely upon those actions. Rather, his desire was to illustrate how the endorsement of such a document by London Yearly Meeting would excite controversy and create a 'stumbling block to the faith of ... an influential minority'. The Declaration, dealt 'with questions of solemn and tremendous impact, requiring the most careful thought ... ' yet it seemed to have been 'adopted with less discussion than is given to the Articles of Association of a trading company.' As an example of the numerous points that were 'either strangely presumptuous or misleading', Rowntree cited the Declaration's judgement 'that the punishment of the wicked and the blessedness of the righteous shall be everlasting'. Would such a statement, which was unacceptable to many good and pious Quakers, henceforth become 'required of all, and ... those who could not adopt it should not presume to be Friends?'[99]

Joseph Rowntree acknowledged J. B. Braithwaite's attempts to dispel fears about the effects of the Richmond Declaration by noting that it had never been the purpose of those who drew up the Declaration to make it 'a preliminary to Church membership,

---

[97] 'The Richmond Conference', *FQE*, (1888), 148–9.

[98] Ann Vernon, *A Quaker Business Man: the Life of Joseph Rowntree, 1836–1925* (London 1958), 94–100 and Roger C. Wilson, 'We shall never Thrive on Ignorance', in *A Quaker Miscellany for Edward H. Milligan*, ed. David Blamires, Jeremy Greenwood and Alex Kerr (Manchester 1985), 153–60.

[99] *Memorandum on the Declaration of Christian Doctrine issued by the Richmond Conference, 1887* (York 1888).

or to the holding of any office in connection with the Church'. And, indeed, after Richard Westlake published J. B. B.'s article on the Richmond Declaration in the *Friends Quarterly Examiner*, he acknowledged that Braithwaite had gone a long way toward relieving his own fears.[100] Joseph Rowntree was not so easily convinced. Noting that Braithwaite's article had presented the Declaration as a bulwark against 'unsound and dangerous doctrines' in a world where the Church was 'in a state of discipline and warfare', Rowntree asked whether the professed beliefs of any Friend that went outside the doctrinal limits of the Declaration would cause that individual to be reckoned unsound or accused of joining with the forces of the enemies of the Church?[101]

The fate of the Richmond Declaration in Britain was decided by London Yearly Meeting in late May 1888. John W. Graham provided his sister Agnes with a lively description of the proceedings: 'The Creed Debate was a glorious success, and my mind is immensely relieved and really quite jolly! There were, on my own counting, 1100 people of both sexes, crowding every seat & aisle & doorway of the large Meeting House.'[102] The debate lasted for over five hours and more than sixty individuals 'made definite speeches', including Graham himself who spoke for

about 10 mins . . . and felt intensely relieved & much backed up by feeling the sympathy of all the younger people in the galleries round. My voice seemed to fill the Meeting easily . . . At intervals the Clerk [Joseph Storrs Fry] stopped the men and asked some lady to speak. On the whole the women speakers helped us; & their presence certainly did. The minute was most satisfactory. It gave no shadow of sanction to the document & said why—(1) We had never decided before the deputation went [to Richmond] that we wanted a creed. (2) We are not allowed to change this. (3) Many Friends object to its contents.[103]

Graham's exultation at his personal success and that of the progressive cause obviously contrasted with Joseph Bevan

[100] Joseph Rowntree, *Memorandum*, 10 May 1888; J. B. Braithwaite, 'Richmond Conference', 285; and [Westlake], 'Richmond Conference', 151n.

[101] Joseph Rowntree, '*Memorandum*', 10 May 1888 and J. B. Braithwaite, 'Richmond Conference', 277–8.

[102] J. W. Graham to Agnes [Graham], 31 May 1888, Box 7, JWGP.

[103] Ibid. At this time female Friends usually met separately from the regular Yearly Meeting. See Chapter 6 below.

Braithwaite's reaction to the debate, but not so sharply as might have been expected: 'there were some[,] to me, very *painful* exhibitions, from *W. S. Lean*, Jno. W. Graham, Edwd Grubb & some others, yet we were helped through better than might have been expected. The prejudice has been stimulated in a high degree against a "creed"; the Declaration is printed in the body of our proceedings, but no judgment is made upon it.'[104]

But a judgement had been made and it changed the British Society of Friends forever. The Angry God of the Age of Atonement had been ushered out of the large Meeting room at Devonshire House and replaced by a kinder, gentler but infinitely more elusive Deity. The process by which this transformation took place was more gradual and less traumatic than has sometimes previously been depicted. It was natural rather than revolutionary, a product, not of startling theological innovations, but of changing social and educational standards. The portrayal of an isolated and embattled youthful minority swaying their elders through the eloquence of their words and the depth of their sincerity also needs to be modified. The young women and men who opposed the Richmond Declaration may have been on shaky historical ground, but they were on the winning side, and, for the most part, they would continue to be insofar as the theological and social drift of British Quakerism was concerned. The successful struggle of liberal Friends against the imposition of a credal statement, a pastoral system and other evangelical innovations as well as the expanding influence of 'modern thought' gave progressive young Friends increasing assurance that they were not only in tune with the times, but also with the future of British Quakerism.

---

[104] J. B. Braithwaite, 'Journals, 1883–1890', 21 June 1888, 289, LSF. Ted Milligan recalls Joan Mary Fry (1862–1955) saying she felt rejection of the Richmond Declaration was still in doubt until William S. Lean expressed his opposition. Interview with Edward Milligan, 26 May 1994, Friends House, London.

4
Prophetic Vision

HOME MISSIONS AND HIRELING MINISTERS

Younger opponents of the Richmond Declaration always characterized its defeat as a dramatic turning point in their own lives as well as in the history of the Society of Friends.[1] Supporters like Richard Littleboy (1819–95) were, on the other hand, deeply chagrined by its rejection. Littleboy feared that sincerely held, long-standing beliefs were 'now stigmatized as dogma' by proponents of a new theology who could 'hardly be aware of the danger of aggressive action in propagating tenets which appear to strike at the root of our faith, which tend to foster doubt, and give rise to rash judgment and unsettled opinion'.[2]

No doubt many Friends who wished to retain a biblically based Quaker faith shared Littleboy's anxiety, but, in fact, the rejection of the Richmond Declaration did not signal the final overthrow of evangelical influence. The machinery of London Yearly Meeting was still effectively controlled by elderly evangelical Friends who were in no mood to compromise with the proponents of the new liberal theology.[3] During the late 1880s and early 1890s, the struggle between liberal and evangelical Quakers continued and found its fullest expression, not over questions of Higher Criticism or Darwinian science, but with regard to the Friends' Home Mission Movement, the most dynamic manifestation of late nineteenth-century Quaker social activism.[4]

---

[1] Edward Grubb asserted on several occasions that he would have left the Society if the Richmond Declaration had been endorsed by Yearly Meeting. *TF*, 27 Jan. 1939, 68 and interview with Richenda Scott, 30 May 1976, Friends House, London.
[2] Richard Littleboy, 'The New Theology', *FQE* (1891), 568, 571.
[3] Wilson, 'The Road to Manchester', 147 and Greenwood, *Friends and Relief*, 169.
[4] Professor Richard Braithwaite, grandson of J. Bevan Braithwaite, made the point that the struggle between liberal and evangelical Friends was seriously joined for the first time on the issue of Home Missions. Interview with Richard Braithwaite, Cambridge, August 1986.

The impetus that gave rise to the establishment of the Friends' Home Mission Committee in 1882 was connected to an earlier and highly successful Quaker experiment, the Adult Schools. As noted above (see Chapter 1), the Adult School Movement was founded in Birmingham during the 1840s by Quaker reformer and philanthropist Joseph Sturge. The concept of Adult Schools was simple and the aims modest: a Sunday morning meeting to teach reading and Christianity to the unlettered working classes using the Bible as primer. Adult Schools, whose teachers were predominantly but not exclusive Quaker, thus combined learning and religious instruction in a rather undifferentiated fashion and sometimes featured activities, including formal readings from Scripture and hymn-singing, that were outside regular Quaker religious practice, although they no doubt helped to put working-class attenders at ease. Whatever form it took, the Adult School movement seems to have provided considerable spiritual stimulation to Quaker teachers. Beyond giving young, middle-class Friends something to do and affording them the opportunity to meet working-class people on a regular basis, the Adult Schools had the added virtue of providing Quakerism with a unifying vehicle for Christian witness. In 1847 the Friends First-Day School Association (FFDSA) was established to co-ordinate the work of Quaker volunteers. By 1870, 1,200 Quaker Adult School teachers were instructing over 15,000 pupils (a larger number than was in membership with the entire British Society of Friends) in the rudiments of literacy and Christian doctrine. The first national FFDSA Conference was held in conjunction with London Yearly Meeting in 1872. Thereafter, the FFDSA met concurrently with Yearly Meeting and annually reported to it while remaining independent of its direct control. This arrangement provided FFDSA Friends with a convenient means for directing and expanding their endeavours while keeping their organization clear of possible questions by or debates with conservative Friends about the unQuakerly methods employed in some First-Day Schools.[5]

London Yearly Meeting had reason to be proud of the FFDSA's accomplishments, but for all its success in attracting students for whom practical as well as spiritual services were provided, a nag-

---

[5] Wilson, *Manchester*, 43 and 'Friends in the Nineteenth Century', 358. Also see Edward Grubb, *Quakerism in England: Its Present Position* (London 1901), 12.

ging question remained: Why did so few Adult School pupils join the Society of Friends? Many Quakers would probably have agreed with the reason given by a young lawyer, Joseph Gundry Alexander (1848–1918), in the early 1870s. Friends, Alexander said, were failing to attract new members because of a 'radical unsoundness' which permeated their Religious Society. Its defects were reflected not only in 'the want of life and freshness in much of the ministry heard in our meetings' but also in the fact 'that we are not, as a whole, a Christian Church, but a great club—professing... to advocate certain principles, but exacting of those who grow up amongst us [with] no indication of personal allegiance to them'.[6]

Alexander's criticism was more social than theological. He believed that the Adult Schools should provide something more than an outlet for youthful energy. Rather, they should be a means for drawing souls to Christ through the unique and consoling message of Quakerism. As Caleb Kemp noted in 1873, 'unless their [sic] is a change in this respect we shall lose our place of usefulness in the Church & in the country...'[7] The first apparent step toward the sort of change Alexander and Kemp had in mind occurred in 1875 with the appointment of a Committee on General Meetings.[8] The idea of the General Meeting was an American import, a product of the Revivalist Movement among western Friends.[9] The spirit of these gatherings was frankly evangelistic, an occasion for teaching, preaching, and discussion which would involve 'vigorously evangelical younger Friends' in the sort of spiritual outreach that might not only rekindle the fire in local meetings but also, as in America, bring substantial numbers of new members into the Society. Certainly one major influence on the appointment and subsequent activities of the Committee on General Meetings was the nearly continuous presence of travelling American evangelical ministers in Britain.[10] Conservative Friends

[6] Joseph G. Alexander, 'Our Social System', *FQE*, (1871), 439–41.

[7] C. R. K., 'Journals', IV, 19 Oct. 1873, 43, LSF. Also see Barclay, *Inner Life*, 583–4.

[8] The members of the Committee on General Meetings, originally 23 and increased to 28, were chiefly evangelical ministers; they are listed by Malcolm J. Thomas, 'The Committee on General Meetings, 1875–83', in *A Quaker Miscellany* for Edward Milligan, eds. David Blamires, Jeremy Greenwood and Alex Kerr (Manchester 1985), 143.

[9] The best discussion of the Revivalist Movement is Hamm, *Transformation*, 74–97. Also see Isichei, *Victorian Quakers*, 93, 99 who incorrectly credits the Moody-Sankey revival tour in Britain (1873–5) as the inspiration for General Meetings.

[10] Edwin Bronner notes that thirty American ministers carrying certificates from their home meetings visited London and Dublin Yearly Meetings during the 1870s. See

were apt to be offended by the aggressive, biblically-based ministry of many of these American visitors and, as in the case of James Owen's visit to Manchester in the late 1860s, local difficulties might be reignited or exacerbated by their brash, undiplomatic approach.[11]

Still, General Meetings were attended with some success in England, although the Committee's annual reports to Yearly Meeting invariably asserted that while General Meetings were attracting souls, they were not keeping them within the Quaker fold. In 1879, for example, the Committee on General Meetings reported

numbers of people have been truly converted to Christ through this instrumentality... In several cases, however, through there being no provision for shepherding the flock, many have joined other denominations; but we fear that many have also gone back to the world that might have been preserved... [T]here appears to be a serious need for the sustained efforts of Friends.[12]

Supporters of the aggressive evangelism manifested in General Meetings believed that some more permanent arrangement had to be made to buttress the work. On the other hand, traditional Friends, suspicious of the prepared sermons, Bible reading, hymn-singing and emotional atmosphere that inevitably accompanied General Meetings, expressed the fear, not, perhaps, unmixed with middle-class snobbery, that Quaker worship services might actually deteriorate into something along the lines of a Moody and Sankey revival. In 1882, Yearly Meeting devised a compromise of sorts by creating the separate Home Mission Committee. (The Committee on General Meetings was officially laid down in 1883.)[13]

Smaller in size but more ambitious in scope than its predecessor, the new Committee's members incorporated several stalwart evan-

---

'American Friends in Transition, As Viewed Through British Quaker Periodicals, 1865–1880', in *The Lamb's War*, 138 and *passim*.

[11] See Chapter 2 above.

[12] Quoted by Thomas, 'General Meetings', 138.

[13] Ibid. 139–41. John Punshon notes that because British Friends tended to come from 'the upper reaches of a stratified society... [they] were paternal rather than comradely in their approaches to the unchurched'. *Portrait in Grey*, 192.

gelical holdovers from the Committee on General Meetings, including J. B. Braithwaite, Caleb Kemp and Richard Littleboy. One of the earliest objectives set forth by the Home Mission Committee was to provide monetary and other support which would allow Friends 'having a gift in the Ministry' to settle in a promising area and to devote themselves on a full-time basis to evangelistic work on behalf of the Society. This work might take the form of reopening meeting houses that had been closed or of attempting to establish entirely new meetings in places where General Meetings had produced hopeful results.[14]

One of the first mission workers to apply to the Home Mission Committee for support was William Jasper Sayce (1857–1946) of London. Upon examination of Sayce's application,[15] the Committee agreed 'to aid . . . in his desire to devote himself more fully to evangelistic work than is at present possible' and to provide sufficient maintenance 'so as to liberate him for visiting the poor & undertaking other missionary work under the control of this Committee'. No one could complain, as had sometimes been the case with General Meetings, that Sayce's labours in London were not sufficiently supervised (he was under the scrutiny of *five* older evangelical Friends).[16] Still, from its inception, the operation of the Home Mission Committee proved to be 'a fruitful source of friction'.[17] In this case, the opposition was not so much concerned with methods of proselytizing or even added expense, but with the more fundamental point that the Committee's paid Mission workers represented a direct threat to the traditional Quaker proscription against hireling ministers, an especially sensitive issue in light of the growth of a pastoral system among American Friends. Supporters of the Home Missions concept justified the payment of spiritual workers on the ground of results. Not only did the missionaries bring new recruits to the fold, but they might also help revive defunct meetings, as in the case of William Hobson, a Home

[14] The Committee, with ten appointed members, first met on 1 June 1882, see *Minutes*, Friends Home Mission Committee (FHMC), 1882–1884, 1 June 1882, 1–14, LSF. Also see 'Is There Not a Cause? The Society of Friends and the Late Home Mission Conference' [Hereinafter ITNAC] (London 1893), 9–13, 20 and Wilson, 'Road to Manchester,' 146.
[15] The Committee doubtless approved of Sayce's doctrinal position. The *DQB* entry for Sayce notes his belief 'that the Bible is to be accepted as a whole, and from it there is no appeal'.
[16] *Minutes*, FHMC, 1882–84, 23, LSF.
[17] Grubb, *Quakerism in England*, 15.

Mission worker in and around St Ives, who was instrumental in the reopening of Cambridge Meeting in 1884.[18]

As Home Mission work expanded in scope (there were six workers receiving support from the Committee in 1886), some advocates began to see this type of proselytizing as a compelling new *raison d'être* for the entire Society. In 1886 Henry Stanley Newman (1837–1912), a member of the Home Mission Committee, commented: 'Our justification for continuing to exist does not rest on the advancement of any theory, however good, BUT IT RESTS WITH THE PRACTICAL WORK WE ARE DOING, and when that work ceases, it will be time to set our house in order, and die'.[19] J. B. Hodgkin, one of H. S. Newman's colleagues on the Home Mission Committee, while cautioning that the fundamental reason for Quakerism's separate existence was still 'its practical testimony to the reality of the guidance of the Holy Spirit', agreed that 'the evangelization of the world is the *primary* work of the Church, and... all other church work will be better done by being placed in its proper subordinate position'.[20]

There were other Friends, however, who wondered if the separate identity of their Religious Society was not being subordinated to the vision of an aggressive element bent on transforming Quakerism's historically unique message into a warmed-over version of mainstream Protestantism. Progressive Friends, of course, believed that their Society had been and should remain a 'living' faith, able to incorporate the most up-to-date discoveries of science and history into its structure precisely because it did not require adherence to any form of dogmatic creed. John William Graham caught the spirit in a somewhat jocular letter to J. B. Hodgkin urging him to 'give up the mechanical non-literary artificial quasi-miraculous theory of [biblical] inspiration & come over to the view for which we are now called heretics...' Graham's advice to a younger sister was more serious: 'we shall have to give up the idea that the Bible was intended as a manual of science or of History. That sort of thing we have the brains to study for ourselves.... But

[18] Ibid. and Phillipson, 'Quakers in Cambridge', 27–9. Also see John W. Graham, 'Reminiscences of... Cambridge Meeting', 31–2, 59–60.

[19] Henry Stanley Newman, 'Gospel Ministry', *FQE*, xx (1886), 526–37.

[20] J. B. Hodgkin, *Three Phases of Quakerism* (London 1889), 3, 5, 11.

we may well believe *Christ,* and obey what he says about God . . . *Jesus* we can understand & love.'[21]

William Pollard warned that while arrangements for a paid pastorate might seem innocent and even practical, the experience of the early Church showed that a separate ministry was 'poisonous fruit' which inevitably led to 'the establishment of a separate clerical Order, that arrogated to itself the name and authority of the Church'.[22] Pollard's former collaborator Francis Frith enlarged upon this same theme in an article published in 1892. Ostensibly a plea for tolerance and charity among those who differed in their interpretation of Christ's saving message, Frith's essay was more fundamentally a defence of those 'more liberal and reasonable views' which, far from tending 'to undermine . . . the foundation of Christian faith', had in many cases,

saved from an almost total wreck of faith, those who have been repelled by the 'iron creed' of some of the Churches. Our souls' peace does not depend upon the acceptance or rejection of certain intellectual definitions of religious truth, but upon 'repentance toward God, and faith towards our Lord Jesus Christ'; upon the persistent devotion to His will and person, and faithfulness to the interests of His kingdom.[23]

Opponents of the new thrust of Home Mission activities perceived an ominous development in the Committee's apparent determination to build up a new form of Quaker ministry, programmed, premeditated and paid, waiting not upon the Light but upon the fashions and fancies of an alien religious tradition. In an article entitled 'An Evangelical Ministry', one concerned Friend noted a disturbing tendency among Home Mission enthusiasts to 'cast upon any who speak in our meetings for worship, a responsibility of evangelising, or preaching gospel sermons, which their Lord and our Lord may not have laid upon them'.[24]

---

[21] J. W. G. to J. B. Hodgkin, 25 August 1890, Box 3, and to Lena, 28 May 1887, Box 7, JWGP.

[22] William Pollard, *Old-Fashioned Quakerism: Its Origins, Results and Future,* (Philadelphia 1889), 42–3.

[23] Francis Frith, 'On Intellectual Differences Among Christians', *FQE,* (1892), 115–21, 123.

[24] Edward Pearson, 'An Evangelical Ministry', ibid., (1886), 446.

Picking up the same theme, Edward Grubb noted that many existing meetings were failing to hold the allegiance of 'a considerable portion of the more thoughtful of our younger members'. This situation had arisen, he said, from two factors: 'the extension of . . . quantity at the expense of quality', as if the number of speakers at worship services was the best reflection of a meeting's spiritual condition; and the fact that conscientious members were spending too much time and energy on Adult School and mission activities. 'It is hard to see how the inner life of Quakerism is to be maintained without a large share of energy being devoted to our own meetings.'[25]

Despite such objections, discussion at Yearly Meeting in 1887 seemed to reveal, as John W. Graham reported to his parents, that the Home Mission Committee had the preponderant support of those attending. But the following year, during the same Yearly Meeting which refused to endorse the Richmond Declaration, Graham noted that the forces attacking the work of the Committee were 'greater than ever before; and there was a decided majority against the continuance of the Committee . . .'[26] Graham's sense of an anti-Home Mission consensus was certainly biased, for supporters of the Committee successfully defended its activities and preserved its influence. Still, year by year, evangelical Friends felt the heat of a growing opposition led by well-educated, self-confident younger men like Graham and Edward Grubb. Sometimes evangelical response to this concern was overtly hostile as in an incident Graham recounted to his parents. While speaking in Manchester Meeting, he was interrupted by an older woman (Graham called her 'a fanatic sort') who said she would leave the gathering unless he desisted from denying Christ's redeeming sacrifice. Graham sat down in the interest of peace, disclaiming any wish to 'tickle the Evangelicals', but his friend, E. Vipont Brown, was apparently spoiling for a showdown. He 'wrote a letter of remonstrance' to the woman who had attacked Graham (Mrs Benson Woodhead) believing that the time had come to deal with such reactionary challenges whenever and wherever they occurred.[27]

[25] Edward Grubb, 'On the Ministry in Our Meetings', *FQE*, (1888), 366–9. Also see Wilson, 'Friends in Nineteenth Century', 362.

[26] J. W. G. to parents, 26 May 1887 and 29 May 1888, Box 7, JWGP.

[27] J. W. G. to parents, 23 and 29 Oct. 1890, Box 3, JWGP.

The widening gulf between evangelicals and liberals on the question of Home Missions was reflected in an article written for the American evangelical journal *The Christian Worker* in 1891 by Frederick Sessions (1836–1920), one of the pioneers of the British Home Mission movement. Noting an increasing 'prejudice against aided ministers for the good old teaching of Christ and His Apostles', Sessions was anxious lest individual members who felt called to preach the Gospel as a 'resident labourer' might not become discouraged or intimidated by attacks on Home Mission activity. He warned that unless the bias against missionary work could be overcome and individuals of high calibre induced to take up the burdens, 'the Society will never be built up on the only possible lines on which it can be revived in these days'.[28]

Here Frederick Sessions touched upon a vital question that would engage British Quakers for the next two decades. Nearly all Friends, excepting the staunchest surviving conservatives, seemed to agree that their Society needed reviving. But what, in fact, were the means to its revitalization? Evangelicals believed the answer lay in the same redeeming Gospel message that had rescued early nineteenth-century Quakerism from the dead end of torpid quietism. Proponents of the New Theology also believed that Quakerism, properly channelled, could achieve boundless growth among a spiritually destitute population waiting, as seventeenth-century Westmoreland Seekers had awaited George Fox, to hear the simple, saving message of primitive Christianity. But, they asked, how could their Society survive and grow by casting aside every principle that was uniquely Quaker while simultaneously denying every proposition that was explicitly modern? The battle lines were clearly drawn and, for a time, the Home Mission question was the major front upon which the struggle would be fought.

At this crucial juncture proponents of 'liberal and reasonable views' gained a significant new forum for the propagation of their message. In 1891 William E. Turner, a co-author of *A Reasonable Faith*, became owner/editor of the *British Friend*. The transformation of this long-standing organ of conservative Quakerism into a voice for advanced opinion was clearly reflected from January 1893 when its masthead verse was altered from Jeremiah 6:16: 'Stand ye

---

[28] Fred Sessions, 'Our Letter from England', *Christian Worker*, 23 April 1891, 259–60.

in the ways, and see and ask for the old paths, which is the good way to walk therein' to 1 Corinthians 4: 20: 'For the Kingdom of God is not in word but in power.'[29]

Advocates for change were not slow to take advantage of the opportunities offered by the refurbished *British Friend*. In April 1892 J. W. Graham warned his parents that they would find the latest edition of that journal 'very full of meal' ground by the forces of religious progress in preparation for the impending Yearly Meeting. Graham himself provided some grist for the mill in a letter on 'The Paid Pastor at Work', attacking the 'flimsy and... egoistic creaturely ministry' which had grown under Home Mission auspice until it encompassed forty-two 'workers' receiving annual payments of nearly £3,500. 'It is in the way of dogmatism', Graham said, 'that meetings have suffered... from the Pastorate.' The attack was joined by William Tallack who complained of the 'great and painful prominence given to "hell", "hell-fire" and "damnation"'' in the preaching of Home Mission workers, 'even amongst children'.[30] The final stinging critique was offered by J. B. Braithwaite, Jr., the eldest son and namesake of the Home Mission Committee's most influential member. Characterizing the Committee his father had sponsored and directed for over a decade as unrepresentative in its membership, 'a failure' in its work, and a danger in its methods, the younger Braithwaite proposed that the forthcoming Yearly Meeting summon a special Conference to reassess the place of Home Missions' work in the life of the Society.[31]

The succeeding issue of the *British Friend* published a series of articles and letters which depicted the work of the Home Mission Committee as a source of 'increasing disunity and estrangement'. Correspondents characterized the growth of a paid pastorate as a 'most noteworthy departure from precedent', a 'false step' leading inexorably toward the creation of a separate class of preaching

---

[29] The reasons for the revised Scriptural message in the masthead were explained in *BF*, January 1893, 1. It should be noted that the *British Friend*'s conservatism was theological rather than social or political. Martin Ceadel, *The Origins of War Prevention* (Oxford 1996), 322–3 notes that the early *BF* 'freely espoused liberal and moral-radical causes', even endorsing appearances by the militant American abolitionist William Lloyd Garrison.

[30] *BF*, 1 April 1892, 94–96; J. W. G. to parents, 9 April 1892, Box 7, JWGP; and 'ITNAC?', 29. Tallack was effectively a defector from the evangelical camp. See Chapter 2 and Bronner, 'Moderates', 367, 370.

[31] *BF*, 1 April 1892, 93–4.

Friends, and an innovation that threatened the 'very existence of the Society of Friends as we know it'.[32]

Perhaps the most authoritative and certainly the most ominous warning concerning the direction in which the Home Missions Committee seemed to be taking British Friends came from a highly-respected American minister Joel Bean (1825–1914). Of moderately liberal views, Bean had been hounded out of Iowa Yearly Meeting (where he had been Clerk in 1877) mainly on account of his opposition to revivalism and a paid ministry.[33] British Friends, said Bean, should consider whether they wished to follow their American brethren in an arrangement whereby fitness for the ministry was determined, not by the spiritual condition of the minister, but by formal training of selected individuals in Bible Institutes. It was difficult to contemplate, Bean said, 'how such a transformation can take place . . . without a total change of base, and the tacit confession that Quakerism itself has been a mistake'.[34]

When London Yearly Meeting gathered in late May 1892, strong sentiments for calling a special conference on the lines proposed by J. B. Braithwaite, Jr. were expressed, but weighty evangelical Friends demurred. J. B. Hodgkin, for one, warned that any disruption of the Home Mission Committee's work might set the Society back fifty years. J. W. Graham responded by implying that such a reversion might have merit since the theology which had come to be connected with the work of paid Home Missioners was narrower than that of the Society at large and seemed not to encompass many vital aspects of traditional Quakerism, let alone modern thought. How, he asked, facetiously, would the Committee react if one of its paid preachers felt the need to remain silent for six months? In the end, a Conference on Home Missions was duly arranged for the autumn, its attenders to be determined by each Quarterly Meeting. Thus, victory seemed to lie with the proponents of reform, although defenders of Home Missions won a concession in the fact that members of the Committee

---

[32] 'The Yearly Meeting and the Home Mission Committee', *BF*, 2 May 1892, 98; Alfred H. Brown, 'The Home Mission Committee', ibid. 115; and William Heaton, 'The Paid Pastor', ibid. 113–15.

[33] For an excellent summary of 'Bean Case' and its influence on British as well as American Quakerism, see Hamm, *Transformation*, 139–46. Also see below Chapter 5.

[34] Joel Bean, 'What is True Preparation for the Ministry?', *BF*, 2 May 1892, 105–7.

were automatically included as delegates, 'irrespective of the representatives of the Quarterly Meeting'.[35]

When the 300 delegates selected for the Conference gathered in
early November 1892, their discussion centered on whether paid
mission workers were performing a service vital to the well-being
of British Quakerism or whether their novel form of ministry 'was
at variance with some of the most cherished principles of
Friends...' and ought therefore to be restrained or even abol-
ished.[36] A summary of the proceedings kept by J. W. Graham
reflects the deep theological, and to some degree generational,
divisions that had arisen over the Home Mission issue. In Graham's
view, opponents of a paid ministry were forced to struggle against
not only the arguments of Home Mission advocates but also
'against the Clerk [Joseph Storrs Fry], who behaved most unfairly'.
According to Graham, Fry committed the ultimate Quaker breach
of trust by allowing his personal opinions to override the sense of
the Meeting, thus 'preventing the majority... from getting a
minute... declaring against the... Resident Pastorate'. Graham
was, however, consoled and encouraged by an 'outburst of true
Quakerism' from amongst the younger opponents of the Home
Mission Committee.[37]

The official report of the Conference played down the differences that had emerged, simply noting that while many Friends
were not entirely satisfied with the actions of the Home Mission
Committee, 'the Conference feels assured that it has been their
earnest concern to uphold the view of Gospel truth which has
distinguished our Society'.[38] The upshot of the Conference's
deliberations was a Quakerly sort of compromise by which
Home Missions work was preserved but its organizational structure
transformed. A new Committee, composed entirely of individuals
nominated by the seventeen Quarterly Meetings, was created and
assignments of paid workers were to be subject to the approval of
the local Friends 'amongst whom they labour, as if they were

---

[35] See *BF*, 3 June 1892, 127–32 for a summary of the discussion and *Minutes*, FHMC, 27
May 1892, 201.
[36] ITNAC, 5–6, 29 and Wilson, 'Road to Manchester', 148.
[37] 'Notes on 1892 HMC Conference', Box 3, JWGP.
[38] *Minutes*, FHMC, 1893, 1–2. Also see 'ITNAC', 6–7 for a summary of statements by
Committee members 'to dispel the alarm' about British Friends following in the path of their
American cousins to a paid ministry.

ordinary members of the Meeting, so that they may be kept in their right place, and preserved from the danger of constituting a separate class'.[39]

While the Conference's settlement appeared to offer something to both sides, John William Graham would not be appeased. In a letter to Joseph Storrs Fry citing Jesus' advice 'to attempt a private understanding if we have anything against our brother', Graham expressed the opinion this longtime Clerk of Yearly Meeting (1870–75, 1881–89) who had formerly been one of Graham's idols, was

unequal to the moral strain put upon a Clerk. I honestly cannot conceive how a Clerk whose aim was to interpret the wish of the Meeting, could fly in the face of such an overpowering expression of opinion ... A Quaker assembly is not adapted for a conflict with its Clerk. And destructive to Quakerism as I believe a paid Pastorate to be, I think it is not more destructive of our historic *tone* than it would be if we had to abandon our trustful plan of deciding matters by speeches and a Clerk.[40]

J. S. Fry's response to this screed is not extant, but however wounding it must have been for a tribal elder to be thus chastised by a cocksure youthful upstart, Fry may have taken consolation in the fact that even as Graham wrote the Home Mission Committee was coming into possession of an £11,000 legacy from the Quaker industrialist John Horniman (1803–93), specifically earmarked for the continuation of Home Mission activities. Significantly, this largess arrived at a time when the embattled Committee's books showed a deficit of £100.[41]

[39] *Minutes*, FHMC, 1893, 2–7 and Wilson, 'Road to Manchester', 148. Members of the new committee were officially appointed by the Yearly Meeting after nomination by Quarterly Meetings, a formality consistent with tradition.

[40] J. W. G. to Joseph Storrs Fry (copy), 16 May 1893, Box 3, JWGP.

[41] *Minutes*, FHMC, 1893, 15. John Horniman's entry in the *DQB* (LSF) lists, in addition to the Home Mission grant, the following Horniman legacies:

Peace Society	£ 5,000
Friends Foreign Mission Association	£ 12,500
Syrian Missions	£ 12,500
Bedford Institute Association	£ 5,000
Friends First-Day School Association	£ 2,000
Friends Christian Fellowship Union	£ 2,000

Nearly concurrent with the announcement of the Horniman bequest was the appearance of '*Is There Not A Cause?: The Society of Friends and the late Home Mission Conference*', an anonymous tract attacking the activities of the Home Mission Committee. The author has not been identified, but both its style and content indicate that it was produced with the knowledge and complicity of John W. Graham. Consisting of carefully arranged extracts from the statements of various Home Mission proponents, the pamphlet implied the existence of a master plan (or conspiracy) to lead London Yearly Meeting in the direction of a paid and separate clerical establishment. The *pièce de résistance* was a long excerpt from an article by Dr William Nicholson of Kansas suggesting that the pastoral system represented 'the foreseen transformation of Quakerism . . . . The Rubicon has now been passed . . . The eaglet is out of its shell and will not return to it . . .' Nicholson admitted that this drastic change was 'a great trial to many' but counselled the troubled ones to 'keep still and sweet and obey the pastor . . .'[42] Whether these deliberately chosen, highly provocative words represented any sort of consensus among British evangelical Friends, their confrontational tone set the stage for the momentous Yearly Meeting of 1893, wherein the control of the machinery of British Quakerism by a clique of elderly evangelical Friends was decisively challenged.

NEW FACES, A NEW THEOLOGY

As 1893 Yearly Meeting approached, J. B. Braithwaite noted in his 'Journal': 'I have for several years past been desirous that some of my dear younger Friends might be . . . introduced into the service [of the Epistle Committee] . . . it is very important that a fresh mind should be trained [?] under this important service.'[43]

Whether these thoughts were merely coincidental or whether J. B. B. had actually begun to feel uncomfortable about growing pressure for change, it became clear, once Yearly Meeting convened, that some younger Friends could no longer be satisfied by soothing promises of being permitted to sit at the feet of tribal elders as a tolerated but permanent minority. Beginning with an

[42] 'ITNAC', 38–48, quoting from the *Friends Review*, 24 November 1892, 278.

[43] J. B. B., 'Journals, 1890–1905', 28 May 1893, 93.

unusually lengthy and heated discussion on 'the State of the Society', which the *Friends' Quarterly Examiner* called 'a remarkable occasion', many young and some older members expressed the 'feeling of unrest and insecurity which haunts so many spirits in the present day . . . that much of the teaching from the gallery is out of harmony with the experiences of the younger minds of this age'.[44]

William Tallack, whose youthful evangelicalism had moderated considerably with advancing age, began with a statement of his concern about the delicate condition of British Quakerism. What truly threatened the Society, Tallack said, was not the nascent agnosticism that had temporarily gripped some conscientious younger members. Such doubts were the normal expression of an earnest search for truth. The real danger, Tallack believed, was rooted in persistent attachment to outmoded 'orthodox' principles 'based upon old theories of Roman legalism, and not upon that which answered the craving of the human soul . . . .' What modern Quakerism needed was not some obsolete form of Calvinism, still obsessed with saving humanity from the wrath of an angry God,[45] but a theology which would evoke the honesty and courage necessary to deal with 'the great questions', i.e., the right relationship between God and man and the right understanding of the Divine message to humanity. Surely, Tallack said, the great spiritual issues with which Friends were grappling could be further illuminated by the light of modern scientific and historical knowledge.[46]

The atmosphere warmed considerably when J. B. Braithwaite responded to Tallack's attack upon the core of his doctrinal position with a ringing declaration on the indispensability of a faith founded upon the Rock of Christ's atoning sacrifice. But before J. B. B. could receive the endorsement of evangelical allies, 24-year-old John Wilhelm Rowntree (1868–1905) rose to deliver an ardent plea that marked the beginning of his emergence as 'one of the most potent influences in the life of the Society of Friends'. In nearly all standard accounts, this scion of the York chocolate family is credited with providing focus and vision to the restless, often negative protests of younger, reform-minded Quakers and is

---

[44] 'Thoughts on Yearly Meeting', *FQE*, July 1893, 324.
[45] Tallack may, in fact, have been referring specifically to J. B. Braithwaite's legalistic 'Thoughts on the Atonement' published in *FQE*, 1890, 103–20.
[46] *TF*, 2 June 1893, 348.

remembered as the 'leader and spokesman for the newer life embodied in the Quaker Renaissance in Britain'.[47]

The crux of Rowntree's message was that for all the obvious sincerity and apparent spiritual contentment of the Society's leaders, they could not continue to ignore a deeply disturbing 'want of spiritual life amongst young Friends'. This void, he said, was being generated by the general belief of younger Friends that they were 'not able to receive the truth as it was uttered from the minister's gallery' of their local meetings. Many young Quakers, himself included, felt 'bound hand and foot, so that they could have no service in the meeting' because there seemed to be no one to whom they could turn for understanding or sympathy. Rowntree insisted that he had no wish to cause pain to beloved and respected elders who were spiritually at ease, but he pleaded with them to begin to come to grips with the issues that troubled his generation.[48]

At first the response to Rowntree's plea was more puzzled than pained. William White (1820–1900), former Lord Mayor of Birmingham and a stalwart pioneer in the First Day School Movement, announced that he had experienced great difficulty in following what young Rowntree was trying to say. Taking this cue from the apparently bewildered White, William Charles Braithwaite (1862–1922), another of J. B. Braithwaite's sons, responded that the inability of some older Friends to grasp the meaning of J. W. Rowntree's protest spoke volumes about the reasons why young people, who were 'no longer . . . secluded from the influences of the world . . . [nor] the scientific spirit of the age', might come away from their local meeting for worship feeling that their religion had become 'a burden rather than a help'. Because the generations had somehow lost the ability to communicate with one another, Braithwaite said, the needs of the day 'might require . . . a fresh costume for the form of truth' which each group sought to illuminate.[49]

This blunt criticism of what W. C. Braithwaite considered an increasingly irrelevant Quaker ministry was supported by several older Friends. A venerable conservative Friend, Joseph Armfield

---

[47] Ibid. 349. The quotation is from Elfrida Vipont [Foulds], *The Story of Quakerism*, (2nd edn. Richmond 1977), 234. Also see A. Neave Brayshaw, *The Quakers: Their Story and Message* (London 1921, 3rd ed. reprinted 1982), 313 and Wilson, 'Road to Manchester', 149.
[48] *TF*, 2 June 1893, 350.   [49] Ibid.

(1821–94), noting the younger men's allusions to Barclay's *Apology*, agreed 'that adherence to the ancient doctrines of Friends was necessary to meet the needs of the present day'. William Scarnell Lean concurred with the need for new ideas and new forms of language in the Society's meetings for worship. Others, however, including Joseph Storrs Fry who had been Clerk of London Yearly Meeting eighteen times between 1867 and 1889, were less sympathetic. In Fry's opinion the problem was not necessarily with those who ministered but might lie with those who 'were not sufficiently open with the ministers as to their feelings and needs and personal convictions'.[50]

Fry's patronizing admonition was too much for Silvanus P. Thompson (1851–1916), a distinguished educator, physicist, and future Fellow of the Royal Society. What many 'revered' ministers of the Society did not seem to understand, Thompson said, was that the young people who questioned them, while they might be in a state of serious spiritual disquiet, were not speaking out of either ignorance or levity but from the conviction that they could not base their religious lives on principles that were neither compatible with reason nor revealed by leadings from the Light. Thompson offered the specific example of Quaker ministers who told young people that they could not be Christian believers unless they accepted the Atonement of Christ as the actual 'sacrifice of the innocent for the guilty... dripping with human blood' to satisfy the fearful vengeance of an angry God. This 'notion of a bloody sacrifice', Thompson declared, 'was a piece of heathenism... [which] simply revolted their whole natures, and raised every fibre of their being, saying this was not the true Gospel.'[51]

After Silvanus Thompson's rejection of the evangelical vision of the Atonement, W. E. Turner, editor of the *British Friend*, exhorted older Friends, 'upon whom God had laid much of the travail and care of the Church, to keep their hearts open in sympathy' to younger people who were becoming more active citizens of this

---

[50] Ibid. 351–2.
[51] Ibid. 352–3. For Thompson, see Jane Smeal and Helen G. Thompson, *Silvanus Philips Thompson, His Life and Letters* (London 1920). Timothy Nicholson, an American Friend, told J. B. Braithwaite he thought Thompson's extravagant language, including his comparing the doctrine of the Atonement with the Jewish rite of circumcision, was '*painful* but *healthful*' since more moderate persons of the 'Reasonable Faith' faction might eschew association with such extremist views. Timothy Nicolson to J.B.B., 4 July 1893, MS Portfolio 17/89. LSF.

world in order that they might better prepare themselves and other members of their religious Society for the next.[52]

In later reflections on his participation in this intense exchange, John Wilhelm Rowntree was encouraged by the fact that he and other young people had been 'heard with wonderful charity' by older Friends.[53] But if there was, in fact, good will between generations, there seemed to be little depth of understanding. J. B. Hodgkin, another pillar of the evangelical establishment, noted that while one might have sincere sympathy for the pleas of younger Friends, 'he could not, when speaking of his crucified and risen Saviour, minimise either the value of His sacrifice upon the Cross, or His power to come home to each individual as a present living Saviour to guide and govern his life'.[54]

Despite continuing difficulties in opening a mutually profitable dialogue between evangelical Friends and their liberal brethren, the discussion initiated by John Wilhelm Rowntree in 1893 has been marked as the beginning of the process through which the purveyors of modern theology eventually achieved a doctrinal realignment that transformed and revitalized British Quakerism. In what remained of his brief, dynamic life, Rowntree assumed the mantle of titular leader of the forces of spiritual progress. Still, he was, in many ways, an unlikely prophet.

When John Wilhelm Rowntree began to take an active part in the affairs of the Society of Friends, few would have seen him as 'the leader and spokesman of the newer life'.[55] Although his family had impeccable Quaker credentials, John Wilhelm had not been a promising youth. Sensitive and temperamental, he grew increasingly deaf, a disability which undoubtedly contributed to his generally indifferent performance in school. Furthermore, as a teenager he was diagnosed with *retinitis pigmentosa*, a degenerative eye disease which causes gradual deterioration of vision.

After leaving school at seventeen, John went to work in his father's factory where he began to show some aptitude as a man of

[52] *TF*, 8 June 1893, 353.

[53] J. W. Rowntree to a friend, 30 May 1893, quoted in *John Wilhelm Rowntree: Essays and Addresses*, edited by Joshua Rowntree (London 1905), p. xxiii. Hereafter cited as *Essays and Addresses*.

[54] *TF*, 8 June 1893, 353–4.

[55] Maurice A. Creasey and Harold Laukes, *The Next Fifty Years* (London 1956), 9; Brayshaw, *The Quakers*, 313; and Rufus M. Jones, *John Wilhelm Rowntree* (Philadelphia 1942), [1].

business and a leader of men. By the time he reached his early twenties, the eldest Rowntree son had achieved modest success, becoming, with his younger brother Seebohm (1871–1954), a partner in the family business, as well as a husband, father, and active member of York Friends Meeting. His easy charm and love of fun attracted a widening circle of mainly Quaker friends, including Constance Naish whom he married in 1892. Their home at Scalby near York became a centre of social life among younger Friends in the vicinity. John Wilhelm had also begun to blossom intellectually, reading widely in theology and philosophy as well as pursuing a serious interest in art, particularly the work of the German Reformation artist Albrecht Dürer.[56]

Despite the apparent success and stability of his life, Rowntree was a spiritually troubled man who seemed in danger of collapsing into agnosticism under the accumulated weight of doubts bred by modern scientific and historical evidence as well as frustrations provoked by his inability to find solace within the Quaker communion. As he told a friend in 1893: 'For two or three years I have been on the verge of resignation, and had it not been that I was favourably circumstanced, should no doubt have left Friends.'[57] At this critical juncture, under the influence of a visiting American Friend, Richard Thomas (1854–1904)[58] of Baltimore, Rowntree experienced a spiritual catharsis which purged him of personal doubt and convinced him that a major part of his life's work should be 'making the Society of Friends . . . a real and living force in the world. I don't see why, if a more earnest spirit is stirred up among our younger members, we should not fill the largest hall in a town; and I do believe ideal Quakerism is the religion for all who are drifting from orthodox Nonconformity.'[59]

So, it was with the zeal of the newly reconverted that Rowntree presented his appeal on behalf of young Friends and, further stirred

[56] Allott, *JWR*, 1–11 and Vernon, *Quaker Business Man*, 76–92 provide information about John Wilhelm Rowntree's (hereafter J.W.R.) early career and home life. Also see *Essays and Addresses*, pp. ix–xxiv.

[57] J. W. R. to a friend, 18 Sept. 1893, quoted in *Essays and Addresses*, p. xii. Also see Rufus M. Jones, *The Trail of Life in College* (New York 1929), 193.

[58] Richard Thomas was one of the most outspoken foes of the pastoral system in America. See *Friends Review*, 13 and 20 March 1890; for the importance of Thomas's influence on the leaders of the Quaker Renaissance, see Jones, *Later Periods*, II, 922 n., 970.

[59] J. W. R. to a friend, 18 Sept. 1893, in *Essays and Addresses*, p. xii. Also see A. Neave Brayshaw, 'Young Friends Movement' in *Swanwick, 1911*, 5 and Rufus M. Jones, *JWR*, 1942), [3–6].

by the surprisingly powerful impact of his message, he began to seek the means for remoulding Quakerism in such a way as 'to make possible, among young Friends[,] a deeper sense of responsibility and a warmer interest in the Society's affairs'.[60]

Shortly after Yearly Meeting in 1893, Rowntree set out to secure realization of his earnest, if somewhat fuzzy, vision for transforming British Quakerism. In a long letter to members of Meeting for Sufferings, he reiterated his belief that among the most distressing circumstances within their Society was the distinct 'Want of Harmony' between generations. John Wilhelm believed that this lack of communication arose from the fact that much of the ministry in local meetings was delivered in 'dead language', confining itself 'too narrowly to the Bible' and ignoring 'the actual problems of our lives'. As a consequence, he said, young people, particularly those who were better-educated, tended to drift away from Friends and even those who stayed out of family loyalty or social pressure exhibited signs of 'spiritual lukewarmness' or 'much worldliness'. What was needed—in addition to 'a liberal measure of Christian tolerance'—was a ministry that was 'direct, practical, thoughtful, and from the heart' as well as opportunities for an active life *within* the Society rather than outside of it. '[W]e want to stir up young Friends . . . to rouse from spiritual torpor those who sleep.'[61]

John Wilhelm's plan may have lacked detail, but he was never deficient in energy. Nor was he alone. In the wake of events at Yearly Meeting in 1893, Rowntree came into contact with a number of reform-minded Friends who had, perhaps for the first time, begun to take him seriously. One of his most important allies was William Charles Braithwaite, the eighth child of Joseph Bevan Braithwaite who had followed his father into the legal profession but not into the evangelical camp. Like Rowntree, W. C. Braithwaite had been greatly influenced by Richard Thomas, who was also his brother-in-law.[62] Following the 1893 Yearly Meeting, Braithwaite joined with John Wilhelm Rowntree in organizing what they rather grandiosely called 'the Yorkshire

---

[60] John Wilhelm Rowntree, 'A Few Thoughts Upon the Position of Young Friends in Relation to the Society', 3 (1893), typescript in LSF.

[61] Ibid. 4–5, 10–12.

[62] Ann Thomas and Elizabeth B. Emmott, *William Charles Braithwaite: Memoir and Papers* (London 1931), 16–17, 83.

Movement', a campaign undertaken by a number of Northern Friends aimed at developing a more vital, practical, and up-to-date ministry which might breathe new life into languid local meetings throughout the North of England. Joining in this effort were John Wilhelm's younger brother Seebohm, later to achieve frame for his study of poverty in York, and Edward Grubb, a persistent critic of the 'poor and thin' ministry in most Quaker Meetings.[63]

A distinctly insider's view of this collaboration has been preserved in the correspondence of W. C. Braithwaite and his fiancée Janet Morland (1867–1936).[64] Like her future husband, Janet Morland was committed to the task of modernizing the Society, but her early letters to 'Mr. Braithwaite' hinted that neither of them seemed entirely certain whether the Rowntree brothers were sufficiently serious or mature to lead such a crusade. But as the Yorkshire Movement continued its progress through northern meetings, from York to Harrogate to Newcastle and Sunderland, William Charles became increasingly impressed with John Wilhelm's ability to inspire young people and lift local meetings which he visited 'to a higher plane'. Braithwaite also sang the praises of Edward Grubb, as 'a fellow of high soul wrought out of much questioning & trial . . . with a strong consciousness of the reality of the spiritual world . . .'[65] Janet Morland, who had not been impressed with Grubb's teaching at the Mount School, believed that his coming into his own owed much to the inspiration of his present company: 'If John had half a dozen supporters as earnest as himself it would be different, but every meeting he holds is preparing the ground. He seems to me to be more wonderful each time I see him, one is almost frightened with the rapidity of his growth.'[66]

---

[63] Grubb, 'Ministry', 366.

[64] The collection includes over thirty letters exchanged between Janet Morland and W. C. Braithwaite from 20 May 1893 to 8 November 1895. This correspondence was preserved by their son, the late Richard Braithwaite (1900–1989), who ended a distinguished academic career at King's College, Cambridge as Knightsbridge Professor of Moral Philosophy. I am deeply grateful for his kindness in sharing these letters as well as his wisdom and insight on other aspects Quakerism.

[65] J. M. to 'Mr. Braithwaite', 30 July 1893 and W. C. B. to J. M, 15 and 28 Aug. 1893, Braithwaite Family Papers (BFP).

[66] J. M. to W. C. B., 14 Sept. 1893 and 18 March 1894, BFP.

Such praise was, most assuredly, a tribute to Rowntree's spark-
ling, magnetic personality. It was also an early contribution, privately and sincerely given, to the Quaker mythology of St John
Wilhelm, the wise and good. There are, in truth, two John
Wilhelm Rowntrees in the lexicography of Quakerism. The first
is a thrice-blessed knight errant, the lost leader cut down in his
prime just as he seemed about to discover what one historian has
sardonically termed the 'Quaker Holy Grail'.[67] According to
standard accounts, the radiant John Wilhelm not only inspired
much of the Modern Movement among Friends but, had he only
lived, might have taken the Society on to yet unattained heights.
The second J. W. R. is a somewhat less glittering young dynamo
who prodded and pushed sometimes reluctant British Friends into
vigorous action in the years between 1893 and 1905. This more
human and more vulnerable John Wilhelm died before he had
formulated a fully-developed view of history, of religion, of modern
society, or of the role that Quakerism should play within that
society. Too often the striving young leader is shunted on to a
side track in favour of the Quaker Superman ready and able to
overcome all manner of disputes and difficulties that bedevilled
Friends. In this version the difficulties concerning the ministry, the
effects of biblical criticism, the changing attitudes toward social
policy, the traumatic transformation of the peace testimony, and a
multitude of other problems but awaited fulfillment through John
Wilhelm Rowntree's amazing vision and astonishing perspicacity.
Unfortunately, such a view transforms an attractive young man
into a plaster saint, robbing him of most of the very human qualities
that made him so appealing to so many of his contemporaries.
Following his premature death in 1905, John Wilhelm was raised
to the exalted status of full-blown Quaker Saint, the White Knight
who rescued the Society from the dead-end of out-dated
evangelicalism and set it on the path to modernity. Whether or
not this rapid canonization was fully deserved, Rowntree's
presence looms sufficiently large in the history of the Quaker
Renaissance to deserve singular attention. However difficult it
has become to separate the man from the myth, John Wilhelm
Rowntree was, in truth, a creative and dynamic force for British

---

[67] See H. Larry Ingle's provocative essay 'On the Folly of Seeking the Quaker Holy
Grail', *QRT*, 25/1 (May 1991), 17–29.

Quakerism throughout his brief public ministry and an inspiring role-model long after his premature death.[68]

J. W. R.'s seriousness of purpose and sense of mission are reflected in a sombre and rather awkward letter written late in 1893 to his cousin Arnold S. Rowntree (1872–1951) on the occasion of the latter's twenty-first birthday. Correctly predicting that Arnold would find his place in the public sphere rather than in religious affairs, John Wilhelm nonetheless admonished his younger cousin never to forget the work that needed to be done: 'to lift up the cross of self-denial and make Christianity more than ever before a living and real force...'[69] According to Arnold Rowntree's children, John Wilhelm always remained one of his heroes. Certainly, as a Liberal MP (1910–18) and High Sheriff (1931) for York, Arnold Rowntree was as serious and diligent a politician as his cousin could have wished.

A case might also be made that, even from the beginning, John Wilhelm Rowntree's influence was corporate as well as personal. It seems plausible, for example, that his message to Yearly Meeting in May 1893 provided the incentive for a group of Friends who in July of the same year protested against the reappointment of Howard Nicholson (1843–1933), an evangelical minister and member of Meeting for Sufferings, to the Ackworth School Committee on account of his propensity for approaching startled school children with questions such as: 'Are you saved?' Such a query, said 23-year-old Samuel H. Davies (1870–1925), was not only fraught with danger for impressionable children but also had no place in 'true Quakerism, where ... liberty to worship God without priestly intervention and where non-intervention with God's own methods of dealing with tender hearts had ever been recognized'. A young female Friend called Nicholson a man 'almost entirely out of touch with a large section of the Society'. Others, including E. Vipont Brown and John William Graham, joined the attack,

---

[68] Stephen Allott's, *John Wilhelm Rowntree* begins the process of adjusting the saintly image for a more balanced perspective. For contemporaneous commentary see Silvanus P. Thompson, 'John Wilhelm Rowntree', *FQE*, 39 (April 1905), 258–68. Also see Kennedy, 'History and the Quaker Renaissance', *JFHS*, 55/1–2 (1985–86), 35–56 and Howard Brinton, *Friends for 300 Years* (London 1953), pp. viii–ix.

[69] John Wilhelm Rowntree to Arnold S. Rowntree (copy), 4 December 1893, Rowntree Family Papers (RFP) in possession of Jean Rowntree and used with her permission.

noting that no one on the School Committee should be 'out of harmony with the traditions of the Society'.[70]

Nicholson was no random target. The producers of the pamphlet 'Is There Not A Cause?' had singled out his defence of a separate paid ministry—'head and shoulders above the people'— at the Richmond Conference as particularly blatant example of how extreme evangelicals intended to use the paid pastorate to undermine Quaker principles and traditions.[71] In this instance, the protest failed and Nicholson was reappointed, but the dissenting message was unmistakable and would be repeated with increasing frequency and, eventually, to considerable effect. On the last day of 1893, J. W. Graham wrote to his wife pledging 'a fresh consecration of life...to God and His Work' during the coming year and expressing thanks for 'lessening evangelicalism' among Friends.[72]

In the meantime, the Yorkshire Movement continued its efforts to produce a more thoughtful and stimulating ministry in Northern meetings for worship. Janet Morland had joined the campaign early in 1894 and her letters to W. C. Braithwaite reveal a sense of exhilaration at the results this spiritual ginger group seemed to be achieving. Much still needed to be done, she recounted in mid-March, but 'I have no fear about this Yorkshire Movement... somehow with John it seems more possible to do it'.[73]

Other young Friends had similar response to the resuscitating powers of John Wilhelm's energy and personality. Among these was Lawrence Richardson (1869–1953) of Newcastle upon Type, one of J. W. R.'s closest friends. While still in his late teens, Richardson heard the editor of *The Friend* (Joseph Sewell) explain the Atonement to Newcastle Meeting by noting that 'as God's justice demanded punishment for Adam's sin, God's love made him inflict that punishment on his Son'. Young Richardson was so revolted by Sewell's depiction of God as a sort of vengeful fiend that he wandered in a spiritual wilderness for several years and

---

[70] 'Ackworth General Meeting', *BF*, August 1893, 223–4, 226.
[71] 'ITNAC', 22. Born in Cumberland, Howard Nicholson lived in Canada and the United States from 1862 to 1888, returning to England in his mid-forties to undertake Home Mission work in Bethnal Green. See *DQB* entry, LSF.
[72] J. W. G. to his wife, 31 December 1893, Box 3, JWGP.
[73] Janet Morland to W. C. B., 18 March [1894], BFP.

might have left Quakerism but for his friendship with John Wilhelm Rowntree.[74]

Beyond this ability to inspire others to work for change within the Society rather than to despair of its changing, Rowntree, in contrast to liberal activists like Graham and Vipont Brown, also seemed to be adept at conciliating those whose ideas and practices he sought to transform. According to Janet Morland, he did not draw distinctions of age or theology but insisted that all Friends, young and old, stretch their frequently underemployed brains by ceasing to arrive at meeting for worship with closed or empty minds.[75]

J. W. R. told Lawrence Richardson that his chief objectives were 'waking up the Society to thought' as well as producing a 'more understanding spirit and some small measure of spiritual stimulation'. Another of the means he choose for attaining these goals was *Present Day Papers*, a periodical he established to try to deal 'with pressing social and theological questions'. The material set out in this journal, he explained, would be 'perfectly straight' and aimed especially at 'those who are [spiritually] out of touch ... to try to get them to energize their ideals in positive action'.[76]

While Rowntree was making plans to launch the *Present Day Papers*, some of his allies were preparing the way for what would be a decisive episode in the broad-based campaign to draw the Society of Friends into the modern world, the Manchester Conference of 1895. Ironically, the impetus for this effort came from the newly reorganized Home Mission Committee. This seems doubly odd considering that many 'progressive' Friends had been disappointed in the fact that fully a third of the new Committee's eighty-four members were holdovers from the previous body, implying a continuing evangelical dominance in its proceedings.[77] When the new Committee first met in October 1894, some of the more impatient liberal reformers in its ranks did not wait to test the

---

[74] Lawrence Richardson, 'Newcastle-upon-Tyne Friends and Scientific Thought: Reminiscences', *JFHS*, 1/45 (Spring 1953), 40–44.

[75] J. M. to W. C. B., 18 March and 4 April 1894, BFP.

[76] J. W. R. to Lawrence Richardson, 17 October 1894, quoted in *Essays and Addresses*, p. xxi; to J. B. Hodgkin, 13 December 1894, MSS Port 42/56, LSF; and *TF*, 17 March 1905, 162.

[77] See the remarks of William Edward Turner in *BF*, June 1894, 168. Members are listed in the Friends Home Mission Committee, *Minute Book*, 1–4, LSF.

waters but plunged in headlong, calling for the abolition of all monetary support to mission workers. This bold thrust, probably conceived by John W. Graham, proved to be a serious tactical error, for it produced a forceful expression of the Committee's obvious consensus that it should continue 'assisting Friends with a definite, religious concern to reside... in given centres of work'.[78]

After this initial set-back, outnumbered reformers adopted a more amiable, and subtle, appraoch which, given the make-up of the Committee, proved remarkably successful not just in restoring harmony but also in transforming this mainly evangelical body into an instrument for change. The events leading up to the Manchester Conference received careful attention from Roger Wilson who gave major credit for this success to the Committee's Acting Honorary Secretary, J. Fyfe Stewart (1845–1908), an unsung hero among Quaker 'emancipators'.[79]

When the Home Mission Committee met in late February 1895, there were no contentious or dissenting resolutions. The Committee concentrated almost exclusively on the practical affairs of the 'mission stations', recording two dozen non-controversial Minutes with regard to their operation and oversight.[80] Late in the day, however, the meeting took a distinctly different tone. Minute 25 departed from the mundane concerns of day-to-day Home Mission activity with a sweeping suggestion that the ensuing Yearly Meeting take up the question of the general 'ignorance and misconception which exists around us as the Society of Friends' and furnish some guidance as to how to aid the Committee in making their fellow citizens of every station and class more aware of 'our distinguishing views'. Having posed the question, the Minute also suggested an answer, noting that if Yearly Meeting should decide that 'a special Conference' was needed properly to inform the

---

[78] FHMC, *Minute Book*, 30. Wilson, 'Road to Manchester', 149–51 notes that the proposal for ending financial support came from two Lancashire members.

[79] Wilson, 'Road to Manchester', 149–54 and private information. John Fyfe Stewart was the son of John Stewart, proprietor of the *Edinburgh Review* and stepson of Louisa Hopper Stewart. Trained as an engineer, he spent his working life in London. In 1892 Stewart was the unsuccessful Liberal candidate for the Parliamentary seat at Hackney Central. He was a member of Stoke Newington Meeting and a recorded minister. See *DQB* entry, LSF.

[80] An earlier minute suggesting that 'a meeting for worship after the manner of Friends' should be held at least once a week in every mission was obviously a reflection of concern about unQuakerly practices by mission workers. It may have rankled, but evangelicals could hardly disagree. See FHMC, *Minutes, 1895*, 8 February, 77.

larger community, 'the Home Mission Committee might be the convenient body' for arranging such an event.[81] This Minute was too singular a departure from the normal business of the Home Mission Committee to have been a spur-of-the-moment inspiration. The initiative for the proposed Conference most likely came from Fyfe Stewart in collaboration with W. C. Braithwaite.[82] It was Stewart who received a special tribute from his colleagues on the Committee after the Yearly Meeting had endorsed the idea of a Conference and accepted the invitation of Lancashire and Cheshire Quarterly Meeting to hold it in Manchester.[83] Fyfe Stewart was also selected as a member of the small sub-committee appointed to make arrangements for the impending Conference. Surprisingly, this group included no prominent representative of the evangelical majority on the full Committee.[84]

As the sub-Committee began laying the groundwork, proponents of change launched a propaganda campaign regarding the topics to be addressed at the impending Conference. Edward Grubb published an article on the theme 'Yearly Meeting, 1836'. In the liberal Quaker tradition, the *Epistle* of 1836, with its endorsement of the supreme authority of Scripture and its virtual dismissal of the Inward Light, marked the beginning of evangelical dominance over London Yearly Meeting (see Chapter 1). Grubb used that occasion as a frame of reference for past damage done to the Society through 'the narrow intolerance and want of sympathetic insight' by those who confused new ideas with 'unsound' faith. 'Happy are they', Grubb concluded, 'who . . . can see through the forms to the truth that lies beneath them, and have faith enough in the vitality of the Truth of God to believe that it is

---

[81] Ibid. 25 Feb. 1895, 77–8. The Minute is also entirely reprinted in *Report of the Proceedings of the Manchester Conference of the Society of Friends, 1895* [Hereafter *Manchester Conference*] (London 1896), 11–12.

[82] The year after Fyfe Stewart's death in November 1908, a pamphlet reprinting his obituary from *The Friend* and celebrating his role in proposing, planning and staging the Manchester Conference was issued. See 'John Fyfe Stewart: Christmas, 1909', 8–9, Box 181, LSF.

[83] FHMC, *Minutes*, 30 May 1895, 110–12.

[84] In addition to Fyfe Stewart, sub-committee members included W. C. Braithwaite, his older brother J. B. Braithwaite Jr. and W. E. Turner, with Joshua Rowntree as chair. FHMC, *Minutes, Executive Committee*, 31 May 1895, 134–6. Wilson, 'Road to Manchester', 154 believed that Joshua Rowntree was the key figure in shaping the agenda for the Conference.

not in danger every time it has to assimilate new additions to the stock of knowledge.'[85]

More directly to the point was W. C. Braithwaite's long essay on 'Some Present-Day Aims of the Society of Friends' published in the summer of 1895. If their Society was to make a difference in the spiritual development of the modern age, said Braithwaite, Friends, moved by 'the breath that vitalized early Quakerism'— the indwelling spirit of God—must understand and embrace the three 'new occasions' which were commanding the attention of thoughtful people looking forward to the twentieth century: 'the growth of the scientific spirit', the pressure of social questions and the *'craving after reality* in religion and life'.[86]

Quakerism was, Braithwaite's said, 'the least unreal of the Churches' and therefore, spiritually, the best prepared to create a true 'fellowship at work for Gods' Kingdom' on earth. By assuming 'a fearless and open mind...towards modern thought'— whether in biology, geology, or historical criticism of the Bible— as 'the revelation which the living Spirit of Christ is making to the world today', Friends could offer a spiritual home to 'many honest doubters...driven to agnosticism or atheism by...insistence on the externals instead of the spiritual realities of religion'.[87]

With regard to the second development, the pressure for social change, Braithwaite pointed to the long-standing Quaker tradition of social action, personified by John Woolman's struggle against slavery but also warned that in the new century it would have to go deeper than 'sentimental philanthropy' or 'transient enthusiasm' to a systematic policy based on stewardship. Finally, Braithwaite said, if Quakerism was to take full advantage of its attractiveness to modern seekers after a spiritual home, the Society must abandon the 'ring-fence of conventions' surrounding it and concentrate on 'the spiritual basis of truth'. The power of God might be *'revealed'* by historical knowledge of the Bible or by an intellectual grasp of theological ideas, but it could only be *'known'* by a true-hearted admittance of the living Spirit of Christ within'. Thus Quakerism, while embracing the new knowledge that was being revealed to humanity, should continue to seek spiritual enlightenment through

---

[85] Edward Grubb, 'Yearly Meeting, 1836', 115–16.

[86] William C. Braithwaite, 'Some Present-Day Aims of the Society of Friends', *FQE*, (1895), 322–5 [emphasis in original].

[87] Ibid. 325–8, 337.

the Inward Light while labouring to reveal to the wider world that this Divine gift was available to Seekers of every stripe. Such, Braithwaite concluded, was the historically unique message through which Quakerism could fulfill its historic mission in working for the Kingdom of God on earth.[88]

While readers contemplated Braithwaite's plea for renewal and modernity, plans for the Conference took definite shape. By early July a special fund had been established to help defray expenses and over thirty individuals had been invited to make presentations on a list of topics determined by the Conference sub-committee.[89] Clearly, then, the agenda for what might possibly be the most important gathering of British Quakers in two centuries was to be decided upon by a tiny group of theologically liberal Friends. What is surprising about these developments was not just the lack of resistance to the process by the evangelical members of the Home Mission Committee but also the lack of information made available to them. For example, on 3 August a minute of the HMC Executive noted that they had received 'No further report' regarding the list of topics to be discussed at the Conference, but shortly thereafter, the August edition of the *British Friend*, whose editor W. E. Turner was a sub-committee member, printed a complete and nearly accurate list of the Conference programme which was not printed in the Home Mission *Minutes* until early October.[90] The only significant change in the final programme was the addition, at the request of the Home Mission Committee, of J. B. Braithwaite to a session on 'The Attitude of the Society Towards Modern Thought'. Obviously, this was a sop to the evangelicals, though it hardly produced a doctrinal balance, for all the other speakers on Modern Thought had revealed decidedly liberal propensities.[91]

Progressive Friends might well feel pleased that a Conference ostensibly arranged by a predominantly evangelical body could produce a list of overwhelmingly liberal speakers to represent Quakerism to the British public. Furthermore, all presentations to the Conference would be widely disseminated by the 'Daily

[88] Ibid. 329–41 *passim*.

[89] HMC *Executive Minutes*, 3 July 1895, 152 and *Minutes*, 4 July 1895, 126–34. The basis upon which invitations were issued was not stated in the Committee's minutes.

[90] *BF*, Aug. 1895; HMC, *Executive Minutes*, 3 August, 158 and 5 September, 178–9; and *Minutes*, 3 October 1895, 144–5. Also see Wilson, 'Road to Manchester', 155–6.

[91] Ibid. 144–5.

press' who were especially invited to attend.[92] In early November Janet Morland wrote to her 'Mr. Braithwaite' expressing a sense of satisfaction that the impending Conference revealed most Friends were no longer willing to leave Home Mission work in the hands of an evangelically-dominated Committee:

I feel . . . the Conference . . . was a necessity, that the strivings after the ideal of Quaker worship & ministry which are obvious in many minds all over the country had to be expressed. We do need, as a Society, to be reminded of our special work . . . If we were all home missionaries, the work c[oul]d certainly be done better than it is at present, & any growing sense that we cannot put all work onto others or pay them to take the responsibility of it, is a hopeful sign.[93]

THE MANCHESTER CONFERENCE, 1895

In late November 1895, Henry Stanley Newman, long-time honorary secretary to the Friends Foreign Mission Association, wrote to Rufus Jones, editor of the *American Friend*, enthusiastically expressing his belief that the recently completed Conference

will mark an era in the history of our Society in England. We have found for some years past . . . that our Church was *losing grasp* of the highly educated & intelligent young men and women belonging to our best old Quaker families who were receiving first class curriculum at College & then drifting theologically. If our Society was thus to lose its best, a few years might settle our fate. Every Christian Church *must* face modern criticism & modern scientific thought . . . This Conference is the effort *for the first time* in our Society to *face* this emergency & I want thee to quietly make the best & fullest use thou can of the double [Conference] number of the [London] *Friend*.[94]

What had transpired at Manchester to make even solid evangelical Quakers like H. S. Newman feel that their Society had taken a decisive turn? The announced objectives of the meeting had been

---

[92] HMC, *Executive Minutes*, 3 Aug. 1895, 179.

[93] Janet Morland to W. C. Braithwaite, 8 November [1895], BFP.

[94] H. S. Newman to R. M. Jones, 25 November 1895, Box 1, RMJP. *The Friend* devoted a special edition to the Conference on 29 November 1895.

to 'to dispel ignorance that . . . exists in the public mind' concerning the Society of Friends and 'to strengthen the attachment of
younger members to its work'. The Conference's introductory
speaker Theodore Neild (1843–1929), a teacher and athlete of
some renown, noted that if these objectives were to be achieved,
all in attendance would have to put aside their fear of discussing
social issues and modern thought. Younger Friends, Neild said,
would have confidence in the usefulness of the Conference only if
controversial topics were seriously 'grappled with'.[95] Such sentiments from a good, grey Quaker like Neild may have puzzled or
even alarmed representatives of the Free Churches of Manchester
who had been invited, as Christian 'comrades', to participate in
Conference. Indeed, 'An Address of Welcome From the Free
Churches of Manchester' had taken special note of the soundness
of Friends' 'testimony on the essentials of the Evangelical faith' and
expressed the hope that such principles would be maintained.[96]
The first speaker in the initial session on 'Has Quakerism a Message
to the World to-day?', Matilda Sturge (1829–1903), did, in fact,
begin her discussion of 'Early Quakerism' with a respectful bow to
the nineteenth-century evangelical revival within the Society,
crediting it with rousing Quakerism from 'apathy and formalism'.
But for the remainder of her address this venerable septuagenarian
minister, temperance worker, and author set the tone for the five-
day meeting, putting forward the entire agenda of liberal, reformist
concerns about the decrepit condition of British Quakerism. Evangelical attachment to dogmatic principles, Sturge noted, had gradually obscured and even undermined the unique ideas and
practices to which early Friends had borne witness. She was particularly critical of the 'blind, almost idolatrous faith in the Bible and
Bible texts' which threatened to fix modern Quakerism in the vice-
grip of the sort of dogmatic principles from which the first Friends
had sought to escape. Concurrent with the danger of theological
rigidity, Sturge said, was the threat of social ossification. The same
laudable virtues which had contributed to Friends' success at business had tended to lead them to false assumptions about the rightness of the existing order and, thereby, produced a general failure

[95] *Report of the Proceedings of the Conference of Members of the Society of Friends held, by
Direction of the Yearly Meeting, in Manchester from the Eleventh to the Fifteenth of Eleventh Month,
1895.* (London 1896), v, 14–15. [Hereafter *Manchester Conference* with page(s).]
[96] Ibid. 22–3.

to address the root causes of social and economic conditions which fostered injustice and inequality. If Quakerism was to meet the challenges of the twentieth century, Sturge concluded, both its theology and social assumptions would have to change with the times.[97]

Neither evangelical Friends nor their guests from the Manchester Free Churches could have been pleased with Maltida Sturge's message. They were no doubt relieved when Frederick Sessions, an evangelical minister and pioneer Home Missioner, presented a corrective rejoinder by asserting the irrefutable authority of the Bible and cautioning against the modern tendency to raise private illumination above the lessons of Scripture.[98]

However heartened by Frederick Sessions' restatement of their fundamental principles, evangelicals would soon realize that it was not to be their day or their Conference. During the question time that concluded the opening session, Dr Edward Vipont Brown of Manchester challenged the sentiments expressed by Sessions, noting that traditional Quakerism was not based on the outward authority of biblical texts but upon 'the breathing of a living spirit into the heart of man . . .'[99] With this statement Brown gave notice that proponents of change would no longer quietly acquiesce in what they regarded as obdurate Calvinism masquerading as true Quakerism. In the days that followed, as liberal theology captured both the rhetorical initiative and the high moral ground, the dominant theme would be the compatibility of modern ideas with Quaker tradition.

Nowhere was this more obvious than during the third day's session on 'The Society of Friends and Modern Thought' when Joseph Bevan Braithwaite was left to bear the evangelical standard alone against an array of liberal Friends, including J. Rendel Harris (1852–1941), newly appointed lecturer in palaeography at Cambridge, Silvanus Thompson, the distinguished physicist, and John William Graham, hammer of the evangelicals. Long a spokesman for and hero of evangelical Friends, J. B. Braithwaite, at his age and in such company, was clearly out of his depth. It was, indeed, a blessing that Braithwaite's indisposition made it necessary for his

[97] Ibid. 31–3. Also see Margaret Allen, 'Matilda Sturge: "Renaissance Woman"', *Women's History Review*, 7/2 (1998), 209–26. I am grateful to Professor Allen for allowing me to read her excellent essay in manuscript.

[98] *Manchester Conference*, 36–9.   [99] Ibid. 52–3.

lecture to be read by his son-in-law, Richard Thomas. Perhaps the most conspicuous aspect of J. B. B.'s address was a lack of freshness, starkly underlined by an admission that the substance of his concluding remarks had been 'written nearly fifty years ago': 'If we duly consider the uncertainty and the shortness of life, we shall think it needful to put a check upon many curious but unprofitable enquiries... and be even content to remain ignorant of many things, because we have neither time nor opportunity here upon earth adequately to search them out.'[100]

The fact that Braithwaite's speech followed hard upon an eloquent and erudite lecture by Thomas Hodgkin, further magnified its musty, archaic tone. The predominant theme of Hodgkin's address had been the advantage which Quakerism provided by permitting Friends to come to grips with modernity without the danger of succumbing to the 'enervating and malarious' excesses of intellectually fashionable movements like aestheticism, pessimism, scientism, and socialism. By way of example, Hodgkin observed that the early Quaker view of 'Universal and saving light' provided a far more efficacious antidote for pessimism than Calvinistic predestination. And, as for science, Hodgkin contended that Friends had surely been 'divinely guided' in their traditional refusal to call the Bible '*The Word of God*' as it had become increasingly clear that Old Testament words spoken 'by the unscientific Hebrew sage [were] no essential part of Christ's message to the world today'. Indeed, he noted, nearly all thoughtful Christians had followed suit and ceased any attempt 'to hem in the scientific enquirer by limitations derived from the supposed necessity of trying to fit the words of those old Hebrew scribes into the discoveries of modern science'.[101]

The remaining speakers on modern thought put a less subtle gloss on the major points of Hodgkin's presentation. The first of these, Rendel Harris, took an uncompromising position in admonishing those Friends who continued to show an aversion to the 'dazzling light of scientific knowledge'. What such individuals failed to appreciate, Harris said, was that they could no longer detach religion from science. The 'doctrine of evolution [was] as applicable to Scriptures, to Churches, and to Sacraments ... as ... [to] the study of the lowest forms of animal life.'

---

[100] Ibid. 217.   [101] Ibid. 204–6, 208–9.

Therefore, he concluded, Quakerism was obliged to set itself in the 'right place amongst the intellectual forces of the world' by incorporating modern ideals into its collective vision.[102]

In addressing the question 'Can a Scientific Man be a Sincere Quaker?', Silvanus Thompson emphasized that there need be no conflict between science and religion since the voice of God spoke to the soul, not to the mind of men. Modern science, he said, might demonstrate what was intellectually false but only the 'guidance of the divine light' could reveal what was 'spiritually true' and lead humanity back to a way of life that was the fullest revelation of Christ's teaching. The great gift shared by all Friends, Thompson noted, was the knowledge that 'creed is not separable from conduct [and] that a man's religion is not that which he professes, but that which he lives...'[103]

The final speaker on 'Modern Thought,' John W. Graham, took the offensive against biblical literalism, noting that the supposed infallibility of the Scriptures rested on nothing 'but the ill-informed view of bishops of the early centuries...' On the other hand, Graham asserted, 'when we cease to be afraid of the competition of other books with the Bible, we shall find out how much it excels them all.'[104]

The rhetorical triumph of the New Theology in the session on 'Modern Thought' was long remembered as a decisive victory for the forces of modernity within British Quakerism. Certainly, there was 'widespread sympathy... especially amongst... younger Friends' for the sentiments expressed by some of the Society's leading modernist thinkers, but one disquieting effect of this liberal victory was the revelation of wounds inevitably inflicted upon the still sizeable evangelical wing of the Society. J. B. Hodgkin, for example, protested that if everything that had been said in the session was represented to the general public as a consensus of Quaker views, 'the position will be exceedingly serious' and could only add to the distress of those who were already deeply disturbed by what they had heard. Furthermore, many Friends, particularly evangelicals, were upset by the fact that the presentations on Modern Thought had gone on so long as to prevent any

[102] Ibid. 218–26 *passim*.
[103] Ibid. 239. Also see David Murray-Rust, 'The Manchester Conference and a Memoir of Silvanus P. Thompson', *JFHS*, 57/2 (1995), 198–207.
[104] *Manchester Conference*, 226–46 *passim*.

discussion of their contents. As chairman, Thomas Hodgkin suggested that the Committee on Arrangements 'provide some time for those who are burdened with what they have heard...' But, in the end, dissenters got no satisfaction. The Arrangements Committee resolved 'to avoid entirely a discussion... which in the nature of things could only be partial and unsatisfactory'.[105]

Evangelical elements were, perhaps, somewhat mollified by the fact that, in keeping with a suggestion of J. B. Hodgkin, the Conference gave no endorsement to any of the papers which had been presented. Still, as Caleb R. Kemp, Clerk of Yearly Meeting, groused to his 'Diary': 'They [the papers] required so much time that none was left for any discussion. The subject was treated "broadly"—more so than I felt to be edifying. Indeed, I had always doubted the wisdom of including it [Modern thought] in the programme.'[106]

The Manchester Conference was conceived of and long remembered as a seminal event in the evolution of modern Quakerism but from the perspective of a century, its *Proceedings*, especially those dealing with 'modern thought', seem rather tame. No doubt, this is because, as one Quaker historian has noted, nearly every bold idea which emerged from the meeting was concerned with theological principles now either commonplace or passé.[107] Still, there were notable developments at Manchester which reflected the direction upon which the Society had set its course. The first of these concerned the place of female Friends. The fact that nearly a third of the speakers at the Manchester Conference were women was in itself unusual for any mixed gathering at the time, religious or otherwise. On the other hand, it was fully in keeping with the tradition of a strong Quaker female ministry and, of course, women still represented a clear majority of the membership of London Yearly Meeting. Quakers naturally took pride in having had, unlike most Churches, the benefit of seeing 'the work of God's spirit when he speaks to the women'. But Gulielma Wallis Crosfield (1851–1945) chided Friends for the complacency inherent in such self-satisfaction. Crosfield reminded the Conference that while 'a large share of the forward work of the world, in moral and religious questions, fall [sic] into the hands of women', Quakerism

---

[105] Ibid. 246–8.
[106] Caleb Kemp, 'Diary', 7 December 1895, 266–7, MS vol. S7, LSF.
[107] Greenwood, *Quakers Encounters, I: Friends and Relief*, 170–71.

was failing in its responsibility to the world by doing little or nothing to advance the position of women in the social and political realm. One of the things most needed, she said, was 'sound judgment and righteousness' in reassessing women's place both in their own Religious Society and in the larger society they were attempting to influence.[108]

No dramatic conclusions were reached with regard to the future role of women in the Society. Still, when, in the midst of a discussion on 'Quakerism's Message to the World', Ellen Robinson (1840–1912) called upon the Clerk to 'kindly silence the men a little bit' so that Friends, in hearing the words of their wives and sisters and mothers, might receive more light and less heat, British Quakers were put on notice of another serious question with which they would be forced to grapple during the impending century.[109]

Another vexations brush with the future that emerged at Manchester concerned what was ostensibly a central theme of the Conference, Friends and Social Questions. One session on the second day was given over to consideration of social problems and their possible solutions, but most presentations on social reform and reconstruction were little more than pious personal summaries of philanthropic deeds illustrating how Friends with a few hours or a few pounds to spare could make meaningful contact with the working classes. For the most part, the discussions of social problems and responsibilities gave off an aura of complacent self-satisfaction. But there were uncomfortable moments.

In the midst of the first day's meeting one incident threw a glaring light not only on the tepid quality of Quaker ideas about social reform but also on the nature of Quaker attitudes toward the equality of believers, at least in the sight of man. During a discussion period following the session on Quakerism's message to the modern world, Kenerie Ward, a barely literate farm labourer, rose to relate how, after years of vainly seeking for spiritual comfort, the silence of a Friends' meeting had become 'the starting point in my life'. But lest Friends wax prideful at the conquest of this humble soul, Ward, whose accent must have struck an odd, even discordant, note amongst solidly middle-class Quakers, went on to describe how he had been treated while seeking closer ties with his fellow

---

[108] *Manchester Conference*, 68–70.   [109] Ibid. 94. See Chapter 6 below.

worshippers. 'I went to that meeting for five months, and only one man . . . ever spoke to me.' Years later, Ward said, even after he had been admitted to membership, some of the meeting's elders had still not uttered a word to him nor even recognized his presence. 'All these things keep people away from *your* Church,' he pointedly concluded.[110]

The immediate response to Kenerie Ward's rebuke must have been stunned silence, as assembled Friends perhaps recalled similar incidents in their own local meetings. Two speakers replied with rather lame accounts of their personal liberality towards the working classes before the discussion shifted back to more spiritually edifying, not to say more comfortable, concerns.[111] This troublesome moment set the stage for a session on the long-standing question of why so few of those who attended Adult Schools or Home Mission meetings joined the Society of Friends. Some practical solutions were put forward,[112] but the crux of the problem still seemed to be, as one speaker noted, the belief of many working-class people that while their presence might 'be good enough for the Lord', they suspected that it might not be 'good enough for Friends'.[113]

If the Manchester Conference did not place the Society of Friends in the vanguard of the movement for social equality, the Conference Arrangements Committee did report its sense of satisfaction that the two major objectives of the gathering, 'the removal of misconceptions on the part of the public' and 'the strengthening of the attachment of young Friends . . . were promoted by the Conference to a somewhat unusual degree'.[114] Almost to a man (there were no women), liberals on the Arrangements Committee had reason to feel gratified that the tone of the Conference, while never startlingly original or innovative, had run strongly in their direction. Doctrines long in decline—biblical literalism, the propitiatory Atonement, absolute human depravity—seemed to be rapidly fading into the shadowy periphery of modern British Quakerism. Still, the waning of evangelical dominance might as easily

[110] Ibid. 87–9 (emphasis added). [111] Ibid. 89–92.

[112] See, for example, J. B. Braithwaite, Jr.'s plan for drawing working-class members into Preparative Meetings as a prelude to full Monthly Meeting membership, ibid. 113–19.

[113] Ibid. 125. The speaker, Harriet Green, was repeating the words of a working-class member in her meeting.

[114] HMC, Executive Comm. *Minutes*, 5 Dec. 1895, 211–12. Also see *TF*, 29 Nov. 1895, 48.

have implied spiritual drift as spiritual renewal. That it ultimately did not was the major achievement of the Quaker Renaissance. The Friends who had conceived and planned the Manchester Conference used the momentum created there to work towards a new spiritual consensus based upon a revival of the 'mystical, practical and experimental nature of Quakerism' which, as they believed, had been diminished, and in some places nearly extinguished, during several generations of evangelical dominance.[115] But if the much-vaunted session on Modern Thought was the key demonstration of the triumph of the New Theology within the Society of Friends, many who recalled the Manchester Conference fixed upon the address of John Wilhelm Rowntree as its decisive moment. Rowntree, while depreciating 'sluggish self-complacency...spiritual pride [and] false respectability' of contemporary Quakerism, also envisioned a revitalized Quaker faith 'deeper in its basis, clearer in its vision, broader in its charity...and as warm in its love' rising out of the 'seeming chaos' of the modern world. 'Friends are not bound by a heritage of creeds, and need not break with their great past to put themselves in touch with the present', Rowntree noted. Therefore, he concluded, new ideas and new challenges should be a source of strength, not weakness.[116] John Wilhelm Rowntree was only 27 when he spoke at Manchester and in the decade of life left to him, his display of 'Christian passion...intelligent imagination and business...skill' in the cause of transforming both the image and reality of British Quakerism would make him the most celebrated Friend of his time.[117]

[115] R. Scott, 'Authority or Experience', 86–7 and Punshon, *Portrait in Grey*, 210.

[116] *Manchester Conference*, 79, 82.

[117] Wilson, ' "We Shall Never Thrive Upon Ignorance" ', 155 and Creasey and Loukes, *Next Fifty Years*, 9–55 *passim*.

5

The New Quakerism

TRANSATLANTIC CONNECTIONS

Quaker communities in the British Isles and on the North American continent evolved along different lines, but never in isolation from one another. There was always a dynamic interaction between them. Some of the most momentous developments in American Quakerism, including the sowing and flowering of evangelicalism among American Friends, the controversies leading up to the Hicksite Separation and the establishment of Gurneyite tenets as mainstream orthodoxy in most American Yearly Meetings, were in large part responses to initiatives brought by British Quakers. Influence did not, of course, move in only one direction; from John Woolman, to Hannah Barnard to a stream of nineteenth-century evangelicals, travelling American Friends had considerable impact, both positive and negative, on events in London and Dublin Yearly Meetings. Not surprisingly, such transatlantic connections were vitally important to the origins and evolution of the Quaker Renaissance in Britain.

When John Wilhelm Rowntree, on the invitation of Rendel Harris, joined a walking tour at Murren, Switzerland in July 1897, he had already established himself as a leader of the British modern movement. Another member of the party at Murren was Harris's former faculty colleague at Haverford College in Philadelphia, Rufus M. Jones (1863–1948). At thirty-seven Jones had attained a considerable, although not uniformly positive, reputation among American Friends. By a conjunction of fortuitous circumstances and skillful negotiations, Jones had recently arranged the merger of the moderately Gurneyite *Friends Review* with the *Christian Worker*, a Mid-western publication with strong holiness leanings. The fruit of that combination was the *American Friend*, a journal which, under Jones' editorship, gradually assumed a progressive theological stance, much to the consternation of many Mid-western holiness Friends.[1]

The trip to Switzerland marked Rufus Jones' introduction to a circle of British Friends who would confirm and encourage his increasingly liberal theological convictions. But the influence was more than one way. Jones was no shrinking violet, having already become involved in a number of controversies as he sought to hold back the twin tides of holiness Quakerism and the pastoral system while simultaneously inculcating progressive theological principles in the minds of American Friends. With his obvious sincerity and simple New England charm, reinforced by a gift for storytelling, Jones made a great hit with his British cousins, especially John Wilhelm Rowntree. Jones and Rowntree were drawn to each other personally by a shared sense of fun and spiritually by their recognition of a common mission as regards the future of Quakerism. J. W. R. had already established close relationship with older American Friends like Richard Thomas and Allen Jay of Indiana,[2] but in Rufus Jones he found a man of ideas as well as a sympathetic friend of his own generation to whom he could open his heart as well as his mind.

For his part, Jones was impressed by Rowntree's 'forward-looking vision' and 'immense fertility of mind'. Jones came to regard John Wilhelm as 'the unique inspiring leader of that epoch of our Quaker history.... He did not come as a rebel...he came as a prophet who reveres the past, lives in the present and forecasts the future...'[3] According to Jones, before they parted in that summer of 1897 he and Rowntree had settled on two important designs: first, that Jones would embark upon a study of

---

[1] Under the control of J. Walter Malone of Cleveland, the *Christian Worker* had considerably larger circulation than the *Friends Review* which Jones had taken over in 1893. Jones' initial editorial approach in *The American Friend* was to balance moderate liberalism with other points of view, but from the beginning many Mid-Western Friends were disturbed by what they saw as a lack of 'real, spiritual, holiness' content in the new journal. See Hamm, *Transformation*, 147–8 and John Oliver, 'J. Walter Malone: *The American Friend* and an Evangelical Quaker's Social Agenda', *QH*, 80/2 (Fall 1991), 67–9 who argues for a distinctive change in Jones' theological position only after his return from Europe in 1897, noting that from 1894 to 1897 Jones' editorials in the *American Friend* had reflected 'the same evangelical Protestant orthodoxy that characterized his writings in the *Friends Review*'.

[2] See Allen Jay's *Autobiography* (Philadelphia 1910), 251–2 and 391. Jay was moderately evangelical by American standards and a close friend to J. B. Braithwaite.

[3] Rufus M. Jones, *The Trail of Life in College* (New York 1929), 195, 197–8 and *John Wilhelm Rowntree*, [1].

European mysticism and its influence on the ideas of early Friends and that J. W. R. would begin work on a definitive history of the Society; second, that they would meet yearly to evaluate their mutual progress and consult on the ways and means of carrying their plans to fruition.[4] This historical scheme, which both men believed was a critical element in the revitalization of Quakerism, provided the crucial tie that first bound them together; and their friendship, deepening in personal affection and intellectual intensity until Rowntree's premature death in 1905, would also be of critical significance in the evolution of the Society of Friends on both sides of the Atlantic. 'Out of that partnership . . . was to come a modern interpretation of the very meaning and universality of spirit of the Quaker Faith as one of the dynamic forms of mystical religion, the religion of life . . . .'[5]

When Rufus Jones returned to America, his exposure to the ideas and encouragement of like-minded English Friends seemed to inspire a new and bolder vision. He was convinced that progressive British Quakers had faced up to the intellectual and spiritual challenges of Darwinian science and Higher Criticism 'in a fearless spirit'. The courage of their convictions, in Jones' view, contrasted most unflatteringly with American intellectual timidity and spiritual impotence in the face of attempts by holiness Friends to reject not only modern ideas but also some fundamental doctrines of Quakerism. A particularly disturbing example of Jones' concern was the above-noted[6] ten-year 'inquisition' against two respected ministers, Joel and Hannah Bean (1830–1909), carried out by holiness Quakers in Iowa Yearly Meeting. During the 1870s and early 1880s, Joel Bean became an outspoken opponent of the holiness-sponsored revivals, general meetings and pastoral system which appeared to be taking Midwestern Quakerism by storm. Bean believed that such activities were not only unseemly and unQuakerly but, more significantly, that they threatened the centrality of the Inward Light in Quaker life and worship.[7] As the holiness faction became increasingly influential in Iowa, the Beans

---

[4] Jones, *John Wilhelm Rowntree*, [9].

[5] Sir George Newman's remarks on Rufus Jones' seventieth birthday, quoted by Elizabeth Gray Vining, *Friend of Life: The Biography of Rufus M. Jones* (New York 1958), 237–8.

[6] See Chapter 3.

[7] For a summary of Joel Bean's complaints against the influence of holiness revivalists, see his article 'The Issue', *BF*, March 1881, 49–51.

sought refuge with like-minded Friends in San José, California. Unfortunately, their San José monthly meeting was under the auspices of an Iowa Quarterly Meeting controlled by holiness Friends who were unwilling to allow matters to rest. After a decade of harassment, both Beans were deposed from their ministry on the charge of holding unsound views. For Rufus Jones, the persecution of the Beans was a disgraceful and ominous illustration that 'it was Calvin and not Fox who was dominant . . . among Quakers, in America . . .'[8]

Liberal Friends in Britain, somewhat inaccurately, perceived of the Beans' treatment at the hands of extreme evangelicals in Iowa as a typical example of the nefarious influence of the sort of creed implied by the Richmond Declaration.[9] In any event, the Bean case was undoubtedly a crucial catalyst to growing concerns in London Yearly Meeting about the extremist nature of American evangelicalism.[10]

In the meantime, Rufus Jones' sense of commitment to a renewal of American Quakerism along modernist lines had been enlarged and deepened by a year of graduate study in philosophy at Harvard under some of the leading American thinkers of the period. Jones was probably most influenced by Josiah Royce's (1855–1916) ideas concerning mysticism as a road to spiritual reality; Royce's neo-Hegelian thought was closely akin to that of the Oxford idealist T. H. Green, whose ideas had inspired leaders of the British Quaker Renaissance. Francis G. Peabody of the Harvard Divinity School, a pioneer of the social gospel movement, also made a deep impression on Jones.[11] The star of the Harvard philosophy department, William James, was in Europe throughout Jones' tenure, but they had previously met at Haverford and Jones used James' *Principles of Psychology* in preparation for a psychology

---

[8] Rufus M. Jones, *The Trail of Life in Middle Years* (New York 1934), 55–61 *passim*. Also see 'The American Declaration of Faith. A Result', *BF*, Nov. 1893, 305–7 and 'Joel Bean and Iowa', ibid., Dec. 1894, 255.

[9] See for example, 'Disownment of Joel Bean and Others', *BF*, Dec. 1898, 305. The anonymous author of this piece believed that Friends in America were 'rapidly becoming two distinct bodies, with diverse interpretations of Quakerism'.

[10] Interview with Edward Milligan, 26 May 1994, Friends House, London. In 1893–94 Thomas Hodgkin organized a campaign to protest against the Beans' treatment; some 400 British Friends sent letters of support and encouragement to Joel and Hannah Bean. These letters, along with correspondence between Hodgkin and Rufus Jones concerning the Beans' case, are in Box U/9, LSF.

[11] See Vining, *Rufus Jones*, 86–7 and Hamm, *Transformation*, 148–51.

course he introduced into the Haverford curriculum. Later, he and other liberal Friends were deeply impressed with James' treatment of George Fox and early Friends in his *Varieties of Religious Experience* (1902), not least because James' work seemed to confirm Jones' own ideas concerning the spiritual origins of Quakerism.[12]

Well before he met John Wilhelm Rowntree, Rufus Jones had developed a theory which traced the ideas of George Fox and other early Friends more or less directly to a brand of Christian mysticism imported to England from the continent at various stages of the Reformation. Jones particularly stressed the thought of the German mystic Jacob Boehme (1575–1624), some of whose works had been translated into English by the 1640s and thus would have been available to early Friends, a fact earlier noted by the Quaker historian Robert Barclay and confirmed by William James.[13] Jones' research, guided by his anti-Calvinist theological propensities, led him to believe that the attractive power of Quakerism lay in George Fox's recognition of the universal and saving Inward Light of Christ which effectively demonstrated his rejection of the doctrines of absolute human depravity and predestination. Such a view also reflected Jones' absorption of neo-Hegelian idealism, stressing the innate goodness of human nature as well as the infinite capacity of reason, properly understood and applied, to lift humankind on to the higher spiritual level in concert with the exalted physical state toward which the laws of nature, expanded and clarified by Darwinian science, seemed to be taking the human race. Thus, Jones saw Quakerism not as a radical spin-off from Puritan Calvinism but rather as a thoroughgoing rejection of it—a life-enhancing spiritual religion fully compatible with the most challenging discoveries of modern thought and science. For him the Atonement did not represent the appeasement of Divinity through the sacrifice of innocent blood but rather 'God Himself taking up the infinite burden and cost of raising men like us into sons of God like Himself; this is the revelation in the face of Jesus

[12] See M. Catherine Albright's enthusiastic review of *The Varieties of Religious Experience* in *Present Day Papers*, V/50 (15 Sept. 1902), 289–92. Albright called James' work 'a treasure-house for "Friends", justifying once more ... their own belief in the "Inner Light" ...' 292.

[13] Barclay, *Inner Life*, 214–15 and James, *The Varieties of Religious Experience* (New York rev. edn. 1902), 315 n. Stephen A. Kent believes that Jones first made the connection between Fox and Boehme from reading James' work and only later read Barclay's *Inner Life*. See Kent, 'Psychology and Quaker Mysticism: the Legacy of William James and Rufus Jones', *Quaker History*, 76/1 (Spring 1987), 1–17.

Christ'. Thus, the Jesus of the new Quakerism was a loving, witnessing God incarnate rather than a bloody sacrificial victim.[14] Jones did not deny the existence of evil in the world nor the human propensity for it, but he believed that he was one with Fox and early Friends in asserting that all human beings possessed a capacity for goodness which, as a reflection of the Divine Seed in all, might, if rightly directed, become the primary motivation for human action and the effective means of salvation.[15]

British Quakers of a liberal persuasion enthusiastically embraced Jones' notion of Quakerism as a mystical faith buttressed by traditions of Quaker life and worship and directly influenced by leadings from the Light. For them, the Light opened the way to both the severance of ties with the harsher aspects of evangelical theology and the pursuit of spiritual answers entirely within the intellectually respectable context of modern, optimistic liberal thought. For those who sought and embraced it, the Light of Christ provided not only a recognition of sin but also illumination in those matters left unclear or incomplete by Scripture. Placing human progress in the vanguard with mystical faith in Christ (they remained steadfastly Christian), liberals in the era of the Quaker Renaissance seemed to have an unbeatable combination—a way open not simply for the survival of Society of Friends as a vital religious community but for its much expanded influence in British, American and, indeed, world society in general.[16]

John Wilhelm Rowntree and Rufus Jones became titular leaders of reformed Quakerism on either side of the Atlantic. What Rowntree brought to the movement was energy, direction, and vision; Jones added the seemingly authoritative confirmation of an

---

[14] Rufus M. Jones, *The Atonement* (Yorkshire 1905 Committee, n.d.), 9–11, #8, Vol. 2, Yorkshire Pamphlets, LSF.

[15] For an illuminating discussion of Rufus Jones's concept of sin, see Wilmer A. Cooper, 'The Influence of Rufus Jones on the Quaker View of Sin and Evil', *QRT*, 66, 22/4 (Fall 1987), 30–6.

[16] This discussion owes much to John Punshon's ideas as set out in *Portrait in Grey*, 226–9 and in private conversation. Also see Daniel E. Bassuk, 'Rufus M. Jones and Mysticism', 17/4 (Summer 1978), 1–26 who believed that 'Jones made his reinterpretation of Quakerism intellectually respectable by attempting to graft it onto the Greek metaphysical tradition of mysticism and by injecting into it affirmations of positive thinking and of the social gospel, thus bringing it into line with late nineteenth century religious liberalism' (23). Christoper J. Holdsworth's splendidly incisive essay on 'Mystics and Heretics in the Middle Ages: Rufus Jones Reconsidered', *JFHS*, 53/1 (1972), 9–30, is more sympathetic towards Jones but also rejects the idea that mysticism significantly influenced seventeenth-century Friends.

implicit, but widespread, belief that Quakerism, centred on the powerful doctrine of the Inward Light, was a mystical as well as a dynamic faith. Under the influence of such a faith modern humanity might cut through the accumulated clutter of contradictory religious ideas and speak directly and meaningfully to God, not as vengeful Patriarch but as loving Father, and to human beings not as depraved sinners but as exalted sharers in God-given Light. Jones believed that early Friends had experienced, in the gathered silence of their meetings for worship, a new and vitalizing form of 'collective' mysticism wherein members together sought and found the guidance of the Inward Light, a form of spiritual authority which surpassed the authority of the human-tainted Bible.[17] Carrying the weight of prevailing theological thought, buttressed by the security of a direct pipeline to the Divinity and proven by history as well as experience, liberal Friends believed that this dynamic New Quakerism could carry all before it. No victory is complete or irreversible, but this generation of reformers had a formidable and timely message, great sincerity and a strategic advantage; such was their apparent success that the historian of Victorian Quakerism has noted the 'rapidity and completeness' of the acceptance of liberal theology among British Friends.[18]

Rufus Jones' conviction that Quakerism originated in continental mysticism was the most innovative theological concept adopted by liberal Quakers. Nearly all of the other ideas associated with the renaissance of Quakerism had been set forth in the previous generation by the authors of *A Reasonable Faith*, by Edward Worsdell, by John Stephenson Rowntree, by Caroline Stephen's *Quaker Strongholds* (1890) and even by the moderate evangelicals who

[17] John Punshon believes that mysticism was more fundamental than the Light to many Quaker liberals because mysticism permitted them to express religious ideas in progressive, non-biblical terms and to affirm the soul's capacity for the Divine in ways that were both emotionally satisfying and rationally acceptable. Interview with John Punshon, August 1986, Exeter.

[18] Isichei, *Victorian Quakers, 39*. Cf. the response of Richard Braithwaite, W. C. Braithwaite's eldest son, to the idea of a rapid liberal triumph: 'Oh, No! No! From 1890 to well... on in the 1920s and 1930s... it took a long time. You see Friends are very long-lived and the Evangelical Friends didn't change their views.' Interview with Professor Richard Braithwaite, August 1986, Cambridge. Also see Brian David Phillips, 'Friendly Patriotism: British Quakerism and the Imperial Nation, 1890–1910', Ph.D. thesis, University of Cambridge, 1989, who argues that the Quaker Renaissance was ephemeral in its influence and that social and political conservatism remained the driving forces in British Quakerism until the First World War.

recognized the need for change and growth in British Quaker-ism.[19] John W. Graham, Rendel Harris and other English Quakers were pioneers in the reforming effort, but John Wilhelm Rown-tree and Rufus Jones were chiefly responsible for shaping a theo-logical consensus. They took the lead in convincing a generation of British Friends that the progressive views they espoused were in harmony with the substance and spirit of early Friends whose revival of primitive Christianity could be replicated if twentieth-century Quakers matched the faith and intensity of early Children of the Light.

What, then, was the doctrinal consensus embodied in the Quaker Renaissance? If reformers had been asked to set out the most important aspects of the renewal, they might have differed with regard to details, but the same four or five prerequisites for renewal would generally have emerged. Leading most lists would be the revival of the Inward Light as the 'great and Fundamental Truth of a living and present Saviour underlying all that early Friends taught...'[20] At the Manchester Conference both W. E. Turner and the American Richard Thomas emphasized the neces-sity of this 'divine impulse' to aid Friends in their special work of rescuing souls from 'the dark places of the earth'. What was needed, said Thomas, was 'a church that knows that God is with it, not one that knows he used to be with it'.[21] Messages for the new century from both elderly Joseph Edmondson (born 1831) and middle-aged Edward Grubb also emphasized that the 'founda-tion principle' of Quakerism was the 'continuous and abid-ing...indwelling of Jesus Christ in the soul...' Grubb added, 'this conception of the dignity of man in the light of Christ's spiritual presence becomes a great moral force, not only in the sphere of *being* but also in the sphere of *action*'.[22]

Another nearly universal theme was the restoration of the Bible to its proper relationship with the Light. Writing for *Present Day*

[19] Caroline Stephen (1834–1909), daughter of Sir James Stephen and sister of Sir Leslie, converted to Quakerism in 1872. Stephen's intense, quasi-mystical view of Quakerism was said to have 'strongly influenced a whole generation of Friends', but her vision of Quakerism probably had more influence outside the Society than within it.

[20] William Pollard, *Quaker Reformation* (London 1889), 7–9.

[21] *Manchester Conference*, 254–7, 281–3.

[22] Joseph Edmondson, 'The Essential Basis of Quakerism and Its non-Ritual Origins', *FQE*, (1899), 353–5 and Grubb, 'The Mission of the Society of Friends', *PDP*, 1 (1898), 35–7.

Papers, Edward Worsdell argued that because so much of spiritual disquiet had arisen from attempts to confer upon Scripture 'a miraculous immunity from error', critical biblical research, by revealing the fallible, human qualities of Scripture, should lead, not to unbelief, but to 'a more thorough appreciation of the Bible as it is, and not as we imagine it to be'. Friends could be confident, said Worsdell, that Fox and Barclay would have welcomed scholarly research into the Scriptures since its purpose was not to disprove Holy Writ but to remove from it 'the veil of misunderstanding and ignorance which for so many had obscured its meaning....'[23] William Charles Braithwaite continued on this theme, noting that once Christians grasped that the Bible was an 'expression of the divine with the help of the human...' the right understanding of progressive revelation would lead to a 'moral perspective' rather than an infallible creed. Thus, the critical study of Scripture could provide 'knowledge of the nature and the will of God which shall inspire our lives and service'. Even if 'the inspired writers often misunderstood the God they were revealing', modern readers might learn to embrace rather than to fear the Truth of Holy Writ. Reiterating this same point, the authors of a 1904 pamphlet written 'to promote the more systematic reading and study of the Bible by children and young people in Friends' families' noted: 'We must teach our scholars to hold fast by the very highest dictates of their own consciences, and never suppose that the Bible when *rightly understood* will lower their standard, although they may often have to account for what is below that standard by the progressive receptivity of man....'[24]

A third point constantly reiterated by liberal revisionists proceeded from their longstanding belief that the future of Quakerism depended on maintaining its tradition of eschewing hireling ministers while developing a ministry that was dynamic and modern as well as 'free'. Such a ministry would draw its inspiration from the Scriptures, as seen through the filter of modern biblical criticism, and its strength from a thorough knowledge of the most up-to-date

---

[23] Edward Worsdell, 'The Restoration of the Bible', *PDP*, 1, (1898), 55–64. Also see Creasey and Loukes, *Next Fifty Years*, 13.

[24] W. C. Braithwaite, *The Inspiration of the Bible*, (Yorkshire 1905 Committee pamphlet, 1905), 1–11 *passim* and Joan Mary Fry, Alfred Kemp Brown, *et al.*, *The Teaching of the Bible in the Family*, (London 1904), 11–13. Also see J. W. Graham, *The Meaning of Quakerism*, (London n.d.), 52: 'So apart are we from Biblical literalism that our chief divergences from other Christians look at first sight like divergences from the Bible also.'

scientific discoveries, while simultaneously conserving an awareness
of the ideas and practices of George Fox and early Friends. For John
Wilhelm Rowntree, no subject was more vital than 'the acute and
difficult problem of maintaining a living, yet free ministry'.[25] The
problem was difficult because an alternative solution, the pastoral
system so widely adopted in America, was, effectively, waiting in
the wings; it was acute because, with Rufus Jones, Rowntree
believed that the system of paid ministers and programmed meetings
was 'eating the heart out of Quakerism in the States'.[26]

In London Yearly Meeting the movement toward a paid pastorate had been nipped in the bud, but, as Rowntree noted, the
Society had never given 'properly sustained recognition of the
intellectual qualifications for a searching ministry'. Writing to
J. W. Graham on the 'lamentable' situation in Yorkshire, Rowntree
had 'no hesitation in saying that in the majority of meetings I have
visited the level of the ministry—mostly feeble . . . deliverance of an
unimaginative Evangelical type, uninfluenced by any great
conception of the Quaker school—is . . . far below the work of the
best men in the other churches.'[27] Rowntree heard few ministers,
whether evangelical or traditional, who addressed themselves 'to
modern needs and conditions' or provided any sort of spiritual
vitality for their meetings.

Not that the question of ministry was ignored by the leaders of
London Yearly Meeting. At Yearly Meeting in 1899 special concern for the ministry produced a document on 'Worship and
Ministry' that was subsequently dispatched to all 376 particular
meetings in Britain (for which there were only 364 recorded
ministers), reminding 'younger members' of their responsibility
'for filling up the ranks and keeping the ministry in touch with
the needs of the day'.[28] Rowntree, however, believed such an

[25] Quoted by Scott, 'Authority or Experience', 89.
[26] Silvanus P. Thompson, 'John Wilhelm Rowntree', 264. For an alarmist view of
combined influence of the pastoral system and holiness practice in North Carolina Yearly
Meeting, see W. C. Allen's 'The New Quakerism', *BF*, Dec. 1898, 305–9, an account of the
'Religious anarchy' Allen had witnessed: 'Hymns were rapidly sung by many. The hysterical
screams of women racked the nerves. Annie Edgerton rushed up and down the aisle
wringing her uplifted hands, weeping and crying, "Oh, God! Oh God!" and imploring
help.'
[27] J. W. R., 'The Need for a Summer School Movement', in *Essays and Addresses*, 153
and J. W. R. to J. W. G., 23 March 1899, RFP.
[28] J. W. R. to R. M. J., 11 Jan. 1899, Box 2, RMJP and Edward Grubb, 'Quakerism in
England', 5–6, 10.

admonition addressed the wrong audience by seeming to place the burden of inadequate ministry on those least responsible for it. Young people were, to be sure, 'drifting away from us'—not because they were deficient in faith, but because ministry in their meetings was largely devoid of content or inspiration.[29] Convinced that 'our future as a Church' depended upon the solution of maintaining a ministry that was at once relevant and free, Rowntree devoted an entire issue of *Present Day Papers* (December 1899) to the question and delivered a paper on the ministry to a Quaker Summer School at Haverford a few months later.[30]

In the meantime, the American pastoral system continued to expand and, in the opinion of its advocates, to provide the sort of consistent spiritual counsel and direction that so many British meetings lacked. Liberals might decry a paid pastorate as seriously at odds with traditional Quakerism, but when pressed for an alternative, they tended to respond with animated appeals to tradition rather than specific plans for the future. In the final number of *Present Day Papers* (1902), John Wilhelm Rowntree issued a dire warning as to the consequences of continued inaction.

So feeble is the witness borne to the freedom of our spiritual heritage, so negative and barren is the interpretation of our testimony, so threadbare and so poor is our simplicity ... that the glory of the Quaker ideal has drawn well nigh to extinguishment.... To *this* generation has been given to decide whether the Free Ministry ... even the Quaker testimony itself, shall survive as a living fellowship.[31]

One reaction to such exhortations was a Conference on Ministry which convened at York late in 1903 to consider possible changes of practice with regard to recognizing, sustaining, and recording Quaker ministers. Nothing fresh or dramatic emerged from these deliberations other than the appointment of a Committee to visit particular meetings throughout the country to assess the state of their ministry. There was an interesting sidelight to the York Conference in that the only noteworthy revisionist proposal

[29] J. W. R. to J. W. G., 23 March 1899, RFP. William Tallack made the same point in, 'Some Thoughts on Ministry, or Service in a Small Meeting', *FQE*, (1896), 227.

[30] J. W. R. to J. W. G., 16 Aug. 1899, RFP; J. W. R. to R. M. J., 19 May 1900, Box 3, RMJP; and J. W. R., 'The Problem of a Free Ministry', in *Essays and Addresses*, 111–34.

[31] Reprinted as 'Pentecost', in *Essays and Addresses*, 227–8.

brought forward, to abolish the practice of recording ministers, was opposed, for different reasons, by both the fading evangelical patriarch J. B. Braithwaite and the 'leader of the new life', John Wilhelm Rowntree. Braithwaite wished to continue recording ministers because he felt that 'no essential change is required in our existing arrangements'. Rowntree believed it would 'unsafe and premature' to do away with the practice of recording, lest the office of minister be further damaged at a crucial time in the life of the Society.[32]

What Rowntree and his allies wanted was not a change in the system but a systematic change in attitude towards the ministry and preparation for it. They believed that the weakness of Quaker ministry arose from 'a deep-seated indolence' encouraged and comforted by the view that what 'was moved by the Spirit could entail no labour of the intellect'.[33] Such Quaker anti-intellectualism, Rowntree noted, was 'closely associated with that strange haziness which characterises the mind of the average Friend when questioned as to the historical and spiritual significance of his Church. Our ignorance, both as to the facts of our church history ...and the want of any adequate conception of our spiritual heritage, is not likely to develop the gifts latent among us.'[34]

The problem, then, was as much educational as spiritual. Its solution was institutional in the sense that the Society, rather than simply admonishing individual members to do their duty, needed to establish some permanent means for producing a ministry that was informed and inspired as well as free. The two most important educational innovations introduced through the reforming zeal of John Wilhelm Rowntree and his collaborators, the Summer School Movement and Woodbrooke Institute, are discussed in some detail below. A third educational concern, the rediscovery of Quaker history, was nearly as important. Reformers came to believe that a comprehensive historical study of Quakerism would help Friends, as ignorant of their past as they were complacent about their future, to understand and appreciate the

---

[32] John Wilhelm Rowntree, 'Memorandum Upon the Recording of Ministers', MSS Portfolio, 23/40, LSF and Joseph Bevan Braithwaite to Conference on Ministry, York, no date, MSS Portfolio, 20/26, ibid.

[33] J. W. R., 'The Rise of Quakerism in Yorkshire', in *Essays and Addresses*, 66–7. Also see J. W. R. to R. M. J., 11 Jan. 1899, Box 2, RMJP.

[34] J. W. R., 'Problem of Free Ministry', 123–4.

significance and continuity of their faith. So informed, they might begin better to appreciate the importance of a modern and dynamic Society to the impending century, which, having achieved unparalleled material advancement, would be searching for more abundant means of spiritual fulfillment. The eventual production of a modern, comprehensive study of Quakerism, based on original sources and placing the Society of Friends into its historical context, also deserves separate treatment.[35]

By late 1903 John Wilhelm Rowntree had determined to devote most of his time to the production of the projected history of Quakerism. His progress was slow, however, interrupted by bouts of illness as well as continued involvement in various aspects of the renewal movement. One such project, completed just before he left for the journey to the United States from which he would not return, was an essay on 'The Present Position of Religious Thought in the Society of Friends', subsequently, and posthumously, published in both the *Friends Quarterly Examiner* and the *American Friend*. This article may serve as a spiritual last testimony of Rowntree's views about the problems and progress of British Quakerism.

In the decade since the Manchester Conference, Rowntree said, the Society of Friends had begun to recognize the debilitating qualities of much of the spiritual baggage it had accumulated over two centuries. But while acknowledging past deficiencies, the Society, as a spiritual fellowship, had not subsequently accepted the responsibility for developing a coherent set of ideas and a comprehensive plan of action that would prepare the emerging generation not just to save their Society from extinction but to 're-assert its positive claim, now so largely historical, if not...myth-ical, to share in the constructive spiritual work that is afoot in the world'.[36] The reason for this abdication of responsibility, Rowntree believed, was a lack of sufficient imagination 'to realize the intellectual chasm which separates the young Quaker of 1905 from the Quakerism of...even...fifty years ago'. The fascinating world of knowledge that had opened to youthful inquiry only

---

[35] See below. Also see R. M. J., *John Wilhelm Rowntree*, [9] and *Trail of Life in College*, 195–96; Kennedy, 'History and the Quaker Renaissance', 35–56; and Scott, 'Authority or Experience', 75–95.

[36] J. W. R., 'The Present Position of Religious Thought in the Society of Friends', *American Friend*, 25 March 1905, 192–3.

underscored the 'deadly dullness' and 'torpor of undeveloped intellectual power' which seemed to characterize so much of Quaker life. Too many Friends, he noted, still regarded their religious faith 'as a collector regards his specimens' and could not or would not comprehend its philosophical content or its spiritual impact. At a time when the means were at hand for their Society to move the religious life of the England of Edward VII as the 'primitive giants' of Quakerism had moved it during the time of Cromwell and Charles II, the average Quaker seemed content to remain a largely 'unintelligent spectator of the greatest revolution in religious thought since . . . the Reformation'.[37]

If Quaker principles were worth anything; if the fire that lived in George Fox, Edward Burroughs, and . . . Isaac Penington was to be rekindled; if it only *could* be rekindled; if Quakerism would only arise from the dust and speak to men in language of the twentieth century, there should be a shaking of dry bones as had not been felt before.[38]

As a result of their Society's ineffective response to the new world of ideas, Rowntree said, young Quakers were finding spiritual and intellectual guidance from non-Quaker sources and outlets for constructive action in non-denominational or inter-denominational movements. He predicted that if such a trend continued, the only possible result could be the extinction of Quakerism. Still, he believed the situation was fraught with great hope as well as great peril. The loss of the Bible as the spiritual court of last resort had, perforce, thrown Friends back upon 'the Inward Voice as the ultimate arbiter—even of the Bible . . . . It may well be that the loss of an infallible book is . . . intended to drive us at last into real and effective union with Him.' The problem was that at this moment of momentous possibility, Friends had not come to grips with the historical or theological meaning of the Inward Light and were, thus, unable to bring its saving illumination to a waiting world.[39]

---

[37] Ibid. 193–4; 'The Wages of Going On', *PDP*, 5/50 (15 Sept. 1902), 255; and 'A Study in Ecclesiastical Polity', ibid. 5/51 (15 October 1902), 302–3.

[38] Silvanus P. Thompson, 'John Wilhelm Rowntree', *FQE*, (1905), 264. The quotation is Thompson's paraphrase of Rowntree's words; emphasis in original.

[39] J. W. R., 'Present Position', 194–5.

The vital point is our basis of belief, our interpretation of the Inward Light, of life, sin, death, and our relationship to God. The truth, clearly grasped and passionately believed, will overcome where the mere tenets of a sect, atrophied by long divorce from the central life, fall unheeded like the dead formalisms they have already become.... We have been delivered from the slavery of denominational narrowness.... But if the Society of Friends is to have a wider... service, if it is to hold its young people, if indeed, it is to have a continued existence at all, it must produce a modern interpretation of its original conception, and lead the world... to a deeper understanding of Jesus Christ.[40]

THE SUMMER SCHOOL MOVEMENT

During the Manchester Conference, George Cadbury (1839–1922), the Birmingham chocolate magnate, known among Friends at least as much for his piety as his business acumen, voiced his concern about 'the dead formality' of so many Quaker meetings. Quakerism would never again flourish, Cadbury asserted, until its members, especially the elders who bore responsibility for maintaining the ministry, 'realised the importance of earnest, life-giving, educated Gospel ministry'.[41] A number of Friends responded to Cadbury's earnest plea, but, at Manchester, as in other settings, pious platitudes about the importance of the ministry were more in evidence than concrete suggestions for improving it. Still, while George Cadbury may have lacked the imagination to devise his own scheme for refurbishing the Quaker ministry, he had both irrepressible fervour and financial means to throw behind any plan he believed might accomplish this aim. Cadbury's strong will and large purse would, eventually, be of considerable significance in the transformation of British Quakerism.

Early in 1897 George Cadbury received a long letter in which John Wilhelm Rowntree set out his scheme for coming to grips with the spiritual and intellectual weaknesses of Quaker ministry. 'If we could get a band of Friends, old and young, together at some country place for a week, 10 days or a fortnight,' John Wilhelm noted, it might 'do much to widen the imagination and

---

[40] Ibid. 195–6.
[41] *Manchester Conference*, 51–2. For George Cadbury see A. G. Gardiner, *The Life of George Cadbury* (London, n.d.).

to stimulate a desire for greater spiritual power and more ability to give it expression.' When Cadbury responded with a promise of monetary support, these chocolate Quakers launched the Summer School Movement, the first sustained dramatic development of the Quaker Renaissance.[42]

Within three weeks of J. W. Rowntree's initial letter, Edward Worsdell, J. W. R's spiritual ally as well as manager of the Rowntree firm's office staff, sent Cadbury a fully developed plan for a 'Summer School of Theology', naming the location (Scarborough), the theme (Quakerism and the Bible), possible speakers ('names of the first rank') and a list of prominent (and mainly non-evangelical) Friends who might assist in carrying out the enterprise. Fearing that Cadbury might feel as if he was being swept into an audacious scheme over which he had little control, Worsdell concluded with a cautionary note, via John Wilhelm's cousin Joshua Rowntree. '[S]tress', he said, 'must be laid on the educational side...as bearing on intelligent First day School Teaching than avowedly on the Ministry lest Friends be frightened.'[43]

Obviously impressed, Cadbury extended his 'almost entire agreement', suggesting only that a few names be added to the committee and that 'two or three...who are considered rather "advanced" in their opinions' be left off. He also expressed gratitude to Worsdell and the Rowntrees for joining the struggle 'to save our Church, which was fast going to destruction'.[44]

By the time London Yearly Meeting gathered in late May 1897, a publicity flyer, signed by over thirty weighty Friends, announced a two-week course of studies to be held at Scarborough in August. The programme, including sessions on the Old and New Testaments, biblical exegesis and church history, was designed to 'stimulate thought, promote helpful reading and study, and...to awaken in the Society a fuller conception of the place in the service of

---

[42] J. W. R. to G. C., 10 Feb. 1897 and G. C. to J. W. R., 11 Feb. 1897, George Cadbury Papers (GCP), Woodbrooke Library (WL), Birmingham.

[43] Edward Worsdell to G. C, 1 March 1897, GCP, WL.

[44] G. C. to E. Worsdell, 2 March 1897, WL. The Executive Committee assembled to plan the Summer School had a decidedly liberal, and Rowntree, flavour including John Wilhelm and his cousin Joshua as well as W. C. Braithwaite and J. Rendel Harris; George Cadbury's interests, and his money, were represented by the treasurer William White (1820–1900), founder of the Birmingham Adult School Movement and a staunch evangelical minister.

Christ of the trained and consecrated intellect'.[45] Information concerning local arrangements, special railway fares, cheap lodging and meals and free afternoons for seaside recreation was also included.[46]

Eventually, over six hundred Friends attended the Scarborough Summer School where featured speakers were about evenly divided between Quakers and non-Quakers. Some of the latter, as one participant recalled, shocked Friends who retained 'old-fashioned views on the literal interpretation of the scriptures...' Professor R. W. Rogers, an American 'authority on Assyriology', and G. Buchanan Gray, Tutor at Mansfield College, Oxford, each gave four lectures on aspects of the Old Testament; T. R. Glover, former Fellow of St. John's College, Cambridge, presented a series on church history; and Professor R. G. Moulton of Manchester University spoke on 'The Literary Study of the Bible'.[47] In addition to these luminaries, the bulk of the Quaker speakers were of decidedly advanced opinions, at least among their co-religionists. The most learned of these, J. Rendel Harris, University Lecturer in Paleaography at Cambridge, proved, by general consensus, to be the star performer. According to one admiring participant, Harris was 'delightful to listen to at all times'. Whether he lectured on 'The Growth of the New Testament' or 'Armenia', Harris was 'the backbone of the whole affair'. Lawrence Richardson recalled that after listening to Rendel Harris, he no longer felt like a fish out of water among Friends. Another young Friend, Laura Jane Moore, was deeply moved by Harris's contributions and 'came away tremendously encouraged in my views, partly owing to a private interview... with.... Harris which confirmed my "Unitarian" opinions about Jesus....'[48]

Laura Jane Moore undoubtedly misread Rendel Harris's message. He was never a Unitarian, but her confusion was indicative of

---

[45] 'Scarborough Summer School', 4 pp., WL. Twenty-five of the thirty-three names were from the original list submitted to George Cadbury by Edward Worsdell.

[46] 'Scarborough Summer School, General Arrangements', WL.

[47] *Time Table*, Scarborough Summer School for Religious Study, 1897, WL.

[48] Dorothy Crowly Brown, *Journal*, 'Impressions of Scarborough Summer School', Wednesday, 4 August–Wednesday, 18 August 1897; L. Richardson, 'Newcastle-upon-Tyne Friends', 43–4; and Laura Jane Moore, 'Reflections', [17]. There is no biography of Rendel Harris, but H. G. Wood gave a brief account of Harris' life and ideas in Robert Davis (ed.), *Woodbrooke, 1903–1953* (London 1953), 19–30. Also see the privately printed *Memories of J. Rendel Harris*, collected by Irene Pickard (no place or date of publication).

why some evangelical Friends, always wary of open-ended discussions of theological ideas, referred to the Scarborough Summer School (SSS) as 'Satan's Sinful Snare'.[49] As another participant noted: 'I wish thou, & all my friends, could have been at the Summer School. Of course many things were said that were startling & that one could not by any means entirely accept—but the reverence & the deep spiritual voice of all the meetings was such as wholly . . . disarms the prejudices with who [sic] many must have approached the lectures.'[50]

Dorothy Brown of Manchester, a young wife and mother whose husband had taken pains to ensure that she could attend for the entire fortnight, left Scarborough believing that the gathering had marked an epoch in the history of Friends as well as pinnacle of her own spiritual growth, giving her 'a more real . . . & true knowledge of God . . . the spiritual life has again become one with the ordinary life'.[51]

Lest the impetus of such salutary responses be lost, a Summer School Continuation Committee was formed, consisting of two dozen mainly liberal Friends. While preparing the way for a self-perpetuating series of Summer Schools, this Committee arranged courses of study and reading circles in local Quaker meetings. Edward Grubb was appointed Secretary to the Continuation Committee and from this position he could exercise considerable influence as regards the development of this new educational initiative. Grubb had also recently become *de facto* editor of the *British Friend*[52] and during the next decade and a half he was probably the most prolific publicist for liberal Quaker theology in Great Britain.[53]

The Summer School Continuation Committee's initial statement of objectives, 'to promote the reverent historical study of

[49] Ruth Fawell, *Joan Mary Fry* (London 1959), 23.

[50] L. G. Hodgkin to J. J. Green, 30 October 1897, MS Port B/3, LSF.

[51] Dorothy C. Brown, *Journal*, Sunday, 3 October 1897. The proceedings of the Conference were collected in *Echoes From Scarborough, 1897* (London 1898).

[52] Grubb replaced William Edward Turner, who was rapidly losing his eyesight, in August 1901 and retained editorship until the journal ceased publication in 1913.

[53] See *TF*, 27 Jan. 1939, 68 and *BF*, Oct. 1897, 263. Also see, James Dudley, *The Life of Edward Grubb, 1854–1939: A Spiritual Pilgrimage* (London 1946) and two of my own articles, 'The Ubiquitous Friend: Edward Grubb and the Modern British Peace Movement', *Peace Research*, 17/2 (May 1985), 1–10 and 'Edward Grubb', in *Biographical Dictionary of Modern Peace Leaders* (BDMPL), ed. Harold Josephson (Westport, Conn. 1985), 366–69.

the Scriptures', seemed modest enough.[54] But J. W. Rowntree and his collaborators had a more ambitious agenda which was reflected in the words of J. W. R.'s esteemed uncle John S. Rowntree who, at Scarborough, had admonished Friends to begin to provide some more meaningful contributions to 'our national life'.

Were we able to set forth the claims of the spiritual kingdom of Christ, by example as by speech... it would carry with it the savour of its own authority, and our own people, and the world, and the Church, would all feel that the message was not a dying echo of Seventeenth century voices, but a veritable Gospel, living, dynamic, catholic—impartially addressing itself to all... whether young or old, rich or poor, learned or unlearned, agnostic or ritualist.[55]

This was a dream worthy of the ambitious, impatient, optimistic group of reformers for whom John Wilhelm provided the spark and George Cadbury the means. While these two benefactors were at a considerable distance on the theological spectrum, the problems they were addressing had more to do with communication than with doctrine. Why did the Quaker ideal of a free, open, and spontaneous meeting for worship so often result in empty silence or in spoken words so narrowly conceived or so lacking in intellectual content as to leave most of the audience wishing that silence had prevailed? Summer Schools could inspire lukewarm or apathetic Friends to a new sense of spiritual awareness or need, but that inspiration often faded when they returned to local meetings where the atmosphere remained insipid or irritating or worse. Obviously, the situation tended to be most trying for younger people searching for some motivation to direct their pent-up energy toward the fulfillment of spiritual goals. If such inspiration did not arise from meetings for worship, from whence would it arise? As Joshua Rowntree had noted at the Manchester Conference, if Quakerism was to be more for its members than 'an

---

[54] Committee members included J. W. Rowntree, W. C. Braithwaite, Edward Worsdell and George Cadbury, who continued to provide most of the funding. In addition to Grubb's appointment as Secretary, William White retained his position as Honorary Treasurer. See Summer School Continuation Committee (SSCC), *Minutes*, First Annual Report, 1898, Summer School Continuation Committee, WL.

[55] John S. Rowntree, *The Place of the Society of Friends in the Religious Life of England* [Three papers read at Scarborough Summer School, 1897] (London [1897]), 60, 62–3.

insurance society, by which they can secure their own personal safety', it had to perform some function and accomplish some task that no other religious organization could or would undertake.

Such was the burden of the message that progressive Friends aspired to spread throughout their Society. The agency for accomplishing their aims, the Summer School Continuation Committee, gathered momentum slowly while planning for the second Summer School which eventually materialized at Birmingham in September 1899.

The Birmingham meeting drew a larger crowd than Scarborough, the majority of whom were women who had not attended the earlier conference. The second Summer School had a similar cast of lecturers and a comparable inspirational effect. Dorothy Brown, who had been so moved at Scarborough, spoke at least as highly of the Birmingham assembly:

The second Summer School is now over.... I feel it to have been a wonderful time...I had got into a common place rut & all spiritual growth seemed hard and slow, and now I feel I have had such a help on the upward road.... Oh for more of the spirit of those mystic souls who lived always so close to God!...As Ted [E. Vipont Brown] was saying, it raises one's ideals to live in such an atmosphere.[56]

During the following year an attempt was made, at the instigation of Rufus Jones, to transfer such an atmosphere across the Atlantic. In the summer of 1900, John Wilhelm Rowntree, W. C. Braithwaite and Rendel Harris spoke to the first American Summer School at Haverford College, offering a dose of the sort of liberal theology that Rufus Jones hoped might provide an antidote to the evangelical tone and pastoral system which continued to dominate Quakerism in the United States.

In the interim, the Summer School Continuation Committee had gathered in the spring of 1900 to consider a question raised by John Wilhelm Rowntree in a series of articles in *Present Day Papers*. Given the success of brief gatherings at Scarborough and Birmingham, Rowntree asked, why not establish a 'permanent Summer School' where, under the direction of a 'peripatetic lecturer',

[56] Dorothy Brown, *Journal*, 'Birmingham Summer School', 4–16 September 1899. There were 736 attenders at Birmingham as against 659 at Scarborough.

Friends could undertake systematic study of the Bible and church history, 'with the definite intention of giving clearness and force to our spiritual message'.[57]

WOODBROOKE

One result of the Summer School Continuation Committee's deliberations in 1900 was the appointment of a sub-committee to investigate the idea of a permanent Quaker Settlement. Nothing was forthcoming, however, until mid-November 1901 when George Cadbury wrote to E. Ernest Boorne (1856–1921), Secretary to the Quaker Central Education Board Re-Constitution Committee, recounting his sense of frustration upon waking one morning to a realization of Quakerism's miserable failure, after more than two centuries, in disseminating the truths preached by George Fox and early Friends. These discouraging reflections pursued Cadbury on his usual morning ride until 'the thought had been strongly impressed upon me' to dedicate Woodbrooke (the estate in suburban Birmingham where his eleven children had been born and raised) for the training and guidance of the 'children of our well-to-do Friends ... filled with the desire to do real earnest aggressive Christian work'.[58]

Mistakenly assuming that Cadbury wished to endow another Quaker preparatory school, Boorne suggested that he hand Woodbrooke over to the Meeting for Sufferings which had overall responsibility for religious education. Somewhat irritated, Cadbury replied that he had not the least interest in some slow-developing scheme for a Quaker boarding school. Indeed, as he later complained to Edward Grubb, Cadbury felt that existing Quaker schools provided inadequate preparation for the sort of 'active aggressive Christian work' that needed doing. What he envisioned was an academy where dedicated individuals would engage in brief but intense study of Scripture and the principles of Quakerism to

---

[57] J. W. R., 'The Problem of a Free Ministry', Sept. 1899 and 'A Plea For a Quaker Settlement', Dec. 1899, *Present Day Papers*, reprinted in Rowntree, *Essays and Addresses*, 111–50 and Third Annual Report, *Minutes*, SSCC, WL.

[58] George Cadbury to C. E. Bourne [sic], 18 Nov. 1901, George Cadbury Papers (GCP), WL. A. G. Gardiner's *George Cadbury*, 179–203, gives a somewhat different version of Cadbury's impulsive decision to make Woodbrooke a Quaker centre for religious studies.

prepare them for apostolic service on the highways and byways, gathering souls for Christ and the Society of Friends. The only place where Quakers were doing anything like this, Cadbury told Grubb, was at the newly established Quaker Biblical Training Institutes in the American Midwest.[59]

Thoroughly alarmed at the prospect of Cadbury impetuously establishing a watered-down theological seminary to prepare professional Quaker pastors, Grubb replied that Friends' schools should not be held accountable for 'the condition of things which at present seems to be general among most educated people'. During his own travels in America, Grubb said, he had found that the 'aggressive Quakerism' of the middle and western states was generally of a 'superficial character' and that teaching in their Bible schools was 'mostly of an extremely crude & ignorantly dogmatic type' tending to 'extremes'. He believed that the best lesson British Friends could learn from the American pastoral system was to avoid it entirely. On the other hand, Grubb felt that Woodbrooke might have an enormous impact if it could be organized to address the needs of younger people 'whose minds ... seem to be developing at the expense of their souls'. Grubb agreed that Friends should engage in 'earnest missionary efforts', but such activities could only be successful, he said, if they involved young Quakers who were capable of combining 'fervent zeal with enlightened spirituality'.[60]

The exchange between Cadbury and Edward Grubb not only had important implications for the future of Woodbrooke, it also revealed a lot about the direction British Quakerism was taking and who was leading the march. George Cadbury, a thoroughgoing evangelical, had, at best, only a nodding acquaintance with early Quaker history and theology. What he wanted was action, the Word aggressively preached to Friend and non-Friend alike. Assertive, self-assured, theologically liberal Friends like Edward Grubb were prepared to take the sort of bold steps Cadbury was

[59] E. Ernest Boorne to G. C, 20 Nov. 1901, G. C. to Boorne, 21 & 26 Nov. 1901, and G. C. to Edward Grubb, 29 Nov. 1901, G. C. P, WL. The section on Woodbrooke in the *Handbook*. *Yearly Meeting, 1908* (Birmingham 1908), 122 suggests that Cadbury was inspired by a pamphlet describing the School for Religious Studies established by evangelical Friends in Cleveland, Ohio in 1892 (now Malone College in Canton, Ohio).

[60] E. G. to G. C., 30 Nov. 1901, ibid.

demanding, but above all else they wished to avoid activities of the 'crude and ignorantly dogmatic type'.

Although Grubb's reputation as an 'advanced' thinker did not recommend him to most evangelical Friends, Cadbury may have felt that Grubb possessed a bolder vision of dynamic Quakerism than his more orthodox brethren were willing to consider. In any case, Cadbury told Grubb that decisions regarding Woodbrooke should remain in abeyance until John Wilhelm Rowntree's return from holiday in the West Indies. Obviously, then, the key element in Cadbury's gradual yielding to the forces of modernity was his growing confidence in John Wilhelm's opinions and judgement.[61]

For the next two years, while the Woodbrooke scheme slowly ripened, John Wilhelm remained George Cadbury's chief consultant. One of the most important results of Cadbury's apparently limitless confidence in him was that the majority of those who played a significant role in Woodbrooke's formation were Rowntree's hand-picked allies. George Cadbury did have a select body of advisors with distinctly evangelical leanings,[62] but nearly all of the innovative ideas about the nature and purpose of Woodbrooke were drawn from a decidedly advanced element, including Grubb, W. C. Braithwaite, Rendel Harris, and Joshua Rowntree as well as the long-distance advocacy of Rufus Jones. Because Cadbury was willing to defer to younger, better-educated and predominantly liberal Friends, Woodbrooke emerged as a breeding ground of the New Quakerism, with a portrait of John Wilhelm Rowntree greeting each new generation of young Quakers who entered its doors.[63]

Woodbrooke took shape with due deliberation, as Rowntree told Rufus Jones, so 'that Friends may not be alarmed... We are seeking to provide a spiritual revival by *means of a settlement* rather than the settlement *as a result* of a religious revival.' For J. W. R., an important aspect of this impending revival was the role he hoped that Jones would play in it. In the spring of 1902, he made a direct appeal to his friend: 'We feel the immediate future of Quakerism is

---

[61] G. C. to E. G., 3 Dec. 1901, GCP, WL.

[62] Cadbury's closest confidants were his wife Elizabeth (Elsie), his sons, George Jr. and Edward, and his friends Henry Lloyd Wilson and Joseph Hoyland as well as John Henry and Mabel Cash Barlow who were living in the house at Woodbrooke while plans were being formulated. See G. C. to J. W. R., 10 Jan. 1902, ibid.

[63] Rowntree's portrait remained a vivid recollection of W. C. Braithwaite's son Richard. Interview with Professor Richard Braithwaite, August 1986, Cambridge.

critical and that earnest and strenuous labour, under the guidance of God and the Spirit of Love can alone save us. "Come over into Macedonia and help us".'[64]

Under Rowntree's urging, George Cadbury sent a similar plea asking Jones to become Woodbrooke's first Director of Studies, if only temporarily. Apparently, John Wilhelm had convinced Cadbury that if Jones would come to England for a year or two to lend his learning and prestige to the Woodbrooke experiment, Friends' contribution to the revival of vital Christianity might be 'a thousand times greater . . . than . . . [it is] today'. Cadbury told Jones that his sole desire was to lift the 'dead weight of formalism' from their Society so that it might become a vital factor in 'hastening . . . the coming of that time "when he shall reign whose right it is" '. Signs were already present, Cadbury added, that his labours were bearing fruit: 'last Yearly Meeting showed a remarkable change in the general feeling of the Society.' Jones' presence in such an environment, he thought, would insure an even more abundant harvest.[65]

Rufus Jones was seriously tempted, especially since George Cadbury included the inducement of a considerable rise in salary. In the end, he decided that he could not, in good conscience, give up his work at Haverford or the editorship of the *American Friend*. Cadbury was sorely disappointed, not only because he believed that Jones was exactly the man who was needed to head up Woodbrooke but also because of problems he perceived with regard to possible alternative choices.

A number of names had been advanced during the formative stages of the project, but the only candidate, besides Jones, upon whom there was anything like a consensus was another American, Richard Thomas of Baltimore. Thomas, the husband of Joseph Bevan Braithwaite's daughter, Anna, was respected by a broad range of British Friends,[66] but John Wilhelm knew that he was even less likely than Jones to accept the position. Therefore, he suggested that the post be offered to Rendel Harris, with Edward Grubb as chief resident teacher. This recommendation received a mixed response. First of all, there was, on theological grounds, 'a somewhat decided expression of opinion against Edward Grubb being . . . resident at Woodbrooke'. Harris, shining light of the

---

[64] J. W. R. to R. M. J., n.d. [late April–early May 1902], Box 3, RMJP.
[65] G. C. to R. M. J., 13 May and 5 June 1902, Box 3, RMJP.
[66] *Minutes of the Settlement Committee*, 5 Dec. 1902, WL.

Summer Schools, touched a more responsive chord. In fact, Rendel Harris had been independently recommended to Cadbury a year earlier by Henry T. Hodgkin (1877–1933), a Cambridge-educated medical doctor, who believed that a world-renowned scholar like Harris 'would be exactly the person . . . [to attract] the educated young men of the Society . . .'[67] Cautious Friends expressed some concern about the soundness of Harris's wife, Helen, who had twice left the Society on doctrinal grounds,[68] but, surprisingly, there was little opposition to Rendel Harris from evangelicals, despite his prominent work in historical and textual criticism of the Scriptures. Cadbury himself believed that Harris was 'thoroughly evangelical' and that 'under . . . a strong local committee[,] Friends would have no fear of his learning carrying him astray with regard to Higher Criticism'.[69]

Finally, in December 1902 Cadbury approached Harris directly pleading with him to resign his position at Cambridge and become Woodbrooke's Director of Studies. The prospect of Harris leaving a prestigious post at a world-renowned University to take charge of a somewhat nebulous Quaker educational experiment seemed remote, but before the end of the year, Harris had accepted the position and effectively written his own ticket as to the role he was prepared to play. To begin, Harris noted that once he was 'adrift from Cambridge', he would lose several sources of income. In these circumstances he thought his salary 'should be a liberal one' and that his wife should have 'some liberty of choice' as regards the house that was to be provided for them, outside the Woodbrooke grounds. Secondly, 'in view of the international position I now occupy in critical science and the importance of keeping up with the work', Harris wanted a definite limit as to the time he would be expected to devote to the Settlement and its students.[70] George

[67] It is not clear if Hodgkin's omission of women was purposeful or incidental. Hodgkin to G. C., 6 Dec. 1901, GCP, ibid.

[68] Helen Balkwill Harris (1841–1914) had resigned from the Society of Friends in 1898. She was also under something of a cloud for supposedly having developed too cosy a relationship with military authorities during the Boer War when she visited South African concentration camps in co-operation with the work of the Friends' South African Relief Fund Committee. She returned to the Quaker fold when her husband took the position at Woodbrooke. See Hope Hay Hewison, *Hedge of Wild Almonds*, (London 1989), 210–11, 223, 348.

[69] G. C. to Henry S. Newman, 6 Dec. 1902, GCP, WL. The quoted passage was crossed out of the copy of the letter in the Cadbury Papers.

[70] G. C. to J. Rendel Harris (J. R. H), 12 December 1902, and J. R. H. to G. C., 31 Dec. 1902, GCP., W. L.

Cadbury apparently did not blink at these demands and within two weeks, Harris was expressing gratitude for 'the extraordinary liberality' of the financial and other arrangements proposed to him. '[I]t will be strange', he noted, enthusiastically if somewhat immodestly, 'if something good doesn't come of it both to the Church and to the world.'[71]

With Harris safely in the fold and plans well underway to launch the new Settlement with a Summer School, John Wilhelm Rowntree told Cadbury he finally felt 'as if some light were breaking on the horizon'. But dawn does not necessarily bring smooth sailing. At its next meeting the Woodbrooke Committee learned that Rendel Harris would be on an archaeological expedition in Armenia during the projected Woodbrooke Summer School. In addition, some evangelical Friends had begun to express serious reservations about the theological tenor of the entire project.[72] Undeterred, the organizers announced in early February that Woodbrooke would commence operations with an extended Summer School (23 July to 3 September) featuring a course of lectures by Rufus Jones. The Summer School would be followed by the official opening of the permanent Settlement in October, combining opportunities for study, worship, and Christian endeavour with a view to 'deepening and strengthening . . . religious life'.[73]

The final step in preparing the way for the Quaker centre of religious study and training was a conference in Birmingham, hosted by George and Elsie Cadbury.[74] In April 1903 a group of weighty Friends of every theological stripe gathered at the Cadburys' Northfield manor house to hear George Cadbury's description of the spiritual objectives and practical arrangements of the new Settlement. Acknowledging the absent John Wilhelm Rowntree 'as the parent of the scheme', Cadbury depicted Woodbrooke as a collective response to deeply-troubling trends in British Quakerism. First, Cadbury said, there was the growing spiritual indifference among Friends repelled by their own 'untrained,

[71] J. R. H. to G. C., 13 Jan. 1903, GCP, WL.
[72] J. W. R. to G. C., 7 Jan. 1903; *Minutes*, Settlement Committee, 14 Jan. 1903; and G. C. to E. G., 7 Feb. 1903, WL.
[73] *TF*, 13 Feb. 1903. Also see material on 'Summer School for Religious Study' in Woodbrooke Library. There had been a third British Summer School at Windermere in the summer of 1902.
[74] See J. W. R. to Claude Taylor, 28 March 1903, WL.

uneducated' ministry; secondly, despite the efforts of Quaker
Home Missionaries and other earnest souls, many Friends were
troubled that their Society was contributing 'practically nothing' in
the struggle 'to save our country from heathenism . . .' What was
needed to rescue Quakerism from this combination of debilitating
apathy and humiliating impotency was not only the realization
'that our young men and women should have the opportunity to
prepare for Christian work' but also some agency through which
that preparation could be systematically accomplished. This was the
role he hoped that Woodbrooke would fill.[75]

To set this process into motion, the Cadburys officially donated
Woodbrooke as a permanent Quaker Settlement to be maintained
at their expense. In addition, £12,000 worth of preferred shares
in *The Daily News*, Cadbury's national newspaper,[76] would constitute an endowment in support lectureships and scholarships,
providing tuition and expenses for a term in residence to a number
of younger Friends. Also, as a means of putting Quaker educational
institutions in touch with 'the best life and aspirations of our
fellowship', an anonymous Northern Friend (probably Joseph
Rowntree) offered to support teachers from Friends' schools 'for
one term during the experimental year'.[77]

The discussion that followed Cadbury's presentation was chiefly
a festival of unity and good-feeling. William Charles Braithwaite
called Woodbrooke 'a natural extension of . . . our Summer
Schools' and Rufus Jones, in a letter read by Elsie Cadbury, looked
to Woodbrooke as a means for 'spiritualising English Quakerism'.
There were also cautionary statements on the dangers of dogmatism, lest the new Settlement become a theological seminary
espousing some new 'special orthodoxy'. Cadbury responded that
while some of the local Woodbrooke Committee, himself
included, might be characterized as 'ultra evangelical', all of its
members, recognizing the damage previously inflicted by 'bigotry
and uncharitableness', were imbued with the principle that 'where

[75] 'Report of the Conference at Manor House, Northfield', 18 April 1903, GCP, WL.
[76] During the 1890s Cadbury had taken control of four weekly suburban Birmingham
newspapers; in 1901, during the South African War, he purchased the *Daily News*, his first
venture into the national press, in order to ensure an anti-war voice among London daily
newspapers. See Gardiner, *George Cadbury*, 204–27.
[77] Ibid. For a summary of the financial arrangements, see G. C. to J. Glaisyer, 7 May 1903
and George Cadbury's deed establishing the Woodbrooke Settlement, 8 Oct. 1903, GCP,
WL.

the spirit of the Lord is, there is liberty'.[78] Birmingham Committee member, Henry Lloyd Wilson (soon to be installed as Clerk of London Yearly Meeting), affirmed Cadbury's vision of Wood-brooke as a place to 'bring the spiritual, the intellectual & the experimental experience together... in saving men, in building up Christian character and in strengthening... [the] work that the Society of Friends has branched out into in the last 30 years.'[79]

The long-waited Woodbrooke Summer School was to consist of three two-week sessions, the first two anchored by Rufus Jones' ten lectures on 'Present-Day Ideas of God and the Spiritual Life'.[80] Then, suddenly, the atmosphere became shrouded in melancholy when word was received of the death of Rufus Jones' son Lowell while the parents were *en route* to England.[81] Despite this stagger-ing personal tragedy, Jones determined to deliver the first set of lectures before returning to America. His decision had a deeply moving effect on those attending, but in the circumstances it was hardly an auspicious beginning.[82]

When the Summer School ended in September, the opening of Woodbrooke's first regular term was only six weeks away and a number of important questions remained unresolved. First, a last-minute crisis had arisen when Rendel Harris received the offer of a Chair in Ancient Christian Literature from the University of Leyden in Holland.[83] After Harris eased fears by renewing his commitment to Woodbrooke, the Continuation Committee responded with a pledge to 'widen the scope of the Settlement' and 'to reserve a certain number of places for those unconnected with Friends'. During Woodbrooke's first year, three theological students from Leyden became the first of dozens of Dutch Reformed ministers who eventually studied there.[84]

---

[78] 'Report of the Conference at Manor House, Northfield', 18 April 1903, GCP, WL.

[79] Ibid.

[80] See the lecture programme in 'Summer School for Religious Studies', WL.

[81] Lowell Jones, the only child of Jones' first marriage (Sarah Jones died in 1899), was in good health when his father and stepmother left for England but died a week later as the result of reaction to a diphtheria vaccination. See Barbour and Frost, *Quakers*, 227.

[82] See *Seventh Annual Report*, 1904, SSCC, WL and Catherine Albright to RMJ, 5 August 1903, RMJP, HCQC.

[83] In *Hedge of Wild Almonds*, 223, Hope Hewison notes that the offer was at least partly a result of Harris' outspoken opposition to the Boer War.

[84] *Minutes of the Woodbrooke Committee*, 26 August 1903, WL and Pickard, *Memories of J. Rendel Harris*, 11–12.

While the Committee were assured of Rendel Harris's presence, they had yet to determine his chief associates. Since Harris was to reside outside the Settlement and be available to its students on only a part-time basis, the institution required a live-in Warden to act as co-ordinator of events and chief spiritual advisor. As of mid-September, no suitable candidate had emerged. Edward Grubb's name re-emerged and he was once again passed over as 'associated with views too advanced for many Friends'.[85] Another widely-mentioned possibility was Joan Mary Fry (1862–1955), a daughter of Sir Edward Fry, who had been active in the Summer Schools and was also a member of the Continuation Committee. But when the Committee decided against 'a lady warden', the position fell, temporarily and almost by default, to John Wilhelm Rowntree's cousin Joshua and his wife, Isabella.[86] As a former Mayor of Scarborough and Liberal MP, Joshua Rowntree was sufficiently respected and weighty to dispel opposition on personal or theologcial grounds.

Woodbrooke opened on 13 October 1903 with twenty-six students, ten of whom were in residence. Lectures on religious subjects were to be given by Rendel Harris with the assistance of Alfred Neave Brayshaw (1861–1940), B.A., L.L.B., a former teacher at Boothham and outspoken liberal reformer. Brayshaw possessed a singular dedication to the revitalization of Quaker ministry and a passionate, outspoken distaste for evangelical ideas and practices. No one could have been more sincere, more earnest, nor, for some, more annoying.[87]

Not long after the beginning of Woodbrooke's first term, Neave Brayshaw dispatched a somewhat alarming report to John Wilhelm Rowntree: 'Joshua and I are anxious . . . ' he said, 'we are

---

[85] Joshua Rowntree to Henry Lloyd Wilson and M. C. Albright (copy), 16 Sept. 1903, GCP, WL.

[86] Ibid. Also see Fawell, *Joan Mary Fry, passim* and Richenda Scott's *Notebook*, 'The Woodbrooke Permanent Settlement', a gift from Roger C. Wilson in possession of the author.

[87] Brayshaw had not been a success as a teacher at either Oliver's Mount (1889–92) or Boothham (1892–1903). Because of his tendency, when frustrated or otherwise moved, to dissolve into tears, unsympathetic students had christened him 'Puddles', a name that stuck. He had a strong interest in Gothic architecture and his excursions with schoolboys to view cathedrals in the English countryside or in Normandy became famous. For the important role he played in the Edwardian and wartime periods, see Chapters 8 & 9 below. Also see A. Neave Brayshaw, *Memoir and Selected Writings* (Birmingham 1941) and A. J. P. Taylor *A Personal History* (New York 1983), 49–51.

disappointed in Rendel *so far.*' The chief complaint seemed to be Brayshaw's perception of a casual, even careless Director of Studies: 'He seems to have made no preparation at all—but drifts in and asks one or two questions—and from the answers he gets he just plays around for the rest of the time.'[88] Furthermore, because Harris refused to be pinned down, it was left to Brayshaw and Joshua Rowntree to 'hammer out a scheme' for a more substantial curriculum. When Brayshaw's lectures on George Fox and early Quakerism went badly, Harris' well-intentioned attempt to intervene apparently made matters worse. These developments not only frustrated Brayshaw but also, by his account, frequently put Joshua Rowntree into a 'state of annoyance'. At the same time, some of the students were proving to be less than satisfactory by Brayshaw's criteria: 'Sims the missionary is a violent Chamberlainite...just a conventional jingo...';[89] other Woodbrookers showed an 'alarming tendency to collect together to sing hymns...' a proclivity deeply disturbing to Brayshaw's sense of acceptable Quakerly worship.[90]

On the other hand, Brayshaw perceived hopeful signs as well. George Shann, whom Neave identified as 'one of Edward Cadbury's helots', came in to teach economics and other social subjects. Brayshaw did not attend Shann's lectures but had on reliable authority that there was 'some good stuff and a lot of it...'[91] He

[88] A. N. B. to J. W. R., 20 Oct. [?] 1903, (copy), RMJP, Box 4, HCQC. In light of these comments, Harris' description of his teaching philosophy is of interest: 'The whole art of lecturing is to be *en rapport* with your audience'. Harris believed that a teacher had to recognize the background and interests of his students by asking questions and developing a connection by answering them rather than by sticking to some rigid theme. See Davis, *Woodbrooke*, 27–8 and Pickard, *Rendel Harris*, 15.

[89] A. N. B. to J. W. R. (copy), 20 Oct. 1903, Box 4, RMJP, HCQC. John and Emily Sims were involved in the Friends Foreign Mission Association (FFMA) project in Madagascar for over forty years. See Greenwood, *Whispers of Truth*, 64–5, 80 and Henry T. Hogdkin, *Friends Beyond Seas* (London 1916), 100 n.

[90] Ibid. The fact that George Cadbury had personally introduced hymn-singing in Bournville Friends' meeting was clearly an omen of future difficulties between the two men. Brayshaw strongly opposed all things evangelical, including the Adult Schools which were so dear to Cadbury's heart. See Gardiner, *George Cadbury*, 185 and GC to W. C. Braithwaite, 13 November 1906, GCP, WL.

[91] A. N. B. to J. W. R. (copy), 20 Oct. 1903, Box 4, RMJP, HCQC. George Shann, a Yorkshireman of working-class origin and educated at Glasgow University, remained at Woodbrooke considerably longer than Neave Brayshaw, acting as lecturer on 'social subjects' until he joined the Army in 1916. He was also active in the Labour party and served as a Labour member on the Birmingham City Council. He died in 1919. See Davis, *Woodbrooke*, 38–9, 47.

also appreciated George Cadbury's continued efforts to make Woodbrooke attractive, 'sending down tennis balls & rackets & laying out a golf course . . . it is wonderful'. Despite his uneasiness, Brayshaw remained confident, if slightly subversive: 'We are going to win, but I should not like certain social and intellectual classes of Friends to know us just yet.'[92]

John Wilhelm Rowntree conveyed Brayshaw's reservations about Rendel Harris to Rufus Jones, but it is unlikely he said anything to George Cadbury. Certainly, nothing untoward can be detected in Cadbury's early reflections on Woodbrooke. From the moment the Settlement opened, Cadbury spoke of it loftily as 'a school for prophets' that would bring 'fresh life' to the Society. Under the ministry of sound Friends and 'the guidance of the Holy Spirit', the 'dry bones' of Quakerism would be roused up and 'members of our Society [turned] into channels of practical work on behalf of the ungodly around them'.[93]

After the first term, the Rowntrees were replaced as Wardens by William Littleboy (1853–1936) and his wife, Margaret. The change had been pre-arranged and had nothing to do with Joshua's apparent reservations about Rendel Harris. Still, if the Director of Studies had been an occasionally distracting irritant to Joshua Rowntree, he would prove a much heavier cross for the solid and serious William Littleboy. Theological as well as temperamental differences between Harris and Littleboy were illustrated by an earlier incident during the planning for the first Woodbrooke Summer School. Rendel Harris, for all of his apparently serendipitous approach, always projected 'a strong streak of Quaker mysticism'.[94] With Rufus Jones and others,[95] Harris had been deeply impressed with William James' psychological cum mystical interpretation of early Quakerism in the *Varieties of Religious Experience* (1902). When John Wilhelm Rowntree broached the idea of inviting William James to speak on the psychology of religion at the Woodbrooke Summer School in 1903, William Littleboy, who had become 'seriously alarmed' after reading James' work,

[92] A. N. B. to J. W. R. (copy), 20 Oct. 1903, Box 4, RMJP.
[93] G. C. to Rendel Harris, 30 Nov. 1903, GCP, WL and G. C. to R. M. J., 18 Jan. 1904, Box 4, RMJP.
[94] Interview with Rendel Harris, *The Examiner*, 16 March 1904.
[95] See Chapter 4 above.

successfully organized opposition to the idea.[96] Littleboy rejected the notion, implied by James, that adherence to Quakerism required some sort of mystical experience or rapture to authenticate the presence of a universal and saving Light. For while Littleboy did not doubt that individuals like Rendel Harris were capable of emotionally satisfying spiritual exhilaration, he was fearful that emphasis upon such experiences would cause potential believers to feel that Quakerism was limited only to a spiritual élite capable of intimately perceiving the Divine Presence.[97] At the same time, Littleboy also had a sense of being called to the work of revitalizing Quakerism. As he told Rufus Jones prior to assuming his new post:

I do believe that this absence of spiritual sunshine—this failure to grasp experimentally and consciously the love of God in our lives—is a very much more common difficulty than is often supposed. If one can be used to help such as those who have this disappointing experience to recognize some bright points amid the general greyness of the inner life, one feels that it is some compensation for being without conscious enjoyment of the deep Christian privileges oneself.[98]

The impetuous, fun-loving Harris, who once described Woodbrooke as 'a kind of permanent Chautauqua', would probably have thought such sombre words an odd approach to discovering 'bright spots'. Still, Littleboy, who had all the qualifications for the Woodbrooke position—intellectual ability, emotional maturity, and business success as well as considerable education—no doubt provided solace for those students who found Rendel Harris alternatively too giddy or too far above their heads.[99]

Amidst such divergences, the beginning of Woodbrooke's second term was accompanied by an editorial in *The Friend* which forthwith associated the Settlement with the 'regeneration of the Society of Friends and the coming renaissance' which had brought

[96] J. W. R. to R. M. J., 2 and 11 Dec. 1902, Box 3, RMJP and *Minutes of the Woodbrooke Settlement Committee*, 10 Dec. 1902, WL.

[97] For a thorough discussion, see William Littleboy, *The Appeal of Quakerism to the Non-Mystic* (Harrogate [1916]), published by the '1905 Committee of Yorkshire Q. M.' (Reprinted as a 'Quaker Classic' in 1964).

[98] William Littleboy to R. M. J., 23 December 1903, Box 4, RMJP.

[99] Davis, *Woodbrooke*, 32–3 and *The Examiner*, 16 March 1904.

'our . . . membership into much closer touch with the great moral and social problems of our time'. In making Woodbrooke 'a centre of educational influence of the highest order . . . We realise far more than did some of our fathers that intellectual culture, careful and accurate thought are essential to the true and permanent advance of a religious community.'[100]

After the successful completion of the first year's operation, the Settlement Committee determined that if Woodbrooke was 'to draw into its sphere of influence those who . . . desire an all-round equipment for religious service', it required a substantial expansion in personnel. In searching for additional staff, Rendel Harris emphasized his desire to sign on the brightest minds that could be secured, regardless of denomination. The Committee, recognizing the importance of 'the expository and historical treatment of religious subjects, as distinguished from a strictly dogmatic presentation', followed Harris' lead, adding Robert S. Franks, a Congregational minister, and Herbert G. Wood, a Cambridge-educated Baptist, to the staff. Franks would stay on until 1910; H. G. Wood spent most of the rest his life at Woodbrooke, becoming, in turn, a convinced Friend, the second Director of Studies and one of the most influential Quaker thinkers of the twentieth century.[101]

Such expansion also reflected Cadbury's vision of Woodbrooke's dual role: to equip young people for more effective teaching in Adult Schools and to revitalize Quaker meetings for worship. The entire world, he believed, was a field ripe for harvest wherein every Christian had a duty 'to turn men from darkness to light . . . If this real aggressive Christian work is conducted in connection with the Society of Friends, we shall see a great revival, & possibly even millions brought into it.'[102] In both the growing willingness of young members to take a 'wider view of our responsibilities as a church' and 'the marvelous awakening that is coming over the people of England', Cadbury perceived the time was ripe for a great spiritual revival and hoped that Woodbrooke might be the

---

[100]   *TF*, 22 April 1904, 257–8.
[101]   *Minutes of the Woodbrooke Committee*, 6 July 1904, WL and Davis, *Woodbrooke*, 38–48 *passim*. Also Richenda Scott, *Herbert G. Wood: a Memoir of His Life and Thought* (London 1967).
[102]   G. C. to J. W. R., 18 July 1904, GCP, WL.

catalyst for such a movement.[103] To this end, Cadbury enthusiastically supported Seebohm Rowntree's recommendation that
Woodbrooke add a resident lecturer on social subjects (economics
and sociology) so that Friends there could be instructed on the
relationship between religious ideals and social responsibilities.
Seebohm Rowntree and a group of reform-minded Friends had
established the Friends Social Union (FSU) in 1902 to give direction the Society's efforts to grapple with the sort of social disintegration which reflected a deeper spiritual malaise in modern
society.[104] They believed that Woodbrooke needed to supply the
raw material to make the work of the Friends Social Union socially
meaningful. In late 1906 the Woodbrooke Committee appointed
J. St George C. Heath (1882–1918) of Corpus Christi College,
Oxford, as a lecturer on social subjects, his salary to be paid by a
group of Yorkshire Friends represented by Seebohm Rowntree.
Heath arrived in 1908 and introduced a regular course of study for
students planning careers in social work. The programme established by Heath, who joined the Society of Friends in 1910, was a
pioneering effort in English education and a considerable expansion of the original idea of a short-term centre for Quaker Religious Studies.[105]

As Woodbrooke enlarged both its staff and its horizons, questions arose as to whether such expansion might not be leaving its
intended student body behind. A report prepared by William
Littleboy in 1906 indicated that of the 223 students who had
matriculated (165 of these were Friends) 'only 36 had any pretensions to scholarship', and, of these, twenty-nine had been from
Leyden.[106] Two years earlier John Wilhelm Rowntree related to
George Cadbury that although the Hollanders tended 'to raise the
standard of the work' and to provide Rendel Harris with 'students
of a calibre worthy of his scholarship', he was concerned lest the
Dutchmen 'swamp the settlement'. To prevent such a 'fatal' development, Rowntree pushed for an endowment to support '*six* male

    [103] G. C. to J. S. Rowntree, 26 Nov. 1904 and to Mr. Barlow, 27 Feb. 1906, GCP, WL.
George Cadbury associated this new spirit with the Liberal Party's landslide electoral victory
in January 1906.
    [104] See below Chapter 8.
    [105] *Minutes of the Woodbrooke Committee*, 14 July 1905, 14 June 1906 and 7 Nov. 1906 and
G. C. to Mrs. Wilson, 8 June 1906, WL. Also see Davis, *Woodbrooke*, 38–40.
    [106] G. C. to William Charles Braithwaite (W. C. B.), 22 October 1906 and [William
Little boy] 'Memorandum on Woodbrooke after 3 yrs.,' October 1906, GCP, WL.

American friends of any section'. This could not only 'meet the Dutch difficulty... [but] unite Friends now held apart by old out-worn controversies & it would unite young English & American Quakerism... I should like to see Woodbrooke as a Quaker Mecca...'[107]

Cadbury responded to John Wilhelm's plea by funding six scholarships 'to enable American Friends of the Other Branch [Hicksites] to reside at Woodbrooke'. At the time, there were already three Hicksites studying at Woodbrooke, probably recruited by John William Graham who had strong, and for some, disquieting connections within the American Hicksite community.[108] George Cadbury's conclusion was that though 'we [evangelical Friends] believe more fully in the Atonement', these Hicksites seemed 'just the kind of men the world needs'. John Wilhelm, however, apparently had second thoughts about harbouring too many members of the Other Branch. Late in 1904 he was urging Rufus Jones to 'induce some... Philadelphia and Pastoral Friends' to take up the scholarships. 'I am anxious that the Settlement should not get the stamp of Hicksism on it. We want Woodbrooke to be catholic.'[109]

At the end of Woodbrooke's third year, William Littleboy submitted a somewhat troubled assessment of results. Those who had studied at the Settlement, he believed, probably represented a fair cross-section of the Quaker rank and file 'which the original Promoters... had in mind', but these students' 'knowledge of most of the subjects dealt with... was elementary in the extreme'. Repeating the tone earlier struck by Neave Brayshaw, Littleboy concluded that the curriculum should be made more integral and systematic, with adequate arrangements for closer personal tutoring and supervision, including an emphasis on writing, a skill which he felt had been neglected.[110]

All of this seemed to imply criticism of Rendel Harris' free-wheeling, mercurial style, but from Harris' own perspective, as

---

[107] J. W. R. to G. C., 14 July 1904 (private), GCP, WL.

[108] In 1904 Meeting for Sufferings refused to issue a travelling minute endorsing John W. Graham's visitation to American Hicksites meetings. See correspondence on this incident in the JWGP.

[109] G. C. to J. W. R., 18 July 1904, and to J. R. H., 14 July 1904, GCP, WL; Richenda Scott's 'Notebook', citing '8th Annual Report', SSCC, June 1905; and J. W. R. to R. M. J., 24 October 1904, Box 4, RMJP.

[110] 'Memorandum on Woodbrooke after 3 yrs', Oct. 1906, WL.

related to William Charles Braithwaite, he was fighting 'to save Woodbrooke from becoming a Friends Boarding School...' For his part George Cadbury, still footing most of the bills, believed Harris was the 'greatest man' for ensuring Woodbrooke's survival and future development and that, as Director of Studies, he should be fully backed by the Settlement Committee.[111] But for all of Cadbury's efforts, not everything at Woodbrooke was to Harris's liking. In addition to his differences with William Littleboy, he was apparently unhappy about some of the individuals appointed to the Woodbrooke Consultative Committee early in 1906. He even inquired of W. C. Braithwaite if there had been some hidden 'malice' in their selection.[112]

In any case, William Littleboy's 'Memorandum' made clear the necessity for some resolution of the friction between himself and Rendel Harris and shortly after submitting this report, he wrote to Braithwaite, as Chairman of the Woodbrooke Council, asking to be released from his duties as Warden as soon as a suitable replacement could be found. Littleboy noted that his wife's health was a factor in his decision which caused him 'pain and deep regret. My years at Woodbrooke have been in many ways the happiest of my life.'[113]

George Cadbury appears to have felt that Littleboy's decision was a necessary, if unfortunate, development which ought to be accompanied by other changes as well. Cadbury's appreciation of William Littleboy's past service and obvious sincerity made it difficult to criticize him, but, as he told Braithwaite, 'we are at a turning of the ways & a responsibility rests upon us to do what will lead to the best results for the Society...' adding in exasperated tones:

I am quite sure much of the good that would have resulted has been counteracted by the presence of an equally good but very injudicious man, Neave Brayshaw. He has allowed his dislike of Adult School & other Mission Work to interfere with the good that he might have

---

[111] J. R. H. to W. C. B., 2 March 1906, 'Quaker Principles', Box 3 and G. C. to J. R. H., 21 October 1904, GCP, WL. As a reflection of his desire to keep Harris happy, Cadbury had, early in 1906, sent him what amounted to a bonus to cover unexpected expenses, G. C. to J. R. H., 15 March 1906, ibid.

[112] J. R. H. to W. C. B., 2 March 1906, 'Quaker Principles', Box 3, WL.

[113] William Littleboy to W. C. B., 1 Nov. 1906, WL.

accomplished. We shall not, of course, entertain his being allowed to give any more lectures after this term is over . . . I fully believe in his sincerity & excellence, but one has to look at the interests of the Society of Friends which may yet be a great power for good in the land.[114]

In November of 1906, it was determined that the Littleboys should be succeeded as Wardens by Isaac and Mary Snowden Braithwaite, Rendel Harris' favourite candidates. At the same time, curriculum matters, a serious bone of contention, were effectively placed under the direction of a sub-committee headed William Charles Braithwaite. George Cadbury expressed relief and even a sense of 'Divine guidance' in the new arrangements at Woodbrooke, believing that with these alternations 'prejudice against Woodbrooke would be very largely removed' and way opened to allow the Society of Friends to continue enlarging its role in the moral regeneration of British society.[115]

Still, to fully justify the Settlement's continued existence there needed to be proof of its larger service to the Society and the nation. This concern was taken up at a joint meeting of the Woodbrooke Settlement and the Summer School Continuation Committees during the summer of 1907. First, those present decided to amalgamate their two bodies into a single Woodbrooke Council. This new Council then established a Settlement Committee to deal with institutional questions and an Extension Committee to wrestle with looming questions of resuscitating a vocal ministry that was still 'deplorably weak' and discovering 'the best way of supplying more adequate teaching in Biblical and Social subjects . . . for many of our Meetings, and . . . Adult Schools'. Several of the meetings in question seemed to be in imminent danger of dying out unless steps were taken to remedy their situation.[116] The point was made that the problem of reviving moribund meetings might be more adequately addressed if Woodbrooke could become something akin to a University Extension, with the

[114] G. C. to W. C. B., 22 Oct. and 13 November 1906, GCP, WL.
[115] G. C. to W. C. B., 22 Oct. 1906 and to Joshua Rowntree, 20 November 1906, GCP, WL.
[116] John H. Barlow, Sec., Woodbrooke Committee and Edward Grubb, Secretary, Summer School Continuation Committee, to Committee members, with accompanying 'Memorandum with respect to teaching on Biblical and Social subjects', 20 June 1907, and Minutes of a Joint Meeting of the SSCC and the Woodbrooke Committee, 26 July 1907, WL.

Fig. 5   William Charles Braithwaite (1862–1922), historian of
British Quakerism, taken about 1920

Committee dispatching members of 'a staff of salaried lecturers' to
individual meetings throughout the country as the need arose.
Such a system could, of course, only operate if Woodbrooke
provided an adequate supply of knowledgeable individuals trained
in the rudiments of teaching. Also, if endangered meetings could
be induced to send a member or members to Woodbrooke for
even a brief period, such individuals might be instructed in 'various
means to arouse a sense of need in the meetings . . .' This seemed a
simple and sensible means to begin coping with a serious challenge,
but it also raised the question of whether prepared 'teaching' by
especially trained individuals might not undermine 'the unique
character of the meetings for worship'.[117]

---

[117] Proceedings of Conference with respect to teaching on Biblical & Social subjects, 12
July 1907, WL.

To avoid exacerbating such fears, the Settlement Committee laid stress on Woodbrooke's tendency 'towards practical training in religious and social work'.[118] The Extension Committee accentuated other positive developments, noting a growing demand for Summer Schools under the auspices of Quarterly or Monthly Meetings as well as for weekend 'lecture schools'. The most ambitious project had been the Extension Committee's organizing of Summer Schools for Free Churches at Cambridge under the patronage of the National Free Church Council. (Rendel Harris was the President of the NFCC.) So, five years after Woodbrooke opened, its Council was satisfied that 'the benefit... accruing to the cause of spiritual religion in the world can hardly be over-estimated'.[119]

Given the apparent value of the work being done at and through Woodbrooke, the Council no doubt felt justified in asking for an increase in annual subscriptions from £750 to £1250 to deal with existing deficits and to finance expanded extension work, including Rendel Harris's idea of establishing a scheme for training students by correspondence for the Bachelor of Divinity examination at the University of London.[120] George Cadbury had to be pleased by these developments. At the same time, his continuing concern about finances made him wonder if he had 'made a mistake in not taking rather more active part in the management' of the Settlement despite his immersion in other interests, especially the *Daily News*, which, like Woodbrooke, persistently ran at a deficit.[121] In this regard, Cadbury did receive substantial help from the Rowntrees of York who in 1907 collectively paid Woodbrooke's accumulated debt. In a letter to Arnold Rowntree thanking the family for its generous gesture, Cadbury expressed his continued conviction that the work being done at Woodbrooke was well worth whatever material sacrifice they might be called upon to make. By way of illustration, he cited the case of a Hicksite Woodbrooker who had 'lost all faith and... become practically an

---

[118] *Minutes*, Woodbrooke Council, Nov. 1908, WL.
[119] Ibid. [120] Ibid.
[121] G. C. to W. C. B., 24 Nov. 1906, GCP, WL. For a discussion of Cadbury's struggle to make the *Daily News* a paying proposition as well as a force for advancing the Liberal Party and the moral tone of British national life, see Gardiner, *George Cadbury*, 204–27.

agnostic' until he was rescued from the slough of despond by 'the teaching of Rendel Harris and others'.[122]

Arnold Rowntree might have responded in kind by noting the case of Foster Brady, a middle-aged Yorkshire Friend whose year at Woodbrooke had been 'of the greatest possible benefit to him' and had led to his employment by the Yorkshire 1905 Committee as a lecturer and organizer who would spend 'two or three months at a time in Meetings which were not in a very satisfactory state' in the effort to pump life back into them.[123]

Such were the small victories to which George Cadbury could point in hopes they might inspire Friends in general not only to support Woodbrooke but also to assume more of the burden for supporting it. As he told Rendel Harris: 'I want the institution to be running alone before my death . . .' Although he was apparently disappointed in the immediate response to his plea for wider patronage, Cadbury never ceased to believe that Woodbrooke would fulfil the vision that John Wilhelm Rowntree had invoked when he initiated the idea of a Quaker Settlement for Religious Studies. Early in 1909 while musing on the imminent prospect of his seventieth birthday, Cadbury reminded Joshua Rowntree: 'For our light affliction, which is but for a moment, worketh for us a far more exceeding and eternal weight of glory.'[124] In a letter to Warden Isaac Braithwaite later in the same year, he remained confident that 'we cannot doubt for a moment that very much more good will be done . . . It rather reminds one of the disciples who were scattered everywhere preaching the word. The seed sown at Woodbrooke will probably take root in many other countries and bear abundant fruit to the glory of God, and in the end a much greater work will be accomplished.'[125]

[122] G. C. to Arnold Rowntree, 7 Nov. 1907, GCP, WL.

[123] *Minutes*, Yorkshire 1905 Committee, 23 July 1908, Brotherton Library (BL), Leeds. Foster Brady (1859–1944), resident at Woodbrooke during 1907/8, was remembered as 'in [the] truest sense evangelical'. He served as Assistant Secretary and later Field Secretary to the Yorkshire 1905 Committee before moving to London in 1921. See entry, *DQB*, LSF.

[124] G. C. to J. R. H., 2 April 1909 and to Joshua Rowntree, 13 Feb. 1909, GCP, WL.

[125] G. C. to Mr [Isaac] Braithwaite, 14 June 1909, GCP, WL.

HISTORY AND QUAKER RENAISSANCE

Between 1909 and 1921 William Charles Braithwaite and Rufus Jones produced the seven volumes of the so-called Rowntree Series.[126] Except for the broad refutation of Rufus Jones' fixing of the origins of Quakerism in continental mysticism,[127] the series retained its reputation for solid archival scholarship and as the necessary starting place for serious study of Quakerism. Sponsored and financed through a Charitable Trust established by Joseph Rowntree, both the name of the series and the books that comprise it have their roots in the life and work of John Wilhelm Rowntree. In keeping with his vision, these works have not only made Quakerism available to generations of historians and general readers, they have also had an important influence on the evolution of London Yearly Meeting.

According to Rufus Jones, turn-of-the-century Friends knew surprisingly little about their church's past because they 'were not historical-minded and no historian had yet traced the slow transformations through which the Society of Friends had passed in two centuries'.[128] Jones argued, for example, that while most British and American Quakers paid homage to George Fox as their most prominent spiritual ancestor, many of these same Friends adhered to views that Fox had explicitly denounced because contemporary Quaker religious thinking was 'shot through with Calvinistic doctrine'.[129]

For his part, John William Rowntree, even before his meeting with Rufus Jones in 1897, had concluded that a key element to the

---

[126] Rufus M. Jones was overall editor of the series, originally published by Macmillan. Jones's contributions are *Studies in Mystical Religion* (London 1909); *Spiritual Reformers in the 16th and 17th Centuries* (London 1914); *The Quakers in the American Colonies* (London 1911), with Isaac Sharpless and Amelia M. Gummere; and *The Later Periods of Quakerism* (London 1921), 2 vols.; William Charles Braithwaite wrote *The Beginnings of Quakerism* (London 1912) and *The Second Period of Quakerism* (London 1919).

[127] In 1955 a new edition of W. C. Braithwaite's *The Beginnings of Quakerism* was published without Rufus Jones' original 'Introduction'. In a brief Foreword, L. Hugh Doncaster explained that recent studies on the roots of Quakerism had placed its origins 'in a rather different light', p. vii. For further discussion see below, 258.

[128] Jones, *Middle Years*, 56–7. Also see Dr Seth Mills, 'Friends in History, and the Need of a Written History of Friends', *AF*, 18 Sept. 1894, 199–200, who made the same point.

[129] Jones, *Middle Years*, 56–7. Obviously, the success of the evangelical revival and holiness renewal movements in America had led Friends there to embrace 'Calvinistic doctrine' more readily than in Britain.

revitalization of the Society of Friends was in rescuing Quaker history from the obscurantism and neglect in which it had languished for nearly two centuries. Rowntree was convinced that the prevailing lack of solid historical knowledge, especially among young Friends, represented one of the gravest dangers to survival of the Society as a vital religious community. He believed that the rising generation had broken more completely with the ideas and attitudes of their fathers and grandfathers than any previous body of Friends. But if these young people rejected the evangelical tradition, the only one most of them had been taught, what else was there in a Quaker communion, seemingly sunk into 'a torpor of undeveloped intellectual power', to hold their allegiance?[130] There was, he surmised, the glorious history of their Society: 'the voice of God, many tongued', as he once described it in an effusive moment.[131] Rowntree was confident that a 'fresh and sound historical interpretation of the entire Quaker movement', incorporating the most up-to-date canons of historical research, could lead to a vibrant reclamation of the long-submerged spiritual heritage of Quakerism. No child 'educated in a Friends' school, should leave it . . . without at least a knowledge of the history, and of the broad underlying principles, of our religious Society'. Not only Friends but religious seekers everywhere awaited the inspiration of 'Quaker History . . . worked out, not simply with the view of presenting biographical sketches, and interesting historical data, but in order to bring out . . . "the practical, spiritual, and non-sacerdotal aspects of Divine truth" in relation to individual and national life'.[132]

Rufus Jones' first contribution to the campaign for historical enlightenment, *A Dynamic Faith* (1901), was published shortly after his year at Harvard. This was followed three years later by *Social Law in the Spiritual World*, which was dedicated to John Wilhelm Rowntree. Neither book made much impact in Britain. Indeed, the latter was so disdainfully treated in *The Friend*

---

[130] J. W. R., 'The Present Position of Thought', *Essays and Addresses*, 237, 240. Also see Amelia Mott Gummere, 'The Early Quakers and Parental Education', *PDP*, 5/50 (Sept. 1902), 284.

[131] J. W. R., 'God in Christ', *Essays and Addresses*, 279.

[132] Jones, *Life in College*, 195; J. W. R., 'Problem of a Free Ministry', *Essays and Addresses*, 126, 130–31; and 'Present Position', ibid., 249.

Fig. 6 Rufus M. Jones, (1863–1948), c. 1920, American
Prophet of liberal Quakerism

that Edward Grubb characterized the review as 'beneath contempt'.[133]

Still, if Jones' early efforts were little noticed or appreciated by
British Friends of an evangelical bent, there were evangelicals who
also saw historical research as a means to renewal and reconciliation. A vital contributor to the revival of Quaker history during
the Edwardian period was Norman Penney (1858–1933). Deeply
influenced by the American holiness movement, Penney stood at
the opposite end of the theological spectrum from Rufus Jones,
J. W. Rowntree and their allies. Before he was appointed as the
first paid full-time librarian for London Yearly Meeting, Penney
had spent sixteen years working as a Home Missioner. As librarian,
he was assigned the formidable task of organizing a research

---

[133] The anonymous reviewer in *TF*, 16 Dec. 1904, 829, noted that the 'world awaits a
competent expounder of the theme'. [emphasis added] See E. Grubb to R. M. J., 12 Jan. 1905,
Box 5, RMJP. Also see Holdsworth, 'Rufus Jones Reconsidered', 9–30.

collection which had gathered dust at Devonshire House, the Society's headquarters in south London, since the Great Fire of 1666.[134] Because Norman Penney's tenure as librarian was concurrent with perhaps the first serious revival of interest in Quaker history for other than antiquarian purposes, a number of researchers, working at Devonshire House, in local Quaker meeting records and in other public and private collections, made significant contributions to the systematic gathering and cataloguing of Quaker historical documents. Encouraged by Isaac Sharp (1847–1917), Recording Clerk of London Yearly Meeting for nearly thirty years (1890–1917), Penney had, from the bicentennial of George Fox's death in 1891, begun to organize manuscript materials at Devonshire House. These documents, together with other newly uncovered documents, would become the basis for Penney's seminal edition of the writings of *The First Publishers of the Truth* (1907), a book whose impact one Quaker historian calls 'still staggering'. Without the pioneering work of Norman Penney and his associates, the early history of the Society might have continued to languish in obscurity awaiting studies based on solid archival evidence.[135]

Penney was also a founding member of the Friends' Historical Society (FHS), established in 1903 'for promoting research in a field hitherto but imperfectly worked', just at the time that John Wilhelm Rowntree was becoming seriously involved in his projected History of Quakerism.[136] Nearly every important leader of the modern renewal movement was listed among the original members of the Friends Historical Society. In the spring of 1904, the second issue of the Society's *Journal* published a notice of J. W. Rowntree's intention 'to trace the development of Quaker thought and organization . . . with a view to the practical bearing upon current Quaker problems'.[137]

The founding of the Friends Historical Society was a significant expression of the new spirit sweeping through London Yearly Meeting. Accordingly, Joseph Bevan Braithwaite's 'Journal', reflecting perhaps his heightened sense of losing control of affairs

[134] Punshon, *Portrait in Grey*, 223–4 and T. Edmund Harvey, 'Looking Back', 56–7, 57 n.
[135] Punshon, *Portrait in Grey*, 224 and interview with John Nickalls, Welwyn Garden City, August 1986. Nickalls was appointed as Norman Penney's assistant after the First World War and replaced him as Librarian when the headquarters of London Yearly Meeting moved to Friends' House in 1925.
[136] 'Forward', *JFHS*, 1/1 (1903), 1.   [137] Ibid., 1/2 (May 1904), 50.

he had directed for so long, expressed anxiety about this latest innovation. The early literature of Quakerism, Braithwaite noted, was produced in 'an age of religious excitement . . . scarcely paralleled either before or since'. He feared that members of the Historical Society might not show sufficient wisdom and caution to prevent misunderstanding and mischief. At the same time, J. B. Braithwaite was brooding over possible harm from historical revelations, John Wilhelm Rowntree wrote to Norman Penney seeking to borrow 'a series of Reports . . . asked for by Yearly Mtg. at the beginning of the 18th century . . . on the first bringing forth of truth to their respective districts'. Neave Brayshaw had stumbled upon these papers at Devonshire House and Rowntree believed they would prove invaluable in recording 'the very beginning of Friends all up and down the country'.[138]

Unlike J. B. Braithwaite, John Wilhelm and his associates were not concerned about where historical research might lead them. Because they were convinced that a balanced and meticulous history of Quakerism could only enhance their Society's role in the Christian community, they were preoccupied with the desire to pursue every source that would illuminate the 'inner life' of Quakerism. Rowntree urged Friends to follow him into the 'pages of sprawling and faded writing . . . ' 'Do not be angry if they are dry . . . There is a fascination, hard to describe in these musty books, written by men who knew persecution, not by hearsay, but by experience; who perhaps saw and heard Fox, Dewsbury and Whitehead in the flesh, and who . . . were our spiritual ancestors . . . '[139]

John Wilhelm's own work began in earnest during the summer of 1903 on a trip to the United States, where he managed, with the aid of Haverford College librarian Allen Thomas, to acquire 200 essential volumes. As he told Norman Penney, even though his thinking was still in a 'crude raw state', he was anxious to embark on his project.[140] Within a month, however, Rowntree's work was interrupted by a physical setback, 'unpleasant heart symptoms,

---

[138] J. B. Braithwaite, 'Journal', 10 Sept. 1903, IV, MS Vol. S, 293–6, L.S.F. and J. W. R. to Norman Penney, 21 Oct. 1903, Box 4, RMJP. Also see Punshon, *Portrait in Grey*, 224.

[139] J. W. R., 'The Rise of Quakerism in Yorkshire', *Essays and Addresses*, 43–4.

[140] J. W. R. to Norman Penney (copy), 3 July 1903, Box 4, RMJP. Rowntree personally collected nearly 2,000 volumes and pamphlets for his history, see *Essays and Addresses*, p. xxxvii and A. Neave Brayshaw, 'J. W. Rowntree Biographical Notes', *TF*, 17 March 1905, 165.

threatening angina pectoris'. This illness, in turn, seems to have induced a fit of depression which settled on him 'with the blackness of night'. Still, by the end of the year, after a rest-cure in Switzerland, he was back at his desk, and with the aid of a newly acquired secretary, finding 'queer things' but 'making headway'.[141]

Throughout the first nine months of 1904, Rowntree warmed to his work, corresponding with Quaker scholars for advice and approval. 'My desire', he informed one of these, 'is to strip my mind as far as possible of all prejudice and to examine the past in a scientific and impartial study, not an *ex parte* statement representing one school or another.'[142] In late July he confessed to Rufus Jones that he had 'got so closely absorbed in my Quaker History that I am finding it increasingly difficult to give time or thought to the mere outer world'.[143]

John Wilhelm expected to spend ten years at research and writing before his study would be ready for publication—a legitimate prospect for most men of thirty-five. But, in fact, these few months in 1904 were the only period of sustained historical work he was to be allowed. Fortunately, his labours did reach some fruition because of a promise to deliver a series of lectures on 'The Rise of Quakerism in Yorkshire' to a Summer School at Kirbymoorside in September 1904. Preserved and printed, these lectures provide the sole material for a critical assessment of Rowntree's skill and insight as a historian.[144]

Not surprisingly, the Yorkshire lectures at times reflect the enthusiasm and naïvety of the newly initiated, but their defects do not obscure Rowntree's literary ability, his historical imagination or his powerful sense of mission. His absorption in the words and deeds of early Friends convinced him more than ever of the depth of their spiritual power, the courage of their relentless practice and, most significantly, the soundness of their saving

---

[141] J. W. R. to R. M. J., 11 Aug., 28 Sep. and 4 Dec. 1903, Box 4, RMJP. Rowntree's secretary was Emily Jane Hart, whom he described as 'a cultured Church woman . . . who brings the invaluable criticism of an interested & valuable outsider to bear on the work'. J. W. R. to R. M. J., 22 Jan. 1904, ibid. Emily Hart would later also provide assistance to W. C. Braithwaite when he took over the history project.

[142] J. W. R. to Fielden Thorp (copy), 20 Jan. 1904, and J. W. R. to William Tallack, 28 Oct. 1903, Box 4, RMJP.

[143] J. W. R. to R. M. J., 27 July 1904, ibid.

[144] Jones, *John Wilhelm Rowntree*, [14] and J. W. R., 'The Rise of Quakerism in Yorkshire', in *Essays and Addresses*, 3–76.

message—not simply to the seventeenth century but to seeking, striving humanity of every place and time. First and foremost, his historical work gave him a fresh appreciation of the religious insight of George Fox. Fox's genius, Rowntree told Rufus Jones, was made manifest, not in the originality of his conception of Divine guidance (the Inward Light was not a new idea), but in the logical way that he worked out his beliefs as regards social attitudes and church organization. Just as important, Rowntree felt, was the escape Fox offered from the 'terrible shadow of predestination'. The 'sunlight and fragrance of the best Quaker character', he said, 'would have been impossible but for this emancipation'.[145]

Rowntree's enthusiasm for 'Fox's day', when 'the molten metal had not congealed', did not, however, blunt his criticism of subsequent developments.

Those were great days of high courage, noble sacrifice and rich fruit. It is hard to come back to the present without discouragement, for the promise of the past has failed. But there is still the future.... We can afford to study the history of the great decline and to take its lessons to heart, because we have hope in the future and faith in the great renewal.[146]

In the early years, Rowntree noted, the life of Friends was in the open. They would not do hat honour; they would not swear oaths; they would not meet in secret; they would not fight. 'It was impossible to ignore the Quaker because he would not be ignored.' But, by the same token, it was impossible, 'to whitewash eighteenth-century Quakerism' for as it progressed,

the life that was in the open is in secret. Timidly the Quaker peeps over his hedge of prickly cactus, willing that his plain coat of sleek broadcloth should testify for simplicity, but loath indeed to take it off, like the Methodist, and preach to a storming crowd at the street corner. He is . . . ponderous in the sobriety of his language and the dullness of his

---

[145] J. W. R. to R. M. J., 28 Sept. 1903, Box 4, RMJP; Thompson, 'John Wilhelm Rowntree', 262–66; and J. W. R. 'Rise of Quakerism', 69.
[146] J. W. R., 'Rise of Quakerism', 40, 43, 61.

intellect. His culture is narrow, his outlook small; his dinners are good, and his worship somnolent.[147]

Rowntree's survey was kinder to early evangelical Friends; they had, after all, roused Quakerism from a century of slumber. Still, he blamed Gurneyites for their too frequent rejection of 'humane learning' which had 'worked incalculable mischief throughout the Society'. Evangelicals had accomplished the necessary repudiation of quietism and reawakened the vigour of Quaker spirit, but in their zeal to ensure that soundness remained within the narrow confines of scriptural infallibility, they had diminished or abandoned most of the unique aspects of Quakerism that had caught and held the first Friends. The result, he said, could best be summarized in the words of Thomas Hancock's critique of mid-Victorian Friends: 'In 1658 there was not a Quaker living who did not believe Quakerism to be the one only true church of God. In 1858 there is not a Quaker living who does believe it.'[148]

Despite his discovery of much that was 'sad and gloomy' in the first two centuries of the Society's existence, Rowntree scorned the idea that Quakerism was 'unsuited to the masses' or that its message had been assimilated by larger, more popular churches. His last Yorkshire lecture concluded with a ringing declaration of the mission of his historical and spiritual quests:

Quakerism absorbed? . . . No! . . . There is room yet for the teaching of the Inward Light, for the witness of a living God, for a reinterpretation of the Christ in lives that shall convict the careless, [and] language that shall convince the doubting . . . There is room yet for a fellowship, all-inclusive in its tender sympathy, drawn close in the loving bondage of sincerity and truth, for the noble simplicity of life and manners . . . for a freedom that scorns the flummeries of rank . . . because it knows the worth of manhood and loves the privilege of friendship . . . Climb Pendle Hill with Fox and see once more his vision—'a great people to be gathered' . . . and in the spirit of his message face the future that lies before you.[149]

---

[147] J. W. R., 'Rise of Quakerism', 59, 62–3, 65, and 'The Outlook', *PDP* (1899), 9.

[148] The quotation is from Hancock's *Peculium*, second prize winner in the 1859 essay contest on the reasons for the decline of Quakerism. J. W. R., 'Rise of Quakerism', 66, 73.

[149] J. W. R., 'Rise of Quakerism', 59, 73, 75–6. Also see Thompson, 'John Wilhelm Rowntree', 267–8.

Fresh and confident from the success of his Yorkshire lectures, John Wilhelm sailed for America in late February 1905. For him, the future of Quakerism seemed as hopeful as the recent past had been stormy. As Rufus Jones recalled: 'Every dream was coming true. His impact on the youth of the Society of Friends was everywhere in evidence. It seemed as though a new Epoch was dawning.' Then, suddenly, in mid-Atlantic Rowntree was stricken with pneumonia. After several days drifting in and out of consciousness, he died on 9 March 1905 in a New York hospital. Jones, who had met the ship and was with his friend when he died, remembered how pitiful it was 'to hear him dwell in the delirium of fever, upon the great literary plan of his life'. John Wilhelm Rowntree was buried, and remains, in the graveyard of Haverford Friends Meeting House.[150]

Rowntree's death profoundly shook the British Society of Friends. His cousin Arnold remarked that no single event had 'moved the Society, as John's death has done, for 200 years'.[151] Edward Grubb called Rowntree's passing 'the bitterest sorrow I have ever had to bear'; another British Friend published a long elegiac poem depicting John Wilhelm as 'the pure boy knight... our Gallahad'.[152] Others, to greater purpose, called upon his mourners, especially those 'possessing the historical spirit', to set themselves to completing the sort of history that John Wilhelm had hoped would 'weld and unify... the Quaker faith... and... generate throughout the Society new life and vigour'.[153]

Rowntree's immediate family were the first to respond to his death in this positive sense. Within a few days, his father Joseph, his brother Seebohm and his wife Constance set about erecting appropriate memorials. First, they arranged for the collection and publication of his *Essays and Addresses*, to be edited by his cousin Joshua; then they began to sound out Quaker scholars

---

[150] Jones, *John Wilhelm Rowntree*, [15] and 'John Wilhelm Rowntree', *TF*, 31 March 1905, 198.

[151] Arnold Rowntree to R. M. J., 4 April 1905, Box 5, RMJP. Rowntree was quoting his uncle Joshua Rowntree. Also see Henry Bryan Binns to R. M. J., 16 April 1905, ibid.

[152] Edward Grubb to R. M. J., 21 March 1905, ibid., and I. A. R., 'In Memoriam, John Wilhelm Rowntree—a Poem', *Friends Intelligencer*, 62/13 (1 April 1905), 193.

[153] 'John Wilhelm Rowntree', *FQE*, 39/154 (April 1905), 128–31. Also see obituary for J. W. R. in *JFHS*, 2/2 (April 1905), 46; George H. Newman (*FQE* editor) to R. M. J., 15 July 1907; and Edward Grubb to R. M. J., 12 Jan. 1906, Box 5, RMJP.

who might make a contribution to the completion of his history.[154]

At Scalby in early September 1905, members of the Rowntree family met with Rufus Jones, William C. Braithwaite, Neave Brayshaw and others to discuss the Quaker History project. What emerged from this conference was a plan to combine Jones's proposed study of European mysticism as well as a history of Friends in America with John Wilhelm's projected chronicle of British Quakerism to form a multi-volume series named in his memory.[155] Several of those at the Scalby meeting indicated willingness to help, but, in the end, the bulk of the work fell to Jones as overall editor and to William Charles Braithwaite. For the next sixteen years Jones and Braithwaite gave substantial time from already fully-occupied lives to ensure the fulfillment of John Wilhelm's dream.

The two authors co-ordinated their efforts in a way that was both refreshing in their approach to the material and fascinating for the ghost that hovered over each step they took. In resolving questions that arose as to how a particular topic should be handled, Braithwaite and Jones always referred to the outline and notes that Rowntree had left, but they did not feel obliged to follow slavishly after John Wilhelm's largely undigested plan. Braithwaite altered many of the major topics Rowntree had proposed and eliminated others as unsuitable to a comprehensive history of early Friends.[156] From their first tentative feeling out of problems to their later, more confident, consideration of the evidence, the correspondence between Jones and Braithwaite offers a model of industry, honesty, and expanding historical insight.

Braithwaite set the tone by setting out a series of troublesome questions with which he felt they would have to deal:

1) Why had George Fox 'allowed himself to be treated in private letters ... from Margaret] F[ell] and others as a Messiah ... ' much as James Naylor had done publicly?

---

[154] Joseph Rowntree to R. M. J., 29 March and 28 April 1905; B. Seebohm Rowntree to R. M. J., 1 June 1905; and Constance Rowntree to R. M. J., 31 March 1905, Box 5, ibid.

[155] Jones, *Middle-Years*, 85–7 and Vining, *Friends of Life*, 115–17.

[156] Joseph Rowntree to R. M. J., 14 Sept. 1905, Box 5, RMJP. There is a typewritten copy of J. W. R's five-page outline entitled 'A Study of the Development of Quaker Thought and Practice', Box 4, ibid.

2) How far did the doctrine of perfection lead early Friends to 'sublime assurance' and how far into 'exaggeration'?

3) To what degree was the intolerant denunciation of others by early Quakers justified; and to what degree was it an actual cause of persecution?

4) How should 'the miraculous or quasi-miraculous manifestations which attended some of the first publishers...' be treated?[157]

Braithwaite's own response was that he could 'see nothing... but careful, detailed, historical work if the rise of Quakerism is to be correctly delineated on a correct background'. As he perused the manuscripts and letters assembled at Devonshire House, Braithwaite seemed genuinely astonished by the fact that the significance of these sources was 'only apparent to a person who is already in possession of other material into which the new piece of information fits. It is like rebuilding structure out of dilapidated ruins.'[158] 'Possibly J[oh]n Wilhelm had historical discussion a good deal in mind, but I am sure he would have made sure of his groundwork of facts first and would have given us a vivid history illuminated by historical discussion and not subordinated to it.' A really adequate history of the early movement, Braithwaite said, could only be worked out from 'contemporary sources of the best kind... involving a great deal of detailed co-ordination of dates & facts but resulting in a vivid & in many respects fresh presentation...'[159]

John Wilhelm would also probably have applauded Braithwaite's refusal to tone down 'the extravagances of the movement' (the fact, for example, that some early Friends, male and female, demonstrated their rejection of creaturely things by parading naked through northern English towns). Joseph Rowntree, for one, was concerned lest the 'ordinary reader... fasten upon these and let them bulk too large in his mind...' confusing them perhaps with libertine Ranter eroticism. But neither Braithwaite nor Jones was deterred; they published the story of early Friends, 'going naked' and all.[160]

---

[157] W. C. B. to R. M. J., 12 Nov. 1905, Box 5, RMJP.

[158] W. C. B. to R. M. J., 6 Feb. 1906, Box 5 and 5 Dec. 1909, Box 6, ibid.

[159] W. C. B. to R. M. J., 6 Feb. 1906, Box 5 and 10 Jan. 1908, Box 6, ibid.

[160] Joseph Rowntree to R. M. J., 29 Aug. 1907, Box 5, ibid. For the early Quaker practice of 'going naked as a sign', see Braithwaite, *Beginnings of Quakerism*, 148–151, 158

Despite cautious concerns, which he never pressed beyond query, Joseph Rowntree's contribution was also crucial. Having organized the Rowntree Charitable Trust to subsidize the publication of the Series, he consistently urged the authors to 'spare no expense' in ensuring that the History would be 'a standard work broadly based upon full knowledge'.[161] The production of the Quaker history series also revealed Quaker access to élite elements of Edwardian society. When Rufus Jones expressed the wish that a draft chapter on John Wycliffe and the Lollards could be read by G. M. Trevelyan, recently acclaimed for his study of *England in the Age of Wycliffe* (1899), Joseph Rowntree replied that 'Seebohm knows Charles Trevelyan the M. P. (I forget the historian's first name) . . . and Seebohm tells me . . . that he would have no difficulty in asking him to pass on this request to his brother, the historian.'[162]

Given the depth of his personal, intellectual, and spiritual friendship with John Wilhelm Rowntree, it seems fitting that Rufus Jones should have made the greatest contribution of time and effort to the completion of the Quaker history series. After his friend died in his arms, Jones said, 'his life in some sense went into mine', and he vowed to work 'in every way I could . . . toward the fulfillment of his interrupted plans'.[163] Jones discharged this pledge by producing five volumes of the series as well as providing a long introduction to Braithwaite's *Beginnings of Quakerism* which incorporated his fixing of the roots of primitive Quaker thought and action in the work of continental mysticism. Jones believed that this interpretation would provide a link between volumes of the series and 'to bring home to Friends and others the vital lessons of the history'.[164]

where he made clear that this practice 'was not disowned by Quaker leaders'. Also see Kenneth L. Carroll, 'Early Quakers and "Going Naked as a Sign"', *Quaker History* 67/2 (Autumn 1978), 69–87.

[161] Joseph Rowntree to R. M. J., 30 July 1907, Box 5 and 28 April 1910, Box 6, RMJP. For the origins and functioning of the Rowntree Charitable Trust, see Joseph Rowntree to R. M. J., 29 March and 14 Sept. 1905, Box 5, ibid. Joseph Rowntree noted that while he was 'responsible for all expenses . . . if there is any profit it will, of course, go to you'. Rowntree to R. M. J., 3 Sept. 1908, ibid.

[162] Joseph Rowntree to R. M. J., 18 May 1908, ibid. It is not clear if G. M. Trevelyan actually read Jones' section on Wycliffe.

[163] Rufus M. Jones, *A Way of Life and Service* (Oberlin, Ohio 1939), 1–2; *Studies in Mystical Religion* (London 1909), v–vi; and *Middle Years*, 188–191.

[164] Joseph Rowntree to R. M. J., 15 June 1908, Box 6, RMJP. After the publication of Jones' first volume *Studies in Mystical Religion* (1909), he was contacted by Theodor Sippell of

Immediately before the publication of *The Beginnings of Quaker-ism*, Braithwaite told Jones that he thought the introduction 'quite admirable' and 'of great service in giving coherence to the study' as well as illuminating 'the main lesson that our Quakerism of today needs to learn'.[165] Still, it is interesting to note, in light of subsequent challenges to Jones's exegesis, a passage in one of Braithwaite's letters written well before the Introduction was set out: 'The inward light itself [was?] the artificer of the Society of Friends though of necessity coloured by the Puritan medium thro' which it was transmitted for the children of Light remained in many things the children of their age.'[166] When subsequent editions of Braithwaite's volumes were issued (in 1955 and 1961) Jones's introduction was omitted on the ground that the views represented therein had been largely refuted by subsequent scholarship.[167] Still, as one commentator noted, contemporary Friends 'cannot understand who we are unless . . . we realize how much the way we put things today is colored by our reaction to Rufus Jones and to his generation'.[168]

Of that generation, John Wilhelm Rowntree has been acknowledged as the most important representative. Not only did he give

the University of Marburg in Germany who told Jones that he had independently reached conclusions supporting Jones' ideas on the origin of Quakerism. See Sippell to R. M. J., 27 Feb., 10 March, 21 July, and 17 Dec. 1910 and Joseph Rowntree to R. M. J., 28 April and 7 July 1910, noting Rowntree's willingness to provide financial support for Sippell's work if Jones thought it important. Jones' daughter, Mary Hoxie, believes that Sippell's endorsement was a great boost to her father's conviction that he had correctly identified the roots of Quakerism. Interview with Mary Hoxie Jones, Haverford, Pa., August 1983.

[165] W. C. B. to R. M. J., 26 March 1911, Box 7, ibid.

[166] W. C. B. to R. M. J., 10 Jan. 1908, Box 6, ibid.

[167] See L. Hugh Doncaster's 'Forward' to the second edition of *The Beginnings of Quakerism*, p.vii. As noted above, most modern interpreters of the origins of Quakerism depict early Children of the Light as offspring of the Puritan Movement. See Geoffrey Nuttall, *The Holy Spirit in Puritan Faith and Experience* (Oxford 1996) Alan Simpson, *Puritanism in Old and New England* (Chicago, 1955); and Hugh Barbour, *The Quakers in Puritan England* (New Haven, 1964), p.ix. 260–1. A recent study supporting Jones' view is Richard Bailey, *New Light on George Fox and Early Quakerism* (San Francisco 1992), Chapter I. Other scholars who defend the usefulness of Jones' interpretation are Melvin B. Endy, Jr., 'The Interpretation of Quakerism: Rufus Jones and His Critics', *Quaker History* 70/1 (Spring, 1981), 21, and Donald F. Durnbaugh, 'Baptists and Quakers—Left Wing Puritans?' ibid. 62/2 (Autumn, 1973), 67–82.

[168] Chris Downing, 'Quakerism and the Historical Interpretation of Religion', *Quaker Religious Thought* 3/2 (Autumn, 1961), 4. H. Larry Ingle's thoughtful and provocative Presidential address to the Friends Historical Society, 'The Future of Quaker History', provides, among other things, an enlightening discussion on current views of the origins of Quakerism, *JFHS*, 58/1 (1997), especially 2–7.

life to the implementation of practical reforms that allowed British Quakerism to escape from two centuries in a religious backwater, but his vision of the revitalizing effects of a 'fresh and sound' approach to Quaker history also inspired one of the most important intellectual achievements among Friends since the seventeenth century. Questions about what the Rowntree histories might have been if John Wilhelm had lived or what his leadership might have contributed to Edwardian Quakerism or to Quaker resistance during the First World War are, however intriguing, irrelevant. Suffice to say that John Wilhelm Rowntree's influence did not cease with his death and that his presence was distinctly felt among Friends of the succeeding generation. On the fiftieth anniversary of J. W. R.'s death, Maurice Creasey, Director of Studies at Wood-brooke, noted: 'It can be truthfully said that such stability and sense of direction and points of growth as the Society has possessed in recent years, are due in large measure to the influence and teaching and guidance of the Friends whom John Wilhelm Rowntree inspired.'[169]

---

[169] Creasey, *Next Fifty Years*, 22. After the end of the First World War, Wilfrid Littleboy (1885–1979), a future Clerk of London Yearly Meeting (1934–42), still jailed as an absolutist conscientious objector, wrote that J. W. Rowntree was 'wonderfully a spiritual father to many of us'. Wilfrid E. Littleboy to his parents, 17 Dec. 1918, Littleboy Papers seem through the courtesy of W. E. Littleboy's daughter Margaret E. Nash.

6

'Kindly Silence the Men a Bit': Women in the Society of Friends, 1860–1914

FROM HELPSMEET TO SMOTHERED CRY

Among George Fox's most radical teachings was his conviction that Christ incarnate, bringing the gift of spiritual indwelling to all, had restored women to their original place of equality with men.

For man and woman were helpsmeet, in the image of God and in righteousness and holiness . . . before they fell . . . after the Fall, in the transgression, the man was to rule over his wife. But, in the restoration by Christ, into the image of God and His righteousness and holiness again . . . they are helpsmeet, man and woman, as they were . . . before the Fall.[1]

Accordingly, women were drawn to early Friends in considerable numbers and some of them gained prominence among Fox's earliest preacher-followers. While rejecting the ministrations of hireling priests, Quakers had always maintained that Christian ministry was not a male preserve but was rather based on a diversity of God-given gifts to be shared by all who composed the universal priesthood of believers. Thus, according to their gifts, male and female Friends shared equally in the ministry of the word. At least a dozen women were among the so-called 'Valiant Sixty' who began Quaker missionary activities in the north of England during the

---

[1] Quoted in Braithwaite, *Second Period*, 273. Phyllis Mack, 'Gender and Spirituality in Early English Quakerism, 1650–1665', in *Witnesses for Change: Quaker Women Over Three Centuries*, edited by Elisabeth Potts Brown and Susan Mosher Stuard (New Brunswick and London 1990), 39 notes: 'A primary tenet of early Quakerism was that the hierarchical character of gender relationships, indeed of all social relationships, was a product of human sinfulness, an outcome of the original Fall from Grace.'

1650s.[2] Among these were Elizabeth Hooton, recognized as Quakerism's first female preacher, and Margaret Fell, who later married George Fox, and who emerges from the recent work of Bonnelyn Young Kunze as something like the co-founder of the Society of Friends.[3] In 1666 Margaret Fell wrote a tract entitled *Women's Speaking Justified . . .* which, Kunze notes, 'defiantly reassessed the Pauline injunctions against women speaking in Church'. According to Kunze, Fell's activities as well as her strong influence on George Fox were important reasons why 'women . . . approached equality in the spiritual sphere in early Quakerism, probably to a greater extent than in other sectarian movements of the [seventeenth] century'.[4]

But if Quaker women did, in fact, have something like spiritual equality in worship and ministry, this never carried over into the business of directing the day-to-day affairs of their Religious Society. During the 1670s both London Yearly Meeting, as it was developing into the chief legislative organ of British Quakerism, and Meeting for Sufferings, as the working executive committee, were fashioned as exclusively male organizations. After their marriage in 1669, both George Fox and Margaret Fell urged the setting up of separate women's monthly meetings with special concern for charitable activities.[5] This was apparently done in most places,

---

[2] Ernest E. Taylor, *The Valiant Sixty* (London 1947), 43–4. Also see Hugh Barbour, 'Quaker Prophetesses and Mothers of Israel', in *Seeking the Light*, edited by J. William Frost and John M. Moore (Wallingford, Pa. 1986), 41–60; Janet Scott, 'Women in the Society of Friends', in *A Quaker Miscellany* 125–31; and Mack, 'Gender and Spirituality', 33, 58n. who has traced the names of over 250 female preachers and writers between 1650–60. One of early Quakerism's severest critics, John Bunyan, put Friends in the same category as Ranters because both countenanced female preachers. See Bunyan, *Works*, I, 21 & II, 664. Baptists and other gathered churches also had female ministers.

[3] Bonnelyn Young Kunze, ' "Walking in Ye Gospel Order" '. Margaret Fell and the Establishment of Women's Meetings', paper read at the seventeenth Berkshire Conference on the History of Women and ' "Poore and in Necessity": Margaret Fell and Quaker Female Philanthropy in Northwest England in the late 17th Century', *Albion*, 21/4 (Winter 1989), 559–80. Cf. H. Larry Ingle, *First Among Friends*, 252–3, 345 n. who does not believe Kunze's evidence fully supports her assertions.

[4] Kunze, 'Gospel Order', 5, 11. An important study with valuable insights on the role of early Quaker women is Phyllis Mack, *Visionary Women: Ecstatic Prophecy in Seventeenth Century England* (Berkley 1992). Also see Scott, 'Women in the Society of Friends', 127 and Elaine C. Huber, ' "A Woman Must Not Speak": Quaker Women in the English Left Wing', in *Women of Spirit: Female Leadership in the Jewish and Christian Traditions*, edited by Rosemary Ruether and Eleanor McLaughlin (New York 1979), 153–81.

[5] Mary Jane Godlee, 'The Women's Yearly Meeting', in *London Yearly Meeting During 250 Years* (London 1919), 97 and Braithwaite, *Beginnings*, 341–2 and *Second Period*, 273–4. The

especially in the north of England. Sometime between 1675 and 1680, the Lancashire Meeting of Women Friends sent out a letter 'to be Dispersed abroad, among the Women's meetings every where' with the intent of justifying women's meetings, offering suggestions as to how they should be organized and defining tasks they might undertake.[6] George Fox himself had a hand in the formation of the Box Meeting in London, a body which, independent of any male control, dispensed aid to needy female Friends in London and Middlesex Quarterly Meeting and continues to this day.[7] Apparently, 'Fox's unremitting advocacy' for Women's Meeting's was considerably in advance of many of his co-religionists for it caused 'much bitterness' among early Friends. The idea of separating men and women's meetings was a major point of dispute in a separation of Westmoreland Friends during the 1670s under the leadership of John Wilkinson and John Story, who wished for women to meet with men but to remain silent.[8] Fox's obdurate response was to warn

all of you, that are against women's meetings . . . and say, 'you see no service for the women's meetings,' and oppose them, you are therein out of the power of God, and His Spirit live not in . . . Therefore, keep in the power, that ye may stand up for your liberty in Christ Jesus, males and females, heirs of him and of his gospel, and his order.[9]

In 1676 Fox wrote an 'Encouragement to all the Women's Meetings in the World', a tract of nearly a hundred pages encouraging the formation of Women's Meetings as 'in the Time of the Law

latest study is Margaret Hope Bacon, 'The Establishment of London Women's Yearly Meeting: A Transatlantic Concern', *JFHS*, 57/2 (1995), 151–65.

[6] 'From our Country women's meeting in Lancashire to be Dispersed abroad, among the Women's meetings every where', partially reprinted in the 'Introduction' to Brown and Stuard, *Witnesses for Change*, 25–8.

[7] See Irene L. Edwards, 'The Women Friends of London: The Two Weeks and Box Meetings', *JFHS*, 47/1 (Spring 1955), 3–21. Arnold Lloyd, *Quaker Social History* (London 1950), 109 notes that the Box Meeting was 'an independent body of women trustees, possessed of considerable funds and landed property and answerable to no man'. The Women's Two-Weeks Meeting, another exclusively female gathering in London, was established around the same time as the Box Meeting.

[8] Ingle, *First Among Friends*, 261–4 provides the first scholarly assessment of the Wilkinson-Story controversy since Braithwaite's, *Second Period*, 290–323.

[9] *The Journal of George Fox*, 2 vols. (8th edn. London 1901), II, 249–50.

and the time of the Gospel' and denouncing 'Selfish and Unholy Men [who] may seek to Discourage them'.[10]

Despite the efforts of Fox, Fell and others, however, the Pauline tradition was sustained in London Yearly Meeting, at least as regards the governing of church affairs. In the late seventeenth century women ministers in London began to meet with male ministers on Saturday to discuss which local meetings they should attend the next day, but in 1701 the Men's Morning Meeting of Ministers banned this embryonic gathering because, they said, female ministers spoke too long in meeting. '[i]t is a hurt to Truth for women Friends to take up too much time, as some do, in our public meetings, when several public and serviceable men Friends are present and are by them prevented in their serving... the women Friends should be tenderly cautioned against taking up too much time in our mixed public meetings'.[11]

Despite these setbacks, there were intermittent and unsuccessful attempts, especially encouraged by visiting American Friends,[12] to establish a parallel Women's Yearly Meeting. Women did continued to gather separately in conjunction with Morning Meeting and Yearly Meeting, but their deliberations were quietly ignored. The *Minutes* of the London Box Meeting contain a document dated February 1746 and signed by six female ministers asking consideration for a 'National Meeting for the women' to be held at the same time as the Men's Meeting and attended by two or more 'solid well-concerned women' from each Quarterly Meeting. There is no record of a reply to this plea.[13] A few years later York Women's Quarterly Meeting called attention to 'a noble spirited remnant of our sex' who might play a part in the 'needful reformation & Regulation of our Discipline'. Through the establishment of 'an Annual Women's Meeting', they noted, 'Quarterly and Monthly Meetings would be Strengthened and Encouraged in their faithful Endeavors...' While this effort also came to nought as regards a separate Women's Meeting, in 1754

---

[10] Braithwaite, *Second Period*, 314–15. Lloyd, *Quaker Social History*, 54 believed that one of Fox's major concerns for establishing Men's and Women's Meetings was 'strict enforcement of the marriage procedure'.

[11] Quoted in Braithwaite, *Second Period*, 287. Also see Lloyd, *Quaker Social History*, 118.

[12] See Bacon, 'Women's Yearly Meeting', 153–5.

[13] 'Considerations upon the service of the Discipline of the Church in general & the loss sustained by the want of extending the same amongst the women in particular', inserted in the Box Meeting *Minute Book*, 1748–60, LSF.

Yearly Meeting did exhort all subordinate meetings to establish women's meetings for discipline.[14] Also, from 1759 a *Minute Book* exclusively devoted to the annual gathering of women Friends was begun, but the Women's Meeting remained an unofficial body. During the following decade a proposal to create an officially recognized Women's Yearly Meeting was rejected on the ground that there was an insufficient number of women Friends 'of suitable abilities to carry on so weighty and important a work'.[15]

Finally, in 1784, again much influenced by the words and work of American Friends, a separate and official Women's Yearly Meeting was agreed to. It began to function the following year, although it was endowed with no legislative functions and took no part in establishing the rules of discipline. Indeed, the authority of the Women's Meeting was so limited as to preclude the possibility of its performing any meaningful role. As one male Friend noted a few years after the Women's Meeting was set up, the willingness of women Friends 'to be invested with greater power . . . was somewhat limited by the prudence of the Men'.[16]

So, while the Men's Meeting remained authoritative in Britain, female Friends continued to constitute a sizeable proportion of those who ministered in all Quaker meetings for worship as well as to be liberally represented among the elders and overseers who governed local meetings and supervised their ministry. As Mary Jane Godlee, who would become the first female Friend to preside over London Yearly Meeting, testified early in the twentieth century, the slow pace of meaningful female participation in the central governance of the British Society of Friends was 'very curious, and . . . rather painful to those . . . who may have believed in the theory that women Friends have always had an equal place with their brethren in the Church'.[17]

---

[14] Box Meeting, *Minutes*, 12 and 14 June 1753, LSF. Also see Bacon, 'Women's Yearly Meeting', 155–6 and Barclay, *Inner Life*, 528.

[15] Women's *Minutes*, 25 May 1766, LSF. Also see Bacon, 'Women's Yearly Meeting', 156 and Godlee, 'Women's Yearly Meeting', 103, 106–7. Braithwaite, *Second Period*, 286 suggested that women's want of business training precluded their admission to important executive bodies such as the Meeting for Sufferings, but this view is disputed by Lloyd, *Quaker Social History*, 107 f.

[16] Joseph Wood to William Williams, 1787, quoted by Godlee, 'Women's Yearly Meeting', 112. The circumstances of establishing the London Women's Yearly Meeting are fully discussed by Bacon, 'Women's Yearly Meeting', 158–60.

[17] Godlee, 'Women's Yearly Meeting', 93–4. Godlee became Acting Clerk of London Yearly Meeting in 1918, see Chapter 10 below.

Fig. 7   Mary Jane Godlee (1850–1930), first female Clerk in London
Yearly Meeting

When London Yearly Meeting introduced extensive revisions in
its *Christian Doctrine, Practice and Discipline* in 1861, women, who
comprised a clear majority of the Society's dwindling membership,
were recognized as having a distinctive role in the life of the
Society, but this role was clearly designated as subordinate.[18]
Women's standing under the new *Discipline* was summarized in
The Friend in July 1861: 'there is a share in the ministry of the word
for which the female mind is peculiarly adopted . . . [but] "the heat
and burden of the day" should devolve upon the stronger sex,
and . . . when it is otherwise the Church cannot be regarded as in its
healthy normal condition'.[19] Males did more than bear the heat,
they decided every important local and national question

---

[18] John S. Rowntree, 'Facts and Figures', *FQE*, I (1867), 569 and *Christian Doctrine,
Practice and Discipline* (London 1861), 156–8, 170.
[19] 'What is Quakerism?', *TF*, July 1861, 182.

without reference to women's meetings or women's opinions. As Elizabeth Isichei has noted in *Victorian Quakers*, female Friends, like most other middle-class Victorian women were 'shut out by . . . social disabilities . . . from any adequate exercise of [their] highest facilities'. A famous illustration of such shutting out was the 1840 British and Foreign Anti-Slavery Society Conference in London, where women were excluded from the proceedings largely through the influence of the male leaders of London Yearly Meeting.[20]

On the other hand, Quaker women were not denied access to the extensive in-house educational system in which Friends took considerable pride. The dozen or so boarding and day schools available for the female children of Friends provided educational opportunities unavailable to most Victorian women, even in the middle class. Probably the best of these, with regard to both teaching and curriculum, was the Mount School in York, established in 1831 and dedicated to 'the education of Friends' daughters in the middle walks of life'. 'The Mount' subsequently became a centre for training female teachers. By 1870 its 'simple, economical and unostentatious' curriculum had produced 140 teachers, over a third of whom still remained in the profession.[21] For all of that, the education of Quaker girls was generally inferior to that provided for males and, at least until the last quarter of the nineteenth century, Friends schools were uniformly cautious and generally drab. As John Reader pointed out in his Swarthmore lecture on Quaker schools: 'Friends must . . . divest themselves of the flattering notion that, as a body, they have been pioneers in education.'[22] Upper-middle class Quaker women taught at home by private tutors were doubtless the best educated females in the Society,

---

[20] Isichei, *Victorian Quakers*, 95 and Punshon, *Portrait in Grey*, 180. One of the those excluded was the American Hicksite Lucretia Mott who many believe was the real target of the Gurneyite Friends who pressed for the exclusion of women. In any case, Mott thereafter joined with fellow-excludee Elizabeth Cady Stanton to help forge the Women's Rights Movement in America. See Otelia Cromwell, *Lucretia Mott*, (Cambridge, Mass. 1958), 76–153 *passim*.

[21] 'Training of Teachers', *FQE*, IV (1870), 60–1.

[22] John Reader, *Of Schools and Schoolmasters: Some Thought on the Quaker Contribution to Education* (London 1979), 53. For recent insights on the education of Quaker women, see Kerri Allen and Alison MacKinnon, ' "Allowed and Expected to be educated and intelligent": the education of Quaker girls in nineteenth century England', *History of Education*, 27/4 (1998), 391–402.

although the possibilities for putting education to use was limited even for these children of privilege.[23]

The contrast between the Quaker ideal of full female equality and the realities of powerlessness for most Victorian Quaker women caused bitter resentment for some. One disabused, ex-Quaker woman accused her sisters of sitting in meeting week after week like so many 'images in marble' submissively accepting whatever unjust treatment, unrewarding duties or limited opportunities were meted out to them by righteous male leaders.[24] But, in fact, female Friends never suffered entirely in silence. Whether from a modicum of education or the residuum of spiritual equality, some Victorian Quaker women did publicly speak their minds. After the founding of the moderately progressive *Friends Quarterly Examiner* in 1867, they were provided increasing opportunity to do so. A steadily expanding commentary on the condition of Quaker women and women in general began to appear in the *Examiner*, although not all such articles dealt with the backward condition of female Friends. Some, indeed, were strong reaffirmations of the counsel of patience and long-suffering likely to appear in other Quaker publications.[25] One female author warned her sisters against complaining about their tiresome duties and humble places, lest they sink into spiritual self-seeking. 'The heart is deceitful', she reminded readers, and might lead the women astray unless they remembered that 'we are, each of us, in that situation wherein we may really serve the Lord better than any other; if otherwise, he would not have placed us there.'[26]

Many of the articles concerned with women in early issues of the *Friends Quarterly Examiner* touched upon the waning of the central role female Friends had always played in 'the ministry of the Word'. During Yearly Meeting in 1867, Sybil Jones, an influential American minister, had visited the Men's Meeting to decry a growing 'tendency towards a discouragement of women Friends devoting themselves to public ministry'. After hearing Sybil Jones, a number of male Friends gave 'testimony of the value of public

---

[23] Allen and MacKinnon, ' "Allowed and Expected" ', *passim*. For the general topic of Quaker education see W. A. C. Stewart, *Quakers and Education* (London 1953).

[24] *Mary Howitt, An Autobiography*, edited by Margaret Howitt, 2 vols. (London 1889), I, 203.

[25] See, for example, *TF*, January and March 1873, 15, 35, 202–3 and 226–8.

[26] Sarah S., 'On Doing the Will of God', *FQE*, II, (1868), 192–6.

spiritual gifts of women, for which they feared the education now received by the daughters of Friends is somewhat unfavorable'.[27] The fact that many women Friends were 'turning aside from the self-denying service' of public ministry was doubly unfortunate both because of special need for softening female influences in a society hardened by materialism and because female mission work had, historically, 'done more to reinstate the sex in its true position as "members of the body of Christ" than any abstract arguments that we might advocate'.[28]

In an article which ostensibly spoke to the question of female ministry, Louisa H. Stewart (1818–1918), widow of the proprietor of the *Edinburgh Review* and a pioneer suffragist, forcefully addressed a much broader range of social concerns.[29] It had, said Stewart, become 'the rule amongst various classes' that most women's lives were so limited in scope that they had ceased to believe themselves capable of anything useful and so wasted their abilities for fear of 'the charge of eccentricity, or the laugh of ridicule'. Even in the churches, she noted, women who attempted to assert themselves 'have only met with the humiliation of being virtually ignored' or with 'the imputation of incapacity'. This situation, she asserted, was a serious religious and social deficiency with which Quakerism should be vitally concerned. 'Friends as a body', Stewart declared, 'should be forward in all outward movements' and, given the fact that their Society afforded females 'so much liberty and training' in the ministry of the Gospel, Quaker women should be 'a medium of evangelization to the people at large' and especially 'amongst the shackled women . . . who are bound down by forms of opinion to the most contracted spheres of influence, and regarded less as helpsmeet for man than as his proteges or tools'. Because, Stewart concluded, not without a

---

[27] Alfred W. Bennett, 'The Yearly Meeting', *FQE*, July 1867, 374.

[28] Rebecca Thursfield, 'Home Mission Association of Women Friends', *FQE*, I (1867), 74–8; Alfred W. Bennett, 'The Yearly Meeting', ibid., 374; and 'On the Ministry of Women', ibid. II (1868), 301–3. Alfred Bennett was editor (1858–9) and the publisher (1859–67) of *The Friend*.

[29] Louisa Hopper was disowned in 1855 after she 'married out' to John Stewart, a non-Quaker widower with five children; however, when he died in 1862, *FQE* published a lengthy 'Memoir of John Stewart', I, (1867), 147–65. Louisa Stewart also published a book on female emancipation entitled *The Missing Law; or Women's Birthright* (London 1869). In old age she dictated her childhood memories to her granddaughter Evelyn Roberts who eventually published them as *Louisa, Memories of a Quaker Childhood* (London 1970).

touch of irony, 'the principles upon which the constitution of our Society is founded...shelter its female members from...[such] tyranny,' Quaker women should, 'for the world-wide interest of humanity', become missionaries who acted out their Christian principles 'in a spirit of sisterly readiness'.[30]

Louisa Stewart was obviously evangelizing about more than Gospel ministry. Other female writers followed her example in speaking directly to the ways in which Friends might aid in the setting aside of female disabilities. In the wake of J. S. Mill's unsuccessful attempt to insert the word 'person' in the place of 'man' in the franchise qualifications of the Second Reform Act (1867), an anonymous article under the *nom de plume* 'Vega', renewed the call for the enfranchisement of women on the same basis as men: 'Things will be very different when Englishwomen enter thoroughly into whatever concerns their country... when...the theory of "spiritual influence"...is used to inspire and promote, instead of to deaden, a true patriotism and public spirit in the men, and to strengthen their hands in intelligent sympathy.'[31]

If 'Vega' believed the pace of change to be moving too slowly, there were other Quakers who apparently surmised that British society in general and the Society of Friends in particular were about to be overborne by a dangerous wave of radical feminism. In 1870 J. Firth Bottomley (1842–89), a young Quaker solicitor active in London and national politics,[32] used the occasion of the passage of the Married Women's Property Act (1870) to call attention to what he perceived as a veritable 'onslaught upon the system of legal subordination', a circumstance that Bottomley, for one, viewed with considerable alarm. The *Friends Quarterly Examiner*, had given Mill's *The Subjection of Women* a somewhat mixed review,[33] but

---

[30] Louisa Stewart, 'A Word to Our Sisterhood', *FQE*, I (1867), 576–83, *passim*.

[31] 'Vega', 'Should Women Be Admitted to the Exercise of the Parliamentary Suffrage?', *FQE*, II (1868), 444–56.

[32] Joseph Firth Bottomley (1842–89) took the surname Firth in 1873 in accordance with the provisions of the will of his uncle, Joseph Firth. He was admitted to the bar that same year. As J. F. Bottomley Firth, he was Liberal MP for Chelsea, 1880–85 and for Dundee, 1888. A leading advocate of reforming London municipal government, Firth was elected Deputy-Chairman of the London County Council in 1888. He died while mountaineering in Switzerland. See John H. Nodal, *The Bibliography of Ackworth School* (Manchester 1889).

[33] Richard Westlake, 'The Social Position of Women', *FQE*, 3 (1869), 432–41. Westlake, whose brother William edited the journal, thought Mill set out the case for female equality with 'consummate ability' but also believed that he exaggerated the past ill-use of women.

Bottomley was in no way ambiguous about it. In a lengthy anti-feminist and, indeed, anti-female screed, he labelled Mill's work a 'text-book of the agitation' in which the author had confused equality with equity and thus encouraged the likes of radical feminist Lydia Becker[34] to call upon all forces in heaven and earth to bring 'the final end of that Philistine supremacy of the male minority which has lasted so long'.[35] What neither Mill nor Becker seemed to grasp, said Bottomley, was the historical and moral fact that 'the subjection of the female to the male is an universal law'. Bottomley's underlying message seemed to be a warning to male Friends that their women, traditionally the recipients of special spiritual privileges and superior educations, might on that account be persuaded 'to look somewhat kindly upon... the political enfranchisement of women', and thus to support a programme of agitation and legislation that would violate 'the immutable laws of nature'.[36]

There was no direct response, male or female, to Bottomley's harangue, but it may be assumed that his opinion was not unique among male Friends. Indeed, a conference on 'The State of the Society' was convened in 1873, and women were refused admission. This exclusion inspired John Bright's oldest daughter, Helen Priestman Bright Clark (1827–1940), to complain to *The Friend* that while Quaker women were often told of their fortunate state of equality, they could not help but be 'painfully conscious of the unreality of their meetings for discipline [where]... they have no voice in the management of affairs'. Her call for a general discussion of the status of women in the Society elicited no response.[37]

On the other hand, he had only praise for Mrs J. (Louisa) Stewart's *The Missing Law* and united with her in believing that equality of the sexes would 'be conducive to the well-being of mankind'.

[34] Lydia Becker (1827–90) formed the Manchester Women's Suffrage Committee in 1866. For Becker's pioneering work in the cause of female suffrage see Susan Kent, *Sex and Suffrage in Britain, 1860–1914* (Princeton, N.J. 1987), 185–8.

[35] J. Firth Bottomley, 'Public Questions: IV—The Position of Women', *FQE*, iv (1870), 560–65. Bottomley was correct in assuming that some Quaker women were being influenced by Lydia Becker. Mary Jane Hodgson responded enthusiastically to Becker's 'capital' lecture on women's rights in Manchester in 1871. Mary Hodgson to Elizabeth Green, 15 Nov. 1871, Portfolio A 60, LSF.

[36] Bottomley, 'Position of Women', 570–87 *passim*.

[37] *TF*, August 1873, 203. Sandra Holton and Margaret Allen have used the occasion of female exclusion from the 1873 Conference as the jumping off place for a discussion of 'Offices and Services: Women's Pursuit of Sexual Equality Within the Society of Friends, 1873–1907', *Quaker Studies (QS)*, 2/1 (Summer 1997), 1–29.

Still, strong-willed female Friends refused to relent in their efforts to improve the circumstances of women within their religious community. In 1874 Matilda Sturge compared the 'learned leisure' so precious to male Friends to 'the privilege of perpetual interruption . . . for numerous domestic incidents' granted to their wives, leaving the women with little or no time to pursue their own intellectual or artistic interests. 'What women really want', she noted in a subsequent essay, is 'free trade and fair play: the right . . . to do all they can and as well as they can, without fear or favour, or the necessity for self-assertion, which is always unpleasant and unbecoming'.[38] Hannah Maria Wigham (1828–1907) added that most unmarried Quaker females were trapped by the general acceptance of the idea that genteel women were 'lowering' themselves by working for money and thus apparently were only fit to be 'supernumeraries awaiting the chance of marriage.'

How are women to rid themselves of . . . this burden of enforced idleness . . . which lies like a nightmare on their lives, and shuts them out from much of the enjoyment and usefulness intended for them? . . . In the heart of many a fair young creature . . . there is a smothered cry for something higher and better, a longing to be of some use in the world. . . . This is . . . a real, actual misery . . . adding many a bitter drop in the brimming cup of the world's woe.[39]

By the end of the 1870s, the growing intensity of such female concerns may have precluded any bold male Friend from broadcasting the sort of public declaration of the continued necessity for female subordination so boldly set out by J. Firth Bottomley earlier in the decade. Still, Bottomley's view apparently retained vigorous life.[40] During the final quarter of the nineteenth century, London Yearly Meeting made no major and few minor concessions to the principle of female social or political equality.

---

[38] 'Spectator', 'View from Southampton' *FQE*, VIII (1874), 331–2 and Matilda Sturge, 'A Few More Words About Women', ibid. XI (1877), 469–76.

[39] Hannah Maria Wigham, 'Women's Work', *FQE*, XI (1877), 192–6.

[40] John Bright supported J. S. Mill's amendment to enfranchise women on the same basis as men, but by the early 1870s he had become convinced that female suffrage would be a setback for politically progressive forces throughout Great Britain. See John Bright to E. M. Sturge, 12 Dec. 1871, Bright MSS, Friends Historical Library, Swarthmore, quoted by Holton and Allen, 'Offices and Services', 7.

FRIENDS AND THE WOMAN QUESTION

When *A Reasonable Faith* was published in 1884, the thrust of its message was the need to replace outworn theological principles embedded in Quaker thought and practice with ideas and actions compatible with expanding human knowledge. On the question of women's role in the Society of Friends, however, this liberal Quaker classic was as silent as the latest edition of London Yearly Meeting's *Discipline*.[41] But, during the same Yearly Meeting in which the propriety of *A Reasonable Faith* was gravely debated by male Friends, recommendations for advancing the role of women in the affairs of their religious Society were being discussed in the Women's Meeting. A minute of Bristol and Somerset Women's Quarterly Meeting incorporated two proposals: 'That women Friends should be eligible as members of the Meeting for Sufferings' and that the Men's Yearly Meeting should bring subjects of mutual interest before the Women's Meeting 'for their consideration and approval'. These matters were discussed but, in the end, the counsel of patience prevailed and neither proposition was sent forward to the authoritative Yearly Meeting. Both languished for more than a decade before being revived.[42]

Other women were less inclined to patience. In a strident and uncompromising essay published by the *Friends Quarterly Examiner* in 1886, Jane E. Taylor's argued for a 'Women's Place in the Christian Economy' with all the urgency of a Hebrew prophet. Taylor began by contrasting the Old Testament centuries when women were 'degraded to a position of subjection by a tyranny that was as barbarous as it was unnatural', with the onset of the Christian era when the Redeemer Himself struck the 'key-note of her emancipation ... and the chords of sweet harmony that he began, vibrated loudly ... in the hearts of his faithful followers'. But, as the structure of the early Church grew increasingly rigid and patriarchal, its artificially nurtured male hierarchy 'sought to rob woman of her new given liberty' and the sexual harmony

---

[41] In 1883 a new edition of the *Christian Discipline of the Society of Friends* was issued without substantially altering the subordinate role assigned to women by the *Discipline* of 1861.

[42] See Vipont, *Quakerism*, 239; Godlee, 'London Yearly Meeting', 119; and Holton & Allen, 'Offices and Services', 13–14.

revived by Jesus 'gradually melted away into so faint an echo, that its notes were lost amidst the din of sectarian strife and the noisy upheaval of sacerdotal pride and usurpation'. For centuries, Jane Taylor asserted, church leaders, including by implication male leaders of the Society of Friends, had employed every scurrilous device, including the misuse of Holy Writ, 'in defence of errors and abuses that advance masculine interests, feed masculine pride and increase masculine power'. But although Satan—'true originator of women's subjection'—was attempting to aid in the sinister struggle to keep women in bondage, Taylor saw a new day at hand: 'the voice of Truth is once more...clearly heard...[and] Woman's emancipation from creature thraldom is plainly decreed by the loving father.' In such a time of renewal, Taylor concluded, the duty of all women was to prepare themselves for 'gentle, loving ministry' since 'the hideous evils that affect society will never be overthrown until feminine influence and power are fully exercised'.[43]

Fervent pleas for Quakerism to take its rightful place in the forefront of the movement to emancipate women aside, rearguard resistance to seating of females members in Meeting for Suffering was sustained for ten years after Jane Taylor thought she beheld the dawning light of equality. During the 1890s, while liberal theology and progressive opinion advanced steadily in the Quaker communion and female Friends continued to play an integral part in fostering this new agenda, the idea of expanding women's role in the affairs of the Society was all but lost in the shuffle. As one exasperated woman pointed out, when 'Women's Meeting...is chiefly occupied with reading aloud extracts from *The Book of Discipline*, to fill up the time till men Friends come out, some reform is certainly needed.'[44]

Apparently most male Friends, and some females as well, did not feel the same sense of urgency. In 1893 John Wilhelm Rowntree complained that the assembled Yearly Meeting of male Friends had spent 'twenty-five minutes debating whether the women should be [temporarily] admitted to the men's meeting. It was Quaker

---

[43] Jane E. Taylor, 'Woman's Place in the Christian Economy', *FQE*, (1886), 116–23.

[44] Jane E. Newman, 'About Monthly Meeting', ibid. (1891), 267–70. Holton and Allen provide a similar response from the 'Diaries' of 14-year-old Alice Clark in 1889; 'Offices and Services', 15.

caution and love of detail running to seed.' [T]he spectacle,' he concluded, 'was not inspiring.'[45]

The question of women's place in the Society was not part of the official agenda of the Manchester Conference, but it inevitably rose to the surface from time to time during the gathering. One male speaker at Manchester, J. B. Hodgkin, noted that Quakerism had provided a striking example of the strength that could be drawn from female ministry and that the Society might make a signal contribution by reminding the larger Christian community of 'the great loss the Church of Christ has sustained through all these centuries by quenching the work of God's Spirit when He speaks to the woman instead of the man'.[46] In keeping with the tradition of female ministry, fully a third of the speakers at Manchester were women, although the remarks of most of these were largely confined to traditional questions of piety, ministry, and service. One speaker who broke that mould was Gulielma Crosfield (1851–1945) of Cambridge who reminded the Conference that Friends were doing little to advance the position of women and, in the name of 'sound justice and righteousness', ought to do much more.[47] Still, no *Minute* which emerged from the Manchester Conference mentioned the status of female Friends.

The continued paucity of meaningful advances for women had, however, already evoked some stirring among normally quiescent bodies of Quaker women. *Minute 10* of Lancashire and Cheshire Women's Quarterly Meeting, dated 18 April 1895, squarely articulated this concern:

We realize and deeply value the privileges, which we have always understood we possessed, of equality with our brethren, in all matters affecting the well-being of the Society; but we feel that it would be an advantage not only to Women Friends but to the Society at large, that this essential principle of our constitution should be more fully recognized and acted upon.

We hope that the Women's Yearly Meeting will give the whole subject its serious consideration, and will see its way to take steps by which clear understanding may come ... as regards the position that we actually hold,

---

[45] J. W. R. to a friend, 9 June 1893, *Essays and Addresses*, pp. xxiii–xxiv.
[46] *Manchester Conference*, 57–8.   [47] Ibid. 69–71.

both in our Yearly Meeting and in the other Meetings for the transacting of the affairs of the Church.[48]

When this concern was presented to Yearly Meeting, it seemed, at long last, to have attracted some meaningful attention. Still, the Quaker idea of deliberate speed ensured that, subsequent to the appointment of a Committee to Consider the Position of Women Friends, a full year would pass before the Men's and Women's Yearly Meetings jointly gathered to discuss 'Women Friends in Meetings for Church Affairs'.

In its report to the joint Yearly Meeting of 1896, the Committee on women's concerns made three significant recommendations: 1) that in the future women Friends be considered a constituent part of all Meetings for Discipline; 2) that all Monthly and Quarterly Meetings should henceforth determine how much of their business should be considered jointly by women and men; 3) that Meeting for Sufferings should have female members.[49] The discussion which followed was long and occasionally tense. It began with Joseph Bevan Braithwaite's recommendation that discussion of such 'serious and far-reaching proposals' be delayed until the following Yearly Meeting. Braithwaite's position was supported by Charles Thompson, whose independent religious principles had made him a theological adversary of J. B. B. for three decades; in this matter, they were, for once, in full agreement. On the other hand, one of J. B. Braithwaite's staunchest allies, Yearly Meeting Clerk Caleb R. Kemp, ruled that there should be a full and free discussion of the question.

Women Friends who supported the proposals represented them as a matter of simple justice. Margaret Tanner led off by noting the 'deep measure of concern' many women felt over their exclusion of the meaningful business of the Society, 'except at the will of the men's meeting'. John Bright's daughter, Helen Bright Clark, was

---

[48] *Minutes*, Lancashire and Cheshire Women's Quarterly Meeting, *Minute 10*, 18 April 1895, 20–21, Lancashire Record Office, (LRO), Preston. These *Minutes* give the impression that the women's Quarterly Meeting chiefly acted as a sort of female auxiliary handling the difficult and unrewarding tasks that the men's meeting did not have the time or interest to sustain.

[49] *BF*, 5 June 1896, 160–1. Also see Holton & Allen, 'Offices and Services', 18–19 who point out that the Report also took a step backward in recommending that the *Minutes* of the Men's Yearly Meeting should remain the 'official record' of Yearly Meeting discussions and proceedings.

more blunt. She asked if male members could summon-up sufficient imagination to put themselves in the place of those who
wondered why it should be necessary to conduct a discussion
about whether women ought to be a constituent part of their
own religious Society. Such an insight, she noted, might inspire
sufficient courage to support a change which would make future
discussion of the question unnecessary.[50]

Male response was divided. The weighty banker/historian
Thomas Hodgkin was equivocal, but Joshua Rowntree, a
former MP, believed that the Men's Meeting 'would be doing
themselves a great injustice by continuing to act as if they... alone
constituted the Society of Friends'. When one Friend expressed his
fear that 'busy men' would be overborne by ceaselessly chattering
women, J. Fyfe Stewart replied that the meeting in which they
currently sat had amply demonstrated 'that it would not be the
women who would occupy the greater part of the time in
speaking'.[51]

In the end, Yearly Meeting approved a *Minute* confirming 'that
in future women Friends be recognized as forming a constituent
part of our Meetings for Church affairs, equally with their brethren, and that they should be eligible for appointment as members
of the Meeting for Sufferings.'[52]

George Fox had been dead for over two centuries by the time
(1898) constitutional equality of the sexes was established by British
Friends.[53] One might suppose that this long-sought victory, coming in near-conjunction with a revival of agitation for female
suffrage, would have placed Friends in the forefront of the Edwardian Women's Movement. The *British Friend*, writing in support of a
1897 bill to extend the parliamentary franchise to females, seemed
to anticipate such a development: 'it would be peculiarly fitting
that the year when... women Friends really constitute a part of
Yearly Meeting, [and] when our Queen completes the sixtieth
year of her reign—should be memorable for the political

---

[50] *BF*, 5 June 1896, 161 and *TF*, 29 May 1896, 358.
[51] Stewart was responding to R. Hingston Fox, *BF*, 5 June 1896, 164.
[52] Ibid., 165. Also see Godlee, 'London Yearly Meeting', 120 and Jones, *Latter Periods*, 1, 117.
[53] Most American Yearly Meetings had established equality for women in meetings for discipline and representative meetings (the American equivalent of Meeting for Sufferings) by 1877. See Bacon, 'Women's Yearly Meeting', 162.

emancipation . . . [and] . . . the dawning of hope for the women of our land.'[54] Surely the Society of Friends, which, as the *Free Press* noted, always prided itself on the fact that its members, 'exercise more influence—social, political, moral and religious—than any other religious body',[55] could significantly influence the process of political and social advancement for British women if it threw its moral weight solidly behind the woman suffrage movement. Historians of the women's movement certainly present Quaker women as among the leaders in this long, bitter struggle.[56] Since the 1880s Quaker women had been instrumental in the establishment of women's Liberal societies in cities like York, Darlington, and Bristol; indeed, the Women's Liberal Federation was founded in Mrs Theodore Fry's home in London. Such groups formed a strong lobby for women's rights within the Liberal Party.[57]

For all these hopeful signs, British Quakerism, as represented by its official pronouncements and active press, said little and did less in furthering the cause of female suffrage. A careful reading of the text of the Yearly Meeting *Epistle* of 1899 provides a hint of the Society's subsequent reticence, as a Society, regarding the woman question: 'Membership in the royal priesthood is not conditioned by the distinction of age or sex. Especially, though by no means exclusively, in the ministries of home life are Christian women called to fulfill their spiritual priesthood, and we desire earnestly to urge them not to be neglectful of this holy calling.'[58]

Perhaps the intent of such an admonishment was to quiet the concerns of nervous Friends who believed that even deliberate speed might carry Quakerism too rapidly into the twentieth century. In any case, the discrepancy between ideal and action with regard to women was not lost upon suffragists Friends like Emily Manners, who in 1906 commented to the *British Friend*, a journal

[54] Henrietta Brown, 'Help for Women', *BF*, May 1897, 116–17. After women were admitted to Meeting for Sufferings, sentiment for abolishing the separate Women's Yearly Meeting grew until its demise in 1907. Also see Holton and Allen, 'Offices and Services', 20–21.

[55] Quoted in *The Friend*, 19 October 1906, 708–9.

[56] See Olive Banks, *Faces of Feminism. A Study of Feminism as a Social Movement* (Oxford 1981), 23–6; Rae Strachey, *The Cause. A Short History of the Women's Movement in Great Britain* (London 1978, reprint), 44; Roges Fulford, *Votes for Women* (London 1957), 37–8, 52, 94; and Jeffery Weeks, *Sex, Politics and Society: The Regulation of Sexuality Since 1900*, 2nd edn. (London 1981), 161.

[57] See Fulford, *Votes for Women*, 93–4.

[58] Quoted from *Christian Life, Faith & Thought* (London 1923), 106.

of progressive opinion on nearly every contemporary question, on the curious fact 'that our journals have never in any way advocated the granting of Parliamentary Franchise to women'. On the contrary, she said, they seemed to have joined in the conspiracy of 'contemptuous silence on the question ... adopted by both the political parties and the press'.[59]

Emily Manners had good reason to believe that such protests were not making much impression on either the Quaker press or on the general attitude of male Friends. Three years later she was again complaining to the *British Friend* that beyond some expression of disapproval of the militant tactics of the Women's Social and Political Union (WSPU), she could recall 'no allusion to the subject [of Women's Suffrage] in your paper since my letter of eighteen months ago'. Other correspondents followed in expressing their disappointment that the Society of Friends had evinced 'but lukewarm interest, if not cold indifference' to the question of female suffrage.[60]

Were such critics overstating their case? Women's rights did take a back seat to issues like peace and war, 'new liberal' social reform, or temperance, but suffrage and the movement for female emancipation were not totally ignored by the Quaker press. When the woman question was discussed, it was nearly always presented with an assumed sense of broad agreement with any measure that would bring justice and equality to women rather than in support of specific measures that might accelerate female emancipation. At one point Edward Grubb, editor of the *British Friend*, apparently seeking to explain his paper's meagre coverage of women's issues, noted that he could not understand how anyone brought up in the Quaker tradition of sexual equality could be other than an avid supporter of women's suffrage.[61]

---

[59] *BF*, Dec. 1906, 338. Emily Manners (1857–1934) was a Poor Law Guardian, a county magistrate and the author of a biography of *Elizabeth Hooton: First Quaker Woman Preacher (1600–1672)* (London 1914). For an excellent recent discussion of the Society's curious reticence on the matter of women's rights, see Pam Lunn, ' "You Have Lost Your Opportunity": British Quakers & the Militant Phase of the Women's Suffrage Campaign, 1906–1914', *QS*, 2 (1997), 30–56.

[60] *BF*, July 1909, 200 and Dec. 1910, 333. To illustrate the point, it may be noted that between 1906 and 1914, *Friends Quarterly Examiner* published only two articles on female suffrage.

[61] *BF*, March 1907, 73.

To do him credit, Grubb probably believed in the self-evident truth of his assumption, but, in fact, his remarks brought a chorus of disapproval from Friends who resolutely denied any connection between spiritual equality and political or social privileges and expressed deep resentment at the implication that adherence to Quakerism made female suffrage a quasi-religious issue to which true Friends should give automatic assent. One opponent of votes for women invoked the sacred memory of John Bright, citing that Quaker paragon's determined resistance to extending the franchise to the 'weaker sex' (this, as one respondent noted, despite the fact that Bright's female relatives had long been among the most assertive and outspoken supporters of the women's rights movement).[62] Another famous Friend, Caroline Stephen, late-Victorian Quakerism's most illustrious recruit as well as the female Friend best known to the British reading public, was also a standard-bearer of the Quaker anti-suffragist faction. Stephen's *Quaker Strongholds* (1890) had praised the harmony that apparently arose from the condition of spiritual equality among Friends, noting: 'The admission of the ministry of women seems naturally to flow from the disuse of all but spontaneous spiritual ministrations. For such ministrations experience shows women to be often eminently qualified.'[63] But as regards the 'difficult as well as serious question' of votes for women, Stephen, as a founding member of the National Women's Anti-Suffrage Society, claimed to speak for the 'silent multitude of women' who opposed 'any redistribution as would assign to women an increased share in the outer work of the world', away from the 'central work' in the home.[64]

Quaker feminists generally greeted Caroline Stephen's anti-suffrage statements with embarrassed silence until she died in 1909. Still, when the WSPU began to employ increasingly militant

[62] Georgina King Lewis (an opponent of female suffrage) to *BF*, Oct. 1909, 285–6. Also see ibid., April 1907, 109–10 and Sept. 1909, 260. John Bright's daughter Helen Priestman Bright Clark (1840–1927) and her daughters Esther Bright Clothier (1873–1935) and Margaret Clark Gillett (1878–1962) were among the strongest Quaker advocates of female parliamentary suffrage. Holton & Allen, 'Offices and Services', provide revealing examples of the differences between John Bright and his female relatives, see especially Priscilla McLaren [Bright's sister] to Helen Clark, 5 Nov. 1883, 13.

[63] Caroline E. Stephen, *Quaker Strongholds* (London 1890, 3rd ed 1891), 111.

[64] Ibid., 56, 111; Stephen to Lyra T. Wolkins, 1 Jan. 1907, Lyra Wolkins Papers, Temp. MSS 584, LSF; 'Women in Politics', *Nineteenth Century*, LXI (Feb. 1907), 227–36; 'A Rejoinder', ibid., (April 1907), 593–4; and 'The Representation of Women', ibid., LXIV (Dec. 1908), 1018–24. Caroline Stephen never married.

tactics, in clear violation of Quaker peace principles, lukewarm Friends had another excuse to remain on the fence, while opponents of women's rights were wont to associate all attempts to secure female suffrage with extremist violence. Indeed, one letter by a 'male Friend' made the point that violent conduct by suffragettes was 'sufficiently symptomatic of a wide-spread lack of mental balance [among females] to form a serious factor in the question'.[65]

The best responses to such indictments were arguments for simple justice based on Christian principles. As one female correspondent to *British Friend* noted: 'Parent Law, Marriage Law, the Poor Law are all unjust to women.... [and] a disgrace to our Christian profession.' This situation would continue, she said, until women had a direct voice in making and changing the laws of the land. Lucy Morland had made the same point a few months earlier: 'the consciousness of the terrible hardships in the lot of so many women, just because they are women, has taken hold of the women of this generation and they must fight for political equality which will be the first step to social equality.'[66]

The growth of women's suffrage as a national issue did occasion a more forceful public advocacy of women's rights by some female Quakers. A Conference of Women Friends on Suffrage held immediately prior to Yearly Meeting in 1910 emphasized the 'spiritual power of the Suffrage Movement... [as] part of the great struggle for justice and liberty in which Friends have taken so large a share'. In the aftermath of this gathering, several dozen female Friends appealed to Meeting for Sufferings for

an opportunity... for the women members of our Society to express their united sympathy with the cause of women's suffrage—a cause which we consider... vital to the well being of our country... and we should like to show in some united way our sympathy & interest... adding our testimony to those who are working in a constitutional way for the cause we have so much at heart.[67]

---

[65] *BF*, Sept. 1909, 260.

[66] Madeline Grubb to *BF*, May 1910, 129 and Lucy F. Morland to ibid., Nov. 1909, 314.

[67] Edith M. Williams and Evangline Barratt to *BF*, May 1910, 130 and 'Appeal From Women Friends for Consideration of Women's Suffrage at Y. M., 1910', Box 2/16, LSF. This appeal was signed by Anna M. Priestman as Clerk and seventy-five other Quaker women.

The question was duly considered during Yearly Meeting in 1910, but despite the fact that two women, Mary Jane Godlee and Margaret Irwin, sat as assistant Clerks (Godlee had been the first female assistant Clerk the previous year), the time was judged not ripe for an official Quaker endorsement of women's suffrage. One older women expressed the view that the Society, as a body, could hardly endorse social movements to which many members were conscientiously opposed.[68] Feminist response to this argument stressed the fact that some fundamental questions, slavery, for example, 'went deeper... into the ethical and religious foundations of life' and that while Friends had once been divided on slavery, events had illustrated they ought not to have been. In the same way, the future would demonstrate that spiritual ideals like the 'divine worth of every human soul... were intended to find expression in laws and institutions' if Friends were to fulfill their obligation to work for the establishment of the Kingdom of God on earth.[69]

During the next Yearly Meeting the matter of a general endorsement for female suffrage was again brought to the fore and, again, it failed because Friends remained 'much divided on the subject' which many deemed a 'political question'. The Yearly Meeting of 1911 did, however, approve a new edition of the *Christian Discipline of the Society of Friends* which forcefully re-emphasized the principle of spiritual equality in the 'freedom of the Gospel' where there was 'neither Jew nor Greek... bond or free... male or female', concluding, in apparent absence of mind, that 'all are one *man* in Christ Jesus'.[70]

One response to London Yearly Meeting's continued indifference to the cause of female suffrage was the formation in 1911 of the Friends' Council (Friends' League after 1912) for Women's Suffrage. Concurrently, Gulielma Crosfield, who later became president of the League, published a pamphlet '*Friends and the Women's Movement*' which, while decrying the language and the actions of the militants, cited the need to give public demonstration to Quakerism's longstanding commitment to equality

---

[68] Anne W. Richardson to *BF*, 25 Nov. 1910, 793.

[69] *BF.*, Dec. 1910, 333, Jan. 1911, 49 and June 1911, 174–5.

[70] *BF*, June 1911, 161 and *Christian Practice*, Part II of *Christian Discipline of the Society of Friends* (London 1912), 33–4 [emphasis added].

between the sexes.[71] But the League's existence did little to change existing views among anti-suffragist Friends, most notably Joseph A. Pease, President of the Board of Education in the Liberal Government, who refused even to meet with a delegation from the League.[72]

In the meantime, a statistical study published in *The Friend* (1912) revealed that while women Friends still substantially outnumbered men and made up two-thirds of attendees at all meetings for business, their authority within the Society was actually diminishing. Women constituted a majority in nearly every type of meeting, but all seventeen Quarterly Meeting Clerks as well as seventy-four of eighty Monthly Meeting Clerks were males. Since the author of this article interpreted his figures as showing that females lacked the capacity for leadership, it scarcely seemed a harbinger for substantial improvement in either women's role within the Society or the Society's endorsement of female suffrage.[73]

Still, in 1913, following an impassioned address by Philip Bellows, who had also written 'An appeal to the "Quaker Conscience"',[74] Yearly Meeting at long last addressed the question of female suffrage through a passage in the *Epistle* which spoke at length on the blessings which the full recognition of women's dignity and abilities had brought to Quakerism. Friends were called upon 'to bear our share in bringing this movement to its full fruition, and . . . saving it from the serious dangers with which it is threatened', but Yearly Meeting still avoided any corporate testimony as to the justice of the suffragists' cause and any endorsement of equal rights of citizenship.[75]

---

[71] (London 1911), *passim.*

[72] See *TF*, December 1912, 870. A politician and mine owner in Durham, Joseph Albert Pease (1860–1943), the grandson of Joseph Pease, the first Quaker MP, was elected to Parliament in 1892; he served briefly as Liberal Chief Whip (1910), as President of the Board of Education and as Postmaster General (1916). In 1917 he was created Baron Gainford of Headham. For his political career, see Cameron Hazlehurst and Christine Woodland (eds.), *A Liberal Chronicle: Journals and Papers of J. A. Pease, First Lord Gainford, 1908–1910* (London 1994).

[73] Harold Marsh, 'Women in the Church', *TF*, 22 March 1912, 179–81. Also see Lunn, ' "You Have Lost Your Opportunity" ', 43.

[74] See Philip Bellows, *An appeal to the 'Quaker Conscience' of England*, (Wigan 1913) and *TF*, 30 May 1913, 358.

[75] *TF*., 6 June 1913, 375–6.

The inability of the Society of Friends, as a body, to provide support for a movement whose objectives seemed closely to parallel its own historical principles was a reflection of the general unwillingness in British society to bridge the gap between traditional prejudices and the obvious requirements of the modern world. But Friends would seem to have had fewer and less satisfactory excuses for refusing to act in advancing the movement for female emancipation. On the whole, Quaker women were better educated, more comfortably situated, more widely read and more experienced in assuming responsibility than almost any other comparable group of females in British life. Still, even the weightiest Friends were challenged when they used the historical standing of Quaker women as an argument for advancing the position of women in general. Early in 1914 John Henry Barlow, Clerk designate of the next Yearly Meeting, requested that Meeting for Sufferings appoint a Committee for communicating to other Christian groups the 'remarkable results' of Friends having accorded 'liberty of expression and action' to women. Barlow's request was vigorously challenged by Henry Marriage Wallis (1854–1941), a member of Meeting for Sufferings. What Barlow had done, Wallis asserted, was to commit the Society willy-nilly to the women's movement and all its works and all its pomps simply because: 'Our lady friends were upon their feet and assured us that the Time was Ripe and that Wider Horizons than those of this country awaited the Light...' In fact, Wallis asserted, Englishwomen, even Quaker women, were not yet equal to the demands of public life. 'They do not understand how to play the game, how to give way, or when to stop.' Apparently, Wallis's arguments were successful, at least to the extent of preserving the *status quo*. At the last pre-war Yearly Meeting, *Minute 104* admonished Friends that it would be 'wise to leave political action... to the judgment and conscience of individuals'.[76]

Liberal Friends who supported women's suffrage may have derived some comfort in assuming that the Society's unwillingness to stand firmly for political and social justice to women reflected the residual strength of evangelical forces within the Society and that opposition to women's suffrage represented another of their

[76] H. M. Wallis to *TF*, 13 Feb. 1914, 114–15; *LYM*, 1914, 187; and interview with M. M. Barlow, 13 August 1986, London.

reactionary, last-ditch stands. Certainly, many liberal Quakers could be found in the suffrage ranks, working to bolster 'this great movement for the Freedom of Womanhood'.[77] In 1912, for example, a book co-authored by William Charles Braithwaite and Henry T. Hodgkin spoke of an emerging 'Messianic hope': 'Woman's place in the universe in equal fellowship with men. Surely we can stand for that. We have expressed that in our Church life long before it came as a great hope to the mass of the people.'[78] And schoolmaster/social worker Gerald K. Hibbert (1872–1957) delivered a 'weighty and solemn address' to the Friends League for Women's Suffrage in October 1913, pronouncing his vision of a community of men and women working together in 'full and free equality'.[79]

Thus, surviving evidence might seem to establish a connection between liberalism in theology and support for female emancipation. But things are not necessarily as they seem. Take the example of John William Graham, Principal of Dalton Hall of the University of Manchester and one of the most prolific liberal Quaker publicists of his day. Graham's public pronouncements on the women's question stressed the way in which Quakerism had been immeasurably enriched by 'using the gifts of women' to provide their religious Society with 'a family completeness' that other churches lacked.[80] Still, opinions about the political and intellectual capacities of women in Graham's private papers would seem to place him in at least a collateral line of descent from Victorian misogynists. In mid-1913 Graham wrote to his son Richard at Balliol College, Oxford, advising him against joining the local women suffrage society. Despite the 'natural chivalry of youth', said the elder Graham, 'at thy age it is not possible to have a very wise judgment on Women's Suffrage'. The question was 'vexed' to be sure, but among many women, even Quaker women, 'it is very largely a fashionable fad . . .' 'Unfortunately,' Graham continued, 'what they largely want is to get out of the natural duties of women . . .' Indeed, nature seemed to be a most

---

[77] 'Women's Suffrage: Its Deeper Aspects', *BF*, Nov. 1913, 300–301.
[78] W. C. Braithwaite and Henry T. Hodgkin, *The Message and Mission of Quakerism* (Philadelphia 1912), 52.
[79] *TF*, 7 Nov. 1913, 736–7.
[80] John W. Graham, *The Faith of a Quaker* (Cambridge, 1920), 193; much of this book was written before 1914 but it was not published until the end of the war.

serious consideration for Graham and in a section of the letter
marked 'private' he reminded his son:

There is a very solid physiological reason why women for one quarter of
their life [sic] in unmarried life have no ability of judgment required for
voting... This is particularly, in the unmarried, accentuated towards
middle life. In old age there is sometimes a freedom from it, but too
often the mind has permanently suffered by the physical change....

Nor was this all. For noble as it might seem to be on the side of the
female franchise, Graham concluded, there was, for Friends who
wished to adhere to their traditional peace testimony, still another
question, 'seeing that the balance of opinion is entirely that
women will vote for conscription and for war in a large number
of cases ... One cannot trust the working women...'[81]
  Of course, no British electors, let alone working women, were
given the opportunity to render a decision about war and conscription. When decisions by the great and powerful caused these
things to come to pass, most British women followed their men
folk in supporting what they believed to be the national cause and
by contributing so significantly to that cause that the parliamentary
franchise could no longer be withheld from them. From a Quaker
perspective, most women were equally sound in their rejection of
the war and the compulsory military service that war eventually
brought. Like the women who replaced men in shop, factory, and
farmstead, Quaker women, most of them veterans of the struggle
for equal rights, took their places on the front line of their Society's
clash with the Warrior State, gaining in times of violence and war
an equality never afforded them in the long years of peace and
tranquility.

  [81] J. W. Graham to Richard Graham, 2 June 1913, JWGP, JRL. A similar point had been
made in 1907 by Lewis Thompson of Bridgewater who told the *British Friend* that 'income-
tax payers do not feel in a hurry to extend the franchise more widely, and perhaps be called
on to pay for wars voted by a Jingo proletariat'. *BF*, April 1907, 110.

7

Never to Fight with Carnal Weapons

THE PEACE TESTIMONY, ORIGINS AND LEGACIES

George Fox might have obtained an early release from Derby gaol, where he spent most of 1650, if he had accepted a proffered captaincy in the Parliamentary Army, but, as he recorded in his *Journal*: 'I told them I lived in the virtue of that life and power that took away the occasion of all wars, and I knew from whence all wars did rise, from the lust according to James's doctrine . . . I told them I was come into the covenant of peace which was before wars and strifes were.'[1] According to longstanding tradition, Fox's personal testimony was not publicly expressed as a basic tenet of Quaker belief until January 1661 when, soon after the Restoration of Charles II and in the wake of a rising by Fifth Monarchy Men in which some Quakers were allegedly implicated, a group of prominent Friends, including Fox, issued a *Declaration from the Harmless and Innocent People called Quakers* . . . :

All bloody principles and practices, we . . . utterly deny, with all outward wars and strife and fightings with outward weapons . . . this is our testimony to the whole world . . . the spirit of Christ, which leads us into all Truth, will never move us to fight and war against any man with outward

[1] *Journal of George Fox*, edited by John L. Nickalls (London 1952 rep. 1986), 65. Fox's biblical reference is James 4: 1–3. Also see *Christian Practice* (London 1925), 131–2. While he was writing *The Beginnings of Quakerism*, W. C. Braithwaite told Rufus Jones that he believed Fox's response at Derby 'gives . . . the ground of the Quaker testimony against War'. W. C. B. to R. M. J., 1 Jan. 1908, Box 6, RMJP. Recently, a Quaker archivist has asserted that although, in retrospect, George Fox wished it to seem as if this statement was the real origin of Friends' peace testimony, other evidence points up his ambivalence about pacifism throughout the 1650s. See Rosemary Moore, 'Evaluating the Evidence: the Reliability of Sources of Information for Quakerism Before 1660', *FQ*, 27/8 (October 1993), 365–6. Also see Ingle, *First Among Friends*, 121–2, 172–3 & 192–6 who notes that prior to 1661, Fox had defended magistrates' use of force against evil and ungodly persons.

weapons, neither for the kingdom of Christ, nor for the kingdoms of this world.[2]

That seemed clear enough. Certainly, this *Declaration* was prominently cited by Quaker pacifists during the First World War as the foundation of their Society's traditional refusal to fight with carnal weapons. But the citation was somewhat misleading. Modern scholarship has revealed that the document most frequently cited by early twentieth-century pacifist Friends had been culled out of obscurity during the revival of historical research inspired by the Quaker Renaissance and appeared as an official Quaker document only in the 1911 edition of Friends' *Christian Discipline*. Furthermore, the *Declaration* of 1661 'broke no new ground' since it had been preceded by similar declarations, including one signed by Margaret Fell and others in June 1660.[3]

Many late twentieth-century historians of Quakerism, pacifism and the English Civil War support the view, espoused by Christopher Hill, that the peace testimony became central to Friends' witness only after the Restoration and then largely 'as a stratagem for survival' following the defeat of the Good Old Cause to which most Friends had remained devoted throughout the Interregnum and for which some were apparently willing to take up arms. Accordingly, these scholars see the *Declaration* of 1661 not as the clarification of a fundamental Quaker doctrine but as a public renunciation of political objectives and a pledge to withdraw from worldly concerns.[4]

---

[2] This Declaration was signed by Fox, Richard Hubberthorne, Francis Hogwill, and others, but not by militants like Edward Burrough and Isaac Penington nor by Margaret Fell or any other Quaker woman. The complete text is reprinted in Nickalls, *Journal of George Fox*, 398–404 and partially cited in somewhat different form in *Christian Discipline*, Part II (1911), 139–40. Also see Peter Brock, *Quaker Peace Testimony 1660–1914* (York 1990), 24–7 and Horace G. Alexander, 'The Growth of the Peace Testimony of the Society of Friends', (2nd. edn. London 1956), 3–5.

[3] Richenda C. Scott, *Tradition and Experience* (London 1964), 37–41 and Richard L. Greaves, 'Shattered Expectations? George Fox, the Quakers, and the Restoration State, 1660–1685', *Albion*, 24/2 (Summer 1992), 249. Also see Hugh Barbour, 'The "Lamb's War" and the Origins of the Quaker Peace Testimony', in *The Pacifist Impulse in Historical Perspective*, edited by Harvey Dyck (Toronto 1996) 144–58 who notes (150) that Edward Burrough, the early Friend most often cited as ambivalent concerning peace principles, had 'announced' a peace testimony even before Margaret Fell's 'Declaration'.

[4] Hill, *World Turned Upside Down* and *The Experience of Defeat: Milton and Some Contemporaries* (New York 1984), Chap. 5 and Barry Reay, *Quakers and the English Revolution*,

This view has been disputed by several students of early Quakerism. In his study of *The Quaker Peace Testimony* (1990) Peter Brock faults Hill for failing to take into account the spiritual basis of early Quakerism. Brock maintains that pacifism was always integral to Quakerism, even if all early Friends were not pacifists.[5] Richard L. Greaves supports Brock but takes a somewhat different slant, denying the peace testimony was part of a strategy of withdrawal and insisting, quite the contrary, that it reflected an overall Quaker policy of 'constructive engagement' with temporal power on behalf of social and political justice.[6] Quaker scholar Hugh Barbour agrees, arguing that these declarations, taken together, were an integral component of the 'Lamb's War': 'The Quakers' turning inwards, which for Marxists has seemed a turning back from revolution, was actually its intensification.' Douglas Gwynn finds Hill's representation of 'early shifts in the Quaker movement as a sudden transformation into sectarian quietism' irritating, especially in light of Hill's 'over-interpretation of the Quaker movement's [close] relationship with the Army'.[7]

Quaker pacifism has been given still another twist by Meredith Weedle who views the early peace testimony as an 'intensely personal' witness based upon scriptural injunctions and more concerned about the souls of those who engaged in violence than about any injury or injustice inflicted upon its victims.[8] The idea that the early Quaker witness for peace was based on biblical

---

106–7, 121 and 'Quakerism and Society', in J. F. McGregor and B. Reay (eds.), *Radical Religion in the English Revolution* (Oxford 1984). Martin Ceadel in his impressive study of *The Origins of War Prevention* (Oxford 1996), 150–51 takes the position that while the *Declaration* did mark a withdrawal from political involvement, many prominent early Friends were moved to convince the world of the rightness of their pacifist vision.

[5] Brock, *Quaker Peace Testimony*, 9–23. Brock concedes that there was 'tension' between Quakers' desire for justice and peace principles but still believes that the peace testimony was fundamental to early Quakerism.

[6] Greaves, 'Shattered Expectations?', 237–59, *passim*. Greaves concludes that Barry Reay is wrong in implying that the peace testimony was 'virtually forced' on the Quakers; rather, he says, it 'emerged through the conviction . . . that divine power, not temporal weapons, changes the course of human affairs' (250).

[7] Barbour, 'Peace Testimony', 150 and Douglas Gwyn, *The Covenant Crucified: Quakers and the Rise of Capitalism* (Wallingford, Pa. 1995), 218 and 222 n.

[8] Meredith Baldwin Weedle, 'Conscience or Compromise: The Meaning of the Peace Testimony in Early New England', *QH*, 81/2 (Fall 1992), 74–5, 82–4. In contrast to Weedle, Larry Ingle believes that Fox and his contemporaries were deeply attached to the idea of earthly justice as well as eternal salvation, at least prior to the Restoration. See 'George Fox, Millenarian', *Albion* 24/2 (Summer 1992), 261–78.

authority rather than any mystical or ethical concept has also been endorsed by some contemporary Quaker historians and theologians.[9] Such views fly in the face of the usual justification for pacifism when it became a central feature of Quaker belief before and during the First World War, i.e., the sacredness of human life.[10]

Whatever the precise origins of their testimony, most Friends lived out their devotion to non-violence and non-resistance during the two and a half centuries between the Restoration and the Great War. The courageous but passive response of early Quakers to the brutal enforcement of the Quaker and Conventicle Acts cost them dearly in lives, limbs, and fortunes.[11] The moral fortitude to suffer stripes and imprisonments without retaliation arose, no doubt, from the belief, so artlessly expressed by ex-soldier William Dewsbury, 'that the Kingdom of Christ was within, and the enemies was within, and was spiritual and my weapons against them must be spiritual, the power of God. Then I could no longer fight with a carnal weapon against a carnal man.'[12]

For all of this, the peace testimony maintained an inconspicuous place in the lexicon of essential Quaker tenets. Robert Barclay's *Apology* (1676), the classic exposition of seventeenth-century Quaker ideas and beliefs, deals only briefly with issues of peace and war (although what Barclay does say seems decisive).[13] London

---

[9] See especially John Punshon 'The Peace Testimony, an Ethic Derived from a Metaphysic via an Experience', *QRT*, 68–9, 23/2–3 (Summer 1988), 55–73 and Eva I. Pinthus, 'The Roots of the Peace Testimony in the Message of the Bible', *FQ*, 26/2 (April 1990), 54–63.

[10] See especially Margaret E. Hirst, *Quakers in Peace and War* (London 1923), who notes that the peace testimony 'grew inevitably out of the conception of the inward light' which led Friends to the conviction that wars and strife 'were contrary to the Spirit of Christ', 41, 114–15, 522.

[11] For the general background see Ronald Hutton, *The Restoration 1658–1667* (Oxford 1988), 210–90, *passim*. The best study of the persecution of early Friends is Craig Horle, *Quakers and the English Legal System* (Philadelphia 1988).

[12] William Dewsbury's *Works* (London 1689), 55. Cf. with *Friends and War: A New Statement of the Quaker Position* (London 1920), 6: 'It is no accident that this now historically famous peace testimony came to be an inherent and indissoluble part of the Quaker way of life. It never was "adopted". It was hardly discussed...Like everything else that was fundamental in primitive Quakerism, this testimony seemed to the first Friends to be a "revelation" to them.'

[13] See *Barclay's Apology in Modern English*, edited by Dean Freiday (Newberg, Oregon 1991), 391, 425–35. Quaker supporters of the First World War, while making much of Barclay's apparently cursory treatment of the peace testimony, choose to ignore Barclay's powerful admonitions against violence: 'it is impossible to reconcile war and revenge with

Yearly Meeting made no specific pronouncement on the peace testimony until 1730. When the witness for peace was finally included among the 'Queries' directed by Yearly Meeting to each Monthly Meeting as a means of discovering the 'state of the Church', it was, for some time, attached to the prohibition against the payment of tithes.[14] Still, as early as 1693 the Yearly Meeting Epistle had specifically and strongly condemned the arming of Quaker-owned vessels, although some Friends apparently did not adhere to this prohibition.[15] Furthermore, throughout the eighteenth century the consistent refusal by Quakers to perform service in the militia was punished by distraint of property or by imprisonment, generally brief, if the accused had insufficient property to pay the fine.[16]

The crisis of the Revolutionary and Napoleonic Wars caused considerable ambivalence among Friends. For while the *Epistle* of 1804 admonished Quakers to remain consistent in fulfilling their 'awful' responsibility 'to stand forth to the nation as advocates of inviolable peace', the *Epistle* for the following year demonstrated only 'pale enthusiasm' for the peace testimony, advising Friends not to discuss 'the calamitous subject of war' but to pray that God would 'breathe the spirit of reconciliation into the hearts of His erring and contending creatures'. Still, before the war ended London Yearly Meeting (1812) had dispatched an Address to the Prince Regent condemning the conflict, an act Martin Ceadel calls a 'rare

Christian practice' or 'War is absolutely unlawful for those who would be disciples of Christ'. See Chapter 9.

[14] Reference to the peace testimony was first included in the *General Epistle* of 1730; this was repeated in 1742, 1744, 1746, 1757 and 1760. During the wars against Revolutionary France and Napoleon, the standardized 'Eighth Query' read: 'Are you faithful in maintaining our Christian testimony against all War, as inconsistent with the precepts and the spirit of the Gospel?' *Book of Discipline* (3rd. edn., London 1834). Ceadel, *Origins of War Prevention*, asserts that 'pacifism as a publicly declared position was virtually synonymous with Quakerism', 160 while Richenda Scott, *Tradition and Experience*, 40–1 maintained that it was only in the early nineteenth century, with the growth of humanitarian ideals, that Friends, in general, adopted the view that the taking of human life by anyone, for any reason, was always wrong.

[15] Bacon, 'Women's Yearly Meeting', 151 reveals that in 1752 Susanna Morris of Bucks County Pa. criticized English Friends not only for their immodest use of tobacco and alcohol but also for 'their justification of defensive war'.

[16] Brock, *Quaker Peace Testimony*, 33–46 *passim*. In 'The History of the Peace Testimony', in *The Peace Testimony of the Society of Friends* (London [1920]), Margaret Hirst says that Friends without property for distraint were not imprisoned until after 1786.

crystallization of their peace testimony into criticism of an actual war'.[17]

At the end of the Napoleonic Wars, the British Quaker William Allen (1770–1843) was instrumental in the establishment of the London Peace Society and, in his meetings with the Russian Tsar Alexander I, revived, to no great effect, the Quaker tradition of speaking truth to power.[18] Another Friend who achieved some prominence for peace advocacy during this same period was a young linen-draper, Jonathan Dymond (1796–1828), whose essays on the incompatibility of war and Christianity were widely influential among Quakers and other seekers after peace during the nineteenth century.[19] Dymond's pacifist arguments were broadly Christian rather than distinctly Quaker but founded on Quaker traditions and practices. A central thesis of Dymond's argument was that the New Testament's 'dispensation of Christ' had replaced the 'dispensation of Moses' revealed in the more bloody-minded passages of the Old Testament. Because he died young, Dymond's hedging on biblical literalism was never effectively challenged, even as the Society of Friends was being drawn closer to the evangelical mainstream. Subsequently, Jonathan Dymond was much honoured for keeping the Quaker peace banner flying during a period when peace was seldom a burning issue, but his essentially rationalist approach is still found wanting by some Friends.[20]

William Allen's Peace Society, with the majority of its membership and the bulk of its monetary support coming from Friends, remained active through the 1840s, holding public meetings and publishing anti-war tracts. The leading role of weighty Quakers

[17] *Christian Doctrine, Practice, and Discipline* (1861), 110 and Ceadel, *Origins of War Prevention*, 199. Also see Margaret E. Hirst, 'Limitations of the Peace Testimony', *FQE*, May 1918, 300 and Joshua Rowntree, *Social Service: Its Place in the Society of Friends* (London 1913), 56–7.

[18] For detailed discussion of the London Peace Society see Ceadel, *Origins of War Prevention*, 204 ff. and Peter Brock, *Freedom From War: Nonsectarian Pacifism, 1814–1914* (Toronto 1991), 20–35.

[19] Dymond's major works were *An Inquiry into the Accordance of War with the Principles of Christianity* (1823 reprinted New York 1973) and *Essays on the Principles of Morality...* (1829).

[20] Cf. Brock, *Quaker Peace Testimony*, 257–64 who characterizes Dymond as 'a seminal influence on the peace movement' with a somewhat hostile evaluation by T. Vail Palmer, Jr., 'Quaker Peace Witness: The Biblical and Historical Roots', *QRT*, 23/8 (Summer 1988), 48–53. Palmer believes that Dymond's work 'lacks the overall perspective of a truly systematic thinker...' and misrepresents Quaker peace testimony by not acknowledging its biblical basis (51).

like Joseph Sturge in the affairs of the Peace Society may have influenced London Yearly Meeting's decision in 1841 to issue its first peacetime declaration on the 'Unlawfulness of All Wars and Fightings Under the Gospel'. But while many Quakers were willing to give their money to the Peace Society, few gave much of their time.[21] By the late 1840s the thrust of the Peace Society's activities had shifted from an implicit pacifism which condemned all war toward what Martin Ceadel has termed liberal 'pacificist' internationalism or working to prevent the always deplorable results of war but admitting its necessity in some extremities. This latter view was much influenced by Richard Cobden and his Quaker ally John Bright, whose vision of Friends peace testimony was, as noted below, always idiosyncratic.[22]

Under Cobden's leadership, the British peace advocates took the lead in organizing a series of international Peace Congresses beginning at Brussels in September 1848, where Quakers made up a majority of the British delegation, and culminating in London in 1851. But the hopes raised by what *The Friend* confidently termed a 'moral revolution' in the search for international peace[23] were dashed by the growth of an aggressive Russophobia ultimately consummated with the outbreak of the Crimean War. Quakers may well have swelled with pride at the mission of Joseph Sturge, Henry Pease, and Robert Charlton to present a plea for peace prepared by Meeting for Sufferings to the Tsar, but this venture brought little credit and much hostility toward presumptuous Quakers, 'too fond of keeping company with the great.'[24]

Still, for all the hostility and discomfiture engendered by the failed Quaker peace mission, John Bright upheld the Quaker ideal through his politically courageous stand against the bloody and futile struggle in the Crimea.[25] Bright based his opposition to the

[21] See Ceadel, *Origins of War Prevention*, 222–413 *passim*.
[22] For an analysis of 'pacificism' and a discussion of Cobden and Bright's adherence to it, see ibid. 35–44 & 348–55.
[23] *TF*, Sept. 1849, 175.
[24] For an account of this incident, see Stephen Frick, 'The Quaker Deputation to Russia: January–February 1854', *JFHS* 52/2 (1969). Frick elaborated on Quaker opposition to the Crimean War in a series of articles in *JFHS*, see 52/3 (1970), 53/3 (1974) and 53/4 (1975). The quote is from a letter of Cobden to Sturge, cited by Ceadel, *Origins of War Prevention*, 512. Also see Brock, *Quaker Peace Testimony*, 267–9.
[25] For Bright's denunciation of the conflict, see Gregg, 'John Bright', 8–30; Keith Robbins, *John Bright* (London 1979), 124–40; and G. M. Trevelyan, *Life of John Bright* (London 1913), 230–52.

Crimean War on pragmatic and humanitarian rather than religious scruples. Nonetheless, he undoubtedly impressed his fellow Quakers, one of whom noted at the Yearly Meeting of 1856 that Friends had become more united on the peace testimony since the war began.[26] In the aftermath of Crimea, the war-scare of 1859–60 and the near-hysteria of the Volunteer Movement that accompanied it, Friends became sufficiently aroused to include a specific proclamation in the *General Epistle* of 1859:

The Christian and truly scriptural testimony of our Society against all war is as precious to us as ever it was . . . all war, defensive as well as offensive, is unlawful for the followers of the Lamb: but how is this change to be brought about unless by faithfulness in word and deed . . . to the principles and practices of inviolable peace?[27]

When the Queries addressed to monthly meetings by the Yearly Meeting were revised in 1860, what had been the Eighth Query was replaced by a newly sculpted Sixth Query: 'Are Friends faithful in maintaining our Christian testimony against all war?' The question seems simplicity itself until one realizes that Yearly Meeting spent an entire hour struggling with the matter of whether the query should read '*a*' or '*our*' Christian testimony.[28] Shortly thereafter, even as the Angel of Death beat her wings over the bloodied battlegrounds of the American Civil War, John Bright was unable to condemn this struggle against slavery and chose the lesser of two evils in praying for the victory of Mr Lincoln's Armies. If this seemed a violation of the recently adopted standard for Quaker testimony 'against *all* war', Bright made no apology and indeed

[26] Josiah Foster, 'Memoranda Respecting London Yearly Meeting', 1856, MS Vol. S 76, LSF. Brock, *Quaker Peace Testimony*, 275 believes that the 'politicisation' of Quaker peace testimony during the Crimean War as well as Friends' tendency to associate war relief with war resistance made that conflict a landmark of British Friends' stand against war.

[27] *Christian Doctrine, Practice, and Discipline* (1861), 113; John S. Rowntree, 'Yearly Meeting, 1859', MS Vol S 368, LSF and *Minutes*, 4 Dec. 1859, 8 Jan. 1860 and Feb. 1861, Hardshaw East Monthly Meeting (HEMM). For studies of the war scare and the Volunteer Movement, see Michael J. Salevouris, '*Riflemen Form*': *The War Scare of 1859–1860 in England* (New York 1982) and Ian F. W. Beckett, *Riflemen Form: A Study of the Rifle Volunteer Movement* (Tunbridge Wells 1982).

[28] *TF*, 8 June 1860, 104–5 and *Christian Doctrine, Practice, and Discipline*, 169.

admitted that he could not logically support a condemnation of all violence in a contest between good and evil.[29]

John Bright cannot be accused of lacking the courage of his convictions, but there is, at times, some difficulty in pinning down exactly what his convictions, or those of other Victorian Friends, really were with regard to the extent of their peace testimony. The admirably scrupulous Caleb Kemp might give witness to peace principles by attempting to convince a soldier he met on the train to recognize the 'Gospel standard of love' or by refusing to share in the profits from cement sold by his firm for the building of naval fortification of Portsmouth Harbour.[30] But while Quakers might agree to expel the occasionally blatant miscreant who took up arms or urged others to do so,[31] they lacked any consensus as to what constituted a positive peace testimony, except positively avoiding attempts to carefully define one. The reasons for such waffling are understandable, if not admirable. Because no British Government dared to impose conscription, Victorian Friends were never faced with the challenge of having to choose religious principles over the commands of the State or the defence of home and hearth. One Friend, warning against a selective sort of spiritual pride as regards the peace testimony, put the matter in perspective:

We live in a well-ordered State, where persons and property are . . . secure from the hand of violence, and in a country where the presence of a foreign enemy has not been felt for centuries. It is no trial of faith for us to abstain from the use of arms . . . and to refuse to engage in military service. . . . It therefore becomes us, at the present day, while steadfastly supporting the Christian doctrines which we believe to be right, to speak with deference, as never having really had our principle put to the test.[32]

Still, there were repeated occasions when Quakers were filled with 'great zeal' to work for the cause of peace. The Franco-Prussian War was certainly one of these, but, as J. S. Rowntree

---

[29] For Bright on the American war, see Robbins, *John Bright*, 155–68 and Trevelyan, *Life of Bright*, 296–326. Bright's statement on the limitations of non-resistance was made with reference to the Indian Mutiny.

[30] C. R. K., 'Journals', II, 25 Nov. 1859, 268 and III, 19 April 1861, 115–16, MS Vol. S 4, LSF.

[31] For example, in Feb. 1861 Joseph Nodal of Manchester was disowned for joining the Volunteers. *Minutes*, HEMM, 1861–3, 8–9.

[32] Pacificus to *TF*, 1 Nov. 1859, 208–9.

noted at the time, there was always, 'great difficulty... in knowing what to do'. In this instance the Meeting for Sufferings took the lead by establishing the Friends' War Victims Relief Committee to alleviate suffering in the war zone and by issuing 120,000 copies of an address on 'Christianity and War' to rally the Churches in support of peace.[33] Such actions helped to keep Friends foremost in public view as propagators of peace principles, but some Quakers believed that their Society ought to go a step further by combining with non-Friends and entering into the public arena in the struggle against the 'political evil' of wars being fought 'with the approval of popular Christianity'.[34]

Such calls for united political action against State-sponsored and Christian-supported militarism were, for all effect, shouted into the wind. In 1882, for example, the *British Friend* lamented the igno-minious failure of ten Quaker MPs to support Henry Richard's effort to block a £2.3 million grant to finance the calling up of Reserves for the Egyptian campaign.[35] This disgraceful perfor-mance was mitigated to some extent by John Bright's resignation from the Cabinet in protest of the shelling of Alexandria. Still, as Caleb Kemp reported in his diary a few months later, 'fearful bloodshed in the Soudan' was a 'humiliating spectacle for a Christian country'. The failure of Friends to mount any effective protest against the Egyptian campaign caused the exasperated *British Friend* to question 'whether of late years the society, as a united body, has really taken any practically active step... in working against war'.[36]

One Friend who had attempted to take such a step was Pricilla Hannah Peckover (1833–1931) of Wisbech in Cambridgeshire. In 1879 Peckover founded the Local Peace Association, a non-denominational Christian pacifist organization for women. By

[33] See J. S. Rowntree, 'Yearly Meeting, 1871', and Punshon, *Portrait in Grey*, 185–6 who believes the setting up of 'War Vics' was 'a watershed... [in] the development of that earnest dedication to peace work... characteristic of modern Friends'. Also see *Christian Discipline of the Religious Society of Friends* (London 1883), 157–8.

[34] David Duncan, 'John Woolman', 6–7 and William Pollard, 'The Peace Question', *FQE*, v (1871), 443–9.

[35] Quaker Liberal MPs in 1882 were John Bright, William Fowler, Lewis Fry, Theodore Fry, Edward A. Leatham, George Palmer, J. W. Pease, Arthur Pease, James Richardson, and T. Richardson.

[36] *BF*, Sept. 1882, 241; Oct. 1883, 246; and C. R. K., 'Journals', v, 5 August 1883, 57, MS Vol. S 7, LSF.

the early 1890s, P. H. Peckover, whose brother became a Baron (and the only Lord Lieutenant in England to perform his duties in civilian attire), claimed to have enlisted over 15,000 members in Britain and Europe. While Peckover became a fixture at European Peace Congresses for decades and continued to head the LPA and edit its newspaper, *Peace & Goodwill*, until her death in 1931, the organization appears to have had little impact on either the Society of Friends or the larger society.[37]

By the mid-1880s, amidst the proliferation of small but costly imperial skirmishes, Quakers seemed to be in some disarray as regards the extent and meaning of their witness for peace. In 1882, for example, young John William Graham while resident at Kings' College, Cambridge, wrote to *The Friend* criticizing as 'untenable' the idea that it was always sinful for a Christian government to engage in warfare. Two years later Graham wrote in a similar vein, implying that future 'Prospects for Peace' depended less on the triumph of pacifist principles than on the expansion of British influence, and presumably the British Empire, throughout the globe. 'If all Europe were English,' said Graham, 'the peace of the world would be secure.'[38] On the other hand, Quakers were prominent among those already protesting attempts to create a race of imperial warriors by inculcating school boys 'with a military spirit' through the 'dangerous innovation' of introducing military drill into London Board Schools.[39]

Did the Empire, in fact, deserve defending or was it merely the playground of British militarism? If it was of benefit to mankind, it would presumably need soldiers to police and protect it, but the recent fate of Zulus, Afghans and others seemed to belie imperial benevolence.[40] An editorial in the *Friends Quarterly Examiner* in 1885 expressed the 'uneasy feeling' that Friends, perhaps overly influenced by 'political complications and party sympathies', were not as a body doing their 'duty in relation to this ancient testimony'

[37] The Papers of the Wisbech Local Peace Association are located in the Swarthmore College Peace Collection, Swarthmore, Pa. For the origins of the WLPA see *Peace and Goodwill* (*P&G*), 1 April 1882, 3 and *TF*, 18 September 1931. Also see the brief biographical sketch in *BDMPL*, 736–8.

[38] John W. Graham, 'The Distant Prospects of the Peace Party', *FQE*, (1884), 82–96, 161–71.

[39] *P&G*, 15 Jan. 1884, 110 and *BF*, Sept. 1885, 214–5.

[40] In this context, Graham's article, cited above, made oblique reference to 'stationary races... merely awaiting extinction'. 'Peace Party', 83.

against all war.[41] In that same year, Meeting for Sufferings, no doubt moved by events in the Sudan, did endeavour to reiterate the Society's peace testimony by setting out 'a clear and outspoken declaration against all war . . . confining itself to the broad principles of the New Testament . . . '[42]

For some reform-minded Friends, however, the idea of a peace testimony founded chiefly on scriptural injunctions was simply another reflection of the way in which the society's evangelical leadership had bound Quakerism into a strait-jacket of biblical literalism. In the light of the increasing influence, at least on enlightened Protestants, of historical and textual criticism of the Scriptures, would-be Quaker reformers believed that attempts to justify rejection of all wars and strife, or any other Christian principle, solely on the foundation of human-tainted biblical texts was perilous to the faith of increasingly better educated young Friends. Furthermore, both the fresh revelations of liberal Christianity, stressing the Incarnation rather than the Atonement, and renewed emphasis on the Inward Light, encouraged leaders of the Quaker renewal in the belief that they had discovered the means for restoring the vitality of their Religious Society and placing it at the forefront of the morally progressive forces.

Indeed, the historian of Victorian Quakerism has noted that the restoration of Inward Light theology struck late nineteenth-century reformers 'with the power of a new discovery'. In their search for the authentic historical roots of Quaker spirituality, leaders of the Quaker Renaissance perceived that if that which was of God dwelt equally in every person, then every human life must be equally sacred. For them, the Inward Light was not only the chief means by which God revealed Himself and His message, but also an unimpeachable verification of their Society's historic refusal to fight with carnal weapons.[43]

Renewal of emphasis on the Light provided progressive Friends with a fresh and challenging modern interpretation of their peace ideals and a higher level of rhetoric, but with regard to adding new depth and breadth to the Quaker witness against war, no consensus emerged despite the creation of a separate Friends Peace Committee in 1888. Most assuredly, the Quaker press, the Meeting for

---

[41] 'Peace or War', *FQE*, (1885), 153–4.
[42] Richard Littleboy, Clerk, Meeting for Sufferings, 'Address on War', ibid., (1885) 294.
[43] Isichei, 'From Sect to Denomination', 175–6.

Sufferings, its new Peace Committee and the Yearly Meeting itself intermittently addressed various perceived threats to peace such as rising military budgets, continued imperial expansion, the military training of youth, and the perceived threat of conscription. In 1889, for example, Meeting for Sufferings protested that

Whilst Lord Wolseley is glorifying war and urging the establishment of conscription, and Professor Seeley is arguing that war and trade have gone hand and hand . . . and Lord Lytton is announcing that nations are not to be bound by the moral law of God in their transactions with other nations, we need to take fresh courage and testify, in the name of the Prince of Peace, against the iniquity of the present military system and in favour of Peace which is the fount of righteousness and just government.[44]

Such sentiments were clear enough, but a real plan of campaign was not. Quaker groups continued to voice concern about the warlike statements or actions of successive Governments. Friends wanted to believe that protests by Yearly Meeting had some effect in restraining aggressive policies or that pamphlets published by the Peace Committee really improved chances for international peace and reconciliation.[45] But when, for example, in the spring of 1894, Meeting for Sufferings sponsored a resolution calling for international arbitration and disarmament and asked leave to present it to the Prime Minister and Foreign Secretary, Lords Rosebery and Kimberley 'declined to receive a deputation at this period of the session'.[46] The response of Friends to this snub at the hands of a Liberal Government was more akin to that of lambs than of soldiers in the Lambs' War and while such insults did not stop Friends from attempting to influence Government policies, the question of how explicitly to challenge the apparently unrighteous

---

[44] *LYM*, 1889, 81–2. Lord Lytton became a particular target of Friends. In Oct. 1895, for example, the *British Friend* (252) protested his 'policy of domination, extension and petty conquest' as Viceroy of India; York Quarterly Meeting later condemned what it perceived to be Lytton's ruthless treatment and oppressive taxation of native peoples.

[45] Some recent scholarship reflects the questionable view that the sporadic peace propaganda issued by the Peace Committee was efficacious in itself, proof of a strong commitment to the peace testimony and perhaps even useful in maintaining international peace. See Margaret McKechnie Glover, 'Aspects of Publishing by the Peace Committee of the Religious Society of Friends (London Yearly Meeting), 1888–1905', *QS*, 3 (1998), 27–51.

[46] *Minutes*, Peace Committee, 11, 20 Feb., 9 April, 2 May and 23 August 1894, LSF.

practices of British Governments would trouble Quakers right up to the outbreak of the Great War.[47]

Perhaps the lack of an immediate diplomatic crisis in Europe or the Empire explains why the peace testimony was not seriously addressed at the Manchester Conference in November 1895, but the paucity of discussion on this supposedly fundamental principle at a Conference devoted to Friends and Modern Thought seems most curious.[48] In any case, early in 1896, in the aftermath of the Jameson Raid, John William Graham, having apparently modified his earlier vision of the spread of British influence throughout the globe as enhancing prospects for peace, expressed his concern about the 'passive' nature of the Quaker stance. 'Our Peace Principles', Graham said, 'are held in these days without any very obvious sacrifice on our part... "Peace" costs us only a perfunctory subscription.'[49] For his part, Graham hoped that Friends would begin to play not only a more active but also a more practical role in the peace movement. He suggested that Friends co-operate with *every* group advocating peace, whether or not they were Christians or absolute pacifists so that Quakers might help to build a peace alliance which could give effect in some aspects of their struggle against war.[50]

Graham's vision of 'an energetic and self-sacrificing peace policy' struck a responsive chord among some co-religionists, who saw it as a manifestation of the recent 'great awakening of earnest thought among us on this subject... a shifting of views and opinions... leading to a belief which has become vital and

[47] The question of London Yearly Meeting's too cosy relationship with English and European royalty, social élites and civil authorities is critically addressed by Brian Phillips in his Ph.D. thesis 'Friendly Patriotism: British Quakerism and the Imperial Nation, 1890–1910', (Cambridge 1989).

[48] The only speakers who introduced consideration of the peace testimony as an issue for modern Friends at Manchester were Samuel J. Capper and Priscilla H. Peckover. Peckover was a member of the Peace Committee, but Capper (1840–1904), while obviously one of the most active Quaker peace advocates (he spoke to fifty-six peace meetings during the first five months of 1896), was, rather curiously, not accepted as a member of the Peace Committee because he was not a 'member of this meeting'. See *Manchester Conference*, 48–50, 64 and *Minutes*, 11, Peace Committee, 16 May 1896, LSF.

[49] John W. Graham, 'Whence Comes Peace', *BF*, Feb. 1896, 27–9. Graham was referring to frequent Quaker practice of joining Peace Societies without taking an active role in their activities.

[50] *BF*, Feb. and April 1896, 27–9 and 77–80. Half a century earlier Joseph Sturge had suggested collaborative efforts for peace even with those whose opposition to war might be on 'lower ground' than Friends. See Ceadel, *Origins of War Prevention*, 438.

active . . . '[51] As an aspect of such vitality, Friends could also cite Meeting for Sufferings' decision early in 1898 to issue 'AN APPEAL TO THE NATION', partly in response to the 'warlike character of the procession . . . to celebrate the sixtieth year of the Queen's reign', a reign inauspiciously marred by thirty-eight wars: 'We cannot shut our eyes to the fact that the pomp and show by which the nation testifies to its loyalty is chiefly military . . . that the growth of imperial feeling has not been accompanied by a corresponding development of the higher sentiments of national duty . . .'[52]

European nations, said the 'APPEAL', were groaning 'under the crushing burden of their military establishments'. But if the masses could be released from the onerous grip of militarism while their governments began to act on the basis of Christian principles, 'what new age would dawn for the world, and how beautiful upon the mountain would be the feet of that messenger who should herald the promised peace'.[53]

For all such proclamations, the official agencies of British Quakerism consistently held back from any serious confrontation with secular power. When, for example, a member of the Peace Committee proposed, in the wake of the Spanish-American War (1898), that Meeting for Sufferings address President McKinley on 'the unrighteousness of war', the Committee deferred, thinking it better to wait for some 'spontaneous action' by Yearly Meeting. Such delays inevitably banked the fires of righteous indignation; when Meeting for Sufferings finally issued an 'Address to Lovers of Peace in America', the document was sufficiently watered-down to avoid giving serious offence.[54]

---

[51] *BF*, letters from M. L. Cooke, March 1896, 69 and from Frances Thompson, April 1896, 92–3. Still, at times, Quakers exhibited an irritating penchant for remaining righteous in the eyes of both God and Mammon. For example, in August 1895 the *British Friend*, 204 noted that Hodgson Pratt's International Arbitration and Peace Society was not well supported by Friends 'inasmuch as it does not assert the doctrine of the theoretical unlawfulness of all defensive wars'. The next year the Peace Committee withdrew its support from a peace demonstration by the Internationalist Socialist Workers when it discovered that body would offer a Resolution of 'a strongly Socialist character'. *Minutes*, Peace Committee, 11, 2 Sept. 1896, LSF.

[52] *LYM, 1898*, 90–2 and *BF*, July 1897, 182. *P&G*, 4/14, July 1897, 200 listed all thirty-eight armed conflicts in which Britain had been involved during Victoria's reign.

[53] *LYM, 1898*, 92–3.

[54] *Minutes*, Peace Committee, 11, 4 May 1898, LSF and *LYM, 1899*, 129. The Address was issued in August 1898. Also see *BF*, Aug. 1898, 203 and Jan. 1899, 5.

Similarly, the *British Friend* deplored the 'positively loathsome' language of British newspapers in describing 'the sickening slaughter of Dervishes at Omdurman' and looked in vain for condemnation from 'any influential Christian quarter' for General Kitchener's apparent acquiescence in these atrocities. But when the ensuing Fashoda incident brought Britain and France to the brink of war and Ellen Robinson, a tireless peace advocate, drafted a tract condemning Britain's part in creating the crisis, the Peace Committee felt 'the matter too controversial' to sanction publication of Robinson's protest.[55]

Ellen Robinson's was not the only voice calling upon Friends to stand collectively against popular opinion. Readers of religious literature might have taken note of John Stephenson Rowntree's fierce attack on Britain's 'deplorably heathenish' native policy in South Africa. In the course of his lectures to the Scarborough Summer School, Rowntree noted that Britain's method of dealing with black Africans seemed to be 'To steal their country, debauch them with vile spirits, when they resist to call them rebels, and mow down "the niggers" with Maxim guns, and finally give sites of stolen land for mission stations . . . a policy as despicable as it is wicked.' If they failed to condemn such outrages, Rowntree said, Friends were, in effect, treating their peace testimony 'as an isolated piece of social amelioration, which can be detached from the whole body of Christian faith and practice'.[56]

Other Friends were moved 'to denounce a foreign policy of greed and aggression as dishonouring to our country'. Using *The Present-Day Papers* as their forum, William Charles Braithwaite and John Wilhelm Rowntree pointed out that there was 'a great difference between holding peace principles in the vagueness of tradition and grasping them with the intelligent conviction that comes from personal examination'. Friends, said Braithwaite, needed the courage to face up to those who might accuse them of being unpatriotic and to remember that erstwhile patriots 'who drag their country's honour in the mud by "Jameson raids" and the oppression of native races' made patriotism 'a word with sinister connections'.[57] J. W. Rowntree took up the same theme:

[55] *BF*, Oct. 1898, 253–4 and Nov. 1898, 278 and *Minutes*, Peace Committee, II, 30 Nov. 1898, LSF.
[56] J. S. Rowntree, *Place of Society of Friends in Religious Life of England*, 58–9, 61–2.
[57] [William Charles Braithwaite], 'Work for Peace', *PDP*, II, June 1899, 5–12.

We need patriots who will wage unceasing war with all that lowers moral vitality—with the luxury that enervates it, the militarism that stints it, the greed that freezes its force, the pride that fevers it—it is here that the issues of life and death are found, and on the outcome of this struggle hangs our country's fate.[58]

Within a few months after Rowntree issued his challenge, the Anglo-Boer War would provide ample opportunity for testing the moral vitality of the Quaker peace testimony. Friends failed the test. Their response to this crisis was not an occasion for unity, but rather pointed up deep differences as to what constituted both true patriotism and a meaningful peace testimony.

'LET US BE EARNEST AND DO OUR PART'

As early as May 1897, the *British Friend* had warned of the 'danger of race-war in South Africa', and when war did come, an editorial predicted that national humiliation and bitterness would follow in its wake.[59] Events soon justified this assessment and the Society of Friends would discover what an ample legacy of bitterness and humiliation the South African conflict could bestow. At first, Quaker response to the war seemed both predictable and, from the peace lover's perspective, satisfactory. Friends were represented in the activities and especially the financing of the South African Conciliation Committee (SACC) formed in mid-January 1900 to work for the restoration of goodwill between Boer and Briton.[60] Monthly meetings throughout the country issued statements pledging their faithfulness to the peace testimony, not 'traditionally or negatively, but ... with life and true spiritual vigour'.[61] In this regard, Meeting for Sufferings published 'A Protest Against Compulsory Military Service', appealing to fellow-Christians to join Friends in checking 'the spirit of military imperialism'. Indeed, the

---

[58] [John Wilhelm Rowntree], 'The Unlawfulness of War to the Christian', *PDP*, 11, (May 1899), 18.

[59] *BF*, May 1897, 101 and Nov. 1899, 287–90.

[60] Hewison, *Hedge of Wild Almonds*, 109–10 and Greenwood, *Friends and Relief*, 151. Also see Richard A. Rempel, 'British Quakers and the South African War', *QH*, 64 (Autumn 1975), 81 and *BF*, Feb. 1900, 25.

[61] *LYM, 1900*, 171–5 and *Minutes 1 & 8, Minutes*, Lancashire and Cheshire Quarterly Meeting, LRO.

idea that the war might bring conscription and martyrdom seemed positively enticing to some Quakers. *The Friend* noted that if compulsory military service were introduced: 'We shall find out once and for all whether our refusal to share in the patriotism of the day has been dictated by conscience or by indolence;' the *British Friend* added: 'we believe it would not be at all a bad thing for us to have to suffer again in some degree for our principles.'[62]

A few martyrs might indeed have helped to rescue British Quakerism from the trouble and turmoil that eventually engulfed it. But conscription was never in the cards and the suffering endured by a few Friends at the hands of patriotic mobs, most notably the attack on the houses and businesses of the Rowntree family at Scarborough, was insufficient to rally the Society to a united anti-war standard.[63] In the aftermath of the Scarborough incident, *The Friend* perceived a growing 'intensity of moral conviction rising to maintain an unmitigated protest against the present war-fever and all its cruel results'.[64] No such intensity was reflected in the official pronouncements of London Yearly Meeting. When the Peace Committee prepared a 'Memorial' to the Government calling for immediate peace in the Transvaal, Meeting for Sufferings declined to adopt the document, recommending instead that the Committee reissue the 'Christian Appeal' circulated during the Crimean War as more applicable to the South African crisis.[65]

When Yearly Meeting gathered in late May 1900, many Friends undoubtedly united with Ellen Robinson's plea that the 'whole world seemed to be crying out for some one to deliver it from the monstrous yoke of militarism ... crushing the life out of the nations. Let us be earnest and do our part.'[66] But when Yearly Meeting finally approved a new appeal entitled 'Christianity and War', the document proved to be more a cause for division than

---

[62] *TF*, 23 Feb. 1900, 122 and *BF*, Feb. 1900, 26.

[63] See *BF*, April 1900, 74–87 *passim*; Rempel, 'British Friends', 83–4; and Hewison, *Hedge of Wild Almonds*, 116–18 for the attacks on Rowntree property following the appearance of pro-Boer Samuel Cronwright-Schreiner in Scarborough. Members of the family subsequently issued an 'Address' to the community promising not to bring action against any person or to make any charge for compensation against the Borough Fund.

[64] 30 March 1900, 189–90.

[65] *Minutes*, Peace Committee, 11, 29 Nov. 1899, 3 January, 4 April and 8 June 1900, LSF.

[66] *BF*, 8 June 1900, 156–7.

for unity. The *British Friend* noted that while the first Yearly Meeting of the twentieth century should have been chiefly remembered for 'clearing up the Society's position on . . . War and Peace', a small group of Friends (all older evangelicals) had 'astonished their brethren' by protesting against the inclusion of the phrase 'the brotherhood of man and the Fatherhood of God' in the plea for peace.[67] After some discussion the Clerk agreed to the omission, much to the disgust of the *British Friend* which expressed the view that those who rejected the concept of the brotherhood of man under the Fatherhood of God were '*not* Friends *at all*' and, indeed, could scarcely be called Christians.[68] In its printed 'Report to Friends' for 1900, the Peace Committee had to admit that while 'a great number of Friends have done all in their power to oppose and protest against the present deplorable war . . . many others have felt unable to take active part in upholding the testimony of Friends'.[69] Such a pusillanimous performance gave currency to *Reynolds Weekly Newspaper's* assertion in March 1900 that the Society of Friends was 'no longer to be regarded as a strenuous and united peace organisation'.[70]

This conclusion was reinforced by the early defection of the distinguished Quaker publisher, lexicographer and Peace Committee member, John Bellows (1831–1902). Bellows, a man of strong convictions and boundless energy, was given to passionate advocacy of a somewhat bewildering array of causes, including the American Confederacy, the relief of Franco-Prussian War victims, the rescue of Russian Dukhobors, Ulster Unionism and, finally, the crushing of the Boers.[71] Bellows produced a series of diatribes largely given over to the vilification of the Afrikaners, most notably in a tract entitled 'The Truth About the Transvaal War, and About All War'.[72] The fact that the backsliding Bellows had been a much-admired attender at the Hague

---

[67] Ibid. 150–1, 180–2. Also see *LYM, 1900*, 64–69.

[68] *BF*, 8 June 1900, 151 [emphasis in original].

[69] 'Report of Friends' Peace Committee, 1900—To the Meeting for Sufferings'. This printed document is included in the Peace Committee's *Minutes*, LSF.

[70] *Reynolds Weekly Newspaper*, quoted by Rempel, 'British Quakers', 77.

[71] See Kate Charity, *John Bellows of Gloucester, 1831–1902* (York 1993) for Bellows' extraordinary career as a printer, scholar, champion of the oppressed, and purveyor of eccentric opinions.

[72] See *BF*, May 1900, 119–20 and J. Rendel Harris to Margaret Clark, 16 May 1900, 'Quaker Principles', Box 3, WL.

Peace Conference early in 1899[73] would seem to lend support to Brian Phillips' argument that most of the prominent Friends who were part of what Phillips calls the European 'high-life' peace circuit were more eager 'to establish the Quaker point of view as an undisputedly patriotic one' than to testify against the sinfulness of fighting with carnal weapons.[74]

Not that Bellows was let off easily. One of his severest critics was acting editor of the *British Friend*, Edward Grubb, who later recalled: 'If *that* war could be condoned by so-called Pacifists... I was sure that *any* war could be...'[75] Grubb concluded a series of attacks on Bellows in the *British Friend* by noting that 'our Friend has grievously compromised the Society by writing in support of the war *avowedly as a Friend* [and] used his position... of influence to do... irreparable injury to the Society of Friends and the cause of Peace'.[76]

Still, Bellows had some outspoken Quaker supporters, including Caroline Stephen, Victorian Quakerism's most illustrious convert. Her influential *Quaker Strongholds* (1890) is generally accounted a harbinger of the Quaker Renaissance.[77] However, immediately after it was published there were Friends who expressed serious concern about Stephen's rendition of the peace testimony. A review in the leading American Quaker evangelical journal noted that while it was all very well and very flattering for Caroline Stephen to depict Quakerism as an oasis of Light amidst the materialistic darkness of the modern world, she appeared unconcerned with major sources of that darkness like the arms race and militarism. For all her personal serenity within the Quaker communion, Stephen, the author believed, had too little regard for the centrality of the peace testimony in the spiritual witness of the Society.[78]

[73] See *The Autobiography of Andrew Dickson White*, 2 vols. (New York 1905), II, 272–3 which depicts Bellows as 'a thoroughly good man—sincere, honest, earnest, and blessed with good sense'.

[74] Phillips, 'Friendly Patriotism', 67–8.

[75] Edward Grubb, 'Some Personal Experiences', *FQE*, 72 (Oct 1938), 307.

[76] 'John Bellows and the War,' *BF*, Dec. 1900, 307–9. For other protests against Bellows, see ibid., Sept. 1900, 236–8; Oct. 1900, 263–6; Nov. 1900, 4 pp. Supplement; and Dec. 1900, 312–4.

[77] See Jones, *Later Periods*, II, 967–70 and Chapter 5 above.

[78] William Edgerton, 'Have Friends a Testimony Against War?', *Christian Worker*, 21/14 (2 April 1891), 212–13.

A perusal of *Quaker Strongholds* reveals the legitimacy of this concern:

It is commonly supposed that Friends have some special scruple about the use of physical force . . . This I believe by no means true of the Society at large, although . . . very likely to be founded on fact as regards individuals . . . I came to understand that the Quaker testimony against all war did not take the form of any ethical theory of universal application . . . as to the 'unlawfulness' of war . . . I personally cannot but recognize that . . . certain wars appear to be not only inevitable but justifiable . . . . I cannot, therefore, regard all war as wholly and unmitigatedly blameable . . . [79]

Stephen added that she could 'hardly imagine any war which does not both come from evil and lead to evil', but there is nothing distinctly Quaker about that, especially when most citizens tend to assume that the national enemy will, by nature, both be evil and do evil.

When Caroline Stephen appeared with John Bellows at a meeting of the Cambridge Peace Society to defend the justice of the South African conflict, one witness to their performance, J. Rendel Harris, told a friend: 'It was very sad to have our cause given away, as it was by Caroline Stephen and John Bellows . . . There is no doubt in my own mind that we are betrayed in the citadel itself.'[80]

Bellows and Stephen were only two of the most prominent public Friends who defected to the war camp. Perhaps even more jolting was the pro-war stance of Thomas Hodgkin, the pre-eminent public Quaker of his day. Hodgkin not only supported the war effort but also depicted the Boers as monstrous oppressors of both natives and Uitlanders, unworthy, even incapable, of maintaining a civilized state.[81] The controversy aroused by Thomas Hodgkin's forthright support for the war engulfed other members of his family, most notably his son Robin, a student at Balliol, who wrote to *The Friend* implying that many Quakers who

---

[79] Stephan, *Quaker Strongholds*, 122, 130, 15, 139.
[80] J. Rendel Harris to Margaret Clark, 23 Feb. 1900, 'Quaker Principles', Box 3, WL. Also see C. Stephen to L[ucy] H[odgkin], 19 Feb. 1900, MS vol. 128, LSF.
[81] *TF*, 17 Nov. 1899, 760 and T. Hodgkin to R. M. Jones, 21 Jan. 1900, RMJP. Thomas Hodgkin's attitude was probably influenced by the extreme hostility toward the Boers of his brother-in-law, Sir Robert Nicholas Fowler, a former Lord Mayor of London. See Hewison, *Hedge of Wild Almonds*, 106–7.

were not convinced of the immorality of the Transvaal War were nevertheless continuing to take shelter behind the peace testimony, thus 'bringing on the Society the shadow of hypocrisy'. To illustrate the courage of his own convictions, Robin Hodgkin became an officer in the Northumberland Fusiliers.[82]

What especially rankled anti-war Quakers about the Hodgkin family's declarations was not so much their assumption of superior knowledge as their insistence, in the words of one critic, 'that they must be strictly regarded as very true Friends' whatever they said or did.[83] John Wilhelm Rowntree expressed his indignation to Rufus Jones:

You would hardly believe your eyes if you came over here. Thos. Hodgkin's son a Lieutenant, though still a nominal Quaker, heads a procession to burn Kruger in effigy, T. Hodgkin makes the speech and Lily [Lucy?] Hodgkin lights the faggots . . . the spirit of war, stalks the land naked, unashamed & our leading Quaker gives his benediction! . . .

There has been such a moral debacle as I would not have deemed as possible two years ago. Our 'Khaki' election [November 1900] has shaken my belief in democracy & has opened my eyes to the terrifying power of the press . . . As for our pulpits, they have been beneath contempt . . . we have suffered a great moral disaster . . . Until we can exorcise the 'Imperialist' demon—goodbye to real progress.[84]

Rowntree believed 'this wretched war' had cast a pall over the future of the peace testimony:

I feel that one lesson of the war . . . is the need for the proper instruction of our *own* people. Each generation has to recapture for itself its spiritual heritage, and we need to seize upon the opportunity this war gives us for the restatement of our principles . . . It is quite a mistake to assume that

[82] TF, 16 Feb. 1900, 104–5 and Hewison, *Hedge of Wild Almonds*, 129–30. Caroline Stephen told Robin Hodgkin's mother that there was 'much of nobleness . . . much that appeals to all one's best feelings' in what her son had said and done. C. Stephen to L[ucy] H[odgkin], 19 Feb. 1900, MS Vol. 128, LSF. Robert H. Hodgkin (1877–1951) survived the war, resigned from Friends, and enjoyed a distinguished academic career in modern history at Queens College, Oxford, eventually becoming Provost of the College (1937–46).
[83] Shipley N. Brayshaw to *TF*, 9 March 1900, 153–4.
[84] J. W. R. to R. M. J., 6 Feb. 1901, Box 3, RMJP.

our young people will grow up 'right upon the war question', unless we take the proper steps to inculcate our principles.[85]

It was, Rowntree continued,

no time for soft speech. There are elements in our national character which call for stern condemnation . . . Our testimony against war, if it is to be vital, must not be mere testimony against the use of armed force—it must cut at the roots of war, at the pride of Empire, the narrow . . . popular patriotism rendered ignoble by its petty hatreds and the insatiable hunger for wealth which visibly threatens our ruin.[86]

Stirred, perhaps, by such rhetorical flourishes, as well as by widening public indignation against the results of farm burning and concentration camps which Friends had some hand in exposing,[87] Quaker protests gradually became more firm and more united. Early in 1901, after Meeting for Sufferings had issued a 'Memorial to the Government' condemning 'the methods by which the deplorable war in South Africa is now being prosecuted',[88] W. Evans Darby of the Peace Society approached the Quaker Peace Committee asking Friends to organize a Conference of Churches to consider the question of war from a Christian perspective in conjunction with a Peace Congress to be held in Glasgow. With public protest against British tactics rapidly heating up, the Peace Committee leapt at the opportunity to form the centre of an anti-war phalanx. Weighty Friends were enlisted to speak at Glasgow and, in May, Yearly Meeting issued a 'Plea for a Peaceable Spirit', noting the baleful influence of the continuing conflict: death and devastation in South Africa, and in Britain, 'the

---

[85] J. W. R., *Essays and Addresses*, p. xxxii [emphasis in original].

[86] *TF*, 26 Jan. 1900, 56–7. Also see *BF*, June 1901, 134. Rowntree's remarks were directed toward an earlier article by Anne W. Richardson, 'A Quaker View of War', *TF*, 12 Jan. 1900, 19–23 which counselled 'passive resistance' and 'patient consistency'.

[87] Two official Quakers deputations toured South Africa. The first consisted of Joshua Rowntree, mayor of Scarborough and former MP for Yorkshire, his wife and nephew, Harold J. Ellis, the son of J. E. Ellis, MP; the second was an investigatory committee of the Friends South African Relief Committee (FSARC) led by Lawrence Richardson and W. H. F. Alexander. See Hewison, *Hedge of Wild Almonds*, 165–224 *passim*; Arthur M. Davey (ed.), *Lawrence Richardson: Selected Correspondence (1902–03)* (Cape Town 1977); and *BF*, April 1901, 89–90.

[88] Reprinted in *BF*, Jan. 1901, 9. Also see *LYM, 1901*, 109.

reign of prejudice, the fever of passion, the riots, the orgies in our streets, the preaching of vengeance by the Press and even from some pulpits . . . In condoning militarism the Christian church destroys with one hand the . . . ideal of righteousness and love as the bond and foundation of empire.'[89]

Before and after Yearly Meeting the Quaker press provided thorough and sympathetic coverage of Emily Hobhouse's dispatches and speeches on the calamitous conditions in South African concentration camps. During June and July of 1901 Quakers were among the most prominent supporters of Hobhouse's speaking tour on the horrors of British concentration camps. Indeed, in towns like Hull and Scarborough Quaker meeting houses were the only venues permitted to her.[90] The Friends South African Relief Committee reported that the work of its representatives in the camps had 'resulted in the alleviation of bodily and mental suffering, and in the spread of the spirit of peace'. But a lingering controversy over the refusal of the FSARC to publish the correspondence of all its representatives led to accusations that the letters of Georgina King Lewis and others had been suppressed because they were insufficiently critical of the camps.[91]

In the wake of this new bout of divisiveness, Friends needed a morale booster, and although the Glasgow Peace Congress in September 1901 was indisputably a case of preaching to the converted, the prominent role played by Friends there helped provide the required uplift.[92] When the war ended in May 1902, the Society of Friends emerged, if not united, at least in somewhat less obvious disarray and with a widely felt need to define more precisely the Society's position with regard to its peace testimony. The Yearly Meeting which gathered shortly after the signing of the Treaty of Vereeniging seemed to be responding to this renewed sense of urgency when it agreed to the appointment of a special Deputation charged to visit every Monthly Meetings in Britain

---

[89] *Minutes*, Peace Committee, 20 Feb., 15 April, 2 May and 6 June 1901, LSF; *BF*, 10 June 1901, 148–9; and *LYM, 1901*, 115. The Peace Committee reported in 1902 that 250,000 copies of 'A Plea for a Peaceable Spirit' had been circulated, LYM, 1902, 125–6.

[90] See *BF*, July 1901, 181; August 1901, 211, 220; Sept. 1901, 233–4; Nov. 1901, 286–7; and Dec. 1901, 213–4. Also see Hewinson, *Hedge of Wild Almonds*, 193–200.

[91] See *BF*, Feb. 1902, 40–1; March 1902, 50; and April 1902, 77. Also see Hewison, *Hedge of Wild Almonds*, 214–24.

[92] *BF*, Sept. 1901, 234 and *LYM, 1902*, 128–9.

'with a view to arousing our members to their responsibility . . . of maintaining our "testimony of peace" . . . '[93] This 'most important' resolution galvanized John Stephenson Rowntree to address a special memorandum to Meeting for Sufferings. J. S. Rowntree stressed that circumstances required this Visiting Committee to play a central role in rescuing the Society's peace testimony from its status as 'little more than a pious opinion', which was separated from and 'almost independent of the other parts of Christian truth'. Special care should be taken, he said, to place the testimony in its historical setting as well as to address the specific modern causes of its weakness, so that in the new century Friends might truly be prepared to answer 'the cry of humanity, groaning beneath the load of militarism . . . [and] demanding from the advocates of Peace, prayer and labour in her holy name'.[94]

REVIVING THE PEACE TESTIMONY

The Peace Deputation appointed in 1902 to visit every British Monthly Meeting for the purpose of strengthening Friends' attachment to peace principles made its final report to Yearly Meeting in 1904. In the course of its travels, the Committee had been encouraged by indications of a renewed awareness the peace testimony's importance, by the 'warm response' of the general public to appeals for peace and, most especially, by the 'self-denying and untiring effort of younger Friends' in giving practical application to their peace principles.[95]

The self-satisfied ambience of this and other official pronouncements of Edwardian Quakerism has been severely criticized by Brian Phillips in his study of 'Friendly Patriotism'. Early twentieth-century Quakers, Phillips believes, were not so much a religious body attempting to come to grips with historic principles as 'an essentially conservative, respectability-conscious community with no real appetite for risky political struggle . . . trading something of . . . [their] subversive theological origins for a bland set of

---

[93] The resolution was brought by Bristol and Somerset Quarterly Meeting. See *BF*, June 1902, 154.
[94] John Stephenson Rowntree, 'Memorandum on the Peace Committee, LYM 1902', 12 pp. BOV H1/12, LSF.
[95] *LYM, 1904*, 33–5.

doctrines which gave offence to no one'.[96] Furthermore, Phillips asserts that this self-righteous, self-congratulatory tone has persisted in 'the inevitable parochialism of "in-house" denominational scholarship' which, he says, has dominated twentieth-century Quaker historiography.[97]

Phillips' strongly argued thesis certainly reveals some unflattering and even distressing tendencies within the Edwardian Society of Friends. No one writing about early twentieth-century Quakerism can ignore his critique of a Quaker 'peace elite'—prominent Friends inevitably listed among the delegates to sundry highly-publicized and officially-sponsored Peace Conferences—engaged in 'unctuous posturing before the thrones of Europe' while failing to develop any 'critical, realistic perspective on the limitation of monarchical conversion' to the peace movement. Quaker 'hubris', Phillips says, 'drastically diminished the Society's effectiveness in the crucial foreign policy debates leading up to the First World War'.[98] As regards the Society's unquestionably radical official stance during the Great War, Phillips explains this as a sort of last-minute conversion experience inspired by a combination of Norman Angellism—'the very salvation of a flagging Quaker Peace Testimony'—and the clear-headed, tough-minded leadership of young men like Phillip Noel-Baker (1892–1982) and Horace Alexander (1889–1989). Both of these men would attain international prominence as peace advocates in the inter-war period, but neither adhered to the absolutist position which was supported by Meeting for Sufferings and became the standard by which the twentieth-century Quaker peace testimony has come to be defined.[99]

Still, if Phillips' explanation for the emergence of the stalwart official wartime stance of British Quakerism is less than persuasive, his censure of Edwardian Friends has, to a degree, been given credence by other historians of the period. In James Hinton's study of early twentieth-century *Protests and Visions*, he maintains that the British peace movement was 'deeply scarred by often

---

[96] Phillips, 'Friendly Patriotism', 76, 333.

[97] While Phillips, ibid. 22–4, 27 cites the work of the late Roger Wilson, former Clerk of London Yearly Meeting (1975–77), as an 'in-house' historical perceptive, neither of the other historians specifically mentioned, Elizabeth Isichei and Thomas Kennedy, are members of the Society of Friends.

[98] Phillips, ibid. 155, 158, 199.

[99] Ibid. 307–42 *passim*.

unrecognized imperialist assumptions . . . [which] struck deep roots in the British political culture' and haunts pacifists even to this day.[100] Validations of Hinton's view can be found in public or private examples of Edwardian Friends giving apparently whole-hearted approval to the aims and ends of European, and especially British, expansion. The tone might be fervently congratulatory, as in the *British Friend*'s satisfaction that British rule had resulted in freeing the slaves of Zanzibar and Pemba, 'one more solid piece of work . . . The value of such an influence among that child race can hardly be overestimated.' Or, Friends might take an eminently practical approach to empire, as in Edward Grubb's review of Benjamin Kidd's *Social Evolution*: 'The civilised peoples will not, and ought not to, consent to see the richest regions of the earth remain permanently unused. If they could be properly developed, it would not only supply *us* with more abundant food and raw material, but it would afford a far wider market for *our* goods.'[101] Finally, Quaker comments might be merely condescending, as in a report on the inroads Christianity was supposedly making into traditional Japanese religious beliefs: 'as Christianity *proves itself*, by its superior moral efficiency . . . it is likely to take hold of the thinking and enquiring minds of the East.'[102]

Still, for every example of Quaker support for the potentialities or results of British imperialism, two others might be found that questioned or protested against imperial adventures. Ellen Robinson, one of those Phillips includes among the fawning and super-ficial Quaker 'peace elite', personally addressed eighty peace meetings in 1898. The tone of her remarks to these gatherings might be discerned from an article she published in the *British Friend*: 'the main trend . . . of the history of colonization has been in the direction of oppression and injustice towards native races . . . I long that our own Society should take a more prominent and active part in seeking to right some of the great wrongs that are being done. . . .'[103] A year later John Wilhelm Rowntree, whom Phillips depicts as 'not exempt from the spell of national respect

---

[100] James Hinton, *Protests and Vision: Peace Politics in the Twentieth Century* (London 1989), pp. 2 and viii.
[101] *BF*, May 1897, 101–2 and E. Grubb, 'The Future of the Tropics', ibid., March 1899, 53–4 [emphasis added].
[102] *BF.*, Sept. 1899, 236.
[103] Ellen Robinson, 'Colonization and Native Races', *BF*, Nov. 1899, 294–6.

and reputation which so captivated the Society', condemned the hypocrisy of those who, 'under the plea of accepting the white man's burden . . . exploit the lands of savages for the sake of dividends'. Rowntree called upon Friends 'to be heralds of the "peaceful Gospel" . . . and to combat the insidious evil which masquerades as "Imperialism"'.[104]

The point, of course, is that while there were many weighty and venerable Quaker voices, none of these spoke for the collective Society of Friends. Whether they were discussing the Empire, the Temperance Movement, Free Trade, the Liberal Party, Irish Home Rule, socialism, or the peace testimony, individual Friends disagreed. Only London Yearly Meeting and its executive, Meeting for Sufferings, could make or approve pronouncements that represented the sense of the Society. To be sure, in normal circumstances, statements by either of these bodies tended to be bland and inoffensive, full of earnest pleadings and pious generalities. When you combine, as Phillips does, the customarily innocuous resolutions of Yearly Meeting with the usually cautious pronouncements of Meeting for Suffering and add in the occasional obsequious reference to royalty or naïve complacency of individual Quakers, the result cannot not fail to be disconcerting, especially for those who have come to think of Friends as the one Christian community that inevitably spoke truth to power and always maintained the integrity of its convictions. Of course, such a view asks too much, even for so small and tight-knit a body as the Society of Friends. A meaningful evaluation of the fealty of any body of believers to the principles they supposedly live by can only be made in time of crisis. Although many individual Friends faced personal or spiritual dilemmas regarding the peace testimony during the Edwardian period, the peace witness of the Religious Society of Friends was not fundamentally challenged until the Great War began in 1914 and not truly tested until the passage of the Military Service Acts of 1916. Only then did a choice have to be made between visions of God's will and the facts of earthly necessity. Prior to that crisis the more useful question is: How did those who stood the test during the Great War prepare for the trial that awaited them?

---

[104] Phillips, 'Friendly Patriotism', 74; JWR, 'Plea for a Quaker Settlement', 135, 143; and 'What has Jesus to Say to the State?', 373–4 in *Essays and Reviews*.

What follows is an attempt to trace the development of Quaker peace witness during the early years of the twentieth century. Public manifestations of the Quaker peace testimony included protests against the administration of the British Empire (its abolition was apparently never considered), against the threat of conscription, including the compulsory military training of British or imperial youth, and against the growth of popular militarism in both domestic and foreign affairs. Obviously, these combined efforts were insufficient in widening the circle of pacifist true believers, but for an historian of Quakerism the critical question must be whether or not the Friends who engaged in these activities were motivated by genuine devotion to their historic peace testimony.

In the midst of the Anglo-Boer War, the Friends' Peace Committee was forced to admit that many Quakers were not upholding their Society's peace testimony. Still, nearly all Friends and, indeed, most of the general population would have agreed that enforced military service, in South Africa or anywhere, was anathema. Thus, when Meeting for Sufferings addressed a 'Protest Against Compulsory Service' to the Prime Minister (Lord Salisbury) and the Foreign Secretary (Lord Lansdowne), it could be confident of expressing the Society's entire opposition to 'any attempt to enforce compulsory military service [as]...an infringement of the liberty of conscience which...is one of the greatest privileges of citizens of this country'.[105]

While any overt threat of conscription certainly ended with the Treaty of Vereeniging in May 1902, William Charles Braithwaite simultaneously reminded Friends that peace in South Africa would not terminate the 'Imperial policy of self-aggrandizement and lust after gold' that had caused war in the first place. To illustrate his message Braithwaite pointed to two recent and ominous developments: the founding of the pro-conscriptionist National Service League and the Board of Education's recommendation that schools adopt a 'Model Course' for physical training 'taken in the main from the Infantry Drill Book of the British Army'.[106] For his own

---

[105] 'Report of Friends' Peace Committee, 1900, to the Meeting for Sufferings', LSF; *Minutes*, Peace Committee, 11, 1 and 28 Feb. 1900, ibid.; and *LYM, 1900*, 169–70.

[106] W. C. B., 'Youth and Militarism', 34, 6, pamphlet (8 pp.) in Temp Box 4/1, LSF.

part, Braithwaite's response was a motion presented to the Eighty-Sixth Annual Meeting of the Peace Society deprecating 'the strenuous efforts...being made for the...converting of the whole manhood of the nation into a huge fighting machine...' The motion was, of course, 'carried with applause'.[107]

In the meantime, the Friends' Peace Committee determined to meet the threat of military drill for school children by offering cash prizes to young scholars who wrote the best essays on 'Peace and War' in the hope 'that young people shall learn for themselves that...patriotism finds its highest tasks in the development and uplifting of national life...We desire that they...recognize statesmen are most worthy...who labour to cheapen food, reduce taxation, improve education...and generally to effect social and moral improvement.'[108] This was, in fact, also an expression of the hope that young Quakers would, like their fathers, continue to support the Liberal Party and its policies. But in the first years of the century, the Liberals were out of office and in apparent disarray, and, for their part, Friends retained a lingering fear of what the *British Friend* called 'a wide-spread and deep-laid plot...to get military drill introduced into all schools of the nation...'[109]

Since the founding of the Boys' Brigade in the early 1880s, the Quaker and pacifist press had expressed concern about the 'dangerous innovation' of military drill being incorporated into the educational system as 'the thin edge of the wedge of conscription, which grinds so terribly in Continental nations...'[110] By late 1902 such spectral fears had been given substance by Admiral Lord Charles Beresford's amendment to the Education Bill that would have made military drill compulsory for all schools receiving public funds. While the Beresford Amendment was subsequently declared out of order, many believed that there remained 'a real and immediate danger of having our schools "captured" by the War Office'.[111] Indeed, the opponents of military drill managed to unearth a letter from General T. Kelly-Kenny, one of the King's

[107] *The Herald of Peace*, new series, 633, 2 June 1902, 253–5.

[108] Minutes, Peace Committee, III, 3 July 1902, LSF.

[109] *BF*, Dec. 1902, 319; Jan. 1903, 3, 21–2; and Feb 1903, 31. Also see *Minutes*, Yorkshire Quarterly Meeting, 29 Oct. 1902, 289 and 28 Jan. 1903, 294–5, Brotherton Library, Leeds University.

[110] *BF*, Sept. 1885, 214–5 and *P&G*, 15 July 1886, 19–20.

[111] *TF*, 9 Jan. 1903, 21–2 and 13 Feb. 1903, 98. Also see *BF*, Jan. 1903, 3.

hunting companions, indicating that some school inspectors were hinting at reduction of Government grants for schools that did not 'place themselves under the local drill-sergeant' for training in the so-called Model Course. London Yearly Meeting addressed this threat with a Memorandum to educational authorities protesting that the so-called Model Course had been 'born in the War Office' for the purpose of 'fostering the military spirit'.[112]

Opponents of military training for youth breathed somewhat easier after an inter-departmental committee found the Model Course 'so unsuitable for the physical instruction of children... that it cannot even be amended'.[113] Still, the Quaker press remained uneasy about attempts to militarize the Nation's youth and, in fact, such fears were not entirely chimerical. Many military men, some politicians and not a few clergymen saw the military training of youth as an inexpensive counterweight to what they believed was a growing physical and moral degeneracy threatening Britain's survival in the inevitable 'struggle for national existence'. In November 1903, for example, Admiral Sir John Fisher made the point that 'military drill should be compulsory as part of the national school system, and but little is required to extend this, so as to include rifle practice for a certain portion... it would be a most economical expenditure!'[114]

In the years following the South African War, Quaker leaders became increasingly sensitive to the relationship between domestic militarism and the defence of Empire, especially when the South African War brought forth the 'Mafficking'[115] tendencies of the 'ordinary layman' in whose mind 'the British constitution, the Bible, the national flag are hopelessly confused as being... the private properties of the Anglo-Saxon... or British God...' In the Spring of 1902 the *British Friend* arranged for John A. Hobson, Britain's premier anti-imperialist, to publish a series of articles on 'Imperialism and the Lower Races' which addressed the question of how the inevitable involvement of Western nations in the

---

[112] *TF*, 3 April 1903, 218; *BF*, April 1903, 86–7; and *LYM, 1903*, 129–33.

[113] *BF*, May 1904, 118.

[114] 'An Addendum' to J. Fisher's 'Notes for Consideration' written for the Committee on the Re-organization of the War Office, Nov. 1903, Arthur Balfour Papers, Ad. Mss. 49710, British Library. Alan Penn, *Targeting Schools: Drill, Militarism and Imperialism* (London 1999), addresses the question of military drill in British schools from 1870 to 1914.

[115] 'Mafficking' refers to the hysterical patriotic celebrations in major British cities set off by news of the lifting of the Boer siege of Mafeking on 18 May 1900.

development of the tropical lands 'may be so conducted as to yield a gain to world civilisation, instead of some terrible *débâcle* in which revolted slave races may trample down their parasitic and degenerate white masters.' Hobson argued that the fate of undeveloped places could not be left in the hands of unscrupulous freebooters like Cecil Rhodes. The past results of 'barbarous dereliction of a public duty towards the cause of humanity' could be witnessed in the moral and physical destruction of the Congo Free State or the slaughter of native peoples by the agents of chartered companies released from all legal or moral restraint. What was needed, Hobson said, was some 'International Council to accredit a civilised nation with the duty of educating a lower race'; in the meantime, the reality of imperialism was 'selfish, materialistic, short-sighted, national competition, varied by occasional collusion'.[116]

This analysis of Western expansionism prepared the ground for glowing reviews in the Quaker press of Hobson's classic study of *Imperialism* (1902) as the tool of avaricious capitalists seeking more favourable fields of investment and sheltered, at public expense, by thoroughly co-operative political and military establishments.[117] Hobson's arguments most certainly added force to the increasingly hard line taken by Quaker journals and journalists against 'the boastful and aggressive spirit of imperialism' and the maltreatment of native peoples that accompanied it.[118] Early in 1903 the *British Friend* produced a series of articles asserting that 'Imperialism necessarily means Militarism' and 'the prospect of hopeless ruin [which] . . . inevitably awaits the present rivalry in armaments . . . How any of our friends can support Imperialism, either here or abroad . . . and yet profess to maintain the Quaker "testimony against war" passes our comprehension.'[119]

While Quaker journalists like the *British Friend*'s editor Edward Grubb did not advocate abandonment of responsibility for the 'backward races' by the 'progressive races' who ruled over them, the *British Friend* offered the example of William Penn's relations

---

[116] John A. Hobson, 'Imperialism and the Lower Races', *BF*, March, April and June 1902, 53–5, 81–3, 129–32.

[117] For favourable reviews of Hobson's *Imperialism*, see *TF*, 21 Nov. 1902, 764–5 and *BF*, Dec. 1902, 314–5.

[118] *TF*, 'Economic South Africa', 16 Jan. 1903, 33–4 and ibid., 'True Imperialism', 34.

[119] *BF*, 'A Grave National Peril', Feb 1903, 31–2; 'Imperialism at Work', (an attack on the American campaign against the Moro in the Philippines), March 1903, 50; and 'Notes and Comments', June 1903, 135–6.

with American Indians as a prototype for imperial trusteeship. Grubb believed that if native peoples could be guided along the path of moral virtue and political responsibility rather than simply exploited and degraded, the Empire might, in the end, prove of great value to humanity. But, if the Empire could 'only be maintained by iniquitous methods, we would rather it perished. The Kingdom to which we owe our first allegiance is the Kingdom, not of England, but of God.'[120]

For perhaps the first time since the seventeenth century, an important section of the British Quaker community held out the hope that the fundamental objectives of their Society—the establishment of universal peace and social justice as well as spiritual righteousness—might actually be achieved on this earth. For these products of the Quaker Renaissance, the great electoral victory of the Liberal Party in January 1906 (including ten Quaker MPs) seemed a portent for the triumph of enlightened Government over shadowy imperialism and international reconciliation over aggressive militarism. This same spirit might also be made manifest in bold and sweeping new social legislation. *The Friend* called the Liberal victory 'a declaration on behalf of liberty... for definite, practical, earnest service on behalf of the poor and the oppressed'.

The last week has witnessed a great peaceful revolution. Deliverance has come. The spirit of the Puritans has found expression at the ballot-box. It is no light privilege to a great nation that such a Revolution is accomplished in peace instead of amid the horrors of anarchy. The patient labour of years of teaching has borne fruit... the constituencies have risen to their long overdue opportunity, they have recognised their power like a strong giant, and... they have won the victory.[121]

How might British Friends assist the Nation in utilizing this peaceful triumph?

---

[120] *BF*, Feb. 1903, 26 and a summary of Grubb's remarks to a public meeting in York, *TF*, 16 June 1905, 397. Also see *BF*, Oct. 1904, 270 and Oct. 1905, 269–70 for examples anti-imperialist commentary.
[121] *TF*, 19 Jan. 1906, 33, 48–9.

8

Renaissance Years, 1902–1914

A SOCIAL GOSPEL?

Much recent historical scholarship on the aftermath of the English Revolution has depicted Quakers during the 1650s as embodying the radical hopes of a radical decade when Quaker religious ideas were part of a millenarian vision for transforming English society into an egalitarian realm based on social justice as well as moral righteousness.[1] There is considerable evidence indicating that many of their contemporaries were frightened by what they perceived to be the aims and objectives of early Children of the Light. One member of the Rump Parliament described them as 'all Levellers, against magistracy and property'. This accuser had perhaps read James Naylor's diatribe against the rulers of England: 'You have exceeded all that ever went before you . . . Covetous and cruel oppressors . . . you grind the face of the poor . . . And when you have got great estates, you say God hath given you them; you are up above them who are made poor by you.'[2]

Quaker scholars have generally eschewed serious investigation of social, political, or economic radicalism among early Friends, but George Fox's latest biographer, Larry Ingle, has challenged prevailing Quaker views concerning the central vision of early Friends. Labelling Fox a 'millenarian' whose message 'targeted the larger society and amounted to a cry for justice from those

---

[1] The pioneering work of reassessing the social and political ideas of early Friends was W. A. Cole's Ph.D. thesis, 'The Quakers and Politics', (Cambridge 1955); also see Cole's 'Quakers and the English Revolution', *Past and Present*, 10 (1956), 39–54. As noted above, Christopher Hill, in both *The World Turned Upside Down* (1972) and *The Experience of Defeat* (1984), viewed early Quakers largely from the perspective of political and social radicalism; Barry Reay continued to advance this viewpoint in *Quakers and the English Revolution* (London 1985) and a number of articles on aspects of early Quakerism.

[2] Quotes from Hill, *World Turned Upside Down*, 240 and *Experience of Defeat*, 139.

who felt left behind in an emerging and unfamiliar world...' Ingle believes that Quaker writers, in pursuit of the theological purity of a 'Quaker Holy Grail', have for too long ignored the social and political context in which Quakerism was spawned. He gives non-Quaker historians credit for having drawn attention to the important role that radical Friends played in the revolutionary decade of the 1650s, although he believes that they are prone to ignore or play down the 'inward' religious principles of early Quakers.[3]

Fox's political and social concerns, Ingle says, grew out of his religious convictions and were similar to those of contemporary millenarians, i.e., the creation in their own time of the Kingdom of God on this earth wherein the mighty would be brought low and the lowly exalted. The name chosen by the earliest Quakers—Children of the Light—evoked the biblical message of the Chosen Few coming to grips with the powers of evil in a world dominated by dark forces. Thus, early Quakers were a body of believers who found the old social and political order wanting and the expansive rhetoric of their leader 'demonstrated how a conviction that the Kingdom was nigh could propel a millenarian into a vision that the world might be subdued with only a bit more effort and a stronger commitment to faith'. The most complete summary of Fox's vision of the Kingdom of God on earth was a 'nearly forgotten' pamphlet written in 1659. Addressed to the Rump Parliament, this declaration embodied fifty-nine proposals, half of which comprised a radical political and social agenda for 'taking away oppressing laws and oppressors'. Proclaiming that it was wrong for rich men, however righteous, to adorn themselves with gold while the poor suffered, Fox called upon the nation to look to the needs of the poor and helpless, 'that there might not be a beggar in England'.[4] This document, according to Ingle, was

---

[3] In addition to *First Among Friends*, Ingle's work on early Quaker radicalism includes, 'From Mysticism to Radicalism: Recent Historiography on Quaker Beginnings', *Quaker History*, 76 (1987), 79–94; 'On the Folly of Seeking the Quaker Holy Grail', *Quaker Religious Thought*, 25/1 (May 1991), 17–29; 'Richard Hubberthorne and History: The Crisis of 1659', *JFHS*, 56/3 (1992), 189–200; and 'George Fox, Millenarian', *Albion*, 24/2 (Summer 1992), 261–78.

[4] George Fox, *To the Parliament of the Common-Wealth of England, Fifty-nine particulars laid down for the Regulating things* (London 1659). Ingle provides an excellent summary in *First Among Friends*, 177–81. Also see 'George Fox, Millenarian', 275.

Fox's response to a deteriorating political and social situation which threatened his millennial hopes.[5]

After the Restoration Fox and most other Children of the Light were forced to defend their religious Society in an increasingly hostile atmosphere.[6] Thus, Quaker calls for a new social order were replaced by the scramble to survive, and this defensive posture, Ingle asserts, was increasingly accompanied by a push for respectability which led to the deliberate suppression of much of the radical social and political material published by Fox and other early Friends during the 1650s.[7] To be sure, George Fox and his lieutenants worked diligently and well to design internal procedures to assist Quakers who became victims of persecution as well as to provide for 'poor Friends', but post-Restoration Quaker leaders produced no more grand schemes for the reordering of human society so as to create the Kingdom of God on earth.

The Society's shedding of the raiment of social radicalism did not, of course, prevent individual Quakers from becoming justly famous for their work in various philanthropic causes during the decades and centuries that followed. Indeed, the historian of pre-twentieth-century Quaker social work claimed that English Friends 'laid the foundation for modern social work long before the abortive character of public poor relief as actually practiced had been recognized at all'.[8] Near the end of the nineteenth century, Bishop Westcott noted in his *Social Aspects of Christianity*: 'The Society of Friends has achieved results wholly out of proportion to their numbers. No religious order can point to services rendered more humanely, more unsullied by selfishness, or nobler in farseeing vision.'[9]

What services had Friends, in fact, rendered? Late-Victorian Quakers could point with pride to a two-hundred-year record of philanthropic achievements. They could begin with the work of

[5] Ingle, *First Among Friends*, 275–6 and 'Richard Hubberthorne', 189–91; and Christopher Hill, 'Quakers and the English Revolution', *JFHS*, 56/3 (1992), 172–3. It was shortly after issuing this document that Fox, suffering for several months from what appears to have been severe depression, withdrew from all public activity.

[6] As noted above (Chapter 7), Richard Greaves, 'Shattered Expectations?', 237, 259 challenges this view, asserting that the 'dominant characteristics of Restoration Quakerism are not withdrawal and quiescence but engagement and vigor.'

[7] H. Larry Ingle, '*On the Folly of Seeking the* Quaker Holy Grail', 19–20.

[8] Augustle Jorns, *The Quakers as Pioneers in Social Work* (New York 1931), 235.

[9] Quoted by Joshua Rowntree, *Social Service*, Swarthmore Lecture, 1913 (London 1913), 11.

John Bellers (1654–1725), wealthy son of one of the first London Friends, who developed an innovative, though ultimately untried, plan for eliminating poverty and was associated with nearly every important reform movement of his time.[10] Certainly, John Woolman's campaign against slavery, taken up by Anthony Benezet (1713–84) after Woolman's death, and subsequently associated, perhaps without full justification, with Quakers generally (London Yearly Meeting did not threaten slave traders and holders with disownment until 1761), put Friends in the forefront of the most morally riveting social reform movement of the age.[11] All would have been aware of the work of Elizabeth Fry (1780–1845), who, inspired by the courageous example of Thomas Shillitoe (1754–1836) and with the assistance of her Gurney and Buxton relatives, made Quakerism a major force in the nineteenth-century prison reform movement.[12] Perhaps the crowning moment of Victorian Quaker philanthropy was the Society's relief effort during the Irish famine of the 1840s. While not large given the scale of the disaster, Quaker endeavours were entirely untainted by the infamous attempts of some Protestant groups to tie food relief with proselytizing among starving Catholics.[13]

Quaker efforts to ameliorate the sufferings of the unfortunate or improve the lives as well as the morals of the sinful were closely linked to the doctrines and practices of evangelical Friends. Elizabeth Isichei noted that '[a]ll the prominent Victorian Quaker philanthropists were evangelicals' and that an understanding of evangelical Friends was central to an understanding of Victorian philanthropy.[14] But if Quaker devotion to charitable activities was

[10] See Jorns, *Social Work*, 75–86 and *passim* and Punshon, *Portrait in Grey*, 110–12.

[11] For the role of Friends in the anti-slavery campaign, see Jean R. Soderlund, *Quakers and Slavery: A Divided Spirit* (Princeton 1985) who concludes that, in general, Quakers were not only slow to follow John Woolman in condemning slavery but also that during the nineteenth century the white abolitionist movement as a whole 'continued . . . the gradualist, segregationist and paternalistic policies developed for almost a century within the Society of Friends', 187. For a more traditional and complimentary view, see Thomas E. Drake, *Quakers and Slavery in America* (New Haven 1950).

[12] See *Memoir of the Life of Elizabeth Fry, with Extracts from Her Journal* (London 1847). The standard biography is Georgina King Lewis, *Elizabeth Fry* (London 1910); the most recent Janet Rose, *Elizabeth Fry* (London 1980).

[13] For an engaging, if uneven, study of Quaker charitable activities in Ireland, centering on the Famine, see Helen E, Hatton, *The Largest Amount of Good: Quaker Relief in Ireland, 1654–1921* (Kingston & Montreal 1993).

[14] Isichei, *Victorian Quakers*, pp. xix, 214.

deservedly praised, it was also decidedly genteel as befits pious Christians with no desire to challenge the *status quo*. In 1889 J. B. Hodgkin, noted, not without pride, that his Society's approach to social concerns had been marked by: 'Honest examination of some of the causes of human misery and patient, business-like endeavours to remove them... [a method] more fruitful of good than visionary schemes, or wild, random speeches.'[15]

During the final decade of the nineteenth century, leaders of the Quaker Renaissance embraced not only the emerging liberal theology that was taking British Protestantism by storm but also an impending interventionist philosophy that would emerge as the 'New Liberalism'. Anxious to incorporate the great intellectual revelations of the nineteenth century into the corporate testimony of a renewed and revitalized Society of Friends and convinced that Quakerism could play a major role in the rehabilitation of a British society blinded by material opulence and spiritual poverty, these liberal reformers swept the field, sinking Quaker philanthropy as well as Quaker evangelicalism in the apparently cleansing waters of modernity.

One of the pioneers among progressive Quaker social reformers, as in so many other things, was Edward Grubb. In 1889 Grubb produced a number of articles and speeches inquiring as to why Friends as a body seemed unwilling even to discuss the causes and effects of poverty: 'There appears to be no recognition that as a church we have any duties whatever in regard to the destitute multitudes around us...' Quaker devotion to 'individualism' and 'self-help', Grubb said, predisposed Friends either to assume poverty was nearly always the result of drink, or to mumble shibboleths about the poor being always with us, or, in extremity, to ease troubled consciences with donations to some benevolent organization, probably headed-up by one of their prominent co-religionists. In point of fact, Grubb asserted, 90 per cent of all poverty 'can be traced directly or indirectly to the ignorance, apathy, and selfishness of the upper classes...' It was long past time, he said, for Quaker complacency to be replaced by a policy of 'joint action for the good of all... [I]f their Gospel was worth anything it must be a social as well as an individual Gospel, that the Kingdom of Heaven was meant to be realized here below.' As a first step, Grubb

---

[15] Jonathan B. Hodgkin, *Three Phases of Quakerism* (London 1889), 8.

suggested the establishment of a Friends' Social Union to under-take a systematic study of the causes and cures of poverty.[16]

The fact that nearly a generation passed before Friends felt ready to take this 'first step' speaks volumes about Quaker reticence and caution. In the interim, the question of Quaker responsibilities in the social realm was kept alive by Grubb and a few others who believed Quakerism should play a role in shaping British social values and policies in the impending century.[17] In the run-up to the Manchester Conference, William Charles Braithwaite argued that one of 'Present-Day Aims of the Society of Friends'

should be to cease approaching social problems with merely sentimental philanthropy or gushes of transient enthusiasm . . . The time has come for us to declare . . . the fundamental principles which should control the relations of men to one another in social life. We owe it to England to lift up, amid the confused battle which rages about social questions, the spiritual banner given to our keeping.[18]

Still, in the course of the Manchester Conference, not even Braithwaite himself gave a meaningful response to his own call. The reformers were effective in pronouncing and defending the principles of liberal theology, but as regards breaking new ground on social questions, they seemed to have little to offer beyond the inspiring but general admonition set forth by Joshua Rowntree that Quakers attitudes toward social reform should based upon 'true, real, earnest freedom from the trammels of conventionalism and worldlyism, and with spirits lighted by love of Christ and of our fellow man'.[19]

During the session on 'The Society of Friends in Relation to Social Questions', Henry Brady Priestman (1853–1920), director of the Friends Provident Institute and a noted platform speaker,

[16] Edward Grubb, 'Our Mission, II. Social,' *FQE*, 23 (1889), 63–82, *passim*. Quotation from 'T. Edmund Harvey', 5/3, unpublished manuscript by Edward H. Milligan in LSF; used with permission. Also see William H. Marwick, 'Quaker Social Thought', *Woodbrooke Occasional Papers*, 2 (1969), 11–12.

[17] See *Social Aspects of the Quaker Faith* (London 1899), a collection of Grubb's lectures and articles on social reform, most of which had previously appeared in the *British Friend*.

[18] *FQE*, 29 ([July] 1895), 329–30.

[19] *Manchester Conference*, 151. Ormerod Greenwood, *Friends and Relief*, 170–1 calls attention to the timidity of liberal Friends on social questions as compared to the boldness of their theological pronouncements.

exhorted the Manchester Conference to make 'an earnest effort to find ways and methods' of applying their spiritual message to daily life that might match 'the passionate demand for justice which animate and inspire [sic] socialist writers...'[20] But the ensuing discussion was almost embarrassingly tame. Edward Grubb probably caused a brief fluttering of the dovecotes when, notwithstanding an earlier speaker's Spencerian warning against the 'new tyranny of state socialism',[21] he pointedly referred to 'the socialistic side' of Quaker principles and traditions, but instead of an exegesis on collectivism, the remainder of Grubb's address was largely devoted to methods of moralizing private property. The speakers who followed Grubb were invariably orthodox in the social sphere and the earnest discussion that concluded the session scarcely rose above *noblesse oblige* and the 'new philanthropy'. Until, that is, Samuel G. Hobson took the floor.

Sam Hobson (1870–1940), an Ulsterman of considerable bulk and acid tongue, was, at age 25, one of the most politically radical Quakers of his day. He had joined the Fabian Society early-on and served as private secretary to Britain's first independent socialist MP, Keir Hardie. Socialism, as espoused by Hobson, was not a theory which many Friends found congenial, although, in 1893 one member had warned London Yearly Meeting that socialism might prove an attractive alternative for young Friends who found that contemporary Quakerism did not speak to their condition. While at the time such an idea may have seemed preposterous, barely two years later Samuel Hobson was addressing the Manchester Conference on precisely this point, claiming personal knowledge of forty to fifty young male Quakers, himself included, who could find no scope for their social ideals within the Society of Friends and had 'been absolutely forced to work outside...the dilettante circles of eminently Quaker society'. Hobson went so far as to suggest that these lapsed Friends might be returned to the fold along with a host of new converts, if Quakerism, beginning at this momentous Conference, could make 'some great corporate pronouncement...for social progress'. Socialism's struggle on behalf of the labouring classes, Hobson declared, was 'essentially a non-dogmatic religious movement. It only needs the guidance

[20] *Manchester Conference*, 72–3. For Henry Priestman, see 'DQB', LSF.

[21] This speaker, Eliza Pickard, a Conservative Friend, also cautioned 'against the new dogmatism of modern science'. *Manchester Conference*, 161.

of Friends of leisure and culture to give it that religious enthusiasm which can alone secure a great future for social progress.'[22] Hobson's dramatic appeal aroused no enthusiastic response. Indeed, other than his being 'eldered' by the weighty Thomas Hodgkin who firmly disavowed any connection between Quakerism and the idea 'of a ... forcible abstraction of the superfluous wealth of the rich to bestow it on the needy ... ' none of those who spoke after Hobson even addressed any of the questions he had raised.[23] At the conclusion of the discussion on Friends and social questions, a minute was adopted counselling members to seek 'more simplicity of life and more sympathetic relations with those around us'. Hardly the ringing 'corporate pronouncement' Samuel Hobson envisioned.[24]

Throughout the last years of the nineteenth century, discussions concerning some systematic Quaker approach to social questions remained peripheral as meaningful debate remained focused on how Quakers should respond to the theological and scientific ideas that were fashioning modern thought. At the Scarborough Summer School in 1897, John Stephenson Rowntree warned his audience that Quakerism required more than 'philanthropic work' to offset the not unjustified charge that their Society's religious testimony was mainly confined to 'matters of tradition—whilst they had been almost silent on that which most wanted testifying against ... the excessive love and worship of wealth, and the devotion to its acquisition'.[25] But however cogently J. S. Rowntree spoke to the general condition of late nineteenth-century Friends in the social arena, he offered no specific means for correcting their collective deficiency.

One Quaker more than willing to speak to this challenge was the redoubtable Samuel Hobson. In an article published by the *Friends Quarterly Examiner*, Hobson asserted that a 'spirit of doubt and hesitancy' prevailed in Quaker circles because most Friends still embraced an 'effete' Liberal synthesis that lay dead in the social backwater while an invigorating wave of socialist ideas swept toward the future. Anything that remained vital within the

[22] *Manchester Conference*, 197–9. Also see Hobson's autobiography, *Pilgrim To the Left: Memoirs of a Modern Revolutionist* (London 1938).
[23] *Manchester Conference*, 206–7.   [24] Ibid. 202.
[25] J. S. Rowntree, *Place of the Society of Friends*, 56–7, 60.

outworn social creed of liberalism, he concluded, could be useful only if it were merged 'into the splendor of an ampler system... It is to Socialism we must look for a new crusade.'[26]

Reflecting a penchant for remaining at the cutting edge of every aspect of advanced thought, Samuel Hobson believed that the swing toward socialism was an aspect of 'the inevitable struggle for existence' and part of 'a conscious effort to hasten the advent of a higher organism and to alleviate its inevitable birth pangs'. This would be accomplished most safely and effectively, he asserted, if it occurred within an ethical framework provided by 'the points of contact between Quakerism and Socialism'. Hobson believed that it was no exaggeration to say 'that Socialism is the economic continuity of pristine Quakerism... our doctrine of the "inner light" is but the spiritual manifestation of the Socialist doctrine of economic evolution'.[27]

Still, for all the points of convergence between socialism and Quakerism, including their common stance on questions such as 'sex equality and peace', Hobson feared that innovative ideas would make little headway among Friends since they were too much disposed to 'walk in the old grooves, to pursue the old ideals', preferring the pleasant amenities of the Adult School where they might breed fawning sycophants to 'the rough-and-tumble of Socialist agitation'.[28]

Hobson was certainly correct in predicting that Quakers were not, by and large, prepared to rally round the socialist banner. Still, at about the time his essay 'Concerning Socialism' appeared, seven young Friends formed a Socialist Quaker Society (SQS) founded on their belief that the Universal Brotherhood implied by the Inner Light could not 'be realised under the present competitive system...'[29] Within a year of formation of the SQS, John Wilhelm Rowntree, writing for *Present Day Papers*, had concluded that

---

[26] 'Concerning Socialism', *FQE*, 32 (1898), 195–7.

[27] Ibid. 197–98, 201–03, 205, 207.   [28] Ibid. 208–10.

[29] Socialist Quaker Society, *Minutes*, 2 April 1898, microfilm copy; originals in LSF. Four women and three men were original SQS members. A history of the SQS is T[ony] Adams, 'The Socialist Quaker Society, 1898–1924', M.A. Thesis, Leicester University, 1985 which is supplemented by his pamphlet *A Far-Seeing Vision: The Socialist Quaker Society (1898–1924)*, published by the contemporary Quaker Socialist Society (Bedford n.d.). Peter d'A Jones's discussion of the organization in *The Christian Socialist Revival, 1877–1944* (Princeton 1968), 367–89 is less partisan and generally more useful.

'the eager, investigating, reforming, responsible spirit of Social-ism... [was] the healthiest spirit in modern politics'.[30] However promising John Wilhelm Rowntree found the social-ist spirit, the Premises Committee of Devonshire House, Quaker-ism's London headquarters, could not be persuaded to allow the Socialist Quaker Society the use of a room at the 1899 Yearly Meeting. The SQS did meet concurrently with Yearly Meeting in a nearby schoolhouse, where over a hundred Friends assembled to hear earnest attempts to convince them that socialism was indeed the wave of the future, but these were, no doubt, chiefly curiosity seekers.[31] Although the keepers of Friendly space eventually relented and SQS gatherings become a fixture at early twentieth-century Yearly Meetings, Quaker socialists made little progress in their campaign to enlist members of their religious Society in the serried ranks of the socialist legion. And if the SQS could at last meet on Quaker ground, it was, for many years, refused space in *The Friend* for explicitly socialistic articles. Not surprisingly, SQS membership remained static at a few dozen members throughout most of the pre-war period.[32]

The SQS did manage to attract some attention and to double its membership (to around 120) after issuing an 'Open Letter' to all Friends in 1912. This handsomely produced manifesto, widely distributed and printed in both Quaker newspapers, pointed up the uselessness of working within the capitalist structure to remedy social ills which were, in the main, caused by that rapa-cious system.[33] The impetus for this manifesto—some 9,000 copies were distributed—came from the organization's new Clerk, Mary E. Thorne (1873–1957) who, with her husband Alfred (1870–1922), had joined the SQS in 1909. While Quaker socialists like the Thornes generally pictured themselves as 'a group of young, unestablished, intellectual radicals of moderate means' struggling against the powerful prejudices of Quaker officialdom represented by the 'great, sturdy Quaker business families, deep-rooted,

[30] John Wilhelm Rowntree, 'The Stewardship of Wealth', *Present Day Papers*, April 1899, 15.

[31] SQS *Minutes*, 28 March and 27 April 1899.

[32] The SQS *Minute Book*, 11, 22 Feb. 1910 listed only 52 members. Both the *British Friend* and the *Friends Quarterly Examiner* did publish articles by SQS members. See, for example, *BF*, August 1903, 244 and Mary O'Brien Harris, 'The Socialist Alternative to Poverty', *FQE*, 42 (1908), 408–27.

[33] See Adams, *Far-Seeing Vision*, 11–12.

socially conservative, pious and rich',[34] they were, in fact, never a solitary band struggling for social change among indifferent co-religionists. By the turn of the new century modern, scientific social reform, as opposed to old-style philanthropy, came into vogue among non-socialist Friends. But while positivist theories of a science of society threw out the baby of Divine Presence with the bath-water of traditional religious norms, liberal Quakers, desiring to remain both fully Christian and acceptably *au courant*, dumped over the water but kept the Divine Child to be cleansed by a frenzy of good works accompanied by the latest scientific ideas concerning the evolution of the social order. This new approach was made easier by the vigorous revival of Inward Light theology which created the imperative of infusing secular society with what each individual possessed internally and spiritually. As John Wilhelm Rowntree noted in summarizing Quakerism's future mission:

The war between capital and labour, the bitterness of selfish competition, the Poverty that shames our land, the lovelessness of souls that know no Christ, call with one mighty voice for the labours of self-sacrificing love. May teachers and scholars [in Adult Schools] share the mantle and the staff of this service, and build in their measure, and under God's redeeming power, the City of Happy Souls.[35]

In 1903, the long-anticipated Friends Social Union (FSU) finally came to fruition under the leadership of Seebohm Rowntree, whose study of *Poverty* (1901) in York had already placed him at the forefront of British social researchers. Although the Union did not officially represent London Yearly Meeting until 1910,[36] its Executive Committee was composed almost exclusively of respectable and weighty Quakers. Exceptions were Edward Grubb, whose opinions were still too advanced for many cautious Friends, and Percy Alden, a Fabian and future Labour MP, who was appointed Organizing Secretary even though he was not a

---

[34] Quoted by Jones, *Christian Socialist Revival*, 378; Jones also quotes some indignant responses to the SQS 'Open Letter', 380–81. Also see Adams, *Far-Seeing Vision*, 11–13.

[35] Quoted by Stephen Allott, *John Wilhelm Rowntree*, 18.

[36] See *LYM, 1910*, 155–56. Also see Marwick, 'Quaker Social Thought', *passim*.

Friend.[37] Claiming to be the first Quaker group to undertake a systematic approach to social concerns, the FSU promised 'to encourage the study of social problems amongst Friends... in such a way as shall best evoke the spirit of justice and of social service, and... to apply our religious faith intelligently and consistently to our social and civic life.'[38]

Subscriptions to the Friends Social Union during its initial year were inadequate to support the projected annual budget of £500, but the first *Annual Report* nonetheless indicated involvement in a dozen different areas of social concern, including housing, poverty, unemployed and unemployable labour, constructive philanthropy, labour colonies, and 'How to Form a Social Services Committee'; the FSU's lecture series included such notable speakers as the Revd Josiah Strong (on 'Social Services') and H. Rider Haggard (on 'Rural Depopulation'). While at the end of the first year, some members expressed 'disappointment at the small response from Friends to the appeal for work in the Social field', the Executive Committee believed that the Union's work had the potential for strengthening and deepening religious life in England.[39]

Exuding what Peter Clarke has called 'a common seriousness about the dreadful importance of questions of belief as the source of man's vision of... society', the FSU diligently sought to 'evoke the spirit of Justice and of Social Service, and to apply our Religious Faith consistently to our Social and Civic life....' Certainly, the Union's *Minutes* and published materials revealed an abundance of unwavering moral earnestness. Throughout the pre-war decade the FSU continued to sponsor lectures, publish pamphlets, and appoint an perpetual stream of sub-committees to inquire into the 'correct sphere for social work'.[40] But for all of that, the Friends Social Union as a body produced what can only be called a paucity of meaningful social consequences.[41] The *Minute Book* of the FSU's

[37] Adams, *Far-Seeing Vision*, 8, claims that Alden (1865–1944) joined Friends in 1901, but other evidence indicates that while Alden was 'close to Friends', he was never a member. He was elected to Parliament in 1906 but is not included on a list of Quaker MPs in LSF.

[38] 'The Friends' Social Union', 4, printed flyer in LSF.

[39] London and Middlesex Quarterly Meeting, Committee on Poverty & Social Service, 1904 and FSU, *Annual Report*, 1904, LSF.

[40] Peter Clarke, *Liberals and Social Democrats* (Cambridge 1978), 13 and FSU, *Annual Report*, 1905, LSF. The FSU's *Minutes*, 1904–1915, 1916–17, *Annual Reports* and other *Reports and Pamphlets*, 1904–15 are housed in LSF.

[41] It should be noted that the FSU's failure to arouse enthusiasm among Edwardian Friends should not be construed as an absence of Quaker social and charitable activity. Many

Executive Council is full of references to the proper work to be undertaken and the best people for developing it, but these references are frequently followed by lists of reasons why persistent toil produced so few results. When diligent Friends complained about the 'indefinite nature' of various FSU proposals, of their sense of inadequacy for remedying known evils or even of being 'unable to discover anything that needs to be remedied', leaders of the FSU inevitably responded, not with specific plans of action but with exhortations about the need for more systematic studies of the social ills that were so obviously troubling British society.[42]

The general level of Quaker response to social questions might be illustrated by a pamphlet on the 'Stewardship of Wealth' issued in 1910 by the Yearly Meeting Committee on Social Questions and featuring such bold ideas for social action as 'Christian shopping' and not exploiting one's employees. The Socialist Quaker Society reacted with a scathing barrage of criticism, so biting, indeed, that *The Friend* would not publish it, though it did appear in the *British Friend*. This embarrassing episode may indeed have had some influence on London Yearly Meeting's decision to discharge the Committee on Social Questions and make the Friends Social Union directly responsible to Yearly Meeting with regard to social reform.[43]

Responding to this new status, the Union, in its *Annual Report* for 1912–13, attempted to come to terms with the tendency to temporize and drift (or to be periodically blown hither and yon by the latest vogue in social engineering). While noting that 'much pruning' had been done, the *Report* admitted that 'little constructive work' had been accomplished since the Union's essentially middle-class membership had difficulty realizing the degree to which strained economic circumstances hampered spiritual development among the working classes.[44]

Friends worked hard as individuals or as members of local meetings to alleviate the suffering which arose from poverty and other social ills, but these efforts were mainly in a traditional vein and not in accord with more modern principles of integrated social service espoused by the Union.

[42] FSU, *Annual Reports*, 1904–1913, *passim* and *Minutes*, 1908, 1910–12, FSU/3, LSF.

[43] *LYM, 1910*, 155–6; Jones, *Christian Socialists*, 378–9; and *BF*, Nov. 1910.

[44] FSU, *Annual Report*, 1912–13, LSF. One lost opportunity to provide apathetic or oblivious Friends with examples of the pioneering social work of their Society was the FSU's decision not to sponsor the translation and publication of Auguste Jorns' academic study of *The Quakers as Pioneers in Social Work*, published in German in 1911. In an apparent

So, the Friends' Social Union wafted through the pre-war decade, active and earnest, full of respectably fashionable ideas about ways and means for putting Quakerism to the forefront of the campaign for social justice and moral rejuvenation. The FSU was certainly solid, sensible, and respectable, but, apparently lacking focus and direction, it seemed unable to fix upon any unique role for the Society of Friends in the realm of social action.

In the meantime, late in 1912 the less genteel arm of Quaker social activism managed to launch its own journal, an impressive undertaking for an organization so small and impoverished as the Socialist Quaker Society. *The Ploughshare* was to be 'an independent magazine' which might better fulfill SQS aims 'than by seeking entry—and sometimes not finding it—in the more widely circulated journals of the Society of Friends'.[45] That *The Ploughshare* appeared in eight occasional issues between November 1912 and August 1914 was in large measure due to the dedication and technical skill of its editor, William Loftus Hare (1868–1943), a convinced Friend from Derby and a pioneer in photo-engraving and colour-print processing. Hare guided the journal throughout its stormy seven-year existence and, to a considerable extent, *Ploughshare* projected his intense, passionate, and highly personal brand of Christian socialism.[46] That SQS itself endured was a tribute to the persistent enthusiasm of the band of true believers who, with W. L. Hare, continued to see socialist principles as the political and economic counterpart to Quaker religious precepts. Despite its diminutive size and relative obscurity, the SQS did leave marks on the pre-war Society of Friends, especially among well-educated members of the younger generation.

In 1911 Young Friends' Study Circles, looking to expand the social awareness of their members, had requested that the Friends Social Union draw up an outline programme and syllabus for the guidance of Young Friends as regards social questions.[47] This was agreed to and apparently done, but it is difficult to imagine Young

---

fit of humility, the Union's Executive decided that such sponsorship would seem too self-aggrandizing. See FSU, *Minutes*, 29 June 1913, FSU/3, LSF. Jorns' book was not published in English until 1930.

[45] *The Ploughshare* (hereafter *PS*), 1 (Nov. 1912), 2.

[46] See Adams, *Far-Seeing Vision*, 13–23 for information about Hare and *The Ploughshare*. Also see Chapter 9 below.

[47] *Minutes*, 14 Sept. 1911, FSU/3, LSF.

Friends as a body received much inspiration from the Union's example. The FSU executive met regularly and discussed a wide spectrum of possibilities for action, but concrete progress remained discouragingly slow. In October 1913, for example, the FSU secretary suggested that the next Council meeting should be a colloquium 'to consider the responsibility of Friends towards maintaining simplicity of life', using John Woolman's writings on the issue as a guide to the discussion. It seemed an admirable exercise, but the FSU Executive saw so many potential difficulties with even this modest proposal that it was ultimately decided 'to appoint a special sub-committee . . . to consider the matter thoroughly'.[48] Nearly two decades after the Manchester Conference had attempted to bring the Society of Friends into touch with modern thought, such deliberate speed did not seem calculated to inspire the sort of dedicated commitment to social and spiritual change that many Young Friends were prepared to give. Even so basic a Quaker issue as living simply was not addressed by the FSU until a Conference at Letchworth two weeks before Franz Ferdinand and his wife were murdered at Sarajevo. A report in *The Friend* summarizing one attender's reaction to this Conference was most revealing. Friends, he commented, were still groping toward some meaningful plan of social action, hindered by too much emphasis on self-help, too much concern for the details of social service and too little commitment to 'an absolute and complete surrender to the spirit which was the mainspring of John Woolman's actions'.[49]

Joseph T. Harris, a founding member of the SQS, had also attended the Letchworth Conference; his response was more to the point: 'I have come away . . . with a strengthened sense of the need for the Socialist Quaker Society . . . May the SQS be ready . . . to present our message when the Society of Friends is ready to hear it.'[50] Within a few weeks of this exhortation, the Great War began. Ironically, it was this enduring tragedy which provided Quaker socialists with a unique opportunity for delivering their message to members of their own religious Society as well as to the nation at large.

---

[48] *Minutes*, 29 Oct. 1913, FSU/3, LSF.   [49] *TF*, 12 June 1914, 442.
[50] SQS *Minutes*, 26 June 1899 and 22 Feb. 1910 and J[oseph] T. H[arris], 'FSU Conference', *PS*, I/7, May 1914, 85–6.

THE YOUNG FRIENDS MOVEMENT

Clearly, by the turn of the twentieth century liberal theology, with its emphasis on a God of love reflected by Christ Incarnate, was displacing evangelical preoccupations with Divine Justice inherent in the propitiatory Atonement. But old habits die hard and a more tolerant vision of human goodness and earthly possibilities did not necessarily translate into a more relaxed lifestyle. Most liberal Friends tended to raise their children as they themselves had been brought up. For Edwardian Quaker children this could be trying.

Elfrida Vipont Foulds (1902–1990) was a daughter of Dorothy Crowly and Edward Vipont Brown of Manchester. Her father, a physician, was a liberal in theology and a social democrat in politics (he joined the SQS early on), but for all of that, Elfrida recalled suffering considerable frustration as a small girl in the Brown household. Beyond her resentment of the fact that both her parents spent part of each Sunday away from home, her father with his morning Adult School class and her mother with various charitable activities in the afternoon, she remembered other limitations imposed upon young children, especially in weekends:

Sunday afternoon was beginning to be more interesting to Quaker children... They'd got past the state where you couldn't play with any of your toys, but what you could play with was limited. You could... paint things and you could draw things. But you couldn't possibly play card games and... all the jolly games that [other] children played.

When Elfrida's brothers attempted to get round these prohibitions by developing a Sunday version of one popular verbal game in which phrases like 'Hallelujah' or 'Praise the Lord' replaced more secular responses, their mother refused to acquiesce in the deception. Young Elfrida was 'bitterly disappointed', not so much for love of the game as in distaste for restrictions. 'When you come to think of it, I expect a lot of Quaker children must have felt like that.'[51]

Most local Quaker meetings had begun to allow fidgety youngsters to escape from the prospect of long, and often predominantly silent, meetings for worship by making provision for separate

---

[51] Interview with Elfrida Foulds, August 1986, Yealand Conyers, Lancashire, England.

children's Bible classes. Still, the problem of getting and keeping the attention of young people, especially as they faced the trials and tribulations of puberty, had been a perennial challenge and not just for Friends. Attempts to respond to this difficulty had in the latter half of the nineteenth century led to the development of non-denominational movements like the Young Men's and Young Women's Christian Association and Christian Endeavour societies. English Quakers were generally slow to adopt new innovations, but in this instance British Friends had help from an American cousin. In 1874 Allen Jay (1831–1910), an Indiana minister living in North Carolina, visited London Yearly Meeting and planted a seed for the idea of a Young Men's organization which eventually took shape as the Friends Christian Fellowship Union (FCFU).[52] Females were not admitted to the FCFU until 'a number of years later', but by the mid-1880s the Union's membership had grown to several hundred of both sexes. The FCFU also supported one of the central attractions for young male Friends in London, the Foxes Football Club, a fixture in London amateur soccer for over thirty years.[53] Certainly, the Union was a meeting ground for many of the younger Friends who became involved in shaking Quakerism loose from its nineteenth-century image and practice. As the Modern Movement developed, the FCFU gradually shed its evangelical outer skin. Many leaders in the Quaker Renaissance cut their organizational teeth with the FCFU: William Charles Braithwaite was joint-secretary of the Union for a time and an active speaker on its behalf; Neave Brayshaw and John William Graham were among those who worked to draw the FCFU away from its evangelical roots.[54]

At the Manchester Conference in 1895, John Wilhelm Rowntree's father Joseph called on the Society to loosen restrictions on younger Friends, noting that British Quakerism would only regain its 'freshness and power' if young people were permitted to express spiritual truth in their own way. Edward Worsdell followed with an appeal for more young people to take up the ministry of the word and for the Society as a whole to work for the establishment

[52] See Alan Jay, *Autobiography* (Philadelphia 1910), 250; *Swanwick, 1911*, 4; and Wilson, 'Best Things', 141–2. The best account of the Young Friends Movement is Greenwood, *Friends and Relief*, 167–77.

[53] *Swanwick, 1911*, 5.

[54] 'Journal of Dorothy Brown', 24 March 1899 and Greenwood, *Friends and Relief*, 169.

of the means to prepare youngsters for an active ministry which spoke to the future rather than to the past.[55] A year later, inspired by John Wilhelm Rowntree's 'Yorkshire Movement', a Conference of Yorkshire Quarterly Meeting called upon young Friends to take larger responsibility for 'The Right Use of Our Meeting Houses' by organizing visitations for worship and fellowship throughout the North of England.[56]

In *Present Day Papers*, John Wilhelm himself focused on difficulties facing young Friends:

> We desire to handle the vital questions which vex the younger generation . . . which they must face and solve . . . Our small society will neither maintain nor justify its existence unless its view of life is clearly emphasised, and its young life fired by a worthy ideal. It is here we fail and it is here that it is our duty to succeed . . . The want of any arrangement by which our young people are rightly directed at a critical period of life . . . is already disastrous in its consequences, and calls for immediate action.[57]

Rowntree believed that British Friends were facing 'the most critical years in the history of the Society' and feared for what might occur if they did not come to grips with 'the consequences of past neglect'.[58] During the few years left to him, J. W. R. played a key role in preparing for the crisis he predicted. Yet, ironically, it was in his death rather than during his life that John Wilhelm inspired what was arguably the most important development in providing strength of purpose and direction during the moment of truth that would face early twentieth-century British Quakerism.

When John Wilhelm died at 36, only a year after the equally sudden and premature death of his younger cousin Henry Ernest Grace,[59] one direct consequence of the abrupt removal of these

---

[55] *Manchester Conference*, 268, 276–7.

[56] *Minutes of York Quarterly Meeting*, 'Minute of Conference Held in York', 29–30 April 1896, 126, Brotherton Library, Leeds and Chapter 5 above.

[57] J. W. R., Editorial Note, *PDP*, III [1900], 367–8; 'The Yearly Meeting and the Summer Settlement,' ibid., IV, [1901], 145–6; and 'The Problem of a Free Ministry', *Essays and Addresses*, 129.

[58] J. W. R., 'Religious Education', *PDP*, V, (1902), 128.

[59] Henry Ernest Grace (1870–1904), a chartered accountant in Bristol and an ardent advocate of Adult Schools, was also an outstanding cricketer who, after leaving Bootham school, joined the cricket tour in the west of England for a time. He died of appendicitis, 21 November 1904.

two widely admired young men was the emergence of a revitalized Young Quaker Movement which not only attempted to provide solace for spiritually troubled young people but also to establish what one member called 'a fellowship of service' in which all might participate.[60] As George Newman, editor of the *Friends Quarterly Examiner*, told Rufus Jones: 'O yes, we Quakers have been given something of a vision; if only, if only we w[oul]d proclaim it. We might make the word just a bit nearer to a larger & truer thought of God. Now John Wilhelm has left us, some of us must buck up & do . . . something.'[61]

One group attempting to do the sort of thing Newman had in mind consisted of a number of younger Yorkshire Friends and old Bootham School boys who, after a Whitsuntide weekend gathering at Scalby, the home of John Wilhelm's widow and family, determined to initiate a series of 'tramps' through the north of England for religious service and Christian fellowship. The idea, first proposed by Neave Brayshaw, was to form bodies of young men (female members were eventually added) who would walk from village to village in imitation of George Fox and early Friends. By visiting Friends meetings, organizing religious gatherings and establishing personal and spiritual attachments, young people could both act out the traditions of their ancestors and honour the recently departed in spreading the message of Quakerism.

The first trampers who spread out over North Yorkshire and Lancashire converged on Pendle Hill where George Fox had related his vision of 'a great people to be gathered'. This sort of pilgrimage caught on among young Quakers for obvious reasons, not all of them pious. Tramps not only provided the possibility for the sort of religious service so central to the emerging ideals of liberal Quakerism, they also afforded opportunities for breaking free from what was, for many, a still stifling social atmosphere and spending mainly unsupervised time with young people of both sexes whose interests and problems were similar to their own. In old age, Caroline Stephen grasped the mood of the time and the importance of such a Movement in writing to a young Friend:

---

[60] Henry B. Binns, *PDP* (1900), quoted by Greenwood, *Friends and Relief*, 171.
[61] George Newman to R. M. J., 15 July 1907, Box 5, RMJP.

I think you are having the experience which seems to be almost universal, of a rather difficult time midway between childhood & age—the table-land of life seems generally to make great demands on one's courage & trust & we cannot help one another very much in any direct or conscious way—but indirectly and unconsciously I believe we do, more than we can ever measure.[62]

While Caroline Stephen hoped that the younger generation was 'awakening to the value of... a "prophetic ministry"', she was concerned lest admirers of John Wilhelm Rowntree succumb to 'the danger of letting the intellect have things its own way...' As she believed, the only way to acquire the sort of riveting ministry that would shake the spiritual world as early Friends had shaken it was 'by being taught of God—in the depths, & mostly through suffering—for which time and patience are needed... to be true to our faith to our very heart's core is the only way I can see to real fruit-bearing'.[63]

These were prescient words in light of the events shortly to transpire. Within a decade young Friends would face the trial of a Great War and confrontation with the secular State. In the end, it was not the intellectual thrust of the Quaker Renaissance, however powerful its influence on young Friends, but rather the willingness to suffer, 'even unto death', that bore the fruit of Quaker faithfulness to a renewed and revitalized peace testimony.

Even as Caroline Stephen wrote, the Yorkshire 1905 Committee, a sort of 'ginger group' dedicated to pursuing the objectives which John Wilhelm Rowntree had articulated, was taking shape in Yorkshire Quarterly Meeting. Among other things, this ad hoc committee made arrangements for more tramps of the type recently undertaken. Since these walks over sacred Quaker ground were intended to combine religious with social activities, special concern was taken to ensure sufficient involvement of both male and female Friends. Such tramps, in connection with religious Summer Schools, continued on an annual basis, drawing young people into a 'closer Christian fellowship... based on a conviction of the value of Truths entrusted to Friends'. Such endeavours were

[62] Caroline Stephen to Lyra Trueblood, 1 Jan. 1907, Temp MSS 584, LSF. Also see *Swanwick, 1911*, 6–7.
[63] Caroline Stephen to Hannah Bellows, 6 Nov. 1906, L. Violet Hodgkin Papers, MS Vol. 128/3, LSF and to George Hodgkin, 7 June 1908, MS Vol. 128/4, ibid.

seen as 'a time of great blessing', providing the occasion for more thorough instruction in Quaker principles. There were even ambitious hopes that these ventures could help to resuscitate dormant Quaker meetings or establish new ones and, thus, be a source of revitalization, not just for the young, but for the entire Society.[64]

If John Wilhelm Rowntree had been the chief inspiration for the Young Friends Movement, its leading exponent and nursing father was Neave Brayshaw.[65] At the same time that he took the lead in organizing country walks and archeological excursions, Brayshaw was also at pains to ensure that there was a 'deep spiritual basis for all our work'. While he was determined to root evangelical theology and practice out of Quakerism, Brayshaw also felt that many young people, while rejecting the evangelical ministry of their local meetings, became too absorbed in Adult Schools and other forms of social activism or good fellowship. The purpose of the Young Friends Movement was, Brayshaw believed, not simply to expend excess energy or to make new friends, but to inject renewed life and vigour into meetings for worship, the central spiritual exercise of Quakerism. Over seventy years after Philip Radley first became involved with Young Friends, he remembered that Neave Brayshaw had, for the first time, provided him with 'a sense of what . . . meeting for worship should be'.[66] Brayshaw envisioned not just silent waiting but also the sort of vocal ministry 'where the sweep of the divine tide' would catch and hold a gathered meeting.[67] As he noted in a long letter on the strengths, weaknesses, and prospects of the 'Tramp' Movement:

if our 'tramps' do no more than give each of us a good time . . . they are missing the purpose. It is for us to be centres of light and warmth now that we have known so much of ourselves. . . . With our faces set in this

---

[64] *Minutes*, Yorkshire 1905 Committee, 11 November 1905; printed advertisement for 'Yorkshire 1905 Committee', Yorkshire 1905 Committee Papers (hereafter 1905 Committee), BL and John Hoyland, 'Neo-Quakerism', *FQE*, 176 (Oct. 1910), 460–1.

[65] The Yorkshire 1905 Committee's attempt to ensure female participation in all its activities was in marked contrast to Neave Brayshaw's approach. Some female Friends of the period felt that Brayshaw had little use for women in general. Interview with Jean Rowntree, August 1986, Stone-in-Oxney, Tenterden, Kent.

[66] Interview with Philip Radley, August 1986, Cambridge and *Minutes*, Yorkshire 1905 Committee, 29 January 1908.

[67] A.N.B. to Robert Davis, John S. Hoyland and J. E. Thorp, 16 Oct. 1912, Box T, LSF.

direction we shall be no isolated gloomy company... but we shall know the attractive power of an ever deepening fellowship... rooted and grounded in the love which comes only to those in whom the prayer of Christ is being fulfilled. That they all may be one... one in us.[68]

While he emphasized the spiritual aspects of the Young Friends fellowship, Brayshaw did not ignore material concerns of the larger society to which a spiritually reinvigorated Society of Friends might respond. 'As a Christian fellowship we are bound to be deeply moved at the terrible mass of poverty and wretchedness' which made spiritual life impossible for those who suffered under it, he said. But while Friends as Christians should not tolerate a condition of things that afforded so many human beings so little chance to grow, Brayshaw feared the debilitating influence of what he called 'aesthetic Quakerism' and warned against using the material weaknesses of other people as a reason for taking pride in one's own spiritual strength. Socially and spiritually active Young Friends, Brayshaw said, should 'cultivate the power to go in the love of Christ to the unpopular, the lonely, the disagreeable, the ugly in body or mind who are suffering more than we know for what we might give them'.[69] Above all, he believed, it was essential that religious seekers be freely drawn to Quakerism for the intangible blessings of its unique message, not psychologically coerced by the material potentialities of its penchant for good works. 'We need to be keenly watchful against the self-exultation that is ready to come pouring in like a flood... In particular we shall avoid anything in the nature of being spiritual director of another. Christian communities have been grievously injured in these ways, and we do well to be armed beforehand.'[70]

While it is unlikely that many Young Friends could live up to the standard that Neave Brayshaw envisioned, signs of 'quickening' among the young were becoming obvious. '...a new tide of spiritual life was flowing strong in our Society, loyalty was being deepened, waverers were being recalled, there was a clearer light on perplexing problems, and a more earnest desire to understand

[68] A. N. B., 'Memorandum on strengths, weaknesses and prospects of the "Tramp" Movement', November 1910, Scarborough, Box T1/3, LSF.

[69] A. N. B. to Roderic [Clark], Dec. 1910 and A. N. B. to Trampers, 16 June 1914, Box T 1/3, LSF.

[70] A. N. B. to Roderic [Clark], Dec. 1910, Box T 1/3.

our special work and to do it.'[71] One beneficiary of this vibrant spirit was the Friends Christian Fellowship Union which began to show 'signs of renewed vigour and enthusiasm'.[72] At Yearly Meeting in 1910 the FCFU arranged for a separate meeting exclusively for young people. This gathering was followed in the autumn by a Young Friends Conference at Woodbrooke where many expressed their sense of growing possibilities for Quakerism amidst the transforming influence of modern theological thought. There was, one attender put it,

a crying need for the restatement of Christianity in terms of reality and simplicity . . . a restatement our own Society *should* be pre-eminently able to provide . . . a Neo-Quakerism . . . a fresh understanding both by individual and society of the meaning of our great positive principle—life lived according to the ideal of Christ in close and vital communication with God.[73]

As a step toward providing this new definition, those gathered at Woodbrooke laid down plans for a general meeting of Young Friends which might be employed as 'a magnificent weapon for the service of the Kingdom of God at its present time of crisis'.[74]

This planning session culminated in a gathering of over 400 men and women at Swanwick in August 1911 for the first national Conference of Young Friends.[75] The importance of this Conference for maintaining continuity in the impetus for reform and for underscoring the importance of both social responsibility and the peace testimony cannot be overstated. Many of the speakers at Swanwick were the same Friends, now middle-aged, who had initiated the Quaker Renaissance during the previous generation; the audience to which they spoke was mainly composed of young people who, in a few years, would form the front rank of Quaker resistance to the Great War. Links between the Swanwick Conference and wartime defiance of the State may be illustrated by the fact that at least eight of the eleven young men appointed to the Young Friends' Sub-Committee of the Friends' Home Mission

---

[71] 'The Young Friends Movement', in *Swanwick, 1911*, 5.
[72] Hoyland, 'Neo-Quakerism', 460. [73] Ibid. 462–3. [74] Ibid. 463.
[75] A[lfred] N[eave] B[rayshaw], 'The Young Friends'Movement', *Swanwick, 1911* ([London 1912], 5–10.

and Extension Committee at Swanwick would later be imprisoned or detained as conscientious objectors.[76] Beyond the importance of Swanwick to the revitalization of the peace testimony, there were signs that the Young Friends there were also demanding that their Society adopt a more resolute social policy on a wider range of issues.

Travelling to the Conference in the midst of a strike of railway workers, a number of Young Friends were deeply disturbed when they saw soldiers occupying village railway stations to prevent picketing or other activity by strikers. During the Conference two members of the Socialist Quaker Society, Alfred Barratt Brown (1887–1947) and John Percy Fletcher (1884–1961) moved a resolution 'expressing concern at the use of military forces . . . and sympathy with the workers on their efforts to secure better conditions'. Although their motion eventually failed on the grounds that it 'would not be helpful and might lead to misunderstanding', Brown and Fletcher left the Swanwick meeting as two of the best known and most respected young Friends. In time, they would emerge as leaders in Society's resistance to the Great War and conscription.

Nearly three years passed between the end of the Swanwick Conference and the onset of the Great War which brought on British Quakerism's greatest trial of faith since the Restoration era. A crucial development during this period was the publication in 1912 of William Charles Braithwaite's *The Beginnings of Quakerism*, with its inspiring accounts of the faith, sacrifices, and sufferings of early Friends. But for many young Friends, the atmosphere and inspiration of Swanwick in 1911 was probably the most significant event to give meaning and direction to their faith. Whether or not they remembered the exact words with which Neave Brayshaw set the tone for the gathering, many of them would act out the spirit he was attempting to convey: 'May not we go away from this place strong for the work that lies before us . . . [to] put away all . . . things that keep back the work, and together build the Holy City . . . the way of perfect peace is also the holy war . . . the highest happiness is not known apart from fellowship in the sufferings of Christ.' Therefore, Brayshaw concluded, remembering Albrecht Dürer's

---

[76] See *Swanwick, 1911*, 16 for a list of sub-committee members. For discussion of manifestations of a strengthened peace testimony at Swanwick, see below.

plea to Erasmus to lead the struggle against 'the unjust tyranny of earthly power, the power of darkness... [and] in the face of all the sore need of the world, in this day of the battle of God... Ride forth by the side of the Lord Christ, defend the truth, it may be for some of you, to gain the martyr's crown!'[77]

PEACE TESTIMONY AND *A NATION IN ARMS*

In October 1906, the *British Friend* provided a typically detailed description of the Universal Peace Congress in Milan, concluding that this gathering of peace lovers 'has probably had no equal as regards the extent of its labours, and the lofty and friendly tone which prevailed'.[78] Such gatherings formed an integral part of the liberal internationalists' *Weltanschauung* in the pre-war decade. They were often chaired by Friends—R. Spence Watson (1837–1911) presided at the 1906 Birmingham National Peace Congress while J. E. Ellis, MP (1841–1920), held forth at Scarborough the following year—who fraternized with like-minded celebrities of what Brian Phillips has acerbically dubbed the ' "high-life pacifique" crowd'.[79] In any case, occasions like the Milan Congress or the London International Peace Conference of 1908 focused on many of the deepest concerns of Quaker peace advocates and, thus, tended to be celebrated in glowing terms. The Friends' Peace Committee announced that the 1908 London Conference had given the cause of peace 'a place in the public mind such as it never before had'.[80] In point of fact, as regards meaningful results such conferences were essentially non-events, having little or no impact on the spirit or the direction of international affairs. They inevitably featured a stock cast of performers, many of them Quakers, who spent much of their time praising one another or hob-nobbing with diplomatic or even royal emissaries of various nations.[81]

In his study of 'Friendly Patriotism' Phillips has caustically characterized these gatherings as the self-aggrandizing affectations of 'a movement positively drunk with its own sense of amity and

---

[77] *Swanwick, 1911*, 37–8. Dürer had been the favourite subject of John Wilhelm Rowntree's lectures on religious art.

[78] *BF*, Oct. 1906, 264.   [79] Phillips, 'Friendly Patriotism', 301.

[80] *LYM, 1909*, 80–2.

[81] For a very critical summary, see Phillips, 'Friendly Patriotism', 153–259 *passim*.

virtue'.[82] He has also taken aim at Quaker efforts to promulgate Anglo-German friendship which were, in Phillips' view, based on the immodest belief that if the Kaiser and other prominent Germans could learn to know a representative group of British Friends, conflict between their two 'branches of the Teutonic stock allied to one another by a common faith and long friendship' would become virtually impossible.[83] The Friends who headed the unofficial Quaker delegations on the Edwardian Peace Congress 'circuit' were some of the same people appointed to the Quaker Anglo-German Conciliation Committee which remained active throughout the pre-war decade and had the same nominal effect on events.[84]

Phillips, scathing assessment of Edwardian Quaker peace activities may provide a corrective to personal recollections or historical depictions of early twentieth-century Friends as both individually virtue-laden and collectively prescient with regard to the calamitous results of modern warfare.[85] Some weighty Friends were, no doubt, overly taken with themselves and their supposed moral influence over the great and famous with whom they mingled. Still, the ensuing account presumes that the Society of Friends, for all the posturing complacency of some its members, was a religious community honestly attempting to come to grips with rapidly altered theological developments and wildly fluctuating international circumstances, the effects of which were barely comprehended by Friends or anybody else.

Throughout the Edwardian period a characteristically optimistic Quaker vision of 'the rising tide of social and international brotherhood', especially among the labouring classes, was curiously interspersed with dire warnings of 'the impotence of Europe under the crushing burden of its armaments', of 'the growing militarist tendencies of a large section of the British people' and of the disturbing popular inclination to associate 'militarism with patriotism'.[86] This sort of Jekyll-Hyde image of the world was

---

[82] Ibid. 200
[83] Ibid. 153–8 and *LYM*, 1906, 163–4, quoting a *Minute* of Meeting for Sufferings, 9 June 1905.
[84] *LYM, 1905*, 68 and 1906, 165–6 and Phillips, 'Friendly Patriotism', 256–7 who cites Ellen Robinson, Joseph G. Alexander, Thomas Hodgkin and T. P. Newman as representative figures of the European peace élite.
[85] Phillips, 'Friendly Patriotism', 3–4, 8, 23–4.
[86] *BF*, Feb. 1906, 34, 55, April 1908, 90–1 & May 1909, 133; *TF*, 28 May 1909, 367–8 and *LYM, 1909*, 85–6.

bound up with a deeply-felt, if somewhat stereotypical, concern about 'upper' class propensities to support aggressive imperialism and a warlike foreign policy as natural corollaries to the protectionist creed these same elements wished to foist upon an unwary British populace.

The relationship between free trade and international peace was inevitably accentuated along with the wasteful danger of military armaments, the mistreatment of subject races and the need for international institutions which would regularize peaceful arbitration and promote friendship between peace-loving peoples. Within Britain there were particular concerns regarding overt proselytizing for compulsory military service and covert measures to draw innocent youth toward the glaring flame of militarism through the allegedly innocuous introduction of military drill and training into the educational system. However naïve or inconsequential they may seem in retrospect, Quaker opposition to these diverse dangers to a peaceful world were of real significance in clarifying the Quaker peace testimony and in preparing pacifist Friends for the defining challenge of the First World War.

In February 1906 Lord Roberts of Kandahar, hero of the Boer War and newly appointed President of the National Service League, issued a Manifesto calling for the establishment of universal military training as a first step to the creation of a British Nation in Arms.[87] The Liberal press was critical and even disdainful of the old soldier's ringing declaration on the necessity for compulsory military service.[88] Quaker journals naturally followed suit, believing that one important reason for the recent Liberal electoral victory was 'the deep resentment of the public at the reckless way... the wealth of our country has been squandered' by fruitless military spending. The *British Friend*, reporting on a gathering at Mount Street Meeting House in Manchester 'chiefly composed of working men... to protest against Lord Roberts' propaganda', concluded: 'If the Liberal victory is not to be largely thrown away, the rising tide of social and international brotherhood must be directed into such channels as will keep in check the

---

[87] A copy of this document, dated 16 Feb. 1906 is in the Roberts Papers, R139/15, National Army Museum (NAM), London.

[88] See, for example, the *Daily News* and *Westminster Gazette*, 17 Feb. 1906 and *Truth*, 22 Feb. 1906

militarism which is rapidly growing among the "upper" classes of society'.[89]

This indirect confrontation between Friends as the disciples of peace and Earl Roberts as the Prince of Preparedness set the tone for the Edwardian debate over the most efficient means of maintaining the peace of Europe. The National Service League's motto, 'If you would have peace, prepare for war,' pointed up, said *The Friend*, the need for Quakers to help in organizing an 'energetic effort' to contradict such militaristic views and to prove that the 'best opportunity for Peace . . . is in the days of Peace'.[90]

While most Friends believed, with their Peace Committee, that the 'growing prevalence of the pacific spirit', especially among the labouring classes,[91] augured well for arms reduction and international good will, they also recognized a 'great need for the exercise of unremitting vigilance lest the scheme of Lord Roberts for universal military training or some other scheme tending to foster the military spirit . . . should find favour with Parliament'.[92]

Roberts' tireless efforts in pursuit of the compulsory service certainly gave new sparkle to the cause of the National Service League, but, on the other hand, the old soldier provided opponents of compulsion a convenient target on whom to focus. Early in 1906 one Liberal paper published a cartoon depicting Roberts in full regalia surrounded by armed infants and holding a candy jar labelled 'Bullseyes for Babes'.[93] For the Friends' Peace Committee such drollery reflected its longstanding concern about militarist attempts to make military drill and rifle shooting part of the curriculum of British schools, as with the so-called Model Course.[94] In October of 1906 the Peace Committee reported to Meeting for Sufferings on its renewed efforts 'to combat the growing tendency to introduce the use of the rifle in elementary schools', reflecting the co-ordinated exertions of the National Service League and its new affiliate the Lads' Drill Association.[95]

---

[89] *BF*, Feb. 1906, 55. This meeting was organized by John William Graham.
[90] *TF*, 2 March 1906, 133.
[91] *The British Friend* believed that the fifty working-class members in the new Parliament were 'the surest guarantee . . . of a pacific foreign policy'. Feb. 1906, 34. Also see *P&G*, VII/2, 14 July 1906, 20.
[92] *BF*, March 1906, 78. Also see *TF*, 9 March 1906, 146; and *LYM, 1906*, Report of the Peace Committee of Meeting for Sufferings, 161–3.
[93] *The Winning Post*, 16 March 1906.
[94] See Chapter 7.   [95] *Minutes*, Meeting for Sufferings, 5 Oct. 1906.

Such a danger was made manifest even in a Liberal-dominated Parliament. In the spring of 1907 R. B. Haldane, Secretary of State for War, introduced the Territorial & Reserve Forces Bill which included provision for Officer Training Corps at Universities and public schools. The *British Friend* labelled this 'a thoroughly reactionary measure' aimed at 'linking together the educational and military systems of the country'.[96] Friends in Lancashire and Cheshire Quarterly Meeting protested to their local MPs and to the Press that Haldane's scheme would 'prostitute our universities and schools to the service of militarism . . . [and] do grievous wrong to the rising generation'.[97]

For a time such protests appeared to be crowned with some success. When a Quaker deputation waited on Prime Minister Campbell-Bannerman and Chancellor of the Exchequer Lloyd George to ask them to remove certain offending clauses from the Army Bill, Sir Henry told them that he too 'was against introducing the military spirit into Government schools, and had no sympathy with making little children wave flags and behave like soldiers—it was iniquitous, vulgar and absurd'.[98] The Prime Minister's words, enforced by the Government's announcement that it would provide no financial aid to cadets under sixteen years of age, was reassuring to opponents of military training for the very young. Friends were nonetheless chagrined to learn that Cadet Training Corps were to be duly established at schools and universities as a means of enhancing the supply of qualified officer-candidates for the Territorial Army.[99] Such Cadet Corps proved to be very popular within the educational establishment. When Arthur Rowntree, headmaster of Bootham School, introduced an anti-military training resolution to the Annual Conference of the Incorporated Association of Headmasters in 1910, his motion was voted down, 67 to 8.[100]

While Associated Headmasters were proclaiming their enthusiasm for schoolboy military training, peace lovers perceived still

---

[96] *BF*, May 1907, 136, 141 and June 1907, 147.

[97] *Minutes*, Peace Committee, IV, 2 May 1907, LSF and *BF*, May 1907, 136. Also see Minute from Pickering and Hull Monthly Meeting, 17 April 1907, *Minute 14*, 27 April 1907, *Minutes*, York Quarterly Meeting, 415–6, BL.

[98] *BF*, June 1907, 164. Also see *Minutes*, Meeting for Sufferings, 5 Oct. 1906, LSF and *LYM, 1906*, 46–7.

[99] *BF*, June 1907, 164 and 176.   [100] *BF*, Feb. and April 1910, 49–50, 103–5.

another threat in the form of Colonel Robert Baden-Powell's Boy Scout Movement. While recent scholarship has emphasized the deliberately non-military nature of Baden-Powell's organization,[101] it would have been difficult to convince many Edwardian Friends that the Boy Scouts were not part of a nefarious conspiracy to militarize the nation's guileless youth.[102] Indeed, barely a month after Arthur Rowntree's pacific proposal was overwhelmingly rejected by the headmasters, Sir Francis Vane, formerly a close associate of Baden-Powell, revealed in the *Westminster Gazette* 'A Danger in the Boy Scout Movement' which confirmed the Quakers' worst fears. Most of the Scouts' Council Board, Vane said, including Lord Roberts and Generals Herbert Plummer and Edmund Elles, looked upon the 'movement from the military rather than from the educational standpoint', and unless this trend was reversed, he predicted that 'a system will be introduced into the country under the guise of civil training which will have all the evils of militarism without many of its compensating virtues'.[103] Subsequently, some Quakers co-operated with Vane's attempt to organize the National Peace Scouts with a view to promoting 'international friendship amongst our youth.' Indeed, two prominent Friends, George Cadbury and T. Edmund Harvey, MP, re-enforced Vane's movement by joining the National Council of the Peace Scouts.[104] Not surprisingly, Vane's movement failed to flourish and concerns about the militarization of youth remained a troubling aspect of the Quaker struggle against the National Service League's campaign to secure compulsory military training for young men and boys.

Early in 1908 the Friends' Peace Committee, citing the growth of 'agitation in the country in favour of military service', had asked

---

[101] See Martin Dedman, 'Baden-Powell, Militarism, and the "Invisible Contributors" to the Boy Scout Scheme, 1904–1920', *Twentieth Century British History*, 4/3 (1993), 210–23.

[102] For concerns about the militaristic tendencies of the Boy Scouts, see *BF*, Sept. 1909, 236 & Oct. 1909; *P&G*, 7/15 15 Oct. 1909, 225–26; and *TF*, 24 Sept., 648, 1 Oct., 665, 8 Oct., 680, & 19 Nov. 1909, 776.

[103] Reprinted in *BF*, March 1910, 77–8 and *TF*, 25 March 1910, 192. Also see Richard Westlake Jr.'s letter to *BF* taking exception to that journal's criticism of Baden-Powell's movement, *BF*, March 1910, 77.

[104] See C. Brightwen Rowntree, 'The Adult School and the Boy Scout', *FQE*, 44 (1910), 324–31. In 1914 Quaker MP Arnold S. Rowntree joined the national Boy Scout Council, much to the consternation of some Friends. See *Minutes of the Peace Committee*, 30 April and 4 June 1914, 176–7, 183.

Meeting for Sufferings to ensure that special consideration be given to 'the subject of Peace' during Yearly Meeting. At the same time, the Committee noted its own increased activity, listing seven separate projects on behalf of the 'Peace cause', from promoting Peace Sunday to urging colonial politicians to reject all forms of compulsion. But while such endeavours doubtless involved considerable expenditures of time for earnest peace workers, some sense of the limited scope of the Peace Committee's work may be gathered from its average annual budget of just over £141 between 1905 and 1914. These figures may be compared to the thousands regularly collected and spent by the National Service League to advance the cause of compulsion.[105]

Throughout the Edwardian period, agitation for compulsory service and increased naval expenditure were aided and abetted by recurring alarms concerning the size of the German fleet and the intentions of its statesmen. Amidst such clamour, the Quaker press attempted to ensure that Friends were apprised of the 'pestilent nonsense' embodied in this inexplicable 'outbreak of militarism in a time of profound and growing peacefulness'.[106] *The Friend* struck a hopeful note early in 1909, citing public concern about arms expenditure, the rising power of democracy, the growth of 'higher and saner education' as well as the establishment in 1907 of the Hague Tribunal as developments rendering 'the claims of the militarists ... out of date ... we may therefore look for a growing demand among the nations for reduction instead of increase of armaments'. At the same time, Friends were reminded 'to be earnest in paper' by writing to their MPs to urge support for Quaker member J. Allen Baker's resolution deploring the increased spending on armaments reflected in the Naval Estimates for 1909.[107]

Still, for all the solemn piety and liberal optimism reflected in such Quaker attitudes and activities, there were also disturbing signs from within the ranks. As Quarterly and Monthly Meetings

---

[105] *Minutes*, Peace Committee, IV, 4 Feb. 1908 and Report of the Peace Committee to Meeting for Sufferings, 5 March 1908, *LYM, 1908*, 172–4. Material on the NSL's financial support can be found in both the Roberts Papers at the National Army Museum and the Milner Papers in the Bodleian Library, Oxford.

[106] *BF*, March 1909, 57–8. *The Friend* also expressed alarm at 'a rising wave of militarism ...' 19 March 1909, 175–6.

[107] *TF*, 5 Feb. 1909, 81; 12 March 1909, 160; and 19 March 1909, 175–6; *BF*, March 1909, 58.

throughout the country discussed the role their religious Society should play in the debate over war and preparations for war, questions arose as to whether Quaker resistance to military spending, military service and indeed to war itself could or should be absolute. Letters in the Quaker press posed a number of awkward queries concerning the legitimacy of their public stance given the complexities and dangers of international affairs. Were Friends right in rejecting R. B. Haldane's proposed Territorial Force when such a voluntary body might be 'the only preventive of conscription'? Were not military and naval expenditures merely the equivalent to putting locks and bolts on one's doors? Since Quaker opposition would never result in the abolition of military forces, were Friends really supporting peace by attempting to make such forces less effective? Finally, could those, who claimed liberty of conscience against conscription, 'deny similar liberty of conscience to those who feel free to volunteer for military service'?[108]

Immediately prior to the Yearly Meeting of 1909, an editorial in the *British Friend* responded to such questions by noting that the overwhelming majority of those who apparently wished to modify the peace testimony were 'not younger Friends but... more mature members'. Were such members really prepared to permit their Society's traditional testimony against all war to go the way of plain speech and dress and become a mere eccentricity observed only by the unfashionable and out of touch? Were they willing to support the right of members 'to make fortunes by manufacturing bombshells?' Whatever moral authority Quakers possessed in British society, said the *British Friend*, it had been established through the expression of an enduring vision 'as to what the Christian religion really requires of its adherents...' Unless Quakerism maintained an 'unswerving loyalty to the highest we know, whatever the cost... It had better not speak if it had only platitudes to utter...'[109]

Some Quaker peace activities did seem to produce fruitful results. Notable among these was the publication in 1909 of Edward Grubb's *The True Way of Life*, a collection of essays which initially appeared in the *British Friend* which offered a point by point refutation of *A New Way of Life* by J. St Loe Strachey, editor

---

[108] See letters to *TF*, 8 Jan. 1909, 19, 28 and 2 July 1909, 430.
[109] 'Our Testimony for Peace', *BF*, May 1909, 133–4. This unsigned piece was probably written by Edward Grubb.

of *The Spectator*, a celebration of the social, economic, and moral benefits of compulsion.[110] In a letter pledging any royalties from his book to the National Service League, Strachey told Lord Roberts that his aim was 'not to preach moral righteousness... but... to prepare... a new and more serious type of men and women' who would throw off the 'attitude of smug and easy going optimism' which was imperilling the survival of the British Nation and Empire.[111] Grubb's rebuttal asserted that the growth of individual liberty, common rationality and spiritual perception in modern society was working to 'break down the narrow pagan concept that each nation is... the highest end for which its citizens can live or die'. The alleged duty to fight and kill, Grubb said, violated the Christian's obligation to practice a faith which could 'supply the ideal, the impulse and the moral dynamic, that will one day make Human Brotherhood... a reality'.[112]

Friends, of course, believed that Edward Grubb had much the best of the argument[113] and, in fact, *The True Way* also seems to have won the battle of the book stalls. Whereas Strachey admitted to Lord Northcliffe that the sales of *A New Way* had been 'very disappointing indeed', Grubb reported to Rufus Jones that his book was 'selling fairly well'. Eventually, *The True Way of Life* ran through three editions, aided to be sure by orders like the 400 copies purchased by the Friends Foreign Mission Association for distribution in China.[114]

During Yearly Meeting of 1910, the Clerk, Henry Lloyd Wilson while citing *The True Way of Life* 'as an example of the useful work individuals could do to combat militarism' also referred to a new book called *England's* [sic] *Optical Illusion* as worthy of Friends' consideration.[115] This first official Quaker recognition of Norman Angell's soon-to-be-famous commentary on the disastrous economic consequences of modern warfare between interdependent

[110] J. St. Loe Strachey, *A New Way of Life* (London 1909). *The True Way of Life* was initially serialized in *The British Friend* in Sept. and Oct. 1909, 240–44, 269–74.

[111] Strachey to Roberts, 1 June 1909, Roberts Papers, R 85/27, National Army Museum (NAM), London.

[112] 'The True Way of Life', *BF*, Oct. 1909, 274.

[113] See review of *The True Way of Life* in *BF*, Nov. 1909, 303–4.

[114] *Minutes*, Peace Committee, IV, 6 Oct. 1910; Grubb to Rufus M. Jones, 26 Dec. 1909, RMJP; Dudley, *Edward Grubb*, 97–9; and Strachey to Lord Northcliffe, 12 July 1909, Strachey Papers, House of Lords Record Office, London.

[115] *BF*, June 1910, 165–6.

industrial nations marked the beginning of an informal partnership or, better, marriage of convenience between potential allies who were seeking the same objective from very different perspectives. Actually, the *British Friend* had already reviewed *Europe's Optical Illusion*, noting that while Angell's thesis was 'quite too materialistic for our liking... it may be all the more convincing to many who think that Peace advocates are impractical visionaries'.[116]

After Angell's book was revised and reissued as *The Great Illusion*, it achieved astonishing instant popularity. By then the *British Friend* had discarded all reservations regarding the book which a second reviewer called 'by far the most important contribution to Peace literature which our generation has seen... a really magnificent defence of the maxim that "what is morally wrong will not be found economically right".'[117] The reviewer urged Friends to read and re-read Angell's plea for peace before passing it on to others. To ensure a wider circulation of Angell's ideas, the Yorkshire 1905 Committee announced it would prepare a penny pamphlet summary of *The Great Illusion*. The Peace Committee demonstrated its enthusiastic approval of this project by ordering 10,000 copies for distribution in Friends meetings and Adult Schools.[118]

In the final years of peace, a mutual attraction developed between Norman Angellism and Quaker peace advocates. The *British Friend*, for example, began to feature pearls of pacific wisdom from Angell's works.[119] Furthermore, the message of *The Great Illusion* was in large measure responsible for the establishment of the Northern Friends Peace Board in the wake of a Joint Conference on Peace convened by the five northern Quarterly Meetings in 1913. This new body, whose creation reflected the view of many that the official Peace Committee had grown too cautious and stale, was celebrated in a special supplement to *The Friend* as 'a distinctly forward step in the Society's work for International Peace'. The Chairman of the Joint Conference, Dr Thomas Hodgkin, had stirred delegates by reading from Norman Angell's letter to Quaker MP, Arnold Rowntree:

---

[116] *BF*, Feb. 1910, 30, 42–3.   [117] *BF*, Dec. 1910, 323–4.
[118] *Minutes*, Peace Committee, IV, 1 Dec. 1910; *BF*, April 1911, 113–14. The Peace Committee's original order of 3,000 copies was raised to 10,000 in March 1911.
[119] See *BF*, May 1911, 116.

I feel [Angell wrote] that we have arrived at a point in European civilisation where Quakerism might play...an inestimably useful role, perhaps a determining one, in fixing the direction we are to take in our generation...and I believe that the Society of Friends have it in their power just now largely to determine what English policy shall be...[Therefore] the Society...should take some definite and practical step for seeing that the rising generation is equipped to justify intellectually that faith that is in them...[120]

Angell's message of encouragement elicited an enthusiastic response among the delegates. One speaker exhorted Friends to respond to Angell's challenge by setting up a Central Peace Bureau to unite the struggle against the 'war-organized interests'. John William Graham declared that for too long Friends' testimony against war 'had been as a lighthouse upon the rocks, surrounded by surging waves of military emotion and military preparation' but peace advocates like Angell had added new forms of illumination based upon practical considerations like the falling stocks and 'jumpy bank rates' that resulted from wars and rumours of wars. Such practical arguments were not sordid, Graham said, but, to be truly effective, they required the sort of spiritual base of support that Friends could provide.[121]

Graham seemed the ideal Quaker to respond to Norman Angell's call for an alliance of peace lovers. As a liberal in politics as well as religion, Graham was also well known and highly regarded outside the Society. An ardent campaigner for social justice and smoke abatement as well as for peace, Graham's articles regularly appeared in the *Manchester Guardian*, edited by his friend C. P. Scott.[122] Graham had also recently published his first book, *Evolution and Empire* (1912), which was full of praise for *The Great Illusion* and touched upon many of the same themes.[123] In fact,

---

[120] Supplement to *TF*, 14 Feb. 1913, 1, 4–5.

[121] Ibid. 2, 5–6. The idea for a Central Peace Office was suggested by C. Ernest Elcock, but this body and the Northern Friends' Peace Board obviously reflected the dissatisfaction of some Friends with the limited scope of activities undertaken by the official Peace Committee.

[122] See, for example, 'Industrialism and National Character', *TF*, 14 Jan. 1910, 21–2 and his articles on 'Empire Building', in *BF*, Jan. and March 1911, 6–8 & 69–71.

[123] Graham compared the intellectual impact of *The Great Illusion* with Darwin's *Origin of Species*, see *Evolution and Empire* (London 1912), 193–7. Also see Angell to Graham, 24 May 1912, JWGP, thanking him for a copy of the book and for the support it gave to Angell's work.

Graham's book was, to a considerable extent, a compendium of the sort of ideas popular among liberal/progressive Edwardian Friends. Citing the dangerously unhealthy connections between the aristocracy, protectionism, militarism, and imperialism,[124] Graham's analysis ranged from the positive Social Darwinism of the American peace advocate David Starr Jordan to John A. Hobson's depiction of Empire as the playground of 'unpatriotic financiers' who made 'social welfare and Imperialism . . . two competing ways of living . . .'[125] Still, while he assumed an ostensibly anti-imperialist line, Graham admitted that because Western societies needed the fruits of non-European lands and because 'the natives are too indolent . . . to do the needful work . . . We are driven . . . to the establishment of plantations worked by more or less unwilling native labour'. To be sure Graham expressed uneasiness about the necessity for such continued European control of the tropics,[126] but he seemed unaware (or unconcerned) that questions concerning the abuse and exploitation of native labour had for some time been especially crucial for Friends in light of journalist Henry Nevinson's revelations that native workers in the Portuguese African possessions that produced most of the cocoa for the Quaker chocolate firms of Cadbury, Fox, and Rowntree were kept in conditions of virtual slavery.[127]

Evolution and Empire, for all its faults, contained much earnest goodwill, but the shallowness of Graham's intellectual grasp as well as his self-confident moral superiority would seem to make his book a conspicuous example of 'the Society's ambiguous relationship with Imperialism' as well as the 'Eurocentric racism widespread in pacifist thinking' of which late twentieth-century critics have complained.[128]

---

[124] 'There is . . . the closest alliance . . . those who want Protection and those who want Imperialism. . . . So that a protective tariff is one of the commonest accompaniments of militarism . . .' *Evolution and Empire*, 147–8.

[125] Ibid., 129–31, 173. Graham's book also repeated Hobson's vaguely anti-Semitic tones in criticizing South African Jewish bankers and businessmen.

[126] Ibid. 115–16, 124.

[127] See Henry W. Nevinson, *A Modern Slavery* (London 1906; reprinted with introduction by Basil Davidson, New York 1968), 187–210. For Quaker reactions, see *BF*, Nov. 1907, 303–4 and June 1908, 141. In 1909 the Quaker chocolate firms, observing no meaningful reform at cocoa plantations at San Thomé and Principe, suspended all purchases from those islands, ibid., April 1909, 86. Professor Lowell Satre's study of the cocoa plantations scandal and its impact on Quaker chocolate manufacturers is eagerly awaited.

[128] Hinton, *Protests and Visions*, 29 and Phillips, 'Friendly Patriotism', 7–8 & *passim*.

Certainly, as a conspicuous public Friend and a widely-recognized spokesman for his religious Society John William Graham presents an excellent target for such criticism, but it does not necessarily follow that Graham was always as well received by fellow Quakers as by non-Friends who perceived of him as speaking for the Society. Indeed, the limits of Graham's influence among young Friends had been amply demonstrated at the Swanwick Conference. As noted above, this gathering of Young Friends deserves to be remembered as a seminal event in preparing younger Quakers for the challenge of war and conscription. Attenders at Swanwick shared a deepening seriousness about the importance of religious and social issues in their lives. Graham, as a leader of the Quaker Renaissance generation and a celebrated public advocate for the application of Quaker peace principles to British foreign and imperial affairs, was invited to address the Swanwick Conference on 'Difficulties of the Peace Question'.

The ground for Graham's presentation had been prepared by Neave Brayshaw's introductory remarks reminding Young Friends that 'Our testimony concerning war is not something that we can put in or leave out just as we like . . . it is a necessary outcome of our root belief.'[129] But Graham's lengthy, somewhat tortured speech took on a different tone. Application of the peace testimony within the social and political confines of a modern state, Graham noted, raised serious practical difficulties concerning the role that Friends, particularly young Friends, might be called upon to play in any future armed conflict. For his part, Graham frankly stated his conviction that Quakers should be prepared to assist in defending the Nation—most assuredly as non-combatants—in any war threatening British security. The defeat of British Empire, he said, would mean: 'Materialism and brute force would be enthroned where humanity and freedom and progress have their chief seat; the premier shoot of the climbing ivy of humanity would have been torn from the wall.'[130]

The official record of the Conference reveals that 'Disapproval . . . was keenly present in the minds of many . . . during the

---

[129] *Swanwick, 1911*, 27.

[130] Ibid. 56–75. Two years later Graham told his son, 'I think our duty as citizens compels us to defend the country against an invader . . .' J. W. Graham to Richard, 11 Feb. 1913, JWGP.

lecture... [and] very strongly expressed in the discussion which
followed... a number of young Friends rose... to voice their
uncompromising witness to our principles.' Several young men
protested that they would not be willing to serve even in non-
combatant roles. A female Friend added: 'We women do not wish
men to sacrifice their souls for the sake of our bodies.'[131] Thus, as
the official record noted:

the meeting was confirmed in the desire... to make the supreme venture
of faith, and to prepare our hearts in the spirit of love and peace to the end
that in any emergency... we might be so filled with the spirit and so sure
in faith that violence... [would] become impossible to us, and that the
attitude of peace and prayer might alone be natural.

A final, ironic touch was added when, in a 'quiet and sympathetic
reply', Graham reminded his critics 'to be modest in their expressions about distant contingencies'.[132]

One leader of the Young Friends' Movement recalled Swanwick as 'the outward and visible sign of a great and growing
movement... beginning to make itself felt in the life of our society... To many of us the challenge came... to live out our message and our faith in a way which must cost us dear.'[133] When he
wrote this, 22-year-old Geoffrey Hoyland could not know that the
'distant contingencies' of which John Graham spoke would soon
require that, in their fidelity to the peace testimony, he and many
of his companions would be forced live out their witness for peace
in army guardrooms and prison cells.

Prior to 1914, under Neave Brayshaw's leadership, the Young
Friends Movement increasingly stressed the centrality of the peace
testimony, but there remained wide differences among Friends as
to the exact form that testimony should take. One prominent
example was a long-standing controversy brought on by the discovery that some Quakers were joining the Territorial Army and
justifying this action on the twin grounds of fulfilling their patriotic
duty and preserving the Nation from compulsory military service.
These Quaker volunteers argued that since they shared in the
security and prosperity provided by the military system, their

[131] *Swanwick, 1911*, 175.   [132] Ibid. 175.   [133] Ibid. 12.

consciences impelled them to assume some of the burdens as well.[134]

Response to such arguments was generally negative. One peace advocate maintained that he could have no respect for those who 'go to meeting on Sunday... while they hobnob with... the Territorials in the week'. A *Minute* of the Lancashire and Cheshire Quarterly Meeting asked if there was not 'need for loving caution' for those who by joining the Territorials were 'weakening the Christian ideal'.[135] A *Minute* of Kingston Monthly Meeting reprinted by the *British Friend* spoke directly and decisively to the same issue.

Many of us are seeing more and more clearly that our peace principle is not an isolated tradition, but an organic outcome of our Quaker life; that it flows inevitably out of the rock upon which the founders of our Society built their faith... With all love and sympathy, we submit that this is not the time for weakening our [peace] testimony.[136]

And when a revised version of *Christian Practice*, Part II of London Yearly Meeting's *Christian Discipline* (revised 1906), was published in 1911, it specifically warned Friends 'to beware of joining Territorial or... of undertaking services auxiliary to warfare in positions where they would be under military orders'.[137]

In May 1912 when Yearly Meeting gathered at Manchester, an enlarged Peace Committee created in 1909 out of a concern for the 'growing militarist tendencies of a large section of the British public'[138] presented a document entitled 'Our Testimony for Peace'. The purpose of this document was to define precisely how a witness for peace fitted into the modern practice of Quaker faith. When it was accepted by Yearly Meeting, 'Our Testimony for Peace' became, as the *British Friend* noted, the first official

[134] See especially a letter of Richard Westlake Jr., 'Is Patriotism UnChristian?' in *BF*, July 1910, 194.

[135] *LYM*, 1911, 115 and *BF*, June & July 1911, 161, 189–90.

[136] *BF*, Sept. 1911, 263–4, and 'Friends and the Territorial Army', ibid., Oct. 1911, 292–3.

[137] *Christian Practice* (London 1911), 141.

[138] *LYM*, 1909, 162–3 and *Minutes*, Peace Committee, 3 June 1909. This Committee consisted of 67 Friends, only nine of whom were women. It did not replace the Meeting for Sufferings Peace Committee, but the two bodies merged in 1912 to avoid duplication of effort. The arrangement proved unwieldy and the Committee increasingly ineffective.

document in the history of Quakerism to state explicitly that the peace testimony 'follows necessarily from the foundation principle on which the Society . . . is built . . . our belief in and experience of the Light Within'.[139] This official recognition of an explicit connection between the peace testimony and Inward Light theology represented not only the triumph for the liberal tenets of the Quaker Renaissance but also the creation of a rock upon which future Quaker war resistance would be anchored.

The range of 'Our Testimony for Peace' was comprehensive and its provisions were both specific and timely, incorporating, for example, both the positive Social Darwinist argument that the 'fittest races and nations' were those who 'care most for human personality' and Norman Angell's tenet that modern warfare in an intertwined capitalist world was 'useless and ruinous to both conqueror and conquered'.[140]

We recognise that each generation . . . must face these great questions for themselves . . . [But] to leave our attitude in regard to Peace and War entirely to the individual conscience, means that the Society as such abandons any distinctive testimony on the matter . . . War, with the whole military system, is contrary to the Spirit of the God whose name is Love [and the peace testimony is] not an artificial appendage . . . which can be dropped without injuring the whole . . . [but] an organic outgrowth of our Faith as Christians.[141]

Friends, said the document, were bound in faith to lead and 'to Christianise the opposition' to compulsory military service and thus to 'save it from becoming merely the expression of an indolent and selfish materialism'.[142]

Although 'Our Testimony for Peace' clearly asserted that the acceptance and practice of the peace testimony was a defining characteristic of Quakerism, it concluded on a conciliatory note: 'We do not desire, by hasty acts or harsh judgments, to drive from us those who, feeling themselves attached to our Society and spiritual ideals, yet cannot honestly subscribe to the abstract doctrine that War under all circumstances is wrong.' Still, unlike any

[139] *Minutes*, Peace Committee, May 1912, 134 and *LYM, 1912*, 107, 114.
[140] 'Our Testimony for Peace', *LYM, 1912*, 116–17.
[141] Ibid. 107–08, 112–14.   [142] Ibid. 116.

other Christian body, Friends believed that their testimony for peace could not 'be abandoned without mutilating our whole message for the world'. This message would only be fulfilled through 'an active movement towards the oneness of all humanity and the realisation of the Kingdom of God on earth . . . in a campaign of the most strenuous character against organized forces of evil.'[143]

The Yearly Meeting's acceptance of 'Our Testimony for Peace' was of immense significance in linking the ideals of the Quaker Renaissance to Friends' resistance to war and conscription after 1914. British Friends did not, however, have to wait until 1914 to test the mettle of their revitalized peace testimony. Since early 1909 warnings had been sounded about the danger of conscription being imposed in both Australia and New Zealand.[144] On 1 January 1911 by provisions of the Australian Defence Act (New Zealand soon followed suit), all males from age 12 to 18 were subject to compulsory military training, without exemption for religious or an other type of objection. Many members of the tiny Australian Quaker community determined to resist the Defence Acts and the same Yearly Meeting which endorsed 'Our Testimony for Peace' received a report indicating that some hundreds of young men in Australia and New Zealand were being prosecuted, fined, and imprisoned for failure to comply with the Defence Acts. Yearly Meeting responded by suggesting that British Friends provide not only monetary support for this struggle but also volunteers who would go out to the southern Dominions to organize resistance to the Acts and to agitate for their repeal.[145]

One Friend who took up this challenge was John P. Fletcher, the 24-year-old Yorkshireman and budding socialist who had played a prominent role at Swanwick.[146] After working his passage to Australia in early 1912, Fletcher helped to found the Australian Freedom League which took the lead in organizing agitation against the Defence Acts. Moving to New Zealand in 1913,

---

[143] 'Our Testimony for Peace', *LYM, 1912*, 113, 118. Also see *BF*, July 1911, 189–90; Sept. 1911, 263–4; Oct. 1911, 292; and May 1912, 134. Over 25,000 copies of 'Our Testimony for Peace' were printed and distributed.

[144] *TF*, 8 Jan. 1909, 19 & 23 Dec. 1910, 855; *BF*, Feb. 1910, 54; and *LYM, 1910*, 83 & 1911, 113–14.

[145] *LYM, 1912*, 102–5. Also see *BF*, Jan. 1911, 23–4; April 1911, 113; July 1911, 188–89; and June 1912, 163.

[146] See *Swanwick, 1911*, 80 and photos, 140, 172.

Fletcher's anti-conscription activities brought a brief jail term at Christchurch.[147] In all, Fletcher spent over three years in the Antipodes, receiving financial and moral support from London while gaining the experience that would thrust him into a leading role in Quaker resistance to the Great War.[148]

In the Spring of 1914 during the final, optimistic pre-war gathering of London Yearly Meeting, the Friends' Peace Committee introduced a résumé of Quaker peace activity 'since the close of the lamentable war in South Africa'. Proudly citing the prominence of Friends in the Norman Angell Movement and the financial and personal aid provided to Australasian Friends in their struggle against the compulsory military training, the report concluded that as a result of such 'devoted labour... the peacemaker is no longer an object of ridicule', his numbers in Parliament had grown and 'his voice was heard with attention and respect... The ground is prepared and the good seed sown. Let us then work on, ploughing and sowing in faith and hope.'[149]

And they did work on. In the midst of the beautiful summer of 1914, *The Friend* reported on a campaign undertaken by Sussex Friends 'to place before rural people the evils of militarism'. Sixty to seventy meetings had been held for audiences of up to three hundred and despite the occasional 'rough crowd', as at the Romsey horse-fair, the peacemakers' message had been well-received. 'Surely', said editor T. P. Newman, such sustained and well-organized work would 'have its effect in the promotion of a peaceable spirit and a right understanding amongst those who have not hitherto considered whether there is not "a better way".'[150]

These comments were published on the last day of July, 1914.

[147] See William N. Oats, 'The Campaign Against Conscription in Australia, 1911–1914', *JFHS*, 55/7 (1989), 205–19; Leslie C. Jauncey, *The Story of Conscription in Australia* (London 1935), 65–117; and R. L. Weitzel, 'Pacifists and Anti-Militarists in New Zealand, 1909–1914', *The New Zealand Journal of History*, 7 (October 1973), 123–47.

[148] *TF*, 23 May 1913, 335–6 and *LYM, 1913*, 106, 108–14, 121–2, 215–17. From Jan. 1911 to April 1914 the London Yearly Meeting Committee on Australasian Defence Acts received subscriptions of over £4,300. See *LYM, 1913*, 109 and *1914*, 122.

[149] *LYM, 1914*, 110–16.   [150] *TF*, 31 July 1914, 563.

9
'A Ghoulish Terror of Darkness'

'FRIENDS DO NOT KNOW WHERE THEY ARE'

Where were you when the war began?

sitting on a bench looking out over the Irish Sea as my father talked with breaking heart...about how the world would never be the same again...The beauty of the sea, of the long stretching line of the Welsh Coast, seemed to mock at us. To think that the long & patient work for Peace should bring—this![1]

Two Quaker recollections: a boy of 8 and a middle-aged man, both spending the final hours of peace beside the sea and both equally perplexed as to what had transpired or would come to pass. 'All is bewildering, confused, dark and hidden,' *The Friend* lamented in its first wartime edition, 'some ghoulish terror of darkness or pestilence that wasteth at noonday.'[2] 'Many Friends do not know "where they are",' mused Ernest Taylor (1869–1955), Secretary to the Yorkshire 1905 Committee, three weeks after his return from Wales. Taylor feared that some Quakers, 'caught by the "urgency" and "righteousness" of *this* war', were becoming 'very cold' with regard to peace principles. Colder, perhaps, than he imagined. It may not have been surprising that the two Quaker Conservative MPs, Frank L. Harris and Alfred Bigland, abandoned peace for the national cause. But it must have been something of a shock when Henry Marriage Wallis, recently returned from aiding war victims in the Balkans, announced at the first wartime Meeting for Suffer-

---

[1] Wilson, 'Best Things', 9 and Ernest E. Taylor, 'Diary, 1914–' 3 August 1914, Temp. Box 23/3, LSF.

[2] *TF*, 7 Aug. 1914, 575–6.

ings that he was forthwith appealing for Quaker youth to join the half million recruits needed to crush the Hun.[3]

And they did join. More than two hundred young Quakers enlisted during the first flush of patriotic enthusiasm and eventually nearly one thousand or one-third of all male Friends of military age served; over a hundred of them died.[4] The usual explanation for this considerable defection from the peace camp was that most of these Friendly warriors were birthright Quakers without serious attachment to the religious life of their local meetings: 'Strain proved too much for any whose Quaker principles were not rooted in something far deeper than mere tradition or inherited beliefs.'[5] A study of Quaker response to the war in local meetings has challenged this perception. While largely limited to East Anglia and including one sizeable meeting, Norwich, with any unusually large number of working-class members, this work seems to indicate that many early enlisters were serious, thoughtful Friends who had been active in their local meetings.[6] One scrupulously earnest young Friend who eventually volunteered was John Wilhelm Rowntree's only son Lawrence, who was killed on the Western front.[7] In his post-war history of the *Later Periods of Quakerism*, Rufus Jones expressed the view that many Quakers

[3] Taylor, 'Diary, 1914–', 27 Aug., 4 and 25 Sept. 1914 and Isichei, *Victorian Quakers*, 201–2. A cousin of H. M. Wallis, Horace Alexander, recalled being amazed by the vehemence of Wallis' support for the war. Interview with Horace Alexander, Longwood, Pa., November 1980. In the Spring of 1915 a Committee on Friends and Enlistment reported to Yearly Meeting that fifteen Friends were known to have engaged in recruiting activities, *TF*, 28 May 1915, 408–9. Also see Chapter 11.

[4] *LYM, 1915*, 30; *TF*, 28 May 1915, 408–9; and *LYM, 1923*, 232. Also see Maude Robinson, ' "Lest We Forget" ', 3.

[5] Elizabeth Fox Howard, *Friends' Service in Wartime* (London n.d.), 11.

[6] Lucy Mouland, 'Quaker Pacifism and the First World War' (Third Year Dissertation, Department of History, University of Cambridge), 12, 29–44. The working-class membership of Norwich Meeting was clearly not representative for British Quakerism. Ellwood Brockbank's comment at the Manchester Conference that thirty-five members of the Norwich Gospel Band had recently merged with Norwich Friends Meeting helps to explain the surfeit of working-class Friends. See *Manchester Conference*, 104–05.

[7] After serving for nearly two years in the Friends Ambulance Unit, Lawrence (Laurie) Rowntree enlisted during the summer of 1916 and was killed in Nov. 1917. In a memoir entitled 'A Nightmare', kindly provided by his sister, Jean Rowntree, Laurie reflected upon his combat experience: 'The excitment of it, even the fear is enticing; the glorious feeling when you overcome difficulties . . . and the jolly companionship . . . you get in the face of common danger . . .', 19. Jean Rowntree believes that her brother enlisted because he could no longer watch other men suffer and die while he was largely immune from the hazards they were required to face.

opted for military service because, prior to the Great War the peace testimony remained 'an unexamined inheritance' for the majority of Quakers on both sides of the Atlantic. It was, he said, due only to the stand of a staunch 'remnant' that 'the official position of the Society of Friends remained unchanged'.[8]

Despite their considerable numbers, Friends who enlisted were of little or no significance in the development of an official Quaker position on the war. When they marched away, they relinquished any influence over the stance their Society would take. The official Quaker policy regarding the war was determined by stay-at-home Friends, many of them young and some of them female, who resisted the war and conscription. As for the influence of older home-front warriors like Henry Marriage Wallis, their status among pacifist Quakers was neatly summarized in the recollections of a female Friend: 'One just did not listen to them.'[9]

In addition to that third of the Society who openly supported the Great War, there were an indeterminate number, young and old, who drifted, confused and demoralized about which way to turn 'under the present appalling circumstances'. In the spring of 1915, a *Minute* of Pontefract Monthly Meeting in Yorkshire remarked upon 'the depression...and...perplexity which so many Friends are feeling as to the right attitude to adopt'.[10] Leaders of the Society, individually and corporately, attempted to speak to the condition of these wavering brethren with an outpouring of advice and exhortation. Meeting for Sufferings published an appeal asking members to recall the historic responsibility of Friends to uphold their Christian testimony against war, reminding them that 'our testimony loses its efficacy in proportion to the want of consistency...amongst us'.[11] *The Friend* noted in its mid-September issue that the peace testimony was 'the candle that we must

---

[8] Jones, *Later Periods*, II, 728, 757. Jones does not mention London Yearly Meeting's 1912 document on 'Our Testimony for Peace'. Ceadel, *British Pacifism 1914–1945: The Defining of a Faith* (Oxford 1980), 18 makes the same point concerning the British peace movement as a whole.

[9] Interview with Elfrida Vipont Foulds, Yealand Conyers, Lancashire, August 1986.

[10] *Minute 2*, 28 April 1915, *Minutes of the Meeting of Elders*, Yorkshire Quarterly Meeting, Brotherton Library (BL), University of Leeds and Edward Grubb to *TF*, 4 Sept. 1914, 647.

[11] Taylor, 'Diary, 1914–', 10 Sept. 1914 and *TF*, 18 Sept. 1914, 682, 687–8. The quotation was taken from London Yearly Meeting's *Christian Practice* (1911), 141. The Meeting for Sufferings' *Message to Men and Women of Goodwill*, printed copy in LSF, was issued three days after Britain entered the war; nearly half a million copies were printed.

keep alight in England'. Seebohm Rowntree, attempting perhaps to convince himself as much as others, urged Friends to stand firm in their convictions, so as to become the 'rallying point around which all the friends of peace may gather'.[12]

The need to generate a sense of solidarity, not just with peace-lovers, but with all of suffering humanity, was the burden of most tracts and letters produced by anti-war Quakers in the early months of the conflict. The emphasis was on the peace testimony as a 'direct inevitable outgrowth from the... distinctive message of early Quakerism... the... universality of the Divine indwelling' and, thus, the sacredness of every human personality touched by that which was of God. 'No one', said Wilfred Littleboy (1885–1979) in *The Friend*, 'can honestly take our Quaker stand against all war without being committed to a higher and more exacting service, one leading to love and life and not to hatred and death'.[13]

Soul-stirring words, to be sure. But were young Friends prepared to heed the utterances of a Birmingham chartered accountant while the siren song of Rupert Brooke called out for 'the red/Sweet wine of youth'? As the former MP Joshua Rowntree noted: 'It is very natural that with the seething of the war fever all around some of our young people should long to do something to lessen the misery & prove that they do not shirk enlistment from cowardice.'[14]

Quakerism, both officially and otherwise, did, in fact, attempt to provide alternatives to young Friends. The most famous of these, and doubtless the most immediately satisfying, was the Friends Ambulance Unit (FAU), a volunteer nursing corps that was the brain-child of Cambridge scholar and future British Olympian, Philip Noel-Baker (1889–1982). Eventually, over 1,500 men, less than half of whom were Quakers, served in the FAU, but, in time, the Unit became tainted by the accusation of a too-cozy relationship with the military authorities. Indeed, after the introduction of conscription in 1916, the FAU became the centre of a serious inter-Quaker conflict.[15] Another smaller group of about 300,

[12] 'Friends and Enlistment', *TF*, 2 Oct. 1914, 724. Also see, ibid. 25 Sept. 1914, 713. As one of Lloyd George's chief war-time advisors, Seebohm Rowntree could scarcely be said to have practiced what he preached.

[13] William Littleboy, *Friends and Peace* (London 1915), 6.; Wilfred E. Littleboy, 'Our Peace Testimony and Some of Its Implications', *TF*, 2 Oct. 1914, 722–4 (Wilfred Littleboy was Secretary to the Young Friends' Home Mission and Extension Committee created at the Swanwick Conference); and *TF*, 23 Oct. 1914.

[14] Joshua Rowntree to Henry J. Mennell, 17 Nov. 1914, MS Box 5.114, LSF.

including some women, served in the Friends' War Victims Relief Committee (FWVRC) in France and elsewhere during and after the war.[16]

But it was not only young Friends who needed an outlet for their energy and anxiety. Older men like Ernest Taylor also felt drawn toward what he called 'some supreme act of self sacrifice', some escape into active service which would demonstrate rather than violate his peace principles.[17] The seed for such a movement had, in fact, been planted at the Society's Conference at Llandudno in September 1914.

Long planned as a discussion of 'the discrepancy between the teachings of Christ and the conditions of life in this so-called Christian state',[18] events narrowed the Llandudno Conference's considerations to the challenge that war presented to Christianity in general and to the Society of Friends in particular.[19] The Chairman at Llandudno was Dr Henry T. Hodgkin, who had spent five years (1905–10) as a medical missionary in China. Hodgkin had been one of the delegates forced to scatter from the last pre-war Peace Conference at Constance. On 2 August 1914 in the midst of his flight from the war-threatened Continent, Hodgkin wrote to his father that he felt no anxiety for his own or other peace delegates' safety because the German Emperor, who was 'in full sympathy with the Conference', had given his personal assurances for their well-being.[20]

[15] See below. The official history of the Friends Ambulance Unit is Meaburn Tatham and James E. Miles, *The Friends' Ambulance Unit, 1914–1919* (London [1919]). For a fascinating non-Quaker view of the Unit, see *Talking Across the World: the Love Letters of Olaf Stapledon and Agnes Miller*, edited by Robert Crossley (Hanover, Conn. 1987).

[16] See Peace Committee, *Minutes*, v, 3 Sept. 1914, LSF. For an account of FWVRC (often called 'War Vics' by Friends), see A. Ruth Fry's lengthy account of 'Friends Relief Work Since 1914,' n.d., Temp. MSS 481, LSF. An Emergency Committee for the Assistance of Germans, Austrians and Hungarians in Distress was also convened to aid enemy trapped in Britain by the outbreak of the War. An American Quaker, Dr Henrietta Thomas (1879–1919), made six trips to the Continent to repatriate German and Austrian non-combatants. See the Committee's Correspondence in the Woodbrooke Library and entry for Henrietta M. Thomas, *DQB*, LSF.

[17] E. Taylor, 'Diary', 25 Sept. 1914, Temp. Box 23/3, LSF.

[18] *Memorandum for the Llandudno Conference* (Original copy in LSF), printed at Selly Oak, Birmingham [1914] and *TF*, 11 Sept. 1914, 665.

[19] 'Preface', *Friends and the War* [Proceedings of the Llandudno Conference] (London [1914]), 8–10.

[20] Henry T. Hodgkin (H. T. H.) to J. B. Hodgkin, 2 Aug. 1914, Herbert M. Hodgkin Papers (HMHP), Temp MSS 355, Box I/15, LSF. Also see Herbert G. Wood, *Henry T. Hodgkin: A Memoir* (London 1937), 145–6.

However quixotic and unpromising such an assessment appears to be, in fact, Henry Hodgkin proved to be among the most realistic of British pacifists. It was largely through his initiative and leadership that the Llandudno Conference became a launching pad for what Martin Ceadel has called 'Britain's most thoughtful pacifist society', the Fellowship of Reconciliation. The FOR was not exclusively Quaker, but it was, in its origins and continued existence, a permanent Quaker contribution to the twentieth-century peace movement.[21]

Within the Society of Friends, Hodgkin became a force in moving official Quakerism toward alliance with left-wing opponents of the war, especially the Independent Labour Party.[22] His uncompromising conviction that opposition to all war was 'the very heart of the Christian ethic' won little support from fellow non-conformists, although it did command a certain grudging respect. The Scottish theologian D. S. Cairns wrote that while he could agree with neither the logic nor the theology of Hodgkin's position: 'I am thankful that you and the Friends are there to testify... [to such] an ideal in a mad and wicked world.'[23]

Yearly Meeting in late May of 1915 provided Quakerism with its first opportunity to give corporate witness to the peace ideal. In the run-up to what Henry Hodgkin considered the most momentous gathering of Friends since the death of George Fox, he expressed high hopes to Rufus Jones:

These are great days for us. At the Meeting for Sufferings last Friday I believe that we were really baptized into some spirit of courage instead of... the spirit of fearfulness which has so often taken possession of

---

[21] Ceadel, *Pacifism in Britain*, 35. The proceedings of the Llandudno Conference and other material on the origins of the Fellowship of Reconciliation are in the Herbert M. Hodgkin Papers, LSF.

[22] Henry T. Hodgkin, 'The Church and War', *The Constructive Quarterly*, March 1915, 217. The 'General Review' of the Llandudno Conference, following the recommendation of J. T. Walton Newbold, a member of the ILP and the SQS, urged Friends to establish closer relations with the ILP. See *Friends and the War*, 18, 23. Also see John William Graham (J. W. G.) to Richard Graham (R. G.), 6 March 1915, JWGP for an account of a meeting at the Hotel Metropole in Manchester, attended by Ramsay MacDonald, Charles Trevelyan and others, 'to see if Quaker capital and I.L.P. labour could combine in starting a Peace daily newspaper on labour lines...' The matter was dropped because only £1200 of the needed £30,000 was subscribed.

[23] Hodgkin, 'Church and War', 219 and D. S. Cairns to HTH, 23 Nov. 1914, Temp MSS 355, Box V/49, LSF.

us . . . there is a great awakening among the young people, and a tremendous desire to do something strong. I believe that Yearly Meeting will see a big forward movement . . . when the younger portion of the membership has an opportunity to express itself.[24]

After Yearly Meeting commenced, the reports Jones received on its proceedings seemed to confirm Hodgkin's expectations. 'I am glad to say that Truth is prevailing,' wrote Edward Grubb. Hodgkin himself was carried away with enthusiasm for 'the splendid steadfastness of our young men . . . It does make me hopeful for the future of the Society, say 20 or 30 years hence, when those who have stood this furnace so well shall themselves be the leaders.'[25]

After Yearly Meeting established the young men's Service Committee 'to strengthen the Peace testimony among Friends of military age' and also endorsed a *Minute* recommending that in the event of conscription no exemption be given to Friends that was not equally applicable to non-Quakers, Hodgkin and Grubb believed that war-Friends and their wavering allies had been routed by the steadfast pacifists.[26] In recounting those most firm in upholding Friends uncompromising opposition to the war and conscription, Henry Hodgkin singled out the 'wise steady rulings & solemnly helpful presence' of the Clerk, John Henry Barlow, who had responded to the crisis by rising 'onto an entirely different level from anything I had . . . known in him before'. The stern-featured Barlow, a close associate of George Cadbury who had played a role in launching Woodbrooke, composed the *Minute* which summarized the Society's official position on the war:

We have given prolonged and earnest consideration to our Peace Testimony . . . [which] has been clear and unmistakable from the earliest days of our history to the present and . . . which comes welling up from within. It springs from the very heart of our faith . . . [and] must be a reality in our lives.[27]

[24] H. T. H. to R. M. J, 29 March 1915, RMJP.

[25] E. G. to R. M. J., 22 May 1915 and H. T. H. to R. M. J., 29 May 1915, RMJP.

[26] See *LYM, 1915*, 193–4. For the Friends Service Committee manifesto and the list of original twenty members, see *FSC Minutes, Records of Work and Documents Issued*, 3 vols. June 1915–May 1920, LSF. Also see the recollections of Horace Alexander, an original member, in *Quaker History*, 70 (Spring 1981), 48.

[27] *LYM, 1915*, 112–13; also quoted in Mabel Cash Barlow's unpublished memoir of John Henry Barlow in the J. H. Barlow Papers in possession of Mary Millior Barlow Braithwaite, London.

Barlow continued to play a key role throughout the war years in resisting every effort to soften this unyielding stance. Perhaps because he lacked flamboyance, Barlow has received too little recognition for his influence in keeping the Society faithful to its pacifist traditions during the First World War.[28]

Another of Henry Hodgkin's heroes of the 1915 Yearly Meeting was Alfred Barratt (Barry) Brown whose speech to Yearly Meeting, Hodgkin noted, embodied the 'fire & power & intensity of purpose of the young': 'If they offer us exemption from conscription as Quakers, unless all those who agree with us from conscientious motives are exempted too, the position will be intolerable. We may have to leave the Society to fight it out with them *as men.*'[29] As a member of the SQS, the ILP and the No-Conscription Fellowship (NCF), Barry Brown would, with other left-wing Quakers like Robert O. Mennell (1882–1960), a tea merchant, journalist Hubert W. Peet (1886–1951), and female Friends such as Edith Ellis (1878–1963), Edith J. Wilson (1869–1963) and Dr Henrietta Thomas (1879–1919), help the Friends Service Committee to chart the path for Quaker war-resisters. Eventually, and at times reluctantly, London Yearly Meeting resolved to follow along this same track.

Pacifist Friends were, in general, satisfied that the first wartime Yearly Meeting had had the desired affect. Ernest Taylor noted in his 'Diary' that 'Y. M. did good' in making Friends 'more contented'. Still, Taylor remained deeply distressed by the continued enlistment of young Quakers and by the fact that 'ministers of the Church & of the Sects [are] teaching hate to their people'. Like other pacifists, he was growing restless and searching for the means to take up the fight against war 'in ways that some people call "radical"'.[30] As the threat of conscription grew during the final months of 1915, the opportunity for more radical action seemed at hand. In September, Meeting for Sufferings issued a letter to all MPs protesting against the possibility of compulsory military service and denying 'the right of any Government to compel its

---

[28] The J. H. Barlow Papers contain a group of posthumous commendations by Henry Hodgkin, Hubert Peet, Edward Grubb, Ernest Taylor and others on the vital role Barlow played in preserving a strong peace testimony in the face of considerable pressure to compromise both from the Government and from Friends who wished to accommodate the authorities.

[29] H. T. H. to R. M. J., 31 May 1915, Box 9, RMJP.

[30] Taylor, 'Diary', 14 July & 20 Aug. 1915, Temp. Box 23/3, LSF.

Subjects to do things that their conscience disapproves'.[31] In the meantime, the Friends Service Committee had become an active force both within the Society and in alliance with non-Quaker war-resistance organizations like the No-Conscription Fellowship.[32] In a real way this sort of activity was a blossoming of the seeds planted by Neave Brayshaw and others in the pre-war Young Friends Movement, a fulfillment of the promises made at the Swanwick Conference 'to live out our message and our faith in ways that must cost us dear'.[33]

Fig. 8   Alfred Neave Brayshaw (1861–1940), taken in 1928; spiritual leader for the Young Friends Movement

[31] 'Compulsory War Service—Address to the Members of Parliament', 3 Sept. 1915, Meeting for Sufferings, Frederick Andrews, Clerk, Arnold S. Rowntree Papers (ASRP), 310/5/2, LSF. Also see *LYM, 1916*, 229–30.

[32] See Peace Committee, *Minutes*, v, 3 June 1915 noting the FSC's desire 'to work in harmony' with the Peace Committee and FSC Secretary [F. B. Smart] to Clifford Allen, 26 July 1915, agreeing to join with the No-Conscription Fellowship and the Fellowship of Reconciliation in a Joint Advisory Council of anti-war, anti-conscription organizations.

[33] *Swanwick, 1911*, 12 from remarks by Geoffrey Hoyland, an original member of the Friends Service Committee.

Brayshaw had long been a respected and, for some, a beloved Friend, but in many ways his life prior to the Great War might have seemed disappointing. Forced out of Bootham by an unsympathetic headmaster, Arthur Rowntree, and shoved aside at Woodbrooke as a 'good but very injudicious man' by George Cadbury, Neave appeared to be approaching old age without real accomplishment in his chosen role as a teacher and mentor to young Quakers.[34] But Brayshaw's spiritual leadership in the Young Friends Movement and his unyielding adherence to peace principles during the war make him a truly significant figure among early twentieth-century Friends. In keeping with the tone of his pre-war ministry, Brayshaw consistently upheld 'the uncompromising Quaker standpoint' during the war. His wartime correspondence with 'old boys' from the Movement invariably pursued the theme that the war and the threat of conscription were exactly that trial of faith for which Quakerism had been preserved and that those unequal to the task of facing up to this ordeal had no warrant to continue calling themselves true Friends. In a tract on 'Friends and the Inner Light', Brayshaw noted:

the sole justification for the survival of Friends as a separate body was that it was doing work . . . not being done elsewhere . . . We Friends are something more than a social or semi-religious club . . . We exist not for ourselves but to make our contribution to the world in bearing witness to our belief . . . An impossible position is reached when the claim is made that one who goes out prepared to kill men, in obedience to his 'Light', is as much a 'Friend' as another who . . . would go to prison rather than enlist. This is to turn the back on the whole history and testimony of Quakerism.[35]

Brayshaw's wartime activities were dedicated to the young men who were 'walking in accord with the best traditions of our Society' and who, when conscription was enacted, would fill 'long rolls of honour' by accepting persecution, just as their spiritual ancestors, the first Friends, had done.[36] In the meantime,

[34] See Taylor, *Personal History*, 49–51 and George Cadbury to W. C. Braithwaite (W. C. B.), 13 Nov. 1906, GCP, WL.
[35] A. Neave Brayshaw (A. N. B.), *Friends and the Inner Light*, (London [1915]), 70–2. Also see A. N. B. to TF, 9 April 1915, 78, 81 & 24 Dec. 1915, 961.
[36] From A. N. B.'s address to members of the Friends' Guild of Teachers, 13 Jan. 1915, Box T 1/3, LSF.

Neave urged young people to prepare themselves for the approaching test by becoming 'centres of warmth, and light and life to bring healing into that part of the world where they are'. As he told Philip Radley, a future conscientious objector: 'It is out of this sympathy and drawing near to one another that we can become strong to heal the sickness of the world.'[37] Brayshaw's name appears again and again in correspondence, memoirs and interviews as one of the chief inspirations for Quaker conscientious objectors. Indeed, his efforts to ensure that young Quakers remained loyal to his vision of the peace testimony seems a clear confirmation of Martin Ceadel's conclusion that '[c]onfrontation with the State provided the repressive conditions in which pacifism could rediscover its sectarian roots,' and, as in the case of Friends, to begin defining their pacifist stance with 'unprecedented rigour'.[38] The crisis of conscription, however dramatic, did not finally impel British Friends to reach a genuine consensus as to the lengths to which they should go in resisting the war and the Government that was pursuing it. Rather the war and the imposition of compulsory military service permitted a minority alliance of young radicals and middle-aged zealots to grasp the moment and lead their Society, kicking and screaming as may be, to support a radical interpretation of their historic, but previously amorphous, peace testimony.

As the danger of compulsory service loomed ever larger in the final days of 1915, the Friends Service Committee met to consider what course of action it would urge upon young Quakers. Following these deliberations, the FSC issued a declaration which, in harmony with the spirit of Neave Brayshaw's persistent message, harkened back to the uncompromising religious radicalism of the earliest Quakers:

The stand Friends have always taken against military service has been based on deep conscientious conviction, and not on grounds of expediency. Such considerations as family and business circumstances or state of health are . . . irrelevant . . . we assume the Friends will stand fast to their

---

[37] A. N. B. to Young Friends, 22 Dec. 1914, ibid. and to Philip Radley, 2 May 1915, Radley Papers, Temp MSS 299, ibid. Also see A. N. B. to Young Friends, Sept. 1915, Box T 1/3, ibid. and his personal correspondence with Philip Radley, MS Vols. 243–47 and Temp. MSS 299, LSF.

[38] Ceadel, *British Pacifism*, 60.

belief in the sanctity of human personality, and to the principles of Jesus Christ . . . be the consequences what they may. We must uphold liberty of conscience, a right won by much suffering in the past and not lightly to be relinquished . . . we take our position from no mere individual scruple but because we have envisaged a high future for our nation which our conception of patriotism alone makes possible.[39]

Another matter considered at the FSC's November 1915 meeting was an invitation from the No-Conscription Fellowship, an organization largely composed of anti-war socialists, to join with a deputation visiting certain members of Parliament concerning the possible inclusion of an exemption clause for conscientious objectors in any future conscription bill. The clause favoured by the NCF called for a statutory declaration before a Justice of the Peace verifying conscientious objection to any direct or indirect participation in war or warlike operations. The Service Committee, with the approval of Meeting for Sufferings, agreed to support the idea with the clear understanding that both organizations would strongly oppose not only any exemption which separated Quakers from other COs but also 'any clause providing alternative service to military service'.[40]

CARNAL WEAPONS AND THE COMMONWEAL

War Friends aside, the great majority of British Quakers refused to give open support to the British war effort. Beyond that, however, there was little agreement as to what should comprise the official policy of the Society of Friends. For some, refusal to fight was sufficient proof of their loyalty to religious principle; others, taking the same line as Neave Brayshaw, believed that adherence to the peace testimony required positive steps aimed at bringing the war to an end. This lack of consensus was reflected in the negative

[39] 'To Our Fellow Members of Military Age of the Society of Friends', Friends Service Committee, printed documents, Temp. MSS Box 31, LSF.

[40] FSC, *Minutes*, Vol 1, 'Proceedings of the Friends Service Committee Meeting at Devonshire House', 3 November 1915, 21; Robert O. Mennell (R. O. M.) to Clifford Allen, 10 Nov. 1915; and 'Memorandum Re. Conscience Clause', 18 November 1915, 22, Friends Service Committee Files, Box IV, LSF. For the NCF, see Kennedy, *The Hound of Conscience* and Jo Vellocott, *Bertrand Russell and the Pacifists During the First World War* (Brighton 1980).

reaction of certain weighty Quaker leaders, who were apparently in the vanguard of Society's anti-war element, to the activities and pronouncements of the Friends Service Committee. While the FSC was proceeding on its no-compromise course as regards conscription, one member of that Committee, Arnold S. Rowntree, MP, was consulting with influential Quakers, including two prominent lawyers, William Charles Braithwaite and E. Richard Cross (1864–1916) of York,[41] on the feasibility of attaching a special conscience clause for Friends to any proposed conscription bill.[42] The responses that Rowntree recieved contrasted sharply with the attitudes and ideals of most members of the Friends Service Committee. It was not surprising that lawyer Braithwaite found the exemption clause supported by the FSC and NCF unsatisfactory. Even the staunchest potential war-resister recognized that a statutory declaration would appear to be 'too easy an opportunity for the "shirker"' At the same time, it is somewhat startling to discover that Braithwaite was contemplating a bill that would not only specifically exempt Friends, without further proof of conscientious objection, but would also require that those so exempted 'offer some alternative service approved by the authority'. Among the possibilities Braithwaite listed were hospital service for the Royal Army Medical Corps, mine-sweeping and other 'indispensable work', including munitions manufacturing.[43] Thus, William Charles Braithwaite, a leader of the Quaker Renaissance generation whose *Beginnings of Quakerism* had recently inspired young

[41] Elihu Richard Cross who had come into Friends from Methodism in 1898. After a four-year stint as town councillor in Scarborough, he spent eighteen years (1895–1913) as Clerk of Magistrates in that city, before joining the Rowntree Chocolate firm. He was also business manager of *The Nation* and secretary to the so-called Bryce Group which developed ideas for a post-war League of Nations to preserve the peace. See Henry Winkler, *The League of Nations Movement*, 16 and E. M. Forster, *Goldsworthy Lowes Dickinson* (London 1934) 164.

[42] In mid-1915 Arnold Rowntree had consulted F. W. Hirst, editor of *The Economist*, concerning historical examples of exemptions from conscription; Hirst advised him to consult with G. P. Gooch, 'a walking encyclopedia of historical knowledge'. F. W. Hirst to A. S. R., 10 June 1915, 310/S/2, LSF. Apparently on the basis of one 'dreadful' meeting, Bertrand Russell, who admired many of the Quakers with whom he worked during the war, formed a unflattering opinion of Arnold Rowntree, noting in a letter to Ottoline Morrell: 'If many Quakers are like Rowntree, I understand why they instituted silent meeting.' Russell to Ottoline, 11 Aug. 1914, T. 1069, O. Morrell Papers, University of Texas Library, Austin, Texas.

[43] W. C. B. to A. S. R., 19 Nov. 1915, ASRP, Temp. MSS 558, SR 310/S/2, LSF. Cf. with 'Memo. Re. "Conscience Clause"', 18 Nov. 1915, FSC, *Minutes*, Vol. 1, 22, LSF.

Friends with its gripping accounts of the courage and constancy of
the first Quakers in their struggles against a persecuting State, was
counselling the sort of co-operation with the Government and its
war-machinery that the Friends Service Committee had specifically rejected. He did so because, as he told Arnold Rowntree: 'we
ought to make it easy for the State to get good equivalent service.
Our duty to our country is just as clear a demand on us as our duty
to parents or neighbours, and holds us bound by ties from which
we cannot separate ourselves, and which are part of the relations of
life which are to be discharged in fear of God.'[44]

Richard Cross expressed similar views with an additional note—
even as the FSC strengthened its ties with the No-Conscription
Fellowship—expressing his opinion that because Quaker objection
to military service was 'a matter of high spiritual conviction',
Friends 'ought not to dishonour that conviction by joining forces
with disloyal cranks, who want to enjoin [enjoy?] rights without
performing duties'.[45]

The third Friend approached by Arnold Rowntree, Edward
Grubb, made recommendations for exemption that were more
moderate than the Service Committee's no-compromise position,
but, like the FSC, he was emphatic in asserting that 'Friends should
not *ask* for an exclusive clause'. Grubb had, of course, recently
become Honorary Treasurer of the No-Conscription Fellowship,
the organization Richard Cross so roundly excoriated.[46]

It seems unlikely that Arnold Rowntree revealed the contents of
these letters to his colleagues on the Service Committee. Certainly,
the general sentiments expressed by Rowntree's consultants stood
in marked contrast to the FSC's hard-line policies regarding conscription.[47] In any case, by the end of 1915 it became increasingly
clear that the burden of constructing a serious war-resistance policy
among Friends was shifting from the official Friends' Peace Committee to the FSC. Furthermore, the Service Committee's intract-
able stand seemed to have the support of a considerable majority of
young Quaker men. In a poll of over a thousand male Friends

[44] W. C. B. to A. S. R., 19 Nov. 1915, ASRP, Temp. MSS 558, SR 310/S/2, LSF.
[45] E. Richard Cross to A. S. R., 21 Nov. 1915, ibid.
[46] E. G. to A. S. R. (copy), 4 Dec. 1915, ibid.
[47] In a letter of 13 Dec. 1915 to young Friends, Hubert W. Peet, FSC Secretary, noted
that the Committee was prepared to state its 'unalterable opposition to conscription and to
make it clear that we are working in closest conjunction with conscientious objectors of all
sorts'.

(apparently excluding all who had previously enlisted) conducted by the FSC, over 900 of those who responded, or about 85 per cent (some 700 of these were of military age), affirmed 'their determination to refuse to enlist, to make munitions, or to do work entailing the military oath'. Leaders of the Service Committee were confident this response confirmed the existence of 'a strong and convinced body of young men determined to hold fast to their convictions at all costs'.[48]

If the results of the FSC poll were a reasonably accurate reflection of the opinions of younger Quaker males who had not enlisted in the Army by the end of 1915, they indicated that the opinions of men (and women, as events would show) under 40 had enormous influence on the Society's official refusal to co-operate with the national war effort. And while no important leader of the previous generation openly supported the 1914–1918 war, many of them, like W. C. Braithwaite, worked hard to reach some accommodation with the authorities that would permit Quakers to be at once faithful Friends and patriotic citizens. Such differences were not entirely generational, older Friends like Brayshaw and Edward Grubb upheld the FSC's uncompromising stand, but the discord that emerged on these matters was sufficiently sharp to become a troubling distraction for many Friends. A case in point was that of John William Graham, the well-connected voice for liberal Quakerism, and his son Richard, who was an Oxford undergraduate when the war began.

Quaker historian Elfrida Vipont Foulds (born 1902) related that as a young person attending the Manchester Meeting where J. W. Graham ministered every First-Day, she would never have questioned his whole-hearted commitment to peace. However, she also recalled hearing snatches of grown-up conversation indicating that Richard Graham had kept his father firm on peace in 1914.[49] Graham's papers contain evidence that appears to confirm this impression.

In October 1914 John W. Graham told Richard of his irritation with anti-war comments by his good friend (Elfrida Foulds' father) Dr E. Vipont Brown: 'To Brown the whole business seems simplicity itself, but I confess that I should not be easy to stand aloof

    [48] Robert O. Mennell and Hubert W. Peet (H.W.P.) to *TF*, 17 Dec. 1915, 945 and Ernest Taylor, 'Diary', 20 Dec. 1915, Temp. Box 23/3, LSF.
    [49] Interview with E. V. Foulds, August 1986, Yealand Conyers, Lancashire.

from the Army unless I also found some equally useful work at home.' A few days later the elder Graham wrote: 'If the Government deem it wiser I think that they are also within their rights in demanding compulsory and universal service to repel an invader ... If, however, we can get the Government to relieve us of actual fighting, I feel that this would not be too great a concession on our part to natural and patriotic feeling.'[50]

Richard Graham's responses to his father's waffling are not extant, but apparently, as Elfrida Foulds suggested, the son did steady his father's resolve. By April 1915 the elder Graham seemed to have revised his position on conscription, noting in an article for *The Friend* that if compulsory military service was introduced, 'the refusal to serve from the Society of Friends would be almost universal, and rightly so'.[51] By then, Graham had come to be considered around Manchester as something of a peace crank, speaking and writing against conscription, publishing a pamphlet on *War From the Quaker Point of View* (1915) and taking a prominent part in the activities of the local branch of Union of Democratic Control.[52]

Still, John William Graham never seems to have been entirely comfortable with his position. Horace Alexander, who would later become Graham's son-in-law, and who, with Richard Graham, was an original member of the Friends Service Committee, recalled how the elder Graham, 'in the midst of the ... War, at a time when he was most active in supporting and encouraging C.O.s ... startled me by saying that, of course, it was a good thing that there were not too many pacifists, as that might seriously undermine the strength of the Allies and lead to a German victory.' Alexander charitably concluded that Graham's reflections showed that he was 'not bigoted' in his peace advocacy.[53] A less generous appraisal might be that John William was simply going through pacifist motions in the full knowledge that while he could not

---

[50] J. W. G. to R. G., 12 and 16 Oct. 1914, JWGP, JRL. Graham had, in fact, said almost the same thing even before the war; J. W. G. to Richard, 11 Feb. 1913, ibid., see Chapter 8 above.

[51] J. W. G., 'The State and the Individual', *TF*, 9 April 1915, 267–9.

[52] J. W. G. to R. G., 27 Jan. & 23 Nov. 1915, JWGP and J. W. G. to Rufus Jones, 24 Aug. 1915, RMJP. The Graham Papers contain two large scrapbooks full of J. W. G.'s journalistic efforts, including dozens of anti-war, anti-conscription articles.

[53] Horace Alexander to Michael [Graham], 15 Aug. 1960, JWGP. Also see J. W. G. to R. G., 5 June 1915, ibid.

affect the progress of the war, he could retain his place of honour
and influence among Friends. Probably the most accurate judgement would be that Graham was engaged in a very human effort to
resolve war-induced contradictions between love of God and love
of country, powerfully overladen with fatherly concerns for the
fate of two sons of military age.[54]

By the end of 1915 conscription had become a virtual certainty
and while Britain's first Military Service Act and the exemptions it
might include were being debated in Parliament, the Friends
Service Committee was breathing fiery defiance. Robert Mennell,
FSC Secretary, stated in a letter to *The Times* that because the
Service Committee objected 'to the whole organization for war',
they would never accept alternative services like mine-sweeping or
even the medical corps.[55] During this same period J. W. Graham's
letters to his son continue to reveal the ambiguity of his position as
an outspoken anti-war Quaker, a deeply concerned father and an
earnestly patriotic citizen.

In late January 1916, a few days before Friends were to gather for
an extraordinary 'Adjourned' Yearly Meeting to determine their
collective response to the imminent introduction of compulsory
military service,[56] J. W. Graham provided his son with some 'very
private' information from Lord Derby, director general of recruiting, via Arnold Rowntree. The Government, said Graham, wished
to avoid any implication of religious persecution and were 'perfectly willing to give Friends anything', but they would never
accept the 'political objector'.[57] In other words, by showing special
consideration for Quakers, the Government contemplated driving
a wedge between religious COs and the more numerous and
largely socialist objectors of the No-Conscription Fellowship.
Ultimately, this strategy failed because leaders of the FSC, some

---

[54] The second son Michael Graham eventually enlisted in the Naval Air Service, wherein
his somewhat sheltered upbringing caused him to be profoundly shocked by the ordinary
language of barracks' conversation. See J. W. G. to R. G., 6 June & 1 Nov. 1916 and 13 June
1917, JWGP.

[55] *The Times*, 12 Jan. 1916. Also see *PS*, I/1 (Feb. 1916), 7 and a letter to Cabinet
Ministers from Edward Grubb, Joan Mary Fry and R. O. Mennell, reprinted in *TF*, 7 Jan.
1916, 5.

[56] A Military Service Act which applied to single males between 18 and 41 was passed in
late January 1916; a second Act requiring service of all males between 18 and 41 became law
on 25 May 1916.

[57] J. W. G. to R. G., 26 Jan. 1916, JWGP.

of whom were also socialists, were determined to make common cause with the NCF.

The Military Service Act which became law in late January 1916 offered exemption on the basis of ill-health, grave hardship, continued performance of work of national importance and, most controversially, 'conscientious objection to undertaking combatant service'. Evidence indicates that the Government inserted this 'conscience clause' late in the day so as to preclude any large-scale defection by Liberal MPs.[58] Still, the Act in some measure reflected Quaker influence on the legislative process since it included an amendment proposed by Quaker MPs Arnold Rowntree and T. Edmund Harvey, offering exemption to genuine conscientious objectors who agreed to perform civilian work of 'national importance' in lieu of military service. Because this legislation incorporated the principle of exempting all COs, not just Quakers, from any form of military or quasi-military service, it represented a clear advance on earlier proposals Arnold Rowntree had received from Quaker advisors like W. C. Braithwaite and Richard Cross. Indeed, as finally interpreted, the conscience clause allowed not only exemption for noncombatant military service and alternative civilian work of national importance but 'absolute' exemption as well. This final form of exemption would seem to allow for recognition of even the hardline position of the Friends Service Committee, but events would show that the authorities, for the most part, construed 'absolute' exemption very differently from the FSC and its allies.

When the terms of the Military Service Act became known, John William Graham, no doubt breathing a considerable sigh of relief, advised Richard to apply for absolute exemption, as the law allowed, but to further cover himself by declaring his intention to take up teaching, an occupation that might be defined as 'work of national importance'.[59] The problem with this entirely practical advice was that it ran counter to the decision by a special assembly of 450 Quakers of military age in conjunction with the Adjourned Yearly Meeting. This group of young Friends overwhelmingly endorsed a resolution advanced by the Service Committee that Friends could best give witness to their historic peace testimony by

[58] The best discussion of the passage of the conscription acts is John Rae, *Politics and Conscience* (London 1970), 27–35.

[59] J. W. G. to R. G., 7 and 15 Feb. 1916, JWGP.

appearing before the tribunals established to hear petitions for exemption but refusing to undertake any alternative service and accepting only total exemption from all provisions of the Military Service Act.[60] This decision of the young men's meeting was subsequently endorsed by the entire Adjourned Yearly Meeting in a *Minute* affirming 'Our testimony... as a Society is against all war, and on behalf of the supremacy and liberty of conscience. This we unhesitatingly re-affirm, and where our members are brought into difficulty or suffering through obedience to conscience, we take our stand beside them, and assure them of our loving sympathy and support.'[61]

Despite this and other Yearly Meeting *Minutes* giving support to the FSC's stand, J. W. Graham still believed that the Service Committee's position was unrealistic and short-sighted. It would, he said, not only bring on an unnecessary confrontation with the State but would also create serious internal difficulty for Friends. 'The most that we can hope for from the tribunals is exemption conditioned on useful national service. That is a fair offer.'[62]

A fair offer for John William Graham, but not necessarily to the young bloods of the Friends Service Committee. Indeed, the FSC took the initiative in contacting every preparative meeting in Britain with suggestions as to how to advise local conscientious objectors, both Quaker and non-Quaker, for their appearance before the tribunals. In addition, the Committee dispatched a series of communications to male Friends of military age which, while acknowledging that each individual would have to 'decide for himself what service he can render', emphasized that '[p]ractically all Friends have asked for absolute exemption' and made clear its own sense that anything less than absolute exemption might 'imply a compromise with the militarism which underlies a Conscription Act'.[63] Indeed,

---

[60] FSC, 'Preliminary Communication', 4 Feb. 1916, Temp. MSS Box 31 and HWP to Warren Leurs, 31 Jan. 1916, FSC Files, LSF. Also see Leigh Tucker, 'English Quakers and World War I, 1914–1919', (Ph.D. dissertation, University of North Carolina, 1972), 104–5.

[61] *LYM*, Held in Adjournment the 28th to 30th of First Month 1916, *Minutes* concerning the Military Service (No. 2) Act (printed copy in LSF).

[62] J. W. G. to R. G., 4 March 1916, JWGP. Throughout this time J. W. Graham was acting as an advisor to conscientious objectors, Quaker and non-Quaker, who came to Mount Street Meeting House in Manchester for assistance. See J. W. G. to R. G., 7, 12 & 15 Feb. 1916, ibid.

[63] H.W.P. to Clerks of Prep. Meetings, 16 Feb. 1916, FSC no. 12; R. O. M. & H. W. P. to Friends of Military Age, 22 March & 8 April 1916, FSC nos. 13 & 15; and 3rd Communication, 23 March 1916, FSC no. 14, LSF.

in its desire to ensure the purity of its peace testimony, the FSC eventually went beyond rejecting Government offers and began to question Quaker alternatives as well.[64] When local tribunals began assigning Quakers to the Friends Ambulance Unit while denying that option to non-Friends seeking alternative service, the Service Committee condemned this granting of 'preferential treatment' to Friends as a violation of 'the spirit and concern of the Adjourned Yearly Meeting . . . to unite ourselves to the fullest extent with all conscientious objectors'.[65]

This incident was the first in a sequence of disputes which produced a serious split between the youthful Friends Service Committee and the middle-aged leaders of the Friends Ambulance Unit, especially the Unit's Chairman, Sir George Newman.[66] Many Quakers, including John William Graham and William Charles Braithwaite, looked upon the Friends Ambulance Unit as the crowning jewel in their Society's efforts to provide useful national service for young men while avoiding open support for the war.[67] At one point, Graham offered to contact Sir George Newman on Richard's behalf 'and fix up the Unit for thee without any trouble to thee'. When Richard demurred, implying that Newman was undermining FSC efforts to establish a solid anti-conscription front by pursuing a hidden agenda in collusion with authorities, the elder Graham staunchly defended Sir George's motivations and character. Furthermore, he suggested that his son was being unduly influenced by hardliners like FSC Secretary Robert Mennell whom he labelled 'an outsider' whose radical

---

[64] See FSC, 'Preliminary Communication, The M. S. A., 1916', 4 Feb. 1916, LSF.

[65] 'Notes on Recent Meeting', 20 March 1916, FSC *Minutes*, 11, 1 and R. O. M. and H. W. P. to Friends of Military Age, 22 March 1916, Temp. MSS, Box 31, LSF. This letter is apparently a much toned-down version of one which frankly accused leaders of the Friends Ambulance Unit of compromising the Quaker position 'in direct opposition to the pronouncements of the Meeting for Sufferings and the spirit of the Yearly Meeting . . .' ibid. and H. W. P. to Herbert Corder, 18 March 1916, ibid.

[66] George Newman (1870–1948) was Chief Medical Officer and Principal Assistant Secretary of the Board of Education from 1907 to 1919. He had been knighted in 1911 for his pioneering work in child health care, including his book on *Infant Mortality* (1907). He was also extremely active in Quaker journalism as editor of the *Friends Quarterly Examiner* (1900–43) and literary advisor to *The Friend* (1912–32).

[67] William Charles Braithwaite served as Treasurer of the Friends Ambulance Unit throughout the War. Professor Richard Braithwaite noted that his mother Janet Morland Braithwaite did not approve of her husband's role in the FAU. Interview with Richard Braithwaite, Cambridge, August 1986. Also see Thomas and Emmott, *William Charles Braithwaite*, 75.

views, however admirable in the abstract, paled in comparison to the mature judgement of supporters of alternative service like Sir George Newman and W. C. Braithwaite.[68]

Much to his father's consternation, Richard Graham threatened, in keeping with the FSC's hard-line, to argue his case before the Oxford tribunal solely on the basis of absolute exemption. At the near edge of panic, the elder Graham replied that it would be utter foolishness to 'base a decision carrying with it such large practical consequences upon the temper of the tribunal', which would at best be unsympathetic and more likely be filled with bloody-minded aldermen and town councillors who would not blink at refusing any exemption whatsoever: 'we have not only a moral, but a legal right . . . Whatever holes, therefore, we can pick in their armour of unrighteousness, we are justified in doing, both [sic] in morals, law and equity.'[69]

The Friends' Service Committee had taken the position that, whatever the repercussions, every individual's actions regarding the war and conscription should be based on faithful adherence to his or her own interpretation of the peace testimony. What John William Graham seemed to be arguing was that one should by all means follow the peace testimony but should not allow this fidelity to principle to have 'large practical consequences', such as falling 'foul of a Government which is trying to do well for us', and, as a result, facing the possibility of imprisonment. He believed that if Richard would simply indicate that while non-combatant military service was unacceptable, the Friends Ambulance Unit would satisfy his scruples, he would not only be upholding the Quaker refusal to fight with carnal weapons but maintaining his legal rights as well. 'Friends', the elder Graham concluded, 'may surely be content to serve their fellow men and leave the [wounded] soldier himself the responsibility of what he does when he is well.'[70]

Richard Graham's reply is not extant, but the case his father was arguing lay at the very crux of the emerging differences between the radical pacifists of the FSC and their more cautious elders. The

---

[68] J. W. G. to R. G., 1 & 3 May 1916, JWGP, Graham's remarks about Robert Mennell's being an outsider were inaccurate as well as gratuitous, given the fact that Mennell traced his Quaker ancestry on both sides back to the days of George Fox. See Mennell's obituary in *TF*, 22 January 1960, 103–5.

[69] J. W. G. to R. G., 7, 8 and 14 March 1916, JWGP.

[70] J. W. G. to R. G., 8 and 14 March 1916, ibid.

widening split over the legitimacy of the Friends Ambulance Unit as a special Quaker preserve is a further indication of the Service Committee's role in pushing their religious Society toward a version of the peace testimony, i.e., non-co-operation as well as non-resistance, that was beyond anything previously practiced or even imagined by most Friends, at least since the seventeenth century. For if FSC leaders were saying anything, they were saying that it was *the war* rather than any single action or group of actions arising from the war that the peace testimony was about. The central question, they believed, was not: 'Do Friends refrain from fighting with carnal weapons?' but: 'Were Friends trying by every possible means to stop the war?' Most other Christian conscientious objectors, including the numerically larger Plymouth Brethren and Christadelphians, refused military service because, as they saw it, the conflict in Europe was not their war; they were, however, willing to satisfy the State by engaging in other than combatant service. Quakers absolutists, on the other hand, would not perform even alternative service because the war emphatically *was* their war—the testing time for which their Society had been preparing for two and a half centuries and the one from which it would emerge as a prophet society for transforming the world into the Kingdom of Christ.

The militants of the Friends Service Committee, probably a only bare majority even within that body, were intent on making their line of war-resistance *the* Quaker line, despite the fact that only a very few Friends (not, in the end, to his father's immense relief, including Richard Graham) took so extreme a position as that of the 145 Quaker absolutists who chose prison rather than any compromise with the wartime State. These Friends were joined in their stand by over a thousand other absolutist COs, most of them socialists from the No-Conscription Fellowship. But, as a body, the Quaker absolutists went beyond the NCF and, indeed, eventually divided with it over the question of how the anti-war movement should respond to the imprisonment of conscientious objectors which began in the spring of 1916.[71]

---

[71] For a discussion of the divisions this approach caused both within the peace movement and among Quakers, see below and Kennedy, 'Fighting About Peace: The No-Conscription Fellowship and the British Friends Service Committee, 1915–1919', *Quaker History* 69/1 (Spring 1980), 3–22.

DIVIDED STRUGGLE

In late March 1916, the first conscientious objectors, many of them members of the No-Conscription Fellowship, were being arrested, court-martialled and jailed. At about the same time, Sir James Reckitt, a wealthy Quaker patron of the Friends Service Committee, wrote to FSC Secretary Robert Mennell asking for clarification as to the Committee's relationship to 'outsiders'. Mennell replied that while the Committee worked 'primarily for Friends', they were, in keeping with the wishes of the recent Yearly Meeting, closely co-operating with groups like the No-Conscription Fellowship in order to give assistance to as many COs as possible.[72] Two months later, the Service Committee's report to Yearly Meeting explained that it would continue fraternizing with the NCF because 'Friends were concerned not so much for their own traditional right as for the liberty of the individual conscience wherever deep conviction was involved.' As one of the fruits of this co-operation, the FSC had exercised its influence to secure the use of Devonshire House for an NCF emergency convention in early April 1916. The Service Committee also contributed money to aid the NCF's efforts in collecting information on the arrest, conviction, and sentencing of all conscientious objectors. The FSC even released its paid organizing secretary, Hubert Peet (1886–1951), to help the NCF organize a Press Department.[73]

Eventually, the FSC would adopt a more critical attitude toward NCF activities, but during the early days of the struggle against conscription the Service Committee's leaders seemed unable to find sufficient words to praise their ally. The fact that the ideological emphasis within the NCF was entirely secular and largely socialist was not a concern for prominent Service Committee members like Mennell, Peet, Barry Brown, and John P. Fletcher, all members of the Socialist Quaker Society. When Mennell presented the FSC's report to Yearly Meeting in May 1916, he expressed a 'sense of debtedness' for the privilege of working

[72] Sir James Reckitt to R. O. M., 27 March 1916, H. W. P. to R. O. M., 28 March 1916 & R. O. M. to Reckitt, 29 March 1916, FSC Files, LSF. The Reckitt family firm was Reckitt & Coleman, one of Britain's largest and most successful pharmaceutical companies. Sir James Reckitt's continued support of the FSC was important because the Committee received no direct financial backing from the Society of Friends. See *TF*, 15 Dec. 1916, 981.

[73] R. O. M. to E. G., 28 March 1916 and 'Notes on meetings of the FSC, 1916', 6 April, 4 May, 8 June & 6 July 1916, FSC Files, LSF.

with the NCF and absorbing something of that body's infectious enthusiasm and 'immense energy'. Fletcher told a Conference of Young Friends that this socialist/pacifist Fellowship was a harbinger of 'the religious revival for which the churches were looking'.[74] Even the old-line Liberal John W. Graham reminded readers of *The Friend* that Quakerism might not have been able to cope with the conscription crisis without the help of NCF.[75]

Such expressions of solidarity with this novel ally reflected the mixture of excitement and apprehension that surrounded London Yearly Meeting's deepening confrontation with the State. Quakers, long perceived as paragons of civic virtue, seemed to be reverting, in the company of extreme social radicals, to seventeenth-century patterns of behaviour. Still, by mid-1916 even some anti-war Quakers were becoming quietly wary or openly suspicious about where alliance with the NCF might lead. Six weeks after Yearly Meeting Edward Grubb felt sufficiently concerned about these forebodings to publish a letter in *The Friend* which, in addition to heaping more praise on the NCF and its leader Clifford Allen, assured uneasy Friends that the Fellowship had successfully managed to exclude revolutionary socialists from its ranks.[76] Grubb's somewhat misleading reassurance represented more than an off-hand gesture, appearing, as it did, in the midst what Quaker MP T. E. Harvey called 'a strenuous effort' by certain Government officials 'to discriminate between "political agitators" & real COs'.[77] By automatically classifying religious objectors like Quakers as genuine, the War Office was carrying through with the idea of dividing anti-conscription forces while simultaneously gaining a freer hand in dealing with obstructionist, 'political' COs who professed socialist, anarchist, or other unpopular beliefs.[78]

[74] 'ROM's Observations in introducing FSC Report to Y. M., May 1916', FSC Files, LSF.

[75] *TF*, 10 May 1916, 367, 369. Graham told his son that the speeches delivered to a Manchester peace meeting by NCF leaders Clifford Allen and Fenner Brockway, 'might have been made in Yearly Meeting', J. W. G. to R. G., 6 June 1916, JWGP.

[76] E. G., 'On the N-CF', *TF*, 14 July 1916, 551–2. Although Grubb was Treasurer for the NCF, he was probably not well-informed about the broad spectrum of opinions within the Fellowship which included a fair number of militant socialists who were more anti-capitalist than anti-war.

[77] Edith Ellis (E. E.) to ROM, 18 June 1916, FSC Files, LSF.

[78] This strategy was devised by Lord Kitchener in conjunction with the War Office Director of Personal Services General Wyndham Childs. See 'Conscientious Objectors: 1

For a time, it seemed that this ploy might succeed in splintering the peace movement.[79] In the end, however, it was not the specific principles behind a man's objection that divided war resisters but rather the type of exemption those principles permitted him to accept. At first, the NCF, in keeping with an emotional resolution endorsed at its emergency convention in April, resolved to countenance no plea other than absolute exemption. But, despite clear legal stipulation for total exemption, local tribunals rarely if ever allowed individuals to escape from all provisions of the Military Service Acts.[80] Many COs, facing imprisonment for refusal to accept the decision of their tribunals, chose to embrace the proviso allowing them to undertake alternative work of 'national importance'. Thus, those who refused military service came to be classified as either absolutists or alternativists. While the latter group were a decided majority, some members of the absolutist minority held alternativists in disdain for, as one Quaker put it, 'giving the show away'.[81] Eventually, both the NCF and the FSC somewhat grudgingly came to recognize the legitimacy of less than absolute resistance, but some FSC Friends retained a lingering sense that alternativists had chosen what was 'spiritually "second best" '.[82]

In the end, the FSC would not sanction any corporate action on behalf of those who accepted alternative service, refusing either to set up a sub-committee to find work of national importance for them or to support a legal case challenging the right of tribunals to determine the state of a man's conscience. Although many Friends,

June 1916', Kitchener Papers, 30/57/74 and 'Conscientious Objectors', WO 32/5491, PRO. Also see Kennedy, *Hound of Conscience*, 139–40 and Vellacott, *Russell and the Pacifists*, 71–2.

[79] When the policy was instituted, NCF leaders feared that the Fellowship might 'go under' if the FSC did not support to all types of objectors. E. E. to R. O. M., 18 June 1916, FSC Files, LSF.

[80] Most local tribunals interpreted 'absolute' exemption as meaning release from military obligation to perform work of national importance. Only about 350 COs received and maintained absolute exemption, but tribunals gave some form of exemption to over 80 per cent of the COs who appeared before them. See Rae, *Politics and Conscience*, 130–32.

[81] Interview with Philip Radley, Aug. 1986, Cambridge. The statement, according to Radley, was made by George Sutherland.

[82] Corder Catchpool, *On Two Fronts* (London 1918), 154–55. Catchpool, after eighteen months with the Friends Ambulance Unit, returned to England to plea absolute exemption. When his plea was denied, he served more than two years in prison as a conscientious objector. Wilfrid Littleboy, another Quaker absolutist, commented on the apparent spiritual discontent of the men who had chosen alternative service. Wilfrid Littleboy to his parents, 11 Jan. 1917, Wilfrid Littleboy Papers (WLP).

from the beginning, protested against this sort of hands-off policy, Meeting for Sufferings supported the Service Committee's no-compromise stand.[83] Increasing tensions among Friends over these matters mirrored growing differences between the FSC and the No-Conscription Fellowship as to how to respond to Government treatment of imprisoned COs. Many of those initially willing to suffer imprisonment were deeply shocked by the harshness of the conditions they faced as prisoners in the third division of Britain's penal system, a status reserved for the lowest class of common criminal. In late September 1916, while the FSC met at Jordans, the burial place of William Penn, to decide its 'duty towards the N.C.F. Movement', Edward Grubb used the columns of *The Friend* to issue a plea for unity: 'We cannot afford to divide the Peace party as the Temperance party has long been divided because the extremists... believe that to accept half-measures would put back the cause ... Our right course is, surely, to support the movement, using our best powers to guide it, if possible, into safe channels.'[84]

Grubb's appeal was obviously deeply felt, but there soon were signs that it had fallen on deaf ears within the FSC. When, for example, Robert Mennell responded to a letter from a female Friend suggesting that the FSC and NCF get some 'prominent person' to influence the Home Office to allow special food parcels with 'plum puddings' and other treats to be delivered to imprisoned conscientious objectors, he stated emphatically: 'I do not think the N.C.F. or any of our organizations ought even to suggest this kind of thing. The N.C.F. in the opinion of a good many is already becoming too much a society for the prevention of cruelty to C.O.s.'[85]

---

[83] H. W. P. to Isaac Sharp (Clerk of Meeting for Sufferings), 16 Sept. 1916 and R. O. M. to E. Roffe Thompson, 16 & 28 Sept. 1916, FSC Files, LSF. Thompson wanted the Service Committee to provide legal and financial assistance for his case against the tribunals.

[84] H. W. P. to R. O. M., 18 Sept, 1916, FSC Files, LSF and E. Grubb, 'Short Cuts to Peace', *TF*, 22 Sept. 1916, 737–39. Also see E. Taylor, 'Diaries', 8 Aug. 1916, Temp. Box 23/3, LSF.

[85] R. O. M. to Daisy Harland, 25 Oct. 1916, FSC Files, LSF. Seebohm Rowntree may have been the prominent person Harland had in mind. He had already written an emotionally-charged personal letter to Lloyd George asking him 'as a friend & as an upholder of liberty' to mitigate his treatment of 'sincere but extreme conscientious objectors'. Seebohm Rowntree to Lloyd George, 29 Aug. 1916, E/4/1/35, Lloyd George Papers, House of Lords Record Office, London. Rowntree did not, however, resign from Government service when Lloyd George ignored his plea.

Before the year was out, this private expression of philosophical differences had become a public display of serious discord within an increasingly shaky pacifist alliance. J. P. Fletcher and Barry Brown, who were members of the NCF national committee,[86] believed that the Fellowship's political agitation to redress specific grievances or to push for further exemptions, was in danger of undermining 'the witness for Peace which the Fellowship had cone [sic] into existence to bear'. To accentuate this point, the FSC, in its year ending report to Yearly Meeting, emphasized that the Service Committee had been formed, not to negotiate with the Government for redress of grievances or special considerations, but 'to create a real and strengthening sense of fellowship among those who by their uncompromising fidelity are bearing witness to the Truth'. Political action had never been part of their charge.[87]

Above all, the FSC wished to demonstrate the power of its conviction that the primary struggle was not against any Government policy, however unjust or deceptive, but against the war itself. This did not mean that the Committee could simply ignore the Government, but its yardstick for responding to State actions was whether or not these actions advanced the war machinery Friends were attempting to defeat. While the FSC could not really argue that mistreatment of conscientious objectors actually enhanced the war effort, the Service Committee still refused to take any steps on behalf of those being punished for conscience's sake, asserting that, in any case, soldiers at the front suffered far more than COs in prison. Thus, while the NCF was agitating on behalf of prisoners and the Fellowship of Reconciliation was working up 'a "political scheme" . . . to catch the practical man', the FSC could only feel justified in launching a Peace and Disarmament campaign which, while it might have no effect on the war, could

---

[86] Fletcher resigned from the NCF national committee on this issue in the summer of 1916; Brown stayed on until May 1917 when he stepped down because the Fellowship's policy was 'quite opposed to my conscience and my judgment'. See *The Tribunal*, 3 Aug. 1916 and Brown to Catherine Marshall, 23 May 1917, Catherine E. Marshall Papers (CEMP), Cumbria Record Office, Carlisle. (Microfilm copy seen through courtesy of Jo Vellacott.)

[87] 'Notes of Committee Meeting', 2 Nov. 1916, FSC, *Minutes, Records of Work and Documents Issued*, 11, 16, LSF; 'Friends Service Committee Report' by Robert Mennell, 1 Dec. 1916, FSC Files, ibid.; and *TF*, 15 Dec. 1916, 981.

help its own members to 'raise their ideals' and, it was hoped, to influence the NCF 'to revise its basis'.[88]

This potentially divisive situation was momentarily deflected when David Lloyd George, in one of his first actions as Prime Minister, appointed Neville Chamberlain as Director-General of National Service for the purpose of organizing the civilian population in more efficient prosecution of the war. Members of the anti-war movement, logically though erroneously, saw Chamberlain as a sort of czar commissioned to impose universal compulsory service for industrial as well as military service. For its part, the FSC wished 'to forestall the usual stampede into some wonderful innocent employment which our quaker [sic] M.P.s will probably discover for men between 40 & 60 and for women', and therefore sent a 'Memorandum on Universal National Service' (prepared in conjunction with the NCF) to all Quaker Quarterly Meetings asking them to take a 'firm stand against acquiescence in Industrial Conscription'. United resistance, they felt, might make 'clear to the public the nature of the principles which have led many men to refuse military service on conscientious grounds'.[89]

As events transpired, Lloyd George pulled back from industrial conscription and Chamberlain, without real power or a workable plan, failed miserably in his new post.[90] Within the Society of Friends, however, the crisis over National Service revived animosities concerning what was and was not acceptable Quaker service in wartime. As noted, the example of Sir George Newman and the Friends Ambulance Unit was often cited by those who desired some compromise with the Government to show how Friends might faithfully serve both God and country. When, in early 1917, The Friend published a lead article that not only appeared to welcome the idea of civilian National Service and but also extolled Chamberlain's qualifications, as a civilian, social worker, and

[88] J. P. F. to R. O. M., 29 Nov. 1916; A. B. B. to R. O. M, 12 Dec. 1916; and E. E. to R. O. M., 12 Dec. 1916, FSC Files, LSF. The idea for this campaign had come from the Friends Peace Committee, but the Service Committee took the initiative in implementing it.

[89] 'Notes—Joint Advisory Council', 19 Dec. 1916, FSC, Minutes, 11, LSF; A. B. Brown to R. O. M., 12 Dec. 1916 and letter to Friends from Harrison Barrow and Edith M. Ellis, 31 January 1917, with accompanying memorandum, FSC Files, ibid.

[90] For discussion of Chamberlain's ill-fated assignment, which caused him to harbour permanent enmity toward Lloyd George, see R. J. Q. Adams and Philip H. Poirier, The Conscription Controversy in Great Britain, 1900–1918 (Columbus 1987), 192–95 and Keith Grieves, The Politics of Manpower, 1914–18 (New York 1988), 133–44 and passim.

Nonconformist, for directing the scheme, the debate among Friends heated up again.[91] The reaction from the FSC, already dubious about the FAU's close co-operation with military authorities, was immediate and fierce. Wilfrid Littleboy, in military custody while awaiting court-martial, told his parents that he was 'pretty disgusted' with what had transpired. Robert Mennell and others, similarly confined in Kingston Barrack's guardroom, wrote to *The Friend* that Neville Chamberlain's record of effective public service was no more reason for accepting universal compulsion than Lord Robert's sterling personal character had been a reason for accepting universal military training before 1914. Lloyd George's real purpose, they believed, was to 'complete and make more effective the mobilisation of all national resources'.[92] *The Friend* defended its position by noting that 'public service for the benefit of all was [an idea] . . . which commended itself to Friends' and that those who disagreed with this view should engage in positive discussion rather than negative insinuation. 'We are all fallible,' an editorial pointedly remarked, 'even the youngest of us.'[93] Writing from Wormwood Scrubs prison, the FSC's former Organizing Secretary, Hubert Peet, reminded his wife of an elderly Friend at the Adjourned Yearly Meeting who had 'rejoiced that the spirit was greatly into the dry bones of the Society in its younger members' and regretted that a year later the bones appeared to be drying up once again. Certainly, the divergence of generations as well as opinions was all too clear. As Edward Grubb related to Rufus Jones in late February, 'we are very far from being united here at present', adding, perhaps for consolation, that this had probably always been the case with Friends during times of war.[94]

As if differences among Friends were not sufficient, serious discord re-emerged between the Friends Service Committee and the No-Conscription Fellowship early in 1917. The central issue at

[91] *TF*, 12 Jan. 1917, 17–19.

[92] W. E. L. to parents, 14 Jan. 1912, W. L. P. and R. O. M., Roderic K. Clark & Wm. F. Newby to *The Friend* (copy) 14 Jan. 1917, 19 FSC Files, LSF, published in *TF*, Jan. 1917, 52. Also see ibid., 12 Jan., 19 & 19 Jan. 1916, 57, and J. W. G. to R. G., 23 Jan. 1917, JWGP.

[93] *TF*, 26 Jan. 1917, 56. The articles on national service were probably written by *The Friend*'s middle-aged editor, E. Basset Reynolds (1864–1938), a strong supporter of Sir George Newman and the FAU.

[94] H. W. P. to Esther Peet, 18 Jan. 1917, Hubert Peet Papers (HPP) and E. G. to R. M. J., 25 Feb. 1917, RMJP.

dispute was still the matter of whether seeking relief and redress for imprisoned COs was, in fact, a legitimate activity for organizations whose supposed chief thrust was opposition to the war and conscription. In early March 1917 the NCF's Catherine Marshall told Edith Ellis, who had begun acting as FSC Organizing Secretary after the arrest and imprisonment of Hubert Peet, that she had been deeply 'hurt and disturbed' by the FSC's censure of her activities at the NCF's Conscientious Objectors Information Bureau (COIB). The Service Committee's chief objection was to Marshall's detailed negotiations at the War Office on behalf of absolutist COs who were being repeatedly tried and convicted for refusing to co-operate with military authorities or to perform any non-military work under Government supervision. The FSC, of course, believed the only legitimate pacifist activity was attempting, by vigorous propaganda or silent suffering, to end the war.[95] This damaging split was accidentally but precisely timed with an attack by a disenchanted Quaker prisoner on the Service Committee's determination not to seek redress for prisoners of conscience.

On 11 March 1917 Edward Grubb received a letter from Wilfred G. Hinde complaining about the Meeting for Sufferings' refusal, under the influence of the Service Committee, to take any steps to aid imprisoned absolutists. 'I cannot see that there is any advantage in allowing absolutists to continue in prison. Our lot is undoubtedly better than that of many soldiers but this is surely beside the point. Because one evil is less than another is no reason for allowing that evil to exist.'[96]

In passing Hinde's letter on to the Service Committee, Grubb expressed his own belief that Friends, as a Society, 'ought to register some kind of public protest against the administration of the ... Acts on the ground of penalizing conscience'. Within the FSC, however, some expressed the view that Hinde apparently did not 'realize the breadth of the service for peace rendered in prison', or that he was merely 'beating against the bars & losing something of his confidence'. In the end, after much discussion, the FSC

---

[95] Catherine Marshall to Dr.[Henrietta] Thomas, 1 March 1917, with attached 'REPORT FROM MISS MARSHALL', 23 Feb. 1917; Marshall to E. E., 9 March 1917 and Harrison Barrow to E. E., 12 March 1917, FSC Files, LSF. For Marshall's interaction with War Office officials, particularly Chief of Personal Services General Sir Wyndham Childs, see Vellacott, *Russell and the Pacifists*, 126–29, 178–83.

[96] Wilfred G. Hinde to E. G., 11 March, FSC 'Correspondence', II, 44, LSF.

persisted in the view that it was 'not the function of any pacifist body to agitate for the release of conscientious objectors till public opinion desires it'.[97]

The controversy did not end there. In April, Henry T. Hodgkin, with the support of Edward Grubb, John W. Graham and others, gave notice of his intention to introduce a concern to the next Meeting for Sufferings 'that there should be further action taken by the S. of F. concerning the continuance of penalties upon C.O. members'.[98] Subsequently, however, both Meeting for Sufferings and the Yearly Meeting of 1917 affirmed the FSC's policy of appealing only to the public conscience and not to the Government as such.[99]

This decision left many Friends 'troubled in their minds' not just because COs were continuing to be punished with repeated sentences for the same offence but also because they realized that 'the Government would be delighted if Friends withdrew their support from the NCF'.[100] 'I am afraid', J. W. Graham told Catherine Marshall, 'our C.O. cause resembles the Apostle Paul, in that there are fightings within and fears without'.[101]

So long as the Quaker struggle against the war continued, so did such internal skirmishing. When, for example, Yorkshire Quarterly Meeting gathered at Bradford in July 1917, it approved a Minute urging Meeting for Sufferings to recognize the duty of Friends 'as a Religious Society which has always stood for civil and religious liberty, to press for the absolute and unconditional release of all these men . . . who are now persistently persecuted in a Christian

---

[97] E. G. to E. E., 14, 17 & 22 March 1917 and E[sther] B[right] Clothier to E. E., 26 March 1917, FSC, Gen'l Correspondence, and Notes on FSC Meeting, 29 March 1917, FSC, *Minutes*, II, 48, LSF.

[98] 'Notes of subject for consideration at next M. for S.,' (War Victims' Relief Committee stationery), 20 April 1917, FSC Files, LSF.

[99] Notes on FSC meetings of 29 March and 3 May 1917, FSC, *Minutes*, II, 48, 50 (51); A. B. B. to E. E., 2 May 1917; A. B. B. to Catherine Marshall, 23 May 1917, FSC Files, LSF and *LYM, 1918*, 'Proceedings of the Meeting for Sufferings, Summary, 1917–1918', 45.

[100] E. E. to A. B. B. (copy) and Harrison Barrow (copy), 31 May 1917, FSC Files, LSF. Alexander Cowan Wilson (1866–1955) and Joan Mary Fry (1862–1955), both influential members of Meeting for Sufferings were especially uneasy with the FSC policy. For his part, Wilson attempted, unsuccessfully, to get the Liberation Society to take up the cause of conscientious objectors. See A. C. Wilson to Executives of Society for Liberation of Religions from State Patronage and Control, 11 May 1917, LSF

[101] J. W. G. to CEM, 23 May 1917, CEMP. Also see Marshall to E. E., 30 April 1917, FSC Files, LSF.

country for conscience sake'.[102] Their arguments for some action on behalf of COs were historical as well as libertarian and humanitarian. Critics of the non-intervention policy cited a Quaker Conference of 1675 which had urged, contrary to the advice of saintly Quaker pioneers like William Dewsbury, that when Friends were unjustly imprisoned, the Society should 'take such course to relief and ease to the oppressed as may not be prejudicial to Truth's testimony', including 'bringing the oppression home to the persecutors'. Indeed, Meeting for Sufferings had first been appointed in 1675 'to have oversight of all cases of suffering, whether by persecution or misfortune'.[103]

Overlaying the situation of imprisoned COs was another long-standing Quaker concern, the methods, and even the legitimacy, of the entire British penal system. Ironically, Quaker reformers like Elizabeth Fry had given strong support to the principles of separate, silent confinement and 'reformatory and economic labour [sewing mail bags]', under which COs suffered and about which many persistently complained.[104] The physical hardship and mental deterioration suffered by conscientious objectors under the effects of such supposedly redemptive conditions stunned even the staunchest absolutists. One Quaker prisoner, James Crayshaw, told Edith Ellis that after observing 'the effects of prison treatment . . . on the moral[,] mental, & physical condition' of prisoners, he had reversed his position and sided with the NCF's campaign for relief. After personal experience in the third division, even John Fletcher, the consummate no-compromiser, noted 'the reforming zeal of Howard surely did not intend the solitary system to become—I cannot better describe it—a human dog kennel. . . . Moral disease cannot be cured by treating a man like a dog.'[105]

[102] *Minutes Books, 1893–1920*, Yorkshire Quarterly Meeting, 17 and 18 July 1917, BL.

[103] See Constance Braithwaite, *Legal Problems of Conscientious Objection to Various Compulsions under British Law* (London 1968), 284–85. The quotation on the establishment of Meeting for Sufferings is from Margaret E. Hirst, *The Quakers in Peace and War* (London 1923), 64n.

[104] Isichei, *Victorian Quakers*, 250 cites the example of William Tallack, long-time Secretary (1866–1901) to the Howard League, as a defender of the silence system in British prisons. Also see Michael Ignatieff, *A Just Measure of Pain: The Penitentiary in the Industrial Revolution, 1750–1850* (New York, 1978), 49, 58–9, 148–53.

[105] Crayshaw to E.E., 6 June 1917 and Fletcher to E. E. (extract), 6 Dec 1917, FSC Files, LSF. Four months earlier, Fletcher had written a long letter opposing any petitioning of the Government 'to save ourselves and our friends from personal suffering'. See Fletcher to Thompson Eliott, 16 Aug. 1917, ibid.

Still, even alarming reports of 'mental derangement' did not alter the Service Committee's position that no entreaty to improve the lot of imprisoned conscientious objectors should be made directly to the Government.[106] The FSC did agree that the Society of Friends should appeal to public opinion by issuing a 'clear statement that we regard all penal methods as opposed to the spirit of Christ's teaching'. To this end, the Committee delegated three members 'to draw up a careful statement of the Society of Friends' point of view'. A declaration on 'Friends and Conscientious Objectors' was duly published in *The Friend*, although the Service Committee's apparent presumption in speaking for the entire Society continued to irritate Quakers and others who believed that every possible means should be used to end the travesty of justice represented by the continued punishment of COs.[107] Those who protested against doing nothing certainly represented the majority of conscientious objectors and probably the majority of British Friends as well. And while, officially, the Service Committee never wavered from maintaining the purity of its position, in May 1918 London Yearly Meeting did issue an official *Appeal to the Conscience of the Nation*, characterizing the imprisonment of COs as an assault on freedom of religion which, 'at this dark hour... the nation can ill-afford to condone'. The national conscience as well as the Government remained largely unmoved and absolutists languished in prisons even after the war ended.[108]

---

[106] 'Christianity, Crime & Punishment', FSC, *Minutes*, II, 1917, no author or date; 'Cases of Mental Derangement', 28 Jan 1918, listing twenty-five men, two of whom had already died as a result of the their prison experiences, as examples, FSC Files; and FSC, *Minutes*, 11, 4 Oct. 1917, LSF.

[107] See especially, Bertrand Russell to E. E., 11 Sept. 1917 & E. E. to B. R., 22 Sept. 1917, FSC Files. Also see FSC, *Minutes*, 4 Oct. 1917, 11, 83 & *TF*, 2 Nov. 1917, 838–39; *Minutes*, Yorkshire Quarterly Meeting, 29 Oct. 1917, 113, 24 Jan. 1918, 27 May 1918, 130 & 18 Oct. 1918, 146, BL; FSC, *Minutes*, 5 April 1918, III, 4; and FSC [Arthur Watts] to Rev. Leyton Richards (copy), 24 April, 1918, LSF.

[108] *An Appeal to the Conscience of the Nation*, from the London Yearly Meeting of the Society of Friends, May, 1918, signed by John H. Barlow, Clerk. Copy in LSF. Beginning in December 1917, a numbers of absolutist COs, including Clifford Allen and the saintly Quaker Stephen Hobhouse, were released as 'medically unfit'. This action, supported by Lord Milner and other Cabinet officers, was largely a reaction to *I Appeal Unto Caesar*, a book describing the plight of imprisoned COs attributed to Stephen Hobhouse's mother Margaret, but actually ghost-written by Bertrand Russell. See Rae, *Conscience and Politics*, 207–25; Jo Vellacott Newberry, 'Russell as Ghost Writer, a New Discovery', *Russell*, 15 (Autumn 1974), 19–23 and *The Collected Papers of Bertrand Russell*, Vol. XIV, *Pacifism and Revolution, 1916–1928*, edited by Richard A. Rempel, et al., (London and New York 1995), p. xxxviii. Hereafter cited as *CPBR*, with page.

In the meantime, the FSC and NCF had fashioned an uneasy compromise which limited activities of the NCF Record Office and COIB to '[c]ollecting, recording and tabulating all available information regarding CO's'. Obviously, these guidelines were aimed at eliminating Catherine Marshall's personal mediations with Government officials on behalf of prisoners for conscience.[109] But the partial resolution of one murky internal complication for pacifist allies was soon overborne by another event with universal ramifications, the revolution in Russia. No single event so raised the morale and aspirations of the pacifist movement and none, in the end, was more disillusioning as regards its ultimate effects on peace and non-violence. The much ballyhooed Leeds Convention in early June 1917 had established the machinery for Workers' and Soldiers' Councils in Britain which would, it was supposed, begin the process of ending the war while sweeping away the militarism which had produced it. As one expectant CO wrote from prison: 'Isn't . . . life worth living to be in at the beginning of a new age like this.'[110]

Moved by 'the spirit of Leeds', the executive officers of the FSC, NCF and Fellowship of Reconciliation met for two days in mid-July 'to consider their relation to the International movements for freedom'. As a result of these deliberations, the participating organizations summarized their expectations in a special supplement to the NCF's newspaper, *The Tribunal*. The essence of their collective response was to depict events in Russia as the harbinger of a world-wide non-violent revolution of which the war-resistance movement might grasp moral leadership. 'Only unite and organise your fellows', said Barry Brown for the FSC, 'and you can achieve a revolution by the irresistible methods of non-resistance.'[111]

But, in fact, new complications arose for FSC just because some conscientious objectors, inspired by the Russian example, had ceased to be interested in methods of non-resistance. At a newly

---

[109] FSC, *Minutes*, II, 9 and 30 June 1917.

[110] P. Fletcher to E. E., 19 Aug. 1917, FSC Files, LSF; Fletcher was quoting Hubert Peet. For the Leeds Conference, see 'What Happened at Leeds' (London 1917), published by the Council of Workers' and Soldiers' Delegates; Rempel, *et al.*, *CPBR*, XIV, pp. xxxiv–xxxvii; and Stephen White, 'Soviets in Britain: The Leeds Convention of 1917', *International Review of Social History*, 19/2 (1974), 167–93. Also see Chapter 10 below.

[111] Supplement to *The Tribunal*, 19 July 1917. The articles in the four-page supplement were written by Brown and Edith Ellis for the FSC, Bertrand Russell for the NCF and Henry Hodgkin for the FOR.

reactivated prison on Dartmoor, authorities had gathered a group of COs willing to accept the so-called Home Office Scheme. This policy had been devised by the Government to allow CO prisoners to be released from jail, collected in one location under restricted but not penal conditions (e.g., no locked cells or enforced silence, possibility for weekend leaves, etc.) in order to perform useful civil work under civilian supervision.[112] The Home Office Scheme had been in operation since August of 1916, and while several hundred COs chose 'the scheme' in preference to prison with hard labour, the programme never came close to success. On the one hand, COs complained about the miserable conditions under which they performed useless work. On the other, public opinion was outraged by what one newspaper subbed 'C.O.s Cosy Clubs' where 'coddled Conscience men' continued to whine even as they escaped both the army and prison.[113]

The Dartmoor experiment, which commenced in February 1917, was the Government's attempt to meet criticism from both sides. It proved a dismal failure for many reasons, not the least of which was the organized resistance of what Quaker Stanley Kneeling called the '"rabid" type' of socialists inspired by the Russian Revolution and led by a founding member of the NCF, C. H. Norman.[114] Norman, whom Kneeling called 'a real danger here', and his followers, apparently including some Quakers, 'ate their food, took remuneration, but did nothing to justify it'.[115] The situation was further muddled when Norman threatened to bring legal action against officials who allegedly mistreated him, and the Service Committee, which rejected 'prosecution of those who may have offended us', refused to supply documents pertinent to his case.[116] Writing from prison, Hubert Peet supported this deci-

---

[112] For the Home Office Scheme see Rae, *Politics and Conscience*, 159–86 *passim* and Kennedy, *Hound of Conscience*, 156–77.

[113] For attacks on the Home Office Scheme, see *Daily Mail*, 23–30 April 1917. Also see Thomas C. Kennedy, 'Public Opinion and the Conscientious Objector, 1915–1919', *The Journal of British Studies*, XII/2 (May 1973), 113–14.

[114] Clarence Henry Norman, a radical socialist, publicist, and founding member of the NCF, initiated a number of internal disputes within the Fellowship and later blamed the Quakers for the ineffectiveness of the NCF's wartime protests. See Kennedy, *Hound of Conscience*, 276–7.

[115] Stanley V. Kneeling to Miss [Henrietta] Thomas, n.d. [May 1917], FSC Files, LSF. For Quaker supporters of '*direct action*' in response to the Russian Revolution, see Selwyn Hayes to Henrietta Thomas, 16 June 1917 and Ernest C. Everett to Thomas, 24 June 1917, ibid.

[116] G. R. Rinder to E. E., 20 July 1917 and E. E. to G. Rinder, 20 July 1917, ibid.

sion as an aspect of the FSC's mission 'to educate the Society of Friends, and the much larger circle with whom we are now in touch'. Edith Ellis agreed that it was the sort of thing that might help 'to deepen the spiritual side of the NCF.'[117]

Members of the Service Committee might have felt their efforts to raise the spiritual consciousness of the NCF were crowned with some success when Dr Alfred Salter (1873–1945), a socialist and a convinced Friend, replaced Bertrand Russell as Chairman of the NCF just before Russell was charged with publishing subversive material in *The Tribunal* and subsequently imprisoned.[118] Edith Ellis could only have been pleased when Salter related to her that the idea of securing the release of COs, favored by some NCF leaders as a first step in defeating conscription, 'carries no weight with me at all'. Salter was also instrumental in the drafting of an NCF Manifesto published in mid-1918 which muted any political message while stressing the Inward Light and other religious manifestations of pacifist resistance.[119] Members of the NCF like Clifford Allen, Bertrand Russell, and Catherine Marshall were deeply chagrined by the tone of this document. Immediately before beginning his prison sentence, Russell remarked: 'I should entertain him [Salter] with examples of unsuccessful martyrdoms.' For his part, Allen who had been released from prison because of official fears that he might himself suffer a martyr's death, had come to the conclusion that patience and long-suffering would be no more useful to the pacifist struggle than 'the Quakerism of centuries' and would cause all COs to fall into the 'trap of passivism' which he believed had ensnared too many Friends.[120]

Such criticisms of the FSC position were, of course, accurate in the sense that the idea of embracing a martyr's crown was central to the Quaker absolutists' stand. Neave Brayshaw had made precisely

---

[117] H. W. P. to Service Committee, 27 Aug. 1917, ibid. and E. E. to Stephen Hobhouse, 7 Feb. 1918, ibid.

[118] The best account of Russell's trial and imprisonment is Vellacott, *Russell and the Pacifists*, 223–40.

[119] Alfred Salter to E. E., 26 March 1918, FSC Files, LSF. The NCF Manifesto was printed in *The Tribunal*, 6 June 1918. The Service Committee decided against signing this document but most members were sympathetic with its contents; see FSC *Minutes*, 2 May 1918, III, 6.

[120] Russell to Allen, n.d. [late April 1917] and Allen to Russell, 27 June 1918, Bertrand Russell Archives, McMaster University, Hamilton, Ontario.

this point at the Swanwick Conference;[121] Geoffrey Hoyland, a leader of the FSC absolutist faction, had noted at Llandudno in September 1914: 'I have felt very strongly that the greatest work which many of us can do for Christ in the cause of peace will not be in intellectual argument between ourselves and those who are in strong disagreement with us . . . the root and backbone of our peace testimony lie in the Cross of Jesus Christ.' Traditionally for Friends 'the Cross', as an experience of spiritual struggle, had been the means of bridging the two realms of life—that which is of the creature and ultimately deceptive and that which of God and always authentic.[122] The meaning and importance of the Cross to the resistance of Quaker absolutists may in some measure be grasped by close consideration of the struggle of one middle-class, professional, pious, and previously law-abiding absolutist Friend.

'THEY IN THE LORD WHO FIRMLY TRUST'

On 18 January 1917 from the guardroom of Budbrooke Barracks, Warwickshire, Wilfrid Littleboy (1885–1979), recently qualified chartered accountant, future Clerk of London Yearly Meeting and prospective inmate of His Majesty's prison at Wormwood Scrubs, wrote out for his parents the words that, for him, had become 'a sort of wartime motto':

> They in the Lord who firmly trust shall be like Zion hill
> Which at no time can be removed and standeth ever still.
> As round about Jerusalem, the mountains stand alway,
> The Lord His folk shall compass so, from henceforth and for aye.[123]

---

[121] Brayshaw, 'Introductory Address', *Swanwick 1911*, 38. Also see Anne Wakefield Richardson, 'The Spiritual Application of the Quaker Message', ibid., 139: 'Amid the voice calling for warlike preparation . . . [the Friend] knows that unless he himself is concerned to offer a deeper, more real, more Christian, and more unselfish Service to his country in the common life . . . the spirit that calls men off from war . . .'

[122] Geoffrey Hoyland, 'The Real Argument for Peace', *Friends and the War*, 101 and Punshon, 'Peace Testimony', 65.

[123] Wilfrid Littleboy to his parents, 18 Jan. 1917. Littleboy's prison letters (hereafter WLP) are in the possession of his daughter, Margaret E. Nash, and are used with her permission. For Littleboy's recollections of his wartime experiences, see '1914–1918, "I remember . . . VIII, with the C.O.s in prison", *TF*, 92 (1934), 859–61.

Fig. 9   Wilfrid E. Littleboy (1885–1979), taken 1934;
Quaker prisoner of conscience

Littleboy had taken his watchwords from a Scottish metrical version of the opening verses of Psalm 125; they provide an appropriate starting point for an analysis of the wartime resistance by Quaker absolutists like Wilfrid Littleboy in such unlovely places as Wormwood Scrubbs (where, supposedly, at one point during the war the largest Friends meeting in London was being conducted).[124] Such resistance has been considered in the context of the progressive ideas and impulses, politically and theologically liberal, which influenced the generation of Quakers to which Wilfrid Littleboy belonged and which obviously contributed to the anti-war struggle for which that generation has become justly famous. Ironically, the experiences of many war resisters and

[124] W. E. Littleboy, 'I remember...' 859 and Maude Robinson, 'Lest We Forget': A Memory of the Society of Friends in the War Years, 1914–1918 (London n.d.), 21. One CO wrote that there were 'about 20 Friends' working in the laundry at the 'Scrubbs'. James Jones to William T. Ecroyd, 8 April 1917, William T. Ecroyd Papers in possession of Henry Ecroyd.

prisoners of conscience like Wilfrid Littleboy finally revealed the inadequacy of both liberal religion and political liberalism as guides for the twentieth-century pacifist.

Like most of the Friends who became war resisters, Wilfrid Littleboy grew to maturity in the sort of stable, comfortable, middle-class family to which birthright Quakers typically belonged. After attending Bootham, Littleboy moved to Birmingham and in 1905 spent two terms at Woodbrooke where his Uncle William and Aunt Margaret were Wardens. Certainly, his subsequent career fully justified the hopes of Woodbrooke's founders that the Settlement should be a seed-bed for nurturing the future leaders of their religious Society.

After his year of study at Woodbrooke, Wilfrid set out upon his apprenticeship in accountancy with a Birmingham firm in which he would eventually become a senior partner. After accompanying Thomas Hodgkin's family on a trip to Australia in 1909, Littleboy started his way up the Quaker *cursus honorum* with an appointment in 1910 as secretary to the Sibford School Committee, adding a step in the next year as a member of the Woodbrooke Council. He continued to serve in both these capacities until he was imprisoned in 1917. At the Swanwick Conference in 1911, Wilfrid Littleboy was named secretary to a special Young Friends sub-committee charged to work closely with the Yearly Meeting's Home Missions and Extension Committee with a view to expanding Quaker influence throughout British society.[125]

For Littleboy, as for many young Friends, the Swanwick Conference was a particularly riveting event. One attender recalled that 'the message of the Conference . . . stood out ever stronger and clearer. We were brought face to face with the hard facts . . . Seldom has a call so high and so masterful come to us . . . and we go forth . . . with what seems to many of us . . . strangely little fear.'[126]

Whatever challenges these young Quakers had expected, most of them were profoundly shocked in August 1914 by the sudden cataclysm of violence that broke upon a world that had seemed to be moving, however haltingly, toward the fulfillment of the Quaker dream of an end to wars and strife. But while popular enthusiasm for the war caused an agnostic peace-advocate like

---

[125] Wilfrid Littleboy's entry, *DQB*, LSF and *Swanwick, 1911*, 14–17.
[126] *Swanwick, 1911*, 12–14. The statement was written by Geoffrey Hoyland.

Bertrand Russell 'to revise my views on human nature' and resolutely, even perversely, to set himself against the popular will,[127]
Wilfrid Littleboy responded like a boxer momentarily stunned by a
severe blow, halting briefly to clear his head, then continuing on
toward the infinitely more distant victory to which he aspired. In
an article published in October 1914, Littleboy addressed the
altered circumstances of young Friends, and the fact that they had
to 'be willing to face unpopularity and hard criticism in true
patience and to draw our line of what we may and may not do
absolutely, according to the guidance of our conscience no matter
what the result...'[128]

Such were the circumstances and beliefs that brought Wilfrid
Littleboy, respectable Quaker accountant and apparently model
citizen, into the hands of the military authorities at Budbrooke
Barracks in January 1917. Because he was over 30, Littleboy had
been called to the colours later than many of his fellow Quakers,
some of whom had already served several months in prison by the
time he was arrested by a Birmingham policeman for failing to
report for duty and subsequently court-martialled by military
authorities for refusing to obey the order to don an army uniform.
As a member of the Friends Service Committee, Littleboy had few
illusions as to what awaited him as a prisoner of conscience.

It bears repeating that Wilfrid Littleboy's stand was not typical,
even for Quaker COs, since fewer than 150 or about 5 per cent of
Quaker males of military age ultimately took the extreme or
absolutist position of refusing to co-operate in any fashion with
military or government authorities. In the end, of course, absolutists within the Society of Friends established a moral influence that
far outweighed the paucity of their numbers.[129]

During the twenty-eight months of his imprisonment, Wilfrid
Littleboy's resolve was apparently never seriously shaken. Still, in
letters to his parents, generally written at intervals of about six
weeks, a gradual but perceptible change emerged about the

---

[127] *The Autobiography of Bertrand Russell, 1914–1944*, Volume 2 (London 1968), 17–18 and
passim. When, for example, Russell, a longstanding teetaller, discovered that King George
V had, as a wartime sacrifice, stopped serving alcohol at Royal functions, he resumed
drinking alcoholic beverages.

[128] Littleboy, 'Our Peace Testimony', 722–4.

[129] Tucker, 'English Quakers and World War I', 242–3, 266; *LYM, 1919*, 75; and
Kennedy, 'Quaker Renaissance', 270.

meaning of his experiences. At the beginning, Littleboy found the treatment afforded him so bizarre as to be positively amusing, 'more like a camping opportunity than anything else...I am disposed to laugh at one thing after another...I suppose when wars...are all things of the past, the world as a whole will shout with laughter as we are constantly tempted to do.'[130] But however amused or bemused by his circumstances, Littleboy reported that neither he nor his companions felt a 'shadow of a doubt that we are in the right place; one that we would not wish to alter from our personal point of view, or from the point of view of the cause'.[131]

For Littleboy and his fellow absolutists 'the cause' was not only the general struggle against the war but also the firm conviction that such a struggle could only be effective if it embodied the steadfast refusal to compromise with Caesar. He did not condemn the men who took some form of alternative service, but he did contrast his growing sense of spiritual peace[132] with the uncomfortable anxiety of alternative-service COs he met at intervals between his four courts-martial and terms of imprisonment.[133] As he told his parents: 'You may rely on my not coming out of Scrubs on the Home Office Scheme...I do not see myself coming out except on absolutely unrestricted conditions.'[134]

Littleboy and other Quaker absolutists believed that the war would end only when a sufficient number of people became convinced, by argument or example, that war, as an affront both to human reason and the Divine Will, was always wrong. Therefore, they felt that prisoners of conscience should play out their parts as silent witnesses for truth. As noted above, these Friends believed the No-Conscription Fellowship's policy of conducting a propaganda campaign to protest the repeated sentences and harsh conditions imposed on COs was a purely political stratagem

---

[130] W. E. L. to parents, 2 and 4 Jan. 1917, WLP.

[131] W. E. L. to parents, 18 Jan. 1917, WLP.

[132] For example, W. E. L. to parents, 'a sense of serene peace and contentment', 10 March 1917; 'my real feeling is quite peaceful & confident', 25 April 1917; 'I am full of happiness, peace & contentment', 18 June 1917; 'I have literally not been "off colour" for a day since first coming here,' 30 July 1917, WLP.

[133] W. E. L. to parents, 11 Jan. 1917 and 28 Sept. 1917, WLP and Littleboy, ' "I remember..." ' 860.

[134] W. E. L. to parents, 18 Jan. 1917, WLP.

which, while it might relieve the hardships of COs, would make no contribution to ending the war.[135]

As regards activities to secure the release of COs, Littleboy told Edith Ellis of the FSC that the more he and his companions thought about it 'the more we come to realise that Conscription is absolutely wrapped up with the whole war question. We cannot conceive England or any other country continuing as a war state without some form of Conscription, and therefore . . . calling . . . attention to the evils thereof is really a sort of addendum to the whole question.'[136] Furthermore, he believed that those who had in the past suffered for conscience sake 'would have been the last to call attention to their own sufferings'. While Littleboy believed it was presumptuous to link oneself too closely to 'the great army of those who have suffered for ideals . . . we now know that we are of the same make as they were; and it is the same power that lived in them as shall live in us'. It was, he said, the 'old case of the dreamers of the dream who assure the future . . .' a future that he felt sure was in 'perfectly safe hands'.[137]

As the weeks in prison stretched into months and then years, Littleboy's confidence was not shaken. What did seem to emerge was a growing sense not only that he was personally in God's hands but also that all human efforts were insufficient to resolve the misery of the world, whether that misery arose from war or imperialism or simple selfishness. 'One is driven', he said, 'to feel that one's only hope lies in God . . .' When he heard of someone's saying that God would 'send peace in His time', Littleboy responded that the nations had had the opportunity to achieve God's peace but had been too blinded by materialism and sin to recognize it. So, in the end, mankind would have to do with some imperfect human peace, 'probably a financier's peace . . . This does not mean that it is no good praying for peace . . . only we must realize that the answer to that prayer will not be confined to the actual negotiations at the close of the war, but must be viewed as all a piece of the growth toward the establishment of His will on earth.'[138] The mistake that he and others had made in their spiritual

---

[135] See Kennedy, *Hound of Conscience*, 197–215 and 'Fighting About Peace', 9–20. Also see Rempel, *et al., CPBR*, XIV, pp.xxx–xxxi, 61.

[136] W. E. L. to Edith Ellis, 27 Sept. 1917, FSC Correspondence, 1915–19, LSF.

[137] W. E. L. to parents, 18 and 20 Jan. 1917, WLP.

[138] W. E. L. to parents, 25 April 1918, WLP.

lives during the previous ten years, Littleboy concluded, was to be overly concerned with method and insufficiently aware of content. 'The message . . . must centre in God. We shall grasp it only as we begin to understand Jesus . . .' In the meantime, Littleboy believed that, in their struggle with Caesar, Friends 'must keep our "unmitigated no" in our testimony' to ensure they did not succumb to the 'superficial ebb & flow' of merely human emotions.[139]

Littleboy seemed to have discovered in prison what many in the peace movement never understood or appreciated, that pacifism, Quaker or otherwise, could not be based on a political ideology or an advanced social theory or an optimistic view of human potentialities. Rather, it could only be 'an exacting personal faith'.[140] In other words, Littleboy's pacifism, whatever its starting point, finally came to rest on the acceptance of a martyr's crown and a martyr's fate as his spiritual witness.

Herbert G. Wood, who succeeded Rendel Harris as Director of Studies at Woodbrooke, formulated this same argument to the next generation of Friends during the dark days of 1941. It was not the Inward Light, Wood said, but the 'Cross of Christ' that justified the Quaker stand against war. Only by sacrifice, suffering, or martyrdom in the name of faith could Friends give expression to the Light that was within each of them and thus communicate the pacifist testimony that at some point might convince other (i.e., sinful mankind) that there should be an end to wars and strife.[141]

When Wilfrid Littleboy was released from prison in 1919, he must have recognized that his protest had neither shortened the war by a day nor saved a single human life. This sort of realization led Bertrand Russell, who had lost his academic post and eventually his personal freedom for the cause of peace, to comment bitterly on the futility of efforts undertaken on the strength of liberal ideals that proved woefully inadequate for the task of rescuing humanity from its propensities for irrationality, savagery, and self-destruction. In the aftermath of his experiences, Russell ceased to be either a pacifist or a liberal.[142] Wilfrid Littleboy's pacifism was

---

[139] W. E. L. to Alfred, 12 Sept. 1918 and to parents, 13 March 1919, WLP.

[140] Ceadel, *British Pacifism*, 315.

[141] Herbert Wood, 'Pacifism and Politics', *FQE*, 75 (July 1941), 199–211. Also see Punshon, 'Peace Testimony', 64–72.

[142] Russell, *Autobiography*, 40 and Thomas C. Kennedy, 'Nourishing Life: Russell and the Twentieth-Century British Peace Movement, 1900–1918', in *Intellect and Social Conscience*,

also no longer informed by lingering liberal sentiments, but he expressed no distressing doubts about the value of his wartime experiences. As he told his parents from Dorchester Prison: 'I am quite content in the thought that God will not let my time here be wasted but will continue his preparation and constantly lead me on "to see greater things than these": & whether it be weeks, months, or longer, this stage will end when I can serve His purposes better elsewhere...'[143]

In the end, Littleboy did not dare to hope that by suffering he might somehow aid in a human resolution of the conflict that would produce a better world. Rather, he accepted the daunting prospect of a personal Cross 'as all a piece of... growth toward the establishment of His will on earth'.[144] Through this acceptance came the redeeming power of the absolutists' sacrificial act. In imitation of the Cross of Christ and in the great tradition of Quaker witness, they achieved a smashing victory over militarism, violence, and death. It was not, of course, a universal triumph, any more than Quakerism was a universal faith; but it was this victory, the choice of life over death, that British Friends collectively, whatever their individual degree of war resistance or non-resistance, came to recognize as the most important outcome of the trial of faith imposed by the Great War. It also became, as Martin Ceadel has noted, the standard by which all subsequent pacifist war-resistance would be measured.[145]

Twenty-five years after Wilfrid Littleboy became a prisoner at Budbrooke Barracks, he was Clerk of London Yearly Meeting. His message to Yearly Meeting in 1942, whether recalling Herbert Wood's recent admonition to look to the Cross or his own experiences a quarter of a century earlier, reflected both the persistence of his pacifist faith and the inspiration for it:

The whole world is drawn into common suffering. Is there no way out of its evils but by waging war yet more ruthlessly? War is evil and wrong;

edited by Margaret Moran and Carl Spadoni (Hamilton, Ont. 1984), 232–3. A penetrating study of Russell's dilemma as a secular pacifist is Louis Greenspan, *The Incompatible Prophesies: Bertrand Russell on Science and Liberty* (York, Canada 1979).

[143] W.E.L. to parents, 18 June 1917, WLP.

[144] W.E.L., 'Guardroom notes', 25 April 1918, WLP.

[145] Ceadel, *Pacifism in Britain*, 60.

military victory will not bring true peace. Cannot our common suffering make us aware of our common brotherhood? Let us turn from the terrible deeds we do to one another and seek one another's forgiveness. The way of friendship can overcome evil. We see it perfectly in Jesus Christ. Its cost was the Cross. The loyal spirit which faced the Cross showed us the triumphant power of God. For us as children of a common Father it is time to follow His lead.[146]

[146] *Christian Faith and Practice* (London 1963), paragraph 612. Littleboy's statement was composed at Yearly Meeting during a luncheon break. I am grateful to Edward Milligan for this and other insights into the life and ideas of Wilfrid Littleboy.

10

War and the Social Order

'A CHALLENGE TO MILITARISM'

In late May 1918 John Henry Barlow relinquished the Clerkship of
London Yearly Meeting to Mary Jane Godlee and, in the company
of five other Friends appointed by Yearly Meeting,[1] made his way
from Devonshire House, Bishopsgate, to the London Guildhall
where three members of the Friends Service Committee were on
trial for violating Regulation 27C of the Defence of the Realm Act
(DORA) by refusing to submit a pamphlet called *A Challenge to
Militarism* to the official censor. Yearly Meeting had directed the
Clerk and his companions to attend the trial and make clear that
their religious Society 'desires to share responsibility for the action
of its three members...'[2] In Barlow's absence Mary Jane Godlee
adjourned regular business 'and the assembly sat in reverent and
prayerful silence' which, as Esther Peet related to her imprisoned
husband, Hubert, gave her a sense of 'sharing in the...deep stand
for truth in a way which I have not had a chance to do in public
before'.[3]

John H. Barlow's gesture of solidarity with his indicted co-
religionists not only occasioned the first instance of Yearly Meeting
being presided over by a female,[4] but also represented the most
conspicuous example of direct Quaker confrontation with the
State in over two centuries. Some, indeed, were reminded of the
trial of William Penn and William Meade in 1670. During that
celebrated contest against the Second Conventicle Act, a

[1] William A. Albright, Gulielma Crosfield, J. Thompson Elliott, T. Edmund Harvey, MP
and Edith J. Wilson accompanied Barlow to the Guildhall.
[2] *LYM, 1918, Minute* 11, 9–10.
[3] Maude Robinson, *'Lest We Forget': A Memory of the Society of Friends in the War Years,
1914–1918* (London, n.d.), 26 and E[sther] Peet to Hubert Peet, 4 June 1918, Peet Family
Papers, seen by permission of Stephen Peet, London.
[4] Since 1918, only three other women, Maude Brayshaw (1943–8), Jill Hopkins (1978–
81) and Christine Davis, have served as Clerks of London Yearly Meeting.

courageous jury had refused, even after imprisonment, to accept the judge's directed verdict of guilty, thus freeing Penn and Meade from religious persecution and future juries from the whims of tyrannous judges. Might this new Quaker challenge also produce some legal or moral milestone that would begin to loose the bonds of war from suffering humanity? Friends, as always, had hope.

The defiant Quakers in the dock included the Friends Service Committee's acting chairman Harrison Barrow (1868–1953), a former city councillor and Lord Mayor of Birmingham, who had resigned from his civic offices in 1914 because of his opposition to the war.[5] Also on trial was FSC treasurer Edith Ellis, daughter of the late John Edward Ellis, MP, Cabinet Minister and privy councillor. She had become a commanding presence in the FSC after most of its younger male members were sent to jails or Home Office Camps for resisting conscription. The third defendant, Arthur Watts (1888–1958), secretary to the Service Committee, was an engineer from Manchester and former secretary to the pre-war Australian Freedom League. He had already served several months as a CO prisoner until released from the Army in March 1917.[6] All three had accepted responsibility for violating Regulation 27C which required that material relating to the war be approved by the Government censor prior to publication.[7] The Guildhall trial climaxed months of cautious sparring over censorship between Government authorities and the Society of Friends. Meeting for Sufferings was first approached by the Director of Public Prosecution early in 1917 concerning the Society's possible

---

[5] See newspaper clipping on Barrow's withdrawing from office as Lord Mayor-elect, Temp. Box 23/3, and entry for Harrison Barrow in *DQB*, LSF.

[6] *TF*, 16 March 1917, 203. Watts was apparently released on a technicality because of his previous residence in Australia where he had joined the fight against compulsory military training. In July of 1920, Watts travelled to Russia to engage in relief work for Friends and the British Save the Children Fund. Eventually, he took Soviet citizenship and, except for periodic visits to England, remained in Russia for the rest of his life. See Richenda C. Scott, *Quakers in Russia* (London 1964), 229–84 *passim* and Greenwood, *Friends and Relief*, 240–44 and *DQB*, HCQC.

[7] Leigh Tucker provided valuable accounts of the 'A Challenge to Militarism' case, in both 'English Friends and Censorship, World War I', *QH*, 71/2 (Fall 1982), 114–24 and 'English Quakers and World War I', 170–84. Also see the FSC pamphlet *The Story of an Uncensored Leaflet* (London [1918]) and the section on Regulation 27C in Andrew G. Bone's doctoral thesis 'Beyond the Rule of Law: Aspects of the Defence of the Realm Acts and Regulations, 1914–1918' (McMaster University, 1994), 194–213. Bone believes that 'Regulation 27C was the most vivid illustration of the War Cabinet's deep-seated anxiety about the possible ramifications of unrestricted publicity for a compromise peace' (213).

association with certain materials published in opposition to 'universal national service'. The Friends' executive body denied direct responsibility for the materials in question but also made clear its unconditional opposition to any from of censorship. The battle was not fully joined until the promulgation of Regulation 27C in late November 1917 which occasioned the Friends Service Committee's decision to defy the new Regulation.[8] 'We feel that the declaration of Peace and goodwill is the duty of all Christians and ought not to be dependent upon the permission of any Government Official. We therefore intend to continue the publication of such leaflets as we feel it our duty to put forth, without submitting them to the Censor...' The FSC's action was swiftly endorsed by Meeting for Sufferings which noted the Christian's 'paramount duty to be free to obey... the law of God, a law higher than that of any state'.[9]

The Government took the bait. In February 1918 two women were charged with distributing copies of *A Challenge to Militarism*, a rather innocuous four-page pamphlet explaining the position of absolutist COs and quoting anti-war testimony from some of them.[10] During a subsequent hearing, Harrison Barrow testified that the Friends Service Committee, prominently listed as 'Authors and Publishers', was prepared to take full responsibility for the offending tract. At this point, the three executive officers of the FSC were arraigned and their trial fortuitously set to coincide with Yearly Meeting in May.[11]

When Yearly Meeting assembled, Esther Peet recounted to her husband how representatives of the Service Committee had come 'right bang into the middle of Y.M. & one could feel how the

[8] See *Minutes of Meeting for Sufferings*, MSS Vol. LVII (1916–19), letter of 2 March 1917, signed by Issac Goss, Recording Clerk. Also see J. W. Graham to Richard Graham, 22 Feb. 1917, JWGP wherein Graham promised that he would 'try to get the Meeting for Sufferings to stand by the Service Committee' on the matter of refusing to submit to Government censorship.

[9] The FSC's letter was endorsed by the Peace Committee and forwarded to Meeting for Sufferings. See *Minutes*, Peace Committee, MSS Vol. CVI (1916–21), 6 Dec. 1917, LSF and *Minutes of Meeting for Sufferings*, 7 Dec. 1917, signed by J. T. Elliott, as Clerk, ibid.

[10] According to FSC records, by mid-April 1918 82,000 copies of the pamphlet were printed and 74,000 distributed. *FSC Minutes*, II, 14 April 1918, 4, LSF.

[11] Tucker, 'English Quakers and World War I', 175–7. After the indictment, Edith Ellis was visited by 'three detectives', a somewhat extravagant use of wartime manpower, who confiscated materials relating to the case. See E. E. to FSC members, 1 May 1918, FSC Records, II, LSF.

whole of Y.M. without a doubt—in spite of M[arriage] Wallace—was at the back of the FSC'.[12] Those Friends who left Yearly Meeting to attend the trial gave unvarnished witness to the Society's official support for the defendants by holding an impromptu meeting for worship after the magistrate had retired to consider his verdict. Following a period of silence, they collectively prayed for an end to the war and to the persecution of all who, with Friends, refused to accept the war system as the means to a better world. All the defendants were convicted and sentenced; Barrow and Watts received six-months and Edith Ellis served out a three months' sentence after refusing to pay £150 in fines.[13]

It was a climactic moment for British Quakerism, the culmination of a four-year struggle to maintain, despite the power of the State and the force of public opinion, the continuity of their Society's two-and-a-half-century testimony against all war. Ordinary citizens, reading newspaper reports of the bizarre and provocative behaviour of this tiny sect might, understandably, have been irked or offended or at least seriously puzzled. At the very moment the Germans were pushing ahead with Ludendorff's ominously successful offensive on the Western Front, Quakers, hiding, as it seemed, behind the bulwark of religious toleration, attacked the national cause from a different direction. But the three members of the Friends Service Committee sentenced at the Guildhall for defying Government censorship represented only one aspect of a multi-faceted Quaker challenge to British society at war. In one guise or another the war crisis caused some Friends to confront not just militarism and conscription but underlying features of the entire social order, including the status of women and the legitimacy of capitalism.

'THE GREAT WORK OF FRIENDS'

However much British Friends might deplore the traumatic impact and tragic consequences of the war, for some of them, especially

---

[12] Esther Peet to Hubert Peet, 4 June 1918, Peet Papers.

[13] For accounts of the courtroom scene, see *The Story of an Uncensored Leaflet* (London 1918), and Tucker, 'English Friends and Censorship', 114–24. According to the entry for Harrison Barrow in the *DQB*, LSF, during the time he was in prison, Barrow was awarded the Order of the British Empire for his earlier service on behalf of Belgian refugees and military families.

for women, the conflict provided opportunities never previously available nor even imagined. Whatever form Quaker wartime activities took, aiding refugees, joining the FAU or Friends' War Victims Relief Committee in France, enlisting in the Fellowship of Reconciliation, serving as a 'Quaker Chaplain' to imprisoned COs or becoming involved in some facet of the anti-war movement, the work was often as radicalizing as it was stimulating. For female Friends, as for women in general, the Great War offered the possibility of breaking free to become involved with ideas and movements that, in tumultuous times, seemed capable of changing the world.

When British Friends gathered at Llandudno in late September 1914 to consider their Society's collective response to the war crisis, L. Violet Hodgkin (1869–1954) spoke of war's effect on Quakerism's relation to British society as a whole. Friends, she said, could never again be 'merely the same looked-up to, respected ... easy-going ... Society ... We are going to count either for very much more, or very much less, in the national life.' In responding to this sort of challenge, a group of Quaker women presented their assessment of the situation to those who had assembled at Llandudno: 'We believe that to us, too, a call has come ... It is the time for women to join hands as sisters. Do not let us wait till the darkness is over. This is the creative time in which we must draw together and unite in a conscious effort all the forces which have been entrusted to us ...'[14]

Some of these women were instrumental in making the Llandudno Conference a launching pad for the Fellowship of Reconciliation's battle to restore the spirit of Christian harmony in Europe and the world.[15] But the longer the war lasted and the more destructive of life and liberty it became, the stronger was the tendency among Quaker pacifists to see the conflict as an embodiment of all the dark forces their Society had pledged to overcome in its mission to establish Christ's Kingdom on earth. The Fellowship of Reconciliation, with its emphasis on spiritual witness as the means generating 'a great wave of moral feeling as to the awfulness of ... [war] and the sin of having been led into it,' seemed to some

---

[14] From the published proceedings of the Llandudno Conference, *Friends and the War* (London 1914), 77 & 131.

[15] Ceadel, *Pacifism in Britain*, 35. Also see Herbert G. Wood, *Henry T. Hodgkin: A Memoir* (London 1937), 145–76 *passim*.

an inadequate or at least incomplete instrument for accomplishing this goal.[16] As Edith J. Wilson (1869–1953), a mother of four recently named an Assistant Clerk of Yearly Meeting, told FOR founder Henry Hodgkin early in 1915: 'those of us who take the "uncompromising" attitude about war must think out a scheme whereby our philosophy may be systematically & rapidly spread throughout Europe . . . We want a readjustment of personal lives that will bear witness to an irresistible enthusiasm for rational righteousness.'[17] To accomplish such an exalted aim, many Quaker women, including Edith Wilson, sought to devote their energies to one or another of the more socially and politically radical movements as they confronted what they perceived as rampant forces of evil loosed upon the world.

Fig. 10   Edith Jane Wilson (1869–1953), *c.*1900;
a leader among Quaker absolute pacifists

[16] Henry T. Hodgkin to J. Hope-Moulton, D.O., 27 Nov. 1914, Temp MSS 355, V/49, HMHP, LSF. Also see Wood, *Henry T. Hodgkin*, 157.
[17] Edith J. Wilson to Henry Hodgkin, 2 Jan. 1915, FOR File, HMHP, LSF.

Militarism was, of course, the most familiar and consistent of the evils against which pacifist Friends felt compelled to struggle. Since the Revolutionary and Napoleonic Wars, Quakers and their liberal internationalist allies had warned the nation of the dangers of a growing acceptance of violence as the most efficacious means of resolving personal or national difficulties. As the battle against the war and its attendant horrors lengthened and escalated, new, hitherto less obvious, antagonists emerged. A number of Friends, including women, began, for the first time, to discover an inexorable connection between the war and the social and economic order that had spawned it; others, especially women, came to associate the origins and prolongation of the war with the same principles of force and domination which had kept females in a state of perpetual subjection. For them, feminism and pacifism became inseparable weapons in the struggle for human emancipation. As Helena M. Swanwick of the Women's International League noted in *The Ploughshare*: 'the war has revealed to many anti-suffragists that their political philosophy was precisely the doctrine which . . . all . . . execrate as Prussianism'.[18]

During the course of the Great War, a number of Friends added capitalism and the suppression of women to the list of moral, and mortal, enemies to both human progress and the establishment of God's kingdom on earth. After 1916, the thrust of Quaker pacifist, socialist, and feminist activity was to a considerable extent directed by radicalized female Friends. The focus of much of this activity was the British State's illegitimate use of power to suppress opposition to its reactionary policies. As one Anglican observer at the Adjourned Yearly Meeting in February 1916 noted: 'there were . . . [those] who looked upon the State as an alien, anti-social, and certainly anti-religious organization, leagued with all the powers of evil . . . [and] antagonistic to the efforts of those seeking to establish the Kingdom of God.'[19]

[18] H. M. Swanwick, 'The World After the War . . . Franchise Reform', *PS*, I/9 n.s., Oct. 1916, 278. Also see Jo Vellacott's 'Introduction' to *Militarism versus Feminism: Writings on Women and War*, edited by Vellacott and Margaret Kamester (London 1987), 1–34 for a discussion of the view that the historical relationship between militarism and misogynism made pacifism a necessary aspect of the feminist struggle.

[19] 'The Adjourned Yearly Meeting: A Churchman's Impressions', *PS*, n.s. 1/1 (Feb. 1916), 41.

The association of female emancipation with the triumph of absolute pacifism over the militarist State as well as the victory of democratic socialism over capitalist materialism is reflected in one women's expectations after attending London Yearly Meeting in 1916: 'the Society... is about to be called again to renew and widen its peace testimony, its Social message, its attitude to (and of) womanhood... After this war the triple Labour, Peace and Women's movement... will surely find Friends concentrating their all to the task of human emancipation.'[20] This exalted vision was about to be put to the test.

Shortly after the appointment of the Young Men's Service Committee a separate Women's Service Committee was also created, although, at the time, it seemed merely the traditional afterthought to maintain the appearance of female inclusion in what many assumed to be primarily a male activity. In the first year of its existence, the Women's Committee, however strong its resolution to support the men in resisting conscription, was given little to do.[21] After the passage of the Military Service Acts, the Women's Service Committee, seeking to expand its role, prepared a Minute outlining some 'practical points in which we felt we might be of use to the Men's Service Committee'. Several women who were already working for the Men's Committee, including Henrietta Thomas and Edith Ellis, offered to take on 'more responsibility' for the FSC's operations.[22] When the actual imposition of conscription in the Spring of 1916 brought the inevitable thinning of the ranks of FSC men, female volunteers began to play a more central role in maintaining the Service Committee's affairs. Still, the status of these women remained that of auxiliary 'helpers' rather than co-equal partners in the struggle for peace. This situation became a source of considerable irritation and resentment among female Friends. One outspoken critic of continuing male dominance was Esther Bright Clothier (1873–1935), suffragist, educator, and a granddaughter of John Bright.

---

[20] L[ucy] F. M[orland], 'Impressions of Yearly Meeting: The Society in Unity and "Under Conviction" ', *PS.*, n.s. I/6 (July 1916), 169–70.

[21] *LYM, 1916*, 36 and John W. Graham, *Conscription and Conscience* (London 1922), 161 n. Also see *TF*, 28 May 1915, 417 for a statement of solidarity from young women Friends to young men.

[22] 'Minute to the Men's Service Committee', undated [Spring 1916], signed by Eileen Barratt Brown and Sylvia M. Aggs, FSC, *Minutes*, 1, 85.

In June of 1916 Clothier wrote to Robert Mennell, Chairman of the Men's Service Committee, expressing extreme displeasure at the fact that, despite the impending crisis, the chief recent activity of the Women's Committee had been to 'sit in Lucy Gardner's house praying to God for concerns'.

I don't think it quite sound that it [the FSC] should be a Com[mitt]ee of men only; I think in Friends' things we ought not to exclude either sex... tho' I am quite willing to admit women Friends at present are in a poor and backward way. Still, it is just this kind of treatment that keeps them so... After all, the work the Friends Service Com[mitt]ee is doing is the great work of Friends at present and women have to share in the blessing that comes in such work—I am sick of being told Conscription is a man's question—it isn't—and I know you and probably all the Service Com[mitt]ee would agree.[23]

Within a month of this challenge, despite some lingering hesitation among the men, Robert Mennell told Clothier: 'You will be happy to know that we are inviting the Mens and Womens Service Committees in future to meet as one Committee—an entirely original suggestion of mine!'[24] The Friends Service Committee ceased to be gender exclusive just in time. As more and more male Friends were consigned to prison or detention camps, Quaker women took an increasingly large and ultimately indispensable role in keeping their Society in the forefront of the struggle against conscription and the war.[25]

The presence of women on the Service Committee did not alter the policy of non-co-operation to which the FSC had determined to adhere. On the contrary, the women seemed to sharpen and harden the Committee's resolve to maintain a hard line against the

[23] Esther Bright Clothier to Robert O. Mennell, 11 and 20 June 1916, FSC Files, LSF. Also see Kennedy, 'Quaker Renaissance', 261–2.

[24] Mennell to Clothier, 13 July 1916, FSC Files and FSC *Minutes*, 1, 85. Also see Clothier to Mennell, 16 & 20 June 1916 and Mennell to Clothier, 19 June 1916, ibid., LSF. *LYM, 1917*, 170 lists only thirteen female members, including Esther Bright Clothier, among the thirty-six members of the Service Committee, but by early 1917 most of the Committee's male members were in prison or some other type of detention.

[25] For consideration of the wartime activities of female Friends see Thomas C. Kennedy, 'Quaker Women and the Pacifist Impulse in Britain, 1900–1920', in *The Pacifist Impulse in Historical Perspective*, a *Festschrift* for Professor Peter B. Brock, edited by Harvey Dyck (Toronto 1996), 182–206.

Government and against the pliancy of Friends who seemed willing to compromise. Late in 1916, for example, as older and influential Friends were attempting to strike some bargain with the authorities for a form of alternative service that would bring about the release of imprisoned Quakers and prevent further detention of others,[26] Edith J. Wilson, who had become one of FSC's most active volunteers, addressed the question of Quakers and alternative service in an article for *The Ploughshare*.[27] Although it was, Wilson said, quite natural for older male Friends to try to work out some means by which younger members could avoid both the spiritual inconsistency of military service and the physical unpleasantness of prison, such activities were unacceptable. Once individuals determined to place their religious convictions before the commands of a State engaged, as they believed, in an evil enterprise, such individuals, Wilson said, were no longer at liberty to compromise with that State and thereby, at least implicitly, to condone its evil actions. By arranging schemes for special treatment, older Friends were, Wilson believed, tempting the Quaker conscientious objector to strike a 'bargain with a thing he regards as essentially evil', and, in effect, to become a defector from the battle against militarism. 'It is a tragedy of advancing years that wealth, and honours, and position, and comfort, gain such a hold upon us that it becomes well-neigh impossible to believe that young men are willing to sacrifice all these things, and life itself, in the pure joy of a quest for truth.'[28]

In concert with the absolutist faction of the FSC, Edith Wilson consistently maintained that any attempt by Quakers to gain exemption or concessions from the Government was 'an acknowledgment that the laws of God are not really applicable in the Kingdoms of this world, and therefore it is no use trying to make them universal... it [is] ... an unconscious yielding to the temptation to use a religious conviction as a plea for a political concession rather than as an inspiration to service and to sacrifice.'[29]

Jo Vellacott has noted that female members of the Friends' Service Committee, including Edith Wilson and the FSC's acting

---

[26] See Chapter 9 above.

[27] ' "Alternative Service": Friends and a Perplexing Problem', *PS*, 1/7 n.s. (Aug. 1916), 203–4.

[28] Wilson, ' "Alternative Service" ', 204–5.

[29] Edith J. Wilson, 'Law-Abiding Citizens', *PS*, 11/2 n.s. (March 1917), 62–3.

chair Edith Ellis, generally tended to take a hard and even intolerant position with respect to what constituted legitimate or faithful
conscientious objection. Wilson, Ellis, and other female hardliners
not only insisted that 'true' COs should refuse any form of alternative to military service and accept imprisonment as the logical
result of their stand but also rejected any attempts to mitigate the
sufferings of those, non-Quaker as well as Quaker, who had been
imprisoned.[30] This stand brought few new recruits into the radical
camp; indeed, the FSC's apparent inflexibility was severely criticized even by those who had heretofore been its closest allies.
Bertrand Russell, as Acting Chairman of the No-Conscription
Fellowship, admonished Ellis and the Service Committee for
maintaining a stand which seemed to ignore the 'duty to human
kindness' and to smack of 'the cruelty of fanaticism which is the
very spirit that supports the war'.[31]

Edith Ellis remained unmoved even in the face of such blunt
criticism from a formidable ally.[32] Many, including fellow Quakers,
thought the FSC's refusal to work on behalf of imprisoned COs
smacked of obdurate self-righteousness. Still, if theirs was not an
attractive stance, it accurately reflected their radical vision of the
struggle against the Government and the war as a confrontation
between the forces of good and evil; certainly, it made Quaker
militants far more troublesome to the powers that be than their
minuscule numbers would seem to have warranted. Their faith in
the righteousness of the struggle most assuredly gave Quaker
absolutists the resolve to carry on, but so too did what they saw
as the impeccable logic of their decision not to compromise.

Another aspect of the contribution of Quaker women to the
anti-war struggle was outlined by Dorothy Richardson. The war,
Richardson concluded, had played into the hands of radical feminists 'by demonstrating the social efficiency of women and by
giving unprecedented urgency to the problems of women in

---

[30] See Vellacott, *Russell and the Pacifists*, 196–7 and private information. Also see Kennedy, 'Fighting About Peace', 16–18.

[31] Bertrand Russell to Edith Ellis, 11 Sept. 1917 and Ellis to Russell, 22 Sept. 1917, FSC
Files, LSF. For the same argument earlier advanced by a female Quaker, see E[dith]
J. B[igland], 'Our Own Ruthlessness: A Warning That We Need', *PS*, 1/8 n.s. (Sept.
1916), 232.

[32] See Ellis to Russell, 22 Sept 1917, quoting Barry Brown's assertion that the FSC had
always encouraged 'the human touch' and 'personal sympathy' in its approach, FSC
Files, LSF.

industry'.[33] In the immediate future, she said, women needed to exploit this situation by building

> their power upon the basis of industrial organisation . . . [advancing] in a body, boldly and consciously, taking their old rank as producers . . . [and] doing the world's housekeeping in the world . . . The world must become a home. In it women will pursue socially valuable careers, responsible to the community for an economic status clear of sex and . . . set free from their dependence upon a single masculine pocket for everything they desire . . . .

Only by doing away with 'THE GREAT DOMESTIC CANT', Richardson concluded, would women 'find it possible to live a full life . . .'[34]

So, the urgency of the wartime crisis opened the way for some Quaker women to do things they might not otherwise have done and think thoughts that might not have otherwise occurred to them. In the longer range, however, after the crisis of the war abated and female citizens voted in national elections for the first time, the Society of Friends, if it did not revert to pre-war form, certainly adopted a less than revolutionary approach to the problems of the social order, including the question of female equality. To be sure, during the first world-wide Conference of All-Friends, which met in London in 1920,[35] the point was made that the 'low estate of women has been shown to be always the direct fruit of warfare and a militant society' and that, by way of contrast, Quakers had from the beginning 'taken seriously the view that in Christ Jesus there is neither male or female' and, thus, they had a 'message and approach to the world that is peculiarly modern and timely'.[36] But, in the intervening decades, some female Friends

---

[33] Dorothy M. Richardson, 'The Reality of Feminism', *PS*, II/8 (Sept. 1917), 241–6.
[34] Ibid.
[35] See *All Friends Conference, Official Report* (Hereafter *AFC, Official Report*) (London [1920]) and Thomas C. Kennedy, 'Why Did Friends Resist? The War, the Peace Testimony and the All Friends Conference of 1920', *Peace and Change*, 14/4 (October 1989), 355–71.
[36] Quotes from Report of Commission VII ('The International Service of Friends'), Henry T. Hodgkin, 'The Quaker Movement and the Modern World', 7 and Report of Commission III (Personal Life and Society), 'Introduction', 5, in *The Peace Testimony of the Society of Friends: Reports of Commissions issued by the Committee of the Peace Conference of All Friends* (London [1920])

have felt that the practical results of such pious phases were less than fully realized.[37]

THE WHITE-HOT WAR

Yea, *this* is the white-hot war!.... Who is on the Lord's side?...[in] the greatest, the noblest, the godliest fight man has ever yet put up...The Socialist Movement aims at sweeping away the competition for existence and replacing it by the Christian method of organised co-operation...To this holy war is the Church called.... Have you enlisted in the New Army? Are you doing your bit?

Dr Alfred Salter *The Ploughshare*, Feb. 1916.

In June 1921 *The Constructive Quarterly*, an Oxford-based 'Journal of the Faith, Work and Thought of Christendom', reported that British Quakerism, long thought of as 'an embodiment of middle class virtues', had, as a result of the Great War, awakened 'from its "dogmatic slumbers" in the matter of the industrial system' and undergone a 'silent revolution' which reflected 'not only a widespread discontent with the old social order but an intense mental (and spiritual) activity in planning for a new one'. The chief catalyst for this dramatic metamorphosis, the article said, was a special Quaker Committee on War and the Social Order. Created in a super-heated wartime atmosphere and heavily laced with members of the Socialist Quaker Society, this Committee, according to the *Constructive Quarterly*, had proposed that London Yearly Meeting endorse a radical social and political critique which portrayed an intimate relationship between the capitalist economic system and the modern warrior State and called for drastic material and spiritual modifications of that system and that State.[38]

Christopher Hill has made the point that 'a Quaker of the early 1650s had far more in common with a Leveller, a Digger or a

---

[37] When Yearly Meeting met at Exeter in 1986, the topic for the annual Swarthmore Lecture was the history and role of Quaker women. This 'lecture' took the form of a collective and radical feminist critique of the Society's failure to measure up, in either the present or in past generations, to George Fox's admonition: 'The Lamb of God...is but one in all His males and females, sons and daughters, and they all are one in Christ, and Christ one in them all.'

[38] Herbert H. Horwill, 'A Quaker Socialist Movement', *The Constructive Quarterly*, IX/2 (June 1921), 318–31, *passim*.

Ranter than a modern member of the Society of Friends'.[39] This is undoubtedly true. But in response to the cataclysmic events of the Great War, a small body of early twentieth-century Friends concocted, like their spiritual ancestors, a scheme of non-violent insurgency for transforming both human society and the human spirit. With a view to achieving victory for the new Children of Light over the dark forces of militarism and greed, militantly pacifist Friends, closely connected to absolutist conscientious objectors in both the Friends Service Committee and the No-Conscription Fellowship, were able, for a time, to cajole, push, frighten, or shame the leaders of their eminently middle-class Society toward a political and social agenda reminiscent of the millenarian vision of George Fox and his compatriots during the 1650s.

When the war began, *The Ploughshare*, organ of the Socialist Quaker Society, took a position that seemed almost smug not only in its 'we told you so' demeanour (the journal had warned from its first issue in 1912 that the prolongation of the capitalist system would 'inevitably' bring war) but also with the fact that the war crisis would force capitalist/imperialist Governments to enact numerous collectivist measures for more efficient prosecution of the war.[40] The war, as seen by the SQS, was being fought as 'part of a general struggle to *make profit* out of the industry necessary to maintain life' and could only be ended by those who, like the first Friends, were not averse to turning the world upside down.[41]

While the Socialist Quaker Society was primed for action in what one member called 'the White-hot War' of Haves against Have-nots, the wartime focus of its more moderate counterpart the Friends Social Union was the 'wide-spread desire to grapple with social conditions ... especially ... the relationship between the War & the Social Order'.[42] By February 1915, the Executive Council of the FSU had appointed a special committee charged with introdu-

---

[39] Hill, *World Turned Upside Down*, 14.

[40] *TP*, 7 August 1914, 575–6 and *PS*, 8 (August 1914), 87–96 *passim* and 'War's Alarm', 1 (Nov. 1912), 11–12. Also see 'The Roots of War', ibid., 4 (August 1913), 47–50.

[41] 'The War, the Under-War and the Class War', *PS*, 10 (Feb. 1915), 126 and 'Friends Settlement at Reigate', ibid., 7 (May 1914), 84. Emphasis in original.

[42] The relationship between the war and the social order was first addressed by members of the SQS at the Llandudno Conference in September 1914; see *Memorandum for The Llandudno Conference*, 23–30 September 1914, Temp MSS 355, Box VIII/84, LSF and the Group Report, 'War and the Social Order', in *Friends and the War*, 126–28.

cing to 'respective Q[uarterly] M[eeting]s a minute urging Friends to consider the relations between the War and the prevailing Social Condition'.[43] Believing that Quakerism might 'be called to a great experiment in social reconstruction' which would provide 'the opportunity of making a great step forward towards the realisation of the Kingdom of God on Earth', the FSU's Council also moved to bring the question of building this new social order to the attention of Yearly Meeting.[44]

When the FSU presented its report to the Yearly Meeting in May 1915, that body was sufficiently impressed to call for the appointment of a committee 'to investigate what connection there is between war and the social order ... and to consult with those Friends who have been led, owing to the war, to ... a personal readjustment of their way of life'.[45] The resulting War and the Social Order Committee (WSOC) had thirty-six members (twenty-five men, eleven women), half of whom were drawn from the Councils of either the FSU (seven members) or the SQS (eleven members, including the co-editors of *The Ploughshare*, William Loftus Hare and Hubert Peet). The Committee's membership would change and grow during the course of the war, but, in whatever guise, the WSOC proved to be 'the most lively London Committee' and, in most ways, the most radical as well.[46]

During the first few months of its existence, the activities of the War and Social Order Committee seemed to reflect the moderate influence of the Friends Social Union. Pamphlets on social questions were published and Study Circles were planned to encourage Friends 'to dedicate ourselves to a better way of life, and to a Christ-like endeavour, no matter at what sacrifice ...'.[47] Of course, during the early stages of the war the matter of sacrifice by British Quakers was really a moot question. Unless male Friends of military age abandoned the peace testimony and enlisted in the forces or joined the Friends' Ambulance Unit or War Victims' Relief Committee, Quakers, however much they deplored the war,

---

[43] FSU, *Minutes*, 11 Feb. 1915, FSU/3, LSF.
[44] FSU, *Annual Report*, 1914–15, 4, 5–8.
[45] FSU, *Minutes*, 9 June 1915, quoting from Minute 65 of LYM, FSU/3, LSF.
[46] *LYM, 1915*, 274–75. The War and the Social Order Committee was reappointed each year by Yearly Meeting. The quotation is from a letter of Roger C. Wilson (1906–92), Clerk of London Yearly Meeting in the mid-1970s, to the author, 6 August 1985.
[47] FSU *Minutes*, 9 June, 7 July and 30 Nov. 1915, FSU/3, LSF.

could continue to live much as they had before it began. They were loyal, hard-working, law-abiding citizens; few of them had the sort of German names that might elicit attacks by their neighbours and while they could, as some did, give public speeches or write letters to the press condemning the conflict as a monstrous denial of Christian principles, even then they were not likely to be visited by the police enforcing the more odious provisions of the Defence of the Realm Acts.

However, as illustrated above, with the passage of the Military Services Acts, Friends had to choose whether to make some accommodation with the State or to continue unsullied adherence to their traditional peace testimony regardless of what the authorities might do to them. The extraordinary Adjourned Yearly Meeting of late January 1916 decided upon an official policy of resistance to conscription and non-co-operation with the war effort. Thus, pacifist Friends were placed into a position *vis-à-vis* the Government not unlike that of their ancestors during the Restoration when the imposition of the Quaker and Conventicle Acts threatened the free exercise of their faith.

While some Friends were uneasy about this adversarial relationship, the radical socialists of the SQS celebrated the opportunity to expose the war as a conspiracy to preserve capitalism by sacrificing the lives and fortunes of the working classes. From February 1916 the Socialist Quaker Society trumpeted its struggle against the capitalist war machine in an enlarged and expanded version of *The Ploughshare*, which the editor of one radical American journal called 'a beautifully printed, admirably written, [and] very impressive paper'.[48]

The first issue of the new series of *The Ploughshare* depicted anti-war socialists, representing the interests of all humanity, as confronting 'the Real Armageddon . . . not a war *between* the Kingdoms of the earth but *against* them all: We believe that the greatest of all issues—the Armageddon issues—are becoming clearer than they have been for many a long day, and they who perceive them will infallibly fight on the right side in all the lesser wars here below.'[49]

---

[48] Floyd Dell, editor of the Marxist paper, *Masses* (New York), quoted in *PS*, I/6, July 1916, 196. Monetary support for the enlarged version of the SQS paper was provided by anonymous anti-war Friends.

[49] 'Commentary: The Seven Wars', *PS*, I/1, Feb. 1916, 3.

Who were these Friends pronouncing an apocalyptic vision in hopes of moving their Society to reaffirm its radical roots and once again to become Children of the Light righteously struggling against the dark forces that blocked the way to the realization of the Kingdom of God on earth? In the main they were members of the Socialist Quaker Society, which in September 1916 could claim all of seventy-five male and fifty-two female members. The males were usually under 40 and middle class, with rather better educations than most Quakers. Nearly all were of military age but most would have eschewed any relationship between their vulnerability to military service and their militant social and political opinions. SQS women tended to be slightly older than their male counterparts, although just as solidly middle class; many were veterans of the pre-war suffragist movement. As was the case with the Friends Service Committee, female members of the SQS came increasingly to the fore after a considerable number of their male counterparts were arrested and detained as conscientious objectors.

How, then, might the radical vision of this tiny Socialist Quaker Society be effectively transmitted to London Yearly Meeting and through Yearly Meeting to the inarticulate masses seeking spiritual and material relief from capitalist-induced poverty and war? The most obvious agency for spreading their message to the Society was the War and Social Order Committee. After the imposition of conscription, socialist members of the WSOC insisted that any Quaker scheme for transforming the moral and social order of British society must include the dissolution of the competitive capitalist system which was, in their view, the handmaiden of all wars and strife. The effect of this tiny but doggedly insistent minority on wartime developments within London Yearly Meeting was not insignificant. Jonathan Edward Hodgkin (1875–1953) may serve as a case in point. Scion of an old and weighty Quaker family, a consulting engineer and successful businessman, J. E. Hodgkin, who would eventually serve as chairman of sixteen companies and as a director of four others, seemed an unlikely social revolutionary. Yet during his tenure as Chairman of the War and the Social Order Committee, Hodgkin became the chief advocate for many of the radical proposals advanced by socialist members of the WSOC.[50]

---

[50] J. E. Hodgkin (1875–1953), a brother of Henry T. Hodgkin, was one of the last English Friends recorded as a minister (1907) as well as a town councillor in Darlington and a

Early in 1916, J. E. Hodgkin set out his vision of the Committee's objectives for readers of *The Ploughshare*:

We feel that . . . the present social system has as its outcome a state of international . . . warfare. It is to a new way of Life that men are looking, if we can embody in practical life an example of the testimony we hold, not only *against* all war, but for a new World Order, we shall surely have made an effective contribution to our day and generation.[51]

The Ploughshare maintained that because the capitalist warrior State was, by its very nature, 'antagonistic to the efforts of those seeking to establish the Kingdom of God', winning the sort of legacy Hodgkin envisioned would require direct confrontation. The front-line fighters coming to 'grips with present-day evils' were young men and women willing 'to suffer in an unpopular cause'; the inspiration for their sacrifices would be 'those early Quakers who did and dared everything for the right to express the truth which was working through them. . . . The days of the Apostles and the primitive Quakers are with us once again,' one Friend noted. For socialist Quakers, at least, the role model was less George Fox than Gerard Winstanley who, 'whilst voicing the religious views of Friends, had a practical expression . . . far beyond anything of which . . . our forefathers dreamed'.[52]

When the War and the Social Order Committee met in April 1916 at Jordans in Buckinghamshire, the burial place of William Penn, to prepare its first report to Yearly Meeting, the struggle against conscription had barely begun, but socialist members of the Committee sounded an aggressive tone, pressing for a general endorsement of their view that 'Universal Brotherhood cannot be established under the present competitive system of industry'. Many Friends believed that the Committee's ensuing report, entitled *Whence Come Wars?*, went a considerable way towards

---

magistrate on the Durham County Bench. The *DQB* describes him as a large man, mentally and physically, with a 'dominating personality, impatient of opposition and not always quick to understand any point of view but his own'.

[51] J. E. Hodgkin, 'War and Social Order Committee', *PS*, 1/1, Feb. 1916, 33–4. Also see *Minutes, WSOC*, 3 Feb. 1916 written by Hodgkin and stressing the need 'to look at the whole question of our social relationship in light of our testimony against *all* war'.

[52] *PS*, 1/2, March 1916, 40–2, 52–4; 1/3, April 1916, 99; 1/4, May 1916, 105; and 1/8, Sept. 1916, 237.

fulfilling this SQS objective, although not all WSOC members accepted 'the root thesis that competition is itself an evil thing...' Still, in addressing what many believed to be the most important Yearly Meeting in the history of Quakerism, Hodgkin, as Committee spokesman, posed the question: 'Is the Society... content to remain a highly respected body of spiritual epicures, or is it realising, as in the stirring days of its early history, that it has a message for the world which must be given, cost what it may?'[53]

Yearly Meeting provided no definitive answers to J. E. Hodgkin's searching inquiry. *Whence Come Wars?* was received with thanks and discussed at length but finally acknowledged only as 'the first stage' of the Committee's work. Some Friends were disappointed at the indeterminate nature of Yearly Meeting's deliberations on the relationship between War and the Social Order; others were impressed with what they perceived to be a sense of urgency 'to work for and with their brothers for a *new* social order'; still others left Yearly Meeting 'unsettled, shaken... [that] one of Yearly Meeting's own committee's was asking whether this comfortably middle-class Society... was either relevant or useful' if it did not rise to a new level of resistance.[54] For its part, *The Ploughshare* was pleased that the WSOC had 'directed attention to the theoretical and historical efforts of a more or less revolutionary kind in the realm of industry and the social order'. At the same time, the paper warned that: 'The Banks, the Tribunals, the Press, the Army and the Churches are all against us, and the people are still unawake to the truth that we wish to tell them.'[55]

Some Quakers who were, in the deepening crisis, rediscovering their radical sectarian roots might indeed begin to see their confrontation with the Government as a long-awaited revival of the struggle between the forces of darkness and Children of the Light. For them at least, the eschatological implications of this vision were reflected in the perception of one Friend who saw Yearly Meeting as 'actually engaged in the age-long battle with "forces that control

---

[53] *PS*, 1/4, May 1916, 106, 128 and 1/9, Oct. 1916, 290–1.
[54] M[orland], 'Impressions of Yearly Meeting', 168–70 and Tucker, 'English Quakers and World War I', 141–2.
[55] ' "War and the Social Order": A Study of the Committee's Report', *PS*, I/5, June 1916, 146–8.

and govern this dark world—the spiritual hosts of evil arrayed against us in heavenly warfare" '.[56]

Too much can be made of this apocalyptic vision. As would soon become obvious, it represented nothing like a majority response among Quakers. Still, most members of the Socialist Quaker Society looked upon socialism as a faith within a faith whose enduring principles included the necessity for overthrowing those dark forces of Mammon which continued to advocate and advance wars and strife for the sake of profits and power.[57] As more and more Quaker and socialist war resisters were arrested and incarcerated, *The Ploughshare* evoked the image of capitalist warmongers as the worshippers of the 'mighty giant Mammon-Moloch, whose food is gold and whose drink is blood'. For socialist Friends, conscription was not just an attack on freedom of conscience but an attempt to forge the final link in the chain with which capitalism had bound the working classes and would eventually shackle all who resisted its rapacious grasp. They perceived of themselves, as 'conscientious objectors to our whole social system, and our whole life...must be that of Christian revolutionaries'.[58]

While the movement to radical or revolutionary solutions was a distinctly minority crusade representing the cutting edge of left-wing Quaker political and social opinion, it also reflected, among Quakers of military age, liberalism's impending fall from grace as the political agency for creating the Kingdom of God on Earth. Redrawing the ideological boundary so as to exclude private ownership for profit (self-help had been effectively expelled by the New Liberalism), socialist members of the War and the Social Order Committee viewed all props of the old order as irredeemably compromised. The capitalistic Warfare State had, with the support of most Churches and other social institutions, appropriated for itself the accoutrements of traditional morality and proceeded to make a mockery of them. It was beyond salvation.

The next opportunity for the War and Social Order Committee to attempt to establish new ground rules for Quaker social action was a four-day Conference on 'Friends and the Social Order' held

[56] M[orland], 'Impressions of Yearly Meeting', Ibid. 169–70.
[57] 'Commentary', ibid. 1/9, Oct. 1916, 261.
[58] 'Christian Revolutionaries', ibid. 1/7, Aug. 1916, 227.

in London during October 1916. As J. E. Hodgkin noted in his introduction to *Facing the Facts*, the printed proceedings of the Conference, this gathering marked the first time British Quakerism had officially set itself 'to consider the implications of the Christian testimony in relation to the far too easily accepted social conditions in which we live'.[59] Hodgkin believed that, on account of the war, the collective conscience of their religious Society had been, in the parlance of early Friends, 'tendered', and that while in this spiritually sensitive condition Quakerism might expiate 'the depths of humiliation and repentance for a past . . . in which our witness has been hopelessly compromised by our ready acceptance of the standards and ethics of the non-Christian world'.[60]

Hodgkin may have hoped that collective remorse and a tender conscience would help Friends achieve a strong consensus on social and economic concerns, but what actually transpired was considerably less auspicious. John William Graham's keynote address on 'War Spirit in the Social Order' might well have been delivered in 1906 for all its appreciation of altered circumstances. In the course of a long paean to good intentions, good works, free trade, and liberal moderation, Graham, much to the chagrin of Quaker socialists, issued two peremptory 'cautions'. First, he declared that '[W]ar and capitalism are different in character and require different treatment'; next, he announced that a graduated income tax would be 'Socialism enough to keep us all busy for some time to come'.[61]

In response to Graham's ringing defence of liberal principles and practices, *The Ploughshare*'s impatient editor, W. L. Hare, depicted the speaker as 'a matador . . . [come] to slay the bull . . . let loose in the ring' by the War and Social Order Committee. After that wild beast had been duly dispatched 'and buried in the presence of one solitary mourner and a host of sightseers', Hare noted, the Conference's pusillanimous programme committee decreed that there would be no further discussion of the foregoing proceedings. Hare

---

[59] J. E. Hodgkin, 'Introduction', *Facing the Facts: Being the Report of the Conference on The Society of Friends and the Social Order Held in London, 19–22 October 1916* (London [1916]), [8]. Also see Horwill, 'Quaker Socialist Movement', 320.

[60] Hodgkin, 'Our Complicity in Perpetuating Admitted Evils: Have We Faced It?', *Facing the Facts*, 34, 39–40.

[61] Graham, 'The War Spirit in the Social Order', ibid. 21 and *passim*.

was certainly not the only Friend upset by Graham's counsel of moderation, but the mandate of silence was simply a standard Quaker ploy for avoiding serious disputation within the fold. In fact, during the remaining days of the Conference an entire range of social and political issues were seriously debated. Still, *The Ploughshare* characterized the discussion as reflecting 'an excessive nervousness' and concluded that 'the Conference and the Society are not facing the facts but shirking them'.[62]

Most assuredly John William Graham marched to a different drummer than W. Loftus Hare and socialist members of the War and Social Order Committee. But who among these was in step with the majority of their fellow Quakers? Like most Friends, Graham was a sincere opponent of the war, but whatever horrors the terrible conflict might impose at home or abroad, he would not abandon the Liberalism of his youth. As Graham was a patriot, he sought to create circumstances wherein Quakers in wartime could serve both God and Mammon with rectitude and grace; as he was a Liberal, he worked to reform the social order to make it what it should have been before the war, not to create the Brave New World of socialist dreamers. And for all the displeasure this position caused the SQS and other radical Friends, Graham was probably in advance of the rank and file British Quaker with regard to social policy. Of course, ordinary Quakers were not, generally speaking, as ordinary folk. They tended to be comfortable and well-situated within the economic and social systems that the SQS seemed bent on casting into the outer darkness. Therefore, most Friends, hovering somewhere between bemusement and indignation, responded to radical statements at the War and the Social Order Conference as might be expected from any group of honest, earnest, affluent citizens. They opposed the war (or at least deplored the fact that it had to be fought) as a product of mankind's inability to see and embrace the Light, but most believed that labelling the capitalist system as the principal source of human suffering and sin was merely an obsessive fantasy. There had been wars long before the emergence of capitalism and even most anti-war Friends were not prepared to substitute economic propensities for spiritual weak-

---

[62] W. L. Hare, 'Friends and the Social Order', *PS*, 1/10, Nov. 1916, 297 and ' "Facing the Facts": The Report on the Conference on the Society of Friends and the Social Order', ibid., 11/2, March 1917, 60–1.

nesses as the chief causes of violence and strife. In their view, only realistic recognition of sin and humble submission to the Divine Will were sufficient guides for alternating and improving the human condition. This position was coherently summarized at the London Conference by Wilfrid Irwin (1858–1928) of Cockermouth, an employer of labour and former Council member of the Friends Social Union. Given the realities of human nature, said Irwin, war or no war, 'the best thing to do was to patch and improve the present system'.[63]

While young SQS firebrands might have audibly groaned at Wilfrid Irwin's words, his statement pointed up the problem of trying to achieve consensus in even so small a body as the Society of Friends in even so galvanizing a crisis as the Great War. In the end, the social radicals, like their allies the absolutist war resisters, listened, patiently or otherwise, to their less militant brethren and then proceeded to attempt, by hook or crook, to take control of the machinery of their religious Society for the purpose of making their point of view *the* Quaker position, however imperfectly it reflected any consensus among Friends. An editorial in *The Plough-share* summarized this position, noting that those who

shrink from swallowing the bitter pill of economic criticism... would ... rather put all this chaos down to the devil or the evil of man's nature ... [but] the evil system which issues ... inevitably and periodically in war has its roots in a false materialistic view of life ... we do not know how to change man's nature, but we do know how to change his economic system.[64]

So, even amidst the depressing prospect of a seemingly endless war, a growing list of imprisoned or interned conscientious objectors and the continuing refusal of many anti-war Friends to attach the tail of a radical social or economic agenda on to the spiritual principles of their peace testimony,[65] socialist Friends attempted to maintain the impetus of their anti-capitalist crusade. In the final

---

[63] *Facing the Facts*, 121.

[64] 'Economics, War and Philosophy', *PS*, 1/8, September 1916, 230.

[65] See, for example, Edith Ellis to R. O. Mennell, 12 Dec. 1916, 'FSC Correspondence', 1915/16, LSF in which Ellis, the virtual backbone of the FSC's struggle against conscription during the final two years of the war, complained that Dr Henrietta Thomas, a member of

days of 1916, *The Ploughshare* took pains to remind members of the War and Social Order Committee, and Friends in general, of the link between the contemporary message of Quaker socialists and the spiritual heritage of their Society. As early Friends had employed the weapons of faith against an unrighteous state to preserve the precious gift of religious liberty, so latter-day Quakers were bound to enlist as non-violent fighters in the decisive struggle for universal peace and human dignity. Drawing upon both 'Revelations' and Greek mythology, W. L. Hare painted a picture of the ultimate Quaker warrior, 'the Armageddon man', who when the world refused to embrace his righteous cause, 'turns to Heaven, where are the sources of a higher rightness than any here below; there he takes his stand armed, with weapons that are not carnal . . . a mystic trumpeter is calling to the spiritual Armageddon, a mighty battle between the old Titans who have ruled us and the new Gods we shall yet adore.'[66]

Three months after this pronouncement, one of the old Titans toppled from the Russian throne. When Yearly Meeting gathered in May 1917, Quaker socialists, basking in the still-inspiring glow of the first Russian Revolution and its Petrograd Formula of 'no annexations and no indemnities', had reason to be confident that their Society might at last be willing to take a bold step in the direction of non-violent social transformation. For one thing, the Friends' Social Union had been virtually merged into the War and Social Order Committee. Although the FSU maintained a vestigial existence for fear that the WSOC 'might become a mere annexe of the Quaker Socialist Society [sic] . . . ', members of the SQS could only have been pleased to see the lingering dregs of liberal reformism being cast aside in the wake of a more realistic assessment of social and economic ills.[67] Socialist members of the WSOC also believed that, despite some criticism of the Committee's work, 'there is a large & growing body of awakened seekers' who were

---

both the FSC and the WSOC, was preaching State Socialism 'which to some of us seems an unFriendly point of view'.

[66] 'The Tragedy of Right Against Right', *PS*, I/11 Dec. 1916, 325.

[67] *Minutes, WSOC*, 2–5 Feb. and 8–9 June 1917; [A. H. Bayes], Act. Sec., FSU, to W. H. Sturge, n.d. [May–June 1917]; and W. H. Sturge to FSU Council, 9 June 1917, FSU 3/4. About £10 was left in the FSU's Treasury to allow for the revival of the Union 'in case the War and Social Order Committee should be discharged, or . . . the policy of the Committee should widely diverge from the objects for which the Friends Social Union was founded'.

prepared to follow their lead.[68] But despite *The Ploughshare*'s exhortations that Yearly Meeting should 'cross the Rubicon of doubt and indecision', and strike at the roots of war by declaring for ' "a really new world" of economic relationships', no decisive pronouncements on social policy were forthcoming.[69]

Disappointed Quaker socialists wanted to believe that Yearly Meeting had failed to join the advanced guard in the march toward a new social order because most Friends had not really heard the call to spiritual combat. On the other hand, no one who attended the famous Leeds Conference held shortly after Yearly Meeting could have missed that call. Organized by British enthusiasts for the Russian Revolution and attended by most Quaker socialists who were not yet imprisoned as conscientious objectors, the delegates at Leeds resolved to work for an end to capitalism and militarism by establishing Workers' and Soldiers' Councils on the Soviet model throughout Great Britain.[70]

When the War and Social Order Committee met immediately following the Leeds Conference, its now dominant socialist faction sought to raise the tone of revolutionary rhetoric. Barry Brown, who had already suffered repeated imprisonment for anti-war activities, noted that while the workers and soldiers councils did not in themselves mean revolution: 'Nothing short of Revolution, in the best sense of the word, would bring the better day for which we long.' Other WSOC members spoke of the increasingly obvious relationship between the labour movement's idea of 'Co-operative Commonwealth & [the] Quaker ideal of the "Kingdom of God" '.

In the light of the movement towards social revolution exemplified at the recent conference in Leeds, we have again considered our duty... in relation to both parties in the struggle between Capital & Labour as well as to our own Society. We feel that we have still work to do in clearing up and adjusting our personal attitude before we can make our right contribution to the present situation.[71]

---

[68] *Minutes, WSOC*, 2–5 Feb. 1917.

[69] 'Is Christian Civilization Possible?', *PS*, 11/5, June 1917, 133–6.

[70] *What Happened at Leeds* was a pamphlet published by the Council of Workers' and Soldiers' Delegates (London 1917). Also see White, 'Soviets in Britain', 167–93.

[71] *Minutes, WSOC*, 8–9 June 1917.

Noting, with chagrin, the Society of Friends' past connections with the sort of philanthropic ventures that had allowed Quakers to expect and receive obsequious deference from the working-class recipients of Friendly largess, socialist Quakers called, in the spirit of Leeds, for the incorporation of more working-class members into their Committee. As one speaker noted, 'the right revolution' would require doing away with the idea of a 'servile class'. Dr Henrietta Thomas added that closer Quaker connections with the working-classes would better accommodate future revolutionary mandates 'to renounce possessions willingly when demanded by revolution and so obviate a bloody struggle'.[72]

The level of rhetorical bravado continued to rise throughout the summer of 1917. Indeed, when War and Social Order Committee met at Letchworth in September, Britain was in the early stages of what has been called the 'only mass agitation to halt the European conflict... that verged on revolutionary resistance to the government'.[73] At Letchworth William C. Anderson, an MP for the the Independent Labour Party, reminded the Committee that while 'revolutionary feeling was growing in the country... the people still endured oppression far too patiently'. A socialist member of the WSOC took up this theme, nothing that 'our ideals should be to so re-arrange control of industry that every worker should enjoy the experience... of feeling his fingers on the pulse of the world'. Moved perhaps by such oratorical flourishes, the Committee approved a *Minute* which, among other things, called upon Friends 'to do their utmost to promote... the transfer of "capital" from private to public control'.[74]

This was heady stuff. But for all the earnest passion in such pronouncements, there was about them the same ring of unreality as pervaded the columns of *The Ploughshare*. Suspended between deepening discouragement over a war that could not be drowned even in its own blood and inspirational reports of an emerging Bolshevik socialist republic, the SQS's newspaper concluded that 'nothing short of revolution... can save the world', adding, omi-

---

[72] Ibid. 20–22 July 1917.

[73] Howard Weinroth, 'The Dilemma of British Socialists during the Great War: Revolutionary Peace or Pacifist Reconstruction', in *Doves and Diplomats*, edited by Soloman Wank (Westport, Conn. 1978), 193–4. Also see Hinton, *Protests and Visions*, 261–7.

[74] *Minutes*, WSOC, 7–10 September 1917.

nously, that the successful resolution such a global upheaval would require 'stern work'.[75]

Sterner, certainly, than Quakers, socialist or otherwise, were likely to accept. When the War and Social Order Committee met at Manchester early in 1918, the Bolshevik Revolution had already begun to reveal its penchant for bloody-minded repression. The crucial episode at this gathering was the presentation of a paper on 'Quakerism and Capitalism' by J. Walton Newbold (1888–1943), an SQS member who would, after leaving Friends, become Britain's first Communist MP.[76] The central theme of Newbold's address was a proposal to give trade unions (the producers) rather than consumers (the people) control over economic policy in the postwar socialist State he envisioned. His audience, which consisted of only thirty of the WSOC's eighty-two members, was not convinced. Perhaps attendance at Manchester was low because so many of the WSOC's younger, and presumably more radical, male members had been imprisoned or interned as COs. In any case, the minority who did attend entirely repudiated Newbold's undemocratic proposition. Furthermore, the Committee also agreed that the so-called 'Letchworth Minute' on transferring capital from private to public hands should not, in future, be considered an accurate expression of the WSOC's position.[77] In the meantime, the news from the Front, from CO prison cells and from Russia could scarcely have been more gloomy. Still, *The Ploughshare*, having, in the interim, become resolutely anti-Bolshevik, soldiered on in its mission to convince the Society of Friends 'to stand for the economic truth that modern wars are stages in the struggle for the economic hegemony of the

---

[75] 'On Plough', *PS*, 11/10, Nov. 1917, 287.

[76] In his *Personal History*, 37, A. J. P. Taylor recalled Newbold as 'the English Lenin, at any rate in his own eyes', and remembered his disappointment upon meeting Newbold to discover that he was 'fat with a sickly complexion like a great slug'. A birthright Friend, Newbold resigned from the Society after adopting Communism but returned to Quakerism in 1932 when he supported Ramsay McDonald's National Government and, finally, resigned again as a militant supporter of Winston Churchill and the Second World War. See *The Friend*, 24 Feb. 1943, 7.

[77] *Minutes, WSOC*, 4–7 January 1918. Also see Tucker, 'Quakers and World War I', 253–6 for an account of a Quaker-sponsored Conference of Employers in April 1918 called by J. E. Hodgkin, at the behest of Arnold S. Rowntree, MP to consider employers' role in reshaping a new social order. Not surprisingly, its recommendations, later discussed by Yearly Meeting, were mild and unthreatening to the existing order.

world... and... [to] generate from the clouds flashes of lightning to startle... the people who walk in darkness'.[78]

Some Friends may indeed have been startled when in May 1918, after much serious lobbying by social activists in the Quaker press,[79] London Yearly Meeting accepted the War and Social Order Committee's list of eight 'Foundations of a True Social Order' as the blueprint for post-war Quaker social policy.[80] These Foundations might usefully be compared to the 'four pillars' of a new social order envisioned by the Labour Party Conference held shortly after Yearly Meeting. Articles three and four of the Quaker 'Foundations', emphasizing the need for full development of every member of the community to free them from 'the bondage of material things', are roughly equivalent to Labour's first pillar, a universally enforced National Minimum. Again, the fifth and sixth articles of the Quaker document were entirely compatible with Labour's second pillar, Democratic Control of Industry. Articles seven and eight of the 'Foundations', stressing service to humanity above material gain and the proper regulation of land and capital so 'as best to minister to the need and development of man', were along the line of Labour's call to use 'Surplus Wealth for the Common Good'. Friends, of course, were in the end pleading for a moral revolution rather than the 'Revolution in National Finance' which Labour demanded. Still, the economic provisions of the 'Foundations of a True Social Order' reflect just how far to the left the wartime Society of Friends had moved with regard to social policy; on the other hand, the 'Foundations' represented 'a practical & reasonable programme', rather than the radical transformation of society envisioned by more zealous Quaker socialists. Moderating influences were reflected in the decision of Yearly Meeting to adopt a new procedure for determining membership on the War and Social Order Committee. Obviously this represented a sop to cautious Friends who believed that militantly anti-capitalist members of the Socialist Quaker Society were over-represented on the WSOC.

[78] 'Is Man the Measure of all Things?', *PS*, 11/12, Nov. 1917, 339–40.
[79] See, for example, Robert Davis, 'Friends and Social Reconstruction', *The Friend*, 22 March 1918, 183–4.
[80] *LYM, 1918*, 78, 80. The 'Foundations' were reprinted in *Christian Life, Faith & Thought in the Society of Friends* (London 1923), 121–2 and are still included (23.16) in the current edition of *Quaker Faith and Practice* (1995).

Not surprisingly, *The Ploughshare* expressed strong disappointment at the continuing unwillingness of British Quakers to take some definitive step toward refashioning the social order. An editorial pointed out that the Society, while 'keenly sensitive to questions of religious significance', remained 'dull and antiquated in connection with those urgent matters of social reconstruction which it, year in, year out, lightly touches with its finger-tips'. As idealists, said W. L. Hare, Friends should stand ready to crown Karl Marx as a 'true prophet' by working for what he had predicted, 'the inevitable social revolution . . . affected entirely by peaceful and legal means'.[81]

The end of the Great War further curtailed the influence of those hot-blooded Friends whose moral intensity and willingness to sacrifice had briefly endowed them with influence and authority all out of proportion to their numbers or experience. The Socialist Quaker Society had managed, for a time, to gain effective control of the War and Social Order Committee, but the SQS could not persuade Yearly Meeting to adopt its radical social agenda. This failure may be contrasted with the success of the Friends Service Committee in pushing for the acceptance of a radically new but spiritually powerful version of the Quaker peace testimony. Radical pacifism was not carried over into the social realm. As the crisis of war and conscription wound down, a combination of weariness, relief, and caution induced a palpable suspension of the quest for the imminent creation of God's Kingdom on earth along socialist lines.

Undaunted, *The Ploughshare* strove to carry the struggle into the post-war era, altering its masthead in March 1919 from 'A Quaker Organ of Social Reconstruction' to 'A Quaker Organ of Social Revolution'. Still, by November 1919 dreams of a new social order had faded and, surrendering to the inevitable, the journal severed its tenuous connection to both the SQS and Society of Friends and again altered its masthead. For the brief remainder of its existence, *The Ploughshare* was 'A Journal of Hope'. That hope, whatever its dimensions, was never realized. Unable to sustain an independent existence, the paper ceased publication in June 1920. In his editorial swan-song William Loftus Hare expressed a personal vision of

---

[81] 'Responsibility for Idealists', *PS*, III/5, June 1918, 117–20 and an editorial comment on Yearly Meeting, ibid. 143.

how the seed scattered by the sturdy ploughers of the Socialist Quaker Society had fallen on good ground and would 'germinate, thirty-fold, sixty-fold, yea, even a hundred fold. We can see the delicate green blades coming up, and look for the good harvest if there are labourers to reap it.'[82]

Such reapers never appeared. But despite its ultimate failure 'to reconcile the accepted principles of Quakerism with suitable ideals of Social Revolution',[83] the SQS did leave its mark on the Society of Friends as a socially committed and politically significant body of believers. During the war, more and more Friends, like other pre-war progressives, drifted away from the Liberal Party and alighted, somewhat awkwardly perhaps, among the Labourites. This was not because any large number of Quakers had been convinced by the SQS's pleas for Christian socialism but rather because only Labour had remained relatively untainted by militarism and because, among the post-war parties, Labour alone seemed interested in the sort of social justice a new generation of Friends were increasingly seeing as an obligation of their birthright. Furthermore, as the sort of family firms associated with nineteenth-century Quaker business activities were gradually replaced by large-scale conglomerate corporations, those who remained in the world of business tended to be alienated from Quakerism and those who remained Friends tended to move from business to the professions, just as they had moved from Liberalism to Labour. As a mid-twentieth-century commentator on Quaker social and business practices noted: 'It is often deplored that Quakerism fails to appeal to the proletariat; it would seem that it also fails to hold the capitalist.'[84] The Socialist Quaker Society had helped begin this process of transformation and perhaps made it easier for some Friends, but, lacking the *raison d'être* of a war crisis or impending social revolution, few Quakers of the post-war period were attracted to a separate body of Quaker socialists and the SQS was duly laid down in 1924.

Before its demise, however, some SQS members had a final opportunity to make a meaningful contribution to a dialogue

---

[82] *PS*, v/5, May/June 1920, 118.

[83] *PS*, III/8, Sept. 1918, 204 commenting on Lucy F. Morland's 1918 Swarthmore Lecture, *The New Social Outlook* (London 1918).

[84] William H. Marwick, 'Some Quaker Firms of the Nineteenth Century', *JFHS*, 48/3 (Spring 1957), 258–9.

about the future direction of the Religious Society of Friends. In the course of its 'Report' to London Yearly Meeting in 1916, the War and the Social Order Committee had voiced its concern that 'an opportunity... be provided for consideration of the nature ... of our "Testimony against all War" ', and for reflection upon the social and political spheres in which future Quaker witness would be continued throughout the world.[85] This was the opening call for what would eventually become the first World Conference of All-Friends which met in London in August 1920. The London Conference's consideration of the relationship between Personal Life and Society would provide a final forum for the Socialist Quaker Society and reveal both the extent and the limitations of its influence on the future of the British Society of Friends.

[85] *LYM, 1916*, 103–4. Also see *Minutes, WSOC*, 2–5 Feb. and 4–5 May 1917.

11

Abiding Wounds, 1918–1920

TORN ASUNDER: WAR FRIENDS AND THE PEACE TESTIMONY

During the Great War the Friends Service Committee and its supporters maintained that Quakers who resisted war and conscription, even in the face of imprisonment or death, were 'serving the truest interests of the country and of mankind'.[1] Such a statement at least implied that those Friends who did not oppose the warring State were failing to act in the best interests of the nation and the world, let alone according to the tenets their religious faith. This radical version of the peace testimony was repeatedly endorsed by both the Meeting for Sufferings and Yearly Meeting. And when the Service Committee refused to submit the text of 'A Challenge to Militarism' to Government censors, its defiance of civil authority was fully sanctioned by these official agencies of British Quakerism. The Government's subsequent prosecution of three FSC officials was clearly intended to put the Society of Friends on notice that there were limits to war resistance, even by highly respectable, traditionally pacifist religious bodies.

Then, in July 1918, newspaper accounts of an appeal hearing for the 'Challenge to Militarism' defendants reported the appearance at court of solicitor Cecil Whitely claiming to represent 'a large number' of Britain's 'real' or 'patriotic' Quakers. These Friends, lawyer Whitely declared, 'did not identify themselves in any way with . . . the attitudes of the defendants' nor, as one of their number had put it, with any other 'glib theorists . . . now claiming the right to speak for the Society of Friends'. On the contrary, Whitely's clients believed that by supporting or even participating in a struggle to defend the British Empire and Christian civilization from Hunnish barbarism, they were sustaining their Society's his-

---

[1] 'A Challenge to Militarism', [1].

toric peace principles.[2] This was not the first collective declaration of support for the war effort offered by dissenting Friends. Shortly before Yearly Meeting in May 1918, one prominent war-Friend, lawyer and stockbroker J. B. Braithwaite Jr., wrote in the *Friends Quarterly Examiner* that the Society 'must recognize that the use of force against evil is not only permissible, but necessary'. After Yearly Meeting characteristically ignored Braithwaite's admonishment, he and twenty-five others, including three women, wrote to *The Times* proclaiming their bona fides both as patriots who supported the war and as Quakers who rejected the extremism of Friends Service Committee.[3]

Quaker pacifists were prone to suggest that many war-Friends became actively involved in the Society's affairs only 'when the outbreak of the present war disclosed their wide divergence from the position of Friends as held throughout long years of trial'.[4] But such an assertion was difficult to sustain given the number, and sometimes the stature, of those who claimed to be moved by a conviction of the Inward Light which embraced the national cause. There were, in fact, significant defections from the peace camp in nearly all of the eighty British monthly meetings, often from amongst ancient and distinguished Quaker families. In February 1915, for example, the overseers of Darlington Monthly Meeting reported that two members of the wealthy and politically prominent Pease family had taken commissions in the Army.[5] At Birmingham, Bournville Meeting was confronted with the fact that Egbert Cadbury, youngest son of George Cadbury, the meeting's founder and dominant member, had enlisted in the Royal Naval Air Service. (He was subsequently decorated for his role in helping to bring down two Zeppelins.) George Cadbury managed to remain aloof from controversies regarding the 'authentic' Quaker response to the war, but he never disavowed his son's decision.[6]

---

[2] *TF*, 12 July 1918, 442. The 'glib theorists' quotation is from H. Sefton-Jones, 'Reply', *FQE*, 51 (Oct. 1917), 444.

[3] J. B. Braithwaite, Jr., 'The Society of Friends and the Limitations of its Peace Testimony', *FQE*, (April 1918), 202–20 and *The Times*, 4 June 1918.

[4] Henry T. Hodgkin to *TF*, 17 Dec. 1915, 944.

[5] *Minutes*, Darlington Monthly Meeting (DMM), 11 Feb. 1915, 469 noted the cases of Joseph and Henry A. Pease, but no action was taken against them. (I am grateful to John Lockett, a member of Darlington Meeting and the Friends Historical Society, for bringing these *Minutes* to my attention and making these and other documents available to me.)

[6] Gardiner, *George Cadbury*, 250–56 and Richenda Scott, *Elizabeth Cadbury, 1858–1951* (London 1955), 123–24. At the All-Friends London Conference in 1920, Elizabeth Cadbury

The Cadbury firm would not engage in even the indirect production of war materials nor allow recruiting on its factory grounds, but the company took pains to ensure the welfare of the families of the hundreds of Bournville workers who joined the forces and rehired any war veterans who sought their old jobs after they were discharged.[7]

At Oxford, banker Arthur Gillett (1876–1954), although thwarted by age and physical condition in his efforts to enlist, was from beginning to end an outspoken war supporter. Some of the earliest recollections of Gillett's son Nicholas, born in 1914, were the wartime visits to the family home by General Jan Smuts, a member of the War Cabinet, who had befriended his mother, the former Margaret Clark (1878–1962), when she accompanied Emily Hobhouse on a relief mission to South Africa in 1905. However, despite her husband's stand and her friendship with General Smuts, Margaret Clark Gillett remained, according to her son, 'an ordinary Quaker pacifist' firmly opposed to the war. Apparently even such a fundamental difference between parents did not disrupt the tranquility of the Gillett household nor alter the strictly traditional Quaker upbringing of the children, including instruction on peace principles. On occasion General Smuts accompanied the Gilletts to Oxford Friends Meeting wearing his military uniform. Surely eyebrows were raised, but the presence of this worshipping warrior never caused the meeting to dissolve into chaotic discord.[8]

Some Quakers who served in the forces or otherwise supported the war resigned their membership to avoid bringing 'reproach to the name of Friends';[9] others maintained a discreet silence. But there was a noisy and troublesome body of war Friends who

made the point that young Friends who enlisted prior to conscription chose the hardships of soldiering over the comfort of the home front and expressed the view that 'the message of the Society had been strengthened rather than weakened by the diversity of opinion expressed during the war'. *AFC, Official Report*, 134.

[7] For an illuminating discussion of Cadbury's 'Company Culture', including its wartime policies, see Charles Delheim, 'The Creation of a Company Culture: *Cadburys, 1861–1931*', *The American Historical Review*, 92/1, (Feb. 1987), 13–44.

[8] Interview with A. Nicholas Gillett, Exeter, August 1986. For Margaret Clark Gillett's activities in South Africa, see Hewison, *Hedge of Wild Almonds*, 238–9, 263–4, 314–18 and for Smuts' comments on the futility of the suffering endured by anti-war Quakers, see *Selections from the Smuts Papers*, 4 vols., edited by W. K. Hancock and Jean Van Der Poel, (Cambridge 1966), III, 835.

[9] See Percy Brigham to Darlington Monthly Meeting, *Minutes*, DMM, 10 Oct. 1914, 436.

remained within the Society throughout the war years. Their influence on the thrust of official Quaker policies was, as events showed, negligible, but they were never reduced to embarrassed or disheartened silence. Henry Marriage Wallis remained a member of Meeting for Sufferings, maintaining a steady, if ineffective, barrage of pro-war rejoinders to nearly every pacifist pronouncement issued by Friends while simultaneously 'encouraging young fellows to enlist'.[10]

The vaunted Quaker traditions of broad tolerance and free expression ensured that prominent war Friends like Wallis, J. B. Braithwaite, Jr. and Herbert Sefton-Jones would receive a hearing in the Quaker press. When the threat of conscription began to loom large in the final months of 1915, a steady stream of letters appeared in *The Friend* denouncing the Society's refusal to give any support to the war effort and advocating active war service for Quaker youth.[11]

Anti-war Friends responded in kind, mincing no words. The elderly evangelical J. B. Hodgkin, a former major of Darlington, was shocked by statements made by war supporters in the Quaker press: 'I am amazed at the apparent inability of some... correspondents to understand the position of the Society of Friends in relation to Peace and War.'[12] Exchanges became more heated after the passage of the first Military Service Act early in 1916. A group of sixteen 'dissenting Friends', many bearing ancient and venerable Quaker names and all claiming to represent a 'large body of [Quaker] opinion', announced in *The Times* that they, at least, would 'stand by our country in her hour of peril with other loyal citizens'.[13]

The Friends Service Committee was a particular target of Quaker war supporters, who also also poured scorn on Meeting for Sufferings' apparently unwavering endorsement of every policy the FSC chose to pursue. When young Quakers began to be

[10] See *TF*, 19 Nov. 1915, 871–3 for a letter complaining about Wallis's promoting war and killing as virtuous activities. Also see Ernest E. Taylor, 'Diary, 1914–', 4 Sept. 1914, Temp. Box 22/3, LSF.

[11] For examples of letters from war Friends, see *TF*, 20 Aug. 1915, 652–4; 3 Sept. 1915, 686; 10 Sept. 1915, 707; 5 Nov. 1915, 844–5; and 19 Nov. 1915, 871–2.

[12] Ibid. 19 Nov. 1915, 872–3 and 26 Nov. 1915, 887.

[13] *The Times*, 3 March 1916. Also see *The Ploughshare*'s attack on this letter as an 'exhibition of...low motives' by individuals who should have known better. *PS*, April 1916, 70.

imprisoned for refusing all forms of service, J. B. Braithwaite, Jr. accused the FSC of causing unnecessary suffering as well as bringing the Society into public disrepute. Yearly Meeting, said Braithwaite, had 'never authorised the Service Committee to act as a general stirrer up of strife on its own account', especially in the company of radical political organizations like the No-Conscription Fellowship. Braithwaite also claimed that the extract from George Fox's declaration of 1660 inserted into the 1911 edition of the Society's *Christian Discipline* by which the Service Committee claimed to justify its militant pacifism was a 'garbled' misrepresentation of the views of early Friends. To illustrate his point, Braithwaite reproduced Edward Borrough's 1655 statement to parliamentary soldiers that they should 'not strengthen the hands of evil doers, but lay your swords in justice upon every one that doth evil'.[14]

Amidst these attacks on both the activities of the FSC and the historical validity of its pacifist position, a convinced Quaker from Saffron Walden noted in *The Friend* that when he entered the Society and affirmed his belief in the statements set forth in the *Book of Discipline* and the 'Queries', he had assumed that all Friends were expected to abide by these principles, including the peace testimony. When, he asked, had Quaker ideas about Peace and War been placed in a different category from other fundamental Quaker beliefs?[15]

An answer to this question was published in the *Friends Quarterly Examiner* by Herbert Sefton-Jones (1855–1929), patent attorney, world traveller, recorded minister and former Clerk of London and Middlesex Quarterly Meeting. In support of J. B. Braithwaite Jr.'s assertion that the FSC was misrepresenting the peace testimony of early Friends, Sefton-Jones claimed that Quakers had always affirmed the right to use force against evildoers. Careful study of Robert Barclay's remarks on war and fighting, he said, would inevitably lead one to the conclusion that 'our foremost Quaker theologian ranked war with cockfighting, bull-baiting, may-pole dancing, bell-ringing and other popular amusements of his day... far less offensive in the sight of God than Hireling Ministry, Oaths, or Payment of Tithes'. Given such historical evidence, Sefton-Jones concluded that the Society ought to take the 'earliest possible

[14] *TF*, 30 March 1917, 246.   [15] Ibid. 246–7.

opportunity of restating in language corresponding to fact our present doctrine regarding war'.[16]

Responding to what he believed were false and dangerous misrepresentations of early Friends' views, Edward Grubb noted that if the Society were to abandon its fundamental principle that war was '*never*... necessary', it would simply be following the example of most other Christian churches and placing itself 'at the mercy of the Government... and popular opinion, which always makes out that each war, as it arises, is necessary'. Did Sefton-Jones truly wish to see Friends drift into the sort of nebulous moral condition assumed by sects like the Christadelphians and Plymouth Brethren—that this war was wrong for them, but not for the State—'a position at once non-Quaker and antisocial'.[17]

Such censures had little affect on the activities and statements of Quaker war supporters, but, in a practical sense, their challenges to the Society's anti-war stance were invariably overruled or ignored. At Yearly Meeting in 1918 Sefton-Jones protested against the reappointment of the Friends Service Committee. The FSC, he correctly asserted, represented only one small faction within the Society and was engaged in 'political activities of which many Friends did not approve'. These remarks were inevitably seconded by both J. B. Braithwaite, Jr. and Henry Marriage Wallis, but the most apparent effect of their collective protest was a Yearly Meeting decision to place the FSC directly under its own auspices rather than under Meeting for Sufferings. Such an action implied not only wider support for the Service Committee but also less direct supervision of its activities.[18]

Because unity of ideals and purpose were thought to be a major source of strength in opposing the war, most pacifist Friends deplored public exchanges with Quakers war-supporters as unseemly and fractious. Still, however disturbed or embarrassed by public divisions within their religious community, pacifist Quakers could and did point with pride to the fact that members

---

[16] H. Sefton-Jones, 'The Eighth Query', *FQE*, April 1917, 216–27. See Ingle, *First Among Friends*, 194 who notes that right up to the issuing of the 'Declaration' of 1660 Fox had acknowledged 'that a magistrate who bore a weapon might permissibly use it in a just cause'.

[17] Edward Grubb, 'Eight Query: Reply', *FQE*, July 1917, 349–57.

[18] See *TF*, 31 May 1918, 344 for the discussion.

who refused to support the Society's official opposition to the war
and conscription were not drummed out of their meetings but
rather given a fair hearing and 'sympathetic care'.[19] This oft-
repeated assertion of tolerant forbearance straightaway established
itself as a part of Quaker wartime mythology. Like most myths, it
requires modification and correction.

In a post-war book intended to clarify Quakers beliefs and
practices to the general public, Edward Grubb admitted that a
'few' who had felt duty-bound to join the Forces 'were disowned
by their Monthly Meetings'.[20] Since none of the post-war statistical tables on Quaker war service provided a figure for disown-
ments, discovering the exact number who were cast out would
require close study of the *Minute Books* of eighty Monthly Meetings, assuming all still survive. As it stands, there are only painful
bits of anecdotal evidence as, for example, the bitter resentment of
former Liberal MP Alfred E. Pease that his son Christopher, who
enlisted as a matter of conscience and died on the Western Front,
had been stricken from the rolls of Guisborough Monthly Meeting.[21] In these circumstances, it may be useful to discuss one well-
documented disownment of an economically and politically
prominent Friend. The case may not be typical but it can be
instructive as regards the sorts of distinctions that could be made
in dealing with those who failed to uphold peace principles.

Walter Trevelyan Thomson (1875–1928) was a successful and
respected Middlesbrough businessman as well as a birthright Friend
claiming Quaker connections back to the days of George Fox.[22]
After a thoroughly Quaker education at Ackworth and Bootham
schools, Thomson, in partnership with his father, established himself as an iron merchant in Middlesbrough where he, his wife, and
daughter were members of the local preparative meeting. In 1914
W. T. Thomson seemed a model Quaker citizen, active in Home

[19] Elizabeth Fox Howard, *Friends' Service in War-time*, (London, n.d.), 36–7.
[20] Edward Grubb, *What is Quakerism?* (London 1917; 3rd. ed. 1929, reprinted 1942),
128.
[21] A. E. Pease, *My Son Christopher*...(Middlesbrough 1919), 226. Also see Mouland,
'Quaker Pacifism', 42.
[22] Walter Trevelyan Thomson claimed direct lineage from John Reckless, High Sheriff of
Nottingham and one of George Fox's earliest followers. W. T. Thomson to the Clerk of
Darlington Monthly Meeting (J. Edward Hodgkin), copy in *Minutes*, DMM, 9 Dec. 1915,
516.

Mission work, co-founder of a social and recreational club for boys and President of the Ackworth Old Scholars' Association.[23]

When the war began, Darlington Monthly Meeting, to which Middlesbrough preparative meeting was attached, took a strong anti-war stand. Following the lead of its formidable Clerk, J. Edward Hodgkin, soon to gain prominence as chairman of the War and the Social Order Committee, the Monthly Meeting not only circulated Meeting for Sufferings' warning against 'undertaking any service . . . which involves becoming a part of the military machine' but also prepared its own message to local Friends 'reiterating our protest against all war as contrary to the spirit of Christ'. The Darlington letter emphasized 'our belief as Friends that *no* war can be defended' and counselled members to ask themselves 'if any participation in or preparation for . . . [war] can harmonize with our allegiance to Christ'.[24]

In mid-January 1915 J. E. Hodgkin received a letter from Walter Trevelyan Thomson which, while attesting to Thomson's continued belief that war was contrary to the Spirit of Christ, also indicated his intention to resign his membership in the Meeting:

If the Society of Friends as a society is prepared to maintain that our country should not have sent troops to the assistance of Belgium . . . If . . . there is not room in our Society for any difference of opinion on this vexed question then I must regretfully tender my resignation, although on all other matters I am in complete accord with the tenets of Quakerism.[25]

Thomson's proffered withdrawal was held in abeyance until he was visited by a Monthly Meeting Committee to whom he admitted that while he had thus far been rejected as too old for active military service, he had done the next best thing by helping to secure recruits for the Army. When it was revealed that in the course of this recruiting activity, Thomson had publicly identified himself as a member of the Society of Friends, he insisted that this revelation was in no way an attempt to associate his opinions with

---

[23] For a biographical sketch of W. T. Thomson, see Ackworth School *Memorial Notices*, 106.

[24] *Minutes*, DMM, 17 Sept. 1914, 438 and 8 Oct. 1914, 441–2, emphasis in original.

[25] W. T. Thomson to the Clerk of Darlington Monthly Meeting, 7 Dec. 1914, copy in *Minutes*, DMM, 14 Jan. 1915, 463.

those of any other member of the Society. Thomson also claimed that despite his obvious disagreement with the position taken by his Monthly Meeting, he really had no wish to resign his membership and would only do so if the Monthly Meeting believed, as he obviously did not, that 'testimony against all war is an essential part of the Society's principles'.[26]

Since Darlington Monthly Meeting had clearly stated that the peace testimony was a fundamental tenet of Quakerism, it 'reluctantly, and after prayful consideration,' decided to disown Walter Thomson. Darlington's decision to cast out the erring member was based on the Meeting's consensus that while actual military service might be forgiven as an expression of honest convictions, however misguided, appearing on recruiting platforms and attempting to convince others to join in acts of war and killing went over the line. Thus, when Thomson asked for an enumeration of the precise reasons for his disownment, the Meeting cited his public refusal to adhere to the peace testimony as well as 'his action in appearing on a public platform in support of recruiting for the army'.[27]

At this point, Thomson dug in his heels and refused to acquiesce in the decision of the Monthly Meeting, giving notice of his intention to appeal to Durham Quarterly Meeting, the next highest authority. This appeal was apparently part of a general offensive Thomson had determined to wage against the decision of London Yearly Meeting to adhere to its traditional peace principles even as the Nation was in grave peril. While he sparred with Darlington Monthly Meeting, Thomson also used the occasion of his Presidential Address to the Ackworth Old Scholars Association to air the case for his maintaining membership in the Society in spite of his support for the war.

At Ackworth, Thomson seemed to be on more favourable ground for disputing the views of Quaker pacifists. The wartime record of Quaker boarding schools in upholding the peace testimony was ambiguous at best. One post-war commentator on Quaker education noted that although Friends had depended on their schools to champion the Society's ideals and principles, 'they

---

[26] W. T. Thomson to the Clerk of Darlington Monthly Meeting, 7 Dec. 1914, copy in *Minutes*, DMM, 14 Jan. 1915, 464.

[27] Ibid. 11 Feb. 1915, 468 and 13 March 1915, 473–4.

failed us . . . in the recent crisis'.[28] Statistics indicated that old boys from Friends' schools who served in the forces heavily outnumbered not only war resisters but also those engaged in non-military alternative service. At Ackworth, for example, nearly 500 former students joined the army or navy as compared with 192 who joined the FAU or Friends War Victims Relief Committee; only nineteen went to prison. The figures for Bootham were similar, with 227 serving in the forces and 103 in Quaker war relief bodies, while thirteen took the absolutist position.[29]

An obvious reason for this imbalance was the fact that Quaker schools had long since begun admitting non-Friends. One of these, the historian A. J. P. Taylor, a student at Bootham during the war, recalled Headmaster Arthur Rowntree's wartime fence-sitting as 'a remarkable exercise in Quaker flexibility'. One Sunday evening a lecture would be delivered by a Quaker CO, to be followed the next week by the bellicose exhortations of a soldier lately returned from the front.[30]

A printed account of the Ackworth Old Scholars Association (AOSA) meeting over which Walter Thomson presided in the Spring of 1915 supports Alan Taylor's recollections. Prior to Thomson's presidential address, the AOSA Secretary's Report was presented by Malcolm Sparkes, a Quaker socialist later jailed as a conscientious objector. Sparkes' Report detailed wartime services of Old Ackworth scholars, ranging from the founding of the Friends' Ambulance Unit by Philip Noel-Baker to a Lieutenant Malone's continuing service in the Royal Irish Rifles.[31] Sparkes concluded his presentation by reminding Old Scholars that, whatever path they chose 'whilst civilisation itself is being trampled underfoot in the terrible military struggle', all were obliged to

[28] Charles E. Stanfield, 'Problems of Education in Relation to Testimony', *AFC, Official Report* (London 1920), 139.

[29] Mouland, 'Quaker Pacifism', 49. About 5 per cent of all Friends of military age took an absolutist stand; the figure for Ackworth was less than 3 per cent and, for Bootham, less than 4 per cent.

[30] A. J. P. Taylor, *Personal History*, 48.

[31] See *Thirty-Fourth Annual Report of the Ackworth Old Scholars' Association*, edited by Albert G. Linney (York 1916), 11–13. Sparkes became a celebrity among Friends as founder of the Parliament of the Building Industry and originator of the plan upon which the Whitley Councils for settlement of industrial disputes were based. See Graham, *Conscription and Conscience*, 95, 243.

prepare themselves to contribute to 'the great re-construction that must follow the conclusion of the war'.[32]

President Thomson began his own presentation by nothing how 'the whirligig of time' had forced him to come to grips with the question of a possible conflict between his obligations to God as a Quaker and to country as a citizen. Given the desperate situation facing the Nation, he believed that 'the only safe course . . . [was] to follow Geo. Fox's advice and let each ascertain for himself with the guidance of the Holy Spirit what is the Will of God for us in this matter'. Having thus placed himself in the august company of the Founder, Thomson went on to provide 'an excellent summary of the arguments against an absolute peace testimony, from the 17th century through to John Bright and Caroline Stephen', repeating verbatim many of the points he had made in his letter to Darlington Monthly Meeting.[33]

Thomson concluded his address by noting that as a loyal Briton, he was hard put to 'divorce my responsibilities of citizenship from any obligations as a Quaker'. In his opinion, the Society's decision to embrace a narrow interpretation of acceptable wartime service was 'creating a new precedent' in seeking 'to ostracise and excommunicate . . . members who think the present war justifiable . . . as . . . the lesser of two evils'.[34]

No one in that audience rose to dispute Walter Thomson's conclusions, and resolutions of thanks, if obligatory, seemed entirely genuine. Indeed, Ackworth's Headmaster, Frederick Andrews (1850–1922), sitting Clerk of Meeting for Sufferings and a leader among Friends who opposed the Boer War, headed off the possibility of any awkward disputations, declaring 'it is altogether necessary at such a critical moment in our country's history, and also in the history of the Society of Friends, that we should approach this question with an open mind, and be prepared to go wherever truth leads us'. With that, Andrews moved that discussion of the topic be deferred until an impending informal conference would provide the opportunity 'to sift all

---

[32] *AOSA Report*, 13.

[33] Ibid., 18–19; W. T. Thomson to Clerk, DMM, 7 Dec. 1914, *Minutes*, DMM, 14 Jan. 1915, 463; and Malcolm Thomas to John Lockett (copy), 31 July 1995, (seen through courtesy of the author).

[34] *AOSA Report*, 32.

arguments . . . in hope that it may help us to arrive at the real truth . . .'[35]

In the meantime, while W. T. Thomson's appeal of his disownment was being considered by Durham Quarterly Meeting, Darlington Monthly Meeting issued a letter to members who had enlisted in the forces nothing that while 'we feel that patriotism should not lead us to actions incompatible with higher service under the Prince of Peace . . . We have decided to take no further disciplinary action in the case of those members who have taken up arms.'[36] Two months later the Yearly Meeting's Peace Committee issued a similar Minute expressing its 'earnest hope that no question of disciplinary treatment' for serving members be considered by Yearly Meeting. The Peace Committee also spoke directly to those who had enlisted, noting that while they had taken a step which had cut them off from other Friends, their convictions could be respected in the spirit 'of love and true sympathy'.[37]

Obviously, a consensus was developing to avoid taking any action against serving members. Responding to this conciliatory spirit, Durham Quarterly Meeting set aside Walter Thomson's disownment, restoring his membership. This judgement caused considerable consternation in Darlington where the Monthly Meeting's *Minutes* reiterated its opinion 'that the position taken by the appellant, and his repeated appearance at recruiting meetings, are utterly inconsistant [sic] with the principles we profess on the question of Peace'. Still, while expressing 'much regret' over the Quarterly Meeting's action, the Darlington Monthly Meeting decided, in keeping with the 'general desire in the Society', not to pursue the matter any further.[38]

For his part, Thomson was not appeased by the meeting's reluctant forbearance. In December 1915 he rejected reinstatement on the ground that the majority of the Darlington's members 'regard my association with them as a thing to be deplored'. Expressing regret at the setting aside of that 'broad spirit of

[35] Ibid., 33–4. For Frederick Andrews' opposition to the Anglo-Boer War, see Hewison, *Hedge of Wild Almonds*, 139.

[36] *Minutes*, DMM, 13 March 1915, 474.

[37] *Minutes*, Peace Committee, v, 6 May 1915 and 'To Members of the Society of Friends Who have Enlisted', June 1915, LSF.

[38] *Minutes*, DMM, 12 Aug. 1915, 495–6.

tolerance' which characterized early Friends, Thomson uncondi-
tionally resigned from the Society and immediately enlisted in His
Majesty's forces. If Walter Thomson's service with the Royal
Engineers severed his connection with Friends, it also elevated
his stature in the local community as well as with the Liberal
Party constituency organization. His wartime efforts culminated
with his election as MP for West Middlesbrough in December
1918. There was apparently no post-war reconciliation with
Quakerism, but Thomson proved to be a worthy MP, with a
special interest in slum clearance, whose electoral majorities regularly increased until his untimely death in 1928 at age 52.[39]

Darlington Monthly Meeting's thwarted decision to cast out
Walter Trevelyan Thomson was unusual and may have, to some
degree, reflected the strong opinions and personality of its Clerk, J.
Edward Hodgkin. Another factor in Thomson's disownment was
the general consensus that while actual military service might be
forgiven, appearing on recruiting platforms and attempting to
convince others to join in acts of war and killing could not be.
The fact that other Friends, including Marriage Wallis, were not
disciplined for recruiting activities reflects the strong measure of
autonomy permitted to monthly meetings. In the end, of course,
Durham Quarterly Meeting decided that even punishing this
offence was a breach of the Quaker spirit of tolerance and reconciliation.

Such a spirit apparently prevailed in most Quaker meetings.
John Henry Barlow, Clerk of Yearly Meeting, told his wife of a
Committee appointed in Birmingham Monthly Meeting to advise
whether some action should be taken against members who had
enlisted. In the end this Committee decided to avoid punitive
measures, 'but to say frankly we regret their decision and state
more strongly than ever our belief in the unlawfulness of war'.[40]
When, at Yearly Meeting in 1918, the elderly pacifist William
Littleboy expressed the hope that Friends would hold out 'the
right hand of fellowship' to all conscientious objectors, Quaker
and non-Quaker, when they were released from prison, a female
Friend urged that this same cordial hand be extended to 'those who

---

[39] W. T. Thomson to Clerk, DMM copied in *Minutes*, DMM, 9 Dec. 1915, 516 and
AOSA. *Memorial Notices*, 196.

[40] M. C. Barlow to Mary Millior Barlow, 1918, John Henry Barlow Papers, London, in
possession of M. M. Barlow Braithwaite.

were actually engaged in the fighting'. No one disputed her sentiments and, so far as may be ascertained, the usual post-war practice
of local and monthly meetings was to welcome returning soldiers
without comment or criticism.[41] There were, however, some
limits to what might be tolerated.

After John W. Graham presented the Peace Committee's
Report to Yearly Meeting in 1918, J. B. Braithwaite, Jr. inquired
as to whether British Quakers were 'now prepared to take a
definite step towards international peace'. This might be done,
Braithwaite said, if Yearly Meeting announced its support for
President Woodrow Wilson's plan to establish a League of Nations
as an international instrument for enforcing peace. Like William
Penn's seventeenth-century *Proposal for the Present and Future Peace
of Europe*, Braithwaite said, Wilson's scheme was based on the
recognition that 'any plan for abolishing war must depend upon
the power of coercion of those who would not comply'.
Braithwaite believed that by endorsing the League in all its details,
Quakerism could 'take its place at the head of the great peace
movement in the world'. Herbert Sefton-Jones seconded
Braithwaite's remarks, calling the question of support for the
League of Nations the 'most important subject the Society has
ever had before it'.[42]

Yearly Meeting was not convinced. Certainly, some may have
seen the appeal of these pro-war Friends to this sparsely attended
gathering as a subterfuge for manoeuvring the Society, which had
maintained its peace testimony at considerable cost, into accepting
the righteousness of force when peace finally came. Henry T.
Hodgkin expressed the view that Friends were first and foremost
a religious body whose mission was 'to bring back the Churches to
uncompromising loyalty to Jesus Christ'. Their success in pursuing
this spiritual quest, Hodgkin noted, 'might help to call forth a real
League of Nations of which brotherhood would be the key'. Clerk
John H. Barlow, who had just returned from the 'Challenge to
Militarism' trial, closed the discussion by ruling that J. B.
Braithwaite's proposal had not received sufficient support to justify
Yearly Meeting's endorsement of the League of Nations.[43]

The Clerk's pronouncement, which seemed to reflect the view
that to be pro-League was to be, in effect, pro-war, settled the

---

[41] See *TF*, 31 May 1918, 346 for the discussion.   [42] Ibid. 346–7.   [43] Ibid.

matter for the time being. But Quaker supporters of the League were not so easily put off. In September 1918 they inserted an advertisement in *The Friend* endorsing the League of Nations and claiming the active support of over three thousand Quakers, a figure representing 15 per cent of the entire membership of London Yearly Meeting. Subsequently, a Friends' League of Nations Committee (FLNC) was formed, with Lord Gainford (J. A. Pease), colliery owner and long-time Liberal MP, as president[44] and J. B. Braithwaite, Jr. as chairman. The avowed purpose of the FLNC was to secure Yearly Meeting sanction for the League of Nations. If war Friends could accomplish this objective, they would also effectively validate their argument that morally righteous force was, in extreme circumstances, the only possible path to lasting peace. Certainly, this was the stance assumed by J. B. Braithwaite, Jr. in the final wartime issue of *The Friend*. Beginning with the assertion that 'the whole tenor of Scripture justifies the use of force for the restraint and punishment of evil', Braithwaite noted that nations representing 84 per cent of the world's population had combined to frustrate the designs of a 'great evil power' bent on world conquest. With peace in sight these allied states proposed 'to enter into mutual obligations which shall render war as nearly impossible as human arrangements can achieve'. Friends who claimed to oppose this arrangement on account of their peace principles obviously had, Braithwaite asserted, 'failed to grasp the vital distinction between the use of the sword for conquest and its use for the restraint of evil . . . tyranny'.[45]

Another prominent Quaker proponent of the League was Sir George Newman, who, as President of the Friends' Ambulance Unit, had clashed repeatedly with the Friends Service Committee. Ten days after the war ended, Newman chaired a Conference on the League of Nations which met at Devonshire House. Picturing the League as the only viable means for ensuring the future peace of the world, Newman expressed his hope that the Society of Friends would 'give a sincere, a united and a determined support to the idea and the principle of a League of Nations'.[46]

[44] For J. A. Pease, see Chapter 6 above.

[45] *TF*, 8 Nov. 1918, 669. See ibid. 10 Jan. 1919, 14 for announcement of the Friends' League of Nations Committee.

[46] *TF*, 29 Nov. 1918, 699–700.

Such declarations by well-known Friends moved the Peace Committee to raise the alarm. Even before the war ended, this Committee had written to Meeting for Sufferings expressing its concern that the Friends' of the League of Nations Committee might 'seriously embarrass' the Society if the press and public assumed it had some official capacity.[47] Within a few weeks these apprehensions were fully realized. When Woodrow Wilson stopped in London on his way to the Versailles Conference, the Friends of the League of Nations Committee managed to secure an audience. FLNC President Lord Gainford introduced his associates to Wilson as a delegation from the Society of Friends who, while traditionally opposed to war and violence, 'realized that as a last resort the employment of force for the realization of great ideals might be unavoidable and necessary'.[48] Many Friends, including Isaac Sharp, the Recording Clerk for Yearly Meeting, expressed serious consternation with the fact that while the press had apparently gone out of its way to portray Quaker supporters of the League as official representatives of the Society, no member of pro-League delegation had taken steps to correct this harmful misconception.[49]

Eventually, Meeting for Sufferings, perhaps as much chagrined by the spectacle of publicly aired differences among Friends as by possible association with supporters of the League of Nations, appointed a group of representatives to meet with Lord Gainsford's Committee and resolve differences. When, however, Edward Backhouse reported back for this ad hoc committee, he noted that reconciliation had again been smashed upon the rock of military force, adding 'it would be nothing short of a calamity if, as almost the only religious body which stands for a practical belief in the potency of the Gospel message of good-will to all men though Jesus Christ, we should . . . now publicly affirm that military force is, on certain occasions, the ultimate remedy for wrong.'[50]

In 1919 Yearly Meeting rejected 'the scheme of the League of Nations . . . embodied in the Paris Treaty'.[51] And although the League was discussed at some length at the All-Friends Conference

[47] *Minutes*, Peace Committee, MSS Vol CVI (1916–21), 31 Oct. 1918, LSF.
[48] *The Times*, 30 Dec. 1918, 4. Also see Tucker, 'English Quakers and World War I', 220–26 for a discussion of Quaker differences over support for the League of Nations.
[49] See *TF*, 10 Jan. 1919, 14–16 for a lengthy summary of the debate.
[50] See *LYM, 1919*, 62–3.   [51] Ibid. 60.

of 1920, London Yearly Meeting never established an official position regarding that body. In any case, the threat of further embarrassing disputes as to who spoke for British Quakerism diminished as the Friends' League of Nations Committee was gradually absorbed into the League of Nations Union. Both Lord Gainford and J. B. Braithwaite were elected to the Council of the LNU in 1919 and Braithwaite served on its Executive Committee as well. While neither exerted much influence on the future direction of Yearly Meeting, both remained Friends into honoured old age.

TOGETHER AGAIN? THE ALL-FRIENDS CONFERENCE, 1920

London Yearly Meeting's firm and persistent opposition to the war and conscription tempered and hardened Friends' peace testimony, adding strength and clarity to twentieth-century Quaker pacifism. In British society as a whole the question of what one did in the war became a sort of crude litmus test for patriotism; within the Society of Friends, by contrast, the manner in which one resisted the war provided a rough guide to individual influence during the inter-war period. Those who suffered most, the absolutist conscientious objectors, came to be most highly regarded, and some level of resistance was almost a necessity if a member was to carry any real weight. As historian Leigh Tucker noted, post-war leaders 'came from those who remained true to their beliefs and had done so through personal experience and . . . example. These formed the meristematic point of a Society which was still vital.'[52]

The resolute adherence of British Friends to peace principles had another positive affect on the larger, world-wide body of Friends. The admiration and sympathy with which Quakers in the United States viewed the war resistance of their British cousins allowed many evangelical American Friends to put aside concerns about the growing influence of liberal religious ideas in Britain and to extend a hand of unity in the struggle against war. This process had begun in 1915, when New York Yearly Meeting wrote to London

---

[52] Tucker, 'English Quakers and World War I', 266. Also see Howard, 'Friends' Service', 11, 30.

offering its aid in 'any joint enterprise for peace'.[53] On the British side, the initial inspiration for a post-war congress of Friends which would attempt to define the Society's role in the post-war world may have come from a special subcommittee of Yearly Meeting appointed in 1915 under the leadership of Henry T. Hodgkin and John William Graham. Unfortunately, other than a widely distributed pamphlet, *Looking Towards Peace*, nearly all of this subcommittee's papers have been lost and, thus, its influence in shaping the Conference is difficult to measure.[54] In any case, the idea of a post-war reassessment of Quakerism as a world religion touched a responsive cord among British Friends. At Yearly Meeting in 1916, a proposal was put forward for a post-war conference 'of all those who bear the name of Friend with the object of giving full consideration to the deeply important subject of how to secure a general and lasting peace'.[55]

In November 1916 Meeting for Sufferings acted on this proposal by appointing a Special Committee, chaired by Edward Grubb, to consider the prospects for a Peace Conference of all Friends.[56] Amidst the disorder and uncertainty of war, it was difficult to make precise plans, but by April 1917 the Committee reported that 'it had communicated with American Friends of all branches [including Hicksites], who had given warm welcome to the project'. On the strength of this response the Committee proposed a 'World Conference' of Friends, to meet at Devonshire House as soon as possible after the end of the war, with four hundred places allotted for Friends from outside London Yearly Meeting. The projected cost for such a gathering was £2,500, an expenditure Edward Grubb felt was justified in the fact that this would be 'the most important Conference ever called by Friends . . . designed not only to clear and deepen the Peace testimony of our Society, but to bind together its scattered branches in common work for the

---

[53] Roger C. Wilson, 'The Best Things in Ye Worst Time', in *Quakerism: A Way of Life*, edited by Hans Erik Aarek and others (Kuekerforlaget, 1982), 144.

[54] Horace G. Alexander, the last surviving member of this subcommittee (he died in 1990), brought this information to my attention in a letter of 23 November 1985, together with his unpublished essay 'British Friends and the War of 1914'.

[55] *AFC Official Report*, 36.

[56] Other member of this Committee were John H. Barlow, Charles Stansfield and Edward Backhouse, the Honorary Secretary.

coming of the Kingdom of God.'[57] So, British Quakers, who had begun the war years at Llandudno by declaring the unshakable moral imperative imposed by their peace principles, would end the years of conflict with Quakerism's first world-wide conference on the themes of 'permanent universal peace' for the world as well as reconciliation and unity for all previously divided Friends. After the war ended, four delegates from London travelled to Philadelphia and on to Richmond to co-ordinate final arrangements for this first Quaker world conference.[58]

Nine hundred and thirty-six delegates[59] assembled at Devonshire House on 12 August 1920 to begin discussion of 'their historic Testimony and its application to the conditions of the world today'. Obviously, they held out high hopes for this extraordinary gathering.[60] These expectations were ably summarized by Henry T. Hodgkin who was about to return to his missionary work in China:

> During the war, we have all passed through deep waters and out of our struggle and sorrow new convictions have been won and ... old ones have been strengthened. For ourselves, the War has meant a certain measure of isolation and misunderstanding, but also a great fellowship with many very fine spirits in various circles. Even more important, it has led us to see that the way for social renewal is the way of Christian adventure, the full acceptance of all risks entailed in the way of love ...[61]

Although the peace testimony was the organizing theme around which deliberations would go forward, William Charles Braithwaite's introductory address stressed that the 'fuller vision of a true way of life for men will take us beyond the formal statement of our Peace testimony to the far-reaching issues of social

[57] Greenwood, *Whispers of Truth*, 215; *TF*, 6 April 1917, 255; and William C. Braithwaite, 'The Conference: A Vision of Its Possibilities', *All Friends Conference, London, August 12 to 20, 1920: A Guide and Souvenir* (London [1920]), 5.

[58] Greenwood, *Whispers of Truth*, 215; *AFC, Official Report*, 31.

[59] Of the official delegates to the Conference 497 (53%) represented London Yearly Meeting, 336 (36%) were from North America, including seven Canadians, and 57 (6%) from Dublin. The remaining forty-six (5%), came from Australasia (10), China (8), India (5), Norway (5), Japan (4), South Africa (4), Denmark (3), Syria (3), France (2), Madagascar and Jamaica.

[60] *AFC, Official Report*, 31.

[61] Henry T. Hodgkin, *Letters* (London n.d.), Letter No.1, August 1920, 1–2.

and international behaviour that belong to it...'[62] To explore and develop these issues, Preliminary Commissions, seven each in Britain and North America, had been appointed to report to the conference on topics ranging from the 'Fundamental Basis of the Peace Testimony' to 'Methods of Propaganda' to 'International Service'.[63] The reports of each of the fourteen commissions, incorporating several hundred pages and presumably embodying 'the most thorough and exhaustive study' of the application of peace principles to Quaker belief and practice, were separately printed, bound, and made available to the delegates.[64] Obviously, much time and trouble went into the formulation of these *Reports*, but for all of their direct influence on proceedings, they might never have been written. Still, they make interesting reading as regards the perceptions of post-war Friends and especially for the considerable differences between British and American impressions.

Overall, the contributions of the American Commissions are clear, reasonable, pragmatic, and optimistic. They seem to have been written by practical men, and a few women, and are, as a rule, devoid of deep spiritual reflection. In contrast, the British *Reports* tend, at times, to be slightly fuzzy, leaning toward the mystical, while in other instances recommending daring, even radical, ideas and programmes. The problem, of course, was in trying to incorporate the findings of fourteen Commissions into the Conference's deliberations, as no systematic method was developed for relating their conclusions to the daily sessions. Despite the time available for preparation, apparently no serious thought had been given to the necessity for a weighty steering committee to guide the proceedings toward the completion of the carefully developed agenda. One Quaker historian has asserted that, as a result, the

[62] W. C. Braithwaite, 'The Conference', *AFC, Guide & Souvenir*, 5 and *AFC, Official Report*, 31.
[63] The topics investigated by the Commissions were: I. THE FUNDAMENTAL BASIS: II. NATIONAL LIFE AND INTERNATIONAL RELATIONS; III. PERSONAL LIFE AND SOCIETY; IV. PROBLEMS OF EDUCATION; V. THE LIFE OF THE SOCIETY OF FRIENDS VI. METHODS OF PROPAGANDA; VII. THE INTERNATIONAL SERVICE OF FRIENDS.
[64] *AFC, Official Report*, 26–31, 61–66. The *Reports* of the seven British Commissions were published as *The Peace Testimony of the Society of Friends* (London [1920]).

conference stumbled along in a desultory fashion, 'at no very high level'.[65]

This difficulty may be illustrated by comparing the tone of the reports of the British and American versions of Commission III on 'Personal Life and Society'. The American *Report* was filled with lofty generalities emphasizing truth, justice, and goodwill. It did go so far as to criticize 'the unearned wealth of inheritance' and to deprecate a system of production that had been 'so diverted as to leave an insufficient supply of necessities for the poorest and weakest'.[66] Yet what the American Friends may have believed to be bold declarations appear pale and thin when compared to the conclusions of the British Commission which included a majority of members from the Socialist Quaker Society. The British *Report* declared, in the spirit of SQS's confrontational wartime stance as well as its recent attraction to guild socialism, that the world-wide temper of the working classes was increasingly one of revolt, 'not only against capitalist management and Trade Union officialism, but also against the increasing bureaucracy of the State'. What was needed, said the *Report*, was 'a social revolution...to redress inequality and injustice' and to create a 'system which assures to every human being enough bread and goods for a full and finely-developed life'. The *Report* called upon Friends actively to participate in 'a radical transformation of the social and industrial system...to ease the coming of the impending revolution...Let us take now a further advance to the greater ideal of social justice and the fellowship of free men, which is the only earthly ex-pression of "the glorious liberty of the sons of God"!'[67]

Most American Friends, particularly Midwestern Republican merchants, manufacturers, and farmers, were scarcely prepared to countenance a message so laden with socialist rhetoric as the basis for the collective social and political position of world Quaker-ism.[68] Thus, although the conference's official 'Minute' on Person-

---

[65] J. Ormerod Greenwood to the author, 20 September 1985 and Greenwood, *Whispers of Truth*, 215–16.

[66] Report of American Commission III, *Personal Life and Society* (Philadelphia 1920), 7, 12.

[67] Report of Commission III (British) *The Implication of the Testimony in Personal Life and Society* (London [1920]), 3–4.

[68] The British radical social message was perhaps not entirely without affect. On 23 September 1920 an editorial in *The American Friend* noted: 'We trust and believe that many of us [Americans] had our horizons of understanding...widened by our contacts in Lon-

al Life and Society expressed a sense of the meeting that went beyond the timidity of the American report, it in no way reflected the radical implications of the British Commission's presentation. Without the ground being carefully prepared, there was simply too great a diversity of opinion to develop meaningful collective principles on subjects like social and economic reform. The same could be said for the conference's discussion of the proper Quaker attitude toward such contemporary issues as the League of Nations, free trade and protectionism, the British government's suppression of Irish nationalism, or the conference's endorsement of the Council of Action organized by the Labour Party to prevent British intervention in the war between Poland and Soviet Russia. The *Official Report* spoke of how 'harmony and good feeling prevailed ... [and] carried through ... differences to practical unanimity of judgment ...' But in point of fact, on larger questions such as those concerning the League, no positive guidance was forthcoming. On other emotionally charged issues—like the supporting the Council for Action to halt aid to enemies of Bolshevik Russia or protesting British 'coercion' in Ireland—minority opposition was largely ignored.[69]

Still, if the conference was unwisely diverted by contemporary issues and seriously weakened by puerile, inane or ill-considered individual contributions, it did manage to achieve a considerable measure of agreement concerning the peace testimony, the overriding issue for which it had been called into being. Here, at least, Friends did not fall into the trap of turning their discussion of peace principles into a self-congratulatory celebration of the nobility of Quaker wartime resistance. For one thing, the Conference had the advantage of Margaret E. Hirst's *Historical Introduction* to the peace question.[70] The thrust of Hirst's essay was that while the Society of

---

don ... that Liberalism, even Socialism, is not *prima facie* evidence of mendacity or diseased mentality.'

[69] 'Personal Life and Society', *AFC, Official Report*, 33–4, 72–4, 115–18 and Wilson, 'The Best Things', 144. Also see 'A Message to the Irish People', *AFC, Official Report*, 165, 195 and 'Letter to the Council of Action', ibid. 165, 197. Also see Francis, Beatrice and Robert Pollard, *Democracy and the Quaker Method* (London 1949), 136–143, which points to the Conference's messages to the Council of Action and Ireland as examples of the success of the Quaker method of conducting business.

[70] *Historical Introduction to the Reports of the Commissions Regarding the Peace Testimony of the Society of Friends* (London 1920). Hirst later expanded this work into a long-time standard on the peace testimony, *The Quakers in Peace and War* (London 1923).

Friends had faithfully maintained its testimony against all wars and strife, prior to the twentieth century the power of that testimony had atrophied from lack of use. In keeping with the theological vision of the Quaker Renaissance, Hirst emphasized that the revival of this historic testimony had not been based on scriptural evidence but 'grew inevitably out of the conception of the inward Light...' With obvious reference to those Quakers who had supported the recent war,[71] she noted that while some Friends still held that peace principles were 'a mere individual preference to be held or abandoned by Friends at their pleasure...', the record of history revealed that faithful Quakers had consistently woven the twin threads of love of God and love of man 'into the web of their belief and practice'.[72]

When Joan Mary Fry presented the first paper in a session on 'The Character and Basis of Our Testimony for Peace', she not only endorsed Hirst's view of the peace testimony as 'an integral part of our reading of Christianity', she also provided some insight as to the path British Friends would follow for the remainder of the twentieth century. Because the peace testimony had proved to be a singular vision of fundamental Christian principles, Fry emphasized the Society's obligation to demonstrate to their fellow Christians and to the world the universal truth of their vision. This could not be accomplished by standing aside from the world as Friends had previously been wont to do, but by embracing the 'tangled mass of social reform' as a means of easing the path to peace and reconciliation.[73]

The next speaker was Rufus Jones, who emerged as one of the shining stars of the Conference. Taking up a major themes of the Quaker Renaissance, Jones asserted that Christian acquiescence in war was a result of the fateful substitution of 'the theology of the Church... for the way of life which Christ inaugurated'. Theologians had turned humanity's gaze from the Divine commandment to establish the Kingdom of God on earth toward a 'heavenly Zion already built' to which even warriors could ascend. The role of Quaker peacemaker was to return men's attention to the original

---

[71] Among the British delegates were war Friends Edgar Collinson and Herbert Sefton-Jones; the latter spoke in defence of his views on the peace testimony, AFC, *Official Report*, 66.

[72] Hirst *Historical Introduction*, 26–8.   [73] AFC, *Official Report*, 38–40.

task. Theirs was a faith, he said, which could 'overcome the world as it had been and turn it into the world that ought to be'.[74]

In the discussion that followed, several speakers acknowledged personal and corporate failures. 'We were all to blame', said former Liberal MP T. Edmund Harvey, 'for our indolence in accepting conditions that led to war.'[75] Edward Grubb added that if, prior to 1914, he and other Friends had not given way 'to ... apathy and weakness, things might have been different'. J. E. Hodgkin noted that even the struggle against the war, which had provided the Society with 'the greatest opportunity in its whole history ... to show the world the reality of our testimony for Peace,' had been inadequate because Friends 'did not present the united front against the forces of militarism which some of us had fondly assumed ... as a matter of course'.[76]

When questions arose as to Friends' attitudes toward those who did not believe that pacifism was a fundamental tenet of Christianity, most speakers attempted to put the best face on wartime divisions and warned against recriminations or bitterness. Still, John P. Fletcher, a leader of the Friends Service Committee, apparently felt the need to underscore its wartime message: 'the fundamental basis of Quaker Christian truth [is] that man must not kill his fellow man ... we must as a Christian Society keep to this spiritual testimony.'[77]

In the end this view prevailed. War Friends were, 'in a spirit of love and humility', to be fully reconciled with their pacifist brothers and sisters; but there could be no backing away from the principle that the peace testimony was 'an organic part of our faith as Christians ... a sure and inevitable outcome of our belief in the sacredness of human personality' which could never be abandoned but must be 'broadened, deepened and enriched by a larger vision of the needs of the world, and a keener insight into the realities of the spiritual order'.[78]

---

[74] Ibid. 45–7.   [75] Ibid. 52.

[76] *TF*, 20 Aug. 1920, 524–5; Edward Grubb, 'The Life of the Society in Relation to Its Testimony', *AFC, Official Report*, 122; and John Edward Hodgkin, 'The Testimony in Personal Life and Society', ibid. 94.

[77] Ibid. 48–51.

[78] *TF*, 20 Aug. 1920, 524; 'Life of the Society of Friends', *Peace Testimony*, 26, 12–13; and Herbert Corder, 'Methods of Propaganda', *AFC, Official Report*, 181–2.

The same point was emphasized by the Report of the British Committee on 'The Life of the Society of Friends', which noted that the Quaker witness against war could never again be simply a rejection of or withdrawal from the world: 'The Church is in the world in order to transform it into the Kingdom of God . . . we are to work as well as pray for the coming of that Kingdom and the doing of God's will on earth . . .'[79]

The wartime experience of British Friends had convinced many of them that their peace testimony was a political as well as a religious necessity. As the British Report on the 'Life of the Society' noted, 'the way of Peace is within, and not outside, the domain of "practical politics".' Quakers could not wait in the silence of their meeting houses for converts to drift into the peaceable kingdom but were bound to venture out on to the highways and byways, teaching the message of peace that the world awaited.[80] There was, the Report noted, 'a real place and an urgent need for a prophet Society, a body of moral pioneers, committed to the upholding of a truth which, though unpopular now, will one day be accepted by men . . .'[81]

As noted above,[82] not all Quaker war resisters and conscientious objectors were convinced that political and social activism would be the most efficacious lesson learned from their wartime experiences. They had, indeed, concluded that pacifism could never be based on a political ideology or social theory but was rather an act of personal faith resting, in the end, upon one's willingness to take up the Cross as Christ as a sacrificial victim and witness to a better way. Still, the majority obviously hoped that a collective statement of Quakerism's unwavering adherence to the peace testimony would be the best means of winning a larger audience for this view. To secure this objective, the Conference authorized the publication and widest possible distribution of a pamphlet entitled *Friends and War*.[83] This document, a modified version of the report of the American Commission on 'The Fundamental Basis of the Peace Testimony', was written by Rufus Jones and remained the standard Quaker statement on the peace testimony throughout

[79] 'Life of the Society of Friends', *Peace Testimony*, 6–7.
[80] Ibid. 5, 9, 31–33.   [81] Ibid. 21–2.   [82] See Chapter 9.
[83] [Rufus M. Jones], *Friends and War: A New Statement of the Quaker Position* (London, 1920).

the inter-war years. It also contained a convenient summary of the reasons why Friends resisted the Great War and would continue to resist in future wars. They did so, Jones said, because of their agreement upon and devotion to 'the Christian way of life revealed in the New Testament, the voice of conscience revealed in the soul, [and] the preciousness of personality revealed by the trans-forming force of love . . .'[84]

One of London's melancholy, though generally unperceived, monumental ironies stands on an otherwise barren square in front of Euston Station. It is a simple obelisk memorializing the sacrifice of '3,719 men of the London and Northwestern Railway Com-pany who . . . served and died in the Great War . . . for their Coun-try, Justice and Freedom'. From its steps one can look across Euston Road into the tranquil little garden beside Friend's House, a citadel of British pacifism, and imagine the two south-facing statues in infantry garb childing gentle Friends: 'We know why we fought. Where were you, mate?' Would the war resisters attending All-Friends Conference have felt comfortable with their Society's attempts to answer that question? Would the 3,719 dead railway men have understood or appreciated any of those explan-ations? Unanswerable questions, no doubt. But live Quaker and dead soldier might have agreed about and identified with Rufus Jones's last, and least Quakerly, justification for refusing to fight with carnal weapons: 'the irrationality revealed in modern war-fare . . .'[85]

It may be true that the All-Friends Conference of 1920 was, in the words of one critic, an 'utter failure' in respect to its goal of forging a path that would lead humanity to 'permanent universal peace.' But for all its lack of success in arriving at 'a united judgment about future work for peace',[86] the conference did mark an historic turning point for British Quakerism. Once and for all, it affirmed that for British Friends, the peace testimony was 'the fundamental basis of Quaker Christian truth, that man must not kill his fellow man, and that this shall take pre-eminence over the claims of any other order of any other group of people'.[87] Since

[84] Ibid. 24 and E. W. Orr, *The Quakers in Peace and War, 1920–1967* (Eastbourne, Sussex, 1974), 23–7. *Friends and War* was reprinted by the Friends Peace Committee in November 1931.
[85] *Friends and War*, 22–4.   [86] Greenwood, *Whispers of Truth*, 216.
[87] John Percy Fletcher, *AFC, Official Report*, 51.

the day of this reaffirmation, Quakers have been prominent in nearly every peace society and larger peace movement that has emerged. Although not every Briton who claimed to be a Friend adhered absolutely to this fundamental basis, the world at large defines Quakerism chiefly in pacifist terms, and the Society of Friends in Britain could scarcely survive as a separate religious body if it were to disavow or seriously weaken its peace testimony.

This principle, at least, was strongly reaffirmed by the inter-war generation of Young Friends who gathered for a separate conclave four days after the close of the All-Friends Conference.

JORDANS CONFERENCE OF YOUNG FRIENDS, 24–30 AUGUST 1920

The International Conference of four hundred Young Friends that convened at Jordans was the first general gathering of the Young Friends Movement in Britain since Swanwick in 1911. Many believed that the roots of British Quakerism's determined resistance to the late war could be traced to a dramatic episode at Swanwick when, according to the official record, 'young Friends rose one after another to voice their uncompromising witness to our principles of non-resistance'.[88] By 1920, the wartime witness of young Friends and the support given that witness by Yearly Meeting had elevated the peace testimony from a theoretical position to the organizing principle of Quakerism's first World Conference and for the remainder of the twentieth century, pacifism would endure as the rock upon which Friends stood to face a warring world. Could the post-war generation of British Quakers make an equally meaningful contribution to the spiritual strength of their Society and to its continuing struggle for peace and reconciliation?

There were elements of continuity between the pre-war and post-war gatherings. An official convener at Jordans, Wilfrid E. Littleboy, recent veteran His Majesty's prisons and a future Clerk of Yearly Meeting, had been one of the leading lights at Swanwick.[89] Neave Brayshaw, who at Swanwick had called upon

---

[88] *Swanwick, 1911*, 175.

[89] Other official conveners at Jordans were A. Mabel Holdsworth (1878–1963), a member of Meeting for Sufferings and soon to be Clerk of Cheshire Monthly Meeting, and Paul Furnas of New York Yearly Meeting.

Young Friends to be prepared to 'gain a martyr's crown' in defence of their faith, was also at Jordans. Still, the war years had effected substantial changes in the outlook and demeanour of the young men and women who convened in 1920. For one thing, the reticence and reserve characteristic of so many generations of Quakers was to a considerable extent a thing of the past. Henceforth, social and political activism would be a hallmark of British Quakerism. Another indication of changing attitudes may be gleaned from a letter sent in 1920 by John H. Barlow, Clerk of Yearly Meeting, to his 16-year-old daughter Mary Millor. Commenting on the political scene, Barlow expressed his enthusiasm for Norman Birkett, an 'exceptionally good Liberal candidate' who had been chosen to stand in their Birmingham constituency at the next election. 'I am very interested', he added, 'that you are Labour.'[90] Notwithstanding the fact that Mary Barlow would not be permitted to vote for any parliamentary candidate for another decade, she was not simply a defiant or disaffected young person rebelling against parental authority or standing apart from the pious Quaker crowd. She had, in fact, joined the majority of her peers in rejecting the support Quakers had traditionally given to the party of Gladstone which had, as many young Friends believed, lost its nerve as the party of Asquith and its soul as the party of Lloyd George.

In the end, the Jordans Conference may not have been so memorable nor so inspiring as Swanwick, but its proceedings can provide insight into the nineteenth-century ideas and practices that were being left behind as well as the principles and actions that would give direction to London Yearly Meeting during the inter-war years. One of the key points to emerge at Jordans was a vision of Quakerism as more than simply a Society standing righteously apart from the madding crowd. Many Young Friends believed that, henceforth, their Society was obliged to leap into the fray as a social and political force truly seeking to create the Kingdom of God on earth.

The question of the Society's role in the modern world was confronted straight on in the opening address by the liberal American Friend Henry Cadbury: 'Quakerism's religious contribution to our generation is not merely in its revolutionary

---

[90] H. Barlow to M. M. Barlow, n.d. 1920, J. H. Barlow Papers.

theological and ecclesiastical aspects . . . It is our ethical revolution that . . . the world needs. . . . We are wont to look upon the great crisis through which we have passed as the testing time of Quakerism . . . [but] the real crisis of Quakerism is in the opportunity that is yet before us.'[91]

During the discussion that followed, the point was made that the Society should prepare to embark on a new world-wide crusade 'comparable to that undertaken by Early Friends'. Quaker detachment and exclusivity must become relics of the past. If their wartime stand was to be more than an isolated incident of martyrdom or special pleading, they were obliged to reach out to the Labour Party and other emerging movements wherein they had an 'opportunity to bring the Quaker pacifist message to bear upon what was perhaps the most dangerous problem of the hour'.[92]

Rufus Jones, very much the man of the hour, re-enforced his fellow American's message:

The Society of Friends has been awaiting this generation of Young Friends for 250 years . . . We must . . . get down to the great constructive principles underlying our Quakerism instead of having superficial peculiarities . . . The Inner Light is in danger of becoming an abstract phrase . . . we need . . . to incarnate what we mean by the Inner Light and carry it into human and living experience . . . We must *know* the Inward Light in terms of experience if we are to meet the world's troubles today.[93]

These sentiments were certainly indicative of the triumph of the liberal theology which, asserting its dominant influence over a third generation of English Friends, would cast British Quakerism in a new mould. The speech most indicative of the altered dimensions in Friends' social and political thinking was delivered by Walter H. Ayles, a member of the Amalgamated Society of Engineers and future Labour MP. A Friend by convincement, drawn to Quakerism while serving four sentences as a conscientious objector, Ayles was a man of humble origins and a socialist.

---

[91] 'The Upshot of the War: World Problems', in *Jordans, 1920: Being the Report of the International Conference of Young Friends held at Jordans, August 24–30, 1920*, edited by Bertram Pickard (London [1920]), 15–17
[92] Ibid. 20–1.   [93] 'The International Quaker Church', ibid. 21–2.

He was also representative of an emerging breed of British Friend, unconnected with the Society by birth and without much sense of or interest in historic Quakerism, but socially active and staunchly pacifist.[94]

Despite his status as a recent convert, Ayles was obviously confident of the support of his new co-religionists when he declared that the most pressing post-war task for Quakerism was to bring about God's Kingdom on earth by liberating 'the "wage-slave"' through 'common ownership of the Land and Capital of the world'. 'We must, Ayles concluded, "go into politics and Christianize them, and at the same time we must socialize Christianity. In short, we must live dangerously..." '[95]

Walter Ayles' point stuck home. The official *Report* of the conference claimed that 'there was absolute unanimity in the belief that the present social system is fundamentally anti-Christian' and that the best means of changing that system was 'by evolutionary methods', even if such 'evolution may be tantamount to revolution. We need not fear revolution, so long as it was of the right kind.' *The Report* concluded that only way to achieve such a revolution was for Friends to break free from the stand-offish timidity of the past, face the Social Problem head on and pay the cost of their revolutionary Quaker convictions by getting 'out into politics... in the true sense of the organisation of life'.[96]

To demonstrate the genuineness and the immediacy of these convictions, the conference dispatched a message to the Home Secretary pleading for the release of Terence MacSwiney, the Lord Mayor of Cork, recently jailed for alleged IRA activities.[97] It was a heartfelt but futile gesture—MacSwiney had already commenced the hunger strike that would kill him after ten agonizing weeks— and it illustrated the difficulties inherent in the attempt of a tiny minority, however respected, to use its moral force to procure political ends. Still, young Friends would never be more willing or eager to bring the weight of their convictions, recently vindicated by communal defiance and individual suffering, to bear on any situation, however removed by geography or circumstance

---

[94] Walter Ayles (1879–1953), a founding member of the No-Conscription Fellowship, was Labour MP for North Bristol (1923–4, 1929–31) and for Southall, (1945–53) as well as the organizing secretary for the No More War Movement, 1926–32. See *BDMPL*, 43–5.
[95] *Jordans, 1920*, 30–1.   [96] Ibid. 31–2.   [97] Ibid. 101–2.

from their individual experiences. Another convinced Friend who supported the spirit of this sort of commitment addressed the problem of how a sectarian body might influence not only domestic events but global affairs as well.

Carl Heath (1869–1950) had, like Walter Ayles, joined Friends during the Great War. In August 1914 Heath, as Secretary to the National Peace Council, had been shocked to discover that Quakers were nearly the only members of that erstwhile pacifist body to retain their convictions. At a Friends conference of 1917, shortly after his acceptance into the Society, Heath introduced a proposal to establish 'Quaker Embassies' in the great cities of post-war Europe as 'growing points of the spirit', directed by a 'Friends Foreign Office' and spreading the message of reconciliation and peace.[98] Yearly Meeting approved of Heath's plan in 1918 and the next year a Council for International Service (CIS), eventually headed by Heath himself, was established to implement a modified version of his plan.[99]

At Jordans, Heath attested to the practicality of his proposal by demonstrating the historical example of a religious community affecting international events. Citing the traditional influence of the Church of Rome on the international scene, he admitted that, historically, the Catholic hierarchy had too often used their Church's spiritual authority to preserve or advance its worldly status rather than to seek the Kingdom of God. But with the dawning of the new Age of Democracy, Heath envisioned a means for directing world events along the path to peace through 're-discovery of a Christianity which will prove to be a practical mysticism closely akin to essential Quakerism'.[100] 'If Quakerism is to have a part in the corporate life of a new age it is not as a small sectarian Church. God forbid! It is rather as a witness to that inward power in the common man which, rightly directed may mould the politics of the new world in righteousness, freedom, and the joyful corporate life of a religious international.'[101]

---

[98] *TF*, 20 April 1917, 298. See Heath's pamphlet *Quaker Embassies* (Privately printed [1917]). Also see Greenwood, *Quaker Encounters*, III, 198–202 and *BDMPL*, 390–92 for brief accounts of Heath's career.

[99] Quaker agencies, called 'centres' rather than embassies, were set up in Berlin, Vienna, Paris, Geneva, and other places. In 1927 the CIS merged with the Friends Service Council, of which Heath remained Secretary until 1935.

[100] *Jordans, 1920*, 33–6.   [101] Ibid. 37–8.

The discussion that followed Carl Heath's speech centred on the idea of Quakerism as the possible 'germ' of a great international Fellowship which 'might rise to that place of moral supremacy... of which the Roman Church had given us a glimpse in the Middle Ages,' was, according to the official *Report*, the most elevated and inspiring of the conference.[102]

Neave Brayshaw was the final speaker at Jordans. That he should have had the last word was a special honour and well deserved. More than any other, Brayshaw had nurtured and shaped the pre-war Young Friends Movement which had played such a vital role in ensuring Friends' official corporate adherence to the peace testimony. During the war his words and letters braced up many young men who were unsure about or frightened of the implications of the stand they were attempting to make. By 1920, however, some of those present at Jordans may have felt that Neave, for all the value of his past services, was looking back to where Young Friends had been rather than forward towards where they might wish to go. Still, the themes Neave pursued were akin to those which had dominated both the post-war conferences.

If the Society of Friends was to make the most of the spiritual strength built through its wartime resistance to violence and hatred, Brayshaw said, Quakers must relinquish that 'certain reserve', in which Friends of previous generations had taken an almost perverse pride, and mingle with a broader company of humanity, for if God was truly in every human person, then love of God and love of man could not be separated. Their faith must be a living thing and in putting that faith into practice as a means of healing the world of the sickness of hate, Quakers could not simply help the victims of wrong but must also minister to the victimizers. To accomplish this monumental task, he said, young people would need to draw upon the spiritual strength of their Quaker ancestors as well as the example of their courageous contemporaries. Wielding these weapons of the spirit, they might, by action and example, build, he concluded, a 'Holy City... of living stones, living members, that it may be true to the words of the prophet contemplating his plan of the ideal Jerusalem, the name of the city... shall be "The Lord is there" '. The fulfillment, indeed, of God's Kingdom on earth.[103]

---

[102] Ibid. 38–40.   [103] *Jordans*, 65–6.

The British Friends, young and old, who drifted—energized, inspired, exhausted, disappointed, or indifferent—back to their several meetings and separate lives from the first international gatherings of their Religious Society, were most assuredly of a different breed from the grey-clad, bonneted Quakers who had departed London Yearly Meeting six decades earlier. To use a Darwinian analogy, those Victorian Friends were like the finches of the Galápagos archipelago, isolated, inbred, out of touch with the wider world. Three generations later, their descendants, and the strangers who had flown in to join them, were less peculiar, less shy and, leaving nature behind, less pious than the odd birds whose great London nest they still occupied.

In 1861 the *Christian Doctrine, Practice, and Discipline* warned against 'the attendance of places of diversion' and 'the temptations of music' or other 'indulgence in the vain amusements of the world. In mixing in public companies . . . our minds may be gratified, but our quick perception of spiritual instruction may be weakened . . . Love not the world or the things of the world . . . The prize is before you: it is a prize not of earth but of heaven . . .'[104]

Sixty years later the Yearly Meeting *Epistle* admonished young Quakers to go out into the world with eyes wide open 'to the oppression caused by . . . economic and other privileges . . . we have often taken for granted', but with firm resolve to 'break down the social and educational barriers . . . which mar the fellowship of the human family'. Life for Friends was no longer to be apart from the world but rather a part of 'the joyful adventure of establishing that commonwealth . . . which Jesus proclaimed as the reign of God upon earth'.[105]

So, guided by the renewed authority of the Light of Christ Within, armed with a rejuvenated peace testimony more powerful than the commands of the State and moved by a quickened sense of social and economic justice for all women as well as all men, the British Society of Friends faced the world of the twentieth century resolved to create the Kingdom of God on Earth. That they have so far failed to do so comes as no surprise; nor should anyone be amazed that they have never ceased to try.

[104] *Christian Doctrine* (London 1861), 81, 98.
[105] *Christian Life, Faith and Thought in the Society of Friends* (London 1923), 88.

12

Legacies of the Quaker Transformation

What was different about the British Society of Friends which hosted Quakerism's first World Conference in 1920 and the Society which had begun the process of transformation around 1860? What difference had this transformation made in the condition of British Friends? What influence did the changed condition of Quakerism have with regard to relations between Friends and the British State? Why is any of this important in the history of religion in modern Britain? What difference does any of this make to anybody who was not a Quaker? These are some of the questions to be answered in the following recapitulation. To the reader's satisfaction it is to be devoutly hoped.

Whether or not the religion practiced by early Victorian evangelical Friends had strayed significantly from ideas and practices established by George Fox and his followers in the 1650s, whatever energy and creativity flowed out from the Society of Friends during the first half of the nineteenth century derived from its evangelical wing. By 1860 the urgency and vigour of evangelical Friends had induced the leadership of London Yearly Meeting to embark upon a series of significant reforms, the first among British Quakers in over a century. But while internal provisions for easing dress, speech, and marriage regulations began the process of bringing British Quakers out of their 'closed-in hedge of prickly-pear', Friends were inevitably slow to respond to new ideas or attitudes, even those that might be shaking the foundations of the world outside the Meeting House. Thus, during the decade of the 1860s the leaders of British Quakerism were beginning to make compromises with ideas that had been fresh in the 1830s and 1840s. At the same time, an increasing number of younger Quakers were being educated in the world of 'creaturely' things and becoming entangled with the thoughts and ways of that world. Because this mid-Victorian generation was being exposed to theological and scientific ideas which could not be accommodated by evangelical beliefs and practices, difficulty and upheaval were inevitable.

The events in Manchester surrounding the putative revolt of David Duncan and his followers reflected a widening gap between the assertive, progressive vision of better-educated, more worldly-wise Friends, and the cautious posture of the evangelicals who dominated London Yearly Meeting. David Duncan was sufficiently learned and egotistical to challenge the powers that were, locally and nationally, to a showdown on a broad-based agenda of modern thought. He failed miserably not simply because he was premature in his vision of what might be acceptable to Friends but also because he had no following outside Manchester. Had Duncan lived long enough to challenge his disownment from Manchester Meeting in some national Quaker forum, he might have made a beginning as the prophet of the new, liberal vision of Quakerism. Still, given his obvious Unitarian tendencies, it seems improbable that he could have provided the leadership for an early blossoming of the Quaker Renaissance. Most likely, Duncan would have carried his devotees out of the Society of Friends into some short-lived, long-forgotten theistic congregation.

What Duncan did do, however, was to bump up the level of argument among thoughtful Quakers who were prepared to debate the case for change within a solidly Christian context. These were the reform-minded Friends who engaged the attention of moderate evangelicals who were willing to consider the possibility of change as a product of long study and deep reflection. During the 1870s and 1880s the path toward serious transformation was prepared by Friends who, like David Duncan, had absorbed many of the lessons of liberal theology and modern science but who, unlike the Manchester rebels, operated within an unassailably Christian framework. The authors of influential books like *A Reasonable Faith* and *The Gospel of Divine Help* had sound credentials among Friends as well as broad knowledge of and accomplishments in the wider world. They set out the theologically liberal foundation stones upon which the Renaissance of Quakerism was erected between 1890 and 1914.

The Manchester Conference of 1895 has been depicted as the decisive moment in the triumph of the ideals and principles of that Quaker Renaissance. There is a sense in which this is true. At Manchester the forces of liberal modernity obviously outshone and outmanoeuvered their evangelical brethren, at least to the satisfaction of most younger members of the Society. Modern ideas of both the secular and religious variety were openly embraced for the first time. Even more important was the emergence of a discernible group of leaders, John Wilhelm Rowntree, W. C. Braithwaite, Rendal Harris, Edward Grubb and others, who had the courage of their convictions and the energy to spread their views, in person and in print, throughout the confines of London Yearly Meeting, and even beyond. The Summer School Movement, the founding of Woodbrooke, the opening of a serious dialogue with the liberal American Quakers led by Rufus Jones, the deepening interest in Quaker history and the more effective organization of Young Friends were all vital by-products of the spirit of Manchester. Yet some questions and concerns which were basic to the spirit of the Quaker Renaissance, including the peace testimony, social policy and the role of women, were scarcely discussed or totally ignored at Manchester.[1] Each of these issues, under the influence of both secular and spiritual liberal idealism, took on a life of its own after 1895 and each, in its own way, would generate fundamental changes in the twentieth century Society of Friends.

Most of the significant alterations that took place within the Society of Friends during the course of the Quaker Renaissance could be termed progressive in both a social and theological sense. Those responsible for implementing these modifications viewed them as representing positive movement, from traditional preoccupations to modern thought, from antiquated philanthropy to sound social policy, from self-consciously outside the intellectual and social mainstream to comfortably within it. By the end of the nineteenth century, as the Society slowly recovered its numerical strength, the progressive moulders of the Quaker Renaissance had apparently emerged triumphant. Under the growing influence of a better-educated, socially sensitive and theologically up-to-date generation, Quakerism had not only undergone an intellectual revival but had also created a new theology, fusing modern thought with the inspirations of early Friends. Entering a new century, Friends seemed to possess a clearer sense of who they were and where they were going, to be a religious community that had

---

[1] For consideration of the Manchester Conference, see my essay 'What Hath Manchester Wrought? Change in the Religious Society of Friends, 1895–1920', *JFHS*, 57/3 (1996), 278–83.

come to grips with the challenge of modernity and emerged, if not with unanimity, with, at least, a broadly optimistic consensus concerning future prospects, both spiritual and material.

Still, for all of their emphasis on aligning the Society of Friends with the most important and influential aspects of modern thought, there were still ways in which even the most liberal or radical members of the transformed British Quaker community were unwilling to accommodate modern society and the modern state. In an age when imperialism and militarism were propagated and celebrated as natural results of the universal struggle for survival of the fittest, and at a time when the socially and morally debilitating effects of widespread poverty were being starkly and systematically revealed, many Friends were acutely aware of a need to resist the cynical, materialistic impulses of the day. A key development for the leaders of the modern Quaker movement was the failure of London Yearly Meeting to uphold Friends' traditional peace principles by presenting unified opposition to the war in South Africa. In the wake of what they considered to be a humiliating spiritual debacle, activist Friends undertook a serious inquiry into the origins and meaning of their Society's historic peace testimony, which appeared to them to have grown languid from lack of testing. The ensuing re-emphasis upon and revitalization of Quaker peace principles during the Edwardian period was a crucial development that would, with the coming of the Great War, again transform both the image and reality of British Quakerism.

The First World War presented the British Society of Friends with its greatest crisis since the Restoration, severely testing the principles and practices that had emerged during the Quaker Renaissance. For while most British Quakers remained at least nominally opposed to the war and the threat of enforced military service, a considerable body of war Friends chose to support the national cause. At the same time, wartime decisions by London Yearly Meeting brought Quakerism into direct conflict with State authority for the first time since the seventeenth century. In truth, this defiant resistance to secular power did not reflect a broad-based consensus. Even the majority of Friends who refused to support the war, if left to their own devices, would probably have been willing to make some accommodation with the Government, so long as they were not forced to take up carnal weapons. The policy of non-co-operation as well as non-resistance officially adopted by

London Yearly Meeting represented the determination of a small but spiritually powerful minority of British Friends, all products of the Quaker Renaissance, to maintain unwavering adherence to the traditional but long untested Quaker peace testimony. Thus, in the extremely significant question of the duties of citizens to the modern State during wartime, the Society's stand, as a Society, was a throwback, not just to early Quaker practice but to the pacifism of primitive Christianity. Furthermore, British Quakerism's redefining of its peace testimony in the crucible of the Great War was not only a logical extension of the message of the Quaker Renaissance but was also a giant step on a journey from which there is not likely to be a return. For all that British Friends did between 1860 and 1914 to accommodate themselves to the social, intellectual, and political conventions of modern industrial society, London Yearly Meeting defiantly resisted the commands of the Warrior State during the Great War, a position British Quakerism has maintained in the face of the British State and the warring world throughout the twentieth century.

At the same time London Yearly Meeting was challenging the right of the State to place its security over the majesty of conscience, socialist Friends, whose voices were powerfully amplified by the extraordinary events of the Great War, seriously called to question the prevailing social, political, and economic systems which had served their fathers and grandfathers so well. The glaring social injustices produced by an apparently triumphant capitalist system caused these Friends to embrace radical social and political ideals. The founding of the Socialist Quaker Society (SQS) in 1898 marked the first significant step away from both the *laissez-faire* liberalism and placid philanthropy characteristic of nineteenth-century Quakerism. The SQS remained small in numbers and influence before 1914, effectively neutralized by a more weighty and respectable product of the New Liberalism, the Friends Social Union. Still, this small body of socialist Friends created a spark of radicalism that would burst forth amidst the tempestuous events of the war years. Inspired as much by Levellers and Marxists as by Holy Writ or George Fox, these men and women sought to transform the Society of Friends from a socially conservative, eminently respectable, politically Liberal body of believers into a truly radical organization, advocating revolutionary political, social and economic changes. In the end, socialist

Quakers never managed to establish their own distinctly minority view as the Quaker standard. For while the post-war Society made a discernible shift to the political left and drastically reorganized itself for the implementation of social action programmes, this realignment brought most British Quakers only so far as a somewhat uncomfortable alliance with the Labour Party. They supported Labour, not because of its socialist principles, but because it seemed the only significant political body to have maintained its moral integrity during the war years.

After the war ended, British Quakers sought to assess the implications of their newly asserted peace testimony and social activism in conjunction with other Quaker communities, especially those in North America. The ensuing London All-Friends Conference of 1920, called to consider the place of Quakerism in the emerging twentieth-century world, marked the first world-wide gathering of the followers of George Fox. While in many ways the All-Friends Conference failed to fulfill the expectations of its organizers, it did manage effectively to establish a sense of the validity of unwavering Quaker resistance to war and conscription, the necessity for Quaker social action, at home and abroad, as an aspect of the Society's spiritual mission and the primacy of liberal theology as the organizing principle for British Quaker spirituality.

What were, then, the most important results of Quakerism's transformation? To begin, the focus of Quaker theological concern had shifted from the uneasy mid-nineteenth-century combination of biblical fundamentalism and conservative quietism to an emphasis on Inward Light theology as the key to personal and collective spiritual fulfillment. Furthermore, the triumph of liberal theology was increasingly accompanied by a sort of ideological tolerance which would have been unthinkable for nineteenth-century Friends, as the example of the Duncanites revealed. In the course of becoming associated, almost against their will, with radical resistance to State authority, British Friends found themselves yoked to some curious allies—militant socialists, liberal freethinkers, eccentric anarchists. Earlier generations had consistently resisted such alignments, but the Quaker experience during the Great War had a two-pronged effect. Not only were Friends more ready to associate with unbelievers but a fair number of social and political militants, some of them without any attachment to Christianity, were drawn to Quakerism.

Now, in the late twentieth century, a rising chorus of neo-evangelical and neo-conservative Friends have asserted that in the decades since the First World War the Society's largely liberal leadership, in both its acceptance of an increasingly nebulous Quaker theology and in its tolerance of ideas and practices brought to Friends from various fringe movements, has put the Society of Friends, both in Britain and North America, in danger of losing contact with its vital centre and, indeed, its identity within the Christian community. Much of the current discourse among Friends concerning the legacy of the liberal-inspired Quaker Renaissance in Britain, which advanced in tandem with Rufus Jones' vision of Quakerism as a mystical religion, revolves around the question of whether the results of the changes inspired by Jones and British liberals were a good thing or a bad thing. For the most part, liberal Friends continue to believe that the transformation thus effected was salutary because it greatly expanded the horizons of Quakerism in the modern world.[2] Both neo-evangelical Quakers[3] and the back-to-our-roots New Foundation Movement[4] believe that the liberal Renaissance has had negative repercussions because, whether by accident or design, the tolerant atmosphere it helped to create opened the Society of Friends to an influx of left-wing humanists, assorted social radicals and ethical universalists who envision Quakerism as an agency for social change or a forum for radical idealism rather than a community of faithful Christians.

As it seems to me, many of those who now argue for or against one or another contemporary version of Quakerism and point to the liberal reformers of the Quaker Renaissance as the progenitors of either great success or serious deterioration, ignore centrally important historical truths about the British Society of Friends in the twentieth century. The critical, life-sustaining revitalization of

---

[2] For a vigorous recent defence of a broad-based Quaker communion (including Friends who practice a form of witchcraft), see Chuck Fager, *Without Apology: The Heroes, the Heritage and the Hope of Liberal Quakerism* (Media, Pa., 1996).

[3] For a spirited example of contemporary criticism of liberal British Quakerism, see Martin Davie, 'Quaker Theology Since 1895', *FQ*, 30/3 (July 1996), 131–43. Less strident and more convincing is John Punshon's, *Letter to a Universalist* (Wallingford, Pa. 1989).

[4] The New Foundation Fellowship, emphasizing the prophetic nature of authentic Quakerism, was in large measure a response to Lewis Benson's *Catholic Quakerism* (Philadelphia 1966). Its ideas and aims are most lucidly and powerfully set out in Douglas Gwynn's, *Apocalypse of the Word* (Richmond, 1986).

the London Yearly Meeting during the last years of the nineteenth and first two decades of the twentieth century not only changed the theological disposition of British Quakerism, it prepared London Yearly Meeting, spiritually as well as socially and politically, to deal with the great crisis of the First World War, the most decisive test of the character of Quaker faith in 250 years. In Britain, at least, that test was passed and Quakerism was greatly strengthened thereby. Without the very early twentieth-century reawakening of the need for a revitalized peace testimony, an obsessive point for many Quaker liberals, the London Yearly Meeting would not likely have taken the defiant stance it assumed between 1914 and 1918. What difference would it have made if British Friends had decided, as many wished, to compromise with the State by accepting some special status in exchange for muffling official protests against the war and conscription? Who can say? What one can say is that with regard to the extremely significant question of the duties of citizens to the modern warring State, during the Great War the Society of Friends, liberal or otherwise, represented a throwback, not just to seventeenth-century post-Restoration Quaker practice but to the pacifism of primitive Christianity. That expression of what Wilfred Littleboy called the 'Everlasting No' to the State's commands for even passive support of fighting and killing was as great a triumph as Quakerism has won in its three-hundred-year history. And there's the rub.

Quakers as a body seem to have problems dealing with history. From an historical perspective it is difficult to imagine authentic Quakerism without the centrality of the Inward Light, for it was from George Fox's revelation that only the Inward Light of Christ could speak to the human condition that Quakerism emerged as a separate, unique religious community. Yet throughout much of the nineteenth century many who accounted themselves true Friends believed that the concept of an Inward Light was a seventeenth-century 'delusion' which ought to be discarded. These Friends denied the historical relevance of the Inward Light because it seriously impinged upon the validity of their evangelical theological posture. On the other hand, it seems impossible for the historian to conceive of the Society of Friends as other than a Christian body of believers. But in the late twentieth century there are those who hold themselves to be perfectly good Quakers while at the same time denying the necessity of any connection between

Quakerism and Christianity. The positions of both nineteenth-century evangelicals and twentieth-century universalists would have to be judged at least as a-historical, if not anti-historical.

Historians, on the whole, reject the old saw that history somehow repeats itself, but most agree that instances of historical continuity can be identified. In this light, the negative response of some late twentieth-century Friends to what is seen as the insidious, if unintended, influence of liberal theology on contemporary Quakerism appears in many ways to be a circular repetition of the same sort of argument used a century ago by liberal Quakers against their evangelical brethren. Reformers during the era of the Quaker Renaissance passionately believed that most evangelical Friends, overwhelmed by the emotional intensity and biblical literalism of mainstream Protestantism, had lost sight of the original spiritual principles of their Religious Society, adopting a pinched and stifling Calvinistic creed that would have utterly repelled early Friends. A century later there is deeply felt concern, and not only among evangelical Friends, that as John Punshon has put it, Quakerism is becoming 'a form of religion that is so open that it seems unable to provide clear guidance in the things that really matter'.[5] There is much to be said for the pertinence of the criticisms of anomalous forms of Quaker practice during both nineteenth and twentieth centuries, but to the critically admiring outsider there would seem much to be gained if more Friends acquired a deeper understanding of and appreciation for both high and low points in the history of their most remarkable and highly esteemed religious Society.

As for the impact of Quakerism in Britain and around the world since 1920, the revitalized peace testimony has remained the most important social and political consequence of the Quaker Renaissance. To a considerable extent, modern British Quakerism is identified, at least by those outside the fold, with peace principles delineated in the early decades of the twentieth century and officially, if not individually, maintained by British Friends since that time. Indeed, the late twentieth-century Society of Friends could hardly survive as a separate religious communion if it were to

---

[5] John Punshon, 'Some Reflections on Quakers and the Evangelical Spirit', in *Truth's Bright Embrace*, edited by Paul Anderson and Howard R. Macy (Newberg, Oregon 1996), 217.

abandon or seriously weaken its peace testimony. The really new and vital element of twentieth-century Quaker commitment to peace was the Society's insistence on positive action to prevent war rather than purely negative resistance once war had begun. In this regard, one significant inter-war Quaker innovation was the establishment of 'embassies' or Council Centres in various European capitals from which unofficial Quaker ambassadors of peace ventured forth to offer their services in conflict resolution and humanitarian aid programmes. Of course, Friends were no more able to prevent the Second World War than they had been capable of stopping the First. Still, the good work that was done and continues to be done by the Friends Service Council and other Quaker agencies on behalf of the weak and the persecuted planted the seeds which have begotten not just new recruits to the Quaker fold but helped to bring to the attention of people of goodwill throughout the world the efficacy of the Quaker model of serving life rather than ministering to death.

As for Quaker influences within British society and politics, the decision of Friends as a corporate body to accede to the demands of their faith rather than to accommodate the dictates of the State raised serious questions about the role of conscience in a free and democratic society. During the inter-war period loathing over the results of the Great War and fear about the onset of an even greater catastrophe elevated former Quaker prisoners for conscience to positions of moral superiority in the minds of many. Ultimately, even the British Government responded by establishing provisions for more flexible treatment of war resisters and thus avoiding a repeat of the worst abuses of the Great War period. For while the legitimacy of every claim of conscientious objection to war and military service was still severely tested, the right of genuine resisters to special consideration became a principle of law and a point of national pride. In the end, then, the most important effects of the transformation of Quakerism on the British nation were its contribution to the preservation of religious freedom and civil liberty.

The Quakers had been heard because they would not allow the voice of conscience to be silenced. That voice still resonates out from the London Friends House on Euston Road and from hundreds of meetings in large cities and tiny villages with a 'Message to

Friends and Fellow Seekers', which represented the deep faith and earnest hope of the makers of twentieth-century Quakerism:

Day by day... [to] seek out and remove every seed of hatred and of greed, of resentment and of grudging in our own selves and in the social structure about us... Surely this is the way in which Christ calls us to overcome the barriers of race and class and thus to make of all humanity a society of friends.[6]

[6] 'To Friends and Fellow-Seekers', *AFC, Official Report*, 201.

Bibliography

MANUSCRIPT SOURCES

Quaker Collections

Friends Historical Library, Swarthmore College
Priscilla H. Peckover Papers

Haverford College Quaker Collection
Rufus M. Jones Papers.

Library of the Society of Friends, London
A. C. Wilson to Executives of the Society for Liberation of Religion from State Patronage and Control, 11 May 1917
'Appeal From Women Friends for Consideration of Women's Suffrage at Y.M.', 1910, Box 2/16.
Arnold S. Rowntree Papers, Temp. MS 310/5/2
Box Meeting, *Minute Book*, 1748–1760.
Braithwaite, Joseph Bevan, 'Journals and Commentaries', 4 vols., MS. vol. S 293–6, Ports. 17/89, B/39, 81/26.
—— 'Thoughts on the Atonement', 11 April 1872, MS. Port. 8/126.
—— to Conference on Ministry, York, MS. Port., 20/26.
Braithwaite, William Charles, 'Youth and Militarism', Temp Box 4/1.
Committee to Assist Lancashire and Cheshire Quarterly Meeting, 1870–1872, SR 4 Lan.
Committee to Consider the Position of Women Friends, Letters and Papers, MS. Box X3/3b.
Correspondence to Thomas Hodgkin relating to Joel and Hannah Bean (1894–1899)
Forster, Joseph B., 'Memoranda in reference to the action of the Committee of the Manchester Institute, 1858 to 1869', 25 September 1870, MS Box 9.6 (2), LSF.
Forster, Josiah, 'Memoranda Respecting London Yearly Meeting from 1828–1870 (with some exceptions)', MS. vols. S 26 and 76.
Francis T. Howith to John Hodgkin, 10 Nov. 1868, MS. Port. C/130.
Friends Home Mission Committee, *Minutes*, 9 vols.

Friends Service Committee, *Minutes, Records of Work and Documents Issued*, June 1915–May 1920, 3 vols.
Friends Social Union, *Annual Reports*.
—— *Minutes*, 1904–1915, 1916–17.
—— 'Reports and Pamphlets', 1904–1915.
Fry, Ruth A., 'Friends Relief Work Since 1914', Temp, MSS. 481.
Herbert M. Hodgkin Papers, Temp. MS. 355.
John Bright to J. B. Braithwaite, 26 December 1859, Temp. Box 10a/11.
Kemp, Caleb R., 'Journals, 1853–1908', Temp. Box 2414, Port. C/127, MS. Vol. S.3 to S.8.
L. Violet Hodgkin Papers, MS vol. 128.
Lyra T. Wolkins Papers, Temp. MSS. 584.
'Manchester Crisis', MS Box 9/1–10.
Mary Hodgson to Elizabeth [Green], 7 March 1864, 12 Aug. and 15 Nov. 1871, Port. A/58–60.
Meeting for Sufferings, 'Message to Men and Women of Goodwill', [August 1914].
Meeting for Sufferings, *Minutes*.
'Meeting on Quaker Literature, its History and Aims', London Yearly Meeting, 1907, Box R2/13.
Milligan, Edward, 'T. Edmund Harvey', unpublished manuscript.
Peace Committee, *Minutes*.
Peace Committee Publications, Box U/7.
Penney, Harrison, 'Account of Yearly Meeting, 1870', MS. Box P1/8.
Philip Radley Papers, Temp MS 299.
Rowntree, John Stephenson, 'Account of Yearly Meeting, 1859', MS Vol. S 368.
—— 'Account of Yearly Meeting, 1871', MS. Vol. S 270.
—— 'Memorandum for Peace Committee, London Yearly Meeting, 1902'.
—— to Norman Penney, 10 October 1905, MS. Port. 81/35.
—— to Elizabeth [Rowntree], 14 July 1858, MS Port. 42/56.
Rowntree, John Wilhelm, 'Memorandum Upon the Recording of Ministers', MS. Port., 23/40.
Satterthwaite, George to John Hodgkin, 13 Jan. 1868, Port. C/136.
Septuagenarian [Thomas Tonge], 'Fifty Years Ago', *Manchester City News*, 3 August 1921, in Vol. vv/75.
Socialist Quaker Society, *Minute Book*, 1898–1909, MS Vol. S 275, 1910–1913, MS Vol. S 171.
Stewart, John Fyfe, 'Christmas 1909', Box 181, LSF.
Taylor, Ernest E., 'Diary', Temp. Box 23/3.
'To Our Fellow Members of Military Age of the Society of Friends', FSC printed documents, Temp. MS S. 31.

Woodbrooke Library, Birmingham
George Cadbury Papers
Minutes of the Settlement Committee
Summer School Continuation Committee Papers
Woodbrooke Settlement Committee Papers

Archival Collections

British Library, London
Arthur Balfour Papers, Ad. Mss. 49710

Brotherton Library, University of Leeds
Minutes of the Meeting of Elders, Yorkshire Quarterly Meeting.
Minute Book, Yorkshire 1905 Committee.
Minutes, Yorkshire Quarterly Meeting, Minute Books, 1893–1920, II/
12–14.

Cumbria Record Office, Carlisle
Catherine Marshall Papers (Microfilm copies seen by courtesy of Jo
Vellacott)

House of Lords Record Office
David Lloyd George Papers
Andrew Bonar Law Papers
J. St Loe Strachey Papers

John Rylands Library, University of Manchester
John William Graham Papers

Lancashire Record Office, Preston
Minutes, Lancashire and Cheshire Quarterly Meeting, 1855–1879
Minutes, Lancashire and Cheshire Women's Quarterly Meeting,
1893–1924

MacMaster University, Hamilton, Ontario, Canada
Bertrand Russell Archives

Manchester City Library, Manchester
Minutes, Hardshaw East Monthly Meeting.

National Army Museum, London
Lord Roberts of Kandahar Papers

Public Record Office, London

Lord Kitchener Papers, 'Conscientious Objectors: 1 June 1916', 30/57/94

War Office Papers, 'Conscientious Objectors', WO 32/5491.

University of Texas Library, Austin

Ottoline Morrell Papers

Private Collections

John H. Barlow Papers, in possession of Mary Millor Barlow Braithwaite, London.

Braithwaite Family Papers, in possession of Richard Braithwaite, Cambridge.

Dorothy Crowly Brown, 'Journal, 1897–1901', typescript in possession of Elfrida Vipont Brown, Yealand Conyers.

William T. Ecroyd Papers, in possession of Henry Ecroyd, London.

Hubert S. Peet Papers, in possession of Stephen Peet, London.

Wilfrid E. Littleboy Papers, in possession of Margaret Nash.

Joseph Rowntree Papers, in possession of Michael Rowntree, Kirkby-moorside.

Hodgkin Family Papers, in possession of Robin Hodgkin, Torquay.

Laura Jane Moore, 'Reflections, 1870–1955', in possession of Henry Ecroyd, London.

Rowntree Family Papers, Jean Rowntree, Stone-in-Oxney.

Rowntree, Lawrence, 'A Nightmare', unpublished manuscript.

Scott, Richenda C., 'Notebook on Summer Schools', gift of Roger C. Wilson to the author.

INTERVIEWS

Alexander, Horace, Longwood, Pa., November 1980.

Braithwaite, Richard, Cambridge, August 1986.

Braithwaite, Mary Millor, London, August 1986.

Ecroyd, Henry, Friends House, London, August 1986.

Foulds, Elfrida Vipont, Yealand Conyers, Lancashire, August 1986.

Gillett, Arthur Nicholas, Exeter, August 1986.

Greenwood, J. Omerod, London, August 1986.

Hewison, Hope Hay, Exeter, August 1986.

Hodgkin, Robin A., Torquay and Exeter, August 1986.

Jones, Mary Hoxie, Haverford College, September 1983.

Milligan, Edward, Friends House, London, May 1994.

Nash, Margaret, Exeter, August 1986.
Naish, Richard, Stoney-in-Oxney, Kent, August 1986.
Nickalls, John, Welwyn Garden City, August 1986
Punshon, John, Exeter, August 1986.
Radley, Phillip, Cambridge, August 1986.
Rowntree, Jean, Stone-in-Oxney, Kent, August 1986.
Rowntree, Richard, Exeter, August 1986.
Scott, Richenda, Friends House, London, May 1976.
Sturge, Roger, Exeter, August 1986.
Wilson, Roger C., Yealand Conyers, Lancashire, August 1986.

PUBLICATIONS, THESES, AND OTHER PRINTED SOURCES

Abbreviations of Journals

AF	*The American Friend*
BF	*The British Friend*
CH	*Church History*
FQ	*The Friends Quarterly*
FQE	*Friends Quarterly Examiner*
HOP	*The Herald of Peace*
JFHS	*Journal of the Friends Historical Society*
MF	*The Manchester Friend*
PDP	*The Present Day Papers*
PS	*The Ploughshare*
QH	*Quaker History*
QRT	*Quaker Religious Thought*
QS	*Quaker Studies*
TF	*The Friend (London)*
TRIB	*The Tribunal*
VS	*Victorian Studies*
W&P	*War and Peace*

A Challenge to Militarism (London: The Friends' Service Committee [1918]).
'A "Conservative" View of London Yearly Meeting, 1846', *JFHS* 181/1 (1921), 28.
'A Declaration Issued by the Committee Appointed by the Yearly Meeting of the Religious Society of Friends to Visit Lancashire and Cheshire Quarterly Meeting', reprinted as Appendix A to LYM, 1872, 32–5.

A.B.C.D. [anon.], 'Ideal Quakerism or Undogmatic Theology', *BF* (1 Aug. 1871), 201.

Aarek, Hans Eirek (ed.), *Quakerism: A Way of Life: In Homage of Sigrid Aellieson Lund* (Kvekerforlaget: Norwegian Quaker Press, 1982).

Adams, R. J. Q. and Philip H. Poirier, *The Conscription Controversy in Great Britain, 1900–1918* (Columbus, Ohio: Ohio State University Press, 1987).

Adams, T[ony], 'The Socialist Quaker Society (1898–1924): A Consideration of the Factors Influencing the Origins of the Socialist Quaker Society', (MA thesis, Leicester University, 1985).

Adams, Tony, *A Far-Seeing Vision. The Socialist Quaker Society, (1898–1924)* (Quaker Socialist Society, n.d.).

'Adjourned Yearly Meeting: A Churchman's Impressions', *PS*, 1/1 (Feb. 1916), 41.

'Adjourned Yearly Meeting: A Churchman's Impressions', *PS*, 1/2 (March 1916), 40–42.

Albright, M. Catherine, 'Review of *The Varieties of Religious Experience*', *PDP*, V/50 (15 Sept. 1902), 289–92.

Alexander, A. T., 'Yearly Meeting Attenders—Familiar Personalities', *JFHS*, 27 (1930), 15–16.

Alexander, Horace G., 'British Friends and the War of 1914', (typewritten personal memoir kindly provided by Horace Alexander).

—— 'Documentation and Correspondence' *QH*, 70/1 (Spring 1981), 47–50.

—— 'The Growth of the Peace Testimony of the Society of Friends', (London: Friends Home Peace Committee, 1939) 2nd edn. 1956.

Alexander, Joseph G., 'Our Social System', *FQE* (1871), 437–43.

Allen, Kerri and Alison Mackinnon, ' "Allowed and expected to be educated and intelligent": The Education of Quaker Girls in Nineteenth Century England', *History of Education*, 27/4 (1998), 391–402.

Allen, Margaret, 'Matilda Sturge: "Renaissance Woman" ', *Women's History Review*, 7/2 (1998), 209–26.

Allen, W. C., 'The New Quakerism', *BF* (Dec. 1898), 305–09.

All Friends Conference, London, August 1920: A Guide and Souvenir (London: Friends Bookshop [1920])

Allott, Stephen, *Friends in York* (York: Sessions, 1978).

—— *John Wilhelm Rowntree, 1868–1905* (York: Sessions Book Trust, 1994).

'The American Declaration of Faith—A Result', *BF* (Nov. 1893), 305–7.

'An Appeal to the Conscience of the Nation' from the London Yearly Meeting of the Society of Friends, May 1918.

[Anon.], *Observations on a Lecture Delivered at the Manchester Friends Institute by David Duncan, Entitled* Essays and Reviews, (London: A. W. Bennett, 1861).

Ash, Edward, *Quakerism* (London: A. W. Bennett, 1865).

—— 'The *Beacon* Controversy and the Yearly Meeting Committee of 1835–37', *TF* (Sept. 1870), 207–11 and Nov. 1870, 256–7.

Atkinson, Joseph, 'Institutionalism, the Last Stronghold of Priestcraft', *MF* (15 Aug. 1872), 136.

Bacon, Margaret Hope, 'The Establishment of London Women's Yearly Meeting: A Transatlantic Concern', *JFHS* 57/2 (1995), 151–65.

—— *Mothers of Feminism: The Story of Quaker Women in America* (San Francisco: Harper & Row, 1986).

Bailey, Richard, 'Making and Unmaking of a God: New Light on George Fox and Early Quakerism', in Michael Mullet (ed.), *New Light on George Fox and Early Quakerism*, (York: Sessions, 1993).

Barbour, Hugh, 'The "Lamb's War" and the Origins of the Quaker Peace Testimony', in Harvey L. Dyck (ed.), *The Pacifist Impulse in Historical Perspective* (Toronto: University of Toronto Press, 1996).

—— 'Quaker Prophetesses and Mothers in Israel', in J. William Frost and John H. Moore (eds.), *Seeking the Light: Essays in Quaker History* (Willingford & Haverford, PA: Pendle Hill Publications & Friends Historical Association, 1986).

—— *The Quakers in Puritan England* (New Haven, Conn.: Yale University Press, 1964).

Barclay's Apology in Modern English, ed. Dean Freiday (Newberg, Oregon: Barclay Press, 1991).

Barclay, Robert, *The Inner Life of the Religious Societies of the Commonwealth* (3rd. edn. London: Hodder and Stoughton, 1879).

Bassuk, Daniel E., 'Rufus Jones and Mysticism', *QRT* 17/4 (Summer 1978), 1–26.

Bean, Joel, 'The Issue', *BF* (March 1881), 49–51.

—— 'What is True Preparation for the Ministry', *BF* (2 May 1892), 105–7.

Bellows, Philip, *An Appeal to the 'Quaker Conscience' of England* (Wigan: Roger & Pennick, 1913).

Bellows, William L., '*Barclay Vindicated*': *A Review of Robert Charleton's Thoughts* (Manchester: Wm. Irwin, 1868).

Bennett, Alfred W., 'The Yearly Meeting', *FQE*, (1867), 359–76.

Benson, Louis, *Catholic Quakerism* (Philadelphia: Philadelphia Yearly Meeting), 1968.

Besse, Joseph, *A Collection of the Sufferings of the People Called Quakers* (London: Luke Hinde, 1753).

Birkel, Michael and John W. Newman (eds.), *The Lamb's War: Quaker Essays to Honor Hugh Barbour* (Richmond: Earlham College Press, 1992).

Bittle, William G., *James Naylor, 1618–1660: the Quaker Indicated by Parliament* (York: Sessions, 1986).

Blamires, David, Jeremy Greenwood and Alex Kerr (eds.), *A Quaker Miscellany for Edward H. Milligan* (Manchester: David Blamires, 1985).

Bone, Andrew G., 'Beyond the Rule of Law: Aspects of the Defence of the Realm Acts and Regulations, 1914–1918', (Ph.D. thesis, McMaster University, 1994).

Bottomley, J. Frith, 'Public Questions: IV—The Position of Women', *FQE* (1870), 560–87.

Bowen, Desmond, *The Idea of the Victorian Church* (Montreal: McGill University Press, 1968).

Brady, George S., *Lumen Siccum (An Essay on the Exercise of the Intellect in Matters of Religious Belief* (London: F. Bowyer Kitto, 1868).

—— 'Thoughts Supported by Darwin's "Origin of Species" ', *MF*. April 1872, 73–5.

[Braithwaite children], *Joseph Bevan Braithwaite: A Friend of the Nineteenth Century* (London: Hodder and Stoughton, 1909).

Braithwaite, Constance, 'Legal Problems of Conscientious Objection to Various Compulsions under British Law' (London: Friends Historical Society, 1968).

Braithwaite, J. B., 'Notes on the Richmond Conference, 1887', *FQE* (1888), 272–88.

—— 'Thoughts on the Atonement', *FQE* (1890), 103–20.

Braithwaite, J. B., Jr., 'The Society of Friends and the Limitations of its Peace Testimony', *FQE* (1918), 202–20.

Braithwaite, William Charles, 'The Adult School Movement', in Richard Mudie-Smith (ed.), *The Religious Life of London* (London: Hodder and Stoughton, 1904), 331–33.

—— *The Beginnings of Quakerism* (Cambridge: Cambridge University Press, 1955; 2nd. edn.).

—— 'The Conference: A Vision of Its Possibilities', in *All Friends Conference . . . A Guide and Souvenir*, 5.

—— *The Inspiration of the Bible*, (Yorkshire 1905 Committee Pamphlet, 1905).

—— *The Message and Mission of Quakerism* (Philadelphia: J. C. Winston, 1912).

—— *The Second Period of Quakerism* (Cambridge: Cambridge University Press, 1961).

—— 'Some Present-Day Aims of the Society of Friends', *FQE* (1895), 321–41.

—— 'Work for Peace', *PDP* (11 June 1899), 5–12.

Brayshaw, Alfred Neave, *Friends and the Inner Light*, (London: Headley Bros., [1915]).

Brayshaw, Alfred Neave, 'J. W. Rowntree, Biographical Notes', *TF* (17 March 1905), 165.

—— *Memoir and Selected Writings* (Birmingham: Woodbrooke Extension Committee, [1941]).

—— *The Quakers: Their Story and Message* (London: Swarthmore Press, 1921; reprinted York: Sessions, 1982).

Brinton, Howard, *Friends For 300 Years* (London: George Allen & Unwin, 1953).

Brock, Peter, *The Quaker Peace Testimony, 1660–1914* (York: William Sessions, 1990).

Bronner, Edwin B., 'Moderates in London Yearly Meeting, 1857–1873: Precursors of Quaker Liberals', *CH*, 59/3 (Sept. 1990), 356–71.

—— *'The Other Branch': London Yearly Meeting and The Hicksites, 1827–1912* (London: Friends Historical Society, 1975).

Brown, E. Vipont, 'The Renaissance of Quakerism', *FQ*, 514 (Oct. 1951), 201–06.

Brown, Henrietta, 'Help for Women', *BF* (May 1897), 116–17.

Carroll, Kenneth L., 'Early Quakers and "Going Naked as a Sign" ', *QH*, 67/2 (Autumn 1978), 69–87.

—— *John Perrot: Early Quaker Schismatic* (London: Friends Historical Society, 1971).

Catchpool, Corder, *On Two Fronts* (London: Headley Bros., 1918).

Ceadel, Martin, *British Pacifism; 1914–1945: The Defining of a Faith* (Oxford: Oxford University Press, 1980).

—— *The Origins of War Prevention: The British Peace Movement and International Relations, 1730–1854* (Oxford: The Clarendon Press, 1996).

Charity, Kate, *John Bellows of Gloucester, 1831–1902: A Many-Sided Man: Quaker Printer, Lexicographer, and Archaeologist: His Life and Letters* (York: Sessions, 1993).

Charleton, Robert, *Brief Thoughts on the Atonement* (Bristol: Ackland & Son, 1869).

Christian Discipline of the Religious Society of Friends (London: Samuel Harris, 1883).

Christian Discipline of the Religious Society of Friends of London Yearly Meeting, 2 vols. (London: Friends Bookshop, 1911)

Christian Doctrine, Practice, and Discipline (4th edn., London: Friends' Book Depository, 1861).

Christian Faith and Practice (London: Friends Book Centre, 1963).

Christian Life, Faith, and Thought in the Society of Friends (London: The Friends Bookshop, 1923).

Christian Practice (London: Friends Bookshop, 1925).

Church Government (London: Friends Book Centre, 1931).

Clark, J. Edmund, ' "The *Beacon*" Letters of James Clark', *JFHS*, 16/1 (1919), 129–33.

Clarke, Peter F., *Liberals and Social Democrats* (Cambridge: Cambridge University Press, 1970).

Clarkson, Thomas, *Portraiture of the Society of Friends*, 3 vols. (New York: Samuel Stansbury, 1806)

Cole, W. Alan, 'Quakers and the English Revolution', in T. Ashton (ed.) *Crisis in Europe* (1970 edn.), reprinted in *Past and Present* 10 (1956), 39–54.

Conference of All Friends: American Commissions I–V, VII. Report of American Commissions of the Conference of All Friends (Philadelphia: American Friends Service Committee [1920]).
I *Fundamental Basis of the Peace Testimony*
II *National Life and International Relations*
III *Personal Life and Society*
IV *Education: The Road to Peace*
V *The Relation of the Life of the Society to the Peace Testimony*
VII *The International Service of the Society of Friends*

Conference of All Friends Held in London, August 12 to 20, 1920: Official Report (London Friends Bookshop, 1920).

Cooper, Frederick, *The Crisis in Manchester Meeting: With a Review of the Pamphlets of David Duncan and Joseph B. Forster* (Manchester: Wm. Irwin, 1869 [not published, for private circulation in the Society of Friends]).

Cooper, Wilmer A., 'The Influence of Rufus Jones on the Quaker View of Sin and Evil', QRT, 22/4 (Fall 1987), 30–36.

Corder, Herbert, 'Methods of Propaganda', in *AFC, Official Report*, 178–84.

Creasey, Maurice, 'The Theology of Robert Barclay with Special Reference to his Apology', (B. D. thesis, University of Leeds, 1951).

Creasey, Maurice A. and Harold Loukes, *The Next Fifty Years* (London: Friends Home Service Committee, 1956).

The Crisis of the Quaker Contest in Manchester (Manchester, London & Bristol: 1836/7).

Cromwell, Otelia, *Lucretia Mott* (Cambridge, MA.: Harvard University Press, 1958).

Crosfield, Gulielma, *Friends and the Women's Movement* (London: Headley Bros., 1911).

Crossley, Robert (ed.), *Talking Across the World. the Correspondence of Olaf Stapleton and Anges Miller, 1915–1920*, (Hanover & London: United Press of New England, 1987).

Crowther, M. A., *Church Embattled: Religious Controversy in mid-Victorian England* (Newton Abbot: David & Charles, 1970).

Damrosch, Leo, _The Sorrows of the Quaker Jesus: James Naylor and the Puritan Crackdown on the Free Spirit_ (Cambridge, MA.: Harvard University Press, 1996).

Darton, Lawrence, 'The Baptism of Maria Hack, 1837: An Episode in the _Beacon_ Controversy', _JFHS_, 46/2 (1954), 67–77.

Davey, Arthur M. (ed.), _Lawrence Richardson: Selected Correspondence (1902–1903)_ (Cape Town: Van Riebeeck Society, 1977).

Davie, Martin, 'Development of British Quaker Theology since 1895', (D. Phil. thesis, Mansfield College, Oxford University, 1992).

—— 'Quaker Theology since 1895', _FQ_ 30/3 (July 1996), 131–43.

Davis, Robert (ed.), _Woodbrooke, 1903–1953_ (London: The Bannisdale Press, 1953).

Dedman, Martin, 'Baden-Powell, Militarism, and the "Invisible Contributions" to the Boy Scout Scheme, 1904–1920', _Twentieth Century British History_ 413 (1993), 210–23.

Dewsbury, William, _Works_ (London: 1689).

'Disownment of Joel Bean and Others', _BF_ (Dec. 1898), 305.

Doncaster, L. Hugh, _Quaker Organization and Business Meetings_ (London: Friends Home Service Committee, 1958).

Downing, Chris[tine], 'Quakerism and the Historical Interpretation of Religion', _QRT_ III/2 (Autumn 1961), 3–14.

Drake, Thomas E., _Quakers and Slavery in America_ (New Haven: Yale University Press, 1950).

Dudley, James, _The Life of Edward Grubb, 1854–1939: A Spiritual Pilgrimage_ (London: James Clarke & Co., 1946).

Duncan, David, _Can an Outward Revelation Be Perfect? Reflections Upon the Claims of Biblical Infallibility_, (2nd edn., London: F. Bowyer Kitto, 1871).

—— _Essays and Reviews: A Lecture Delivered at the Manchester Friends Institute_, (Manchester: 1861).

—— _John Woolman: A Paper at the Friends Institute, Manchester, 20 Jan. 1871_, (Manchester W. Hale, 1871).

—— _National Life_ (A Lecture read at Manchester Friends Institute, 22 April 1870, London: F. Bowyer Kitto, 1870).

—— 'Quakerism Past and Present', _MF_ (15 March 1872), 57–8.

Durnbaugh, Donald F., 'Baptists and Quakers—Left Wing Puritans?' _QH_, 62/2 (Autumn 1973), 67–82.

Dyck, Harvey L. (ed.), _The Pacifist Impulse in Historical Perspective_ (Toronto: University of Toronto Press, 1996).

[Dymond, Jonathan], _An Enquiry into the Accordancy of War with the Principles of Christianity_, reprint of 1823 edn., ed. Naomi Churgin Miller (New York: 1973).

Echoes From Scarborough, 1897 (London: Headley Bros., 1898).

Edgerton, William, 'Have Friends a Testimony Against War?', *Christian Worker*, 21/4 (2 April 1891), 212–13.

Edmondson, Joseph, 'The Essential Basis of Quakerism and Its non-Ritual Origins', *FQE*, (1899), 350–65.

[Edmundson, William,] *A Journal of . . . William Edmundson* (London: J. Sowle, 1715).

Edwards, Irene L., 'The Women Friends of London: The Two Weeks and Box Meetings', *JFHS*, 47/1 (Spring 1955), 3–21.

Ellegard, Alvar, *Darwin and the General Reader: The Reception of Darwin's Theory of Evolution in the British Periodical Press, 1859–1872* (2nd edn., Chicago: University of Chicago Press, 1990).

Endy, Melvin B. Jr., 'The Interpretation of Quakerism: Rufus Jones and His Critics', *QH*, 70/1 (Spring 1981), 3–2 1.

—— *William Penn and Early Quakerism* (Princeton, N.J.: Princeton University Press, [1973]).

Epistles From the Yearly Meeting of Friends Held in London, 1681–1858, 2 vols. (London: Edward Marsh, 1858).

Facing the Facts: Being the Report of the Conference on 'The Society of Friends and the Social Order' Held in London, 19–22 October 1916 (London: Headley Bros., [1916]).

Fager, Chuck, *Without Apology: The Heroes, the Heritage and the Hope of Liberal Quakerism* (Media, Pa.: Kimo Press, 1996).

Fawell, Ruth, *Joan Mary Fry* (London: Friends Home Service Committee, n.d.).

Forbush, Bliss, *Elias Hicks, Liberal Quaker* (New York: Columbia University Press, 1956).

Forster, Joseph B., 'David Duncan and His Reviewer', *BF* (2 Sept. 1861), 224–5.

—— 'Dread of Controversey', *BF* (2 Dec. 1861), 287–8.

—— *On Liberty: An Address to the Members of the Society of Friends*, (London: F. Bowyer Kitto, 1867).

—— *The Society of Friends and Freedom of Thought in 1871* (London: F. Bowyer Kitto, 1871).

Forster, Josiah, *Letters to the Younger Members of the Religious Society of Friends*, (London: R. Barrett & Sons, [1869]).

Fox, George, *To the Parliament of the Common-Wealth of England, Fifty-nine particulars laid down for the Regulating of Things* (London: n.p., 1659).

Francis, Mark, 'The Origins of *Essays and Reviews*: An Interpretation of Mark Pattison in the 1850s', *Historical Journal* 17 (1974), 797–811.

Friends and the War (London: Headley Bros., 1914).

Friends Service Committee, *A Challenge to Militarism* (London: FSC [1918]).

The Friends' Social Union, *Annual Report*, 1904.

The Friends' Social Union, *Reports and Pamphlets, 1904–1915*.

Frith, Francis, *Evangelicalism from the Stand Point of the Society of Friends* (London: Samuel Hards & Company, 1877).

—— 'On Intellectual Differences Among Christians', *FQE* (1892), 5–23.

Fry, Agnes, *A Memoir of Sir Edward Fry* (Oxford: Oxford University Press, 1921).

Fry, Elizabeth, *Memoir of the Life of Elizabeth Fry, with Extracts from her Journal* (London: Charles Gilpin, 1847).

Fry, Joan M., Alfred Kemp Brown, and other Friends, *The Teaching of the Bible in the Family* (London: Headley Bros., 1904).

Fulford, Roger, *Votes For Women: The Story of a Struggle* (London: Faber & Faber, 1957).

Gardiner, A. G., *The Life of George Cadbury* (London: Cassell & Co., n.d.).

Gilbert, Alan D., *Religion and Society in Industrial England: Church, Chapel and Social Change, 1780–1914* (London: Longman, 1974).

Glover, Margaret McKechnie, 'Aspects of Publishing by the Peace Committee of the Religious Society of Friends (London Yearly Meeting), 1888–1905', *QS* 3 (1998), 27–51.

Godlee, Mary Jane, 'The Women's Yearly Meeting', in *London Yearly Meeting During 250 Years* (London: Society of Friends, 1919).

Graham, John W., *Conscription and Conscience: A History, 1916–1919* (London: George Allen and Unwin, 1922).

—— 'The Distant Prospects of the Peace Party', *FQE* (1884), 82–96, 161–71.

—— 'Empire Building', *BF* (Jan. & March 1911), 6–8, 69–71.

—— *Evolution and Empire* (London: Headley Bros., 1912).

—— *The Faith of a Quaker* (Cambridge: Cambridge University Press, 1920)

—— 'Industrialism and the National Character', *TF* (14 Jan. 1910), 21–2.

—— *The Meaning of Quakerism* (London: Headley Bros., n.d.).

—— 'Reminiscences of the Beginning of Cambridge Meeting', *BF* (Feb. 1895), 31–2.

—— 'The State and the Individual', *TF* (9 April 1915), 267–9.

—— 'Whence Comes Peace?', *BF* (April 1896), 77–80.

Graves, Michael P., 'Robert Barclay and the Rhetoric of the Inward Light', QRT, 26/2, 80 (March 1993), 17–32.

Greaves, Richard, 'Shattered Expectations? George Fox, the Quakers and the Restoration State, 1660–1685', *Albion* 24/2 (Summer 1992), 237–59.

Greenwood, John Ormerod, *Quaker Encounters*, 3 vols. (York: Sessions, 1975–8).

Vol. 1 *Friends and Relief* (1975).

Vol. 2 *Vines on the Mountain* (1977).

Vol. 3 *Whispers of Truth* (1978).

—— *The Quaker Tapestry* (London: Impact Books, 1991).

—— (ed.), *The Quaker Tapestries* (London: Quaker Home Service, 1987).

Gregg, Howard, 'John Bright: Called to the Lord's Service', QRT, 24/3 (Summer 1990), 8–30.

Grieves, Keith, *The Politics of Manpower* (New York: Oxford University Press, 1988).

Grubb, Edward, 'Eighth Query: Reply', FQE (1917), 349–57.

—— 'The Evangelical Movement and its Impact on the Society of Friends', FQE (1924), 1–33.

—— 'The Future of the Tropics', *BF* (March 1899), 53–4.

—— 'John Bellows and the War', *BF* (Dec. 1900), 307–9.

—— 'The Life of the Society in Relation to Its Testimony', *AFC, Official Report*, 199–225.

—— 'The Mission of the Society of Friends', *PDP* I (1898), 35–7.

—— 'On the Ministry in Our Meeting', *FQE* (1888), 366–76.

—— 'Our Mission, II. Social', *FQE* (1889), 67, 78, 81–2.

—— 'Our Testimony for Peace', *BF*, (May 1909), 133–4.

—— *Quakerism in England: Its Present Position*, (London: Headley Brothers, 1901).

—— 'Seventy Years Ago', *FQE* (1928), 294–316.

—— 'Short Cuts to Peace', *TF*, 22 Sept. 1916, 737–9.

—— *Social Aspects of the Quaker Faith* (London: Headley Brothers, 1899).

—— 'Some Personal Experiences', *FQE* (1938), 307.

—— *The True Way of Life* (London: Headley Bros., 1909).

—— *What is Quakerism?* (3rd edn. London: George Allen & Unwin, 1929, reprinted 1942)

—— 'Yearly Meeting, 1836', *FQE* (1895), 99–116.

Grubb, Mollie, 'Abraham Shackleton and the Irish Separation of 1797–1803', *JFHS* 56/4 (1993), 262–71.

—— 'The Beacon Separation', *JFHS* 55/6 (1988), 190–98.

—— 'Tensions in the Religious Society of Friends in England in the Nineteenth Century', *JFHS*, 56/1 (1990), 1–14.

Gummere, Amelia, 'The Early Quakers and Parental Education', *PDP*, V/50 (Sept. 1902), 284.

Gwyn, Douglas, *Apocalypse of the Word: The Life and Message of George Fox* (Richmond: Friends United Press, 1986).

—— *The Covenant Crucified: Quakers and the Rise of Capitalism* (Wallingford, Pa.: Pendle Hill Publications, 1995).

Hamm, Thomas D., 'The Problem of the Inner Light in Nineteenth Century Quakerism', in Michael L. Birkel and John W. Newman (eds.), *The Lamb's War: Quaker Essays to Honor Hugh Barbour* (Richmond: Earlham College Press, 1992), 101–17.

—— *The Transformation of American Quakerism, Orthodox Friends, 1800–1907* (Bloomington: University of Indiana Press, 1988).

Hancock, Thomas, *Peculium* (London: Smith, Elder & Co., 1860).

Handbook. Yearly Meeting, 1908 (Birmingham: n. p., 1908).

Hankin, E. H., 'The Mental Ability of the Quakers', *Science Progress* 16 (1921–22), 654–64.

[Harris, J. Rendel], *Memories of J. Rendel Harris*, collected by Irene Pickard (no publisher, place or date of publication).

Harris, Mary O'Brien, 'The Socialist Alternative to Poverty', *FQE*, (1908), 408–27.

Harris, Terry, 'Matthew Arnold, Bishop Joseph Butler, and the Foundation of Religious Faith', *VS* 31/2 (Winter 1988), 189–208.

Harrison, Frederick, 'Neo-Christianity', *Westminster Review* (Oct. 1860).

Harvey, T. Edmund, 'Looking Back', *JFHS*, 45/2 (Autumn 1953), 51–9.

Hatton, Helen E., 'Friends and Famine Relief in Ireland, 1846–49,' *QH* 76/1 (Spring 1987), 18–32.

—— *The Largest Amount of Good: Quaker Relief in Ireland, 1654–1921* (Kingston & Montreal: McGill-Queen's University Press, 1993).

Heath, Carl, *Quaker Embassies* (Privately printed, [1917])

Hewison, Hope, *Hedge of Wild Almonds* (London: James Cuney, 1989).

—— 'Human Progress and the Inward Light: the Position of Thomas Hodgkin (1831–1913), in Relation to His Contemporaries', *JFHS* 56/2 (1991), 126–47.

Hill, Christopher, *The Experience of Defeat: Milton and Some Contemporaries* (New York: Viking, 1984).

Hill, Christopher, 'Quakers and the English Revolution', *JFHS* 56/3 (1992), 165–79.

Hill, Christopher, *The World Turned Upside Down: Radical Ideas During the English Revolution* (London: Penguin Books, 1972).

Hilton, Boyd, *The Age of Atonement. The Influence of Evangelicalism on Social and Economic Thought, 1785–1865* (Oxford: Clarendon Press, 1988).

Hinton, James, *Protests and Visions: Peace Politics in the Twentieth Century* (London: Hutchinson Radius, 1989).

Hirst, Margaret, 'The History of the Peace Testimony', in *The Peace Testimony of the Society of Friends* (London: [Friends Bookstore, 1920])

—— *The Quakers in Peace and War* (London: The Swarthmore Press, 1923).

Hobhouse, Margaret [Bertrand Russell], '*I Appeal Unto Caesar*' (London: George Allen & Unwin, 1917).

Hobson, John A., 'Imperialism and the Lower Races', *BF* (March, April, June 1902), 53–5, 81–3, 129–32.

Hobson, Samuel, 'Concerning Socialism', *FQE* (1898), 195–210.

Hobson, S.[amuel] G., *Pilgrim to the Left: Memoirs of a Modern Revolutionist* (London: Edward Arnolds & Co., 1938).

Hodgkin, Henry T., 'The Church and War', *The Constructive Quarterly* (March 1915), 213–30.

—— *Friends Beyond Seas* (London: Headley Bros, 1916).

—— 'The Quaker Movement in the Modern World' in *The Peace Testimony of the Society of Friends*, vol. VII.

Hodgkin, J. B., *Three Phases of Quakerism* (London: The Beford Institute, 1889).

Hodgkin, J. Edward, 'The Testimony in Personal Life and Society', *AFC, Official Report*, 94–100.

—— ' "War and the Social Order": The Committee's Recent Conference at Jordans', *PS*, n.s. 1/4 (May 1916), 128–9.

Hodgson, William, *Selections from the Correspondence of William Hodgson, with Memoirs of his Life* (Philadelphia 1886).

Holdsworth, Christopher J., 'Mystics and Heretics in the Middle Ages: Rufus Jones Reconsidered', *JFHS*, 53/1 (1972), 9–30.

Holton, Sandra Stanley and Margaret Allen, 'Offices and Services: Women's Pursuit of Sexual Equality Within the Society of Friends, 1873–1907', *QS* 2 (1997), 1–29.

Horle, Craig, *Quakerism and the English Legal System, 1660–1688* (Philadelphia: University of Pennsylvania Press, 1988).

Horwill, Herbert H., 'A Quaker Socialist Movement', *The Constructive Quarterly* (June 1921), 318–31.

Howard, Elizabeth Fox, *Friends' Service in Wartime*, (London: Friends' Council for International Service, [1920]).

Howitt, Mary, *Mary Howitt, an Autobiography* (London: Wm. Ibitser, 1889).

Hoyland, Geoffrey, 'The Real Argument for Peace', in *Friends and the War* (London, 1914).

Hoyland, John S., 'Neo-Quakerism', *FQE* (1910), 460–64.

Huber, Elaine C., ' "A Woman Must Not Speak": Quaker Women in the English Left Wing', in Rosemary Ruether and Eleanor McLaughlin (eds.), *Women of Spirit: Female Leadership in the Jewish and Christian Traditions* (New York: Simon and Shuster, 1979).

Hutton, Ronald, *The Restoration, 1658–1667* (Oxford: Clarendon Press, 1988).

I. A. R., 'In Memoriam, John Wilhelm Rowntree—A Poem', *Friends Intelligencer*, 62/13 (1 April 1905), 193.

I. K., 'Scientific Notes', *TF* (Aug. 1861), 210–12.

Ignatieff, Michael, *A Just Measure of Pain: The Penitentiary in the Industrial Revolution, 1750–1850* (New York: Pantheon Books, 1978).

Ingle, H. Larry, *First Among Friends: George Fox & the Creation of Quakerism* (New York: Oxford University Press, 1994).

—— 'From Mysticism to Radicalism: Recent Historiography on Quaker Beginnings', *QH*, 76 (1987), 79–94.

—— 'The Future of Quaker History', *JFHS* 58/1 (1997), 1–16.

—— 'George Fox, Millenarian', *Albion* 24/2 (Summer 1992), 261–78.

—— 'On the Folly of Seeking the Quaker Holy Grail', *QRT*, 25/1 (May 1991), 17–29.

—— *Quakers in Conflict: The Hicksite Reformation* (Knoxville: University of Tennessee Press, 1986).

—— 'Richard Hubbersthorne & History: The Crisis of 1659', *JFHS* 56/3 (1992), 189–200.

'Interview with Professor Rendel Harris', *The Examiner* (16 March 1904).

Irwin, William, *Brief Remarks on the Past and Present Condition of the Society of Friends*, (Manchester: Wm. Irwin, 1867).

—— *A Refutation of William Tallack's Remarks on Barclay's* Apology *and the Manchester Schism as Contained in his Book Entitled* George Fox, the Friends, and the Early Baptists, (Manchester: Wm. Irwin, 1868).

—— *Some Suppressed Facts Respecting the Recent Conference on Christian Work*, (Manchester: Wm. Irwin, 1867).

Isichei, Elizabeth, 'From Sect to Denomination Among English Quakers', in *Patterns of Sectarianism*, ed. Bryan R. Wilson (London: Heinemann, 1967), 161–81.

—— *Victorian Quakers* (London: Oxford University Press, 1970).

James, William, *The Varieties of Religious Experience*, (New York: Longmans, Green, 1902).

Janney, Samuel M., *An Examination of the Causes which Led to the Separation of the Religious Society of Friends in America in 1827–28* (Philadelphia: T. Ellwood Zell, 1868).

—— *History of the Religious Society of Friends*, 4 vols. (2nd edn., Philadelphia: Hayes & Zell, 1860).

Jauncey, Leslie C., *The Story of Conscription in Australia* (London: George Allen & Unwin, 1935).

Jay, Allen, *Autobiography of Allen Jay* (Philadelphia: John C. Winston Co., [1910]).

Jay, Bill, *Victorian Cameraman: Francis Frith's Views of Rural England, 1850–1898* (Newton Abbot: David and Charles, 1973).

'Joel Bean and Iowa', *BF* (Dec. 1894), 225.

Jones, Peter d'Alroy, *The Christian Socialist Revival, 1877–1914: Religion, Class and Social Conscience in Late Victorian England* (Princeton, NJ: Princeton University Press, 1968).

Jones, Rufus M., *The Atonement*, (Yorkshire 1905 Committee, n. d.), 9–1
11, No. 8, Vol. 2, Yorkshire Pamphlets, LSF.

[———], *Friends and the War: A New Statement of the Quaker Position*
(London: Friends Bookstore, 1920).

——*John Wilhelm Rowntree* (Philadelphia: Committee on Education
General Conference, 1942).

—— *The Later Periods of Quakerism*, 2 vols. (London: Macmillan, 1921).

—— *The Trail of Life In College* (New York: Macmillan, 1929).

—— *The Trail of Life in Middle Years* (New York: Macmillan, 1934).

—— *The Way of Life and Service* (Oberlin, Ohio: 1939).

Jorns, Auguste, *The Quakers as Pioneers in Social Work*, [published in
German in 1912] trans. Thomas Kite Brown, Jr. (New York: Macmillan Co., 1931).

Kamester, Margaret and Vellacott, Jo (eds.), *Militarism Versus Feminism:
Writings on Women and War* (London: Virago Press, 1987).

Kennedy, Thomas C., 'An Angry God or *A Reasonable Faith*? The British
Society of Friends, 1873–1888', *JFHS* 57/2 (1995), 183–198.

—— 'Fighting About Peace: The No-Conscription Fellowship and the
British Friends' Service Committee, 1915–1919', *QH*, 69/1 (Spring
1980), 3–22.

—— 'Heresy-Hunting Among Victorian Quakers: The Manchester Difficulty, 1861–73', *VS*, 34/2 (Winter 1991), 227–53.

—— 'History and the Quaker Renaissance: The Vision of John
Wilhelm Rowntree', *JFHS* 55/1–2 (1983 and 1984 issued 1986),
35–56.

—— *The Hound of Conscience: A History of the No-Conscription Fellowship*
(Fayetteville, Arkansas: University of Arkansas Press, 1981).

—— 'Nourishing Life: Russell and the Twentieth Century Peace Movement, 1900–1918', in Margaret Moran and Carl Spandoni (eds.),
Intellectual and Social Conscience (Hamilton, Ont.: MacMaster University. Library Press, 1984).

—— 'Public Opinion and the Conscientious Objector, 1915–1919', *The
Journal of British Studies*, XII/2 (May 1973), 3–20.

—— 'The Quaker Renaissance and the Origins of the Modern British
Peace Movement', *Albion*, 16/3 (Fall 1984), 243–72.

—— 'Quaker Women and the Pacifist Impulse in Britain, 1900–1920', in
Harvey L. Dyck (ed.), *The Pacifist Impulse in Historical Perspective*
(Toronto: University of Toronto Press, 1996).

—— 'The Ubiquitous Friend: Edward Grubb and the Modern British
Peace Movement', *Peace Research* 12/2 (May 1985), 1–10.

—— 'What Hath Manchester Wrought? Change in the
Religious Society of Friends, 1895–1920', *JFHS* 57/3 (1996), 277–305.

—— 'Why Did Friends Resist? The War, the Peace Testimony and the All-Friends Conference of 1920', *Peace and Change*, 14/4 (Oct. 1989), 355–71.

Kent, Stephen, 'Psychology and Quaker Mysticism: The Legacy of William James and Rufus Jones', *QH*, 76/1 (Spring 1987), 1–17.

Kent, Susan, *Sex and Suffrage in Britain, 1860–1914* (Princeton, N.J.: Princeton Univ. Press, 1987).

Kitching, John, 'On the Rise and First Principles of the Society of Friends', *TF* (February, March & April 1859).

Kunze, Bonnelyn Young, ' "Poore and Necessity": Margaret Fell and Quaker Female Philanthropy in Northwest England in the Late 17th Century', *Albion* 21/4 (Winter 1989), 559–80.

—— ' "Walking in Ye Gospel Order": Margaret Fell and the Establishment of Women's Meetings', paper read at 7th Berkshire Conference on History of Women, June 1987.

Lewis, Georgina King, *Elizabeth Fry* (London: Headley Bros., 1909).

Linney, Albert E. (ed.), *Thirty-Fourth Annual Report of the Ackworth Old Scholars' Association, 1915–1916* (York: privately printed, 1916).

Littleboy, Richard, 'The New Theology', *FQE* (1891), 567–73.

Littleboy, Wilfrid E., '1914–1918, I remember . . . VIII, with the C.O.s in prison', *TF* (1934), 859–61.

—— 'Our Peace Testimony and Some of Its Implications, *TF* (2 Dec. 1914), 722–4.

Littleboy, William, *The Appeal of Quakerism to the Non- Mystic* (Harrogate: Robert Davis, For the '1905 Committee of Yorkshire Q.M.') [reprinted in 1964 as a 'Quaker Classic'].

—— *Friends and Peace*, (London: Friends Home Mission and Extension Committee, 1915).

Lloyd, Arnold, *Quaker Social History* (London: Longman's, Green & Co., 1950).

London Yearly Meeting During 250 Years (London: Headley Brothers, 1919).

Loverance, Rowena, 'Edward Worsdell (1852–1908), *FQ*, 23/8 (October 1984).

Lowndes, Walter, *The Quakers of Fritchley, 1863–1980* (1980).

Lucas, William, *A Quaker Journal . . .* ed. G. E. Bryant and G. P. Baker (London: Hutchinson & Co., 1934).

Lunn, Pam, ' "You Have Lost Your Opportunity": British Quakers & the Militant Phase of the Women's Suffrage Campaign, 1906–1914', *QS* 2 (1997), 30–52.

McGregor, J. F. and Barry Reay (eds.), *Radical Religion in the English Revolution* (Oxford: Oxford University Press, 1984).

Mack, Phyllis, 'Gender and Spirituality in Early English Quakerism, 1650–1665', in Elisabeth Potts Brown and Susan Mosher Stuard (eds.), *Witnesses for Change: Quaker Women Over Three Centuries* (New Brunswick & London: Rutgers University Press, 1990)

—— *Visionary Women: Ecstatic Prophecy in Seventeenth Century England* (Berkeley: University of California Press, 1992).

MacKinnon, Alison, ' "My Dearest Friend": Courtship and Conjugality in Some Mid and Late Nineteenth Century Quaker Families', *JFHS* 58/1 (1997), 44–58.

Maclear, James, 'Quakerism and the End of the Interregnum: A Chapter in the Domestication of Radical Puritainism', *CH* 19 (December 1950), 240–70.

Malmgreen, G., 'Anne Knight and the Radical Subculture', QH, 71/2 (Fall 1982), 100–12.

Manchester Conference, or Report of the Proceedings of the Conference of Members of the Society of Friends Held, by Direction of the Yearly Meeting in Manchester from the Eleventh to the Fifteenth of Eleventh Month, 1895 (London: Headley Bros., 1896).

Manners, Emily, *Elizabeth Hooten: First Quaker Woman Preacher (1600–1672)* (London: Headley Bros., 1914).

Marsh, Harold, 'Women in the Church', *TF* (22 March 1912), 179–81.

Marwick, William H., 'Quaker Social Thought', *Woodbrooke Occasional Papers*, Friends Home Service Committee, 1969.

—— 'Some Quaker Firms of the Nineteenth Century', *JFHS* 48/6 (Autumn 1956), 239–59.

Masterman, L., *C. F. G. Masterman, A Biography* (London: Nicholson and Watson 1939).

Maurice, Frederick, *The Kingdom of Christ*, 2 vols., ed. Alec Vidler, based on 2nd. edn. of 1842 (London: SCM Press 1958).

Maxey, David W., 'New Light on Hannah Barnard, A Quaker "Heretic" ', *QH*, 2/78 (Fall 1989), 61–86.

Meeting for Sufferings, 'Message to Men and Women of Goodwill', printed copy, LSF.

'Memoir of John Stewart', FQE (1867), 147–65.

'Memorandum for the Llandudno Conference', 23–30 Sept. 1914 (Birmingham: Selly Oak, [1914]).

Milligan, Edward, ' "The Ancient Way": The Conservative Tradition in Nineteenth Century British Quakerism', *JFHS* 57/1 (1994), 74–101. (Presidential Address to the Friends Historical Society, March 1993).

—— 'How We Got Our Book of Discipline: The Revision of 1921— From Doctrine to Experience', *FQ*, 25/3 (July 1988), 110–17.

—— ' "In Reason's Ear": Some Quaker and Anglican Perplexities', *FQ* 23/8 (Oct. 1984), 384–96.

—— 'Quaker Marriage', pamphlet in *Quaker Tapestry Booklets* series (London: Quaker Home Service, 1994).

Milligan, Edward,'Quaker Marriage Procedure', Lecture to the Annual Conference of the Institute of Population Registration, Carlisle, 7 June 1993.

—— ' "To Friends Everywhere": Reflections on the Epistle in the Life of London Yearly Meeting', *FQ* 22/11 (July 1982), 724–36.

Milligan, Edward H. and Malcolm J. Thomas, 'My Ancestors were Quakers: How can I find out more about them?' (London: Society of Genealogists, 1983).

Mills, Dr Seth, 'Friends in History, and the Need of a Written History of Friends', *The American Friend* (18 Sept. 1894), 199–200.

Minnear, Mark D., *Richmond 1887: A Quaker Drama Unfolds* (Richmond Ind.: Friends United Press, 1987).

Minutes and Proceedings of the Yearly Meeting of Friends (*LYM*, with year).

Minutes, Darlington Monthly meeting, 1914–1915 (copies provided by John Lockett).

Moore, Rosemary, 'Evaluating the Evidence: The Reliability of Sources of Information for Quakerism Before 1660', *FQ* 27/8 (October 1993), 364–72.

Morgan, Nicholas, *Lancashire Friends and the Establishment, 1660–1730* (Halifax: Ryburn Publishing, 1993).

M[orland,] L[ucy] F[ryer], 'Impressions of Yearly Meeting: The Society in Unity and "under Conviction" ', *PS*, 116 (July 1916), 169–70.

Morland, Lucy Fryer, *The New Social Outlook*, Swarthmore Lecture, 1918 (London: Headley Bros., 1918).

Mortimer, Jean, 'Leeds Friends and the Beaconite Controversy', *JFHS* 54/2 (1977), 52–66.

Mouland, Lucy, 'Quaker Pacifism and the First World War', (Third-year dissertation, Cambridge University, 1990).

Nevinson, Henry W., *A Modern Slavery*, introduction by Basil Davidson (New York: Schocken Books, 1968).

Newberry, Jo Vellacott, 'Russell As Ghost Writer, A New Discovery', *Russell* 15 (Autumn 1974), 19–23.

Newman, Henry Stanley, 'Gospel Ministry', *FQE* (1886), 526–37.

Newman, Jane E., 'About Monthly Meeting', *FQE* (1891), 263–70.

Nickalls, John L. (ed.), *The Journal of George Fox* (London: Religious Society of Friends, 1952; reprinted 1986).

Nodal, John H., *The Bibliography of Ackworth School* (Manchester: Frank Nodal & Co., 1889).

Nuttall, Geoffrey, *The Holy Spirit in Puritan Faith and Experience* (Oxford: Blackwell, 1946).

Oats, William N., 'The Campaign Against Conscription in Australia— 1911–1914', *JFHS* 55/7 (1989), 205–19.

Oliver, John, 'J. Walter Malone: The American Friend and an Evangelical Quaker's Social Agenda', *QH*, 80/2 (Fall 1991), 63–84.

'On the Ministry of Women', *FQE* (1868), 301–2.

Orr, E. W., *The Quakers in Peace and War, 1920–1967* (Eastbourne: W. J. Offord & Sons, 1974).

Our Testimony for Peace, (London Y. M. 1912).

Paquet, Alfon, *The Quakers*, pamphlet reprinted from *Frankfurter Zeitung*.

Palmer, T. Vail, Jr., 'Quaker Peace Witness', *QRT*, 23/2–3 (Summer 1988), 36–55.

Peace Conference of All Friends. Commissions I–VII, *The Peace Testimony of the Society of Friends: Reports of Commissions Issued by the Committee of the Peace Conference of All Friends* (London: [Friends Bookshop, 1920]).

I The Fundamental Basis
II National Life and International Relations
III Personal Life and Society
IV Problems of Education
V The Life of the Society of Friends
VI Methods of Propaganda
VII The International Service of Friends

Pearson, Edward, 'An Evangelical Ministry', *FQE* (1886), 440–6.

Pease, A[lfred] E., *My Son Christopher: Being the Story of the Childhood of Christopher York Pease Esquire* (Middlesbrough: William Appleyard, [1920]).

Penney, Norman (ed.), *The First Publishers of the Truth* (London: Headley Brothers, 1907).

Phillips, Brian David, 'Friendly Patriotism: British Quakerism and the Imperial Nation, 1890–1910', (Ph.D. thesis, History, King's College, Cambridge, 1989).

Phillipson, Laurel, 'Quakerism in Cambridge from the Act of Tolerance to the End of the Nineteenth Century (1689–1900)', *Proceedings of the Cambridge Antiquarian Society*, vol. LXXVII (1988), 1–33.

Pinthus, Eva I., 'The Roots of the Peace Testimony in the Message of the Bible', *FQ*, 26/2 (April 1990), 54–63.

Pointing, Horace B., *Social Thought in the Society of Friends* (London: Friends Book Centre, 1939).

Pollard, Francis, Beatrice and Robert, *Democracy and the Quaker Method* (London: Bannisdale Press, 1949).

Pollard, William, *Old-Fashioned Quakerism: Its Origin, Results and Future* (Philadelphia: H. Longstreth, 1889).

—— 'The Peace Question', *FQE* (1871), 443–9.

Pollard, William, *Quaker Reformation* (London: Swan Sonnuneschein & Co., 1889).

—— 'The Recent Friends Conference in London', *FQE* (1874), 13–24.

—— 'Thoughts for the Next Yearly Meeting', *FQE* (1871), 292–6.

Punshon, John, *Letter to a Universalist* (Wallinford, Pa.: Pendle Hill Publications, 1989).

—— 'The Peace Testimony: An Ethic Derived from a Metaphysic via an Experience', *QRT*, 23/2–3 (Summer 1988), 55–73.

—— *Portrait in Grey: A Short History of the Quakers* (London: Quaker Home Service, 1984).

—— 'Some Reflections on the Quakers and the Evangelical Spirit', in Paul Anderson and Howard O. Macy (eds.), *Truth's Bright Embrace: Essays and Poems in Honor of Arthur O. Roberts* (Newberg, Oregon: George Fox University Press, 1996), 205–20.

Quaker Faith and Practice: The book of Christian discipline of the Yearly Meeting of the Religious Society of Friends (Quakers) in Britain (The Yearly Meeting of the Religious Society of Friends (Quakers) in Britain, 1994).

Rae, John, *Politics and Conscience: The British Government and the Conscientious Objector to Military Service, 1916–1919* (London: Oxford University Press, 1970).

Raistrick, Arthur, *Quakers in Science and Industry* (New York: August M. Kelley, 1968, reprint of 1950 edn.).

Reader, John, *Of Schools and Schoolmasters: Some Thought on the Quaker Contribution to Education* (London: Quaker Home Service, 1979).

Reay, Barry, *The Quakers and the English Revolution* (New York: St Martin's Press, 1985).

—— 'Quaker Opposition to Tithes', *Past and Present* 86 (1980), 98–120.

Rempel, Richard, 'British Quakers and the South African War', *QH*, 64/2 (Autumn 1975), 75–95.

'Report of Friends Peace Committee, 1900, to the Meeting for Sufferings.'

Richardson, Anne W., 'A Quaker View of War', *TF* (12 Jan. 1900), 19–23.

Richardson, Lawrence, 'Newcastle-upon-Tyne Friends and Scientific Thought: Reminiscences', *JFHS*, 1/45 (Spring 1953), 40–44.

Roberts, Evelyn (ed.), *Louisa: Memories of a Quaker Childhood* (London: Friends Home Service, 1970).

Robinson, Ellen, 'Colonization and Native Races', *BF* (Nov. 1899), 294–6.

Robinson, Maude, '"Lest We Forget": A Memory of the Society of Friends in the War Years, 1914–1918', (London: Reprinted for the Peace Committee of the Society of Friends, n.d.)

Rose, June, *Elizabeth Fry* (London: Macmillan, 1980).

Rosman, Doreen, *Evangelicals and Culture* (London: Croom Helm, 1984).

Rowntree, C. Brightwen, 'The Adult School and the Boy Scout', *FQE* (1910), 324–31.

Rowntree, John Stephenson, 'Facts and Figures', *FQE* (1867), 566–71.

—— 'The Friends' Book of Discipline', *FQE* (1898), 457–98.

—— *Quakerism, Past and Present* (London: Smith, Elder & Co., 1859).

—— *The Place of the Society of Friends in the Religious Life of England* (London: Headley Bros, [1897]).

Rowntree, John Wilhelm, *Claim Your Inheritance: Essays on Man's Relation to God* (London: Bannisdale Press, n.d.).

—— 'A Few Thoughts Upon the Position of Young Friends in Relation to the Society', (York: Wm. Sessions, July 1893).

—— 'The Need for a Summer School Movement', in Joshua Rowntree (ed.), *John Wilhelm Rowntree: Essays and Addresses* (London: Headley Bros, 1906), 153–60.

—— 'Pentecost', in Joshua Rowntree (ed.), *John Wilhelm Rowntree: Essays and Addresses* (London: Headley Bros, 1906), 223–31.

—— 'The Present Position of Religious Thought in the Society of Friends', *FQE* (1905), 109–22 and *AF* (25 March 1905), 192–205.

—— 'The Problem of a Free Ministry', in Joshua Rowntree (ed.), *John Wilhelm Rowntree: Essays and Addresses* (London: Headley Bros, 1906), 111–3 4.

—— 'Religious Education', *PDP*, V (1902), 128.

—— 'Rise of Quakerism in Yorkshire', in Joshua Rowntree (ed.), *John Wilhelm Rowntree: Essays and Addresses* (London: Headley Bros, 1906), 3–76.

—— 'A Study of Ecclesiastical Polity', *PDP* 5/51 (15 Oct. 1902), 302–3.

—— 'The Unlawfulness of War to the Christian', *PDP*, II (May, 1898), 287–90.

—— 'The Wages of Going On', *PDP*, 5/50 (15 Sept. 1902), 255.

[——] 'The Outlook', *PDP*, 11 (1899), 9.

Rowntree, John Wilhelm and Henry B. Binns, *A History of the Adult School Movement* (London: Headley Bros, 1903).

—— 'History of the Adult School Movement', *PDP* 5/50 (15 September 1902), 262.

Rowntree, Joseph, *Memorandum on the Declaration of Christian Doctrine Issued by the Richmond Conference, 1887* (York: privately printed, 1888).

Rowntree, Joshua, *Social Service: Its Place in the Society of Friends*, Swarthmore Lecture, 1913 (London: Headly Bros., 1913).

Rowntree, Seebohm, 'Friends and Enlistment', *TF* (2 Oct. 1914), 724.

Rowntree, William Stickney, 'Christianity and War', *FQE*, (1885), 236–45.

Russell, Bertrand, *The Autobiography of Bertrand Russell, 1914–1944* (London: Allen & Unwin, 1968).

—— *Pacifism and Revolution, 1916–1918*, vol. 14, *The Collected Papers of Bertrand Russell*, ed. Richard Rempel, Louis Greenspan, Beryl Haslam, Albert C. Lewis and Mark Lippincott (London & New York: Routledge, 1994).

S., Sarah, 'On Doing the Will of God', *FQE* (1868), 192–6.

Scott, Janet, 'Women in the Society of Friends', in Blamires *et al.*, *A Quaker Miscellany for Edward Milligan*, 125–31.

Scott, Richenda C., 'Authority or Experience: John Wilhelm Rowntree and the Dilemma of 19th Century British Quakerism', *JFHS*, 49 (Spring 1960), 75–95.

—— *Quakers in Russia* (London: Michael Joseph, 1964).

—— *Tradition and Experience* (London: Allen & Unwin, 1964).

Seebohm, Benjamin (ed.), *Memoirs of the Life and Gospel Labours of Stephen Grellet* (London: A. W. Bennett, 1860).

—— *Memoirs of William Forster* (London: A. W. Bennett, 1865).

Selections from the Smuts Papers, 4 vols. ed. W. K. Hancock and Jean Van der Poel (Cambridge: Cambridge University Press, 1966).

Sessions, Fred, 'Our Letter from England', *Christian Worker* (23 April 1891), 259–60.

Simpson, Alan, *Puritans in Old and New England* (Chicago: University of Chicago Press, 1955).

Smeal, Jane and Helen G. Thompson, *Silvanus Philips Thompson, His Life and Letters* (London: T. Fisher Unwin, 1920).

Soderlund, Jean R., *Quakers and Slavery: a Divided Spirit* (Princeton: Princeton Univ. Press, 1985).

Somerville, C. Johan, 'Anglican, Puritan and Sectarian in Empirical Perspective', *Social Science History* 13 (1985), 119.

[Southall, John], 'London Yearly Meeting, 1836', *JFHS*, 17/2 (1920), 82–9.

[——]'London Yearly Meeting, 1838', *JFHS*, 18/1 (1921), 89–92.

'Spectator', 'A View from Southampton', *FQE* (1894), 331–2.

Spurrier, William Wayne, 'The Persecution of the Quakers in England, 1650–1714', (Ph.D. dissertation, University of North Carolina, 1976).

Stephen, Caroline E., *Quaker Strongholds* (3rd edn. London: Edward Arnold, 1891).

—— 'A Rejoinder', *Nineteenth Century* (April 1907), 593–4.

—— 'The Representation of Women I: A Consultative Chamber for Women', *Nineteenth Century* (Dec. 1908), 1018–24.

—— 'Women in Politics', *Nineteenth Century* (February 1907), 227–36.

Stewart, Mrs, J. [Louisa], *The Missing Law; or Women's Birthright* (London: W. Tweedi, 1869).

—— 'A Word to Our Sisterhood', *FQE* (1867), 576–84.

Stewart, W. A. C., *Quakers and Education: As Seen in Their Schools in England* (London: The Epworth Press, 1953).

The Story of an Uncensored Leaflet, (London: Prepared for the Friends Service Committee, 1918).

Strachey, J. St Loe, *A New Way of Life* (London: Macmillan, 1909).

Sturge, Emily, 'Am I My Sister's Keeper?', *FQE* (1888), 489–506.

Sturge, Matilda, 'A Few Words About Women', *FQE* (1877), 469–76.

Swanwick 1911, Being a Report of a Conference of Young Friends Held at Swanwick from August 28th to September 4th, 1911 (Published by Young Friends' Sub-Committee of the Friends Home Mission and Extension Committee, [1911]).

Tallack, William, 'Christian Positivism', *FQE* (1874), 556–64.

—— *George Fox, the Friends and Early Baptists* (London: S. W. Partridge & Co., 1868).

—— 'Some Thoughts on Ministry, or Service in a Small Meeting', *FQE* (1896), 225–9.

Tatham, Meaburn and James E. Miles (eds.), *The Friends' Ambulance Unit, 1914–1919: A Record* (London: The Swarthmore Press, [1919]).

Taylor, A. J. P., *A Personal History* (New York: Atheneum, 1983).

Taylor, Ernest E., *The Valiant Sixty* (London: The Binnisdale Press, 1947).

Taylor, Jane E., 'Women's Place in the Christian Economy', *FQE* (1886), 116–23.

Thomas, Anna and Elizabeth B. Emmott, *William Charles Braithwaite (B.A., LL.B. & D.Th): Memoir and Papers* (London: Longmans, Green & Co., 1931).

Thomas, Malcolm J., 'The Committee on General Meetings, 1875–83', in Blamires, et. al., *A Quaker Miscellany for Edward Milligan*, 133–43.

Thompson, Silvanus P., 'John Wilhelm Rowntree', *FQE* (1905), 258–68.

Thorp, Fielden, 'Consideration on the Genuineness, Authenticity, and Divine Authority of the Holy Scripture', *FQE* (1868), 71–104.

—— *A Review of the Lecture on 'Liberty'*, (London: F. Bowyer Kitto, 1867).

'Thoughts on Yearly Meeting', *FQE* (1893), 321–33.

Thursfield, Rebecca, 'Home Mission Association of Women Friends', *FQE* (1867), 74–8.

Tolles, Frederick B., 'The New Light Quakers of Lynn and New Bedford', *New England Quarterly*, (1959), 291–19.

'Training of Teachers', *FQE* (1870), 60–61.

Trueblood, D. Elton, *Robert Barclay* (New York: Harper, 1968).

Trust-to-Truth [anon.], *Thoughts on the Toleration of Important Differences of Opinion in the Same Religious Community-Respectfully Addressed to the Lancashire Committee* (London: F. Bowyer Kitto, 1870).

Tucker, Leigh, 'English Quakers and World War I, 1914–1920', (Ph.D. dissertation, University of North Carolina, 1972).

—— 'Friends and Censorship, World War I', *QH*, Vol. 71/2 (Fall 1982), 114–24.

Tyrrel, Alex, *Joseph Sturge and the Moral Radical Party in Early Victorian Britain* (London: Croom Helm, 1987).

Vann, Richard, *The Social Development of English Quakerism* (Cambridge, MA: Harvard University Press, 1969).

Vega, 'Should Women Be Admitted to the Exercise of Parliamentary Suffrage?', *FQE* (1868), 444–56.

Vellacott, Jo, *Bertrand Russell and the Pacifists During the First World War* (Brighton: Harvester Press, 1980).

Vernon, Anne, *A Quaker Business Man: The Life of Joseph Rowntree, 1836–1925* (London: Allen and Unwin, 1958).

Vining, Elizabeth Gray, *Friend of Life: The Biography of Rufus M. Jones* (Philadelphia: Lippincott, [1958]).

Vipont, Elfrida, *The Story of Quakerism* (Richmond: Friends United Press, 1977).

'War's Alarm', *PS*, 1/1 (Nov. 1912), 142.

'"War and the Social Order": A Study of the Committee's Report', *PS*, 1/5 (June 1916), 146–8.

'The War, the Under-War and the Class War', *PS*, 10 (Feb. 1915), 126.

Weddle, Meredith Baldwin, 'Conscience or Compromise: The Meaning of the Peace Testimony in Early New England', *QH*, 81/2 (Fall 1992), 73–86.

Weeks, Jeffery, *Sex, Politics and Society: The Regulation of Sexuality Since 1800* (2nd edn., London: Longman, 1981).

Weinroth, Howard, 'The Dilemma of British Socialists during the Great War: Revolutionary Peace or Pacifist Reconstruction', in Soloman Wank (ed.), *Doves and Diplomats* (Westport, Conn.: Greenwood Press, 1978), 193–4.

Westlake, Richard, 'The Social Position of Women', *FQE* (1869), 432–41.

What Happened at Leeds (London: Council of Workers & Soldiers Delegates, 1917).

'What is Quakerism?', *TF* April 1861, 88–9; May 1961, 168–9; July 1861, 182.

Whence Come Wars (London: War and the Social Order Committee, 1916).

White, Andrew Dickson, *Autobiography of Andrew Dickson White*, 2 vols. (London: Macmillan, 1905; New York: Century Co., 1905).

White, Stephen, 'Soviets in Britain: The Leeds Convention of 1917', *International Review of Social History* 19/2 (1974), 167–93.

Why I Am a Conscientious Objector (London: No-Conscription Fellowship, [1916]).

Wigham, Hannah Marie, 'Women's Work', *FQE* (1877), 191–203.

Williams, Beryl, 'Francis Frith (1822–1898)', *FQ*, 23/8 (Oct. 1984), 364–70.

Willis, Kirk, 'The Introduction and Critical Reception of Hegelian Thought in Britain, 1830–1900', *VS*, 32/1 (Autumn 1988), 85–111.

Wilson, Edith Jane, '"Alternative Service": Friends and a Perplexing Problem', *PS*, 1/7 (Aug. 1916), 203–4.

—— 'Law-Abiding Citizens', *PS*, 2/2 March 1917), 62–3.

Wilson, Roger C., 'The Best Things in Ye Worst Time', in Hans Erik Aarek (ed.), *Quakerism: A Way of Life* (Kvekerforlaget: Norwegian Quaker Press, 1982).

—— 'Friends in the Nineteenth Century', *FQ*, 23/8 (October 1984), 353–63, 405.

—— *Manchester, Manchester and Manchester Again: From 'Sound Doctrine' to 'A Free Ministry': The Theological Travail of London Yearly Meeting throughout the Nineteenth Century*, (London: Friends Historical Society, 1990).

—— 'The Road to Manchester, 1895', in J. William Frost and John M. Moore (eds.), *Seeking the Light: Essays in Quaker History Honor of Edwin B. Bronner* (Wallingford and Haverford, Pa.: Pendle Hill Publications, 1986), 145–62.

—— 'We Shall Never Thrive Upon Ignorance', in *A Quaker Miscellany for Edward H. Milligan*, (Manchester: David Blamires, 1985), 153–60.

'Women's Suffrage: Its Deeper Aspects', *BF* (Nov. 1913), 300–1.

Wood, Herbert G., *Henry T. Hodgkin. A Memoir* (London: SCM Press, 1937).

Wood, Herbert G., 'Pacifism and Politics', *FQE* 75 (1941), 199–211.

Worsdell, Edward, *The Gospel of Divine Help: Thoughts on Some First Principles of Christianity* (London: Samuel Harris, [1886]).

Worsdell, Edward, 'The Restoration of the Bible', *PDP*, 1 (1898), 55–64.

Index